WORSHIP AND THEOLOGY
IN ENGLAND

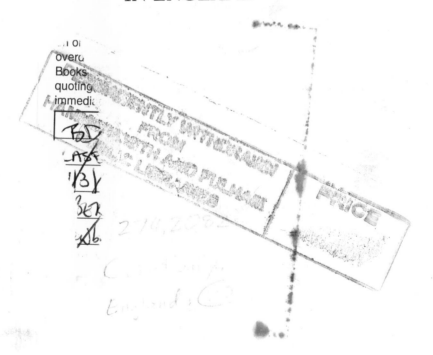

WORSHIP AND THEOLOGY IN ENGLAND

WORSHIP AND THEOLOGY IN ENGLAND

V. *The Ecumenical Century,*
1900–1965

VI. *Crisis and Creativity,*
1965–Present

HORTON DAVIES

WILLIAM B. EERDMANS PUBLISHING COMPANY
GRAND RAPIDS, MICHIGAN / CAMBRIDGE, U.K.

WORSHIP AND THEOLOGY IN ENGLAND
First published in 5 volumes by Princeton University Press:
I. *From Cranmer to Hooker, 1534–1603* (1970)
II. *From Andrewes to Baxter and Fox, 1603–1690* (1975)
III. *From Watts and Wesley to Maurice, 1690–1850* (1961)
IV. *From Newman to Martineau, 1850–1900* (1962)
V. *The Ecumenical Century, 1900–1965* (1965)

VI. *Crisis and Creativity, 1965–Present*
published 1996 by Wm. B. Eerdmans Publishing Co.

The Ecumenical Century, 1900–1965
© 1965 Princeton University Press
Crisis and Creativity, 1965–Present
© 1996 Wm. B. Eerdmans Publishing Co.

Combined edition published 1996 by
Wm. B. Eerdmans Publishing Co.
255 Jefferson Ave. S.E., Grand Rapids, Michigan 49503 /
P.O. Box 163, Cambridge CB3 9PU U.K.

Printed in the United States of America

02 01 00 99 98 97 96   7 6 5 4 3 2 1

Library of Congress Cataloging-in-Publication Data
Davies, Horton.
Worship and theology in England / Horton Davies.
p.   cm.
Includes bibliographical references and index.
Contents: v. 1, [pt. 1.] From Cranmer to Hooker, 1534-1603;
[pt. 2.] From Andrewes to Baxter and Fox, 1603-1690 —
v. 2, [pt. 1.] From Watts and Wesley to Maurice, 1690-1850;
[pt. 2.] From Newman to Martineau, 1850-1900 —
v. 3, [pt. 1.] The ecumenical century, 1900-1965;
[pt. 2.] Crisis and creativity, 1965-present.
ISBN 0-8028-0891-3 (v. 1: pbk.: alk. paper). —
ISBN 0-8028-0892-1 (v. 2: pbk.: alk. paper). —
ISBN 0-8028-0893-X (v. 3: pbk.: alk. paper).
1. England — Church history — Modern period, 1485-
2. Public worship — History. 3. Theology — England — History.
4. Theology, Doctrinal — History — England. I. Title.
BR755.D35   1996
274.2 — dc20   95-4514
CIP

OUTLINE

VOLUME V
THE ECUMENICAL CENTURY

PART ONE: THE WIDE-ANGLE VIEW

PART TWO: THE NARROW FOCUS

VOLUME VI
CRISIS AND CREATIVITY

WORSHIP
AND THEOLOGY
IN ENGLAND

V. *The Ecumenical Century,*
1900–1965

CONTENTS

CONTENTS

PART TWO: THE NARROW FOCUS

ACKNOWLEDGMENTS

THE SCALE of the indebtedness of the writer of contemporary history forbids its adequate acknowledgment. He needs to consult the participants and observers of events. In writing religious history he must also be scrupulously fair to members of traditions other than his own and seek their interpretations of theology and worship. Above all, when he deals with the two handmaids of worship, religious art and music, he requires expert guidance. I have not hesitated to avail myself of much advice, generously proffered in interviews and correspondence, most of which is acknowledged in the footnotes of relevant chapters or in the descriptions of the illustrations.

My special thanks are due to those who have assisted me far beyond the call of duty. I wish to thank Lady Kathleen Epstein for three interviews on the work of the late Sir Jacob Epstein; the Right Reverend B. Christopher Butler, O.S.B., the Abbot of Downside, who invited me to be the guest of the Benedictine Community which has contributed so generously to spirituality and scholarship; the Reverend Dr. Ernest A. Payne, the Secretary of the Baptist Union of Great Britain and Ireland, for helpful correspondence; the Reverend Dr. John Marsh, Principal of Mansfield College, Oxford, in whose home I stayed during Michaelmas Term 1964; the Reverend Dr. Erik R. Routley of Edinburgh, a former Oxford colleague, for his advice in that field which he has made peculiarly his own—Sacred Music; the Reverend Dr. E. C. Ratcliff, Regius Professor Emeritus of Divinity in the University of Cambridge, England's leading liturgiologist, for many kindnesses; the Reverend R. Aled Davies of Croydon, Convener of the Presbyterian Church of England's Assembly Committee on Public Worship, for an unusually full report on the state of worship in that Communion; and the memory of the late Dr. Mortimer Rowe, former General Secretary of the Unitarian and Free Christian Churches of Great Britain, for both letters and the loan of rare books. These and numberless others have been my benefactors in scholarship. It is also a pleasure to thank Mrs. Dan Crawford who typed the manuscript so efficiently, and Mrs. Polly Hanford of Princeton University Press for her careful editorial work on a 'mid-Atlantic' manuscript which was neither wholly English nor American in its spelling or use of idiom. I am also deeply indebted to the consideration shown me by Mr. Herbert W. Bailey, Jr., and Miss R. Miriam

Brokaw, respectively the Director and the Managing Editor of Princeton University Press. My gratitude to my wife is beyond all reckoning.

The Research Committee of Princeton University deserves my gratitude for the award of two grants which made it possible to spend two summers in English libraries. The Trustees of the John S. Guggenheim Memorial Foundation of New York by the award of two Fellowships have accelerated the progress towards the completion of this five-volume project. I am greatly cheered by their encouragement as I press on to complete the two final volumes, I and II.

To all these persons and institutions I express my deep gratitude.

HORTON DAVIES

Easter 1965
Department of Religion,
Princeton University

INTRODUCTION

THE SERIES, *Worship and Theology in England*, of which this volume is the fifth, is being written in the conviction that the study of the cultus of the Christian Churches offers the deepest clue to their interior life, as well as an index to their state of health. Theology and ethics are the conscious faces which the Churches show to the world; worship is the unposed face of the Church turned towards God in adoration and aspiration. Since worship is essentially *common* prayer, it might be argued that it is more truly representative of the life of the Christian community than theology (which is predominantly the work of thinkers operating as individuals within the tradition) or ethics (which vary with changing contexts). Its importance, however, is better judged when worship is seen as an inclusive category; for, being the adoration of the Body of Christ responsive to revelation, it necessarily includes both the knowledge of God (theology) and the strongest motives to fulfill the Divine will (ethics). The value of the cultus as an expression of the dynamic ethos of a community has long been acknowledged by social anthropologists; yet it is far from being recognized as significant by the majority of church historians.

Nonetheless its worth has been recognized by two distinguished English historians, John Selden (the seventeenth century antiquarian) and Professor Herbert Butterfield, Master of Peterhouse, Cambridge. In his *Table Talk*, it is recorded that Selden observed: "To know what was generally believed in all ages, the way is to consult the liturgies, not any man's private writing. So, if you would know how the Church of England serves God, go to the Common Prayer Book, consult not this nor that man."[1] Professor Butterfield observes that serious students, like Lord Acton, have been greatly interested in Church history, but that in considering its institutional impact on an age they have "tended to overlook that more intimate thing, the inner spiritual life of the Church." He adds, perhaps selecting the spiritual low point of 1800:

"The ordinary historian, when he comes, shall we say, to the year 1800 does not think to point out to the readers that in this year, still, as in so many previous years, thousands and thousands of priests and ministers were preaching the Gospel week in and

[1] *Table Talk, 1689*, under "Liturgy."

3

week out, constantly reminding the farmer and the shopkeeper of charity and humility, persuading them to think for a moment about the great issues of life, and inducing them to confess their sins. Yet this was a phenomenon calculated greatly to alter the quality of life and the very texture of human history; and it has been the standing work of the Church throughout the ages—even under the worst of popes here was a light that never went out."[2]

The present volume, then, brings the comparative history of Christian worship in all the major denominations in England up to the present. Like its two predecessors,[3] worship is studied both in a theological and in an aesthetic context. The changes of theology are reflected directly in the preaching of the age and more directly in freer than in liturgical types of worship. This is evident in the comparative neglect of worship when social witness is accorded imperative interest (as in the depreciation of the Lord's Supper in the Free Churches during the predominance of the "Social Gospel" emphasis), or when intellectual and moral discourses freeze the springs of devotion (as in Latitudinarian Anglicanism).

Worship is also greatly influenced by the prevailing modes of architecture, art, and music. To take a single example, one may cite the contemporary struggle between church architects who stand for the principle of *numinosity* and symbolism and those who emphasize the principle of *community-feeling* and functionalism. Since England has in the twentieth century witnessed an artistic and musical renaissance, the wider implications of aestheticism on worship have received fuller treatment in this volume.

This book has proved, in fact, to be the hardest to write of the three so far attempted in this series. The poet Horace rightly observed that to treat of current events is like walking on ashes beneath which the embers are still glowing.[4] Many experiments which excited a passing interest in their day are known to be unimportant to later investigators only because they were rapidly covered by the dust of oblivion; but the historian of current events has to do the sifting for himself. How can he tell whether a liturgical experiment which seems promising is a dangerous *ignis fatuus*, or a mere flash in the pan, or a guiding light? Another difficulty is the sheer bulk of reports, monographs, and periodical

[2] *Christianity and History*, p. 131.
[3] *Worship and Theology in England*, Vol. III: *From Watts and Wesley to Maurice, 1690-1850* and Vol. IV: *From Newman to Martineau, 1850-1900*.
[4] The third ode.

articles printed in our overproductive century on the theme of worship, a theme which has been brought into prominence by the success of the Modern Liturgical Movement. Merely to read them is difficult enough: to digest them calls for a Gargantuan appetite.

In facing these problems, I have had to rely more than in previous volumes on the official reports of the liturgical commissions or worship committees of the English Churches, and on their denominationally sponsored liturgies or service-books, and less on the often brilliant writings of individual interpreters, however creative. Furthermore, my judgment has been confirmed in many cases, but also contradicted in others, by the advice of experts in the fields of worship, art, architecture, and music whom I have interviewed or with whom I have corresponded. Yet, even in a century remarkable for its passionate concern for the establishment of Christian unity which, as Archbishop Temple insisted, was "the great new fact of our time" which argues for a stress on the unity of achievement in worship, I have also tried to do justice to the contributions of individual scholars, preachers, and artists precisely because this has been a period of liturgical experiment and artistic ferment.

My sub-title—"The Ecumenical Century"—has been selected to emphasize the fact that for Christian life in England as elsewhere this marks the decisive difference between the *competitive* character of nineteenth and the *cooperative* character of twentieth century Christianity. The term "Ecumenical" does not merely evoke a nostalgia for the first five centuries of the Christian era, when the Fathers of those Ecumenical Councils declared the apparently[5] unanimous mind of the Church against the heretics and schismatics in a moving demonstration of unity. Rather it points to the undoubted fact that attempts have been made, with renewed vigour by Protestants and Orthodox, on the one side, and more recently by Roman Catholics, on the other side, to heal the wounds of Christendom.[6]

Two events in recent ecclesiastical history symbolize this pas-

[5] See S. L. Greenslade, *Schism in the Early Church*, an important revisionist study.
[6] For a reliable series of accounts of the development of the ecumenical outlook since the Reformation see Ruth Rouse and S. C. Neill, eds., *A History of the Ecumenical Movement, 1517-1948*. Roman Catholic interpretations of Ecumenism are M. J. Congar, Divided Christendom (London, 1939, a trans. of *Chrétiens désunis*, Paris, 1937) and *Aspects de l'oecumenisme* (Bruxelles, 1962) and Hans Küng, *The Council in Action: Theological Reflections on the Second Vatican Council* (trans. C. Hastings, New York, 1964).

sionate concern for reunion. One was the foundation in 1948 at Amsterdam of the World Council of Churches, which had been prepared for by the Faith and Order and the Life and Work Commissions of cooperating Protestants, Anglicans, and Orthodox. The other is the epoch-making first session of the Ecumenical (or Second Vatican) Council of the Roman Catholic Church which was convoked in 1962, and which spoke of Orthodox and Protestants not as heretics but as "separated brethren" and whose representatives were invited as official observers to the Council. This rapprochement of a divided Christendom is most clearly mirrored in worship. In no period since the Reformation but our own would it seem natural and wholly right for an English Free Church minister, E. Romilly Micklem, gratefully to affirm his devotional indebtedness to "his mother the Church of England, his grandmother the Church of Rome, and his great-grandmother the Jewish Synagogue."[7]

At the same time, the success of the Pentecostalist Movement, which has been called Christianity's "Fourth Force" is a warning to the historic churches that Christian Reunion—if it be envisaged as an organization with a vast and impersonal super-structure, blissful only in the eyes of bureaucrats—could be too dearly purchased, at the cost of fellowship, variety, and freedom at the grass-roots level.

This book falls into two parts. The first, termed "The Wide-Angle View," presents a picture of the unparalleled agreement in worship in England of which the Ecumenical Movement in general, and the Modern Liturgical Movement in particular, are both stimulus and expression. The second part, "The Narrow Focus," shows that while there are elements of unity, there are also significant differences in worship. It presents the claim that the techniques of liturgical, free, and silent prayer, hitherto the separate treasures of different traditions, may be regarded as ultimately complementary approaches to the Divine in the Coming Great Church. It is thus hoped that both unity and difference have been given their accurate places in the reconstruction of the worship of the past six and a half decades.

Chapter I provides an account of "The Continental Liturgical Movement and its Influence," as it recounts the successive phases of the Movement in Solesmes, Mont-César, and Maria-Laach, and the appropriation of these insights by Lutherans and Reformed in

---

[7] *Our Approach to God*, p. 148.

Europe, and by Anglicans, Roman Catholics, and Free Churchmen in Britain. What is so fascinating about this Movement is that it has enabled Protestant Churches to recover in part the Catholic liturgical heritage, while the Catholics seem to have appropriated the Protestant valuation of preaching, of shared worship in the vernacular tongue, and the importance of the laity as the people of God. It is an appropriate index of the decreasing insularity of English theological interest.

Chapters II and III are studies in religious aesthetics. The second chapter documents "The Rebirth of Religious Architecture and Art" from neo-Gothic to functional liturgical architecture (exemplified, in part, in Scott's Anglican Cathedral and Gibberd's projected Roman Catholic Cathedral in Liverpool), and assays the contribution of Jacob Epstein, Henry Moore, Graham Sutherland, and others, to religious art. Chapter III records "The Development of Church Music" from Vaughan Williams to Benjamin Britten, and considers anthems, hymns, chants, and psalmody, in the classical and modern manners.

Chapters IV and V describe the changing fashions in English theology, using 1933 as the watershed year. The movement from a revelational to a redemptional and finally to a radical secular-oriented theology is charted. In Chapter IV—"The Early Development of Theology"—particular attention is paid to the theologians of the "social Gospel" (R. J. Campbell), of mysticism (Inge, von Hügel, Underhill), of Incarnationalism (Gore and Temple), and of the *Holy* Fatherhood of God (Forsyth and Oman). In Chapter V attention is given to the influence of Karl Barth, to the schools of "Realized Eschatology" (Hoskyns and Dodd), and of neo-Orthodoxy, and finally to the Cambridge Radicals. The impact that each theological change had on the role of worship in the Church is then analysed.

The first part concludes with Chapter VI, "Trends and Types of Preaching." This mirrors the theological changes in four major types of preaching: apologetical, charismatic, exegetical, and liturgical, as seen in the leading preachers—Anglican, Roman Catholic, and Free Church. Among the vivid figures encountered in this chapter are Monsignor Ronald Knox, Bishop H. Hensley Henson, Drs. Leslie Weatherhead, and W. E. Sangster, not forgetting "Woodbine Willie" and "Dick" Sheppard. They, and especially the two latter, complement the objectivity of worship with the passionate subjectivity of preaching. Other preachers are objective

7

exponents of the Scriptures or of Christian revelation reflected in the Liturgy.

The second part of the book consists of seven chapters, detailing the progress of theory and practice in worship in five traditions. Chapter VII, on "Roman Catholic Worship," tries to show why the Liturgical Movement has made tardy progress in this Communion in England, but also records the liturgical scholarship and spirituality of the English Benedictines, the importance of popular instruction given by some of the English Jesuits, and the liturgical promise of the Second Vatican Council. Chapter VIII, on "Anglican Worship to 1928," attempts to account for the rejection of the 1928 Revised Prayer Book by Parliament. Chapter IX on "Anglican Worship after 1928," tries to assess the consequences, including a closing of party-ranks within the Church, a deeper and more united understanding of the nature of the Eucharist, and a recent remarkable efflorescence of liturgical experiments. Chapter X, on "The Worship of the Free Churches," shows the major revaluations of their traditions of worship undertaken by the English Baptists, Congregationalists, Methodists, and Presbyterians, and questions whether the decline of free prayer is to be considered entirely a gain in worship. Chapter XI, on "Quaker Worship," takes account of modern Quaker defences of corporate silent prayer and considers the contribution this might make as an important ingredient of liturgical worship. Chapter XII, on "Unitarian Worship," notes the liturgical fertility of this denomination, and claims that its radical honesty of thought, its ethical integrity, and its deep understanding of the doctrine of Creation are greatly needed by the more orthodox Churches. Both Chapters XI and XII raise the question whether Quakerism and Unitarianism will pull up the Christological anchor and move out into the wider sea of interreligious theism, or re-establish their basis on historical Christian foundations and come more fully into the Churchly orbit.

The book ends with Chapter XIII, a "Concluding Critique," the purpose of which is to assess the gains in worship achieved during this century and to point to the remaining critical issues which have to be faced.

As I come to the end of this introduction I wonder whether in the pages that follow I have sufficiently stressed that Christianity was, on any statistical analysis, weakening its hold on the life of the nation to the point of feebleness. This century has been for the Church, as for all the British people, a desperate time—a period of crises, of wars, of scepticism, of secularism, and of stupendous scientific advance in technology in inverse proportion to the drastic decline in Church attendance and worship. Twice the lights have gone out in Europe and left a spiritual black-out which did not vanish when the electric lights were switched on again. In nihilistic days when the winds of change swept like hurricanes through the land, the torches of Christians were fewer, less luminous, and more flickering. But if Christ's companies were smaller, they were also more committed and far more united than in the past. The same winds of change have helped to winnow the chaff from the grains of wheat: there is little pride or prestige in Church membership for the natural man in contemporary England. For a remnant, man's extremity has proved to be God's opportunity, and the challenges of society were found to be answerable only in grace. In the call to contemporary faith, the appeals to respectability, to a merely aesthetic experience, to a nominal or half-hearted attachment, are mercifully minimal. So worship is less an escape than an encounter with the living God and a demand to witness in daily life and social service that *hurts*—that is compassion, a sharing in Christ's passion, and a *scandal*.

Even if sensitive English Christians share the sense of being witnesses to a twilight with no earthly promise of dawn, a realistic theology tells them that Western Christianity has failed because it failed to evangelize or only half evangelized. God needed men and men exploited God. For myself, I share this diagnosis of François Mauriac's and with him would affirm: "Whatever happens, even in a world three-quarters blotted out by a weapon of destruction, there will always be in the back part of some cellar a small group crowding around a table and a man anointed who breaks and distributes the Living Bread."[8] As in the earliest days of the Church, its present day worshippers are "perplexed, yet not unto despair."

[8] *What I Believe* (trans. with an introduction by Wallace Fowlie, New York, 1963), pp. 80-81.

9

PART I: THE WIDE-ANGLE VIEW

CHAPTER I

THE CONTINENTAL LITURGICAL MOVEMENT AND ITS INFLUENCE

ENGLISH INSULARITY is often mocked by retelling the fable that a London newspaper once printed the headline: "Fog in the English Channel: Continent Isolated." If England ever was so insular, culturally or spiritually, it is no longer so today.

The English Churches, especially since 1914, have increasingly reflected the four inter-related concerns of European and American Christianity. They have played a notable part in the Ecumenical Movement[1] for the reunion of a divided Christendom. They have shared in the recovery of a Biblical and Patristic theology of depth and relevance.[2] They have, with less theoretical success, been trying to develop a more sophisticated Christian social ethic in the modern technocratic context. Finally, and this is the particular concern of this chapter, they have been greatly influenced by the Continental Liturgical Movement and have made some considerable contributions to the newer understanding of worship as the renewal of the people of God.

1. The Importance of the Liturgical Movement

A provisional definition of a tentative character will provide a skeleton on which the flesh and muscle of the Liturgical Movement (its history, principles, and practices) can later be laid. The Liturgical Movement may be defined as an interconfessional renewal of Christian worship and life which sees in the self-offering of the Eternal Son of God on the Cross a Sacrifice which is both the descent of Divinity and the ascent of the Perfect Humanity, and therefore as the type and pattern of Christian worship in the Eucharist, the nexus of Christian unity, the inspiration of all human talents and labour, and the supreme means of grace. In the narrower sense "Liturgy" refers to the Eucharistic rite (as both Revelation and response in which the Sacrament of the Word is

---

[1] N.B. In this chapter the contributions of a multitude of scholars are mentioned, sometimes without listing all the relevant titles. In most cases the latter can be found in the Bibliography.

The fullest and most authoritative study of the subject is Ruth Rouse and S. C. Neill, eds., *A History of the Ecumenical Movement, 1517-1948.*

[2] For a study of the parallel course of the Liturgical and Biblical Movements, see K. Federer, *Liturgie und Glaube; eine theologie-geschichtliche Untersuchung.*

linked with the Sacrament of the Holy Communion), and the restoration of the Eucharist to its central place in truly corporate worship has been the primary concern of the Liturgical Movement. In the wider sense "Liturgy" has been used to refer to the whole round of the official public worship of the Christian Church, in the Daily Office, and in authorized forms. In this wider sense, moreover, the Movement has been concerned with such major issues as the theological basis of worship, its sincerity and relevance to modern life.

It must be insisted that the Liturgical Movement has been encouraged by the researches of learned liturgiologists as well as by the severely practical concerns of parish priests and ministers. It is not only an organization within the single largest Communion of Christendom (the Roman Catholic Church), but also an inter-denominational reformation of Catholic and Protestant import. It may quite properly be regarded as a movement of the Holy Spirit, since its effect has been to increase the holiness, charity, social witness, and ecumenicity of Christians in a tragically divided world. Its outstanding mark is increasing vitality. Its impact was first felt in a significant manner in Europe in 1840 and its influence on Britain and North America has been considerable, especially in recent decades. If Protestants have led in the theological revival of our times, then Catholics have clearly pioneered in the Liturgical Movement. More important, however, is the fact that the vitality of each movement has had a marked influence on its hitherto opposing ecclesiastical tradition.

A preliminary pointer to the significance of the Continental Liturgical Movement is the assessal of its importance made by non-Roman Catholic scholars in recent years. Between the First and Second World Wars there was the pioneering appreciation of the Movement in the work of the Swedish Lutheran (later Archbishop) Yngve Brilioth in his *Eucharistic Faith and Practice, Evangelical and Catholic* and of the Anglican priest, A. G. Hebert, in *Liturgy and Society*. More recently, however, there have been a series of important studies of the Continental Liturgical Movement, each of which manifests an amazing empathy from the Protestant side. Jean-Daniel Bénôit, of the University of Strasbourg, a French Reformed theologian, has published *Liturgical Renewal: Catholic and Protestant Developments on the Continent* (1958), which was originally given as a series of lectures to Anglican clergymen in the diocese of London. This is an important indication of the interaction of Catholic and Protestant theory and practice in worship. The Anglican liturgiologist and former Dean of Lincoln Cathedral, J. H. Srawley, has produced a suggestive account of the principles of the most recent phase of the Liturgical Movement in *The Liturgical Movement* (Alcuin Club, 1954). Two American clergy, both Episcopalians, Massey H. Shepherd, Jr.[3] in *The Living Liturgy* and in the volume he has edited, entitled *The Liturgical Renewal of the Church*, and Alfred R. Shands in *The Liturgical Movement and the Local Church* (1959), show how deeply sensitive and appreciative is right-wing Protestantism to the new developments of worship on the continent of Europe. Furthermore, an American Lutheran scholar, Ernest B. Koenker, has produced the fullest theological appraisal of *The Liturgical Renaissance in the Roman Catholic Church* from the Protestant side.

An even more impressive testimony to the impact of the Continental Liturgical Movement is to be found in the growing recognition on the part of Protestant Communions (in some cases this is a *recovery* of an earlier tradition) that Holy Communion or the Lord's Supper is the central and climactic act of the corporate worship of the Christian community. This is to be found in certain movements within the Protestant Churches of Britain and America. Many of these movements, though not all, have an official character. These are: the "Parish and People" Movement within the Church of England and the "Associated Parishes" of the American Episcopal Church; the "Church Service Society" and the Iona Community Movement within (and also beyond) the Church of Scotland; the "Methodist Sacramental Fellowship" in England and the newly founded "Wesley Society" in the United States; and the "Church Order Group" among the ministry of the Congregational churches in England and Wales. Moreover, the denominations to which these movements belong have been engaged in important liturgical experiments, some of which have been incorporated in their official books of worship. Lutherans and Episcopalians, of course, already have an honoured Liturgy. That such interconfessional liturgical borrowing and lending which has crossed the Catholic, Orthodox, and Protestant lines is a significant fact of our times can be seen from the most cursory survey of the pages of acknowledgments which preface the texts of most modern liturgies, denominational handbooks or manuals of worship, and devotional compilations.

---

[3] Professor Massey H. Shepherd, Jr. has also written a notable ecumenical liturgical volume, *The Reform of Liturgical Worship: Perspectives and Prospects.*

Besides, a rain-shower of liturgical pamphlets in ecclesiastical journals, and a hail-storm of books, pelting from the presses, ought by now to have drenched the literate minister and thoughtful laymen in the new liturgical climate of our times. Though many are high, few are dry. Possibly only the most Tridentine of Roman Catholics and the most dissident of Protestant Nonconformists remain dry in this deluge, merely because they are stranded on the arid sands of a sixteenth century controversy.

If it be erroneous to refuse to acknowledge the impact of the Liturgical Movement, it is equally so to claim too much for it, as two considerations will bear out. In the first place, far from the influence having been all one way, and the Roman Catholics the donors and the Protestants merely recipients, there has been reciprocal giving and accepting. At first glance the claim that classical Reformed worship has influenced the liturgical thought and practice of the Roman Catholic Church would seem improbable to the point of absurdity; it seems less so when some of the more revolutionary principles of the Continental Liturgical Movement are considered. Many of these principles were once the convictions and are now the commonplaces of Reformed celebrations of the Holy Communion or Lord's Supper. Such principles are: the insistence upon a rite translated from the Latin into the vernacular for the edification of the common people; an insistence upon participation rather than passivity on the part of the communicants, with its correlate of corporate Communion rather than any private Eucharistic devotions (such as the "Forty Hours" or "Benediction"); the manducation of *both* the consecrated Bread and Wine, rather than Communion in *one* kind; liturgical preaching, for which a parallel can be found in the "Communion Discourses" in the Reformed tradition; and the so-called Western or Basilican posture for celebration, in which the priest or minister faces the people across the Holy Table (possible only when the Altar is brought forward from the usual position immediately beneath the East wall and window). All of these principles and practices, for which a pre-Reformation precedent can be found, even if arbitrarily and unconvincingly, are more easily and naturally found as legitimate Reformed protests against abuses of the Sacrament as celebrated in the later mediaeval Western Church, and they have been customary in most Reformed Churches during the past four centuries. Thus it is not necessary to claim Roman Catholic influence for practices

16

which have been characteristically those of classical Protestantism in its worship.

Furthermore, it has been characteristic of English and American life (and not less of English and American theology) to adapt, modify, and mould its borrowings to suit its own needs. While the insularity and moderation of English theology[4] is not as prominent in the twentieth as it has been in the three prior centuries, it is itself a factor which would urge the pragmatic English to be suspicious of Continental importations until they have been thoroughly tested and Anglicized. On the positive side, England can claim that she made her own contributions of singular importance to the renewal of worship. If France urges the claim that the origins of the Liturgical Movement are to be found in a Romantic protest against Rationalism made vivid in the mediaevalism of the novels of Victor Hugo and J. K. Huysmans, or if Germany urges the priority of Schlegel, then Britain demands the palm for Sir Walter Scott's "Waverley" series of novels, or, if the debate is desperate, for the architectural mediaevalism of William Beckford and Horace Walpole. In these "Gothic Games" (if the international competition to discover the earliest pioneers of neo-mediaevalism may be so termed) France can claim that Rohant de Fleury, with his study of the Mass in art, Didron's iconographic monographs, and Viollet-le-Duc's architectural researches and restorations, were at least as significant as the mediaeval restorationism of Pugin, Barry, G. G. Scott, Street, and Butterfield[5] in Victorian England, even though an English nationalist might find it convenient to cite the German Reichensperger's tribute to Pugin that "he was the hero in the fight for Christian art."[6] Though the Oxford Movement was not without Continental influences, it would be an injustice not to regard it as predominantly an indigenous and successful English attempt to renew liturgical and sacramental worship. Thus the ambiguities of origins and the multiplicity of cultural influences, as well as the pragmatic character of English religion, are restraints on exaggerated claims for the impact of the Continental Liturgical Movement on English ways of worship. It must, however, also be insisted upon that English theology became increasingly dependent upon European theology in the twentieth century and that the

[4] See C. C. J. Webb, *A Century of Anglican Theology*, pp. 20-25.
[5] See B. F. L. Clarke, *Church Buildings of the Nineteenth Century*.
[6] Olivier Rousseau, *L'Histoire du Mouvement Liturgique*, p. 132.

impact of the second phase of the Continental Liturgical Movement has been considerable.

What has been said of English theology is also largely true of American theology and worship, which has been profoundly influenced by the free and spontaneous techniques of evangelism in the "Great Awakenings" and on the western-moving frontier, making the very concepts of Liturgy and Church traditions matters of suspicion. Here, too, pragmatism prevails. The "Continental" or European character of the Liturgical Movement will be considered as reference is made to its most important contributions, which came from France in the nineteenth and from Belgium, Italy, the Rhineland, and Austria in the twentieth century.

2. *The First Phase: Solesmes*

Since worship, which he termed the *opus Dei*,[7] was for St. Benedict of Nursia the primary privilege and duty of monks (although both contemplation and manual labour played their important but subordinate parts), it is not surprising that the restoration of the Benedictine order in France was accompanied by an intense renewal of liturgical life. The pre-eminent pioneer in the Liturgical Movement in France was Dom Prosper Guéranger (1805-1875), an ardent disciple of Lamennais. The latter had wished to bring France back to the political and social order of the days of Pope Gregory VII by means of the revival of the Roman Catholic Church. However roseate Lamennais' view of the eleventh century was (and this is a common characteristic of mediaeval religious restorationists), it is understandable. After the political unsettlements of popular revolutions succeeded by dictatorships in nineteenth century France, it was inevitable that an idealized image of the conjoint rule of the Orb and the Cross (of godly emperor and holy pontiff) in the eleventh century, in which Chartres—the sublimest symbol of French Catholic faith—was erected, should glisten enticingly in the minds of devout Frenchmen. It was a case, not of *reculer pour mieux sauter* (for to advance beyond Chartres was unthinkable), but only *reculer pour sauter*. For Guéranger, as for St. Francis of Assisi, the command was to rebuild God's house in ruins.[8] Guéranger's ruins demanding restoration were those of the ancient Abbey of Solesmes, left desolate by the image-

---

[7] There are two instances in the *Regula* of Saint Benedict where this term is employed, once notably in *Caput* LXIII, where it is stated: *Ergo nihil operi Dei praeponat* ("Nothing is to take precedence of the worship of God").

[8] G. Cozien, *L'oeuvre de Dom Guéranger*, p. 43.

18

breakers of the French Revolution. If Lamennais desired a revival of the mediaeval politico-social order, Guéranger longed for the restoration of the Church life of the Middle Ages. His own vocation, he was convinced, was to return to the Church those now desolate sanctuaries of prayer which had nourished saints. The restored abbey of Solesmes would be the type and forerunner of such ecclesiastical renewal.

Solesmes, widely known for its restoration of Gregorian chanting, was the first power-house and dynamo of liturgical renewal, and its Daily Office and its celebration of the Festivals were widely admired and frequently imitated. While relatively few were able to make their pilgrimage to Solesmes and share in its worship, two publications of the greatest influence carried the principles and the scholarship of the abbey to the remotest corners of Catholic Christendom. These were the *Institutions liturgiques* of 1840 and *L'Année liturgique*, issued from 1841 onward. Within sixty years of issuing the first imprint over half a million copies of the *Année liturgique* had been sold and it had been translated into the major European languages. Though Guéranger was the director of this scholarly work, much of the credit for the Greek and Patristic erudition must go to Dom Pitra, one of his monks, who edited classical works on the Greek Liturgy and hymnology and was created a Cardinal in 1863.

The entire aim of Guéranger was the rejuvenation of liturgical piety in an age that was increasingly secular, rationalistic, and individualistic. He believed that the restoration of the Benedictine rule and worship would build up Christian faith to combat secularism, that Christian mysticism was the antidote to rationalism, and that the disciplined community life in the Church would defeat undisciplined individualism. For him the Church was most truly herself in worship, an offering of adoration to God linked with the perfect Offering of the God-man and High Priest, Jesus Christ, with and for humanity. The Divine Liturgy, being the Spirit-prompted response of the Church at worship, was regarded as the essential means of human sanctification and therefore of humanity's renovation and redemption. The conception is romantically conveyed in the preface to his *L'Année liturgique*:

"It is in Holy Church that the Divine Spirit dwells. He came down to her as an impetuous wind, and manifested Himself to her under the expressive symbols of tongues of fire. Ever since that day of Pentecost, He has dwelt in this His favoured Bride. He is the principle of everything that is in her. He it is that prompts her prayers, her desires, her canticles of praise, her enthusiasm and even her mourning. Hence her prayer is as uninterrupted as her existence. Day and night her voice sounds sweetly in the ear of her divine Spouse, and her words are ever finding a welcome in His heart."[9]

Guéranger believed that the temporal cycle of the Liturgy was a providentially inspired means of accommodating in time the eternal mysteries of the Creation of man, his re-creation and restoration through the Incarnation, and his sanctification in the Church by the Holy Spirit. The sanctoral cycle he interpreted as the proof of the Divine renewal, from the first century of the Christian dispensation to his own. Rome was for him the mother of saints and the traditional Roman rite was the path to perfection. Utterly faithful to the Roman *magisterium*, he approved all devotions officially sanctioned by the Roman Church, whether it were the cult of the Blessed Sacrament or of the Sacred Heart.

Although he was deeply concerned to instruct the laity in the meaning of the Liturgy, and, indeed, had translated several parts of it into French (always excepting the Canon of the Mass), he never deviated from the conviction that the Mass must be said in Latin, the "sacred tongue." As a keen Ultramontanist (and therefore the sworn enemy of any attempt to retain or introduce any national variants or "Uses" in the Liturgy), he might be expected to prefer the use of the Latin language, but it was due in part to his excessive antiquarianism and in part also to his view that a partially understood language would preserve the essential element of mystery in Christian worship. (He seemed unaware that such a thesis makes mystery and ignorance equivalents, whereas mystery and transcendence are more properly correlated.)

His profound spirituality (which made him so admirable an expositor of the Liturgy) was nourished upon a love of the Scriptures, themselves illuminated by Patristic examples of exegesis, and upon a high respect for the continuity of tradition. Father Louis Bouyer, critical as he is of the sentimentalism and archaeologism of Guéranger's restoration of the Liturgy, yet acknowledges that his reforms made the monastic worship at Solesmes "one of the most impressive types to be found in modern times."[10] Such devotion and erudition in general, and in particular, the restoration

[9] Vol. I, pp. 1-2, trans. and cited by Dom Olivier Rousseau, *op.cit.* Chap. 1.
[10] *Life and Liturgy* (republished as paperback, 1962), p. 11.

of the Gregorian mode of chanting, austere and yet haunting; a scrupulous observance of all rubrics and ceremonies of the Roman rite; and above all, a sober, uncluttered, untheatrical celebration of the Liturgy, were his abiding contributions to the renaissance of Catholic worship.

Guéranger's importance can also be gauged in his stimulus to others to maintain and to improve upon his own work. His own religious order, the Benedictines, made excellent use of his initiative and example by the prosecution of liturgiology in France, England, Belgium, and in the Rhineland. The first prior of Farnborough, England (itself a daughter house of Solesmes), was Dom Fernand Cabrol, who in the very year of the foundation of the house had published a study of the liturgy of Jerusalem in the fourth century based upon his edition of the *Peregrinatio Silviae* (1895). In 1903 he began to publish the monumental *Dictionnaire d'Archéologie chrétienne et de Liturgie*, with the help of the learned Dom Henri Leclercq. Two other distinguished Frenchmen also promoted the scientific study of liturgies. One was Louis Duchesne, the author of a work translated as *Christian Worship: its Origin and Evolution*, which went into several editions, and the other was Pierre Batiffol, author of the *Histoire du Bréviaire Romain* (1893) and of the popular *Leçons sur la Messe*. In Southern Germany the first centre of revived Benedictinism was the congregation of Beuron, founded in 1863. Its founders had stayed with Guéranger in Solesmes and were greatly attracted by his liturgical ideals, as was evident in the writings of Dom Maurus Wolter.[11] The Belgian Solesmes was the Abbey of Maredsous, a great liturgical centre of Benedictinism which has attained even greater fame in our own day as the promoter of Mont-César near Louvain, a daughter house which had its own profound modification of the Guéranger tradition to offer under Dom Morin and Dom Lambert Beauduin. The second great twentieth century Benedictine liturgical centre is Maria Laach in the Rhineland, renowned for the work of Abbot Herwegen and Dom Odo Casel, which complemented and corrected the work of Guéranger, and was itself complemented by the practical concerns of Abbot Pius Parsch of Klosterneuberg in Austria. A most distinguished English contribution to liturgics was made by the Benedictine lay brother, associated with Downside, Edmund

---

[11] See his *Gertrudenbuch*, St. Gertrude's sixteenth century *exercitia spiritualia* patterned on the liturgical cycle, a massive commentary on the psalms, and the *Praecipua Ordinis Monastici Monumenta* which devotes a chapter to the value of the Divine Office.

Bishop. All these, however much they might and did differ from Prosper Guéranger, were sons that could rise up and call him blessed.

Admirable, even epochal, as was Guéranger's work, it was not flawless. The flies in this liturgical amber were romanticism and Ultramontanism. The sober worship of Solesmes was, indeed, a relief after the theatrical posturings and the dramatic *mise-en-scène* of the Baroque period, but Baroque was a genuine expression of the spirit of its age whereas Solesmes was an artificial and anti-quarian reconstruction of a long buried past, if indeed that past had ever existed in such an idealized form. The mediaevalism it sought to revive was a fancied mediaevalism, as irrelevant as the manufacture of a modern gargoyle in concrete, even if much love-lier. In brief, this was only a splendid fossil, not the contemporary expression of a living tradition of Divine worship. Moreover, it was essentially monastic worship, the "shadowy image of Cluny."[12] It had no direct relevance to the worship of the masses in city or rural congregations in the nineteenth century; it was an idyllic, aesthetic, and disciplined escape for monks.

It was romantic, not only in its roseate reconstruction and ap-parent irrelevance, but also in its sentimentality. The real focus of the Eucharist for Dom Guéranger was the "miracle" of the Divine Presence of Christ, not the sacrificial Action. To put the point directly: Guéranger was impressed by the descent of Christ in a moment of time in the Mass, rather than by the Church's ascent with Christ and inclusion in His perfect and eternal Offering which consummates the whole drama of redemption for the people of God. It was an irruptionist and individualistic conception of the action of God in the Sacrament of Holy Communion, and could naturally accommodate such modern cults as that of the Sacred Heart and the Exposition of the Blessed Sacrament, which suffer from the same excessively subjective emphasis.[13] Different considerations may help to establish the justice of this criticism: notably, the radical revision of the Eastern liturgies demanded by Guéranger in *Les Institutions liturgiques* in order to make them conform to the Roman rite of 1570; the disproportionate emphasis given by his successors to the Feast of Corpus Christi in *L'Année liturgique* (an entire volume is devoted to the theme), and the fact that the

12 Bouyer, *Life and Liturgy*, p. 12.
13 See E. Dumoutet, *Le désir de voir l'Hostie*, for a penetrating criticism of sentimental subjectivism in mediaeval worship.

most genuinely communal worship at Solesmes, celebrated with the most impressive ceremonial, was Benediction rather than the Community Mass.

Guéranger's Ultramontanism (also a legacy from Lamennais) accounted for the liturgical inflexibility that made him consider the 1570 Missal of Pope Pius V as inalterably sacrosanct, assuming it to be the final development of Western worship. He was, therefore, prevented from considering that earlier forms of the Roman liturgy might have been worthier of preservation. Moreover, he was almost as blind to the intrinsic glories of the Eastern rites as he was to the importance of ancient French usages, as distinguished from the neo-Gallican liturgies of the seventeenth and eighteenth centuries on which he poured the vials of his scorn.

The very deficiencies of a Guéranger, however, were to be corrected by his own order, especially in the work of Dom Lambert Beauduin of Mont-César and of Abbot Ildefons Herwegen and Dom Odo Casel of Maria Laach. The Belgian Benedictine saw that the right locus for the liturgical revival was a properly instructed parish congregation; the German Benedictines were the constructive critics of the idiosyncratic and romantic tendencies of revived mediaevalism, and they had their own positive *mysterientheologie* to expound. Both Mont-César and Maria Laach were daughters of the Solesmian revival.

3. *The Second Phase: Mont-César and Maria Laach*

It is during the second phase, that is in the twentieth century, that the Liturgical Movement has made its most impressive contributions, and its influence is far from being spent. The greatest impetus the Movement received was the strong support of Pope Pius X, who became the official propagator of the liturgical apostolate.

The beginning of the second phase of the Continental Liturgical Movement is usually dated from a speech made in 1910 at Malines by Dom Lambert Beauduin. In this he urged that the Liturgy should be understood as the action of the Church as a whole, bringing the whole individual man in the whole community to God. The idea of lay participation in the Eucharist was, however, put forward by another Belgian Benedictine, Dom Gerhard Van Caloen, as early as 1883 at the Eucharistic Congress of Liége; he had given proof of his conviction by the publication in 1882 of a small missal in Latin and French, the *Missel des Fidèles*. It was the Abbey of Mont-César, however, founded in 1897, which became the chief centre of liturgical renewal in Belgium and Beauduin was its leading luminary.

Lambert Beauduin was professed as a Benedictine monk in 1906, after eight important years of experience as a parish priest devoted chiefly to social work. Here was a man who knew the supreme importance of worship, but also the extraordinary difficulty of maintaining the life of devotion in the crowded tenements of the industrial cities of present-day Europe, and with the apparent lack of any nexus between worship and daily work. Realizing that the Liturgy in the Church is the central and integrating act of all parish life, he became convinced of the paramount need for parish priests to instruct their flocks in the meaning of the supernatural life as mediated by the rites and Sacraments of the Church. Thus a parish worship in which an instructed laity shared in the prayers as well as in the praises of the Mass would mean spiritual renewal.

Partly as a result of Beauduin's passionate and intelligent advocacy of these convictions, the Catholic Congress at Malines (1909) resolved on a programme of liturgical reform, which was fully approved by Cardinal Mercier. There was complete agreement, in the first place, on the need to emphasize the use of the Roman missal as a book of popular piety (instead of the usual private devotional manuals), and therefore on the need for a wide dissemination of the complete text of at least Sunday Mass and Vespers in a vernacular translation. It was also proposed to give a definitely liturgical character to popular piety. This aim was to be accomplished by encouraging the laity to recite Compline as evening prayer, to attend parish High Mass and Vespers, to use the prayers of the Missal as both a preparation for and a thanksgiving after receiving Communion, and to restore the ancient liturgical traditions in their homes. It was also agreed to work for a wider and more worthy use of the Gregorian chant, according to the wish of Pope Pius X. Finally, it was agreed to provide annual retreats for parish choirs at a liturgical centre, and thus again fulfil the wish of the Pope, who had founded a *schola cantorum* in Salzano, where he had been parish priest, and who had declared in the frequently cited sentence in *Motu Proprio* (1903): "We must not sing or pray during Mass, but we must sing and pray the Mass."[14]

14 *Motu Proprio* insisted that the public worship of the Church is the principal

In order to give effect to these reforms Dom Beauduin published *La Vie liturgique,* of which 50,000 copies were sold during its first year of publication (1909). After two years his series of pamphlets had developed into the review, *Questions liturgiques,* which was intended exclusively for the clergy.[15] At frequent gatherings of parish priests in retreat at Mont-César Abbey, the ardent monk and former secular priest instructed them in the meaning of liturgical spirituality. Thus the treasures of Solesmes, instead of being hoarded in monasteries, were prodigally scattered to become the common possession of the parochial clergy, and through them of the laity.

Beauduin's teaching was admirably condensed in *La Piété de l'Eglise, principes et faits* (1914), which demonstrated the theological basis of true piety, based upon the Divine action in the life of the faithful. Writing from within the context of a bitter-sweet remembrance of a parish ministry in which he found labouring men and women to be mere driftwood caught by the impersonal industrial maelstrom, "hands" to be used if skilled, and discarded if ailing, old, or redundant, Beauduin insisted that the liturgical revival would enable men and women to know the dignity of human nature. This reality was made known in the Incarnation, which had made possible the lifting up of our callous, sinful, and lonely humanity to God, and the Liturgy was the recalling and renewal of the Incarnation's effects upon the faithful by the power of the re-creating and sanctifying Holy Spirit. Recalling the acrimonious class feuds of his parish, the disdainful patronage of employers, the sullenness or servility of employees, and the desperate need for a charity that would work for social justice and go beyond it, Dom Beauduin maintained that the Liturgical Revival would foster brotherhood by a profound understanding of the Church as the Body of Christ, in which He lives and works, organically uniting the members to Himself and to each other. Furthermore, Dom Lambert insisted that the Eucharistic Sacrifice evoked the spirit of renunciation in the faithful, for here again the Incarnate Christ

---

means of sanctifying the people of God, that worship should be purged of profane music, and that Gregorian chanting should be encouraged. In the Bull *Divino Afflatu* (1911), Pius X insisted on the reform of the Church Calendar, the Psalter, and the Breviary.

15 See Lambert Beauduin, *Mélanges liturgiques recueillis parmi les oeuvres de Dom L. Beauduin, O.S.B.,* which contains his most important articles.

and High Priest makes the perfect Offering of His life to the Father and the "Offertory" requires the participants to offer themselves with Christ for the world. The rich appositeness of Beauduin's teaching was a genuine integration of the liturgy as adoration in the Church and witness in the world.

The stronger theological and historic undergirding of the Liturgical Movement was to come from the German Benedictines of Beuron and especially of Maria Laach. As the historical studies of Guéranger had been applied to the practical needs of parish congregations by Beauduin, so the liturgical researches of Maria Laach were applied to the parishes by Abbot Pius Parsch and the Augustinian canons of Klosterneuberg.[16]

The leadership of Maria Laach in the second phase of the Liturgical Movement coincided almost exactly with the abbacy of Dr. Ildefons Herwegen (1913-1946). The exact beginning of Maria Laach's influence may perhaps be traced to Holy Week in 1914, when a group of Catholic university teachers, doctors, and lawyers asked the Abbot of Maria Laach to advise them on how to encourage the faithful in more active participation in the Mass. It was the research undertaken and promoted by Herwegen and his most able henchman, Dom Odo Casel, which taught the clergy and the more cultured laity the revolutionary implications of the Liturgy for life. This corporate scholarly enterprise included the commencement of the series "Ecclesia Orans" in 1918, with the appearance of Guardini's *Vom Geist der Liturgie*;[17] in the same year the monks of Maria Laach and of other Benedictine foundations in the Rhineland edited and issued *Liturgiegeschichtliche Quellen und Forschungen*, and three years later in 1921 there began to appear the important annual, *Jahrbuch fur Liturgiewissenschaft*. The third of these monuments of scholarship, and the most penetrating, is a memorial to Dom Odo Casel, the outstanding theologian of the entire Movement. In 1931 Herwegen established the important Institute of Liturgical and Monastic Studies at Maria Laach.

It is profoundly significant that this spiritual and intellectual renewal of worship was promoted during a time when Europe was prodigally expending the blood of its manhood in the mud and barbed-wire entrenchments of Flanders, where there were

16 See Pierre Mesnard, *Le Mouvement liturgique de Klosterneuberg.*
17 Translated into English by A. Lane and published together with an additional work under the title *The Spirit and the Liturgy.*

No passing bells for those who die as cattle
Only the monstrous anger of the guns
Shall patter out their hasty orisons.[18]

Our own century was and is peculiarly in need of the integration and wholeness that divided man can recover in the Liturgy by understanding his destiny in the purpose of God, as a part of the people of God, fortified by the grace of God. Maria Laach's task was to demonstrate the "Christification" of man in community.

Many aspects of the Liturgical Movement are illustrated in the researches of Maria Laach and its associated Benedictine monasteries. These include the return to the Biblical and Christ-centred tradition of the Early Church; the recognition of the importance of the vivifying Word proclaimed in the lections and sermons of the Synaxis as well as in the *Verbum visibile* of the Eucharist; the need for an objective and corporate, as contrasted with a subjective and individualistic, liturgical piety; an emphasis on the *communal* offering of the Eucharistic Sacrifice, as well as a complementary stress on the Holy Communion as a commemorative repast; and also the strongly social implications of the Liturgy for the overcoming of class divisions and its potential consecration of Christian art. Maria Laach's chief contribution to the understanding of the Liturgy, however, has been the systematic exposition of it as the efficaciously sanctifying representation of the Christian Mystery of salvation. This is the so-called *mysterientheologie*.[19]

Its chief exponent, Dom Odo Casel, distinguishes three correlated aspects of the *mysterium*.[20] First of all, the supreme Mystery is God in His own Being, the utterly Holy and Unapproachable One. Secondly, the revelation of God in Christ is the personal Mystery of God the invisible revealed in the flesh, and in His humiliation, Incarnation, Sacrificial death upon the Cross, as in His Resurrection and Ascension, God marvellously reveals Himself in a way that far surpasses all human capacities. The third mystery is that of the cult, which is defined as a liturgical action "in which the redemptive act is rendered present in the rite,"[21] and

---

[18] Wilfred Owen's *Anthem for Doomed Youth*, recently popularized by Benjamin Britten's *War Requiem*.

[19] See the over-high evaluation of Casel's work in Alphonse Heitz's article in *La Maison-Dieu*, VII (1946), where (p. 51) he describes as mere "tid-bits" (*amorces*) the contributions of the predecessors of the Maria Laach School.

[20] See *Das Christliche Kultmysterium* (3rd edn., Regensburg, 1948).

[21] *Repraesentatio* or *gegenwartigsetzung* are the words used.

"since the cultic community accomplishes the rite, it shares the saving rite and through it attains redemption."[22]

It must, however, be emphasized that for Casel not only the Passion of Christ but the entire work of redemption is made present again in the Liturgy, from His advent to His second advent. Moreover, this is declared and believed to be not a psychological or subjective reality but an ontological and objective reality, which, though veiled in symbol or image, actually shares in the reality of God's redemptive action of grace for His people.

Related to "mystery" is the term "transfiguration," and these are seminal terms for the Eastern Church as for Maria Laach. The purpose of the Liturgy, as of the Christian religion, is to sanctify, even to deify mankind, bringing transfigured Christians to the Christ of the Transfiguration. Through the bestowal of grace in the Liturgy, man is raised to the supernatural order and therefore into sharing the Divine existence, light, and glory. Not for Maria Laach any individual meditations on the crucified Christ or devotions to the Christ "imprisoned" in the Tabernacle, but a proleptic sharing of the life of the glorified Christ. The focal centre is the Christ in Glory, but with the constant remembrance that this Christ went "from God to God" by the route of the humiliation and the *via dolorosa*.

It will be no surprise, therefore, recognizing the Eastern Patristic provenance of the central theological concepts of Maria Laach's expositors, that the art of Beuron and Maria Laach is Byzantine, not Baroque in character. It is a simplified stylized art in which the symbols point to the universal divine reality that intersects time, rather than the dramatic, tortuous, psychologism (and even naturalism) that characterizes Baroque. The art of the German Benedictines is closer to the Christ in Glory of the tympanum of Vézelay than to the El Greco Christ in the agony of the Garden of Gethsemane. This, indeed, might have been expected from Abbot Herwegen's sharp disjunction in *Kirche und Seele* (Munster, 1928) between the sentimental, subjective, and individualistic piety[23] of the later mediaeval and post-Tridentine Mass and the objective and corporate liturgical piety of the Fathers. In the same book he had also argued that mediaeval romanticism (which, by

[22] *Das Christliche Kultmysterium*, p. 121.
[23] Gallican worship found such floridity attractive (see Gregory Dix, *The Shape of the Liturgy*) and the neo-Platonism of the Pseudo-Dionysius reached its most bizarre and idiosyncratic heights in symbolical interpretations of Gulielmus Durandus.

implication, had been rejuvenated by Guéranger) had shifted the emphasis in the Eucharist from the union of the whole Church with God to a concentration on individual benefits to be derived from the Mass. By such a misplaced emphasis, Herwegen maintained that a Christocentric action of the Church had degenerated into a pious or moralistic passivity of the laity, as individual spectators, who were no longer participants in the Eucharistic action. It is clear that the liturgical work of Maria Laach was as much a revolution as it was a restoration.

The scholarly researches and recovered insights of Maria Laach were made available to the parishes by the Augustinian canons of Klosterneuberg in Austria, chiefly through the work of popularization undertaken by Pius Parsch, which was later to be taken up by the pastor Pinsk in Berlin and the Jesuit scholar Jungmann in Innsbruck.[24] Parsch's deepest insight was to join in promoting the union of a Biblical movement with the Liturgical Movement through the review, *Bibel und Liturgie*, thus uniting the Liturgy with its main source, the record of God's revelation. The Bible itself came alive for many thousands of Catholics perhaps for the first time since the Reformation of the sixteenth century, and in the true context of the Liturgy.

Further developments in the second phase of the Liturgical Movement, accelerated by the work of Maria Laach, are to be found in France. Here the important *Centre de Pastorale Liturgique* was founded in 1943 by a remarkable act of continuing cooperation between Benedictines, Jesuits, Oratorians, and secular priests. This centre has concentrated on making the Liturgy the centre of the mission of the Church in a secularized nation. Elsewhere in France a limitation of the mission of the Church by focussing on the new intellectual pagans or almost exclusively on establishing social justice have aroused more opposition than is inevitable on the introduction of innovation. The critics have argued that such an approach has led to the denial of the importance of the parish as the traditional unit of the Church, that it has disregarded the traditional Liturgy in favour of "para-liturgies" as half-way houses between the outsider and the insider, and that social justice may be a by-product of Christian concern elicited by

---

[24] Joseph Jungmann, S.J., is the author of a masterly historical study, *Missarum Solemnia; eine genetische Erklärung der romischen Messe* (2 vols., 4th impression, Vienna, 1958). This has been translated into English as *The Mass of the Roman Rite, Its Origins and Development*, by F. A. Brunner.

the true fraternity created by the Holy Spirit, but can never be the main end of the Liturgy or the mission of the Church.

Even more significant, as a proof of the pre-eminent importance of Maria Laach's contribution to the second phase of the Liturgical Movement, is the remarkable number of Roman Catholic theologians and liturgiologists who have endorsed, or partly endorsed, the theological and practical insights of Herwegen and Casel. Among these may be mentioned Dom Anscar Vonier, O.S.B., Henri de Lubac, S.J., Jean Daniélou, S.J., P. Doncoeur, S.J., Pié Duployé, O.P., Eugène Masure, and Louis Bouyer, Cong.Orat., all of whom expound the *mysterientheologie*. It is accepted, with some reservations, by François Diekamp, J. Butler, Karl Adam, and Sohngen. It is, however, severely criticized by Joseph Jungmann and Theodore Klauser, as well as by certain members of the hierarchy.

The *mysterientheologie* has been criticized as denigrating the scholastic and mediaeval interpretations of the Mass, as Greek antiquarianism, and as denying the once-for-allness of history in claiming the re-enactment of the crucial historic event in the Liturgy. The debate continues, but it is undeniable that the theology of the Mystery has brought freshness and vigour and, most meaningfully, a sense of the rediscovery of the saving work of Christ, into the worship of scholars and of simple people. Its ecumenical significance is profound. Not only does it provide a bridge between Eastern Orthodox and Western Catholic theology, but it offers a third alternative to mediaeval scholastic and post-Tridentine Eucharistic interpretations, and this has met with an interested response on the part of Protestant theologians. Its revivification of parish life, through emphasis on the Divine initiative and the action of grace in the Liturgy, is its most impressive fruit.

The *mysterientheologie* has many other important implications. Faith, in its view, is more than assent to intellectual propositions, since it requires the commitment of the whole life of the whole man to God. Man is no longer envisioned atomistically, but as a part of the people of God, mystically incorporated into the *Corpus Christi* in the action of the Mass, sharing the life, purposes, and divine energy of God. This theology, furthermore, views man's daily work as worship, the offering which the Christian in the world brings to the company of the transfigured, to be presented in the Offertory of the Liturgy, together with the Perfect Offering of Atonement renewed. The Eucharist itself is transformed also: it is no longer merely a hierarchical offering in which the laity are passively present, but an action of grace in which the general priesthood of the people of God is exercised in response to the gracious Offering and Sacrifice of the Great High Priest, Christ Himself.

4. *A Theological Consensus for Practical Reform*

Despite differences of emphasis in the various countries in which the Liturgical Renaissance has been experienced, there is a broad, general theological agreement which has been sufficient to warrant a platform for liturgical reforms.

If one comprehensive category is sought which may be sufficiently inclusive of the many aspects of the Liturgical Movement, it might well be "Social Salvation." It is a reminder that in our time the rediscovery has been made of the Church as the people of God, the saved and saving society. In its worship the Church reaffirms its utter dependence upon the grace of God as it rehearses the mighty acts which have created and re-created the people of God— the Creation, the Restoration after the Fall in the Incarnation, the Passion and Sacrifice, the Resurrection, the Ascension and continual Intercession of Jesus Christ, the bestowal of the Spirit of renewal and integration (the Holy Spirit), and His witnesses (the saints)—and as it looks forward in hope to the Consummation of the Divine purpose in the Second Advent and the Final Judgment of Christ and the gathering in of the nations. As part of the Church militant on earth the people of God rejoices, even amid its trials, with the veteran victors of the Church triumphant. The Body of Christ offers a *symphonic* sacrifice of praise.

From this conception of social salvation which is the being and the end of the Church, several important liturgical corollaries may be drawn. It follows that true Christian worship can never be an individualistic, idiosyncratic search for personal merit or advantage ("O it will be glory for me") but must be the communal action of the entire *Corpus Christi*. Here there should be no passive performance of an empty, if aesthetically pleasing, rite in which mere spectators are dumb while the priest consecrates the sacred elements in a language of great dignity, mystery, and unintelligibility (such as Latin is for the great majority of the faithful), with his back turned to the people of God. Neither should there be a concentration upon one special moment of time (as at the elevation of the Host) to the comparative neglect of the rest of the action, nor should there be private meditation at the Exposition of the

Mass in a monstrance, as if this were the height of devotion; both are excluded because the Eucharist is a communal and continuously significant rite.

The Liturgical Movement in its variously important emphases teaches the social nature of salvation. That is why it is concerned with a vernacular rite[25] (or, in many parishes also with a Dialogue Mass) to encourage common participation and joint understanding. The sense of the general priesthood of the laity (who are the λαος τοῦ θεοῦ) is made more visible when the priest celebrates in the Western or Basilican posture, facing the people from behind the altar—which is placed centrally in the new churches inspired by the Liturgical Movement—and when provision is made for the faithful to take part in the Offertory procession to demonstrate that their own life and work is to be consecrated with the Perfect Offering of Christ Crucified for their salvation and the world's. It cannot be too frequently emphasized that the Liturgical Movement expresses in all its teaching and reforms the demand that the people of God shall take their full part in Divine worship and that a central altar, vernacular translations of the Roman rite, and the closest relationship between priests and the faithful shall express a common status (though differentiated liturgical functions) of the redeemed and renewed of Christ all participating in the Eucharistic action.

The social nature of salvation is also expressed by the Liturgical Movement in its ecumenical thrust. In delving behind post-Tridentine and mediaeval scholastic Eucharistic interpretations, the leaders of the Movement have recovered the Biblical and Patristic roots of theology and thus opened up a conversation between Catholic, Orthodox, and, to some extent, Protestant Christians. There is renewed appreciation for the hitherto divided insights of a fragmented Christendom. The objective and communal piety of the Church Fathers in East and West is again acclaimed for its profundity and relevance. The understanding of the Liturgy as the representation in time of the eternal action of God mysteriously revealed in the Incarnation, and the adoration paid to Christ the King of Glory, are grateful appropriations of the treasures of spirituality of the Eastern Church. The emphases on the efficacy of grace through the mediatorship of Christ, the importance of edification of the faithful in vernacular rites and liturgical preaching, the

25 See C. Korolevskij, *Liturgie en langue vivante; Orient et Occident*, and C. R. A. Cunliffe, ed., *English in the Liturgy; a Symposium.*

growing sense of the priesthood of all believers shown in the liturgical apostolate, and, above all, the return to vigorous Bible study, all have parallels in classical Protestantism. The increasing openness[26] to such diverse Christian traditions is a manifestation of ecumenical zeal of some protagonists of the Liturgical Movement in working for the better visible expression of the *Una Sancta*. Even more remarkable evidence of ecumenical interchange is provided by the recent foundation of religious communities by Protestants at Taizé and Pomeyrol in France, and at Grandchamp in Switzerland, in which a primary concern is for the restoration of liturgical worship and prayer for the unity of Christ's Church. Such ecumenical reciprocity is at least partly attributable to the growing impact of the Liturgical Movement.

In yet another sense, and a very significant one, the Movement has stressed the social nature of salvation by integrating worship and work, *orare* with *laborare*. Not only have many of its churches, expressing the glory of Creation and Incarnation in modern techniques of art and architecture, been placed in the ugly milieu of industrial slums, but their worship has enabled men and women to discern a purpose in their daily labour as co-workers with Christ the carpenter, whose yoke then becomes easy. Particularly in the Offertory have they learned to lay the products of their labours on the altar, that they and their work and their associates may be hallowed. Moreover, the inspiration for social justice has often been stimulated by their worship of God, the beneficent Creator, the gracious Redeemer of the whole human race, and Sanctifier and Judge. They have learned penitence, forgiveness, and charity—those Divine lenitives for the inevitable abrasions caused by industrial relationships—in the Liturgy. The Liturgical Movement has shown that the Divine Action in the Liturgy provokes corporate human action in and after worship. It is, therefore, the nexus between adoration and sacrificial service.

5. *Lutheran, Reformed, and Orthodox Contributions to the Liturgical Movement*

As we have seen, the Roman Catholic contribution to the Liturgical Movement was important. So was the less easily defined—

26 As evidence of such openness on the Roman Catholic side one has only to recall the researches of Herwegen and Casel into the Eastern rites or Louis Bouyer's *The Spirit and Forms of Protestantism*. On the Protestant side the openness to Roman Catholic liturgy is evidenced in the works of Y. Brilioth, Hebert, Koenker, Bénoît, Thurian, Massey Shepherd, Shands, and many others.

because inter-related—contribution to liturgical understanding and practice made by the Lutheran, Reformed, Orthodox, and other Communions associated in the Faith and Order Commission[27] of the Ecumenical Movement, in what became officially established as the World Council of Churches in Amsterdam in 1948.[28] The Faith and Order Conferences at which official representatives of these different Churches met to discuss their common convictions and to explore their differences in the understanding of the nature and function of the Church, the Ministry, the Sacraments and forms of worship, gave an immense stimulus to the Liturgical Movement. This may be recognized readily by consulting the symposia which were issued by the Commission or its subdivisions. Two of the most notable symposia which before Lund stressed the differences (for after Lund in 1955 the emphasis was to be on the Biblical and Patristic unity underlying differences in the hope of overcoming them) were: *The Ministry and the Sacraments* (1937) edited by R. Dunkerley and A. C. Headlam, and *Ways of Worship* (1951).[29] Such conferences and their conclusions indicate the growth of a common concentration on the worship of the Church of considerable moment and value. Since, however, they are joint reports of committees they are inevitably compromises.

They must, therefore, be supplemented by the significant investigations of individual writers of the various non-Roman Communions. Their contributions to the philosophy, psychology, history, and theology of worship have been considerable, and have helped to stress the primacy of worship in the on-going life of the Christian Community.

The names of Rudolf Otto, Friedrich Heiler, Nathan Söderblom, and Yngve Brilioth are themselves an index of the magnitude of the Lutheran contribution. The first three were phenomenologists who explored the distinctive dimensions of religious experience among many religions in different historical contexts, and par-

[27] See the following official reports: H. N. Bate, ed., *Faith and Order*—the Lausanne Conference proceedings; Leonard Hodgson, ed., *The Second World Conference on Faith and Order*—The Edinburgh Conference proceedings; Oliver S. Tomkins, ed., *The Third World Conference on Faith and Order*—The Lund Conference proceedings.

[28] See W. A. Visser t'Hooft, ed., *The First Assembly of the World Council of Churches*—report of the Assembly held in Amsterdam in 1948. Accounts of later Assemblies of the World Council of Churches are: W. A. Visser t'Hooft, ed., *The Evanston Report* and S. M. Cavert, ed., *The New Delhi Report*.

[29] *One Lord, One Baptism* (Faith and Order Paper No. 29, Minneapolis, 1961) contains a Faith and Order Report on "The Meaning of Baptism."

ticularly in the Christian religion. The fourth was a distinguished Church historian.

Time will permit only the sketchiest account of their work, selecting *Das Heilige* (translated as *The Idea of the Holy*) as typical Otto, *Das Gebet* (translated as *Prayer*) as typical Heiler, and *The Living God* as typical Söderblom. It should be noted that Otto and Heiler even produced rather academic liturgical forms as practical fruits of their researches. The concern of all three phenomenologists was to treat the religious experience as *sui generis*, in the tradition of Schleiermacher, and all three were erudite philosophers and historians of religions. While Otto and Heiler were attracted by mysticism, Söderblom was equally concerned with the institutional aspects of religion (as was the case with von Hügel). Their importance for our purpose is that they refused to subsume religion under either philosophy or morals, though recognizing that the experiences of awe and adoration necessarily issue in intellectual statements and moral practice.

The core of religion, however, according to Otto, was itself *felt*, and in the first encounter with the divine (God or gods) it was experienced as a polarity of attraction and repulsion: a *mysterium tremendum et fascinans*. The fact that it was a mystery indicated that it could not be rationally comprehended because the Divine transcendence exceeds human grasp. It attracts because it is love, but it repels because it is Holy love. Such an analysis, combined with Heiler's study of different religious types of prayer and of mysticism, inevitably encouraged an investigation of worship which is the corporate expression of the affectional response to God. Moreover, all rites of Christian worship explore the alternate rhythms of attraction and repulsion, of adoration and thanksgiving, on the one hand, and of confession, on the other. Furthermore, the work of anthropologists was making abundantly clear that all peoples have practised religious community rites and used ceremonial signs, thus again emphasizing the importance of ritual and ceremonial.

Yngve Brilioth's work as a church historian contributed even more directly to the impetus to ecumenical and liturgical renewal. In 1930 there first appeared in the English translation by A. G. Hebert (himself the pioneer Anglican promoter of the Liturgical Movement), Brilioth's *Eucharistic Faith and Practice, Evangelical and Catholic*. In a wide geographical and historical survey, Brilioth showed that any adequate rite for Holy Communion must contain four basic elements (with the ecumenical complication that every Christian Communion must examine itself to see if any of these complementary elements were missing in its celebration of Mass, Holy Communion, or the Lord's Supper). The first element was *Communion*, which makes the Eucharist the sharing of a community meal. The second was *Sacrifice*: the concept that the Church is pleading the eternally efficacious Atonement and Reconciliation accomplished by the death of Christ now the Ever-living Eternal High-Priest, with which is linked the Church's own offering of its members with the Head. The third essential element was the *Eucharist*, the joyous thanksgiving of the Church which finds its chief expression in the Lord's Prayer offered by him who presides at the worship. The fourth and final element was the *Memorial*, chiefly of the Cross as the culmination of the overflowing of the Divine love, but, in addition, a recalling of God's mighty acts before and after this pivotal event in Sacred history. This was a capital work of ecumenical analysis and synthesis and has been influential in Protestant and even Roman Catholic circles.[30]

Among many Reformed scholars who have contributed significantly to the understanding of worship in our time, one of preeminent importance would be Gerhardus Van der Leeuw, a phenomenologist and distinguished historian of religions. His *magnum opus* was translated as *Religion in Essence and Manifestation* (1938), and gave significant place to the importance of rites in religion. A more recently issued posthumous volume, now in an English translation, *Sacred and Profane Beauty* (1963) has important implications for worship. Perhaps his lasting memorial is the foundation of *Studia Liturgica*, "an international and ecumenical quarterly for liturgical research and renewal" which first appeared in 1962. It is significant that Wiebe Vos, its editor and founder, is introduced by the Bishop of Bristol as "a pupil and disciple of the late Professor G. Van der Leeuw [who] has inherited a deep concern for an ecumenical approach to liturgical matters, in the spirit of that great and gifted pioneer."[31] Numerous other Reformed scholars have been concerned with the Biblical

[30] The importance of this analysis can be seen by the fact that it was accepted by Fr. Louis Bouyer, the Oratorian, in *Life and Liturgy*. Subsequent scholarship would, however, add an additional element, the *Eschatological*, by which the Church at the Communion Service lives, in anticipation, in the completed Kingdom of God, at the end of the ages. This is a dimension of the life of pre-Constantinian Christianity much emphasized in the early Fathers and the importance of which Dom Gregory Dix has shown in *The Shape of the Liturgy*.

[31] *Studia Liturgica* (Rotterdam), Vol. I, No. 1, March 1962, p. 1.

basis of worship, its structure, and its historical development; and the relationship of worship to architecture. They have particularly stressed the coordinate importance of Word and Sacrament.[32]

The contribution of the Orthodox churches to the understanding of worship has been far from negligible. Some indication of this has already been given in the way that this understanding fertilized the Maria Laach mystery-theology. The refugee scholars from the Russian Revolution such as Berdyaev, Zernov, and Florovsky, in their peregrinations in France, England, and the United States have given the West a far deeper understanding of Eastern liturgies and spirituality than was possible before. A symptom of this desire for rapprochement in England was the foundation of the Society of St. Sergius and St. Alban, with a membership from the Orthodox and the Anglican Communions. A desire for closer relationship between the Roman Catholic and Orthodox Communions in England led to the foundation of the Society of St. John Chrysostom in 1926 and to the editorship of the *Eastern Churches Quarterly* by Dom Bede Winslow, O.S.B. The purpose of both societies was to encourage the understanding of the doctrines and liturgy of the Eastern Christians.

Three strong emphases of Orthodox theology and spirituality have had important implications for the theology of worship. As against any atomistic individualism, the concept of *Sobornost*— the Christian life as incorporation in Christ and his Community— has been stressed. According to this view, the mystical Coinherence in Christ is supremely manifested by the worshipping community. Furthermore, the therapeutic view that idiosyncrasies and alienations are overcome in the salvificatory community under its Head is another important correlate of this conception. A second important emphasis has been Solovyev's recovery of the Patristic concept of God-Manhood, so that the purpose of the Incarnate Christ is to take up our humanity to God, in a word, to deify humanity, and this proceeds through the sanctification effected in the Liturgy. Finally, the recovery of the eschatological emphasis owes much to the inspiring writings of Nicholas Berdyaev, in which he empha-

---

[32] Among these would be: J-D. Bénoît, author of *Initiation à la Liturgie*; Jean Cadier, author of *La Cène*; Max Thurian, a prolific writer of Taizé, the French Reformed Church Community; W. D. Maxwell, A. A. McArthur, William M'Millan, A. L. Drummond, T. H. Keir, Howard Hageman, P. Carnegie Simpson, André Biéler, and the important work of the distinguished German church historian, Hans Lietzmann, especially his *Messe und Herrenmahl* (Engl. trans., *Mass and Lord's Supper: A Study in the History of Liturgy*, by Dorothy Reeve, with introduction and supplementary essay by R. D. Richardson, appearing in nine fascicules).

sizes that eternal life is a quality of existence that begins here and now and is not postponed to the hereafter. There again, the Liturgy is where Christians become what they are intended to be and share in the powers of the age to come. Apart from these important theological convictions, the Western world has come to recognize the Biblical basis of worship, the intricate symbolism in the mysteries of the Orthodox Eucharist, and to appreciate as never before the stylistic qualities of their icons as pointers to Eternal qualities. Who can estimate the impact of the visual and musical glory of the worship of the Orthodox Churches—particularly those of the Russian and Greek Churches, and their impressive festivals—on Protestant visitors?

6. *The Influence of the Liturgical Movement in England*

Since the rest of this volume is a testimony to the impact of the Liturgical Movement in England in the present century, our immediate concern is merely to provide the briefest sketch of those who were the leaders of liturgical renewal in the Anglican and Free Churches.[33] Members of the Roman Catholic Church in England have not made a contribution to liturgical renewal comparable with that of Roman Catholic scholars in France, Germany, Belgium, or Italy.[34] Their contributions to worship are considered later in Chapter VII.

Anglican interest in the development of the Liturgical Movement was, as might be expected, close and continuing. In the first place, the Church of England is unique among Protestant Communions in having retained substantially unchanged its vernacular revision of the late mediaeval Western Rite from the mid-sixteenth century to the present day. Furthermore, the Oxford Movement of the nineteenth century reaffirmed the primacy of the Liturgy. It has, therefore, never ceased to be a *liturgical* Church and, moreover, it finds its nexus of unity, its spiritual regimen, its tradition and way of life in the Book of Common Prayer. In addition, the first Book of Common Prayer was an attempt to revise worship on the basis of Scripture and the practice of the Early Church (for

[33] A. H. Couratin in "Liturgiology 1939-1960" (*Theology*, Vol. LXIII, No. 485, November 1960, pp. 451-458) begins with the monitory statement: "In no other branch of theology has interest increased in the last twenty-one years as it has in Liturgy."

[34] This is probably because in a predominantly Protestant country any Roman Catholic stress on a vernacular liturgy, on the table aspect of the altar, and on the active cooperation of the laity, would seem like imitating Protestantism. The pioneers of the Liturgical Movement in English Roman Catholicism were Monsignor O'Connor of Bradford and Eric Gill.

these are its twin foundations as the Elizabethan apologists, Jewel and Hooker, ever maintained).

The Church of England has ever had a succession of scholars researching in the area of the early development of liturgies in East and West. The succession has been maintained in the present century, as the names of F. E. Brightman, W. H. Frere, J. H. Srawley, Gregory Dix, and E. C. Ratcliff will indicate. Furthermore, the services of Anglican liturgical scholars have been required in advising the other Provinces of the Anglican Communion when revisions of the Book of Common Prayer began in India, South Africa, Canada, and in the Caribbean.[35] The very set-back suffered by Parliament's refusal to approve the "deposited" Prayer Book, in 1927 and 1928, released the services of liturgists for overseas recommendations where the other provinces were free from the limitations (and advantages) of Erastianism, and even for the exciting ecumenical revisions being prepared for the United Church of South India. Finally, the consecration of several Anglican religious communities to the primacy of worship and spirituality has benefitted the entire Anglican Communion. It is significant that Father Gabriel Hebert and Dom Gregory Dix belonged, respectively, to the Society of the Sacred Mission at Kelham and to the Anglican Benedictine Community at Nashdom.

The earliest Anglican interpreter of the Continental Liturgical Movement was Father Gabriel Hebert. Learned in the Swedish tongue, he considered it part of his mission to introduce important Swedish theological works into English by his translations. He translated Anders Nygren's *Agape and Eros* and Gustaf Aulen's *Christus Victor*, and also Brilioth's important *Eucharistic Faith and Practice, Catholic and Protestant*. Having undergone this ecumenical work of translation, Hebert showed his own mettle as an interpreter of the Continental Liturgical Movement in *Liturgy and Society: The Function of the Church in the Modern World* (1935). As stimulating as it was profound, the book went through five impressions in nine years, and was the subject of keen theological debate far beyond the confines of his own Communion.

The Preface indicated the strength and breadth of Hebert's outlook. It averred that this "is an essay on the Church and her message, particularly as embodied in the actual order of the Church

---

[35] For these Rites see Bernard Wigan, *The Liturgy in English*. A fine study of the South African Rite is P. B. Hinchcliff's *The South African Liturgy*. The more experimental English liturgies will be discussed later in Chapter IX.

and her liturgy, in relation to the problem of belief and a true social life in the confused order of today."[36] Here was no merely antiquarian or aesthetic approach, but a plea to consider that the Church in her worship was living her theology, and renewing her spiritual life. Here was the claim that the Church was expressing the will of God in a redeemed society which already transcended in principle and partly in reality the divisions of race, nationality, and class that tear the outside world asunder, and was also commissioned to demonstrate this integrating life in the world.

In this pioneering volume, Hebert wrote urgently from a threefold conviction. First, he intended to show that the Church, far from being a collection of individuals or a quasi-legal entity, had its own organic life as the mystical Body of Christ, of which He is the Head and all Christians are members.[37] Secondly, he was concerned to demonstrate that a diluted liberal and accommodating theology had made too easy terms with the times. He opposed the *Zeitgeist* with the Holy Spirit in Bible and Liturgy. Positively he wished to claim that only a reassertion of the Gospel, as recorded in the Bible and witnessed to in the historic Creeds, was both critical and consoling enough to meet the desperate need of man in difficult days, together with the adequacies of Divine and supernatural grace as communicated through Christ and His Church. Thirdly, he was attempting to show that "the Church in England is as much a missionary Church as the Church in India or Japan."[38]

Hebert believed that the Liturgical Revival offered a way of presenting Christianity as more than a system of belief (which a purely theological approach would imply), and as more than an individual way of holiness (as piety had often previously regarded spirituality). Christianity could now be presented "as a way of life for the worshipping community"[39] which was a corporate renewal of faith (through the theology proclaimed in Sermon and Sacrament), of commitment and consecration (through the Offertory), and an incentive to serve and transform the fragmented society outside, as the very mission of the Church. Thus the evangelical, liturgical, and sociological are seen to be three correlated aspects of Christian life focussed in the corporate Christian cultus.

This theoretical programme was to find its practical expression in the Parish Communion, and more popularly in the *Parish and People* movement and magazine. It is a tribute to Hebert's per-

[36] *Liturgy and Society*, p. 7.   [37] *Ibid.*, pp. 12-13.
[38] *Ibid.*, p. 14.   [39] *Ibid.*, p. 64.

suasiveness that his advocacy wrought a fundamental change in many Anglican parishes, so that Communion at eight o'clock in the morning and Matins at 10:30 or 11:00 A.M. were less well attended than the Parish Communion at 9:00 or 9:30 A.M., followed by a Parish breakfast.[40]

The master-work in the interpretation of the history and the significance of Liturgy from an Anglican viewpoint was *The Shape of the Liturgy* (1948), the work of Dom Gregory Dix, the witty, erudite, and very original monk of the Anglican Benedictine house at Nashdom. The work of fourteen years of study and fourteen months of writing, it follows the development of the pattern of the liturgy from its two-fold origin as a combination of the Synaxis (or Liturgy of the Spirit), deriving from the Synagogue, and the Eucharist, deriving from the Upper Room, through its Patristic, mediaeval, Reformation and Counter-Reformation, as well as modern developments, as it takes on the characteristic colouring of different peoples and centuries. Essentially he claims it has a "Four Action" shape: the "taking" of bread and wine (the Offertory); the "giving of thanks" or "blessing" (the Eucharistic prayer with its preliminary dialogue of invitation with its parallel in the Preface of the Prayer of Consecration); the "breaking" or Fraction; and the sharing or "Communion." The most important chapters are the ninth ("The Meaning of the Eucharist" with its stress on the Eucharist as Action, as manifestation, and Eschatology and the Eucharist),[41] and the eleventh ("The Sanctification of Time"), where Dom Gregory shows that in the fourth century worship, since Christianity under Constantine became a *religio licita*, is public and not private, less eschatological and more conscious of time. The worldly contempt for Christianity in several countries may indeed cause the twentieth century to rediscover the pre-Constantinian characteristic of its worship as a mystery which is focussed on eternity; but while the social implications of the Liturgy are recognized there need be no withdrawal except for return, and gathering only for scattering.

The contemporary implications of the Eucharist are finely described in the prefatory account of the concepts of man and society implicit in the Eucharist, which speak to modern man's relation to

40 This is described as worked out in different city, suburban, and rural parishes in the volume Hebert edited, *The Parish Communion.*

41 "The Eucharist is nothing else but the eternal gesture of the Son of Man towards His Father as He passes into the Kingdom of God" (*The Shape of the Liturgy,* p. 266).

society and his need to obtain a sufficiency of material things. "There is," says Dom Gregory, "a Christian pattern of a solution which is expressed for us and by us at the Eucharist."[42] The individual's need of material things even for the good life is emphasized and met, yet the needs are met from the resources of the whole society, which are offered by each of its members for all. This analysis culminates in a *tour de force* which must be cited in full:

"Over against the dissatisfied 'Acquisitive Man' and his no less avid successor the dehumanised 'Mass-Man' of our economically focussed societies insecurely organised for time, Christianity sets the type of 'Eucharistic Man'—man giving thanks with the product of his labours upon the gifts of God, and daily rejoicing with his fellows in the worshipping society which is grounded in eternity. This is man to whom it was promised on the night before Calvary that he should henceforth eat and drink at the table of God and be a king. This is not only a more joyful and more humane ideal. It is the divine and only authentic conception of the meaning of all human life and its realization is in the eucharist."[43]

Though particular parts of Dix's reconstruction and interpretation may be criticized,[44] the extraordinary sweep of the perspective and the verve of the writing, and the perceptiveness and contemporary relevance of this invigorating study are undeniable. In consequence the volume was widely studied in many Christian Communions, more especially as it is a summary of liturgical research for the previous half-century.

A scholar of at least equal erudition and greater caution is Professor E. C. Ratcliff. At Oxford where he was University Lecturer in Liturgiology and Fellow of Queen's College, at London where he was Professor of Ecclesiastical History, and at Cambridge where he was Ely Professor and subsequently Regius Professor of Divinity, Dr. Ratcliff's influence has been considerable. His lectures on early Christian liturgies and on the Book of Common Prayer, which are masterpieces of compressed and lucid

---

[42] *Ibid.*, p. xviii.

[43] *Ibid.*, pp. xviii-xix.

[44] Exception has been taken to the following features in the work: an over-emphasis on the Hellenistic contrast between the eternal and the temporal with insufficient recognition of the Biblical conception of time as fulfilment and *dénouement*; a supposed caricature of Reformed doctrines of the Church and of the Lord's Supper as, respectively, atomistic and memorialist (forgetting Calvin's understanding of the Church as the Communion of the elect and the sacraments as *Sigilla Verbi*), and the presumption that, contrary to Jeremias, the context of the Last Supper was a *chaburah*, not a Passover meal.

erudition, his careful tutorials on the liturgical texts, and his super-vision of research students (or examination of their completed dissertations) now holding scholastic posts in different countries,[45] have been impressive. His advice to revisers or makers of liturgies in other lands, and his membership of the Liturgical Commission of the Church of England, are also indications of a quiet but deeply pervasive and continuous influence. His written works are a mere fraction of his hidden resources. They include an admirable chapter on "Christian Worship and Liturgy" in K. E. Kirk's *The Study of Theology* (1939), another in Nuttall and Chadwick's *From Unity to Uniformity, 1662-1962*, on the Savoy Conference preceding the 1661 revision of the Book of Common Prayer, and yet another assessing Cranmer as liturgist, in *Three Commemorative Lectures delivered in Lambeth Palace* (1956). His books include the magisterial *The Booke of Common Prayer of the Churche of England: Its making and revisions. M.D.xlix—M.D.clxi* (1949) and a superb rationale of the English Coronation Rite.[46]

In our own time, largely because the Church is no longer an established or privileged institution in the secular state, liturgics has come to be a study of the Church's self-understanding, intelligible both to the church member and the interested enquirer. To this necessary task of popularization the Anglican Evelyn Underhill, student of mysticism, devoted disciple of Baron Friedrich von Hügel (a Roman Catholic with strong Anglican sympathies), contributed admirably by her interconfessional study, *Worship*, which appeared in 1936 and which has, in paperback, a continuing widespread influence. Other Anglican exemplars of *vulgarization haute* are: Colin Dunlop in *Anglican Public Worship* (1953); J. A. T. Robinson in *Liturgy Coming to Life* (1961) and a controversial chapter in his iconoclastic volume, *Honest to God* (1963); Basil Minchin in his series *Worship in the Body of Christ* (which

[45] Four may be mentioned: A. H. Couratin, now the Archdeacon of Durham, formerly Principal of St. Stephen's House, Oxford, and Ratcliff's successor as University Lecturer in Liturgiology at Oxford; C. W. Dugmore, Professor of Ecclesiastical History in the University of London at King's College; Professor James F. White, of the School of Theology at Southern Methodist University, author of *The Cambridge Movement*, and Professor P. B. Hinchliff of Rhodes University, Grahamstown, South Africa. Other liturgical scholars who would acknowledge his direct influence are Bernard Wigan, A. Elliott Peaston, C. J. Cuming, and the present writer.

[46] Reference should also be made to two important articles by E. C. Ratcliff, "The Sanctus and the Pattern of the Early Anaphora" in *The Journal of Ecclesiastical History*, Vol. I (1950), pp. 29-36; 125-34, which claim that the primitive consecration prayer was a prayer of thanksgiving culminating in the Sanctus and excluding invocation and oblation.

began in 1958); and the work of the Birmingham trio of J. Gordon Davies, Gilbert Cope, and D. A. Tytler, as well as many others.

Father Lionel Thornton's massive and detailed Biblical and theological studies of the nature of the Church have also had a considerable indirect influence on the understanding of the liturgy.[47]

Nor should the careful scholarly researches into liturgy, spirituality, and hymnody by many other Anglican scholars be forgotten. Two outstanding volumes were Bishop Kenneth Kirk's *The Vision of God* (1934) and G. W. O. Addleshaw and F. Etchells, *The Architectural Setting of Anglican Worship* (1950). Important studies of Anglican liturgical revisions were made by R. C. D. Jasper and G. J. Cuming, A. C. Don and G. Donaldson. The chief researchers into the history of psalmody and hymnody in the English language were John Julian and M. Frost. A. M. Allchin, Martin Thornton, and G. J. Stranks studied the history of English spirituality. Moreover, E. Milner-White and A. H. Couratin were admirable composers of litanies and collects. T. S. Garrett wrote illuminating studies of the Worship of the Church of South India.

A significant feature of this century has been the increasing interest of the "Low Church" or Evangelical wing in the history and theology of worship. Its representatives have made notable contributions in this field, among them C. F. D. Moule, C. W. Bowles, A. B. MacDonald, G. F. Bromiley, D. E. Harrison, and F. W. Dillistone. In its cumulative impact the concentration of so many Anglican scholars in the field of worship has been most impressive.

In the Free Churches the signs of an appreciation of the Liturgical Movement are more difficult to discern[48] because they are discovered more easily in the ferment of discussions on worship in the denominational quarterlies and newspapers, or in the denominational revisions of manuals of worship, than in books that drew widespread attention. One book, however, was a notable contribution to the Free Church reappraisal of worship in the light of the long Christian tradition. It might be regarded as a Free

[47] The following of Lionel S. Thornton's books are pertinent: *The Common Life in the Body of Christ*; *The Dominion of Christ*; *Christ and the Church*, as well as his organic and Whiteheadian conception of the nature of Christ's union with the Father, the Universe, and the Church, in *The Incarnate Lord*.

[48] Cf. *A Free Church Book of Common Prayer*, anonymously edited by J. M. Lloyd Thomas, had already appeared in 1929. It is perhaps one of the few significant contributions of the moribund but fascinating "Free Catholic Movement," of which Lloyd Thomas and W. E. Orchard were the leaders. This movement is studied in Chapter x, Section 3.

Church counterpart to the Anglican compilation *Liturgy and Worship*, edited by W. K. Lowther Clarke. Planned by Dr. Nathaniel Micklem, then Principal of Mansfield College, Oxford, it was entitled *Christian Worship, Studies in its History and Meaning* (1936). The foreword claimed that the book, written by members of Mansfield College, was "A Systematic Study of Public Worship," and hoped that "our historical studies may be accepted as a serious contribution to this great subject and that our later chapters in particular, may serve as an interpretation, and in this sense as a vindication, of the common tradition of our Reformed Churches." The first part dealt with Biblical Studies in which H. Wheeler Robinson, T. W. Manson, W. H. Cadman, and C. H. Dodd contributed chapters. The second consisted of historical studies with chapters by J. V. Bartlet, R. S. Franks, James Moffatt, C. J. Cadoux, J. S. Whale, and A. G. Mathews. The third and concluding part contained contemporary studies by E. R. Micklem, Edward Shillito, Kenneth Parry, and the Editor. It was the first time that as notable a group of Free Church Scholars (Congregationalists, Presbyterians, and a Baptist) had surveyed the history of the great Christian tradition of worship and indicated its primary importance for their Communions, which hitherto had been thought by others (and perhaps even by neglect among themselves) to emphasize preaching to the derogation of prayers and sacraments. Apart from its intrinsic importance, the volume was a portent.

It was not long before several authors in the tradition of the English Free Churches were stressing the importance of worship in their books. Apart from further works by the members of the Mansfield College symposium, contributions made by other Congregationalists were: Bernard Lord Manning (notably in *The Hymns of Wesley and Watts* and *Essays on Orthodox Dissent*); John Marsh (both in his historical introduction to *A Book of Public Worship compiled for the use of Congregationalists*[49] and in his important essay in *Ways of Worship*, edited by Edwall, Hayman, and Maxwell in 1951); James Todd in *Prayers and Services for Christian Festivals* (1951), a companion volume to *A Book of Public Worship*; and Raymond Abba in *Principles of Christian Worship with special reference to the Free Churches* (1957). Erik Routley wrote several important books in the area of church music and the theology of hymnody. The Congregationalists may, indeed,

[49] Edited by John Huxtable, John Marsh, Romilly Micklem, and James Todd.

be regarded as pioneers in England of the Free Church renewal of worship in the present day.

Among English Presbyterians the name of Dr. P. Carnegie Simpson, with his concern for a Catholic Evangelicalism, was pre-eminent. But, of course, the splendid influence of the larger sister Communion, the Church of Scotland, should not be forgotten. There was no Communion during this period to which the English Free Churches turned with greater admiration and respect in the area of theology and worship than the Church of Scotland. The 1940 edition of the *Book of Common Order,* with its splendidly comprehensive First order for Holy Communion was taken as the pattern of Reformed worship. The writings of its liturgiologists such as Millar Patrick, William M'Millan, W. D. Maxwell, Allan McArthur, and D. H. Hislop were as widely read in England, and especially among Free Church ministers, as were the works of its distinguished theologians.

The Methodists contributed to the revival of interest in worship with several interesting historical studies. Many of them seemed to imply that they wished the umbilical knot linking them to the Church of England in the eighteenth century had never been severed. As there were "High Church" Genevans among Presbyterians and Congregationalists, so there were several "High Church" Methodists. R. Newton Flew, Principal of Wesley House, Cambridge, produced a most erudite study of *Christian Perfection* through nineteen centuries in East and West. J. E. Rattenbury wrote *Vital Elements in Public Worship* (1936), *The Eucharistic Hymns of John and Charles Wesley* (1948), and *Thoughts on Holy Communion* (1948), and stressed that John Wesley never ceased to be a high churchman in his evaluation of Holy Communion. In two careful works John C. Bowmer wrote of *The Sacrament of the Lord's Supper in Early Methodism* (1951) and brought the story more succinctly up to the present in *The Lord's Supper in Methodism, 1791-1960* (1961). John Bishop wrote of *Methodist Worship in relation to Free Church Worship* (1950). Perhaps the most popular of all exemplars of the Catholicity of this branch of Protestantism was A. E. Whitham. Three volumes of his which were correlated collections of articles with a wide sale were *The Pastures of His Presence, The Culture and Discipline of the Spiritual Life,* and *The Catholic Christ.* They stressed that Catholic and Protestant saints were united in the *imitatio Christi,* and moreover, of the Incarnate Christ. More recently A. Raymond

George has combined a Biblical and a liturgical interest in *Communion with God in the New Testament* (1958), and is co-editor with J. Gordon Davies of a series of volumes entitled *Ecumenical Studies in Worship*. Gordon S. Wakefield's *Puritan Devotion: its place in the development of Christian Piety* (1957) was a choice of topic unusual for Methodist writers and important in seeing the clear parallels between Puritan and Methodist forms of piety. Geoffrey Parrinder made a welcome contribution to comparative religion in *Worship in the World's Religions* (1961).

Although the Baptists share the same type of polity as the Congregationalists and have shared with them the social indignity and the spiritual rigour of espousing orthodox dissent, yet their differences on the issue of believers' baptism as contrasted with paedo-baptism have tended to keep them apart and to the left of the Congregationalists in their frequent iconoclasm in worship. "High Church" Baptists have had a difficult path to tread. All the more creditable for their courage, therefore, have been the contributions of H. Wheeler Robinson, D. Tait Patterson, Neville Clarke, Stephen Winward, and Ernest A. Payne. No more liturgically advanced directory of worship in any of the Free Churches has been prepared than *Orders and Prayers for Church Worship*, by Ernest A. Payne and Stephen F. Winward (1962). While they do not jettison the flexibility of the Free Church tradition, they undergird it with a traditional theological and liturgical structure. Thus they keep the essential elements of the traditional liturgy of the Word and of the Upper Room, while refusing to become liturgical literalists insisting on sacrosanct and inalterable words and phrases. This achievement is all the more striking as this denomination in England has traditionally, since the time of John Smyth, the first Cambridge don to become a "Se-Baptist," insisted on the priority of the untrammelled Holy Spirit in worship and denigrated the priestly in order to exalt the prophetic. That prophet and priest join hands in this manual is the most striking proof of the triple and interrelated impact of the Biblical, Ecumenical, and Liturgical Movements—in crossing denominational boundaries and overcoming even hard and fast and almost un-examinable denominational traditions which were no longer guides but chains.

7. An Appraisal

It is abundantly clear that the England of the twentieth century has manifested a remarkable interconfessional renewal of worship.

However, when full appreciation is given to the Liturgical Movement as one of the major signs, and indeed a major medium, of the "Twentieth Century Reformation," like all mixed Divine-human institutions it is in danger of claiming too much for itself. Two chief dangers must be guarded against: the first is aestheticism and the second is antiquarianism. It might be thought that Guéranger rather than his successors was in greater danger of falling a victim to these tendencies, particularly as his pioneering work was out of touch with parish life, whereas the Liturgical Institutes, Liturgical Weeks, and Liturgical Years of the present time have in mind the needs of secular priests and their flocks as well as of members of the religious communities. Certainly the dangers are minimized by the emphatic concern in the present phase of the Liturgical Movement for the restoration to the laity of their privileges as participants in the Liturgy; but the dangers are not entirely eliminated.

The danger of antiquarianism is great, although the exponents of the Movement have objected to the fossilization and petrifaction of the Tridentine Liturgy and even to the roseate view of the mediaeval rites, because the repristination of the Patristic ideal without a consideration of the changed circumstances of the present century could be a more dangerous, because a more remote, form of antiquarianism. Furthermore, while the Eastern Church in the early centuries of the Christian era undertook much eleemosynary work for "the household of faith," it was not distinguished for any prophetic attempt to remould the conditions of society into a more just and Christian order. In fact, it was ethically nearly static, so that in the Byzantine Church–State the chosen people became almost the frozen people. A contemporary expression of the Liturgy, while being faithful to the Christian tradition, must apply itself creatively to stimulating the twentieth century's paramount concern for establishing social justice and winning the artisan, in a way that was beneath the contempt of the Byzantine theocratic rulers.

The danger of aestheticism is the greater in the Catholic and Orthodox areas of Christendom because they have ever inspired the visual and plastic arts with the sacramental principle deriving from the Incarnation, whereas Protestantism (with some great exceptions such as Dürer and Rembrandt) has been afraid of absolutising the finite in art and of confusing the Creator with the created (idolatry). The tendency of the Catholic and Orthodox branches of the Church to equate the Church with the Kingdom of God (not to see the Church as the main but not exclusive agent of the Kingdom), and their assumption that the Church is the extension of the Incarnation, leads them into the danger of sanctifying the social *status quo*. Protestantism's danger, on the contrary, is that of a too ready response to the new currents of thought in the world and therefore of contemporary relevance at the cost of diluting the historic faith.

Both Catholicism and Orthodoxy, on the one hand, and Protestantism, on the other, need the criticism of the Gospel, with its prophetic role of exposing the easy conformities and blind idolatries of institutionalism and its aesthetic trappings. The faithful proclamation of the Gospel in its fulness will not permit the making of the finite absolute, or the equation of the symbol with the reality it represents and also veils. The Gospel proclaimed in its freedom and fulness is the countervailing correction of the supposedly inherent efficacy of the most perfect and lovely liturgy, the necessary distinguisher between the Creator and the works of men who are only derivatively creators. While the Liturgy should and often does proclaim the Gospel, it can also mute it, particularly in so-called liturgical preaching where the unbound Word of God is thought sometimes to be a subjective element in an objective rite, and collects and sequences, not the written record of God's revelation, are made the basis of liturgical homilies.

It should not be forgotten, moreover, that even when the term "priesthood" is interpreted to include the laity in the Liturgy, the entire *Sacrificium laudis* is only a human response inspired by the Sacrifice of Him who, besides being the Great High Priest, is also a Prophet and King. His prophetic authority and His kingly rule are made known in the preaching of the Word, witnessed to by the interior action of the Holy Spirit. The ultimate restraint, then, on any aestheticism and antiquarianism in the Liturgical Movement, is the giving of a coordinate place to the Word and the Sacrament. In this way the Liturgy of the Word will reinforce the Liturgy of the Upper Room, and ensure that from worship shall spring mission and the more just re-ordering of the life of the world in its political, economic, and social aspects. Today as never before Liturgy is correlated with Life.[50]

[50] Perhaps the most promising feature of the latest phase of the Liturgical Movement is that in the Roman Catholic Church, accelerated by the Second Vatican Council, "a new period in the history of the Roman Liturgy is coming under our eyes, and that *The Epoch of Changelessness or Rubricism* is over." In this judgment Archdeacon Couratin (*Theology*, Vol. LXIII, No. 485, November 1960, p. 452), referred to the Roman decrees of 1947 and 1955 which introduced the simplification of the rubrics of the Breviary and the Missal, and also the new Paschal Vigil for Holy Week.

CHAPTER II

THE REBIRTH OF RELIGIOUS ARCHITECTURE AND ART

THE BUILDING or embellishment of churches was a marginal activity for most leading architects and artists during most of our period. There were good reasons for this. The chief one was that worship and religious instruction were the fringe concerns of the minority of the nation's population after the First World War. Also, a nostalgia for the past blinded many church building-committees to the needs and the technical opportunities of the present. Hence the creative architects and artists learned to expect abuse instead of encouragement. Inevitably, the result was that most churches erected in the first four decades were tame clichés, mere regurgitated Gothic. The more exotic churches were chaotic evocations of a Byzantine or Baroque past that had only existed overseas, or a gallimaufry of all styles. In the two most recent decades, however, there has been a genuine rebirth of religious art and architecture that is functionally contemporary.

But the reluctance of that rebirth mirrors the confusion of our times. Artists of the twentieth century have had their imaginations sometimes liberated, but more often cluttered, with the artifacts of many civilizations, centuries, and countries. Thus, in the confused consciousness of the modern artist, Japanese colour-prints and icons from Constantinople jostle with Aztec monuments and Melanesian masks, Benin bronzes and Bushmen rock-paintings, T'ang horses with swords recovered from sunken Viking ships, Icelandic animal carvings with mediaeval illuminated manuscripts and ivories from France. El Greco's "Agony in the Garden" vies for attention with Picasso's "The Bombing of Guernica," and the gods of Praxiteles with the Christ and the clowns of Rouault.

Confusion was worse confounded by the successive radical changes of style: post-impressionism, symbolism, vorticism, cubism, naturalism, functionalism, and abstractionism followed fast upon one another's heels to dizzy the pursuer. New materials and new techniques (plastics, pre-stressed concrete, and light alloys) have revolutionised and dazzled the architects and artists of today.

In these circumstances it is not surprising that twentieth century religious architecture and art in England is marked successively by timid traditionalism, blundering syncretism, and pragmatic functionalism. The wonder is rather that England can boast that from this chaos have arisen architects and artists of the finest calibre, whose religious work will engage our detailed attention. The architects are Sir Giles Gilbert Scott, Sir Edward Maufe, Sir Basil Spence, Sir Ninian Comper, and Mr. Frank Gibberd. The sculptors are Sir Jacob Epstein, Eric Gill and Henry Moore. The painters are Sir Stanley Spencer, Graham Sutherland, and John Piper.

1. *Cathedrals and their Functions*

The largest, though not always the most impressive, of modern ecclesiastical edifices are cathedrals. In the nineteenth century they tended to be diocesan museums and their Chapters the fussy custodians of an archaic dignity, despite the vigorous protests[1] of a Pusey or a Howson, and, of course, St. Paul's and Westminster Abbey were great preaching centres. They have had a remarkable renaissance in the twentieth century. The pioneer in their revival was Dean Bennett of Chester, who changed Chester Cathedral from a museum for curious visitors into a home for pilgrims. His pioneering example, in domesticating a cathedral, was widely but not quickly followed.

That is the inference to be drawn from the observation of the anonymous editor of *Crockford* in 1943 that cathedrals were admired more highly as architectural monuments than as religious institutions. "As the latter," he added, "we believe them to be of unique and supreme importance to the whole Church, as the principal repositories of the Anglican faith and worship in a dark and cloudy day."[2]

The functions of a modern cathedral were defined in the Report of the Cathedrals Commission of 1961 as follows:

"These are the visible counterparts of the episcopal system. Just as there has to be a Bishop to ordain and confirm, so there must be a Church which outwardly symbolises the organisation of the family life around a Mother-Church. The Cathedral is the natural centre for ordinations and some other episcopal functions. Besides

[1] See E. B. Pusey, *Remarks on the Prospective and Past Benefits of Cathedral Institutions*, and J. S. Howson, ed., *A Week in Chester Cathedral*. Also, Frank Bennett, *The Nature of a Cathedral* and Roger Lloyd, *The Church of England in the Twentieth Century*, Vol. II, Chap. 8.

[2] In a supplement of 1943 reprinted in *Crockford Prefaces: The Editor Looks Back*. In 1929, however, he had remarked on "the resurrection . . . of Cathedral Churches which has taken place within living memory" (*ibid.*, pp. 83-84).

this, the traditional arrangement whereby the worship of the Cathedral is entrusted to a Dean or Provost and Chapter, provides a ministry of depth and variety which is beyond that normally available in a parish church. The worship offered there is often of an artistic quality higher than is normally possible. Its corporate nature, in which Dean and Canons all participate, preserves in miniature what was good in the monastic tradition of a corporate devotion to the *opus Dei*. . . . Far from being outmoded the Cathedral Churches of England have never before served as living centres of worship for such a variety of ordinary Church members."[3]

The modern Anglican cathedral is thus seen primarily as a "living centre of worship" in which the service of Holy Communion is the climax, but in which also the preaching of the Word, the musical settings of chants, anthems and masses, and the art of the architect, the stone-mason, the glazier, the metal-worker, the weaver, the embroiderer, and not least the sculptor, all assist the people of God to join in His praise, to bless Him for His works of nature and of grace. The cathedral is, therefore, both liturgical centre and home of the diocese.

From this twin concept of its functions are derived important ancillary activities and interests: theological study and scholarship; the improvement and extension of Christian education, as of social and industrial evangelism;[4] and the glorification of God through music, drama, and the plastic arts.[5] Its pulsating life as a dynamo of spiritual power can be appreciated by contrasting a present-day cathedral, such as Coventry or Southwark, with the life of a cathedral a century ago as described by two Broad Church Canons, Sydney Smith and Charles Kingsley.[6] Compassion has replaced petrifaction in most cathedrals, if not yet in Royal Abbey Churches.

---

[3] Pp. 21-22.

[4] Sheffield, Manchester and Coventry specialise in the industrial mission of the modern Church, as also Southwark.

[5] Canterbury and Chichester Cathedrals are renowned for their work in presenting religious drama of high quality, while Coventry and Chichester are distinguished patrons of painters, sculptors, and glaziers.

[6] In 1841 Smith gave the following evidence before the Select Committee on National Monuments: "The whole Cathedral [St. Paul's], excepting the choir and those assembled in it for divine service, is converted into a lobby for fashionable loungers; hundreds of persons come together for no other reason than to make an exhibition of this description; so that what with the pacing of feet, the murmur of voices, the gadding to and fro of figures, every Church-like notion is driven from their minds; the whole thing resembles more a promenade in a ball-room than a congregation in the house of God" (cited by C. K. F. Brown, *A History of the English Clergy, 1800-1900*, pp. 64-65). Charles Kingsley wrote of an afternoon service in the same cathedral in Chap. XVII of his Christian-Socialist novel *Yeast*: "The organ droned sadly in its iron cage to a few musical amateurs. Some nursery-maids and foreign sailors stared about within the spiked felon's

2. *Five New Cathedrals*

The predominant impression left by the new Anglican cathedrals of Liverpool and Guildford and the Roman Catholic cathedral of Westminster is one of traditionalism. The first two are neo-Gothic and the third is neo-Byzantine. Coventry (Anglican) Cathedral, though lacking a central altar, is in most other respects modern.

The Roman Catholic Metropolitan Cathedral of Christ the King being erected in Liverpool is modern through and through. This can be seen both in its polygonal shape with circular sanctuary, and in its tent-shaped exterior, surmounted by a crown (a cylindrical tower with pinnacles of alternating crosses and spikes). By means of ingenious planning the external space is internally reflected, so that the most dominant object, the tower, is over the most significant space, the sanctuary. In the designing, the liturgical concern was paramount: to associate the congregation ever more closely with the celebrant of the Mass in order that the ministers at the altar should be clearly in the sight of the people. The central altar, made of a single block of white Carrara marble, is surrounded on three sides by the congregation, and two thousand people can be within sixty feet of the Sanctuary steps.[7] The problem of a circular plan, that it lacks direction, was solved by forming a principal north to south axis through the building by placing an entrance porch at one end and the most important chapel (that of the Blessed Sacrament) at the other. The east and west entrances form a secondary axis. The Chapel of the Blessed Sacrament and the Lady Chapel project from the perimeter of the cathedral to form extensions of the nave. The eight other smaller chapels are individually designed to contrast with and yet support the vast central space. Some will be secluded spaces for meditation and others will open out into the nave.

Frederick Gibberd, the architect, was selected in an open com-

---

dock which shut off the body of the cathedral, and tried in vain to hear what was going on inside the choir. As a wise author—a Protestant, too—has lately said: 'the scanty service rattled in the vast building like a dried kernel too small for its shell.' The place breathed imbecility and unreality and sleepy life in death, while the whole nineteenth century went roaring on its way outside. . . . Coleridge's dictum that a cathedral is petrified religion, may be taken to bear more meanings than one."

[7] Other dimensions of interest are: external diameter, 288 feet; diameter of Sanctuary, 54 feet; width of base or podium, 315 feet; and height of centre line of cathedral to the top of the pinnacles, 324 feet. This information was supplied by Monsignor Thomas Turner of the Metropolitan Cathedral.

petition for which the assessors were the Archbishop of Liverpool (now Archbishop of Westminster), the architect of Coventry Cathedral, and David Stokes. The architect had to face formidable problems. How was the new building to be related to the massive crypt of Lutyens? How could it best express the aims of the modern Liturgical Movement? Could so vast a space be covered with a cathedral enclosing ten chapels and providing a huge car park at a price estimated in 1959 at no more than a million pounds sterling? Could a symbolism be devised which was authentically Christian, yet recognizably modern? It is, of course, too early to judge the ultimate effect from the architect's model; but already it can be seen that here is an intriguingly imaginative, functional, and elegant design. The crowned tent image is a powerful image of the nature of the Church in the twentieth century as the pilgrimage of faith of the people of God nourished with the iron-ration of the Liturgy.

Gibberd (as was the case with Spence at Coventry) is making use of the talents of distinguished modern artists. John Piper and Patrick Reyntiens are to fill the spaces between the ribs in the cylindrical tower with coloured glass. The cone of the lantern will form three bursts of light, symbolizing the Trinity, set against a background of the colour progression of the spectrum. David Atkins has designed the nave floor with white and grey marble as the foundation, with black and dark grey marble for the intricate motifs. The massive ninety-feet high entrance porch (echoing Marcel Breuer's bell-tower shields of the Benedictine Abbey at Collegeville, Minnesota) and the sliding doors will bear designs of William Mitchell, symbolizing respectively the three crosses and crowns and the four evangelists. These are wholly appropriate for a cathedral dedicated to Christ the King.[8]

In each of the traditional neo-Gothic cathedrals the ideal of liturgical primacy and dignity predominates over the concept of a diocesan family home for the people of God. The very monumentality of the design prefers ultimacy to intimacy. Moreover, a distant altar, as in the cases of Westminster Cathedral and the Anglican cathedrals of Liverpool and Coventry, encourages a passive, not a participating type of worship, and this is contrary to the trend of the modern liturgical movement which stresses a

---

[8] Most of the information in the three previous paragraphs is contained in a kind letter from the architect (December 30, 1963), to whom I was recommended by the courtesy of the Most Reverend John C. Heenan, now Archbishop of Westminster. See Fig. 8.

"domestic" rather than a "theatrical" kind of worship, though discouraging any over-familiarity with God.

Liverpool Anglican Cathedral was built from the designs of Sir Giles Gilbert Scott, the grandson of the eminent nineteenth century Gothic revivalist and restorer, and is one of the most splendid edifices of that nostalgic mode. St. James' Mount, with its commanding view of the mouth of the Mersey and the great ocean-going liners, was the site chosen for the building which began to arise in 1904, and which was unfinished at the architect's death in 1960. Other new cathedrals, such as Sheffield or Blackburn, began their life as adaptations of existing parish churches, with the advantage of possessing vigorous congregations. Liverpool Cathedral, on the other hand, forfeited the advantage of a ready-made congregation for the benefit of an elevated site. It seems that the twenty-two-year-old architect planned on too grand a scale for the financial means of the diocese, though he could hardly have foreseen the disruption created by two World Wars.[9]

Its dimensions fully warrant the literal use of the much-abused epithet "colossal." When completed, it will be the second largest cathedral in Christendom, exceeded only by St. Peter's in Rome. Its great eastern arm (liturgically, not geographically considered) is 138 feet long; its spacious central area at the crossing, which runs the entire width of the building, is 200 feet long, is surmounted by a tower 308 feet high, and constitutes a vast preaching space which can accommodate a mighty throng whose vision is uninterrupted by piers. The aisled nave of three huge bays will terminate in a western narthex. The total length of the completed cathedral, excluding buttresses, but including nave, central preaching space, choir and Lady Chapel, will be 560 feet.[10]

The exterior massing suggests a mighty ship or fortress of the Spirit, while the interior is reminiscent of immemorial cliffs against which the tides of time will batter in vain. No fussy or redundant detail distracts the attention. Such decoration as there is is the more impressive for its restraint, and leaves the walls to speak for

[9] George Pace (*Anglican World*, Vol. I, No. 6, 1961) writes that each new stone added to Liverpool costs twelve times what it did when the building was started, and that Guildford Cathedral was expected to cost £250,000 when the designs were approved, had cost £540,000 at the date of the article and another £200,000 was still needed. Sir Edward Maufe had "nursed his scheme through five episcopates" (p. 23). See Fig. 1.

[10] Information about dimensions from G. H. Cook, *The English Cathedrals through the Centuries*, pp. 337-40.

themselves.[11] The piers of the choir are intricately moulded; there is a traceried parapet atop the central space and immediately below the central tower; there is arcading in the vast bays; but all serve to stress the massive simplicity of the warm stone cliffs of the walls and to accent the symmetry. The reredos, carved in the most discriminating detail, the font with its delicate and soaring cover, the subtle organ case, and the aspiring lines of the Lady Chapel with apse, recall the inspiration of French and Spanish, as well as English Gothic masterpieces. The windows of the cathedral are large and simple, with the exception of the east window with its four lights, huge central mullion, and flowing tracery. Of particular interest is the recently installed Scholars' window, commemorating the scholarship of distinguished Anglican divines, among them the chief author of The Book of Common Prayer, Archbishop Cranmer, and the apologists, Hooker and F. D. Maurice.

Liverpool's notable Consecration Service (of 1924) was based on the sermon of St. Bernard, "On the Consecration of a Church," and was the work of Dean Dwelly, who also designed the unusual and appropriate vestments and robes of clergy and choir.[12]

Another great edifice built in the archaeological manner was Westminster Roman Catholic Cathedral, commissioned by Cardinal Vaughan and designed by Bentley in the Byzantine style, it may be assumed, so as not to compete with the former Benedictine Abbey, Westminster Abbey, its near Gothic neighbour. Its vast brick exterior, with striped campanile tower, discloses the shapes of a huge nave and sanctuary covered with four shallow domes. The interior is, however, far more appealing. The vault of the nave rises to 109 feet (exactly four feet higher than Westminster Abbey vault), and the arches of the nave are 90 feet high. The aisles are sacrificed to the demands of several heavy side chapels. The interior columns of *verde antico* from the Thessalian quarries of Larissa lead the eye towards the central dome, under which is glimpsed first the huge pendent crucifix and beyond it the impressive high altar beneath a *baldachino*, with eight columns of onyx bearing a marble canopy. In the sanctuary the jewelled effect is maintained by the columns of red jasper granite and pavonazza, although the

---

[11] George Pace, *ibid.*, p. 27, refers to "the juxtaposition of starkness with small intricate areas of detail."

[12] See E. H. Short, *The House of God*, p. 289. At the invitation of Dr. F. W. Dillistone (then the Dean of Liverpool), the present writer visited the cathedral in 1960 and perused a copy of Dwelly's superb Consecration Order, a model of its kind.

mosaic work on the central cupola seems timid and uninspired compared with the simple mosaics of San Apollinare in Classe or the more splendid and rich mosaics of Ravenna's San Vitale basilica. In justice it should be said, however, that much more decoration remains to be done.[13]

In this cathedral that evokes memories of Roman Baroque and much earlier basilical models, the English simplicity of Eric Gill's Stations of the Cross carved in limestone low relief strikes a welcome, if incongruous note.[14] Particularly impressive are the first station with its contrast of the bound hands of Jesus and Pilate's hands free only to wash them of concern, the fifth depicting Jesus and Veronica, the seventh contrasting the vigour of the stalwart centurion with the bent back and head of Jesus as He falls a second time, and the thirteenth where the sagging body of Christ is taken down from the cross, while Mary, with folded hands and furrowed cheek, watches. The unsentimental but deeply felt clarity of technique, the variety of the postures, the different angles from which the cross is shown, the changing of the border design for each station, and the hieratic stylization of the whole, not forgetting the fine lettering, is cumulatively most impressive. Perhaps the most haunting single work of religious art in the cathedral is a black metal wall plaque in bas relief depicting a plain nun, with an appealing angularity of design that conveys the meaning of sacrifice more impressively than the rest of the basilica. Spiritually and aesthetically considered, she might well have been one of the sisters commemorated in Hopkins' unforgettable "Wreck of the Deutschland."

The second Anglican cathedral to be built in the present century was Guildford in Surrey, the foundation stone of which was laid in 1936, four years after Edward Brantwood Maufe had won the competition for the best design. Among his earlier experiments in church architecture were St. Saviour's, Acton, and St. Thomas the Apostle, Hanwell. It is possible that the able but unheralded architect, Temple Moore, may have influenced the work of both Sir Giles Gilbert Scott and Sir Edward Maufe, for Scott was apprenticed to Bodley and Moore, and the latter's Middlesborough Church of St. Cuthbert and St. Columba was outstanding in its use of brickwork. Other probable influences on Maufe were the new

---

[13] Most of the information in the above paragraph was obtained from E. H. Short, *op.cit.*, p. 280, supplemented by a visit in July 1963. See Fig. 2.

[14] This work was commissioned in 1914, a year after Gill had been received into the Roman Catholic Church, and was completed in 1918.

churches in Scandinavia and Germany built in the twenties and thirties.[15]

The site of the new Cathedral of the Holy Spirit, which was consecrated in 1961, was Stag Hill, which offers a commanding view of the neighborhood. The cathedral is a simple modern derivative of the Gothic tradition, but the interpretation is severe and restrained, and the effect is much lighter than in Liverpool. Maufe is well aware that he can be charged with traditionalism, in which he glories, but he stoutly maintains that this is not antiquarianism. The latter, he asserts, "is merely a modern feeling [for] it is traditional to be modern; that is to say our forebears built as well as they knew how to suit their own conditions and did not attempt to copy the past—in fact they thought they could build better than the past. They were the modernists of their day."[16] Maufe further claims that the modernism of today is seen in the use of modern materials, and in new methods of construction which are able to provide larger spans and to reduce fire hazards. While recognizing the importance of functionalism, Sir Edward insists that the religious mind "seeks the infinite—the in-finite. Churches must not strike the eye with finality; we should not see everything at once— there should be a certain mystery—there should be spaces in which the imagination can play."[17] Furthermore, he warns that there is a danger that the artists employed to embellish a cathedral or church will almost certainly be specialists and individualists, unused to subordinating their personalities to produce a co-ordinated effect. Therefore there is a need for an architect of "sympathetic and benevolent mind" to direct a team of artists and craftsmen and to maintain the organic unity of the whole. These precepts seem to have been practised first at Guildford before the architect recommended them to others.

The cathedral, of cruciform shape, is 365 feet long, with a great central tower which rises, at the crossing, to a height of 175 feet. It has an eastern choir-arm which is enaisled; its extension is the Lady chapel. The unaisled transepts are shallow. The wide nave has seven bays, with narrow aisles at each side which lead to a narthex at the west end with north and south porches. A forecourt or garth is being added on each side of the western end of the cathedral. The garth is also to be enclosed by an arcaded cov-

15 See George Pace's article, "Modern Power Houses of Faith," in *Anglican World*, Vol. I, No. 6 (1961), p. 27. See Fig. 3.
16 Sir Edward Maufe's *Modern Church Architecture*, p. 4.
17 *Ibid.*, p. 6.

ered way leading to the porch. The five-sided apse of the Lady chapel is raised above a crypt chapel.

In comparison with Liverpool Anglican Cathedral, where the worshipper is lost in the vastness, there is a feeling of sublimity and also of intimacy, the latter probably because the congregation is close to the choir, and the shallow transepts at Guildford contrast with the dwarfing central space at Liverpool. In comparison with Coventry, where individual artistic brilliance (as in the green and gold tapestry and in the coruscating Baptistery window) detracts from the organic unity, the art in Guildford is almost mediaeval in its near anonymity. It is significant that the uncoloured and incised glass of John Hutton is equally effective in both Coventry and Guildford, although the treatment of the angels in the former is freer and in the latter tightly formal. In short, if the danger of Coventry is that of becoming a brilliant showcase of modern religious art, and the danger of Liverpool is that it may reduce man to the measure of an ant, the wonder of Guildford is that it combines a sense of God's majesty with a feeling of the intimacy of His people. Of the three modern Anglican cathedrals Guildford seems most conducive to *common prayer*.

3. *Coventry: Deo Adjuvante Resurgo*[18]

There is no question, however, but that Coventry is the most exciting modern English cathedral to visit. This is attested by the constant flood (even deluge) of week-end visitors, both eager pilgrims and informed aesthetes, and perhaps some looking for a *new* curiosity shop. Many problems and their attempted architectural solutions combine to stimulate and hold the interest.

What kind of cathedral is appropriate for a rebuilt mediaeval city which has become the roaring workshop of the modern automobile industry, and from which cars and buses emerge to cross the English Channel and the Atlantic Ocean? How are the gaunt ruins of the old cathedral to be related to the new one? For the former has a superb mediaeval tower and spire still standing, a gutted nave with sightless windows, and a charred cross with the legend "Father, Forgive," as poignant reminders of Coventry's ordeal by fire in the Second World War, and of that greater agony of Christ's. How are the old essential symbols of the Christian faith and life to be repristinated by the architect and his team of out-

[18] The arms of the new Coventry Cathedral bear this Latin legend, which may be translated, "With God's help I rise again."

standingly brilliant artists, such as Epstein, Sutherland, Piper, and Hutton, so as to be relevant without being idiosyncratic? How can one great edifice express the purpose of the Church in the modern world, giving due place to the liturgical and evangelistic, the ecumenical and diocesan tasks? Can the right combination of tradition and experiment be found? Above all, how can these theological affirmations be made in an age in which they are no longer organic to the culture? It is questions such as these which raise the highest expectations of the visitor or pilgrim on the way to Coventry.[19]

The year after the ending of the Second World War the Cathedral Council of Coventry appointed a reconstruction committee charged with the duty of rebuilding the cathedral. They authorized the holding of a competition open to all the architects of Britain and the Commonwealth, which the three assessors appointed by the President of the Royal Institute of British Architects (including Sir Edward Maufe) declared in 1951 to have been won by the designs submitted by Mr. (later Sir) Basil Spence of Edinburgh and London. Their report stated: "In selecting this design we do not only feel that it is the best design submitted, but that it is one which shows that the author has qualities of spirit and imagination of the highest order. He lets the conditions grow under his hand to produce a splendid cathedral, and as the conditions are unusual, the resulting conception is unusual, revealing the author's ability to solve the problem of designing a cathedral in terms of contemporary architecture."[20] The new cathedral was completed in 1962.

Spence has made the ruins of the old cathedral an imposing forecourt to the new, which is at right-angles to it,[21] and has used the module of the old Church of St. Michael in the new. Links between the old and the new are forged by the use of the same pink-grey sandstone colouring in the new walls, as by the slender

[19] See the partly perceptive, partly ingenuous, and wholly enthusiastic book written by Coventry's architect on his cathedral, Sir Basil Spence's *A Phoenix at Coventry*. See also Figs. 4-7.

[20] Citation from the brochure *The New Coventry Cathedral* (Coventry, edn. of September 1959, p. 5), from which, together with Basil Spence, *op.cit.*, much of the ensuing factual information is derived. Several "angry young" architects were displeased that a more modern design (reproduced in Peter Hammond's *Liturgy and Architecture*) offered in the competition was not accepted, although the assessors recommended it in high terms.

[21] As the architect has planned the main axis of the new cathedral in a north-south direction, the high altar is geographically at the north end of the cathedral. All subsequent references to the new Coventry Cathedral will, therefore, be liturgical (not compass) directions.

flèche atop the crossing of the new cathedral, recalling in miniature the mightier thrust of the old spire above its tower, which reaches to 295 feet. A colossal arch leading to the porch joins the new and old cathedrals.

Apart from the internal arrangement of the nave and aisles with the high altar at the liturgical east end, the break with traditional cathedral building is complete.

The vast nave, 270 feet long, has walls planned in zigzag fashion, so that in each angle of the zigzag there is one wall which is a solid cliff of masonry, while the other is a mullioned and transomed window of multi-coloured lights rising from base to roof height. All the dappled light from these windows is directed towards the high altar. Thus the visitor entering the doors of the great western window-wall, on which John Hutton has engraved thirty-five angels and thirty-one saints,[22] is confronted with an uninterrupted vista of the high altar, and beyond and above it the green and gold tapestry of Graham Sutherland's design representing Jesus Christ the Redeemer in the Glory of the Father. The Aubusson tapestry covers the entire east wall of the cathedral and dominates, if it does not overdominate, the altar. The ceiling is a huge wooden prismatic canopy, supported by two columns of seven slender pillars each, which are star-shaped in section and which taper towards the base. The floor of the nave is of black and white marble with insets of maple leaf motifs to commemorate Canadian generosity.

Other powerful centres of focus are the massively solid "Crusader's Tent" which is entered from the north-western corner of the nave and serves as a chapel of Christian unity. Directly opposite it, in the south-western corner, is the resplendent Baptistery window, designed by John Piper. The south-eastern corner of the nave (immediately adjacent to the south wall of the Lady chapel) has a small chapel for private meditation, named the Chapel of Christ in Gethsemane, affording a glimpse, through a striking metal frame of a crown of thorns, of a gilded mosaic mural of an angel holding a bejewelled chalice. Then, passing this on the left hand, the visitor approaches the steps to the cylindrical Chapel of Christ the Servant, the centre for the cathedral's work for industry. On its black marble floor there is a wide disc or plinth of white

[22] Particularly impressive are the designs for the Madonna and Child, the long-necked Abbess Hilda of Whitby, and an angel practically bursting his cheeks in blowing the trumpet of praise, like an ethereal version of Louis Armstrong. See Fig. 19.

marble, on which rests the *mensa* or table-altar which is supported by four conic shapes. The plinth is inscribed in large golden letters, "I am among you as one that serves." Above the table is a long pendent white cross to which is attached a rough metallic sculpture of hammer, spikes, and nails, which simultaneously suggests the crown of thorns, the nail-making guild for which ancient Coventry was famous, and modern industrialism. The plain windows of the chapel, with the light streaming out from within, is inviting by day and reassuring as a lighthouse by night.

The most striking characteristic of the building has yet to be mentioned. This is the approach along the accordion-shaped nave from west to east, so arranged that the worshipper sitting in the congregation or the visitor walking towards the altar will see no window, unless he turns or looks back, for every window is masked by the portion of the wall behind it. The ten large nave windows, which have been designed by Lawrence Lee, with the help of Geoffrey Clarke and Keith New, and executed by a team of artists and students at the Royal College of Art, are planned on the basis of colour-symbolism representative of the successive stages in life. According to the architect's interpretation, a rather subjective one in this case, the first pair of windows composed in tones of green and yellow symbolizes youth; the next pair, in pink and red, represents adolescence and the age of passion; the next pair, multicoloured, represents the age of experience; then the next pair, in deep blue and purple, represents the age of wisdom; and the final pair, nearest to the altar, is of golden hues. In Spence's words: "As in life, the colour of the windows is revealed only as you reach each stage—the past is known, the future is not. Only when the altar is reached the whole range of colour is seen for the first time."[23] The plan of the fenestration is thus extremely ingenious, if somewhat contrived, and it results in the walls and the floor of the nave being stencilled and dappled with a myriad dyes, varying with the position of the sun and the intensity of its rays. In the ultra-modern nave there are, stylistically considered, two incongruously primitive or "Stonehenge" features. One is the roughly scooped-out Bethlehem boulder-basin which serves as a font at the foot of the shimmering Baptistery window, and the other is the series of stone tablets, with New Testament inscriptions, attached to the walls of the nave.

[23] Citation from the brochure, *The New Coventry Cathedral*, p. 18. For fuller description see Basil Spence, *A Phoenix at Coventry*, p. 119.

Coventry is the most truly modern, and therefore the most controversial cathedral to have been completed in England in the twentieth century. It is on the whole a striking rebuttal of the charge that English religious architecture is excessively tame and traditional. In this great centre of worship and art, there are powerful reminders of the ecumenical, sociological, and missionary concerns of the present Church of Christ in a modern industrial milieu. It links the centuries in Coventry with the Christ of the ages and of the contemporary world. It has encouraged the distinctive gifts of England's major artists, with the notable exception of Henry Moore. The daring ambition of the architect, as it has brought considerable achievements, was also almost bound to produce a few failures.

There seem to be four weaknesses. The first is in the structural dichotomy, by which there is no suggestion that the inner structure (of the prismatic ceiling supported by seven slender pairs of concrete piers) is related to the outer (the pair of ten massive wall panels of local masonry). As a distinguished American architectural historian (himself an Episcopalian) has written, in a predominantly appreciative review of the building, "unquestionably there should be a visible separation and statement here."[24]

A liturgical critic could rightly draw attention to the over-attenuation of the nave and to the lack of a more centrally positioned high altar, in keeping with the sense of God's people renewed about His board. Incidentally this possibility was seriously considered by Sir Basil and the former Bishop of Coventry, and rejected.[25] As it is, there is now a "theatrical" altar for spectators rather than sharers in the Eucharist.

A third criticism might justifiably question whether the brilliant individualism of certain artists had been sufficiently subordinated to the unity of the cathedral. To be specific: do not the brilliance and size of Piper's Baptistery window and Sutherland's tapestry dominate the attention and thus distract it from the organic unity of the whole edifice? And, in this way, are not ancillary emphases (respectively the reredos and the sacrament of initiation) through their aesthetic brilliance overshadowing the primary emphases of the altar and the pulpit, where the Eucharist is celebrated and the Word preached? Or, to put the question in another way: have the

[24] G. E. Kidder Smith, *The New Architecture of Europe*, p. 66.
[25] *A Phoenix at Coventry*, pp. 41-44.

needs of the regular worshippers been sacrificed by the desire to dazzle fascinated pilgrims?

A fourth criticism is that while the Chapel of Christ the Servant seems admirably adapted to its purpose of welcoming the outsider by its illuminated invitation, yet the Chapel of Unity, original as its design undoubtedly is, by its forbidding fortress-like exterior seems to frustrate the ecumenical purpose for which it exists. The strong and even menacing treatment seems ill-fitted to represent a crusader's tent, for such surely was essentially transitory and mobile in character. A possible rebuttal of this criticism would be that the various branches of Christ's Church are being pushed together by the pressures of an increasingly secular world and that ecumenism is best symbolized by such a fortress. In that case, it is still relevant to ask why the rest of the cathedral, with its emphasis on triumph and glory, is so optimistic a portrayal of the role of the Church in the world.

In justice to the architect, however, it must be recognized that it is his generosity which has not only allowed but encouraged distinguished individual artists to compete for attention in the cathedral, and that this may well be inevitable in the twentieth century where the artist is not a part of a guild, as his mediaeval counterpart was.[26]

The place of the traditional cathedral reredos and east window is in Coventry filled by the largest tapestry in the world, 74 feet 8 inches high and 38 feet wide. It was designed by Graham Sutherland and woven at Aubusson by the firm of Pinto Frères under the artistic direction of Mme. Marie Cutolli.[27] Sutherland was asked to design a Christ in Glory and to select his colours to fit in with the general decorative scheme. (It may be recalled that the nave windows nearest to the high altar are of a golden colour, and the tapestry is chiefly in pale gold and variegated greens.) The choice of Sutherland was particularly fitting, for besides being the most eminent modern painter in England, he is a devout Roman Catholic deeply moved by the mysteries of the Christian faith, as

[26] The warning of Sir Edward Maufe may be recalled: "One wishes that the best artists and craftsmen of our day were employed quite simply and naturally in our churches and not brought in as specialists." He continues (referring to the painter): "He has for so long thought that the aim is to compete with others in galleries that he is losing his power to relate his work to the rest of the building" (*Modern Church Architecture*, p. 7). The problem in Coventry was not cooperation, but *size*; Piper and Sutherland worked with the architects' colour-scheme.

[27] Coventry Cathedral has an international quality, both in the sources of its support (the West German government paid for the windows of the Chapel of Unity and Canadians for the organ) and in its artistic contributions: French weaving, some Swedish glass and mosaic, and the "Tablets of the Word" inscribed by Ralph Beyer of distinguished German parentage.

his poignant and stark Crucifixion at St. Matthew's (Anglican) Church in Northampton (Fig. 22) had already shown.

The tapestry, in fact, contains two designs, ingeniously separated and yet related. The upper design, occupying approximately four-fifths of the space, is technically described as "The Christ in Glory in the Tetramorph." The last term refers to the four panels, symbolizing the writers of the four gospels, which are laterally related to the central ovoid panel representing the glorified Redeemer. This part (the upper) is clearly visible to the congregation in the nave, since the lower panel is obscured at least in part by the high altar. The lower panel is a most moving representation of the Crucifixion, exhibiting a pallid, emaciated, and tortured Christ, and it becomes the vivid "reredos" of the Lady Chapel "space."[28] Its blacks and greys strike the right sombre notes for the Christ who passed to His glory through the anguish and desolation of the Cross. It also bears, in a smaller tetramorph, the four casual chalk-marked crosses (or kisses) which make it an expression of contemporaneous love and sacrifice, and which were seen in Sutherland's Northampton Crucifixion painting.[29] This crucified Christ also evokes memories of Grünewald's Eisenheim Christus, of the victims of Belsen, Buchenwald and Auschwitz, and of the preoccupation of the painter with thorns and their effects.

The Christ in Glory represents the vision of a serenely young and compassionate Christ, with both hands raised in blessing. Yet the nail-prints are shown in his feet, between which stands typical man, erect, in that position to which he was raised by Christ after the Fall. Christ's simple white, monk-like garment, swells out in egg-like shape, accented by yellow tints on the white from waist to knees, suggesting that He is the re-creative principle.[30] Beside the central ovoid panel are the four excited witnesses to the Gospel of the crucified and exalted Christ, and their iconography owes much to the Book of Revelation 4:6-8.[31] The theme of redemption is

[28] The term "space" is used to designate the fact that no wall divides the 48 feet separating the high altar from the Sutherland tapestry, and that the Lady Chapel is merely the area of the nave behind the high altar terminated by the Crucifixion panel.

[29] For fuller explanation see Sutherland's article, "Thoughts on Painting," in *The Listener* (issue of September 6, 1952, pp. 376-78) and *The Work of Graham Sutherland*, text by Douglas Cooper, p. 34. See Figs. 22 and 23.

[30] Here the iconography is overweighted. Cooper indicates the subtlety of Sutherland's imagination by citing a letter to him in which the painter states: ". . . I wanted to do a large figure like a Buddha or one of the Egyptian figures in the Valley of Kings" (*ibid.*, p. 36). There are also evocations of Byzantine images and a reflection of early Patristic interpretations of the cosmic regenerative role of the Logos. Not all symbols are, however, compossible, without some confusion.

[31] ". . . and round about the throne were four beasts full of eyes before and

repeated in the small chalice below the feet of the Christ, in which the serpent of evil writhes as it drowns. The symmetry of the oval rectangle and the four rectangles containing the evangelical "beasts" is subtly broken by the figure of St. Michael, the patron saint of Coventry Cathedral. Above the mandorla behind the head of Christ is an effulgence of rays, and right at the very top of the tapestry the dove, symbol of the Holy Spirit, is shown in a small blue triangle, evoking the Holy Trinity. The Glory of the Father in which the exalted Christ lives is suggested by the vigorous rays which develop into an intense bar of light, and by the pale yellow or gold lines that define and link the central oval and the side rectangular panels. The background of the tapestry is green, predominantly a cypress shade but merging into the hue of the first shoots of fern in springtime. The space between the Christ and the oval outline is coloured in greys that vary from pale to gunmetal shades. The background of the beasts in their rectangular boxes varies from sepia to lavender blue. There are significant splashes of blood-red in the upper parts of the panels of the four evangelists, which spill over into the green outside them and provide a link with the theme of the underpart of the tapestry. The variegated colours, however, make verbal description more than usually inadequate, and they are equalled only by the complex richness of the symbolism.

The second great work of art in the cathedral is, of course, the immense, glowing, jewelled wonder of John Piper's Baptistery window.[32] The colour is so daring, and so interpenetrating and merging are the variegated hues, that it defies anything but the baldest description in words. Moreover, since the work is entirely abstract, it defies exact interpretation, while at the same time provoking the most intensely subjective reactions from its beholders. It is made up of 198 lights spaced between the carved mullions. It is flanked by crimson hues, but the eye is first caught by the central circle of pure white light, ringed with gold, which

---

behind. And the first beast was like a lion, and the second beast like a calf, and the third beast had a face as a man, and the fourth beast was like a flying eagle. And the four beasts had each of them six wings about him: and they were full of eyes within: and they rest not day and night, saying, Holy, holy, holy, Lord God Almighty, which was, and is, and is to come." We may note that Sutherland's is one of the few interpretations of the "beasts" to give them the multiplicity of eyes which the text demands.

[32] The coincidence may be noted that Sutherland and Piper were both born in 1903 and both educated at Epsom College. Thereafter their paths diverged: Sutherland studying art at Goldsmith's College, London University, and Piper at the Royal College of Art in London. Sutherland is a Roman Catholic and Piper an Anglican.

leads above into bands of a dark sepia that merge into an irregular rectangle of the bewitching butterfly-winged blue, deepening into purple at its edges, in turn leading to the crimson of the border. Here and there the lights are flecked with brilliant gold. Below, the white circle ringed with gold merges into fresh bracken green, then into a light sepia, and reaches the base in aquamarine tints.[33] There, on an octagonal plinth of black marble, rests the hollowed out primaeval bowl (or font) of Baptism.

For some, the central white circle edged with gold will resemble a pool, fitting symbol of the cleansing of Baptism, and the impact of Christ in life's fever will seem as exhilarating and freshening as a plunge in a Cumberland lake. Others, like the poet Traherne, may interpret the white circle as a symbol of the perfection of eternity and the high blue as a celestial symbol, representing the eternal dimension of Christian living. Yet others, again, will link the blue and white as the virginal colours of chastity and perfection. And some, like the architect, will refer to the earthy colours in the lower half of the panel and the celestial or spiritual colours in the upper half. The sheer brilliance of the window is open to almost any Christian or associational interpretation on the part of the delighted viewer.

The third great work of art appears on the outside of the cathedral. It is the late Sir Jacob Epstein's impressive sculpture of St. Michael and the Devil, his last completed religious work. This bronze group weighs four tons. The figure of St. Michael is 19 feet 6 inches high and the span of his wings extends to 23 feet. In the dedication service, Dr. C. K. N. Bardsley, the Bishop of Coventry, said of the representation of the Devil: "Here is no stupid melodramatic portrayal of an unreal entity—here is a man—fallen man —man as we see him today—man who has missed his mark, man who has cast himself out of heaven." The Bishop went on to describe Epstein (Sir Jacob had died in 1959, the year before the unveiling) as "a very great artist, a man much misunderstood, a giant who had to face the jibes and jeers of the little men."[34]

This bronze group is, indeed, a strong image of the struggle between good and evil. It may perhaps be interpreted more specifically as the struggle between the "athlete" of the Spirit, ever

[33] The glass was made by Patrick Reyntiens, who interpreted Piper's design with sympathetic subtlety. See Fig. 7.

[34] The sculpture was unveiled by Lady Kathleen Epstein, the sculptor's widow, who said: "I am so glad that it is on an outside wall, where the people can see it as they go to their work." The citations from the speeches at the unveiling are taken from the report of *The Times* (of London), issue of January 25, 1960.

vigilant to do the Divine bidding, and the heavy, paunchy, grovelling indulgence of the Devil who once was enormously strong. It bears many of the distinctive qualities of Epstein's major religious works. There is the superb moulding of hands and feet, as of the knotty torso muscles of the lithe St. Michael, with his intense and pointed face. There are also the brilliant feathering of the wings; the subtle wind-blown drapery, emphasizing the bone structure of the ascetical spirit; even the spear, with its triangular tip in Michael's right hand, stressing determination, as does his clenched left hand, calling attention to the spire of the old cathedral.

The chief force of the group derives from a major contrast and a minor correlation. The major contrast is between the vertical *up-thrust* of the angel, with pillar-like body and upright spear, all austerity and aspiration and freedom—as the extended arms and feet indicate—with the cramped horizontal *down-drag* of the proud and sensual Devil with heavy thighs and paunch, barrel-chest, arrogant bull-like head, who is writhing though bound, still protesting with jutting chin and the splayed fingers of the hands twisted behind his back. This embodiment of the double paradox of the freedom of God's servant and the enslavement of the libertine is admirable. Though the figures are separate (presumably for eternity, since there is here no hint of ultimate reconciliation),[35] they are linked, not only as victor and vanquished, but by the correspondence of the anklets of St. Michael and the chains cramping the Devil's feet. It is an exceedingly powerful statement of a significant myth. Even so, it is not perhaps in the very top rank of Epstein's religious works, as are the *Madonna and Child* in Cavendish Square, or the *Christ in Majesty* of Llandaff cathedral.

While Coventry Cathedral is not as convincing an expression of the twentieth century understanding of the nature of the mystery of God as the pioneer pilgrimage chapel of Ronchamps by Le Corbusier, yet the edifice (and the works of art of which it is the brilliant casket) represents an exciting and distinguished achievement and a portent for the future of English Church architecture and art. It comes not very far short of fulfilling the final petition of "A Prayer for the New Cathedral" that "in the end there may come forth from Thee the building of Thine own good pleasure, which may speak to us and to generations to come of Thy majesty and

[35] Had the faces of the devil and the angel borne any resemblance at all, it would have been natural to interpret this powerful group as a symbolic statement of man's inner civil war, the dichotomy that rages within. See Fig. 25.

love in Jesus Christ our Lord."[36] The difficulty for modern man is how to find in threatening and torturing times any immediate relevance in Byzantine-style mosaics and glories, or in mythological angels, or, indeed, in the blazing beauty of the Baptistery window, or in the green and gold of the tapestry (except at its sombre base, largely hidden from the congregation).[37] The stark grey and black Sutherland Crucifixion panel, the overpowering whirl of that high dungeon (the Chapel of Unity), the struggle in the Epstein sculpture, and the vast poignancy of the burned-out old cathedral—these alone speak to many of Christ as our contemporary and of the agony of a despised and rejected Church, and of a bewildered populace, and of what may prove to be the redemptive pain of the present in God's own inscrutable designs. Coventry Cathedral is ingenious, exciting, novel: it is only rarely disturbing. Its serenity and optimism may seem to have been too easily purchased in our day. Yet, and this is its chief importance, it marks the beginning of a technical, if not iconographical, break with the recent past, so dominated by Gothic nostalgia and, therefore, by escapism. It is an important, if only partly successful, experiment, but a welcome portent.

4. Other Churches[38]

Even though domination by neo-Gothic continued to enthrall

[36] *The New Coventry Cathedral* (brochure, edn. of November 1958), p. 28.

[37] See, for example, the strictures of A. C. Bridge on the irrelevance of angels in this century in *Images of God*, p. 28, and of Ian Nairn, the architectural correspondent, in *The Daily Telegraph*, issue of May 18, 1962. The latter writes of Coventry Cathedral and its architect: "Sir Basil is an ebullient optimist designing in what is, in religious terms, a deeply pessimistic century. More than that, he had for Coventry a deeply sombre theme—Christ of the Passions and Sorrows, the hard way of persecution and atonement." Nairn does, however, praise the Chapel of Unity (which he thought would make a better Baptistery) as "a haunting, disorienting room worth matching with the great architectural discordances."

[38] In this section of the chapter it would be impractical, as it is unnecessary, to describe the different styles employed by several denominations for their church architecture in the three periods of the present century as divided by two World Wars. Hence a summary sketch is provided which can be supplemented from the following sources: A. L. Drummond, *The Church Architecture of Protestantism*; Martin S. Briggs, *Puritan Architecture and its Future*; Edwin Maufe, *Modern Church Architecture*; Edward D. Mills, *The Modern Church; Sixty Post-war Churches* (Incorporated Church Building Society, London, 1957); John Betjeman, *Collins Guide to English Parish Churches*, with its admirable introductory historical essay and its accounts of judicious restorations; Peter Hammond, *Liturgy and Architecture* and the same author's *Towards a Church Architecture*; and the general architectural history, Henry Russell Hitchcock, *Architecture—Nineteenth and Twentieth Centuries*. The following periodicals should also be consulted: *Architectural Design, Architectural Review, The Journal of the Royal Institute of British Architects*. A comprehensive interdenominational history of British church architecture in the twentieth century is greatly needed.

most church building committees and ecclesiastical architects throughout the period, there were occasional signs of dissatisfaction. Incongruous as they appeared on the English scene, Byzantine revival churches began to challenge the hold of Gothic.[39] Between the First and Second World War architects of the Free Churches in new housing areas devised the "dual-purpose" edifice, intended to serve as a sanctuary on Sunday and as a social and educational centre during the rest of the week. While often architecturally undistinguished, they represented a serious questioning of the basic functions of churches in the twentieth century, and marked a further dissolution of Gothic nostalgia.[40] Even Gothic itself began to be stream-lined, as in the impressive Baptist Church at Sutton, Surrey, locally and wryly christened "Gaumont-Gothic,"[41] probably because of its superficial resemblance to a cinema, in its functionalism and raked floor.

The first English swallow of the long-delayed summer of the Continental Liturgical Movement's impact on architecture made its appearance in Bradford, Yorkshire. Here, it was the influence of the hero of G. K. Chesterton's "Father Brown" stories—Father John O'Connor—which inspired the architect, J. H. L. Langton, to design the Church of the First Martyrs in 1935. It admirably fulfilled O'Connor's intention to create a building which would express the essential character of the liturgy as a corporate action in which celebrant and laity have their own parts to play. The plan was octagonal, the altar central, and the pulpit was placed behind

[39] Two very simple, dignified adaptations of the basilical style in Surrey, produced in the inter-war period, were the Church of the Peace of God (Congregational) in Oxted and the Ewell Congregational Church. Immanuel, Southbourne, in Hampshire, was also a simple and dignified sanctuary of the same denomination. Examples of "stream-lined Gothic" Free Churches included Purley and Leatherhead Congregational Churches, and St. Andrew's Presbyterian Church, Cheam—all in Surrey.

[40] "Dual-purpose" or "Community" churches were also built in considerable numbers by the Free Churches to replace the over 200 sanctuaries destroyed in World War II. This situation "gave the architects an opportunity to build functionally and economically and, with a great housing shortage, it was often necessary to provide significant social amenities in churches." (E. D. Mills *The Modern Church*, pp. 31ff. See also p. 27 for the author's drawings of Mitcham Methodist "Community Church" which he designed.) Some recent Anglican dual-purpose churches are discussed, with reproductions of several varied plans, in Peter Hammond, *Liturgy and Architecture*, pp. 124-28. See also L. A. Brown and L. T. Moore, *The Dual Purpose Church*. N. Cachemaille-Day, Henry Braddock, and D. F. Martin-Smith have been perhaps the most successful architects of Anglican churches of this type.

[41] Sutton Baptist Church was notable for the strong central communion-table behind which was set a semi-circle of seats for minister and deacons, for its impressive pulpit and sounding-board, and for the unfussy lines of its brick and wood.

the altar on the dominant axis of the church. The Baptistery was located on the left of the church as the congregation of the faithful entered the porch.

Eric Gill was entranced by it, writing: "The altar is right in the middle and the result is very remarkable. The sacrifice is offered not only for the people but by and in the midst of them."[42] Indeed, so impressed was Gill that he designed a Roman Catholic church for Gorleston-on-Sea, Norfolk, in 1939 to embody his conception of "Mass for the Masses." The altar was central because, in Gill's words, "it began as a table around which people sat and partook of the consecrated bread and wine. It remains that thing."[43] Unfortunately these examples were not followed for another two decades, although at the time of writing the Roman Catholic church at Wythenshawe, near Manchester, is one of several recent churches admirably adapted for the purposes of the "Dialogue Mass."[44]

The impact of the Continental Liturgical Movement on Anglican architecture was not felt in any significant way until the closing years of the sixth decade of the century. The determination of advanced theologians and architects to press for genuinely contemporary liturgical churches was marked by the foundation of the "New Churches Research Group" in 1958. It aimed at promoting the cooperation of theologians and architects in various regions to provide direction for diocesan architectural projects.[45]

The Chapel of Queen's (Anglican) Theological College, begun in 1938, interrupted by the war, and dedicated in 1947, was the first Anglican attempt—under the inspiration of its Principal, J. O. Cobham—to build a sacred edifice expressive of the new liturgical concerns. The architect, H. W. Hobbis, was persuaded to erect a church like an early Roman basilica, with rectangular nave and an apse. The impact of the liturgical movement is also evident in the

[42] Walter Shewring, ed., *The Letters of Eric Gill*, p. 351. See also G. K. Chesterton, *Autobiography*, pp. 322-28.

[43] See Gill's *Sacred and Secular*, p. 351. I owe this reference to Peter Hammond's authoritative volume, *Liturgy and Architecture*, and am greatly indebted in particular to the account of liturgy and architecture in the Church of England since 1945 (Chap. 7).

[44] Other interesting Roman Catholic churches were built at Pershore in England and in Glenrothes New Town in Scotland, the architects being Gillespie, Kidd, and Coia. See also new churches in Oxford and East Acton.

[45] See Robert Maguire, *Program and Idea* ("New Churches Group Papers," No. 2); also J. Gordon Davies, who has written widely on theology and architecture and is the founder and director of the Institute for Liturgy and Architecture at Birmingham University—see *Studia Liturgica* (Rotterdam), Vol. I, No. 4, December 1962, p. 265. Nor should the educational value of the influential "Parish and People" Movement, founded in 1950, be forgotten, as it helped to create a climate favourable to architectural change in the Anglican Communion.

Chapel of St. Aidan's (Anglican) Theological College in Birkenhead, where there is a central Communion-table.

Neither of these buildings, however, was the harbinger of theological and liturgical re-assessment in the Church of England. D. F. Martin-Smith, architect of John Keble Church at Mill Hill (1936), had given considerable thought to the location of the choir. Some effect of the "Parish Communion" Movement, associated originally with Fr. A. G. Hebert of Kelham, is probably to be seen in the planning of a nave wider than it is long, in which there was a central space for clergy and choir, surrounded on three sides by the congregation. The altar was, indeed, easily visible, but it was placed against the east wall. Another church in the modern mode—apart from its lack of a central altar—was the star-shaped St. Michael and All Angels, Wythenshawe (1937), designed by a notable innovator, N. F. Cachemaille-Day. It used the diagrid system of reinforced concrete construction, based on a grid of squares "tilted" into diamond shapes. The slender columns do not impede the view of the altar, to which the congregation seems close. A third modern church was the work of J. N. (later Sir Ninian) Comper. St. Philip's, Cosham (1938), is both simple and functional. It is significant that Comper, this brilliant exponent of "unity by inclusion," who so admirably designed Baroque chancels and roods for ancient Gothic churches, here planned a functional church as "a building to house an altar." The fourth century plan, so Comper believed, having a short rectangle with a free-standing altar beneath a ciborium, "is most suitable for the needs of the modern parish, with the altar in the midst of the worshippers," as contrasted with the "mediaeval plan to which we in England still adhere" which is unsuitable, "developed as it was for monastic use."[46]

The influence of the European Liturgical Movement on Anglican architecture is most clearly seen in several fairly recent buildings. All of them emphasize a dominating and easily visible altar, which seems to draw the congregation to itself as to a magnet, despite the fact that the ground-plans are of many different shapes. The basilical or Romanesque plan is employed in All Saints, Bawdesley (1955), whose architect was J. Fletcher Watson, and in St. Cuthbert's, Peterloo, County of Durham (1957), which was designed by the firm of Cordingley and McIntyre. In each case a rectangular nave leads to an apsidal sanctuary.

[46] *Of the Atmosphere of a Church*, p. 21. See Fig. 11.

Cachemaille-Day at All Saints, Hanworth, Middlesex (1951-1957), has designed a church that is an eucharistic room, with a subordinated structure for all ancillary purposes. As his plans for Bishop Gorton Church, Allesley Park, Coventry, and for St. Columba, Bannersgate, Birmingham, show, he has a strong preference for a square in his designs. The Church of St. Michael, Hatfield Hyde, Welwyn Garden City (the architects of which were Denis Clarke Hall, Sam Scorer, and Roy Bright), is also based on a square, but the altar is sited on a diagonal line. Perhaps the most brilliant use of a square is that of Robert Maguire's design for St. Paul, Bow Common, London (1958-1960), "a church of outstanding promise."[47] The major entrance for the congregation forces the people to pass the Baptistery (thereby it is an indication that Baptism is the initiation into the Christian life) and a processional path round the central altar is subtly marked by thin and therefore unobtrusive piers on all four sides. A small supplementary rectangle houses a secondary altar.

Octagonal designs were prepared for the Church of the Holy Cross, Doncaster, by its architects, Henry Braddock and D. F. Martin-Smith, as also for the Church of St. Francis, Locklease, Bristol, by the architects T. H. B. Burrough and F. L. Hannam. The former is remarkable for its exterior shape—that of a vast concrete tent.

A circular plan dominates the project for a housing-estate church at Ronkswood, Worcester, devised by Maurice W. Jones. It features a dais that projects into the circle with a dominating altar, a bishop's seat on the east wall, and twin ambos flanking the altar. The first two rows below the dais are reserved for the choir.

Thus the flexibility of pre-stressed concrete is being increasingly exploited in a fecund variety of plans in modern Anglican churches. It is equally clear that some exciting new architects find liberation from the Gothic thrall a spur to build churches expressive of the understanding of the congregation as the Body of Christ, not the passive watchers of an impressive clerical or choral performance.

Several architects belong to this new school concerned to make relevant "theological affirmations" with ideas, materials, and techniques appropriate to our day. Among them are the partners, Robert Potter and Richard Hare, who designed the Church of the Ascension, Crownhill, Plymouth;[48] St. George, Oakdale, Poole,

---

[47] P. Hammond, *Liturgy and Architecture*, p. 111.
[48] Sir Jacob Epstein had prepared a maquette for an impressive sculpture of

Dorset; and St. Mary, Peckham, London. Another lively and imaginative architect is George G. Pace, architect of the brilliant interdenominational Chapel of the Resurrection in University College, Ibadan, Nigeria, of the Church of St. Mary, Newby, Scarborough, Yorkshire, and of many other churches.[49] He collaborated with Sir Jacob Epstein in designing the cylindrical organ-case, supported by the delicate double concrete bridge, in Llandaff Cathedral, on which is suspended the superb *Majestas*. He is also a most perceptive interpreter of the new liturgical architecture in his writings.

Another interesting partnership is that of Alison and Peter Smithson, who submitted an intriguingly functional design for the new Coventry Cathedral which was referred to earlier in this chapter. This highly praised plan aimed "to place the congregation equidistant from the altar rather than progressively away from it," included ancillary chapels open to the central altar instead of separated from it, and designed "a single block of translucent stone at the heart of the cathedral" as its altar. The latter would have been placed in the diagonal forming the east-west axis of the square plan. The entire space would have been covered by a huge concrete vault, forming an "anti-elastic shell," which was to be tilted up at the east and down at the west.[50] Other church architects in the new mode are Robert Macguire, R. E. Enthoven, and the enduringly fertile Cachemaille-Day, Martin-Smith and Bosanquet (Fig. 12).

The architecture of the Free Churches has greatly improved in the course of the century, but it cannot show a comparable inventiveness nor an ability to attract the talents of gifted painters, sculptors, or designers in glass, metals, and tapestry to work with architects. For this there are many reasons. There is, first, the continuing Puritan suspicion of aesthetics as a substitute for ethics. Another reason is a theological overemphasis on the doctrine of the

---

the Ascending Christ and half of the designs for the twelve hexagonal windows of the east wall of this church, when his death in 1959 prevented their completion. The windows, using a different iconography, were completed by Geoffrey Clarke. This information was supplied in a personal communication (dated August 1, 1963) to the writer from the Rev. Eric Turnbull, Vicar of St. Margaret's Church, King's Lynn, formerly the Vicar of the Church of the Ascension, Crownhill, and a great Epstein enthusiast. I am indebted to him for much information about the religious interpretation of Sir Jacob's work. See Fig. 26.

[49] Pace was architect also of the Church of All Saints, Intake, Doncaster, of the Chapel of St. Michael's College, Llandaff, of the Church of SS. Leonard and Jude, Doncaster, and of St. Mark, Sheffield. He favours single eucharistic rooms and free-standing central altars. See his designs for Ibadan Anglican cathedral, Fig. 9; also Figs. 13 and 14.

[50] P. Hammond, *Liturgy and Architecture*, pp. 135-36.

Atonement to the detriment of the doctrines of Creation and Incarnation. Allied to the latter is a high estimate of the audible Word (as proclaimed from the pulpit) and an insufficient appreciation of the visible Word (in the Sacraments of Baptism and Holy Communion). It should, however, be noted that in several of the Free Churches there is, especially among the younger ministers, a recognition that pulpit and holy table must play complementary, not competitive roles.

There is also a curious reason why the Continental Liturgical Movement, while influential on Anglicanism, which proudly claims to be in the Catholic and the Reformed tradition, cannot in the nature of things have more than a superficial impact on the Free Churches: it is that the English Baptists, Presbyterians, Congregationalists, and the non-Wesleyan parts of the Methodist Church have always adopted the Basilican posture at the Communion, and stressed the maximum participation of the people of God in their sacred ordinances. Thus what was being contended for in terms of sharing and intelligibility by the Roman and Anglo-Catholic protagonists of the Liturgical Movement was a privilege never forfeited by the Churches stemming from the Reformation, except possibly on the part of a few wealthy suburban Free Church communities who aped Anglican "spectator-worship" and the use of the remote altar, in the latter years of the nineteenth and the first three decades of the twentieth century.

Other important non-theological factors which also play their part in the slower renaissance of Free Church architecture are matters of taste and of finance. While historically the Unitarians with their elegant eighteenth century meeting-houses, with exquisite chandeliers, silver goblets for the Communion, and finely carved mahogany, and the present-day Quakers with their "scrubbed simplicity" are proof that different interpretations of taste have been given by the well-to-do, nevertheless there is a close correlation between wealth, culture, and architecture. The plain fact is that for a long part of their history the Baptists, Congregationalists, Methodists, and Presbyterians of England sacrificed generously of their pounds and pennies to build their churches, being unestablished Churches, but what might have been spent on elegant sanctuaries or their enrichments was given to the maintenance of the ministry and of missionaries in foreign lands. Such a tradition, with a sound recognition that it is the people who constitute the Church, not a building, and that ethical obedience and charity to

75

the needy are the proofs of their covenant-relationship to God and to the wider Body of Christ, is rightly cherished. But in recent years, in most cases, it has been realized that a functional building need not be a stark one and that while colour-blindness may be an asset for inter-racial relationships, it is not an essential mark of sincerity in worship.

Setting aside the curious imitations and syncretisms of the earlier half of the period, one of the most hopeful recent developments has been a return to the central concept of the meeting-house tradition in Free Church architecture.[51] Two very different examples of this trend are Christ Church and Upton Chapel, Kennington Road, London, S.E. 1 (1959) and Bromley Congregational Church, Kent (1955-1958).

The architect of Christ Church, Peter Darvall, had an unusual assignment: it was to build on a partly ruined corner site (where Westminster Bridge Road and Kennington Road intersect) a five-storeyed office building (Lincoln House) and a modern church, while retaining the corner Gothic Revival tower and spire of the old church, half the cost of which had been contributed by Americans. The exterior amalgam, apart from a stone lattice screen, is a jarring syncretism of styles. The chief interest, however, is the planning of the simple sanctuary, which is to serve a united congregation of Baptists and Congregationalists. A central dais, with three steps, supports a simple Communion-table and benches. It is surrounded on three sides by rising banks of pews, which clearly emphasize the fact that the people are gathered about God's table. The central space between the pews gives an important and slightly subordinate role to the pulpit, some six feet away from the edge of the dais to the west, but what it lacks in siting it gains in elevation over the table. At the eastern end of the central space is a very small font (small comfort to Congregationalists), and behind several pews a Baptistery of ampler dimensions (a great consolation to Baptists), and an eastern window with a central cross towards which there marches an ecumenical procession of "the named and unnamed saints of the Church Universal" (making everyone happy).[52] There is a suspended ceiling of wood and

---

[51] See my *Worship and Theology*, Vol. III, *From Watts and Wesley to Maurice*, Chap. II.

[52] The phrase is taken from a letter from the Rev. P. G. Saunders, the minister, who sent me his own impressions of this worshipful church, along with a descriptive brochure and an excellent photograph. When he wrote (October 17, 1960) his single criticism was that the light from the latticed stone openwork on the

plaster to carry concealed fluorescent lighting and to outline the central area, serving—tell it not in Gath—the purpose of a balda-chino. There will be spotlights on the table and pulpit. Perhaps the chief significance of this church design is that primacy has been given to the Communion-table as the focal point of worship about which the Christian community is gathered, and this in a Baptist-Congregationalist merger.

The Bromley Congregational Church, formed in 1790, had its third sanctuary and adjacent buildings destroyed by enemy action in 1941, and the present modern buildings were erected between 1955 and 1958. The architect, R. R. Wilkins, is a deacon of the Bromley Church, and he and the minister, the Rev. Eric Shave, a gifted musician, cooperated in planning the shape and uses of the new buildings.[53] "Its shape," the latter writes, "is a modifica-tion in modern materials of our forefathers' Meeting Houses of the post-1689 period—domestic architecture, usually rectangular, with pulpit and table on the long side and pews around the other three sides. Norwich Old Meeting was in some senses the pattern and inspiration for our architect." Architect and minister were "as concerned as our forefathers to emphasize the centrality of the Word and Sacraments by placing the Pulpit and Table in the centre, and the Church as a fellowship gathered around. We also stress the 'audibility' of the Word." There is no gallery, despite the fact that in the time of William and Mary, and afterwards, galleries were often added to accommodate the enlarged congre-gations worshipping in the meeting-houses. The historic precedent was rejected because "a gallery manifestly divides a worshipping community into two sections."[54]

Other special characteristics of the sanctuary are worthy of note. The floor is ramped, indicating the importance of visibility as

back of the preacher's head makes it difficult for the congregation to concentrate on the sermon. See Fig. 18.

[53] The Rev. Eric Shave has provided all the information and the citations are from a letter written by him, dated August 22, 1963, giving an account of the theological and practical principles which were expressed in the architecture. Mr. Wilkins, the architect, was good enough to send me a copy of the plans.

[54] It should be noted that Trinity Congregational Church, Poplar, also designed as a modern meeting-house, uses a three-sided gallery, in contrast to Bromley, but attempts by its low elevation above the floor below to give it a close associa-tion with the body of the sanctuary. This church, built to the designs of C. C. Handisyde and D. R. Stark, was part of the "Live Architecture" section of the 1951 Festival of Britain. See Edward Mills, *The Modern Church*, pp. 94-95. An unusual composition, it combines exterior nobility with interior intimacy. Ultimacy and intimacy are also combined in a fresh way in the polygonal plan of Guildford Congregational Church, Surrey (1964). The latter is a most ingenious modern building, mirroring the "Family Church" conception. See Fig. 17.

well as audibility; the organ pipes are concealed in a special chamber behind the pulpit, and the entire wall is set in a simple mahogany screen containing rectangular frames of "sonic twine" to permit the sound to enter. The organ console is at the front of the pews and slightly to the side, sunk 18 inches, and immediately before the four ranks of choir seats. The stepped dais can be cleared of furniture (pulpit included) for festival occasions and for the presentation of religious drama. An entrance vestibule 35 feet long provides a meeting-place of fellowship on all occasions, especially on Sundays, and is a simple solution of the Free Church dilemma—"the need for silence in Church and for fellowship between the worshippers." As a result, "our church is always a quiet place, but the vestibule is always noisy with conversation." The lighting, too, is of a special character. There is "a flat ceiling, a deep-blue in colour, in which 12 perspex circles are placed through which light is thrown at night. Forty 18 inch lancet windows 30 feet high give white 'sky' light but the long walls on the pulpit side are plain and windowless and face south, so sunlight does not enter to dazzle." Finally, it should be noted, that the buildings "form an integrated whole, designed to reflect in theory and in practice the principles of 'Family Church'[55] and to incorporate the total social life of a Christian community with the place of worship in the centre."

In general, then, it may be said that Free Church architecture, when it was not merely syncretistic and chaotic in its borrowings and imitations, followed three styles from 1930 onwards. First, and most common, was "streamlined Gothic" or simplified Gothic, which was particularly popular among prosperous middle-class "dormitory" communities in outer London or on the fringes of the larger provincial cities. It was highly favoured by Presbyterians and Congregationalists and, in some cases, by Baptists, but most of all by the Methodists, who, because of their eighteenth century

[55] The reference is to the book of the Rev. H. A. Hamilton, *The Family Church*, and to the author's inspired leadership in the attempt to cross the abyss between Church and Sunday School (which previously had met in different buildings). He insisted upon including children in the common worship in the sanctuary at the beginning of Sunday morning worship, and throughout the service for the four great "Festivals of Family Church." He also advocated the provision of "Church friends" with whom children might sit, if their own parents were disinterested in their spiritual progress. This renewed familial concept of the Church also provided many other features to offset the usual sectional weeknight activities in churches. It involved a revolution in Christian education for adults as well as children and was exceedingly influential among the Congregational Union of Churches as well as among individual congregations of other Free Churches.

links with the Church of England, are particularly characterized by Anglican nostalgia.

In the second place, "dual purpose" edifices were widely used by all the Free Churches in new housing estates and in extension charges. The Methodist architect, Edward D. Mills, was outstanding in erecting this type of building. Many dual function buildings were put up immediately after the end of World War II on bombed sites because they were, at the time of a national housing shortage, the most economical way of meeting religious and social needs. Moreover, these very needs had always been strongly stressed by the "gathered church" type for which worship, fellowship, and social obligations have been correlated.

The third and most recent type of Free Church sanctuary has been a return to origins, not in any slavishly antiquarian way, but as a rediscovery of their authentic tradition. Churches in the Puritan tradition, whether Congregationalist or Baptist, have rediscovered the significance of the meeting-house. They are again valuing its simplicity and intimacy, with its central Communion-Table and elevated pulpit, about which the congregation gathers to share in the Lord's Supper, and to receive the lively oracles of God. For their part, the Methodists have most recently recovered a forgotten part of their inheritance from John Wesley—that is, his preference for churches of octagonal shape. The most recent striking example of such a rediscovery is Sale Methodist Church in Cheshire.[56]

As the largest Free Church denomination in England, the Methodist Church exceeds the others in the total number of new buildings erected since the Second World War, and they are far too many to allow for particularisation. A vivid impression of their number and variety may be obtained from the plans and photographs in Edward D. Mills' *The Modern Church*, and especially in E. Benson Perkins' *The Methodist Church Builds Again*, as from the published annual reports of the Department of Church Affairs of the Methodist Church.[57] Methodists may justly be proud of the new Punshon Memorial Church in Bournemouth, with its glass, steel, and brick verticality (Fig. 16).

[56] See *The Manchester Guardian*, issue of September 20, 1963, brought to my attention by the Rev. Kenneth W. Wadsworth, minister of the Congregational Church, Heaton Moor.

[57] The address of the Department of Chapel Affairs of the Methodist Church is Central Buildings, Oldham Street, Manchester, which has been operative since the Methodist Union of 1932. For bibliographical information I am much indebted to the Rev. Professor Frank Baker, now at the Duke University Divinity School, Durham, N.C.

The Baptists, according to Dr. Ernest A. Payne, their General Secretary, have produced several sanctuaries of unusual interest since the last war. These include: Westbourne Park, Paddington; Mare Street, Hackney (both of which were destroyed in the blitz and their successors designed by the same architect, Arthur Bailey); Chatswood, Norwood; Amersham Free Church (where the building was almost entirely planned by the Rev. Neville Clark, notable liturgiologist of his denomination); and New George Street, Plymouth.[58]

The English Presbyterians have built sixteen churches between 1949 and 1960. Many of them were extension charges and such buildings are rarely distinctive, being hampered by the compromise decisions of committees and the limitation of funds. So far as reproductions of the exteriors of a small sample of these provide basis for judgment, the Presbyterian Churches at Rugby (1956) and Gosport (1956), as at Wythenshawe (1959), seem less hackneyed in conception than the run-of-the-mill Free Churches.[59] The most notable recent churches of this denomination are to be found in Lockleaze, Bristol, and in Norwich (Fig. 15).

The Congregationalists, too, have added their quota of interesting churches.[60] The three outstanding churches they have built since the end of the Second World War are, as has been previously mentioned, Trinity in Poplar, Bromley, and Guildford. Others worthy of consideration are Lewes (1954), Goring (1961), and Ifield (1963)—all in Sussex—Grindon, Sutherland (1962), and Henningthorpe, Rotherham (partly completed) in Yorkshire. They are notable for shape, the imaginative use of new materials such as multi-coloured bricks, the mixture of external textures (brick and hardwood), for the impressiveness of the fenestration, and for their Congregational emphasis on the community as the family of God.

In the best of the new Free Churches, however, the table-fellowship aspect of the gathered Church, sustained by the Communion-

[58] This information, with the comments slightly abbreviated, was contained in a most helpful letter of Dr. Payne's written from Washington, D.C., on August 17, 1963. See Chap. x for evidence of the ecumenical and liturgical renewal in the life of the English Baptists.

[59] This information was supplied by Miss R. A. Eyles, secretary to the Rev. A. L. Macarthur, General Secretary of the Presbyterian Church of England, in the latter's absence. Her letter was accompanied by a copy of the *Presbyterian Messenger* (No. 1297—114th year, issue of March 1959), which included photographs of the exteriors of some of the new Presbyterian edifices, which are generally simple, unpretentious, and functional. Some are, frankly, dull.

[60] This information I owe largely to the kindness of a friend, the Rev. Kenneth W. Wadsworth, Minister of the Congregational Church, Heaton Moor.

Service and obedient to the Living Word of God and expectant for the inspiration of the Holy Spirit, is fitly expressed by functionalism in architecture and the absence of fussy, distracting decoration or of any striving for social prestige by imitations of styles alien to their past and irrelevant to their present task. Above all, their twin foci are the central Communion-table and dominating Pulpit, illuminated by the clear light of day, unobfuscated by mimic Gothic windows or made mysterious by the ambiguity of distant, half-hidden sideboards which are neither table nor altar. Their clear functionalism, unpretentious use of modern techniques, and clean lines are re-invigorating in their assertion of relevance both of God and to the demands and needs of the twentieth century.

5. Artists in the Service of the Church

The mutual suspicion of creative artists and churchmen which has befogged their relationships over many years will not easily be dissipated. It is, however, significant that several Anglican clergy have been enthusiastic supporters[61] of creative artists and that two Anglican societies have been founded to further cooperation between architects, artists, clergy, and laity.

Reference has already been made to one of them: the "New

---

[61] Readers may well be able to supply their own additions to this list of clergymen who have worked to cross the abyss separating "artists who love God . . . and Christians who love the arts" (see the dedication of A. C. Bridge's *Images of God*). One of the pioneers was Conrad Noel, vicar of Thaxted, and another is the present Dean of Chichester (the Very Rev. Walter Hussey), who vigorously championed and commissioned Henry Moore and Graham Sutherland in their more controversial days, when he was Vicar of St. Matthew's, Northampton. A great Epstein enthusiast is the Rev. Eric Turnbull, formerly Vicar of the Church of the Ascension, Crownhill, Plymouth, who had persuaded Sir Jacob to sculpt a fifteen-feet high "Ascending Christ" (which reached the stage only of an exquisite maquette), a project defeated by the artist's death in 1959. The Rev. Frank J. Glendenning organized an admirable festival of the arts at Hull in 1957 (see his account of it in *The Church and the Arts*). The Rev. A. C. Bridge, formerly a professional artist, has written engagingly and persuasively about the problem of finding suitable *Images of God* for the twentieth century, and Dr. F. W. Dillistone (lately Dean of Liverpool) and Dr. Gilbert Cope have also concerned themselves with the same problem. (See Bibliographical Index for details.) A former architect, the Rev. Peter Hammond, has written with insight and conviction on the new functional, liturgical architecture in *Liturgy and Architecture*, and edited an important volume, *Towards a Church Architecture*. The Rev. Professor J. Gordon Davies, founder and director of the Birmingham University Institute of Liturgy and Architecture, has written widely and eruditely on the theme. The Rev. Gerald Irvine was notably successful in St. Anne's, Soho, in correlating the Christian faith with contemporary culture in its dramatic, poetic, musical and artistic expressions. Nor should the important contribution of such Anglican laymen as Sir John Betjeman, John Piper, and George Pace be forgotten. These names are only a distinguished fraction of those who are urging the correlation of Christianity and Art in the Church of England.

Churches Research Group."[62] The other important organization is the long-established Council for the Care of Churches which came into being shortly after the end of the First World War, primarily to coordinate the work of the advisory committees in each diocese. Today it conceives its task in a three-fold manner. It exists, first, for the prevention of ruthless church restoration; secondly, to encourage good artists and craftsmen in their work for the churches; and, thirdly, as a centre for the dissemination of education. To fulfil these aims it has provided at All Hallows on the Wall, the headquarters of the Council, a library of church art and architecture, a photographic record which will eventually depict all the churches of the nation, and a collection of colour-slides illustrating church architecture and furnishings which may be hired for lectures. Thus, it is proposed to extend the aesthetic education of the Church of England.

Of particular interest is the fact that under the Guild Churches Act of 1952 sixteen of the churches of the City of London were set aside as centres for some specialized branch of the ministry of the Church of England to daily workers in the metropolis. All Hallows on the Wall was designated a Christian Arts Centre. The eighteenth century church, designed by George Dance the Younger, was damaged by air attack in 1941; it was restored and reconsecrated in 1962 to provide in the unfurnished nave a space for lectures and artistic exhibitions and, in the chancel, daily services of worship. Its aesthetic usefulness is enhanced by its unbroken wall surfaces, and the good illumination which comes from the windows set high in the walls. The exhibitions seek to "preserve a balance between the fine arts and the crafts, between the 'modern' and the traditional, and between treasures we have inherited from the past and the work of living artists and architects." In addition, an attempt is made to exhibit good design in everyday products, and to balance the tribute paid to established artists with the encouragement of those who have yet to win renown.

The sponsors declare: "Not all the exhibitions will be concerned with 'religious art' in the narrower sense; for we recognize no hard-and-fast division between the sacred and the secular. Work of sincerity and depth by an artist not specifically committed may be of more value to the Church than a facile and superficial treatment of conventional themes."[63] This Christian Arts Centre is one

[62] See footnote 43 *supra* and the paragraph to which it refers.
[63] The citations are from a pamphlet entitled "All Hallows on the Wall, a

further promising sign that the Church of England is grappling basically with the problem of communicating the Christian faith in a contemporary idiom, without jettisoning the appreciation of a great tradition of Christian iconography. Its establishment, with open-mindedness towards the future, is an act of faith in the potentialities of modern architects, artists, and craftsmen, as well as in the capacities of the office-workers and shop assistants of the immediate neighbourhood to appreciate lively art.

The last consideration, in this chapter, must be an attempt to sketch, although with the baldest brevity, the contribution that some twentieth century painters and sculptors have made in England to the understanding of the Christian faith and life in our time. The ensuing and concluding sections will be restricted to the most considerable artists of established reputation, with only passing mention of artists of promise, and it will also attempt to indicate the variety of media in which they have worked to the glory of God and for the delight and instruction of men.

6. Three Painters: Spencer, Sutherland, and Piper

There are three pre-eminent painters who have essayed Christian themes: Sir Stanley Spencer, Graham Sutherland, and John Piper. Other painters of religious interest are: Roy de Maistre (born 1894), David Jones (born 1895), Ceri Richards (born 1903), and Hans Feibusch (born 1898).[64]

Christian Arts Centre," on sale at the church, which is to be found in the vicinity of Liverpool Street Station. When I visited the Arts Centre in July 1963, an admirably representative exhibition of Epstein's sculptures, drawings, and designs for stained-glass windows was showing. It had been well selected and mounted.

[64] Roy de Maistre is a friend of Francis Bacon (the latter a brilliant technical painter who is haunted by the horror of a dysteleological universe) and his paintings are cubistically shaped in sombre colours. A Roman Catholic "convert" of deep conviction, his moving Pietà (of 1950) is now in the Tate Gallery, and a Crucifixion painting by him is in the City of Leicester Art Gallery. (See Sir John Rothenstein, *Modern English Painters*, Vol. II, pp. 254ff.)

David Jones is another "convert" to Roman Catholicism, and a disciple of the late Eric Gill. His painting consists of profusely detailed essays in symbolism, depicting other rites as anticipations of the Christian Liturgy and Sacrifice. His *Aphrodite in Aulis* and *Vexilla Regis* are practically pictorial equivalents for the allusive dramatic poems of Charles Williams, though each was independent of the other. (See Rothenstein, *ibid.*, Vol. II, pp. 302ff.)

Ceri Richards is a distinguished abstract painter, who painted the striking altarpiece of the Last Supper for the Chapel of St. Edmund Hall, Oxford, in which Christ is depicted as the contemporary guest in what is perhaps a working-man's home. His paintings are in the permanent collections of the Tate, the National Museum of Wales, and the Canadian National Gallery. (See *Who's Who in Art*, Eastbourne, 12th edn., 1962.)

Hans Feibusch is best known as a muralist, and the author of *Mural Painting*. His representations of Biblical scenes are to be found in many Anglican churches, notably in Chichester Cathedral, St. Elizabeth's Eastbourne, St. John's Waterloo

Stanley Spencer (1891-1959) is considered by many to be an eccentric, and by a few to be a genius.[65] Certainly he was a visionary painter who peopled his native village of Cookham on the Thames with the personages of the Old and New Testament whom he thus makes contemporary. His apocalyptic experience in the First World War in Macedonia fused with his meditation on Christian symbols to produce the series of oil paintings in the Oratory of All Souls, Burghclere, in Berkshire. The most remarkable altarpiece vividly illustrates the meaning of the Resurrection by depicting a huge central mound of white crosses which tired soldiers have thrown down in token of their liberation from mortality. Its weakness is the relative insignificance of the figure of Christ, who is presumably the key to the event. His final works were a series of paintings for a Temple of Love, of which the inspiration was human rather than Divine love, *eros* not *agape*, and which pose the problem of whether his inspiration was Christian in the narrower and traditional sense, or pagan. But of the brilliance and originality of his compositions, the immediacy of their impact, the sheer clarity of his brushwork, there is no question.

It appears that his earlier religious paintings derived their inspiration from the simple evangelical faith of his mother, with whom he attended the Methodist Chapel in Cookham at the turn of the century. It was "in chapel-religion he came to know what it felt like to believe in God and in Christ, without intellect perhaps, but intensely and emotionally, and with a form of imagination to which the events of the Bible were literally and indeed rhetorically ever present."[66]

Of this baptism of the imagination, Spencer himself wrote: "I loved the gentle atmosphere that belonged to the poor slummy people who came to the chapel. I remember Mr. Francis the baker, and think of the years I sat and listened to his sermons, which though a little insipid and sanctimonious, were homely. The comfortable atmosphere of this chapel stimulated me as a painter. Being 'Sanctified' was the way they had of expressing themselves. When they fell in that state, they would go and flop down, just

---

Road, London, and in the parish churches of Southwark, Harrow, Battersea, Bermondsey, Wembley and Exeter. His works are, on the whole, formal, conventional, reverent representations in pastel shades of incidents from the Gospels.

[65] See *Stanley Spencer* by Elizabeth Rothenstein and *Stanley Spencer: A Biography* by Maurice Collis.

[66] Elizabeth Rothenstein, *Stanley Spencer*, p. 2a.

under the auditorium.[67] I felt I should not look, but though my eyes were down I was trying to imagine what shape they were on the sacred piece of ground where they were 'coming to the Lord.' It was a patch of hard linoleum, with room for only one man at a time. It seemed to me the taking off place for a Wesleyan heaven. When I heard someone pass by my pew and get down there, I felt it was a sort of apotheosis of the grocer or confectioner or whoever it was." Yet Spencer imagined them in their apotheosis to be more wholly themselves than before. A grocer, he insisted, would be "more intensely a grocer," as he lay, "crumpled, his face turned up in a wonderful ecstasy, expressive of the Wesleyan conception of goodness."[68]

Thus Cookham and a vivid evangelical, Biblicistic Christianity are the twin sources of the inspiration of Spencer's early religious paintings. In 1915 he painted *The Centurion's Servant*, depicting a bedside scene where four simple villagers are praying beside a brass bedstead on which lies a sick child. They are portraits of four Cookham villagers, himself included, linked by anxiety commingled with faith. In 1919 and 1920 he produced twenty paintings, among them the famous *Christ Carrying the Cross*, now in the Tate Gallery, and *The Last Supper*. The former depicts Christ passing by on the way to the Cross, as Spencer would have viewed the event from the front window of "Fernlea," his Cookham home. The villagers look out from their windows, not in compassion so much as in curious surprise, and the Spirit-blown curtains flanking each of the onlookers suggests that they are angelic witnesses to the scene of cosmic significance. The end of the sacred procession is brought up by two workmen with ladders that form a St. Andrew's cross. The iron railings, each segment of which is topped by a blunt diamond-shape, evoke the memory of spears. The onlookers are all typical villagers, only the Christ, almost hidden by the Cross he carries, and the imagined soldiers are phantasms of Spencer's invention. The mood is not tragedy, but calm wonder that Christ is seen in the Cookham of "England's green and pleasant land."

The same sense of naïve wonder dominates *The Last Supper*.

---

[67] Spencer probably refers to the rostrum or platform where he writes "auditorium."

[68] The citations are from Spencer's voluminous journal, excerpted in the biography of Maurice Collis, *Stanley Spencer*, p. 29. The naïve but deeply impressive Biblicism of Spencer's boyhood is remarkably similar to that experienced by the relations of James Baldwin, so movingly recorded in his novel, *Go Tell it on the Mountain*.

The austere brick room may be the interior of one of the Cookham malt-houses, but it might be anywhere. The thirteen figures are not based on the villagers Spencer knew, being entirely invented on the basis of the New Testament narrative. The climactic moment is the recognition by the disciples that the bread broken by the Christ is *His flesh*, and as St. John eagerly examines the divided loaf his mouth is open with stupefaction. The impression is of simple, gentle faith, responding to a miracle.

After the Burghclere murals, already referred to, the next important work was *The Cookham Resurrection* of 1927. The eschatological awe traditionally sensed in this earth-shaking event as envisioned by the New Testament and the great religious masters in painting is entirely lacking in this picture. What Spencer records is happy Cookham villagers, for whom death has been merely an incorruptible interval of interruption, resuming their calm pleasures. The euphoric scene is Cookham churchyard viewed from the vicarage gate. In the upper left corner there is a Thames excursion steamer filled with trippers. In the centre is the porch of the church, with two vague figures, who are supposedly the Father and the Son. Below are tombstones and headstones, from which the unperturbed dead are rising. Almost all of them are well-known figures in the village, some of them Spencer's relations and friends. His patron Henry Slesser, a distinguished lawyer who had become Solicitor-General in 1924, rises in wig and gown from a flowery tomb in the foreground. Hilda Carline, Spencer's wife, is pictured in five different attitudes. Three of them show her smelling a rose, climbing over a stile, and lying on a central ivy-covered tomb. Her brother Richard appears thrice. Spencer himself is shown twice, once as a nude figure in front of the porch, and a second time as a clothed figure lazily viewing the scene from the bottom right-hand corner.[69] The detail is brilliantly captured, and the entire scene resembles an earthly paradise rather than any apocalypse.[70] As in *The Christ Carrying the Cross*, there is only

[69] For identification, see Collis, *ibid.*, pp. 85-87.

[70] On the evidence of Spencer's journal, Collis argues that this picture is largely the transcript of Spencer's joy in marriage to Hilda and the consequent experience of fatherhood. Further, Collis points out that for the Divine figures in the porch Spencer merely reworked a previous sketch he had made of Hilda and himself, adding, "The presiding deities of *The Cookham Resurrection* are Hilda and Stanley" (*ibid.*, p. 87). Spencer later came to think of this as the first of his sexually motivated pictures, believing that in depicting an awakening to love it also depicted an awakening to the divine. The comment of H. D. Ziman, who knew Spencer, seems apt: "Nor was there any decline in the pantheist ardour— an ardour expressed neither in prayer nor in Christian belief—that he developed

a shadowy and unconvincing representation of the important figures of God the Father and Christ, but the sense of human fellowship and bliss is marvellously conveyed.

What Elizabeth Rothenstein has called Spencer's "pictorial garrulity" is even more pronounced in his Port Glasgow *Resurrection* series, which was done between 1947 and 1950. Spencer had come to love the Clydeside ship-builders and their families, and conceived of producing an immense Resurrection on the cemetery on the hill above Port Glasgow peopled with the Scottish townsfolk. Of this series only *The Resurrection: Port Glasgow* and the *Hill of Sion* (1946) were completed on the vast scale he had originally planned. There is here a fantastic and bewildering fecundity of figures, from angels blowing the good news on their trumpets, to embracing lovers, mothers dandling babies on their knees, daughters combing their mothers' hair, to entire groups waving handkerchiefs, or raising their arms in greeting, or dancing with joy. The prodigality of the inventiveness is staggering, but this is even less of a religious picture than the *Cookham Resurrection*. "There is in it," says Elizabeth Rothenstein, "no sense whatever of the unfolding of a tremendous eschatological destiny or of human beings in the immediate presence of their Creator." This Resurrection only shows "a cosmic euphoria in which, with lighter hearts and greater gusto, people continue to do what they have always done, especially to gossip."[71]

Almost all sense of the transcendental has disappeared in the later pictures, in the riotous exuberation of his frolicking fancy. Not surprisingly, only one religious edifice (excepting the Burghclere Oratory, which is more a consecrated art museum than an oratory) contains a Spencer painting. That is Aldenham School Chapel in Hertfordshire, which has a striking *Crucifixion* (Fig. 24) as an altar-piece. It was painted while he was mortally sick and it shrieks with a violence uncharacteristic of the rest of Spencer's painting. All the energy is concentrated on the Bosch-like brutal figures who drive the nails into Christ's hands. It may elicit a sense of pity for the "King of the Jews," with his bearded, crowned, and

---

as a boy. It was heightened some years later into a permanent identification of divine love with physical love, which gave it an embarrassing force." (*Daily Telegraph*, issue of May 18, 1962. I owe this reference to my sister-in-law, Mrs. G. H. A. Cordwent of Milverton, Somerset.) It is significant that Spencer delighted in the painting and poetry of the visionary William Blake who made a similar identification (see Collis, *ibid.*, p. 54).

[71] E. Rothenstein, *Stanley Spencer*, p. 5a.

lolling head, but there is no mystical sense of redemption found through suffering or of devotion to the *salvator mundi*, such as are found in the crucifixions depicted by Rouault or Graham Sutherland. Pictorial possibilities rather than religious sensitivities are exploited and it is most probably, as was so often the case with Spencer, a passionate transcript of his own experience. Gone is the calm of the early religious pictures, but none of the brilliance of invention or the original angularity of viewpoint. It was given to this strange and immensely gifted visionary painter to transform Cookham into a happy, if not always a holy, suburb of heaven.

Graham Sutherland, a convert to Roman Catholicism, is a deeply religious and a far more reflective painter than Sir Stanley Spencer was. Born in 1903, he attended Epsom College, was apprenticed for a time at the railway-engineering workshops of Derby, and studied at Goldsmith's College of the University of London. Successively, he was an etcher, a poster artist, and a designer of fabrics and ceramics. During the Second World War he was an official artist, producing paintings of devastated buildings, which, as Eric Newton expresses it, revealed "a wild crucified poignancy that gives the war a new meaning,"[72] or studies of steel-workers and miners "who have the anxious and tense look of creatures in thrall to some monster."[73] The most moving emblem of the agony of the war was his *Blasted Oak*, which has "roots as vicious as a vulture's claw," and the top of the trunk has an open formation "which at one moment suggests the fearsome beak of a bird about to tear at its prey, and at another a human head screaming in agony."[74]

From 1945 onwards he has given much of his time to religious themes. His best known works, commissioned for churches, are the altar tapestry of *Christ in Glory* at Coventry Cathedral,[75] the *Noli me tangere* altar-piece painting in the Chapel of St. Mary Magdalen in Chichester Cathedral, the *Crucifixion* in St. Matthew's Anglican Church in Northampton, and the mural of the *Crucifixion* at St. Aidan's Roman Catholic Church, Acton East.[76]

---

[72] See *In My View*, p. 117.

[73] *The Work of Graham Sutherland*, p. 26, text by Douglas Cooper.

[74] *Ibid.*, p. 27.

[75] Previously considered in section 3 of this chapter. See Fig. 3.

[76] I am indebted for information on the interpretation of these works to several sources: to Douglas Cooper's monograph; to a sermon by the present Dean of Chichester (the Very Rev. Walter Hussey) subsequently printed; Sutherland's article, "Thoughts on Painting" (*The Listener*, issue September 6, 1952, pp. 376-78), and my own observation of his work—with the single exception of the Chichester altarpiece of which I have a transparency sent by courtesy of the Dean,

Sutherland was invited by the then Canon (now Dean) Walter Hussey in the autumn of 1944 to paint an Agony in the Garden for a wall on the south transept of St. Matthew's Church in Northampton, as a companion piece to the noble sculpture of the Madonna and Child by Henry Moore in the north transept. Because the painter was reluctant to undertake an ecclesiastical commission, he hesitated, and, being profoundly moved by his experience of war, suggested a Crucifixion as an alternative subject. Sutherland has written:

"The Crucifixion idea interested me because it has a duality which has always fascinated me. It is the most tragic of all themes, yet inherent in it is the promise of salvation. It is the symbol of the precarious balanced moment, the hair's breadth between black and white. It is that moment when the sky seems superbly blue—and when one feels it *is* only blue in that superb way because at any moment it could be black—there is the other side of the mirror— and on that point of balance one may fall into great gloom or rise to great happiness."[77]

Sutherland himself meditated for twelve months before attempting the painting into which he put these meditations, fused with his brooding on the Grünewald altar-piece at Eisenheim[78] which he had only seen in an illustration at that time, on the flesh-ripping power of thorns (then and since an absorbing subject for him), and the photographs he had seen of the horrific victims of the concentration camps of Nazi Germany. The result was a disturbingly stark image of the Crucifixion. The spread-eagled arms of the Christ, his open hands with clutching fingers, the heavy, sagging body whose weight tears the shoulders, and the brute strength of the Cross itself—all create a terrible pathos and an "universal monitory symbol."[79] The symbolic crosses chalked on the wall, apparently by an unknown hand, bring the scene into our vicinity and century.

This unforgettable image of Divine suffering has been criticised for two defects: for the weakness of the lower half of the body and

---

who also despatched a copy of the Address given by Sir Eric Maclagan at the unveiling and dedication of the Northampton Crucifixion. The latter declared of Sutherland's painting: ". . . the painting of the Crucifixion is a worthy match for the [Henry Moore] statue of the Virgin and Child with which you have now grown familiar." See Figs. 22 and 23.

[77] *The Listener*, Sept. 6, 1952, pp. 376-78, "Thoughts on Painting."

[78] Sutherland was, of course, familiar with Picasso's drawings after Grünewald, published in *Minotaure*, No. 1 (1933).

[79] D. Cooper, *The Work of Graham Sutherland*, pp. 34ff.

limbs in comparison with the strength of the upper part, and for the often arbitrary suggestions of shadow.[80] Neither defect is repeated in the vast mural of the Crucifixion which Sutherland has painted on the unbroken east wall of the Roman Catholic Church of St. Aidan in East Acton. The Cross itself is shaped like a Greek letter $\tau\alpha\upsilon$ (the upright terminates in a drooping bow form), as contrasted with the Y-shape of the Northampton Crucifixion, from which hangs an emaciated Christ with the head supported by his right arm. The ribs are clearly delineated, and the thin legs form a diamond shape. At the four corners, adjacent to each arm and leg, are small rectangles placed slightly asymmetrically, each bearing a rudely scrawled criss-cross. This entire space, with the exception of the Cross and the pendent body, is painted in crimson, contrasting with the chill grey of the rest of the east wall. The effect is a complete contrast with the all too common sentimental versions of the crucified Christ: for steel and sacrifice (grey and crimson) are the dominant symbolic colours. This mural, too, is an austere symbol of the costliness of sacrifice and, therefore, of the profound love of Christ, the crucified Redeemer.

Sutherland's originality is even more strikingly demonstrated in the *Noli me tangere*, in which the artist interprets the Gospel incident (John 20:17) where the risen Christ forbids the eager Magdalen to touch him as he is about to ascend to the Father. The entire picture is a study of the mystery of how faith penetrates the lowly incognito of Christ. A stubble-faced Jesus, in a white tunic, with a labourer's maize-coloured hat (suggestive of a halo) is ascending an outdoor staircase or fire-escape. His left hand points heavenwards along the line of the rising balustrade, and his right hand is raised in an ambiguous gesture, which seems both to fend off Mary Magdalen and to bless her. The Magdalen appears to be rising from her knees in a frantic attempt to grasp her Saviour, and the carnal green of her pendulous body contrasts with the ascetical strength of Christ's firm limbs and determined step. The whole is a study in vermilion, with a rectangle of turquoise defining the Christ figure; and a flourish of palm leaves symbolizes his victory over death. Other palm trees behind a metal grille, which the topmost branches escape, emphasize again the note of liberation. An oval aperture in the top right of a castellated wall, with a hint of deep azure, is a token of the ultimate destination and glory of the ascending Christ. The iconography is almost entirely Suther-

---

[80] *Ibid.* Compare Figs. 22 and 23.

land's own and shows a profound mind meditating on a deep religious mystery.

The third of the trio of outstanding painters of religious themes is John Piper, born in 1903. He is a brilliant and subtle colourist, as shown (to select a few examples) in the threatening sombreness of his Druidic landscapes of Wales, in the variety of his topographical and architectural studies, and in the splendour of his sunburst of a Baptistery window in Coventry.[81] He is a master of many styles: naturalistic, symbolical, and abstract. In recent years he has specialised in designs for stained-glass windows which have been executed by Patrick Reyntiens. The Emmaus window at Llandaff Cathedral admirably fits a modern style into the three lights of a mediaeval window frame. Here the ethereal figure of Christ is evoked as a *stranger's* presence dimly recognized by the companions of the way. The semi-abstract technique which he has evolved marvellously divines the awe induced by spiritual presences freed from the limitations of the corporeal. In this window translucent colours are mingled with solid blocks of colour; substance merges into shadow; interpenetrating curves and broken lines as well as vertical shafts of light—all are powerful hints of the transcendental temporarily immanent.

Piper's largest interpretative work, not in the abstract mode, is the group of three windows, each of three lights, designed for Oundle School Chapel.[82] The nine lights contain nine Christological interpretations, and in each of them the Christ figure is more than life-size. These are not nine attempts at realism, but nine essays in catching the abstract and eternal qualities of the Son of God. This is achieved by the different shapes of the Christ figure and by stressing the different objects each Christ figure holds in his hands. Thus the left-hand window exhibits Christ as the Way, the Life, and the Truth, respectively with a star, a cross, and a book. The central window exhibits Christ as the Vine, the Bread of Heaven, and the Water of Regeneration, by means, respectively, of a cup, a wafer, and a bowl. In the right-hand window Christ is exhibited as Judge, Teacher, and Shepherd, holding, respectively, a flail, a rod, and a crook. The effect is as delightful as it is theologically instructive.

[81] The Coventry window was considered previously in the third section of this chapter.

[82] Full information on these windows was obtained from a commemorative, illustrative publication, entitled *The John Piper Windows executed for Oundle School Chapel by Patrick Reyntiens dedicated in the presence of her Majesty Queen Elizabeth the Queen Mother, May 26, 1956.*

Reyntiens has devised new methods to enable him to interpret the subtlety of Piper's lines and colours. For example, he has combined the processes of etching and staining glass, with the superimposition of one piece of glass upon another. Thus the effects are magically translucent, and "gold gleams through green and brown; reds and blues shine through one another as well as merging into radiant purples so sombre as to be on the very confines of black."[83]

Piper's importance consists, therefore, partly in his technical variety and virtuosity, and partly in his capacity to suggest the ambivalent fear and fascination of spiritual presences. He is a supreme colourist.

7. Three Sculptors: Gill, Epstein, and Henry Moore

The Renaissance of religious art in England is demonstrated as clearly in sculpture as in painting or stained-glass. Three very different sculptors have made significant contributions in this area. Eric Gill (1882-1940) was a brilliant typographer, a controversial propagandist of Christian art and Christian socialism, and a sculptor in wood and stone. This ardent Roman Catholic "convert" was the head of a large family and a passionate believer in social justice and the enemy of mass-production of *objets d'art*. He was also an amateur architect. Sir Jacob Epstein (1880-1959), a Jew born in New York City, was haunted all his life by the greatest Jewish religious figure in history, Jesus of Nazareth, of whom he made the most moving and monumental images in our time, with the possible exception of Georges Rouault. This fecund sculptor of the great men of his day and also of the unconsidered poor was passionately interested in religious dimensions and their representation, although belonging to a people that had emphasized the transcendence of God by considering all representations

---

[83] *Ibid.* Other brilliant designers in glass are John Hutton (whose work is to be found in Coventry and Guildford Cathedrals) and Geoffrey Clarke, also a sculptor (whose work is to be found in Norwich, Chichester, and Coventry Cathedrals). The latter has designed the 12 hexagonal windows of the east wall in the Church of the Ascension, Crownhill, Plymouth, in a semi-abstract form, symbolizing the twelve "I am" sayings of Christ. Raw aluminum, rather than lead, is used to bind the designs, which harmonise with the grey and blue stones of the wall in which they are set. The colours of the glass are often doubly glazed and carry their own symbolical associations. The Rev. Eric Turnbull offers the following interpretation of the third window ("I am the Resurrection and the Life"): "Coming out of the ruins, the fallen columns of death, is a shaft of blue, symbolising the risen and living Lord of the Church. On the sculpture of this shaft is a mark as though to remind us of the strife through which the battle was won" (from a typescript of the Rev. Eric Turnbull enclosed in a letter of August 1, 1963). Clarke also designed the strong and simple wrought-iron and free-standing candle-stands for the altar of the Chapel of St. Mary Magdalen in Chichester Cathedral.

of Deity as idolatry. Henry Moore (born in 1898), the son of a Yorkshire miner, has by his strange drawings of cocooned sleepers in the Tube shelters of London during the Second World War, and by his towering archetypal sculptures in metal and stone, imposed his brooding imagination on the retina of the modern world.[84] Both Gill and Epstein have left many works in the religious genre, but Moore only one—the hieratic triumph of the Madonna and Child in St. Matthew's Church, Northampton. Each sculptor is compellingly contemporary, concerned with the sociological and psychological problems of our day,[85] yet each is memorably individual and original in attitude and expression.

Gill's importance was that of a pioneer who protested on behalf of the goodness and truth of the Roman Catholic Church that it required a beauty of comparable magnitude, and should not be satisfied with the banality of so many ecclesiastical furnishings, which were merely the mass products of a crudely materialistic and commercial civilization. In him William Morris seemed reborn as a Catholic. "The Church," he argued, "which has the spending of so much money, might at least employ the best artists even if they be few and eccentric."[86] He set himself to destroy two aesthetic fallacies, as he conceived them to be: the view that a work of art is essentially an imitation of an object in Nature, and the claim that the Beautiful necessarily represents the Good. He insisted that verisimilitude to Nature was exalted only by a people who had lost religion, but that genuine art was not imitative, since "in such activity man cooperates with God in creating it."[87] Beauty, he averred, is absolute, and independent of ethical considerations, whereas loveliness is merely relative. "The Madonna of Cimabue is beautiful with an absolute beauty. The Madonna of Sassoferrato is lovely because it portrays that kind of woman who is lovable to those who love that kind of woman, and in that kind of attitude which is charming to those who are charmed by it."[88]

[84] Moore was awarded the International Sculpture Prize at the 2nd Sao Paulo Biennale and at the 24th Venice Biennale, and his works are in the permanent collections of the leading museums of the world. A Henry Moore group adorns the UNESCO headquarters building in Paris and several may be seen in the Metropolitan Museum of Art in New York City, in the Battersea Open-Air Sculpture Park in South London, and in the Tate Gallery.

[85] Gill's membership of Communities (Llanthony and Ditchling) and his concern for "Mass for the Masses," Epstein's *Social Consciousness* group in Fairmount Park in Philadelphia, and Moore's preoccupation with the basic family unit (whether as mother and child or, later, as father, mother and child) give point to this generalization.

[86] *Christianity and Art*, p. 10.

[87] *Ibid.*, p. 30.   [88] *Ibid.*, p. 27.

It will be apparent that, in preferring Cimabue's Madonna to Sassoferrato's, Gill has introduced a theological-ethical criterion into what purports to be a purely aesthetic judgment. His writings are full of stimulating judgments, frequently perceptive and occasionally wrong-headed. Certainly his whole-hearted devotion to religion was like horse-blinkers: it gave him direction but made him tread too narrow a path.[89]

Eric Gill's woodcuts and carvings almost always reflected the Christian doctrine of creation, the belief that "the natural world is God's present to Himself."[90] It was entirely characteristic of him to write of the Stations of the Cross that he had carved for Westminster Roman Catholic Cathedral: "But I was really the boy for the job, because I not only had the proper Christian enthusiasm, but I had sufficient, if only just sufficient, technical knowledge combined with a complete and genuine ignorance of art-school anatomy and traditional academic style." His patrons, so he believed, "thought I was carving in the Byzantine style on purpose. Certainly I was carving in what might be called an archaic manner; but I wasn't doing it on purpose, but only because I couldn't do it in any other way."[91] In fact, here was a recapturing of a simpler stylized and hieratic Byzantine mode which stressed the dignity of the Son of God and tried to snare the permanent in the passing moment. The lines are clean and streamlined.

One of Gill's most moving major works is the *Crucifixion* of 1910, a stone bas-relief of 37 inches by 31 inches, now in the Tate Gallery. Absolutely naked, this flattened and blood-drained Christ, with the long oval face, domed head and high-arched eyebrows, and vast eyelids closed in death, is most eloquent in his appealing silence. The raised Greek and the incised Latin inscriptions are also masterly. Had Gill lived to see the renascence of Christian art in England, of which he was the forerunner, he might have felt that his writing and carving were worth all the labour, misunderstanding, and criticism that they cost him.

The lot of the creative and controversial artist is hard, and the misprision[92] which Jacob Epstein faced in his early years is a

---

[89] See Sir John Rothenstein, *Modern English Painters*, Vol. II, pp. 299-300, where he states that Gill's religion "led him into some contradictions, absurdities, and even uncharities."

[90] Section II: "Creation—After God," p. 19 of *Christianity and Art*.

[91] *Autobiography*, pp. 200ff.

[92] The information on the religious sculptures of Sir Jacob Epstein I owe chiefly to three informative and gracious interviews with his widow, Lady Kathleen Epstein, in late June and July of 1963, and to the following printed sources:

left-handed tribute to his vitality, prodigality of output, and originality of concept and technique.

Manhattan's teeming East Side stimulated his curiosity about human beings, for there the Irish, the Jews, the Negroes, and the Chinese lived in close juxtaposition. An orthodox Jewish upbringing left him with little interest in ritual and ceremonial, but the imagery of the Old Testament had undoubtedly left its mark upon him, since he returned to it in his drawings illustrating Old Testament incidents and in the alabaster sculptures of Adam and of Jacob wrestling with the angel. It also provided his abiding interest in ethical and social attitudes and opened the way for the appreciation of the foundational figures of the New Covenant, Jesus and Mary of Nazareth. In Paris he met Brancusi and Modigliani, as a result of a commission he received to carve a tomb for the remains of Oscar Wilde. Moving to London, where he made his permanent home, he was for a time greatly influenced by T. E. Hulme, philosopher and art critic, in the direction of abstractionism, and he had a brief "vorticist" phase, of which the *Rock Drill* (1913), which welds man and drill into one romanticized machine, is the token. This abstract impersonalism did not hold him long in its thrall, but some of the residue of deliberate distortion remained in the larger stone carvings and gave his works an important accent and a thrusting emphasis.

The religious works followed one another in rapid succession and with astonishing variety. *The Risen Christ*, begun in 1917, was completed in 1919. In 1926 that daring but tender evocation of the Virgin's humility and trust, *The Visitation*, was completed, and is now in the Tate Gallery. In 1927, using an Indian woman and her small son as models, Epstein completed his first group of *The Madonna and Child*, which is now in Riverside Church, New York City. Between 1929 and 1931 he made a series of drawings of Old Testament incidents and sculpted a *Genesis*, a primordial image of age-long travail. Because it was the antithesis of the sentimental, it brought upon him the revilings of the ignorant and a notoriety that was hardly exceeded by the immoral Rector of Stiffkey, for both *Genesis* and the Rector were exhibited on the

---

Epstein: An Autobiography; Geoffrey Ireland, *Epstein: A Camera Study of the Sculptor at Work*, containing a valuable introduction by Laurie Lee the poet. Lady Epstein has assisted in the preparation of definitive studies, *Epstein: Drawings* and of *Jacob Epstein: Sculptor*, both edited by Richard Buckle. I also found Sir John Rothenstein's introduction to *Epstein: Arts Council Memorial Exhibition* quite invaluable.

sands of Blackpool beach for the titillation of the gaping holiday-makers. In 1935 the Romanesque-style carving of *Behold the Man* was exhibited; this dolorous thorn-crowned Christ, flattened by pain, was a powerful image of suffering, the appearance of which coincided with Hitler's pogrom against the Jews.[93] In 1937 the *Consummatum Est* was completed, and in 1939 the powerful, up-straining *Adam*. In 1941 the dynamic struggle of *Jacob with the Angel* was finished and in 1945 *Lucifer*, that proudly sensual angel.

In 1949 *Lazarus* in his cerements, reluctantly coming back to life, and seeming to topple over, was completed, and is now to be found in the ante-chapel of New College, Oxford. Here it is superbly situated, with its heavy feet towards the west door and its head looking towards the reredos with the multiple images of the saints in the beatitude which Lazarus has left. In 1951 one of the supreme works, the Cavendish Square *Madonna and Child*, commissioned by the Convent of the Holy Child Jesus, was begun; it was unveiled in 1952. In 1953 *Social Consciousness* was completed in clay, and the commission to undertake the Llandaff Cathedral *Majestas* (Christ in Glory) was given. The latter was unveiled in 1957 and is another of Epstein's major works. In 1955 he was commissioned to sculpt the *Smuts Memorial* in Parliament Square and also the *St. Michael and the Devil* for Coventry Cathedral; the former was unveiled in 1956 and the latter was completed a year later. In 1957 the *William Blake* memorial bust was unveiled in Westminster Abbey, and is a fitting tribute from one visionary to another.

A severe thrombosis interrupted several commissions in 1958, and thus Epstein's single attempt to depict *The Ascending Christ* was frustrated, leaving only an exquisite maquette as a hint of a great statue that might have been, ethereal in its face upturned to the Father, its elongated limbs and thin up-pointing hands, and with a rotating action hinted by the wind-blown gown.[94] In 1959 portraits of Dr. Geoffrey Fisher, Archbishop of Canterbury, and of Sir Basil Spence were completed, as well as the two last child portraits (in which Sir Jacob also excelled). The Bowater House Group plaster cast was finished on the morning of August 19,

[93] Lady Epstein told the writer that Sir Jacob intended this as an image of "suffering that never ends." This *Ecce Homo* is now in the possession of Canon C. B. Mortlock. Epstein himself wrote of it: "I wished to make an *Ecce Homo*, a symbol of man, bound, crowned with thorns, and facing with a relentless and overmastering gaze of pity and prescience an unhappy world" (*Autobiography*, p. 144).

[94] In the author's possession. See Fig. 26.

1959, and the casting instructions were given to the bronze moulder. The same night that great sculptor whose large studio had given an aesthetic extension of life to hundreds of famous and little known people and who had revitalised our understanding of the Judaeo-Christian saga, lay dead.

Amid God's plenty space can only be found for the briefest consideration of three religious masterpieces.[95] *The Visitation* (1926) is an arrestingly tender but daring treatment of the Virgin in bronze, which is 65 inches high. The head, with frank and open eyes and slightly parted mouth, is inclined forwards and the two long plaits of hair emphasize the submissive line of the neck. The forearms are raised upwards and forwards from the elbows and the left hand rests upon the back of the right, forming from the front a bridge and from the side a further suggestion of forward inclination. The frontal view of the bridged arms provides, as it were, a pedestal upon which the head and neck seem to rest, and the upthrust of the arms is continued, in slightly asymmetrical fashion, by the plaits. Innocence, gentleness, and the humble submissiveness of "Be it unto me according to thy Word" are expressed in a figure literally bent to the bidding of the divine messenger.

Sir Jacob wrote of the *Madonna and Child* (1951-52): "No work of mine has brought so many tributes from so many diverse quarters."[96] So triumphant a work, sculpturally and emotionally, requires the discriminating praise of a poet to do it justice. This Laurie Lee has attempted in the following tribute:

"The siting is perfect; the design complex and monumentally simple. The two figures float above us with no apparent artifice of support and their relationship to each other and to us is profoundly moving. The Christ child is not the customary babe but a lean lad of some five or six years. The mantled Mother with open hands reveals and offers him to the world. And the child both in expression and design is all prophecy: the robe that wraps his narrow body is also the robe of the tomb; the arms outstretched to embrace the world also assume the attitude of crucifixion; and the face with its large wide eyes and serene brow, looks out with love and knows what that love will cost him. This is one of the finest, most subtle,

<hr />

[95] The *St. Michael and the Devil* on the exterior of Coventry Cathedral was considered in section 3 of this chapter. See Fig. 25.

[96] This 13½ feet high group was cast in lead. It is placed above an arch designed by Louis Osman which connects two Palladian-style buildings on the north side of Cavendish Square in London's West End. Sir Jacob gave it his concentrated attention during six months (*Autobiography*, p. 235). See Fig. 20.

most affectionate of Epstein's works. It is also one of the most original conceptions of this theme."[97]

Only one other contemporary sculpture equal to the theme deserves to be compared with it—Henry Moore's *Madonna and Child*. The latter is, however, a great hieratic archetype, while this is majestically merciful. Moore suggests Deity above us, Epstein Deity for us.

Perhaps the subtlest of all Epstein's religious images is the moving *Majestas*[98] of Christ in Llandaff Cathedral (1953-57). This, too, is superbly sited and mounted, with the collaboration of George G. Pace. When mediaeval Llandaff Cathedral was severely damaged by a land-mine in the Second World War, Pace was placed in charge of the reconstruction, working closely with the then Dean of Llandaff, now the Bishop, Dr. Glyn Simon. It was decided to invite Epstein to sculpt a vast representation of Christ in Glory, which would hang on a great cylinder, bearing the organ pipes, and would be most elegantly raised on the delicate arms of two curving concrete bridges. The Epsteins, accompanied by Sir Stanley Spencer, visited the roofless and window-shattered cathedral in 1953. Discerning its dim outline as the dusk was falling, and making out the dark forms of two cassocked canons with black cloaks, Sir Jacob was impressed by the poignancy of the scene and enthusiastically devoted himself to preparing a symbol of the glorious rebirth of the Church.[99]

This eventually became the 14½ feet high *Majestas*, which was cast in aluminium. In the words of Laurie Lee: "It is a transfixing figure, floating, with pointed hands and feet, the sleeves in flat folds, like wings. The whole vacant column of the body annihilates the carnal world and leads one's eyes inexorably upwards to the face. And here again is one of Epstein's personal creations, a face transfigured, remote, supernatural, yet a face of suffering and love."[100] What is so astonishing about the *Majestas* is that it harmoniously combines three Christological concepts: the impassible Byzantine Christ enthroned in glory, the Semitic suffering Christ with sharp nose and agonising eyes, and the contemporary Christ whose hands plead *Shalom, Shalom*, to a world that does not know

[97] Citation from the unnumbered pagination of the introduction to Geoffrey Ireland, *Epstein: A Camera Study of the Sculptor at Work*.

[98] A photographic reproduction of the *Majestas* appears on the dust-jacket of the present volume and of each other in this series.

[99] Information from Lady Kathleen Epstein's notes in the exhibition brochure *Epstein at King's Lynn* and in a conversation with her.

[100] Ireland, *Epstein . . .*, introduction.

the secret of its peace. In Sir Jacob Epstein we salute a Jew who understood the Biblical faith with profundity and relevance and whose religious works continually renew their claims on imagination and belief.

The last of the trio of sculptors is the most original of all, Henry Moore (born 1898).[101] If a profound concern for man's role in the universe and his relationships with society, or a capacity to evoke feelings of awe and ultimate concern, are what is intended by the term "religion"—then Moore is profoundly religious. If, however, we hold to a more traditional and narrower as well as more explicit definition of allegiance to a historic faith (and in particular to Christianity as a religion of redemption), then only his *Madonna and Child* can be considered, thematically, as Christian art.[102] Moore's *Madonna and Child* (1943-1944) reposes behind a delicate wrought-iron grille in the north transept of St. Matthew's Anglican Church, Northampton. It is magisterially carved in Hornton stone and rises to a height of 59 inches. Its serene and quiet dignity entirely fulfils the sculptor's intention: "I have tried to give a sense of complete ease and repose as though the Madonna could stay in that position for ever (as, being in stone, she will have to)."[103] The Madonna presents her Son to the world on which he gazes with calm benevolence and preternatural wisdom, suggesting that he is, indeed, the *Logos* or Divine Wisdom incarnate.

The image has also profound psychological meaning for Henry Moore, who has concerned himself in a whole series of works with the feminine archetype, as if to redress the balance of a destructive, one-sided, and patriarchal culture. As Erich Neumann has written: "The birth of the feminine archetype in modern man signifies at the same time the development of human relatedness, of his social

101 See *inter alia* the following: *Henry Moore, Sculptor*, by Herbert Read; *Henry Moore*, by Geoffrey Grigson; *Shelter Sketchbook*, London (1944); *Henry Moore: Sculptures and Drawings* introduced by Herbert Read; *Henry Moore: Portfolio of Forty Drawings*; *Henry Moore*, by James Johnson Sweeney; *Henry Moore*, by Guilio Carlo Argan; *Henry Moore, Schriften und Skulpturen*, by Werner Hofman; *The Archetypal World of Henry Moore* (Bollingen Series LXVIII) by Erich Neumann; *Henry Moore*, by J. P. Hodin; and *Heads, Figures and Ideas: A Sculptor's Notebook*, by Henry Moore. See Fig. 21.

102 This is not the place to go into the important theological question of whether works of art may be called "Christian" if their creators repudiate any formal association with any branch of the Christian Church, because they are, willy-nilly, done in the providence of God and by the gift of imagination through which man is a cooperator with the Creator. The present writer would, however, prefer to err on the side of theological and aesthetic latitude, especially as the art works of so many committed Christians can be so conventional, flat, and uninspired.

103 Herbert Read, *Henry Moore: Sculptures and Drawings*, Vol. I, p. xxv.

capacity, and the growing consciousness of the unity of mankind on earth."[104]

8. *Summation*

This summary survey of the slow and reluctant rebirth of religious art in England has tried to do justice to the unimaginative traditionalism, mingled with the stirrings of syncretism, of the first four decades of the present century, in which the pioneer voices of Eric Gill and of Jacob Epstein were either unheard or vilified (as in the case of the latter).[105] During this time English ecclesiastical architecture seemed to be unaware of the liturgical and architectural revolution achieved in Audincourt and Ronchamps, at Vence and at Cologne, or in remoter Finland or Brasilia. In such circumstances, the most that could be hoped for was the inspired conservatism of Guildford or Coventry, though Sir Basil Spence's cathedral became a frame for many artists of compelling distinction, and is more than a frame, and Gibberd's Liverpool "tent of pilgrimage" is functionally, liturgically, and symbolically modern.

The value and the danger of religion is its conservative clinging to the past, a clinging that is all the more passionate when it is challenged by the unparalleled rate of contemporary change. It was, indeed, inevitable that a country with a great historic tradition, compelled to play a secondary political role, should seek for solace in its past, and that churchmen should—for the most part—stress what they believed to be the eternal verities of the Christian faith and look for artists with a traditional iconography and architects who would build in the grand Gothic manner. Moreover, a religion such as Christianity bases its hope for the future on the climactic revelatory acts of God in Christ, believing that B.C. and A.D. form

[104] *The Archetypal World of Henry Moore*, p. 129. This is a fascinating Jungian interpretation of the powerful symbols of Henry Moore, which makes the perceptive criticism (p. 89) that "this Madonna figure and other sketches of the kind lack that drastic contemporary element that makes their eternity *our* eternity. This does not detract from the beauty of these sculptures so much as from their 'aliveness,' which is otherwise the most revolutionary quality of Moore's work."

[105] See Sir John Rothenstein's introduction to *Epstein: Arts Council Memorial Exhibition*, where he elaborates the paradox that the man considered to be an "anarchist" and a "barbarian" was one of the most traditional of the major sculptors of his time. The even greater paradox is that Epstein, who came from a people forbidden to make representations of Divine beings or human beings, created some of the most impressive and moving Biblical images of his time, as did Chagall. See Cecil Roth, ed., *Jewish Art, An Illustrated History*, pp. 17ff., for a discussion of the prohibition of "graven images" and the ways in which this was interpreted in the history of Judaism.

the very hinge on which history turns. There can, in the nature of things, be no new Christianity, but only new forms in which the relevance of the Divine saga or *heilsgeschichte* is made known and contemporized. All this, and the lack of any great master of architecture since Wren, or any great sculpture at all, and indeed the want of a visual tradition that can compare with the most brilliant achievements of Italy, France, the Netherlands, Germany or Spain, makes the traditionalism and the weak syncretism intelligible. But it also makes all the more remarkable the emergence of modern masters like Henry Moore and Graham Sutherland and of a new and passionate interest in art and architecture. Truth further compels the admission that for the most part Eric Gill's strictures have not lost their validity because in too many sanctuaries mass-produced *bon-dieuserie* continues to insult God and real artists.

But equally it must be insisted that there is a growing sense of grave dissatisfaction with this situation, and that the new functional liturgical architecture and the symbolical and abstract religious art of the fifth, sixth, and seventh decades will continue to gain ground. It is not too much to hope from the evidence already present, of which only the most striking examples have been studied in this chapter, that increasingly architects, sculptors, painters, glaziers, metal-workers, weavers, and embroiderers will join with the musicians and poets and the whole people of God in a paean of *contemporary* praise, in a veritable twentieth century *Benedicite*.

CHAPTER III

THE DEVELOPMENT
OF CHURCH MUSIC

THE RENAISSANCE of religious art is paralleled by the vigorous growth of religious music. "In church music," writes Erik R. Routley, "there has been no age so full of surprises, and so full of creative promise, as our own."[1] While this seems a perilous judgment, it is supported by several important considerations. The first is that never since the sixteenth century have so many distinguished musicians in the secular field attempted to write sacred music. This is true of such varied composers on the European continent as Stravinsky, Webern, Poulenc, Krenek, and Messiaen. On the English scene it applies with particular force to such twentieth century composers as Elgar and Vaughan Williams, Bliss and Walton, Howells and Britten. Some of the more popular English Victorian composers, like Sullivan, also wrote church music, but their ecclesiastical work was a kind of "writing down" to the church level, a species of amateurishness. The twentieth century composers, by contrast, use their professional standards and techniques to the full in their church music.

The point is that some of the most distinguished modern music in England is written for the Church and that has not been the case since the golden days of Tallis, Byrd, and Purcell. Furthermore, in the recent decades of the twentieth century any temptation for English church music to be romantically escapist or merely cathedrally sonorous and antiquarian has been rejected by the realistic recognition that the Church is *in* the world. Therefore the Church in its music must be involved in the problems of modern life, including the struggle for faith against the inroads of secularism. The outward prosperity of the Church is a thing of the past, and this has forced the Church into a living encounter with the world. Church music, in the vivid phrase of Routley, must now travel second-class. The most hopeful sign of all is that the most

[1] *Twentieth Century Church Music*, p. 5. I here wish to express my deep gratitude to my friend, Dr. Erik R. Routley, for his great kindness in allowing me to read this volume in proof. It is a superb survey of the period, written in the most engaging style, by this witty and erudite musician, church historian, and expert hymnologist, to whom I am greatly indebted. This chapter has been supervised by Dr. Routley and also by Mr. Myron McLellan, a young composer now a doctoral candidate in the Department of Religion at Princeton University.

recent church music is radically experimental both in high-brow and in low-brow directions. This factor alone accounts for the hazardous as well as the promising condition of modern church music in England.

In the past six and a half decades, three major trends can be discerned in the development of English church music, each of which warrants consideration. First, there was the period in which church music attained to professional standards, and was marked by the work of outstanding craftsmen, most of whom were the organists of the English cathedrals. It was, moreover, a time when several eminent musicians, previously not in the sacred field, turned to composing sacred music. It was also the period of distinguished musical teaching, and of important historical research. The foundations of the highest standards of English church music were then laid down. The second phase of development was a move away from traditional music in both the sacred and secular spheres to music that was radically experimental in character. The most recent phase, though it has not eliminated either of the two earlier trends, shows the Church coming to terms with the social revolution and attempting to produce highly controversial "popular" music, for the missionary purpose of relating to the experience of the modern adolescent influenced by the "Hit Parade."

1. Raising the Standards of English Church Music

This, the earliest phase in the century's development, may be said to have reached reasonable fulfilment with the establishment of the Royal School of Church Music in 1927. With the achievement of a highly professional tradition in English church music, it was possible for Commissions appointed by the Archbishops of Canterbury and York to publish in 1922 a report entitled *Music in Worship* and in 1951 another entitled *Music in Church* (revised edition, 1960). But it is significant that the latter looked back to 1906 and the founding of the Church Music Society, as the pioneer period in which musical standards were raised in church to a genuinely professional level.[2]

The attainment of professional standards involved a serious break with the cult of mediocrity and amateurishness, and with the rather pretentious vulgarity and crude sentimentality which had marked the compositions of some of the most famous Victorian composers, such as Sullivan and Stainer.

[2] *Music in Church*, p. 7.

The pioneers were two close friends, who both honoured and criticized each other, Ralph Vaughan Williams and Gustav Holst.[3] Each won distinction in the wider field of music, orchestrally and vocally. Holst's *Planets* was his single greatest work, but Williams won the greater fame with more compositions. Holst disseminated an appreciation of English music by his lectures, while Vaughan Williams by his musical editorship of English hymnals, his organization and writing for the Three Choirs Festivals, and his researches into English musical history, helped to set the highest standards.

Vaughan Williams proved in the *Sancta Civitas* (1925) that he could combine the strains of the ancients with modern harmonic devices. He also produced superb hymn-tunes, as in his "Sine Nomine" to accompany "For all the saints" or his "Down Ampney" for "Come down, O love divine." He was capable, also, of dramatic composing, as his *Dona nobis Pacem* and *Hodie* (1954) demonstrated. His *Mass in G Minor* showed how this versatile musician could fashion a sensitive setting to the requirements of the Anglican liturgy. Holst's church music is not as well known, nor on so large or varied a scale, but it is exquisite. Two examples are the charming anthem, "This I have done for my true love," based on the Cornish carol, "Tomorrow shall be my dancing day" (published by Augener, 1922), and the music to the Mystery Play, *The Coming of Christ* (1928). Holst also contributed valuable hymn tunes to *Songs of Praise*. Both Vaughan Williams and Holst have the power of evoking religious awe and mystery with a great economy of resources.

Vaughan Williams' importance as the musical editor of two important hymnals, the *English Hymnal* and *Songs of Praise*, will be considered later. What it is important to stress immediately is those qualities in music for which Vaughan Williams and Holst were looking, in their dissent from the harmonic and contrapuntal orthodoxy of the eighteenth and nineteenth centuries and which they found, in part, in Tudor England, in both folk and church music. They dissented from four-part writing, and Williams often preferred two-part and three-part writing. They preferred modal scales to the customary diatonic scale with its regularity. They also delighted in highly melismatic melody, both in the original

---

[3] See their correspondence in U. Vaughan Williams and I. Holst, eds., *Heirs and Rebels*.

sense of using graceful and florid vocalization, and in the narrower sense of having several notes sung to one syllable.

Important as they were, they were by no means alone. The standards of music were also raised by more conservative crafts-men, such as Charles Wood, Edward Bairstow, and Basil Harwood. This group was succeeded by another group of excellent craftsmen, almost all cathedral organists, which included Sydney Nicholson, William Harris, Harold Darke, H. K. Andrews, Thomas Arm-strong, Herbert Sumsion, George Oldroyd, Sydney Campbell, and Ernest Bullock. The only comparable national figure representing Dissent was Eric Thiman, the musical editor of *Congregational Praise* (1951). By their compositions, as by their education of church musical taste among choirs and worshippers, they also helped appreciably to raise the standards.

Among the great teachers was Sir Walford Davies, who popular-ized good vocal music through the medium of the British Broad-casting Corporation as effectively as Sir Henry Wood popularized orchestral music through his "Promenade Concerts" at the Albert Hall. Two other admirable teachers of music in the period were the brothers, Martin and Geoffrey Shaw, instructors and inspectors in the English day schools.[4]

The Free Church musicians had far the greater leeway to make up because Nonconformity had neither the Liturgy nor the Cathe-dral tradition behind it. It had to overcome its own Victorian customs, in which heartiness rather than discrimination was characteristic of congregational singing, and which insisted on congregations singing the anthems as well as the hymns. It was also hampered by the fact that little time or money was spared for music because the high point of worship was the intellectual ser-mon, and money had already been expended on the impressiveness of the building or the preacher's salary. In these circumstances, the work of Eric Thiman in raising standards was extraordinarily important. He was helped by the contributions of other less dis-tinguished, but still notable, Free Church musicians, including the Methodists, Luke Wiseman, F. D. Westbrook, and George Brock-less[5] (the latter being organist of Westminster Central Hall), and the Congregationalist, Richard Aldridge.

It was a further proof that English church music had come of

[4] Routley, *Twentieth Century Church Music*, p. 52, claims that "they made the world safe for music to sail on past them."

[5] The son of George Brockless, Brian, is an experimental composer who wrote the anthem "Now blessed be Thou, Christ Jesu" (1960).

age professionally when composers whose chief experience was outside ecclesiastical music produced church music, knowing that it would be appreciated and worthily interpreted. Herbert Howells, Sir Arthur Bliss, and Sir William Walton are professional musicians who paid this compliment to the improved musical standards in churches.

Howells had written in a vein which was reminiscent of Vaughan Williams in his use of Tudor idioms and in an alternation of romanticism and astringency. His *Four Anthems* (1941-1943) are frequently heard, particularly "O Pray for the peace of Jerusalem" and the vigorous "Let God arise." But his most remarkable work in church music is an ingenious series of cathedral or collegiate services dedicated to particular choirs, bearing in mind their history and their acoustical contexts and resources. The series began with the *Collegium Regiale* setting of the Evening Canticles written for King's College, Cambridge, in 1947. Other settings were composed for Worcester (1953), St. Paul's, London (1954), Westminster Abbey (1956), St. John's College, Cambridge (1958), and in 1958 he composed a Communion setting for Christ Church, Oxford, entitled *Missa Aedis Christi*. A very remarkable Requiem is his *Hymnus Paradisi* (1950). In the main, Howells' work is in the traditional vein.

It was no less remarkable that two symphonists should also have written church music in our period. Sir Arthur Bliss composed the long anthem, "Stand up and bless the Lord," as part of the consecration service for Llandaff Cathedral in 1960, and a large cantata, "The Beatitudes," was part of the consecration celebrations for Coventry Cathedral in 1962. Sir William Walton is "the finest example of a composer not naturally a churchman whose contributions to church literature are remarkable."[6] In 1953 he provided the ceremonial setting for the *Te Deum* at the Coronation of Queen Elizabeth II in Westminster Abbey. His greatest work, a massive *Gloria* for choir and orchestra, was composed in 1961 for the 125th anniversary of the Huddersfield Choral Society. It is full of inventive surprises and splendours. He brings to ecclesiastical music the passion and the irony of the world.

Distinguished musical teachers who have written church music must also be mentioned, however briefly. They include Edmund Rubbra, who has written three liturgical Masses, a setting of *Lauda Sion*, and two ceremonial settings of the *Te Deum*; Egon Wellesz,

6 Erik R. Routley, *ibid.*, p. 64.

the historian of Byzantine music and biographer of Schoenberg, who composed a *Mass in F minor* (1949); and Arthur Hutchings, who composed a *Communion service in G* (1957). Nor should it be forgotten that Herbert Howells was a distinguished teacher of music.

2. *Experimental Music*

What Henry Moore is in the world of art, Benjamin Britten is in music—unquestionably an international figure who has explored the musical possibilities of the human voice as Moore has explored the plastic possibilities of stone and metal. While his reputation is chiefly due to his operas, he has written church music of undoubted originality and depth, even if his is not as advanced a technique as many in the *avant garde*. These important ecclesiastical works include a *Ceremony of Carols*, *Rejoice in the Lamb* (both published in 1943), *Festival Te Deum* (1945), *St. Nicholas* (1948), *Hymn to St. Peter* (1955), *Noye's Fludde* (1958), *Missa Brevis* (1959), and the splendidly indignant *War Requiem* (1962). These works are astonishing in their invention and variety, the brilliance of their technique, and in their humanity. To look for parallels one has to compare him with Purcell in the English tradition for the exploitation of voice and instrument, and to Verdi for the originality of his Requiem, but he is all the time distinctively Benjamin Britten, and no man's imitator.

If his influence is to be seen in those who experiment in new vocal possibilities, dissonance, and economy in rhetorical devices, then Nicholas Maw, Mansel Thomas, and John Joubert, though not disciples, have felt his impact. John Joubert, the composer of *Missa Beati Joannis* (1962) is possibly the most distinguished of those for whom Britten blazed the experimental trail.

Other experimenters are more advanced radicals. The influence of Schoenberg is seen most clearly in Michael Tippett, who composed a *Magnificat* and a *Nunc Dimittis* for St. John's College, Cambridge, in 1961. Messiaen's influence can be discerned in the music of Peter Maxwell Davies, whose most impressive work up to now is a carol sequence, *O magnum mysterium* (1961). Webern's impact is most clearly seen in Harrison Birtwhistle's *Monody for Corpus Christi*. Another experimentalist who is a disciple of Messiaen is Malcolm Williamson, who essays both the high-brow and low-brow manner. *Planctus* (1962) is a contemplation of death in which tenors and basses share alternately in a single vocal line, the

107

two voices only occasionally overlapping. *Wrestling Jacob* (1962) is an ingenious setting of three verses of Charles Wesley's hymn, "Come, O thou Traveller unknown." The mere mention of these experiments is an indication of the liveliness of English church music and its openness to the idioms of the secular music of its age, which have blown rhetorical posturing and every other kind of complacency to the four winds.

3. Church Light Music

A much more controversial development in the modern Church has been an attempt to write "popular" music in order to attract the teen-agers who would otherwise reject church music as entirely "square." It is a deliberate "writing-down" of contemporary church music, which is defended by those who write it or use it as a missionary accommodation, a kind of pre-conversion music in a modernized Sankey mode. It is also defended as a fracturing of the Church's image as bourgeois. It is ridiculed by its critics as an unwarrantable perversion of the standards of the Gospel in terms of a sensuous, superficial, and sentimental musical appeal, and as a failure in its attempt to turr juvenile delinquents into juvenile disciples.

The movement commenced with Father Geoffrey Beaumont's *Folk Mass*, published in 1956. In a Preface to it, Beaumont stated that this setting of the Anglican Liturgy was written at the request of a vicar in the East end of London, who claimed that church music was utterly foreign to most people and that nothing had been written since the time of the Elizabethans which could properly be called a *Folk Mass*. Beaumont asserted that in its title "the word 'Folk' is used literally to mean the normal everyday popular kind of music." The work is commonly, but inaccurately, termed the "Jazz Mass."

While the priest is expected to sing his part of the Liturgy to the familiar Merbecke setting, the congregation's part is sung by "dictation"—that is, each phrase is sung first by the cantor and repeated by the congregation. Thus it can easily be learned by the people, and even sung without rehearsal. The style of the music is that of a revue, and the "catchy" tune that is most easily remembered is that of the "Sanctus." It resembles so-called pop music only in the dull and repetitive bass: it is not saccharine enough, nor sufficiently re-iterative, to compete with popular hits. Nor, it may be suggested, is the musical comedy or revue type of music likely to succeed without those lavish embellishments of stage, costuming, orchestra, and widely advertised personalities, which are characteristic of its secular context.

One can hardly imagine a more unsuitable setting for such a type of music than the rather bare church hall in which this kind of musical mission is attempted.

It is, however, as a portent rather than as an achievement that the *Folk Mass* is significant. It was the incentive for the founding of the *20th Century Church Light Music Group*, which has produced much church music in a style imitating Beaumont's. Perhaps its best known works are Patrick Appleford's *Mass of Five Melodies* and a *Festival Te Deum* by John Alldis. Appleford learned from Beaumont's experiment that the services of a cantor should be dispensed with. Neither musician succeeds in writing truly popular music. It seems that the group is more successful with hymn tunes, for some of them can produce tunes that go with a swing. Beaumont's "Chesterton" is a good example, as also his "Gracias," and it is interesting that these have been included in the *Baptist Hymn Book* of 1962. Others associated with him are less able to produce the "Oklahoma!" type of melodies than he, and often succeed only in sounding like re-activated Gilbert and Sullivan or antiquated "Tin Pan Alley." The two publications of the group in this genre are *Thirty 20th Century Hymn Tunes* (1960) and *More 20th Century Hymn Tunes* (1962). The group has not, however, proved as successful in trying to write words to match its tunes.

In *Rhythm in Religion* (1960) there is a serious attempt made to write popular lyrics which will match "popular" music. The eight songs are all the work of clergy, and one can admire their intentions rather than their achievements. These lyrics are marked by a paternalism which attributes to young people a sense of alienation and a search for direction—perhaps what the clergy hope for rather than find in their charges.

There appears to be only one writer of religious verse in England who is able to produce appropriate lyrics for the new popular music. He is Sydney Carter, an authentic folk-singer, who is unusual in being also a Christian. A record of his collected songs has been made, entitled *Songs of Faith and Doubt*. His expertise may be judged from the fact that his song-writing was added to Donald Swann's repertory in "At the Drop of a Hat." He can use irony and satire in a deeply religious fashion, as in the ballade beginning,

"I danced in the morning when the world was begun." Two of its stanzas go thus:

> I danced on the Sabbath and I cured the lame
> And the holy people said it was a shame:
> They whipped and they stripped and they hung me high,
> And they left me there on a Cross to die.
>
> I danced on a Friday when the sky turned black;
> It's hard to dance with the devil on your back.
> They buried my body and they thought I'd gone.
> But I am the dance, and I still go on.

This has the true character of folk music, and its refrains bring in the important community element. Furthermore, it points to the possibility of twentieth century carols, mingling the sacred and the secular as the mediaeval carols did. There is no doubt that irony and satire can be used in the twentieth century Church as a potent weapon for detecting Pharisaism, and that new carols can convey as the old did the authentic Christian *joie de vivre*.

4. Hymnody

The higher professional quality of craftsmanship in church music in the present century is clearly reflected in the improvement in the hymnals that the various communions have produced. This has been accompanied by a more serious and widespread discussion of those qualities in words and music that constitute a good hymn.

This pedagogical concern is reflected in a distinctive type of twentieth century writing on praise—the hymnal companion or handbook. As in so much else in the period, Percy Dearmer was the pioneer, writing his *Songs of Praise Discussed* in 1933. Kenneth L. Parry and Erik R. Routley produced their *Companion to Congregational Praise* in 1953, and Hugh Martin edited *The Baptist Hymn Book Companion* in 1962. A more historical approach to an important hymn book was W. K. Lowther Clarke's *A Hundred Years of Hymns Ancient and Modern* (1961). The greatest historian of hymnody was, of course, Dr. John Julian, the compiler of the monumental *Dictionary of Hymnology*, the first edition of which appeared in 1891. Other important and informed writers on hymnody were Winfred Douglas,[7] Louis F. Benson,[8]

[7] *Church Music in History and Practice*. Both Douglas and Benson were American ministers whose work was well known in England.
[8] *The Hymnody of the Christian Church.*

and the prolific Erik R. Routley.[9] Their work, as well as that of the writers of hymn book companions, was to educate ministers, organists, and interested laity in the appreciation of the literary, musical, and theological values of hymns.

A typical discussion of the qualities, both musical and literary, to be desired in Christian worship, is to be found in the Anglican report of 1951, *Music in Church*, prepared under the chairmanship of Noel T. Hopkins, Provost of Wakefield. Four general canons are laid down as to the music. It is to be "a fitting expression of the words; the words matter most." As music, it must be good, which is further defined as having "life without levity, and dignity without heaviness," the avoidance of discords, and the keeping to simple harmony. It is further to be thoroughly "in keeping with the spirit of the liturgy." This, again, is defined as music which exhibits nobility and restraint, and freedom from sensationalism and mawkishness. Finally, this music should be "fitted to the conditions existing in the church for which it is designed."[10] This means that a rustic parish church choir should not attempt cathedral-type music, for true worship should aim at the glory of God (rather than that of the choir) and the assistance of the congregation.

These canons are applied to the selection of hymns and hymn tunes in more detail. It is insisted that worth rather than popularity should be the first criterion. It is strongly stated that "the emphasis on sincerity and strength in religion is more than ever apparent in an age that is peculiarly critical of pretence and sentimentality."[11] The need of the hour is for austerity. A succinct definition is given of a good hymn tune. It is "one of which the emotional content is appropriate to its plan and occasion; the harmonized parts, especially the bass, should be interesting and distinctive; the melody should be well drawn, not made up of notes which bear no close relation to one another, nor insisting with a wearisome reiteration on a recurrence of the same note; so that it sounds clear, decided and convincing when sung without harmonies." It is then added that "the rhythm must fit closely to the words, but must be neither trivial nor obtrusive nor dull."[12]

These abstractions are given point by contrasting tinsel tunes with genuinely golden ones. "Maidstone" with its hurdy-gurdy rhythm, and the tawdriness of "St. Bees," are set over against the

---

[9] See *The Church and Music*; *Church Music and Theology*; *The Music of Christian Hymnody*; *Hymns and Human Life*; and *I'll Praise My Maker.*
[10] *Music in Church*, p. 4. [11] *Ibid.*, p. 35.
[12] *Ibid.*, p. 37.

beautiful simplicity of Gibbons' "Canterbury" or "Song 13." The feeble melody of Barnby's setting of "For all the Saints" is contrasted with the vigour and triumphant ring of those by Stanford and Vaughan Williams.[13]

What have been the distinctive contributions of the twentieth century to hymnody? As might be expected, the sense of comradeship in a world-wide Church,[14] as stimulated by the Ecumenical Movement, has been expressed in such hymns as John Oxenham's "In Christ there is no East or West." One hymn from the Liturgy of Malabar and another moving hymn on discipleship translated by Nicol Macnicol from the Indian original are becoming increasingly prized by English congregations. The pre-Kraemer[15] confidence that Christianity is the culmination rather than the criticism of other major religions is fittingly expressed in George Matheson's "Gather us in Thou love that fillest all."

The impact of the "social Gospel" is also strong on twentieth century hymnody,[16] resulting in the importation of many hymns on the subject of the Kingdom of God from the United States, such as "Rise up, O men of God" by William Merrill, a Presbyterian clergyman of Pelagian tendencies. Two written by Englishmen, which bid fair to become classics, are Canon Scott Holland's "Judge Eternal, throned in splendour" and G. K. Chesterton's "O God of earth and altar." Less successful were the hymns purporting to be Christian humanism, like that of Clifford Bax: "Turn back, O man, forswear thy foolish ways," which were, in fact, purely humanistic in their orientation.

Another feature of twentieth century hymnody was the composing of children's hymns which did not treat children as little men and women, or religion as renunciation, as had so many Victorian hymns. Two admirable examples are Percy Dearmer's "Jesus, good above all other" and Charter Piggott's "In our work and in our play."[17]

---

[13] *Ibid.*, pp. 37-38.

[14] Percy Dearmer in the preface to *Songs of Praise* commented: "The hymns themselves show how Catholic we have become in spite of ourselves." Even churches using the same language, however, are still a long way from considering a denominational hymnbook an anachronism.

[15] The reference is to Hendrik Kraemer's work, *The Christian Message in a Non-Christian World*, written from a strongly Barthian standpoint, affirming Christianity's finality, in preparation for the Madras Conference of the International Missionary Council.

[16] See the present author's article, "The Expression of the Social Gospel in Worship," in *Studia Liturgica* (Rotterdam), Vol. II, No. 3 (September 1963), pp. 174-92.

[17] Cited in full in H. A. L. Jefferson, *Hymns in Christian Worship*.

The lead for improved hymnody was given by five important Anglican hymnals. Two were works of scholarship, but three had much wider popularity. Of the first type was the *Yattendon Hymnal* of 1899, compiled by Robert Bridges for the village church of Yattendon in Berkshire. Containing only 100 hymns, it was a selection distinguished by the highest devotional, literary, and musical quality.[18] It clearly enunciated and exemplified a new principle—that the most suitable words must be matched to the most adequate tune. Of the same order was *The Songs of Syon* compiled by the Reverend G. R. Woodward. This collection of 414 hymns indicated a tendency towards authenticity in the choice of words as well as in the music of the finer hymn tunes of the European countries. It has proved to be a rich mine for later musical editors.

The widely influential hymn books were *Hymns Ancient and Modern*[19] (which had first appeared in 1861, but was revised in 1904 and appeared in an important revision in 1950), the *English Hymnal* of 1906 (musically revised in 1933), and *Songs of Praise* of 1925 (enlarged in 1931). The two latter volumes had as their musical editor the incomparable Ralph Vaughan Williams (assisted by Martin Shaw for *Songs of Praise*), and as literary editor, Dr. Percy Dearmer.

The importance of Vaughan Williams for hymnody is three-fold. He researched widely into the psalmody of Geneva, the folk-songs of Britain, the classics of early English hymnody and the tunes of the French Counter-Reformation, and raided these treasures for both *English Hymnal* and *Songs of Praise*. Moreover, when texts had been corrupted, he often restored them. For the earlier volume he contributed three excellent tunes of his own composition: "Sine Nomine," "Down Ampney," and "Randolph," and to the later one "Mantegna," "Marathon," and "Guildford," among others. In addition, he introduced Arnold Bax's "Wonder," Darke's "Cornhill," Patrick Hadley's "Pembroke," and borrowed John Ireland's "Love Unknown" from the *Public School Hymn Book* of 1919.

Dearmer's concern was to publish the hymns as their authors wrote them (not as they had been bowdlerized), to introduce hymns of social service and national reformation, and to make genuine poetry serve the cause of congregational piety. He was responsible for widely popularizing a hymn based on Bunyan, "He

[18] See Winfred Douglas, *Church Music in History and Practice*, p. 220.
[19] See W. K. Lowther Clarke, *A Hundred Years of Hymns Ancient and Modern*.

who would valiant be"; as also the following: Donne's "Wilt Thou forgive"; Milton's "The Lord will come and not be slow"; Christina Rossetti's "In the bleak mid-winter"; G. K. Chesterton's "O God of earth and altar"; Bridges' "Rejoice, O Land, in God thy Might"; and Scott Holland's "Judge Eternal." Some of his more novel selections were, however, anticipated by the catholicity of Garrett Horder's *Worship Song* of 1905.[20] According to Canon Roger Lloyd, Dearmer's *English Hymnal* did more to improve the worship of the Church of England than his *Parson's Handbook*.[21]

Although these three major Anglican handbooks aspire to catholicity in the breadth of their choice, they have acquired partisan associations. The green covers of the *English Hymnal* are linked with the expectation of "Catholic" worship in the churches in which they are used. The dark blue or maroon binding of *Hymns Ancient and Modern* suggests the Anglican *via media*. The light blue covers of *Songs of Praise* hint at a liberal and even modernist outlook in the theology of the contents. In truth, however, the *English Hymnal* has catholicity as well as being Catholic in churchmanship, and is admirably fitted to be a companion to the Anglican Liturgy. *Hymns Ancient and Modern* is rather unadventurous and staid. *Songs of Praise* was deliberately conceived as being "national, in the sense of including a full expression of that faith which is common to the English-speaking peoples today, both in the British Commonwealth and the United States."[22] Each has, of course, been subject to criticisms. The *English Hymnal* has been faulted for the chill of its devotional spirit and for an insular narrow-mindedness.[23] *Hymns Ancient and Modern* has been considered stuffily high-brow and musically tame. *Songs of Praise* was musically adventurous, so it was thought, but doctrinally diluted. Nevertheless, all three greatly enriched the vocabulary of English praise in both words and music.

Yet there was also needed, particularly among Anglicans, a revival of interest in congregational singing. This was a task superbly fulfilled by Sir Walford Davies and Sir Hugh Allen. The former, who came of a Welsh Nonconformist background, used broadcasting for this purpose, and the latter invented the "Hymn Festival" as a device for introducing new hymns. As early as 1912 he collected large congregations in the Sheldonian Theatre in Ox-

20 See William Jensen Reynolds, *A Survey of Christian Hymnody*, pp. 76-77.
21 *The Church of England in the Twentieth Century*, I, p. 163.
22 Citation from Dearmer's Preface.
23 See Dom Anselm Hughes, *The Rivers of the Flood*, p. 137.

ford and provided them with specially printed hymn-sheets to encourage their participation in new hymn tunes.[24]

Hymn-singing had always been popular among the congregations of the English Free Churches, but the quality of their hymns (excepting those of Watts and Wesley) was no match for the cordiality of their singing. Both in theological content and in musical accompaniment there was a great need for the improvement that the century was to mark in their official hymn books.[25] The most recent of them to appear show that they have learned the lessons of Bridges and Dearmer, Vaughan Williams and Martin Shaw.

The unreformed state of things was clearly revealed in A. J. Klaiber's article[26] on a hymn ballot taken among Baptists in 1926, in which votes were cast for 235 hymns, though 112 received only one vote each. A few hymns many would call great were omitted. Those included: "Now thank we all our God"; "Let us with a gladsome mind"; "Glorious things of thee are spoken"; and "Awake my soul and with the sun." Ten per cent of the selections were children's hymns. The most popular in the order of choice were: "O Love, that wilt not let me go"; "Lead, kindly Light"; "Jesus, Lover of my soul"; "Still, still with Thee"; "Rock of Ages"; "Beneath the Cross of Christ"; "The day Thou gavest"; "Dear Lord and Father of mankind"; "At even ere the sun was set"; and "Abide with me." What is common to these choices is an individualistic piety (the persistence of the first personal pronoun singular is striking), romanticism in mood (descending to the eroticism of "Still, still with Thee when purple morning breaketh"), and swooping tunes. What was true of the preferences of the Baptists was almost certainly equally true of those of the Congregationalists, the Methodists, and, to a limited extent, the Presbyterians, whose Calvinistic austerity preserved them from too great a liking for syrup.

By the forties, however, *English Hymnal* and *Songs of Praise* had had their salutary influence on the Free Churches. *The Church Hymnary* (Presbyterian) of 1927 went overboard in its desire to

[24] See Erik R. Routley, *Twentieth Century Church Music*, p. 99.

[25] Many Anglican congregations were also addicted to Victorian sentimentality in words and music. Dom Anselm Hughes writes amusingly about the religious folk-songs of the period, "one of which—'Erbide with me'—is used as the official hymn at football cup-ties, while another—'Eternal Father, strong to save'—much beloved for the saccharine semitones of its tune ('Melita') is sung at 11 a.m. on all our ocean liners in the first-class saloon, quite regardless of the state of the weather" (*ibid.*, p. 136).

[26] See *The Baptist Quarterly*, Vol. III (1926-27), p. 312.

imitate the *English Hymnal* in a dive for status symbols. The *Methodist Hymn Book* of 1933 borrowed less from the same source. The *Congregational Hymnary* of 1916 included "Coutances" and "Deus tuorum militum," but resolutely refused to use Vaughan Williams or to follow his principle of authenticity. Similarly, the compilers of the *Baptist Church Hymnal* (1933) were motivated—in Routley's ribald phrase—by "ignorance-by-decision."[27] But the reformation is clearly in evidence in both *Congregational Praise* of 1951 and the *Baptist Hymn Book* of 1962. *Congregational Praise* had Eric Thiman as musical editor (with Erik Routley as the Secretary of the Committee). They helped to make this the finest of the Free Church hymn books for literary and musical quality. The *Baptist Hymn Book* had Hugh Martin as chairman of its editorial committee and E. P. Sharpe as chairman of the music advisory committee. This hymnal was the first to include two of Geoffrey Beaumont's "pop" tunes, but was quite conservative in its retention of some Sankey gospel songs, in which it was perhaps influenced by the evangelistic crusades of Billy Graham in England. No such concessions to popular taste were made by the editors of *Congregational Praise*, for they argued that the congregations whose churches preferred Sankey would use that selection on week-nights. This was all to the good, as some hymns seem rather to corrupt than commend the Gospel. Dr. Routley argued this in his study, *The Gift of Conversion* (1957) which was a sustained critique of attempts to manipulate the personality in revivalistic services. More recently his views have been incisively summed up as follows: "I contend that it is wrong to reduce evangelism to an operation on the soul of the individual, leaving out his brains and his aesthetic sense and his social sense; that it is wrong to represent salvation as one long rest in bed with an automatically re-heated hot-water bottle; that it is contrary to the Gospel to represent 'peace' of the heavenly kind as a long silence broken only by the drone of a harmonium. . . ."[28]

The least satisfactory people's book of praise to be produced in the twentieth century is the *Westminster Hymnal*, prepared for English Roman Catholics. This is the case despite the fact that its first issue had the benefit of the musical advice of Sir Richard Terry, who had published admirable editions of ancient psalters, and the revision committee, in the preparation of the edition of

[27] Communicated in a letter, dated April 18, 1964.
[28] *Music, Sacred and Profane*, p. 139.

1940, had the literary advice of Monsignor Ronald Knox, a master of English prose and of translation. It is partly attributable to the fact, as admitted by Evelyn Waugh, that "many adult English Catholics do not hear a hymn from one year's end to another."[29] It is possible also that those who miss hymns the most are converts, and therefore their advice is probably suspect. A further dissuasive may be the rather wooden translations from the Latin of some of the hymns. Finally, there is almost certainly a feeling that hymns are an accommodation to the sentimentality of the simpler laity and their love for a catchy tune, as contrasted with the professional preference for Gregorian chants. Routley hardly exaggerates in referring to the music of the day echoed in the unrevised *Westminster Hymnal* as "treacly, instrumental, café-orchestra stuff."[30] Monsignor Knox persuaded the committee for revision to introduce the work of comparatively modern poets such as Francis Thompson, Chesterton, Lionel Johnson, Canon Gray, and "Michael Field." He made 47 translations from the Latin out of a total of 106, and composed four hymns of his own. Even so, the final result of the revised *Westminster Hymnal* of 1940 was the attainment of higher professional standards in both words and music, but at the cost of a decline in popularity. Fortunately, English Roman Catholics have a much better record in the field of popular psalmody.

5. Psalmody

Three different communions in England have three distinctive contributions to make to the use of the psalms in praise. The Presbyterians, following the lead of the Church of Scotland, prefer metrical psalmody sung to the simple and solemn accompaniments of the high Genevan days.[31] The Roman Catholics chant in the Gregorian manner and are learning the Père Joseph Gélineau mode of psalmody. The Anglican chant is a harmonized and stylized development from plainsong, which has been interpreted and performed as emphasizing "speech rhythms," particularly under the aegis of Sir Walford Davies, Dr. Thalben-Ball,[32] and the Royal School of Church Music. The pioneer in the reform of Anglican chanting, who avoided the text-mangling and the four-beat bars of

[29] See Evelyn Waugh's *Ronald Knox*, p. 253.
[30] *Music, Sacred and Profane*, p. 129.
[31] See Miller Patrick's *Four Centuries of Scottish Psalmody* and Maurice Frost's *English and Scottish Psalm and Hymn Tunes*.
[32] See his *Choral Psalter* (1940), which should be compared with the *Parish Psalter* (1930) and the *Oxford Psalter* (1929).

"Hellmost Helmore,"[33] was Madeley Richardson of Southwark Cathedral, just prior to 1908.

Despite the notable improvement in Anglican chanting which the "speech rhythm" school has brought in and which is excellently performed in most cathedrals, and the exquisite austerity and ideational quality of Gregorian chanting, especially as heard in Benedictine Abbeys, such music is too difficult for the purposes of congregational singing.[34] And, while metrical psalmody is simple enough, yet all too often it is doggerel rather than poetry, for the rhymes are false and the syntax is forced. Hence, with one exception, no present method is likely to lead to that full participation of the laity in worship which is one of the central aims of the modern Liturgical Movement.

The promising exception is associated with the work of the Jesuit, Père Joseph Gélineau of France.[35] Gélineau tried to render in French the basic rhythm of the Hebrew text, which had in each line an equal number of stressed syllables but an irregular number of unstressed syllables. As he translated the Psalms into French he arranged the lines of each psalm in its original stanza structure.[36] As Leonard Ellinwood has pointed out, this Hebrew rhythmic system which Gélineau tries to preserve in French, and which is now being adapted to English, has a curious analogue in the "sprung rhythm" of the English poet, Gerard Manley Hopkins, himself also a Jesuit priest.[37] The following illustration will make the principle plain, using Psalm xcii: 11 in Hebrew, French and English, and marking the stresses in italic print:

Sad-*dik* kat-ta-*mar* yif-*rah*
Le *ju*ste poussera comme un *pal*mier.
The *just* man shall *flour*ish as a *palm* tree.

Ke-'*er*-es Ba-le-ba-*non* yis-g*eh*
Il grandir*a* comme un *cèd*re du *Li*ban.
He shall *grow* as a *ce*dar on *Le*banon.[38]

---

[33] See Dom Ambrose Hughes, *The Rivers of the Flood*, p. 132.

[34] See the discussion of the relative advantages of Gregorian and Anglican chanting in *Music in Church*, pp. 32-33.

[35] See the entire Psalms in Père Gélineau's translation in *La Sainte Bible traduite en français sous la direction de l'Ecole biblique de Jérusalem*.

[36] See Dom Gregory Murray's article, "The Psalms, a rhythmic restoration leads to a popular revival," in *The Downside Review*, Vol. LXXIV (April 1956), pp. 95-102.

[37] See Winfred Douglas, *Church Music in History and Practice*, p. 235.

[38] *Ibid.*

Having completed his translations, Père Gélineau composed melodies to which they might be sung by a congregation. They are characterized by the utmost simplicity, with a change of pitch only on accented syllables. For this reason they are well suited for congregational use. They are being used by the Protestant Community at Taizé in the Daily Offices, and have been heard at the High Kirk of St. Giles in Edinburgh. It is ironic that in the Roman Catholic Church, for which they were intended, they may be used generally only on non-liturgical occasions. Such popularity as the Gélineau method of chanting has achieved in Britain is chiefly due to the sponsorship of Dom Gregory Murray of Downside Abbey, who is also an expert in Gregorian chanting.

6. Conclusion

Looking back over sixty-five years of the present century, one can see that, while the congregations were larger at its start, the quality of the hymnody, the psalmody, and the anthems[39] was inferior to what it is today. Piety was often sentimental and individualistic, instead of objective and corporate, and church music was not merely insular and complacent, but it had lost touch with the English past and was unrelated to the European Continent. Vaughan Williams was to reawaken ecclesiastical England to its classical heritage in church music and folk music, and to make it empathetic to the strong simplicity of Genevan psalm-tunes and the richness of Catholic baroque music in seventeenth and eighteenth century France. In due course most of the leading composers of the age were to write church music, so that it was no longer a synonym for tamely conventional echoes of the past reiterated *ad nauseam*. Finally, church music, under the influence of Benjamin Britten and composers of the *avant garde*, became highly experimental in English adaptations of Webern and Messiaen. In a more controversial manner, there were pastoral experiments in popular music.

So lively is the experimentation now proceeding in England in the writing of anthems, hymns, carols, and psalm-settings that this brief survey is fittingly concluded on a note of interrogation. Will modern church music, in becoming secular (that is, in speaking

[39] In the first part of the chapter consideration was paid to some of the most memorable anthems of the period. In a brief chapter a section devoted to them would have become inordinately long if it had attempted to be comprehensive. For further information see Edmund H. Fellowes, *English Cathedral Music*, and Erik R. Routley, *Twentieth Century Church Music*.

with the authentic idiom of its time), rightly cease to be *church* music while becoming in a more relevant sense *religious* music? Will it meet the deeper needs of humanity through raising existential questions to which a contemporary, not a second-hand faith, is the living and hard-won answer?

CHAPTER IV

THE EARLY DEVELOPMENT OF
THEOLOGY (1900-1933)

ABERE DEUM EST COLERE DEUM, said Luther. An abstract principle may be considered, but a living God must be worshipped. Yet the quality of worship in every religion is determined by the worshippers' conception of the nature of their deity.

If Christian theology in a given period isolates one of God's major attributes or activities, to ignore the rest, the change will be felt in the worship. If, for example, his Creatorship alone is emphasized, worship will be pantheistic in character and the Harvest Festival will become the supreme day of the Christian Year. If Divine Judgment predominates in theology, then worship will be characterized by legalistic and scrupulous fear. If the Divine Saviourhood alone is stressed, then worship becomes pietistically sentimental and mawkish. If Sanctification predominates over the other attributes and activities of God, then the Christian life becomes a moral activism and dispenses with worship, except as a didactic reminder of duties to be done. For this reason one cannot hope to understand the developments of twentieth century worship without first engaging in a study of the changing theology of our period.

Furthermore, since theology is not carried on in a vacuum, but is ever sensitive to the currents of the national life, we must first sketch in the background of the dramatic changes which modified the ethos of Britain in the twentieth century.

1. *Changes in the National Ethos*

Three cataclysmic factors have radically changed optimistic imperialistic Edwardian England into the sober, realistic, country of today. The first was the horrifying impact of two World Wars. The second was the change from an opulent centre of empire spanning the seas to the leading partner of a freely associated British Commonwealth of Nations, with the passage of the Statute of Westminster in 1931. The third is the institutionalization of the concept of social justice in the development of the Social Welfare State. In consequence of this searing and apocalyptic revelation of the two World Wars, the humanists committed themselves to a greater humaneness, and the optimistic liberal Christians began to think again about that destructive selfishness in man which an older theology had called original sin, and of man's desperate need of the transformation of Divine grace.[1] Theology, as we shall see, became more realistic, knowing from bitter experience that man is both crucifier as well as redeemable.

The second great change in British life—Britain's reduced political and economic role as the Empire became a Common-wealth—had spiritual results more difficult to calculate. Among them was the desire to seek for a new political and economic grouping in an United Europe with a Common Market, with parallel overtures in which the British Churches renewed contact with their European ecclesiastical cousins in denominational as well as ecumenical conferences. A sense of European spiritual soli-darity is growing apace.

The third, and certainly the most significant, change in twen-tieth century Britain is the establishment of the Social Welfare State. The old England of the two nations, the haves and have-nots, is dying rapidly and is being accelerated by the proliferation of new universities. The fact that this social revolution has been accomplished without bloodshed and in silence is a tribute to the cooperation of humanists and political reformers, on the one hand, and to the impact of Christian socialism and liberalism on the other hand. Many of the more cautiously hopeful Britons look with pride on the establishment of the Social Welfare State as not only the half-way house between the excesses of totalitarian Communism in the East and of relatively unbridled Capitalism in the West, but also as the pattern of the future. On the other side, the baffled look to tradition as their guide in a desperate attempt to create a "Second Elizabethan Age." It is significant that the latter view-point is typical of the middle classes (and often of the elderly members of that class) who are the chief support of the Churches, and that it is the Churches with traditional creeds, liturgies, sacra-ments, and church order (Roman Catholic and Anglican) which are making the greatest strides in contemporary England.

What has been the effect of the Welfare State on English Christianity? There have been advantages and disadvantages. Among the former are the fact that there is a greater awareness of the tenets of Christian faith and ethics in the schools and conse-

[1] See D. R. Davies, *On to Orthodoxy*, p. 27.

quently, as educational levels have arisen, so has the quality of Christian proclamation in pulpit, television and broadcasting. Furthermore, as the State has relieved the Churches of most of their ancient responsibilities for education and social welfare, it has liberated them to concentrate on the preaching and living of the Gospel as the answer to the perennial desperateness of the heart of man faced with his three ancient enemies: the egotism of sin in all its personal and anti-social manifestations, the bitterness of physical and mental suffering, and the tragedy of death. One further advantage is that it has eliminated almost all those nominal Christians who attend worship for the sake of respectability or social prestige. Hence the Church of Christ has been freed to become the more fully committed Church of the remnant, when previously it had been what our forefathers called, with curled lip, a "mixed multitude." Furthermore, although the protection of the State is real and important, it is also very impersonal; so the Churches exist in part to be living centres of community life. In all this there is clear and unmistakable gain. Where, then, is there loss?

A Church no longer allowed to express its love for its neighbour in education and social welfare might degenerate into moralistic pietism, sitting at ease in Zion. Irrelevant on the social questions of the day, or muzzled because of its dependence upon the State's sustentation of its members, it could easily lapse into an euphoric type of worship which was no more than escapism from the here into the hereafter. That fate can alone be avoided by a Church whose preachers will be the watchdogs of the nation's conscience, and the critics of the arrogance, the secularism, the chauvinism, and the unfinished tasks of the State. Happily there are signs that the contemporary Church does not lack men of courage and charity to speak the prophetic Word of God. Such preaching is undoubtedly needed in a period when West Indian and African ghettoes are being established in London and Birmingham, and when fear takes the form of advocating massive retaliation and "overkill" in military strategy.

The cumulative effect of these three significant changes in British life has been to re-establish conviction in the centre, while demolishing the outworks of theology. The latter part of our period has seen the demise of Liberalism in politics and in theology. Moreover, the Christian faith and life have been subjected to the most relentless attacks from Darwin's day to Freud's. In addition, the rapid changes in the political and social maps of Europe, Africa, and the East, not to mention the seismic shock to the conscience caused by Hiroshima and Nagasaki, all counsel caution and moderation, not optimism. Interim judgments and shortened horizons are definitely the order of the day. The dominant note in Christian theology is realism, and the clue for that is found not only in the spirit of the times but in the very centre of the Christian saga. For there the cross of Christ cautions against all facile optimism, and the resurrection of Christ against all desperate pessimism. As we shall see, the development of Christian thought in the first three decades of this century is from theologies of explanation and experience to theologies of redemption, from confidence in man's automatic progress to perfection to confidence alone in God who wrought victory from the apparent disaster of the Cross, from secular utopianism to the rule of God, from the horizontal to the vertical dimension. In short, it is a journey from immanence to transcendence, from general revelation to Biblical redemption.

2. Immanentalism: The "New Theology"[2]

Immanentalism was given impetus from both theological and sociological pressures at the very beginning of the century. Harnack's influential *Das Wesen des Christentums* (1900) appeared in English translation in 1901 as *What is Christianity?* Suspicious of dogma, as the unwarrantable Hellenization of the Gospel, Harnack stressed the religion *of* Jesus, not the traditional religion *about* Jesus, and came to the conclusion that it was essentially the proclamation of the Fatherhood of God and the brotherhood of man. On this analysis, religion was less mystical than moral in character. This very emphasis was the more gladly accepted because it implied that it was the duty of Christians, along with all

[2] The following are the major re-statements of theology in an extreme immanental and experiential direction: K. C. Anderson, *The Larger Faith*; R. J. Campbell, *The New Theology*, *New Theology Sermons*, and *Christianity and the Social Order*; J. Warschauer, *The New Evangel*; T. Rhondda Williams, *The New Theology—An Exposition*; C. H. Vine, ed., *The Old Faith and the New Theology*; and the work of an American theologian, W. L. Walker, *What about the New Theology?* A similar movement in America was termed "The Social Gospel" and its leading exponent was Walter Rauschenbusch. For the impact of this movement on American Protestant worship, see the present writer's article, "The Expression of the Social Gospel in Worship," in *Studia Liturgica* (Rotterdam), Vol. II, No. 3 (September 1963), pp. 174-92. The term "new theology" was first used in a precise sense by the American theologian, Theodore T. Munger, in *The Freedom of Faith* (1883) in which the view was traced through Horace Bushnell to S. T. Coleridge.

men of goodwill, to bring in the Kingdom of God. This notion harmonized perfectly with the demands of Socialism for the establishment of the classless society. Essentially the New Theology was a moral awakening within the Protestant Churches, in which the conception of social justice was expounded as an imperative of the Gospel in contradistinction to the ruthlessly impersonal ethics of competitive industrialism. It had, of course, other characteristic liberal features, including a stress on evolution rather than Divine irruption as God's method. It rejected verbal inspiration of the Scriptures and materialistic ideas of future punishment, and generally accepted the conclusions of modern science which laid stress on the education of character as opposed to revivalism. It made little of the Church, and everything of the Kingdom of God which it interpreted as utopianism.

Its most distinguished, if controversial, English exponent was R. J. Campbell, minister of City Temple, the most influential Free Church pulpit in London, who had been brought up as an Anglican and who, after lamenting the chaos his new iconoclasm had created, returned to the Church of England.[3] But although the leader of the movement defected, its popularity remained undiminished in the Free Churches until the middle of the third decade of the century.

It was born from a belief in the necessity of re-articulating the Christian faith in terms of the indwelling of God in the universe and in mankind. It was conceived that the older orthodoxy had presented the doctrine of the divine transcendence in such a way as "to amount to a practical dualism, and to lead men to think of God as above and apart from His world instead of expressing Himself through the world."[4] The older conception of Deity had indeed fitted God into the Procrustean bed of Greek philosophy, with its stress upon His immutability and impassability. The result was that this distant, almost Aristotelian, Deity was pictured as an absentee God, not as the Biblical God "who visits and redeems His people." Moreover, His infrequent visits were conceived as miraculous irruptions into the natural order, as in the crossing of the Red Sea to deliver the people of Israel or in the Resurrection to deliver the Crucified Leader of the new people of God. Apart from these quite unpredictable incursions, the older evangelicalism believed that He made an equally unpredictable descent into the human soul once in a life-time, at conversion. The new immanence emphasized, in however exaggerated a way, that God's dealings

---

[3] See *A Spiritual Pilgrimage.*   [4] *The New Theology*, p. 4.

with men were continuous, not occasional; that His influence was known in the provident over-ruling of the universe in its constancy and order; that He was the Creator of the moral law that bound human households, societies, and nations together; and that His constant inspiration was the fountain of truth, beauty, and goodness in the universe and in mankind. This countered the old supernaturalism, revivalism, intellectual Philistinism, occasionalism, and individualism. It was undoubtedly a formidable case that the New Theology was able to make against the old orthodoxy.

The New Theology became a crusading theology precisely because it was believed that the significant drift from the Churches already apparent at the beginning of the century was due to anachronistic statements of theology, including dogmatic beliefs about "the Fall, the scriptural basis of revelation, the blood-atonement, the punishment of sin, heaven and hell" which Campbell believed to be "not only misleading, but unethical."[5] Where churches were full, and thus meeting the needs of modern men, Campbell asserted that it was not because of the doctrines they preached, but because of their deep human sympathies. "Religion is necessary to mankind," said Campbell, "but churches are not."[6] Furthermore, the new anti-authoritarianism of the immanental theology was not a revolution in Protestantism alone, it was already being embraced by brave souls within Roman Catholicism. Campbell pointed to Father Tyrrell, the Jesuit and Modernist, to Archdeacon Wilberforce in the Church of England, to the Frenchman Auguste Sabatier, and to T. Rhondda Williams, a Congregationalist—all were swallows of the new theological summer.

Furthermore, Campbell argued that the new theology was essentially a more spiritual Socialism. "The great social movement which is now taking place in every country of the civilised world toward universal peace and brotherhood and a better and fairer distribution of wealth is really the same movement as that which in the more distinctly religious sphere is coming to be called the New Theology." Indeed, the term theology is almost a misnomer for a "moral and spiritual movement" which recognizes that "we are at the beginning of a great religious and ethical awakening."[7]

Why was this form of liberal Protestantism so greatly attracted to Socialism? It was due to a sense of the radical contradiction between the Christian standard of conduct and the impersonalism and ruthless competition of a commercial and industrial society.

[5] *Ibid.*, p. 9.   [6] *Ibid.*, p. 12.   [7] *Ibid.*, p. 14.

Thus "to that end we must destroy the social system which makes selfishness the rule and compels a man to act on his lower motives, and we must put a better in its place. . . . In a word we want collectivism in place of competition; we want the Kingdom of God."[8]

Campbell, in the same year in which *The New Theology* appeared, devoted another book exclusively to the social question. It was entitled *Christianity and the Social Order*. It was a vigorous attempt to demonstrate the correspondence between the principles of Christianity and those of modern Socialism. It began by showing that nearly 75 per cent of the adult population of Britain was permanently out of touch with organized religion. The artisans, as well as the professional and upper classes, had rejected Christianity as irrelevant, leaving the Churches as the haunts only of the respectable bourgeoisie. What was so disturbing to Campbell was the thought that such other-worldliness, as presently taught in the pulpits, was not merely irrelevant, but it was also "totally absent from primitive Christian thought."[9] He recognized that the High Church clergy of the Church of England and the members of the Salvation Army were exceptions to the rule, for both served the poor with distinction. Nonetheless he felt this was to deal with symptoms, not with causes. Charity demoralized the poor; social justice would elevate them. Socialism was welcomed for two reasons: it was a concern for a genuinely international fellowship and the message of hope for the oppressed and unprivileged everywhere. Campbell documents his indictment of the callousness of the ruling classes and the indifference of the middle classes with telling statistics, of which two typical examples may be given. The first makes full use of the fact that "about one-seventieth part of the population of the United Kingdom owns far more than one-half of the entire accumulated wealth, public and private."[10]

The other chilling example is cited from Charles Booth's *Life and Labour of the People of London*, the volume that lifted the manhole lid from the obnoxious sociological sewers of Edwardian London, to the effect that "the classes on or below the poverty line of earnings not exceeding a guinea per week per family number 1,292,737 or 30.7% of the whole population."[11] It was a damning exposure of the hypocrisy of a supposedly Christian nation's failure to fulfil the second Christian commandment to love its neighbour as

8 *Ibid.*, p. 249.
9 *Christianity and the Social Order*, p. ix.
10 *Ibid.*, p. 160.   11 *Ibid.*, p. 171.

itself. The book concluded with a peroration on Socialism, which must be quoted because it expresses so completely the coalescence (and confusion) of Christian and collectivist hopes which was typical of the new theology:

"The normal life should be the life of brightness and joy. And this is the life which is in the gift of that greater day which is already on the horizon, when the motives of greed and fear will have passed away for ever by the coming of a social order in which there shall be no longer any room for them. The rich man will lose nothing that he has now, and he will gain immeasurably in the joy of seeing everywhere around him a contented and happy people, his brothers and equals. To the poor it will mean the fulfilment of the promise uttered in the name of Jesus: 'I am come that they might have life and have it more abundantly.' To all alike it will be the fulfilment of the prayer of Jesus, 'That they may all be one.' "[12]

It must be remembered that the more Catholic theologians in the Church of England were also convinced of the compatibility of Christianity and Socialism. Had not Charles Gore confessed as much in the wry epigram: "Each for himself and God for us all, as the elephant said when he danced among the chickens"?

Was the new theology, then, the historic Christian faith with the substitution of collectivist and this-worldly ethics for the individualistic and other-worldly ethics of orthodoxy and pietism? It was this, but also much more than this. The new ethics required a radical reformulation of the historic theology for its support, and the reconstruction of theology was as controversial as the political colour of the ethics. The new theology involved a new Christology, a new interpretation of sin, a new eschatology with a revised view of man's destiny, and a radical ecclesiology, with profound consequences for the understanding of worship.

In Christology the deity of Christ was repudiated, because it was believed that the Council of Chalcedon was guilty of dualism in defining the historic Christ as a personality in whom were united two different natures, divine and human.[13] Campbell insisted that all Christians accepted in practice the identity of the divine and human in Jesus and potentially in themselves. To the objection that this was to make Christ only a man, he replied: "I make Him the Only Man! . . . We have only seen the perfect manhood once and that was the manhood of Jesus. The rest of us have to get

[12] *Ibid.*, pp. 283-84.   [13] *The New Theology*, pp. 77, 81.

there."[14] Yet the unity between Christ and God was posited exclusively in moral, not in metaphysical terms. This alone could guarantee that Jesus would be humanity's exemplar. Hence the new theology's emphasis was all on the humanity of Jesus. "All honour," Campbell wrote, "to those who have called us back to the real Jesus, the Jesus of Galilee and Jerusalem, the Jesus with the prophet's fire, the Jesus who was so gentle to children and erring women, and yet before whom canting hypocrites and truculent ecclesiastics slunk away abashed."[15] Campbell seemed to be unaware, until the fact was pointed out to him by Bishop Charles Gore, that his virtual denial of the Incarnation of Christ was to remove the only lever great enough to raise humanity from its acquisitiveness, for Divine grace is needed even more than a perfect exemplar of altruism.[16]

Campbell's most scandalous statements, however, were his redefinition of sin as a blundering search for God, as contrasted with the Biblical conception of rebellion against God. He was, perhaps, unfortunate in the examples he chose. He wrote: "The man who got dead drunk last night did so because of the impulse within him to break through the barriers of his limitations, to express himself, and to realise more abundant life." As if this were not a Dionysiac enough interpretation of religion, Campbell continued: "The roué you saw in Piccadilly last night, who went out to corrupt innocence and wallow in filthiness of the flesh, was engaged in his blundering quest for God."[17]

There was more justification for Campbell's reinterpretation of the Atonement in terms of the vicarious principle operative in daily life than for his euphoric interpretation of sin. But this, too, gave offence because of his choice of illustration. "Go," he wrote, "with J. Keir Hardie to the House of Commons and listen to his pleading for justice to his order, and you see the Atonement."[18] Campbell's chief point was to stress that Christianity should not confine itself to a devotional attitude to Christ's sacrifice on the Cross but should issue in atoning action to overcome the inequalities of society. His mistake, however, was to reduce the work of Christ to an illustration from being the act that inaugurated the new relationship between God and men.

[14] *Ibid.*, p. 77.   [15] *Ibid.*, pp. 80-81.
[16] Gore's critique was *The New Theology and the Old Religion.*
[17] Both citations are from a sermon on "More Abundant Life" preached in City Temple on March 18, 1906, and republished in *The New Theology*, p. 151.
[18] *Ibid.*, p. 169.

The radical revision of the orthodox conception of man's destiny as well as the redefinition of the role of the Church is fully contained in the exposition of the key concept of the new theology— the Kingdom of God. This was the characteristic concept of Liberal Protestantism throughout the present century, and none was held more tenaciously by Christian laymen in our time who found in it the sanctification of their secular vocations as service for Christ in the world. And this, despite the fact that Schweitzer's *The Quest of the Historical Jesus*, appearing in English translation in 1910, had entirely shattered the view that the Kingdom of God was the earthly establishment of a kingdom of social betterment by insisting that it was a supernatural and world-denying kingdom to be inaugurated imminently by the Messiah.

The proponents of the new Theology were attracted to the interpretation of the Kingdom of God as the central motif of the teaching of the Synoptic Gospels, for several reasons. They reacted against the Rabbinical and metaphysical subtleties of Paul and held the view that the apostle to the Gentiles had corrupted the simplicity of the Gospel of Jesus, transforming an association for righteousness into an institution with sacraments that bore more likeness to the Graeco-Roman mystery religions than to the preaching of Jesus. They protested against the complacent and otherworldly piety, the restrictive credal and confessional forms, the top-heavy institutionalism, and the bourgeois respectability of the Churches, all of which they believed were responsible for alienating artisans from a commitment to true Christianity. Here, in the Kingdom of God, was a concept profound and simple enough to unite all men of goodwill, and one authentically stamped with the example and teaching of the founder of Christianity, prophet and carpenter. Here was an escape from "cold Christs and tangled Trinities." Here, too, was the basis of the new ethical revolution that the world needed.

The two chief characteristics of the interpretation of the Kingdom of God were its corporate and utopian nature. It chimed with both the collectivistic thinking of the age and the confident belief that universal education and the beneficent impact of the natural, social, and technological sciences were about to usher in an era of unrivalled progress and peace. It was a rigorous attempt to show that Christianity had a here-and-now relevance which orthodoxy had wilfully obscured. Orthodox Christianity had been in error in transferring to a future life the concepts of judgment, heaven, and hell. The so-called "Last Things" could be demonstrated to be operative in the present. "The aim and object of salvation are not the getting of a man into heaven, but the getting of heaven into him."[19]

What, then, becomes of the Church on this view? Campbell maintained that there were two views of the Church held in history, which he described as the *sacerdotal* and *evangelical* concepts. The sacerdotal view was that Jesus founded a religious society to represent Him on earth, which was the ark of salvation, and only members of this Church were saved by being called from a ruined world to a blessed immortality. The gateway was Baptism, the continuing source of grace the Holy Communion, and the essential form of government was by bishops, priests, and deacons, authenticated by an apostolical succession. However influential such a view has been in history, Campbell believed it was founded upon an error: "I am quite sure He [Jesus] never thought of such a thing, and historical criticism of Christian origins does not leave the sacerdotalist much to stand on. Jesus appointed neither bishop nor priest, and never ordained that any mechanical ceremony should be the means of admission to the Christian society or be necessary to the eternal welfare of anyone."[20]

The evangelical view denies that Jesus founded a fixed or rigid organization for His society. On this interpretation the Church is "the totality of the followers of Jesus" and now "most sensible men are satisfied that forms of government matter much less than the kind of life that flourishes in the society itself."[21] It is the strictly functional and instrumental view of the Church as the agent for the Kingdom of God which Campbell preferred, and he and his followers rejected the hierarchical and sacramental view.

They also rejected the view that the function of the Church was to pluck brands from the burning and save them for a future heaven. For them the world was not a city of destruction, as for Bunyan. By contrast they held that the "work of the Church is to save the world and to believe that it is worth the saving."[22] Campbell is sure that, for Christ, "the purpose of the *ecclesia* was to help to realise the Kingdom of God by preaching and living the fellowship of love."[23]

Such, then, was the new theology preached by Campbell and by many other ministers, especially in the Free Churches. Among

19 *The New Theology*, p. 224.   20 *Ibid.*, p. 242.
21 *Ibid.*, pp. 242-43.   22 *Ibid.*, p. 244.
23 *Ibid.*

them the best known were the Rev. C. Ensor Walters, the Methodist crusader who had sat with Bernard Shaw as a vestryman of the St. Pancras ward of London; the chivalrous Silvester Horne, minister of Whitefield's Memorial (Congregational) Church and a member of Parliament in the Liberal interest; the doughty John Clifford, Baptist divine of London, leader of the Passive Resistance Movement against the levy of an education rate to support parochial schools in 1903—that last gasp of the Nonconformist Conscience—and supreme democrat[24] and social reformer. They were a dauntless company and did much to prepare the way for the coming in due time of the Social Welfare State. Certainly they sensitized the consciences of the churchly middle classes to the needs of working men and women. Certainly they insisted that pious attitudes must be translated into social actions and they banished a self-regarding and valetudinarian pietism. But in their main object, to entice the alienated artisans into the Church, they failed and failed miserably. The working-man who played billiards or darts in the settlement churches, or attended lectures on social problems, felt no compulsion to attend the worship or join the membership of the churches. Perhaps this was because apostles of the new theology had taught the lessons of the equivalence of Christianity and Socialism, and the reduction of theology to ethics, and the other-worldly to the this-worldly, only too well. The artisans took them at their word.

The effects of the new theology on worship may easily be imagined. If all sacraments were merely the vestiges of sacerdotalism, and sacerdotalism was an erroneous conception of the nature of the Church, then both Baptism and Holy Communion were merely antiquarian trappings. There was, in any case, little point in baptizing a child into the name of the Holy Trinity, for carpenter Christology had removed the halo of Divinity from Christ, and His Community was merely a human association for the betterment of human relations like any other Ethical Culture society, with perhaps a capacity for generating more sentiment. Holy Communion could not remain, in the traditional sense, a means of grace; it could survive only as a useful social ordinance recalling the vows of fidelity made by the community committed to honouring the ethical standards of Jesus. Hymns, indeed, would be composed

[24] He always travelled third class, he explained, "because there is no fourth class, and it enables me to see the class from which I sprang." See Sir James Marchant, *Dr. John Clifford, C.H., Life, Letters and Reminiscences*, pp. 78-79.

joyously to proclaim the advent of the Kingdom of God—and this was the abiding contribution to worship of the new theology movement. Prayers would confess the corporate sins of anti-social behaviour and intercessions would meaningfully recall the underprivileged children who had previously been conveniently forgotten. Sermons, above all, would ring like bells—the chime of compassion for the poor alternating with the clangour of prophetic denunciation of the callously opulent. But the real thrust of the movement was ethical action. The adoration of God lost its priority and holiness its ultimacy, and the earthly paradise obscured the home of the saints contemplating the vision of God and enjoying the love of God. The tragedy was that worship, on this analysis of priorities, was inevitably regarded as an evasion or postponement of social duty, and the love of neighbour was not thought to require as its absolute prerequisite the love of God. The equation of religion with ethics, of the other-worldly with the irrelevant, of liturgy and sacraments with insincerity, and of piety with the picayune, was to lead to the most appalling triviality, formlessness, and even the glorification of the gauche in Free Church worship for the best part of three decades.

Where there is evident such a weakness in worship it is ultimately traceable to a defective theology. What were the defects of the new theology? The ultimate defect was the utter dominance of the immanental over the transcendental concept of God, so that the mystery, the majesty, and the judgment of God were dissipated. As a consequence there were three other major defects. The imperatives of corporate ethics were aggrandized at the expense of the need for personal transformation and discipleship. The key category—the Kingdom of God—was interpreted in too evolutionary and temporal a manner, ignoring both the Divine initiative in the crisis that brings in the Kingdom and in its transhistorical fulfilment. Finally, the new theology confused the secular utopianism of the day with the historical hope of the Kingdom and grievously undervalued the institutional Church with its corporate discipline and its sacramental life.

The Anglican social reformers wisely chose to make the Incarnation of Christ, rather than the concept of the Kingdom, the fulcrum for social leverage.[25] This safeguarded the divinity of Christ, against the carpenter Christology, provided a high (pos-

---

25 See M. B. Reckitt, *From Maurice to Temple: A Century of the Social Movement in the Church of England.*

sibly idolatrously high) doctrine of the Church as the "extension of the Incarnation," as contrasted with the social gospellers with their instrumentalist approach. It founded the sacraments on the "incarnational principle" and ensured that they remained a perpetual reminder and channel of God's renewal of mankind by grace, as Augustinian conceptions continued to prevail in the Book of Common Prayer against the dilutions of Schleiermacher, Ritschl, and Harnack elsewhere in Protestantism, and they spoke both of a transfigured social order on earth and of the everlasting Communion of the Saints.

The Kingdom of God did offer two advantages, however, for the new theologians: one was the possibility for all men of goodwill to unite in social action, whether inside or outside the Churches. The other was an insistence upon the sovereign freedom of God's Holy Spirit which ceremonialism, sacerdotalism, and an exclusive and hierarchical ecclesiasticism were in danger of forgetting. But these advantages were negatived in part by the double weakness of the concept of the Kingdom of God.[26] It was easily confused with utopian humanism and lent itself to the Pelagianism which sang in a typically popular hymn during this period:

> Rise up, O men of God!
> The Church for you doth wait,
> Her strength unequal to her task;
> Rise up and make her great![27]

3. Immanentalism: The Rediscovery of Mysticism

While the rediscovery of mysticism is, from one standpoint, another indication of the early twentieth century's interest in immanentalism and experience in religion, it is also a deeper because a more authentically *spiritual* phenomenon than the "New Theology" and one that had more enduring influence on the theory and practice of worship. For this evaluation five reasons may be given.

The first is that mysticism locates religion neither in the brain nor in the will (though it is often accompanied with asceticism and

[26] In fairness to Campbell's memory, it should be stated that he bought out the rights of *The New Theology* to prevent it being re-issued and admitted, in *A Spiritual Pilgrimage*, p. 165, that "it was much too hastily written, was crude and uncompromising in statement, polemical in spirit, and gave a totally wrong impression of the quality of the Sermons delivered week by week from the City Temple pulpit." Certainly the 1903 edition of *City Temple Sermons*, Nos. III, IV, XXI, and XXII, all of which are concerned with prayer and its relation to service, bear out the truth of Campbell's contention.

[27] Composed by William Merrill in 1911.

rigorous self- and world-denial), but in the heart. Religion is, for the mystic, essentially the adoration of God and worship is the corporate expression of adoration. In the second place, in an increasingly ecumenical century thoughtful Christians were less interested in the discriminatory theological labels that divide, and more in the experience that unites both Catholic and Protestant. There came to be a renewed interest in the mysticism of Walter Hilton and Dame Julian of Norwich, of St. Bernard and St. Bonaventura, of St. Catherine of Genoa and St. John of the Cross, as representing the Catholic side, and in the mysticism of Boehme and Luther, of Wesley and William Law, of George Fox and John Woolman, as representing the Protestant side. Moreover, the recognition that there had been distinguished mystics in Islam and in Hinduism encouraged the thought that here was indisputable evidence of the universality and of the objective validity of religious experience. Fourthly, the exponents of mysticism in England were not intemperate enthusiasts or hotheads, but historical and critical scholars of intellectual, moral, and spiritual depth and discernment. This was particularly true of William Ralph Inge (1860-1954), for a quarter of a century the famous "Gloomy Dean" of St. Paul's Cathedral; of Baron Friedrich von Hügel (1852-1925), an Austrian Roman Catholic layman of the deepest culture, with many Modernist friends, who settled in England in 1867 and had a long and deep influence on the Church of England; as also of his disciple, Miss Evelyn Underhill (1875-1941), the writer of two classics, *Mysticism* and *Worship*. Finally, each of these authors insisted as strongly on the transcendence of God as on His immanence, and thus corrected the inevitable subjectivity of an exclusive assertion of Divine immanence.

There were special circumstantial reasons for the mystical renaissance.[28] A century of blood-letting was profoundly interested

[28] The immense flood of studies of mysticism may be gathered from the following selection of titles printed in London. The Catholic mystics were translated *en masse*. The three volumes of Fénelon's *Spiritual Letters* were translated by Sidney Lear in 1880, 1892, and 1906. The same author translated the *Spiritual Letters* of St. François de Sales in 1892, while the Salesian *Treatise of the Love of God* was translated by W. J. Knox Little in 1901, and the *Introduction to the Devout Life* by A. Ross in 1925. Madame Guyon's *A Short and Easy Method of Prayer* appeared in English translation in 1901 and her *Autobiography* was translated by Alpen in 1897. Brother Lawrence's *The Practice of the Presence of God* appeared in English in 1906. E. K. Sanders published the following series of studies of Catholic mystics: *Fénelon, His Friends and Enemies* (1901); *Angélique of Port Royal* (1905); *Vincent de Paul* (1913); and *St. Chantal* (1918). Jacob Boehme's *The Way to Christ* was translated in 1911; his *The Aurore* in 1914; his *Six Theosophic Points* in 1919; and his *Confessions* in 1920. William Law's *Liberal*

in the way to achieve interior peace. Grasping materialists were intrigued by those who despised the world and all its successes.[29] Historians turned sceptical by the impossibility of attaining the quest for the historical Jesus, when Harnack and Schweitzer produced such varying reconstructions, preferred the pragmatism of mysticism. Tortured amateur philosophers, weary of idealism's abstractions, turned to the tried and trusty *philosophia perennis* of Christian Platonism. In short, men looked for an exposition of religion to the experts—the saints—after trying the unsatisfactory reconstructions of the philosophers, the historians, and the social scientists. It was the hardest as well as the surest source of religious renewal to be found in a feverish and iconoclastic era.

The three most significant English exponents of mysticism filled three roles. Dean Inge was the pioneer. Baron von Hügel was the philosopher-historian who wisely saw that the institutional and intellectual elements in religion were necessary to undergird the primary mystical element, thus guaranteeing its stability. Evelyn Underhill was the popularizer.

Inge was one of the great and paradoxical personalities of the period. It is possible that he was the most quoted clergyman of his time, for as well as being wise he was witty. Bernard Shaw regarded him as "the greatest intellectual asset of the English Church."[30] It is curious that so urbane and witty a personage should have been attracted to mysticism: yet it was precisely because this witty personality and polymath believed that mysticism was the heart of religion that he gained a hearing for it.

---

and *Mystical Writings* was edited by W. Scott Palmer in 1908 and John Woolman's *Journal and Essays* was edited by A. M. Gummere in 1922. George Fox's *Journal* was edited from the MSS by N. Penney in 1911 (Cambridge), while two admirable accounts of spirituality from Quakers were Rufus Jones's *Spiritual Reformers in the 16th and 17th Centuries* (1914) and Braithwaite's *The Beginnings of Quakerism* (1912). Dom Cuthbert Butler's study, *Western Mysticism*, appeared in 1922, and the greatest volume in the field, Baron von Hügel's *The Mystical Element of Religion*, appeared in the same year as Brémond's superb *Histoire Littéraire du Sentiment Réligieux en France* (6 vols., Paris, 1923). These are but trickles of what was a torrent of works on mysticism which appeared in the first quarter of the present century. It should also be noted that William James in his *Varieties of Religious Experience* (1902) gave a spur to phenomenology and pragmatism, as well as making popular the new study—the psychology of religion.

[29] One recalls the assertion of Chesterton that an age is attracted by the saints that contradict it most, as his explanation of the attraction of the Victorian industrialists for St. Francis the mystic of nature and of the attraction of our contemporary relativists for the massive objectivity of the *Summa* of St. Thomas Aquinas.

[30] Sidney Dark, *Five Deans*, p. 211. Archbishop Temple, however, outshone Inge in constructive intellectual capacity and his influence was more widespread. For an admirable biography, see Adam Fox, *Dean Inge*.

Inge believed in the ultimate coincidence of philosophy and religion: "The goal of philosophy is the same as the goal of religion—perfect knowledge of the Perfect."[31] It was, however, only in a single chapter of the long history of philosophy that Inge found the confluence of rational thinking with a mystical apprehension of God. This was neo-Platonism and its leading exponent was Plotinus. Inge, in fact, became the chief expositor of the Plotinian system and produced the results of his studies in the Gifford Lectures, published in 1918 as *The Philosophy of Plotinus*. In the introduction he stated: "I have steeped myself in his writings, and I have tried not only to understand them as one might try to understand any other intellectual system, but to take them as a guide to right living and right thinking. He must be studied as a spiritual director, a prophet and not only as a thinker. We can only understand him by following him and making his experience our own."[32] For him Platonism was the perennial philosophy and consequently he concluded: "We cannot preserve Platonism without Christianity, or Christianity without Platonism, or civilization without both."[33] The value of thus combining philosophy and mysticism was that the dual search would deliver the modern world from both shallow rationalism and emotional irrationalism.

Inge's pioneering contributions to English religion were, however, made in two earlier volumes, the Bampton Lectures published as *Christian Mysticism* (1899) which excited considerable interest in the University of Oxford, and *Studies in English Mystics* (1907).

Inge began *Christian Mysticism* by defining mysticism as "the attempt to realise the presence of the living God in the soul and in nature, or, more generally, as *the attempt to realise, in thought and feeling, the immanence of the temporal in the eternal and of the eternal in the temporal*."[34] He claimed that it rested on four basic propositions or articles of faith. These were: the soul is the organ of spiritual truth; man in knowing God is a partaker of the Divine nature; sensuality and selfishness are absolute disqualifications for spiritual knowledge; and "the true hierophant of the mysteries of God is love."[35] He concluded the general discussion of mysticism by asserting that the mystic makes it the aim of his life "to be transformed into the likeness of Him in whose image

[31] *Contemporary British Philosophy*, Series I, p. 191.
[32] I, p. 7.   [33] *Ibid.*, II, p. 227.
[34] *Christian Mysticism*, p. 5.   [35] *Ibid.*, p. 9.

he was created." The ladder of perfection, the commonest image for this process, is usually marked by three steps or stages of ascent: the purgative, the illuminative, and the unitive life.

The second chapter deals with the mystical element in the Bible, stressing its great importance for Paul and the author of the Fourth Gospel, the latter being "the charter of Christian Mysticism."[36] The third and fourth chapters describe Christian Platonism and Speculative Mysticism in the East and in the West, respectively. Scholasticism is criticized as "philosophy in chains" and the *via negativa* of the Pseudo-Dionysius as "mysticism blind-folded."[37] The fifth and sixth chapters treat of Practical and Devotional Mysticism. Inge regards the introspective, negative, and quietistic mystics of the Counter-Reformation as being more important historically than intrinsically, believing that "the spiritual Christianity of the modern epoch is rather called to the consecration of art, science, and social life than to lonely contemplation."[38]

The most important seventh and eighth chapters on Nature, Mysticism, and Symbolism show the importance both of the Incarnation and of the sacramental system in Christianity and of the necessity of mysticism for the apprehension of their meaning. "I do not shrink from expressing my conviction," asserts Inge, "that the true meaning of the sacramental system, which in its external forms is so strangely anticipated by the Greek mysteries, and in its inward significance strikes down to the fundamental principles of mystical Christianity, can only be understood by those who are in some sympathy with mysticism."[39] He is equally convinced that the abstract mysticism of the negative way is dangerous to Christian faith and worship, for it insists that all symbols are veils between our eyes and reality and must be done away with.

The final chapter has some significant constructive suggestions to offer. Like von Hügel after him, Inge insists that every religion must have an institutional as well as a mystical element. "Just as, if the feeling of immediate communion with God has faded, we shall have 'a dead Christ,' as Fox the Quaker said of the Anglican Church in his day; so, if the seer and prophet expel the priest, there will be no discipline and no cohesion."[40] Nonetheless, as the older seats of infallible authority, the infallible Church and the infallible Book, are so fiercely assailed, the only alternative authority is that of spiritual religion experienced in life. Thus a renais-

36 *Ibid.*, p. 44.   37 *Ibid.*, p. 148.   38 *Ibid.*, pp. 244-45.
39 *Ibid.*, p. 260.   40 *Ibid.*, pp. 329-30.

sance of mysticism is the primary need of Christianity in the twentieth century.

Studies of English Mystics is a slighter volume, but its importance lies in the fact that it recalled the pragmatic English to their sober, yet tender traditions of mystical piety. The introductory chapter on the psychology of mysticism warned against the two dangers that come from too entire a dependence upon feeling in mysticism: the antinomianism that holds that the sins of the body cannot stain the soul, and the quietism that ends in purposeless passivity. In its day the studies of the *Ancren Riwle*, Julian of Norwich, Walter Hilton, and William Law, were new. That they are now commonplace is a tribute to Inge's instruction and evocation of interest. The inclusion of studies of Wordsworth and Browning, while unusual, was a stroke of genius, for no poets were more popular among the preachers of the day and therefore likelier to win Inge an audience for a more thorough-going consideration of traditional mysticism.

The conclusion of the volume is an admirable analysis of the attractions of mystical religion for thoughtful people. It is precisely those persons who crave for a basis of belief that will not rest on tradition or authority or historical evidence, but on the ascertainable facts of human experience, who find the study of mysticism alluring. For the mystics are the only thorough-going empiricists. "They guide us to the perennial fresh springs of religion, and present it to us as a living and active force, as palpable and undeniable as the so-called 'forces of nature,' though less easy to explain and control. . . . The religions of authority are tottering to their fall; but the religion of the Spirit is still near the beginning of that triumphant course which Christ foretold for it on the last evening of His life: 'When He, the Spirit of Truth is come, He will guide you into all truth . . . He will glorify Me; for He will take of Mine, and will show it unto you.' "[41]

Baron Friedrich von Hügel had a mind of less brilliance, but of more balanced profundity than Inge. Moreover, although he was a layman, no priest was ever a more dedicated director of the souls of the intelligent than he. His religious loyalty to the Roman Catholic tradition was joined to an almost universal charity which could sympathise with the Roman Catholic Modernists such as Loisy and

[41] *Ibid.*, pp. 238-39. In view of the next paragraph it is interesting to read Inge's tribute to von Hügel in *God and the Astronomers*, p. 120: "There is no writer on the philosophy of religion with whom I am more in general sympathy and from whom I have learned more than Friedrich von Hügel."

Tyrrell, on the one hand, and with the mystics of the Islamic and Hindu traditions, on the other. No other religious thinker of the period insisted more strongly than he on the necessity for a triple rope to make religion strong: with mystical, intellectual, and institutional strands. No other thinker of his day was more aware of the fructifying contribution religion has made to culture, nor of the importance of all the intellectual, moral, and spiritual disciplines in their contribution to human culture and well-being. Although a great phenomenologist, as his classical study of *The Mystical Element of Religion as studied in Saint Catherine of Genoa and her Friends* (1909, 1923, and 1961) abundantly demonstrates, the emphasis on the transcendent reality of God increased steadily in the books that followed it. *Eternal Life* (1912); *Essays and Addresses in the Philosophy of Religion* (1st Series, 1921; 2nd Series, 1926); *The Reality of God* (1931) and *Selected Letters* (1933) are overwhelming testimony to this gifted layman's concern to express the mystery and grace of the spiritual life in its historical, theological, and practical dimensions in all his writings.

He analysed the three elements which he believed were disclosed in Western civilization.[42] There is Hellenism, the thirst for richness and harmony; there is Christianity, the revelation of personality and the depth of existence; and there is Science, the apprehension of fact and law. All three of them are necessary to the fulness of human life.

Religion is the apprehension of the reality of God. God is revealed to us in experience, though by no means is the meaning of God exhausted by our experience of Him. Von Hügel lays the strongest emphasis on the Divine transcendence. Yet although God Himself transcends space and time, the religion in which we apprehend Him lies within the context of our life in this world. Consequently von Hügel warns, "There is no such thing for man as a complete escape from history and institutions."[43] Religion, therefore, must manifest itself in historical forms—in institutions like the Church, and through sensuous media such as rituals and sacraments, art and music, and the like. In these the Divine is incarnated, so that the transcendent reality becomes immanent in earthly forms. The finest expression in history of the religious spirit is, for the Baron, the institution of the Catholic Church, with all the

[42] *The Mystical Element of Religion* . . . , Vol. I, Chap. 1. For von Hügel's relations to Catholic Modernism see M. D. Petre, *Von Hügel and Tyrrell*, and A. R. Vidler, *The Modernist Movement in the Roman Church*.
[43] *Essays and Addresses*, Series I, p. 15.

richness of its worship and symbolism. At the same time he will be the last to deny value to any way by which the genuine understanding of God has been historically mediated in any religion. From this all-too-compressed summary of his views, it will be clear that Baron von Hügel's contribution to mysticism has profoundly important effects for worship, for he recognizes it as the corporate expression of adoration, penitence, petition, intercession, and consecration. Moreover, he knows how the liturgy with the subtle aid of repeated ritual, with the harmony of praise, with the visually dramatic actions of the sacraments, together with the great expectations it arouses in the hearts of believers on the great festivals of the Christian Year, is a potent teacher of the Christian faith and a powerful channel of Divine grace.

The chief importance of Baron von Hügel, however, was the great influence of his wise and judicious understanding of many aspects of religion, including mysticism. This was particularly valuable in an age of febrile change, when the latest fashion was apt to jettison the traditional values. He was the great synthetist of the early part of the century. This is finely exhibited in the famous second chapter of *The Mystical Element of Religion*.[44]

Von Hügel argued that a retrospect of man's religious life would show that each individual has been shaped religiously by three modes of apprehension. As a child, sense and memory were the chief means of apprehending religion and at this stage "the External, Authoritative, Historical, Traditional, Institutional side and function of Religion are everywhere present."[45] The youth, however, approaches religion in terms of question and argument, so that "Religion here becomes Thought, System, a Philosophy."[46] The mature man has emotional and volitional, ethical and spiritual powers, and these are fed by the experimental and mystical side of religion. "Here Religion is felt rather than seen or reasoned about, is loved and lived rather than analyzed, is action and power, rather than external fact or intellectual verification."[47] Hence in the religious development of man three essential elements come into play: the institutional, the intellectual, and the mystical.

Von Hügel then demonstrates that each element in the triple strand has special motives for suppressing the other two. The

[44] Von Hügel notes (p. viii of the Preface to the 2nd edn., 1923) that Bishop Charles Gore had asked for a separate publication of the 32 pages of Chapter II, concerning the "Three Elements of Religion."
[45] *The Mystical Element of Religion*, Vol. I, p. 51.
[46] *Ibid.*, p. 52.   [47] *Ibid.*, p. 53.

historical and institutional element is spatially and temporally exclusive in asserting the finality of the revelation and the institution that guarantees it, thus demanding surrender, not analysis, and in the process starving or cramping science and literature, art, and politics. How is this to be avoided? Von Hügel answers: "Through dependence upon the living God cooperating with the living soul!"[48] By this he means relying on the inexhaustible self-interpreting illumination of God. Similarly, there will be the tendency on the part of the newly awakened soul experiencing interior freshness to despise the external aids of religion and to refuse the concrete yoke of the institutional discipline, but only at the cost of the soul becoming unconsciously weak or feverish. But, he warns, "The Church's insistence upon some vocal prayer, upon some differentiated specific acts of the various moral and theological virtues, upon sacramental practice . . . is a living commentary upon the difficulty and importance of the point under discussion."[49]

Furthermore, there will be an attempt on the part of the emotional element, either alone or in combination with the institutional element, to suppress the analytic and speculative elements. The danger will be that it will cling to historical facts and elude critical examination, or will feed intensely on its own emotions, opposing all slow discrimination or mere approximation. Here, again, "the true solution will ever be found in an even fuller conception of Personality and of its primary place in the religious life."[50] The intellectual element of the personality will be able to provide rest, expression, and purification for the moral and spiritual side of human nature. The rest comes from the intellect's neglect of emotions, actions, and persons, to concentrate on abstractions and things. The expression comes from the restating by the intellect of the results of the moral and spiritual activities so that they may be understood by civilization and culture. "Above all, they can help to purify these moral-spiritual activities, owing to their interposing . . . a zone of abstraction, of cool, clear thinking."[51]

Finally, von Hügel anticipates and answers the criticism that this three-fold analysis of religion is excessively intellectual, Pelagian, and Epicurean. He argues that Christianity is not a religion for intellectuals only, while all Christians use their intellects. He splendidly claims that some intellectual virtues, such as moral courage, intellectual honesty, chivalrous fairness, manly renuncia-

48 *Ibid.*, p. 73.   49 *Ibid.*, p. 74.   50 *Ibid.*, p. 76.
51 *Ibid.*, p. 77.

tion of popularity and easy honours, "bear upon them the impress of God and His Christ" as profoundly spiritual qualities. He utterly rejects Pelagianism, claiming that "Every one of our acts, our very physical existence and persistence, is dependent, at every moment and in every direction, upon the prevenient, accompanying and subsequent power and help of God, and still more is every religious, every truly spiritual and supernatural act of the soul impossible without the constant action of God's grace."[52] Yet the actions from without are seen as our volition and are known within as God's energies. Nor is his understanding of religion Epicurean: for it is in the mystical life that the Cross and Renunciation are imitated most deeply.

Although much interested in the Divine immanence in history, von Hügel was even more insistent on the importance of the Divine transcendence. His greatest importance lies in his philosophical balancing of the intellectual, institutional, and mystical elements of religion, as in his ever-repeated stress on the priority and pre-venience of Divine grace and on the significance of eternal life as a present possession and an everlasting hope. The mystics are, for him, ultimately important because they dramatically fulfilled the two necessary conditions for living a fully mature religious life. They are filled with "the vivid, continuous sense that God the Spirit upholding our poor little spirits, is the true originator and the true end of the whole movement" and they possess "the continuous sense of the ever necessary, ever fruitful, ever bliss-producing Cross of Christ—the great law and fact that only through self-renunciation and suffering can the soul win its true self." These are "the two eyes of religion and twin pulse-beats of its very heart" and "have been realized, with magnificent persistence and intensity, by the greatest of the Inclusive Mystics."[53]

Reconsidering his views on religion in the Preface to the second edition of 1923, von Hügel claimed that he now saw with greater clarity that the "Givenness" of all religion worthy of the name is its central characteristic. "The Otherness, the Prevenience of God, the One-sided relation between God and man, these constitute the deepest measure and touchstone of all religion."[54] This prophetic recognition amid the flux of competing immanentalisms is the measure of the greatness of the man, as of his continuing influence after the demise of both Protestant Liberalism and Catholic Modernism and during the resurgence of theologies of revelation and

[52] *Ibid.*, pp. 79-80. [53] *Ibid.*, II, p. 395. [54] P. xvi.

redemption. He had prepared the way to reintegrate transcendence with immanence, and thus opened up a path which later phenomenologists such as Van der Leeuw, Söderblom, and Otto were to follow. In Evelyn Underhill he was to find, in England, the disciple who would make his insights known to the wayfaring pilgrim who could not be expected to grapple with his philosophical profundity and complexity, but who needed his balanced insight into the nature of the religious life.

We turn to Evelyn Underhill,[55] not only because she was a distinguished popularizer (for she was a poet, scholar, and expositor of mysticism in her own right before she met von Hügel), but because she it was who combined an abiding interest in personal mysticism and in public worship and educated the religious public to understand the primary significance of both for the contemporary Church. This educational task was accomplished not only in her published writings but in the many religious retreats of which she was the skilled director, and through her perceptive letters which have been edited with an introduction by Charles Williams.

She wrote thirty-three books, almost all of them concerned with spirituality. Three of them deserve careful attention. These are *Mysticism, A Study of the Nature and Development of Man's Spiritual Consciousness* (1911); *The Mystics of the Church* (1925); and *Worship* (1936). They reveal a mind that found neo-Platonism congenial (as did Dean Inge) in its earlier phase, but which (with the friendship of Baron von Hügel, who had taken the place of Father R. H. Benson as her spiritual director) became increasingly incarnational and more appreciative of the institutional aspects of religion. By 1922 she had become a practising member of the Church of England and belonged decisively to its Catholic wing. The change can be noted in the fact that the first book published after the transition, *The Life of the Spirit and the Life of Today* (1922), included a chapter on "Institutional Religion and the Life of the Spirit," while the next book carried the institutional emphasis in the title, *The Mystics of the Church* (1925). She thus expressed in her own pilgrimage the religious movement of the whole period as it proceeded from immanentalism to transcendentalism, from Liberal Protestantism to Orthodoxy,

[55] See Margaret Cropper, *Evelyn Underhill*, for the facts of her life, and Lucy Menzies, ed., *The Collected Papers of Evelyn Underhill*, for an evaluation by Lumsden Barkway, Bishop of St. Andrews, and for a bibliography of Evelyn Underhill's writings, pp. 37-38. A useful anthology of her writings has been compiled by Thomas Kepler, *The Evelyn Underhill Reader*.

from private mysticism to public worship, from the individual to the institutional expression of allegiance, and from Theocentric to Christocentric faith.

Her first great work was *Mysticism* (1911). It attempted in two parts, the first historical and the second psychological, to "set out and justify a definite theory of man's mystical consciousness."[56] Mysticism was defined as "essentially a movement of the heart, seeking to transcend the limitations of the individual standpoint and to surrender itself to ultimate Reality; for no personal gain, to satisfy no transcendental curiosity, to obtain no other-worldly joys, but purely from an instinct of love."[57] Four basic statements are made about the nature of mysticism: it is practical, not theoretical; it is entirely spiritual; its business and method is love; and true mysticism is never self-seeking.[58] As a definite psychological experience it has two sides: "the Vision or consciousness of Absolute Perfection" and "the inward transmutation to which that Vision compels the mystic, in order that he may be to some extent worthy of that which he has beheld. . . . He has seen the Perfect; he wants to be perfect, too."[59]

Two most important chapters are those on "Mysticism and Theology" and on "Mysticism and Symbolism." The distinction is made between transcendental and immanental mystics and Christian theology provides the best theoretical background, according to Evelyn Underhill, in the doctrine of the Trinity, since it combines the unknowable God with the Wisdom of God (the Son) in a personal principle, while in the doctrine of the Incarnation it explains the nature of the inward and mystical experience where the soul resumes the life history of the race. She wisely adds: "In the last resort, the doctrine of the Incarnation is the only safeguard of the mystics against the pantheism to which they always tend. The unconditioned Absolute, so soon as it alone becomes the object of their contemplation, is apt to be conceived merely as Divine Essence; the idea of personality evaporates and loving communion is at an end."[60]

---

56 *Mysticism*, p. ix.

57 *Ibid.*, p. 84. A more precise definition was supplied in *The Essentials of Mysticism and other Essays*, pp. 4-5: "this adoring and all-possessing consciousness of the rich and complete divine life over against the self's life, and of the possible achievement of a level of being, a sublimation of the self, wherein we are perfectly united with it, may fairly be written down as a necessary element of all mystical life."

58 A summary of statements made on pp. 97, 100, 101, 107, 109.

59 *Ibid.*, p. 108.

60 *Ibid.*, p. 145.

The chapter on "Mysticism and Symbolism" studies three groups of mystical symbols: the image of pilgrimage as the symbol of the Divine transcendence; the image of the lover seeking the Beloved; and the image of the saint seeking purity and perfection. It is strongly asserted that no spiritual experiences are capable of direct description, but they must always be expressed in a symbolic, allusive, and oblique mode, suggesting rather than telling the truth. The importance for worship of the following citation is immeasurable: "The greater the suggestive quality of the symbol used, the more answering emotion it invokes in those to whom it is addressed, the more truth it will convey." Furthermore, a good symbol will use to the utmost "the resources of beauty and of passion, will bring with it hints of mystery and wonder, bewitch with dreamy periods the mind to which it is addressed. Its appeal will not be to the clever brain, but to the desirous heart of man."[61]

The second part of the book is wholly concerned to describe the Mystic Way. Evelyn Underhill elaborates instead of the usual three-fold path a more precise five-fold way. The first stage is awakening or conversion. The second stage is self-knowledge or purgation. The third stage is illumination. The fourth stage is surrender or the dark night of the soul. The fifth and final stage is union.

The novelty of the book consisted in its careful analysis of the five stages of the mystical experience, with many illustrative excerpts from mystics of many religions and centuries, and in the insistence that the state of mystical union does not mean a withdrawal from social duty, but rather that the inclusive mystic is the most active citizen of the Kingdom of God.[62] For the author herself the chief importance of *Mysticism* was that it gained her the friendship of Baron von Hügel.[63]

She granted a positive and educative role to the institution of the Church[64] in her next important volume, *The Mystics of the Church*, conceding that mysticism needs to be tested and corrected by the good sense of the Church, otherwise it grows feverishly emotional, lacking in genial appreciation of other persons, or even narrowly

---

[61] *Ibid.*, p. 151.

[62] See Margaret Cropper, *Evelyn Underhill*, pp. 46-47.

[63] *Ibid.*, p. 5, indicates that von Hügel liked the book but felt it did not do justice to the importance of "liturgical acts, of the Sacraments, of the Visible, of History."

[64] In *The Essentials of Mysticism and other Essays* she had regarded the Church as a necessary nuisance for mystics and was critical of the conservative crudity of the cultus. See esp. pp. 27-28.

intense, combative, and intolerant.[65] In this book she shows for the first time a deep appreciation of Christocentric mysticism. She acknowledges that "Christianity is unique among the world's great religions in this: that its Founder is to His closest followers not merely a prophet, pattern of conduct, or Divine figure revealed in the historic past, but the object here and now of an experienced communion of the most vivid kind." She adds that "Christians claim that this communion has remained unimpaired for nineteen hundred years and is the true source of the Church's undying energy."[66] The persons who have most vividly experienced this communion are, of course, the mystics, and they have been the instruments of making the Church's loyalty to her Master a living thing. Whereas earlier Evelyn Underhill had regarded the Transcendental mystics more highly than the incarnational mystics, now she gives the latter sustained and appreciative treatment.

The fullest recognition of the theological, historical and liturgical role of the Church is provided, however, in her last great book, *Worship* (1936). No book on this theme, treating all its varieties with ecumenical fairness, has been as widely read or as influential in our time in the English-speaking world.[67] Its perspective was that of a "mountain-top view of the longing adoration of man for God."[68] The book was divided into two parts, treating the theory and practice of worship. The first part dealt with the nature of Worship, Ritual and Symbol, Sacrament and Sacrifice, and with the Characters, the Principles, and Liturgical Elements of Christian Worship, as also with the Eucharist and the principles of personal worship. The second part was historical and descriptive, tracing the development of Jewish worship, the beginnings of Christian worship, Catholic worship in East and West, the worship of the Reformed Churches, Free Church worship, and the Anglican tradition. The book demanded careful and objective scholarship, open-mindedness in willing to learn new things, and a capacity to

---

[65] *The Mystics of the Church*, p. 16.

[66] *Ibid.*, p. 24. It had an interesting concluding chapter on modern mystics, including cameo studies of J. W. Rowntree, Charles de Foucauld, and Sadhu Sundar Singh.

[67] Yet she accepted the invitation to write it with great reluctance. See Margaret Cropper, *Evelyn Underhill*, p. 197.

[68] *Ibid.*, p. 197. In a review in *The Christian Century*, Dr. Henry P. Van Dusen declared that "here may be discovered the inner genius of whole branches of Christendom," and *The Times* reviewer acknowledged *Worship* to be "a masterpiece of the spiritual life, free from all professional partisanship and the prejudices of the sacristy—a book that will bear fruit for many years to come among men and women of many different communions."

penetrate beyond labels to realities. Among those whom Evelyn Underhill consulted were Bishops W. H. Frere and Leslie Owen, and Drs. W. Russell Maltby and Nicholas Zernov.

The fine spirit in which it is written may be illustrated from the Preface. She wished to show all traditions, sacramental and non-sacramental alike, "as chapels of various types in the one Cathedral of the Spirit," for each great form of the Christian cultus has as its object "to lead human souls, by different ways, to that pure act of adoration which is the consummation of worship."[69]

For those of the non-sacramental tradition its great value was that it introduced them to the reasons why the Catholic tradition stressed the importance of the sacraments. The universality of sacraments was not, she insisted, as is commonly believed, a witness to the Divine Immanence, but a proclamation of the Divine Transcendence. It is due to man's acknowledgment of the chasm between Creator and creature and "the need of a bridge, an ordained path along which the Eternal Perfect may penetrate time and the things of time." Thus "Here man is pressed by God immanent to prepare the matrix; but it is God transcendent who pours into it His quickening love to cleanse, feed, and transform."[70] Typical also is Evelyn Underhill's pithy distinction between a symbol and a sacrament: "A symbol is a significant image, which helps the worshipping soul to apprehend spiritual reality." On the other hand, "a sacrament is a significant deed, a particular use of temporal things, which gives to them the value of eternal things and thus incorporates and conveys spiritual reality."[71] In consequence sacraments are the expression of an incarnational philosophy. This was a word in season, but only by implication, to the non-sacramental traditions of worship which had lost so much of the sense of wonder, beauty, and mystery in worship by their iconoclasm with reference to symbols and sacraments and by their dry didacticism.

In similar ecumenical fashion, she showed that the Protestant elevation of the Word and the Catholic elevation of the Eucharist were not intended to be alternatives, but are essential and complementary aspects of the Liturgy. She showed that the Christian Year (and it is significant that subsequent to her exposition it became more common for the Free Churches to discard their Puritan opposition to the great Christian festivals) lights up all phases of human experience with the radiance of eternity. Thus, "the helplessness and humility of infancy, the long hidden period of disci-

69 *Worship*, p. viii.   70 *Ibid.*, p. 46.   71 *Ibid.*, p. 43.

pline and growth, the lonely crisis and choice of the temptation, above all the heart-shaking events of Holy Week, Easter, and the Forty Days—all these become disclosures of the Supernatural made through and in man, and therefore having a direct application to man's need and experience."[72]

The book concludes by insisting that ultimately the way of devotion and the way of sacrificial service to others is one way, for both are signs of "Creation's response to its Origin and Lord."[73] The hope for the future is that the true meaning and message of the Incarnation will come to be more perfectly understood, when the demand on man's worshipping love and total self-offering will receive a more complete response—"a response stretching upward in awestruck contemplation to share that adoring vision of the Principle which is 'the inheritance of saints in light,' and downwards and outwards in loving action, to embrace and so transform the world."[74]

After completing *Worship*, Evelyn Underhill gave much time to reflecting on the significance of the Eucharist in another volume, *The Mystery of Sacrifice* (1938). She believed that the Liturgy had become the supreme ritual act of the Christian Family because every aspect of the response which the created order makes to its origin and Lord finds there its sanction and expression. The fully Christian life was, for her, a Eucharistic life. "That is, a natural life conformed to the pattern of Jesus, given in its wholeness to God, laid on His altar as a sacrifice of love, and consecrated, transformed by His inpouring life, to be used to give life and good to other souls."[75]

By her writings Evelyn Underhill taught thousands for whom religion had been ethical idealism, or a set of orthodox opinions, that it was the adventure of holiness, the search for the Perfect Who alone is truth, beauty, and goodness, with the aid of the great guides of the mystics, and with the liturgical and sacramental helps of the Church, and that the greatest bridge between God and men had been thrown across the abyss by the Incarnation.

The concentration on mysticism in the work of Inge, von Hügel and Underhill, and their countless disciples and imitators, was to prove fertile ground for the later growth of orthodoxy in doctrine, the reassertion of the doctrine of the Church as the Body of Christ that was to be recovered in the Ecumenical Movement (both

[72] *Ibid.*, pp. 76-77.   [73] *Ibid.*, p. 343.   [74] *Ibid.*
[75] P. xv.

Protestant and Catholic), and in the renewal of theologies of revelation and redemption in the latter part of the third decade of this century. It cannot have been easy to believe in the ultimate victory of a transcendental concept of God or in a revived ecclesiology when immanentalism was so popular in the Catholic Modernism, the Liberal Protestantism, and the Social Gospel Movement of the first twenty years of the century.

4. The Incarnationalists: Gore and Temple

In Charles Gore (1853-1932) and William Temple (1881-1944), the two leading theologians of the Anglican Communion in the twentieth century, there was to be found the strength of immanentalism. Both emphasized the continuity between the divine operations in providence and grace, and in the consentient witness to God in nature, in history and in conscience, as well as in the recognition of social duty. There was also in both a conviction that faith and truth were ultimately one as guaranteed by the same God who is their originator, and hence they were theologians of revelation and explanation rather than of crisis and redemption. But they also differed very significantly from the extreme Liberal Protestants of the day, or Modernists as they were sometimes called. This can be seen in the significance they gave to the doctrines of the Incarnation, the Church, and the Sacraments. Moreover, such an emphasis strongly undergirded the importance of the cultus, which had been minimized in the ethical and social concerns exaggerated by the Social Gospellers.

This difference is manifest in the devastating critique of immanentalism provided by Gore's *The New Theology and the Old Religion*, which shook Campbell's confidence in his own reconstruction and eventually brought him back to the Anglican fold with the confession that "This poor sad world of ours needs a more strenuous gospel than the assurance that our sins are merely wrong turnings on the upward road, and that all must inevitably come right at the last."[76] The new emphasis is concentrated in Temple's assertion that the Incarnation was the supreme instance of "the immanence of the transcendent."[77]

Our reason for grouping Gore and Temple together, despite the fact that Gore was the leader of the Anglo-Catholics in the Church

[76] *Spiritual Pilgrimage*, p. 173. W. E. Orchard, an early supporter of Campbell, also repented and became a Roman Catholic priest. See his *From Faith to Faith*.
[77] *Nature, Man and God*, p. 290f.

of England and that Temple was not clearly affiliated with any party, is that both were strong incarnationalists and Temple admitted his indebtedness to Gore as a paramount influence. In his dedication to *Studies in the Spirit and Truth of Christianity* (1917), Temple acknowledged his gratitude to Gore as "one from whom I have learnt more than any other now living of the Spirit of Christianity." On many occasions in Temple's public life, when he had to decide whether or not to accept preferments or appointments, Gore was consulted as a second father.[78] While stressing their close affinity, however, it must be emphasized that Temple was far from being an echo of Gore, since he was a brilliant, profound, and independent thinker. Moreover, there were considerable differences in approach between Gore and Temple. Gore was a Biblical and historical scholar by training, while Temple was a philosopher in his approach to the theological task. Furthermore, while each believed in the centrality of the Incarnation and denied any adoptionist Christology, Gore was persuaded to adopt Kenoticism, of which Temple was exceedingly doubtful. Furthermore, while Gore treated the purpose of the Incarnation as the rectification of a fallen world, Temple saw it more positively as the fulfilment of the purpose of creation.[79] Then, again, Temple's experiences brought him into touch with a wider world than Gore's, and he exercised more onerous public and ecclesiastical responsibilities. Finally, Gore was attracted by the Pauline and Temple by the Johannine elements in the New Testament; so that Temple was more sympathetic to mysticism than Gore. This incarnational theology (which Gore preferred to call "Liberal Catholicism") included three essential elements. It combined a deep spiritual devotion mediated by the Liturgy, with an emphasis on candour in Biblical and theological scholarship, together with a passion for social justice. It was, therefore, a subtle combination of devotion, critical independence, and compassion, in which the sacramental devotion of the Tractarians was linked with the Maurician concern for social justice, and both with the Liberal conviction that faith and truth were indissoluble.

In Gore the first element was seen conspicuously in the founda-

78 F. A. Iremonger, *William Temple, Archbishop of Canterbury, His Life and Letters*, pp. 89, 131, 133, 194-95, 262-63, 283, 332. Prestige in his life of Gore (p. 538) credits Temple with the following tribute to Gore: "Though I have had many tutors in Christ, he was perhaps above all others my father; and so far as I can picture Jesus Christ, I picture him as not unlike the father I have lost."
79 See Joseph Fletcher, *William Temple, Twentieth Century Christian*, p. 34.

tion of the Community of the Resurrection in 1887 and in his study of Eucharistic doctrine, *The Body of Christ* (1901).[80] In Temple it was worked out in the sacramental view of the universe in *Nature, Man, and God*, in the two volumes of *Readings in St. John's Gospel*, and in the brilliant account of the Eucharist as the transcript of a redeemed social order on earth in *Hope of a New World*.

The second element of Liberal Catholicism, the correlation of Christian faith with the world's culture, was first seen in Gore's daring essay on Inspiration contributed to *Lux Mundi* in 1889, and the volume was significantly subtitled "a series of studies in the Religion of the Incarnation." Both Biblical criticism and the doctrine of evolution forced him to admit that the knowledge of the Incarnate Lord was limited by the conditions of the first century. He later developed the implications of this acknowledgment in a "Kenotic" view of Christology, by which he meant that the Eternal Logos in becoming man "emptied himself" of the metaphysical attributes of Deity while retaining the moral and spiritual attributes. The approach brought great relief to Christians whose intelligence had hitherto to be strait-jacketed in the confines of unnecessary dogmas. Thereafter Gore aimed at being as open-minded as possible, and often jocularly referred to himself as a "Free-thinker."[81] In fact, however, he held tenaciously to the positions he had maintained in this early period, and so "while in the 1890s he was looked upon as the pioneer of a liberal and progressive theology, thereafter he appeared more in the role of a resolute defender of orthodoxy."[82]

Temple's whole approach, as a philosopher, was to show the rational implications of faith in the spirit of Anselm's *credo ut intelligam*. He claimed in *Mens Creatrix* (1917) and in *Christus Veritas* (1924) that if Reality is sought by the different paths of philosophy, science, and art, they will never meet unless there be a God in whom these values eternally exist. He clearly contends that the most satisfactory explanation of the universe is the hypothesis of its creation by intelligent purpose. Life is seen to have

[80] S. C. Carpenter in *Prophet and Priest, A Lecture given on the Charles Gore Memorial Foundation on 13 November 1952 at Westminster Abbey* writes (p. 15): "Finally, those who knew him, knew also that he was in every fibre of his being, priest of God. His concentration at the altar was amazing. The first time I ever saw him celebrate Holy Communion (it was in a College Chapel), I had the sensation that he was gathering the congregation of young men with a sweep of his arms, and drawing them towards God. And many have testified that it was a revelation to hear him say the Litany."

[81] *Ibid.*, p. 14.

[82] A. R. Vidler, *The Church in an Age of Revolution*, pp. 193-94.

four gradations: matter, life, mind, and spirit, and man is seen as the crown of creation, resembling God, dimly but truly, in his mental and spiritual sensitivities, as in the capacity to understand, to make conscious moral choices, and to live in fellowship. God's intelligence and power are shown in creation and his supreme revelation of Himself is in the Incarnation, which Temple expressed as the concept of the Supreme as servant, and which he believed to be a uniquely Christian insight.

In contributing to the third element of Liberal Catholicism, the concern for social justice, both were equally eminent. Sometimes the fiery words of Bishop Gore as prophet would emerge when they were least expected. When at a formal civic dinner he had pronounced the episcopal blessing, he added, "God forgive us for having all this to enjoy, of which many of our neighbors know nothing."[83] At the age of twenty-six he was the most conspicuous of the university socialists at Oxford, and he was fond of citing A. H. Clough's couplet:

> Thou shalt not covet: but tradition
> Approves all forms of competition.[84]

H. D. A. Major rightly affirmed that Gore had revolutionised the public's concept of the political colour of Church of England clergymen, so that "she who had been aptly described as the Conservative party at prayer, became, as the result of Gore's influence, at least in the person of her Anglo-Catholic clergy, the Socialist party at Mass."[85] Although the son of an Archbishop of Canterbury, and later to attain this highest office in the Anglican Church himself, William Temple showed his concern for the underprivileged by accepting the presidency of the Workers Educational Association, a post which he held from 1908 to 1924. His view was that there was a mental slavery as real as any economic bondage and that "If you want human liberty you must have educated people."[86] His fullest thought on the matter appeared in *Christianity and the Social Order*, a Penguin paperback issued in 1942 which had unusually large sales and earned for him the sobriquet of "the pink Archbishop." It insisted on the Church's

[83] I am unable to trace the exact source of this information, but I believe that the narrator of it was Dr. W. F. Lofthouse in reminiscences recorded in *The Methodist Recorder*, ca. 1960.

[84] G. L. Prestige, *The Life of Charles Gore, a Great Englishman*, p. 71.

[85] *The Modern Churchman*, Vol. XXI (February 1932), p. 583.

[86] F. A. Iremonger, *William Temple*, p. 80.

right and duty to "interfere" in social questions, proved that the right was readily conceded in the past, and expounded the primary and the derivative principles by which any social order is to be judged.

Thus both Gore's and Temple's interpretations of Christianity were heeded precisely because they gave their due weight to the spiritual, the intellectual, and moral-social aspects of man's nature. At the same time they acknowledged the truth of immanentalism in both its Social Gospel and Modernistic forms,[87] while going beyond it to assert that it was the *transcendental* God who was immanent.

It is time to turn to the interpretation of the Incarnation in Gore and Temple, as this was their key category and their distinctive theological contribution. They were, of course, in the main Anglican tradition in stressing the Incarnation, in their loyalty to Patristic thought, their exaltation of reason, and their fidelity to Scripture. But there were three other factors which forced them in this direction. One was that the Incarnation was central in the Biblical and theological researches of Westcott and Hort. In the second place, since the Incarnation stressed the advent of the Logos or Wisdom of God in the flesh, it provided a principle of rationality and coherence, whereby the Christ was the clue both to the ultimate purpose of the Creator and the unique example of the perfect human life. In the third place, the Incarnation as the supreme Sacrament was the authority for the "Sacramental principle," and so for the belief that the Sacraments of Baptism and the Eucharist ministered to the spiritual-physical nature of man.

There was much in common between Gore's *The Incarnation of the Son of God* (1891) and Temple's *Christus Veritas* (1924). Both saw the Incarnation as not only the hinge of history, but also as the climax and crown of Divine revelation. Gore showed that there was a progression in nature from the inorganic to the organic and from the animal to the rational, and this he maintained was a "progressive revelation of God." Temple, too, acknowledged the significance of the same ascending series. Each confessed that the ultimate revelation of God was to be found in the Divine personality

[87] Gore was, however, an unrelenting foe of Modernism, which he conceived to be immanentalism in the most extreme form. The Modernists shared a number of R. J. Campbell's views, but were far better informed on the scientific criticisms of contemporary religion. For Anglican primers on Modernism, see H. D. A. Major, *English Modernism: its Origin, Methods, Aims*; M. G. Glazebrook, *The Faith of a Modern Churchman*, and R. D. Richardson, *The Gospel of Modernism*.

of the Incarnate Lord, who in manifesting the order, moral character, and loving personality of God is thus *Christus Consummator*. But He was more than the exemplar; He was also the Divine force by which Christian character could be realized.

Temple, too, insisted on the necessity of the Incarnation. "It is," he wrote, "the only way in which divine truth can be expressed, not because of our infirmity, but because of its own nature. What is personal can only be expressed in a person."[88] The rationale for the Incarnation is God's own nature as love and man's endowment of spiritual freedom, so that God can attract but never compel men by His love. Also, according to Temple, God did not become a man at the Incarnation, but the Man. Thus there is the assertion of Christ's solidarity with humanity. Furthermore, Temple saw the great importance of the combination of the spiritual and the physical in the Incarnation, as challenging the common belief that the spiritual and the material are mutually exclusive. In consequence Christianity, far from encouraging an asceticism which attempts to flee from the body, or a pietism which escapes the obligations of citizenship, is more this-worldly than most other great religions. This insight he expressed in striking fashion: "Christianity is the most materialistic of all the great religions."[89]

Gore's view of the Church was higher than Temple's. This arose, in part, from the polemical need to counteract Hatch's Bampton Lectures of 1881, which had maintained that the Church was the company of the elect, and therefore invisible. Such visibility as it had, said Hatch, was due to the natural attraction of people with the same aims and beliefs. Gore, on the other hand, argued that the Church was both a supernatural creation and a visible organization. He popularized the idea that the Church is the extension of the Incarnation, a concept he borrowed from Jeremy Taylor who had found it in the early Fathers.[90] To enter the community of the Church is, for Gore, to be incorporated into the life of Christ which is perpetuated by the Spirit in the Church, and the Eucharist is the chief means for perpetuating the life of Christ. His summary of the sacramental principle is that the communication of the life of Christ is done by means of material and social ceremonies. This is, he affirms, analogous to what man knows of the relation of the human spirit to bodily conditions, and of the relation of the indi-

[88] *Readings in St. John's Gospel: Second Series*, p. 231.
[89] *Nature, Man, and God*, p. 478.
[90] James Carpenter, *Gore, A Study in Liberal Catholic Thought*, p. 224f.

vidual to society, and of "the principles of the pre-eminently human and social religion of the Son of Man."[91]

Yet highly as Gore valued the Eucharist, as the chief means of grace, he was far from encouraging, with some High Churchmen, the practice of the exposition of the Reserved Sacrament, since he believed that the main end of the Eucharist was communion and *participation*, and that the true indwelling of Christ was in the members of His Body. He was highly critical of the subjectivism, psychologism, and clericalism that marred the mediaeval celebration of the Mass, some fifty years before Dom Gregory Dix drew attention to these faults in *The Shape of the Liturgy*.[92] Gore himself held that there was no renewed surrender of Christ in the Eucharist. The term "sacrifice" in the Eucharist was appropriately used only in view of its relation to the heavenly altar of Christ's perpetual self-presentation as eternal High Priest. All that the Church can do "is to make thankful commemoration, in His way and in His Spirit, of His redemptive sufferings, and to unite ourselves to His perpetual intercession, where He presents Himself for us in the heavenly places, or as He makes Himself present among us in our eucharistic worship."[93]

By philosophical inclination, by ecumenical mediation, and as Archbishop first of York and later of Canterbury, Temple was to keep much freer from party affiliations in the Church than Gore, the leader of the High Church party. Yet he held the conviction "that the visible order of the Holy Catholic Church of Christ is part of its essence as a sacrament of the Incarnation."[94] Moreover, he deeply valued the Sacrament of Holy Communion, holding it to be a ritual expression of the dialectical unity of spirit and matter in the redemption of the world and of mankind effected by the unity of divinity and humanity in the Incarnation. He wrote: "We usually think of the Holy Communion in association only with God's act in *Redemption*; we must also think of it in connexion with His act in Creation. Then the power that guides and sustains us will be indeed the Holy Spirit proceeding from the Father and the Son."[95]

91 *The Body of Christ*, p. 47.
92 This point is made by E. L. Mascall in *Corpus Christi*, pp. 151-52.
93 *The Body of Christ*, pp. 183-84.
94 This is a summary taken from Archbishop A. M. Ramsey's account of Temple's ecclesiology, in his fine analysis of the development of Anglican theology entitled *From Gore to Temple; the Development of Anglican Theology between Lux Mundi and the Second World War, 1889-1939*, p. 153f.
95 *The Hope of a New World*, p. 69. In the same volume Temple gives a splendid account of the Eucharist as a design of the new world order intended by

Enough of the work of Gore and Temple has been discussed to show how they improved upon the immanentalism of their day by insisting that the only significance of the immanental was that it was the immanence of the *transcendental* God, and that it was not immanence in general that mattered, but the supreme instance of immanence, the Incarnation. By so doing they returned theology to its central basis in the historical witness of the Scriptures and the Creeds, in the ongoing testimony of the Christian community that spans the continents and the centuries, and asserted—for the great benefit of the study and practice of the devotional life—that the Incarnational principle justified the use of the Sacraments as central in the Christian cultus. At the same time they vindicated the place of philosophy, science, and art in the Christian theme of things, without accommodating Christian theology to the beckonings of culture. And they decisively showed the inadequacy of the immanentalism of their day.

It was a great service, but, like all human endeavours, imperfect and incomplete. Even within the tradition of Liberal Catholicism another generation was to question the emphases of Gore and his followers. They were to ask if the concentration on the Incarnation would not inevitably lead to a theology of explanation instead of a theology of atonement, and whether a theology of revelation and explanation did not undervalue the place of faith in the Christian life, and, finally, whether the Biblical categories of crisis, judgment, idolatry, rebellion, forgiveness, and reconciliation had been given their decisive role in Christian interpretation?[96]

5. *From Immanence to Transcendence: Forsyth and Oman*

As the most extreme supporters of immanentalism as expressed in the New Theology were Free Churchmen, it is gratifying that the most radical correction of these errors were made by two creative theologians in the same tradition, Peter Taylor Forsyth (1848-1921) and John Oman (1860-1934). Both were emigrants from Scotland to England and Forsyth became Principal of Hack-

the Creator and thus stresses an eschatological element missing in Gore's account of the Eucharist.

96 The newer Liberal Catholicism used less a historical approach, like Gore, than an analytical. See the work of its leader, E. G. Selwyn, in *An Approach to Christianity* and the admirable symposium edited by Selwyn, *Essays Catholic and Critical*, with the brilliant essays by A. E. Taylor on "The Vindication of Religion" and Hoskyns on "The Christ of the Synoptic Gospels." The terms "Catholic" (in reference to sacramental religion) and "Critical" (in reference to radical approaches to Bible and tradition) were taken with equal seriousness.

ney (Congregational) Theological College in London, while Oman became Principal of Westminster (Presbyterian) Theological College in Cambridge. Just as the Anglican Church by its attraction to the Patristic age tends to found its theology on the Doctrine of the Incarnation, which forms the basis of its liturgical and sacramental life, so the Reformed and Puritan Churches founded their systems on the Protestant Reformers and the *theologia crucis*. Thus the Free Church theologians were in a stronger position to commend Christianity as the criticism of culture rather than its crown, stressing the Biblical discontinuity of judgment and justification by grace, as distinct from the Catholic stress on grace as perfecting rather than destroying nature. Their central category for interpreting Christianity was Atonement rather than Incarnation, and the proclamation of the Cross, as St. Paul well knew, has ever seemed folly to the worldly-wise.

Their importance is that in differing ways they protested against the immanentalism of the age in which God and man, the supernatural and the natural, the Kingdom of God and secular utopianism, were confused. Forsyth began as a liberal, and in the acceptance of Biblical criticism and in the correlation of Christianity with culture and society, continued a liberal, but his thought became increasingly critical of liberalism as it recovered the distinctively Biblical categories. Oman never ceased to be a liberal in theology, but he was a chastened liberal who considered it to be his task to rescue the older and discarded theological terms and to fill them with contemporary relevance. Of the two, Forsyth was the more original and prophetic, so much so that he has been considered a "Barth before Barth."[97] Most of his works are being republished so that they are more widely read forty years after his death than they were in his own day, when their "fireworks in a fog" style and their criticisms of liberal theology caused them to seem brilliantly obscure and irrelevant. Oman was perhaps not as great a theologian, but he was an abler philosopher of religion, capable of sustained systematic exposition, where Forsyth's genius was to provoke, suggest, and stimulate rather than to explain.

In three respects they contributed significantly to the correction

---

[97] Notably by MacConnachie in the foreword to F. W. Camfield's *Revelation and the Holy Spirit*, p. vii. See the catena of tributes to Forsyth's major importance in W. L. Bradley, *P. T. Forsyth, The Man and His Work*, pp. 259-68, and Robert McAfee Brown, *P. T. Forsyth: Prophet for Today*, pp. 9-10. They include tributes from Barth himself, and his son Markus, J. K. Mozley, R. W. Dale, A. R. Vidler, F. W. Dillistone, Theodore Wedel, J. S. Whale, H. F. Lovell Cocks, James Denney, and Nathaniel Micklem.

of the current vapid immanentalism. Each came to feel that religion had been so sentimentalized that it was essential to moralize dogma to give it backbone. In particular, they brought back into the theological domain the concept of "grace," which had been superannuated by liberalism in favour of the weaker and more anthropomorphic term of "love." In the second place, they countered an excessive immanentalism with the restoration of the complementary and more ultimate emphasis on the Divine transcendence. In Forsyth transcendence was moralized in terms of the holiness of God, to include the element of judgment that is essential to the Divine love and which distinguishes it from sentimentality. In Oman's case, there was a deep dissatisfaction with psychological theories of religion which, in explaining religion, explained it away, and a determination to show that the environment of man was as supernatural as it was natural. Thirdly, in reaction from the depreciation of the Church in favour of the all-inclusive concept of the Kingdom of God then current among liberal theologians, Oman showed that the Church rested on the Divine order and Forsyth demonstrated that it was a Divine-human society founded on and sustained by the Gospel of the Redeemer. In brief, both asserted that the Church was called into being by Divine creation, not by human association. Forsyth's originality was seen, ecclesiologically, in his understanding of Catholic claims even where he dissented from them, and in his insistence upon the centrality of the Sacrament of the Word, whether audibly manifested, as in the preaching, or visibly, as in the Sacraments of Baptism and the Lord's Supper. A single citation from Forsyth's greatest book will make plain his profundity and balance, and the correction he made of a one-sided immanentalism:

"God and man meet in humanity, not as two entities or natures which coexist, but as two movements in mutual interplay, mutual struggle, and reciprocal communion. On the one hand we have an initiative, creative, productive action, clear and sure on the part of the eternal God; on the other hand we have the seeking, receptive, appropriating action of groping, erring, growing man. . . . All spiritual action is history. History is action and reciprocal action. It is commerce, and even conflict, with the transcendent."[98]

Oman's greatest success in the recovery of the concept of grace and in the moralization of dogma was achieved in his modern classic, *Grace and Personality* (1917). Here he sought to solve the persistently troubling question that had vexed St. Augustine and

[98] *The Person and Place of Jesus Christ*, p. 336f.

Pelagius, Luther and Erasmus, namely, the relationship between Divine grace and human freedom. His solution was found in a conception of grace as personal, whereby God appeals to human insight and decision. In short, in place of *irresistible* grace Oman put *persuasive* grace. The problem was posed in the following terms: "The essential quality of a moral person is moral independence and an ideal person would be of absolute moral independence. But the essential quality of a religious person is to depend on God; and he must be as absolutely dependent as a moral person must be absolutely independent."[99] Here Oman knew he must do justice both to his Calvinistic inheritance in accepting the sovereignty of God and to his ethical inheritance from Kant in insisting upon the independence of the moral agent. The antinomy can only be solved by recognizing that grace is "neither overriding omnipotence guided by omnipotence" nor as "a sort of love philtre" impersonally conveyed through the Sacraments, but only as "a gracious personal relationship" between God and the human personality through which God persuades us to choose our own good. Grace thus becomes the common basis of religion and ethics, for we "accept God's will, as, by insight, we discover it to be our own."[100] Just as there was a Catholic Liberalism in Gore and Temple and their school, to be distinguished from both Catholic Modernism and Liberal Protestantism, so in Oman and Forsyth we see the lineaments of a Liberal Evangelicalism to be distinguished from Liberal Modernism.

As early as 1892 we find the great Congregational theologian, R. W. Dale, writing to a friend: "Forsyth said a good thing the other day—he thought that 'the time had come to get back the word *Grace* into our preaching'; word and thing have too much disappeared."[101] No term describes more concisely the central concern of the thrusting theology of Forsyth. His subsequent writings are all variations on the theme of "the gracious God," a term he greatly preferred to the more common reference to the "grace of God," as less subject to impersonal interpretation. Forsyth was eager to distinguish his understanding of the term from two other current interpretations of its meaning.[102] He denied, as Oman had done, the Roman Catholic view of grace as an infusion into the individual, as a substance or power "piped" into the individual through the hierarchical administration of the Sacraments. He equally dissented

[99] *Grace and Personality*, p. 58.
[100] *Ibid.*, Chap. x, with citations from pp. 80-90.
[101] A. W. W. Dale, *The Life of R. W. Dale of Birmingham*, p. 636.
[102] *The Person and Place of Jesus Christ*, pp. 331-32.

160

from a left-wing and sectarian view of grace as a cordial benevolence of God, apparently oblivious to sin, as sheer sentimentality. He accepted the Reformation's rediscovery of the Biblical concept of grace as the Divine mercy, never earned but freely given—in short, grace to the malignant in granting forgiveness and the power to become "a new man in Christ Jesus." It is nothing less than the reconciling action of God in Christ. It is all of the Divine initiative. "The gospel descends on man; it does not rise from him. It is not a projection of his innate spirituality. It is revealed, not discovered, not invented. It is a gift to our poverty, not a triumph of our resource. It is something which holds us; it is not something we hold. It is Christ sent to us and not developed from us, bestowed on our need, and not produced from our strength, and He is given for our sin more than for our weakness."[103]

Grace was, indeed, a profound experience for Forsyth; after serving many years in the ministry as a liberal he was converted by grace to a theology of grace. "I was," he confessed, "turned from a Christian to a believer, from a lover of love to an object of grace. And so, whereas I first thought that what the Churches needed was enlightened instruction and liberal theology, I came to be sure that what they needed was evangelization. . . . Religion without an experimental foundation in grace readily feels panic in the presence of criticism."[104]

It was Forsyth's perceptiveness to realize a generation before the rest of Europe's theologians that the true centre of theology was the Atonement, not the Incarnation, so that theology is the challenger of human culture, not at all its agent and instrument. He saw that religion is often misconceived as an achievement by man, instead of being, what the work of Christ showed it to be, wholly the gift of a gracious God to undeserving humanity. Thus for Forsyth the Atonement is the medium through which the Incarnation is to be understood, for the essential nature of revelation is that it is redemptive. It is not the transmission of information primarily but the transformation of personality. Consequently he affirmed, counter to the predominant emphasis of the Liberal Catholics like Gore, that "our faith has much more directly to do with the benefits of Christ than with the nature of Christ . . . it is through the work of redemption that I know the person of the Redeemer."[105] To place

---

103 *Positive Preaching and the Modern Mind*, p. 144.
104 *Ibid.*, pp. 193-94.
105 *The Person and Place of Jesus Christ*, pp. 278-79.

the Incarnation before the Atonement was a reversal of values, to give to explanation the priority before reconciliation.

Theologies of immanence postulate God's identification with the world in such a way as virtually to deny the abyss between Creator and created, and to identify human discovery with Divine revelation and human ideals with Divine deliverances. Oman by his insistence upon the supernatural environment of the personality and Forsyth by his emphasis on the holiness of God accented the discontinuity between God and the world, as between infinite and finite, eternal and temporal, righteous and sinful. This was their second contribution to the correction of the theology of their day.

Oman wished to rescue the term "supernatural" from the opprobrium in which it had fallen in the eighteenth century, when it was thought to involve an arbitrary conception of miracle as the lawless caprice of Deity. He felt that the necessity for its restoration, with a restricted meaning, lay in the fact that Liberal Protestantism in discarding it was inevitably involved in the assumptions of a naturalistic philosophy. Moreover, the latter denied the existence of any transcendent spiritual reality and reduced the meaning of "natural" to either "mechanical" or "material." This act of repristination was performed in *The Natural and the Supernatural* (1931). The first part argues that the experience of the sacred and the holy is not a distinctive or abnormal reaction of the human organism to the natural environment, but a response to the Supernatural Environment overflowing the natural and *regularly open* to experience. Thus for Oman "the Supernatural means the world which manifests more than natural values which stir the sense of the holy and demand to be esteemed as sacred."[106] Experience is partly natural in that its values are comparative and to be judged as fulfilling practical needs, whereas "part of it is Supernatural, in the sense that its values are absolute to which our needs must submit."[107]

The second, or epistemological, part challenges the current naturalism as being due to a failure to recognize that there is any other kind of knowledge other than the abstraction inherent in scientific explanation. In a central chapter on "Awareness and Apprehension" he argues that for the understanding of our environment as a whole, in balance and richness, if not in precision, the

[106] *The Natural and the Supernatural*, p. 71.
[107] *Ibid.*, p. 72.

poet's awareness and the child's naïve perception are more reliable guides than scientific measurements or analyses.

The third part attacks the naturalistic world-view with its idea of a mechanically fixed sequence of cause and effect. He holds that this nineteenth century dogma oversimplifies reality more than the Buddhist concept of retribution or *karma* or the Hebrew assertion of the correlation of sin and suffering. Indeed, the two latter concepts are important summaries of aspects of our universal environment. This section ends with an appeal to the richness, variety, and resourcefulness of life as postulating the reality of human freedom and the personality of God.

The fourth and final section of the book deals with the problem of the relation of the Supernatural to the natural. He finds two major contrasting trends in the history of religion: the pantheistic and the monotheistic. The former affirms the absorption of the many into the One and monotheism affirms the victory of the many. The consequence is that for monistic religion the world is ultimately unreal and mystical world-flight is its corollary; while for monotheistic religion the natural world remains real and sacred as a partial embodiment of supernatural values. The natural consequence of the latter view is a hopeful life and an attempt to create a better natural world through the indwelling power of the Supernatural. In his evaluation of religions he places acosmic pantheism and negative mysticism at the bottom of the ladder; above them, Persian dualism and Jewish legalism; and on the topmost rung he puts the ethical religion of the prophets, with its climax and culmination in the life and teaching of Jesus. Thus by positive and negative arguments he claims a place for the Supernatural in a monotheistic religion of strongly ethical type. It was perhaps as far as a philosopher could go, but it sounded very like Schleiermacher's definition of religion,[108] with a substitution of the ethical value-judgments of Ritschl for the sense of dependence in Schleiermacher. At any rate when the current was running strongly for naturalism, Oman argued well for the place of the Supernatural, by which he intended God.

Forsyth was not so much concerned for the Supernatural in a trans-spatial or trans-temporal sense, as in the ontological sense.

[108] The referen.e is to the English translation of Schleiermacher's *The Christian Faith*, para. 11: Christianity is "a monotheistic faith, belonging to the teleological type of religion, and is essentially distinguished from other such faiths by the fact that in it everything is related to the redemption accomplished by Jesus of Nazareth."

That is, he was concerned for that dimension or depth in the Divine Being by which God is qualitatively different from man, and this he termed "holiness." In this the influence of the great Danish philosopher, Kierkegaard, is to be discerned. It was characteristic of Forsyth that when he considered the problem of human sin his first concern was not the damage sin did to men (as with most other theologians), but what it meant to God and how it affects Him. In framing a satisfactory concept of holiness, Forsyth had to beware of two extremes. He could not permit the cynicism or sentimentalism which affirmed, *Dieu pardonnera, c'est son métier*, nor could he resuscitate the Augustinian, Anselmic, or Calvinist conception of the Divine holiness, which equated it with honour or justice, reducing mercy to an exception for the elect. The Liberals in theology stressed love without justice, but the orthodox stressed justice without love. That was the dilemma.

By the idea of "holy love" Forsyth takes the truth from each view, while avoiding the excesses. Correcting the orthodoxy of the day, he substitutes "holiness" for "justice." In this way he escapes any tendency to legalism because holiness embraces within it the idea of love, whereas justice does not. By the same definition he protects his theology from the dangers of sentimentalism, since he qualifies the idea of love with holiness. The following passage admirably illustrates his meaning: "The holiness of God is His self-sufficient perfection, Whose passion it is to establish itself in the unholy by gracious love. Holiness is love morally perfect; love is holiness brimming and overflowing. The perfection speaks in the overflow. It is in redemption. Love is perfect, not in amount but in kind, not as intense, but as holy. And holiness is perfect, not as being remote, not as being merely pure, but as it asserts itself in redeeming grace."[109]

Forsyth was never tired of insisting that only a holy God takes sin seriously and that His love takes the form of wishing the sinner to be holy. Thus he wrote: "The holiness of God is a deeper revelation on the Cross than His love; for it is what gives His love divine value. And it is meaningless without judgment. The one thing He could not do was simply to wipe the slate and write off the loss. He must either inflict punishment or endure it."[110] God's moral transcendence, His holy love, was always to be found by Forsyth at the Cross. In the older views of the Atonement God was thought to

[109] *Positive Preaching and the Modern Mind*, p. 145.
[110] *The Cruciality of the Cross*, p. 98.

judge by penalising either men or Christ; in Forsyth's view God judges by self-reconciliation, and by the *objective* act of the Cross He changes man's relationship to God by the offering of forgiveness through Christ and the power of transformation. Finally, Christ is Mediator because of His dual office, facing God and facing man. As Lord, Christ confesses God's holiness; as Man, Christ confesses man's guilt. In this manner He fulfils the requirement for a lasting reconciliation.[111] Forsyth's genius is to have recovered the sense of the Otherness of God, which was missing in Liberal theology, yet to have purged its definition from any arbitrary, legalistic, or penal substitutionary accretions, and shown its relevance both to soteriology and to the need for a vertebral Christian ethic.

The third contribution of both Oman and Forsyth is in the field of ecclesiology. Both wrote books on the doctrine of the Church, when it was highly unusual for Free Church theologians to do so. Oman's, the slighter of the two volumes, was entitled *The Church and the Divine Order* (1911). Forsyth's substantial and challenging volume was called *The Church and the Sacraments* (1917).

Oman's book had a three-fold importance. It was the first significant book on its theme to have been written by a minister of the revived Presbyterian Church in England, until it was supplanted by P. Carnegie Simpson's *The Evangelical Church Catholic* (1934) which did greater justice to the Catholic tradition, the Sacraments, and the needs of ecumenism than did Oman. It recalled Free Churchmen to the objective authority of the Divine order in the Community of Christ, and warned them that theirs was a freedom within the Gospel and not outside it, or, as Forsyth would have phrased it, a "founded freedom." Thirdly, it presented in forthright fashion his defence and explication of the Reformed doctrine of the Church as a fellowship of believers united personally to Christ and to each other.

The Church had a double aspect for Oman. Viewed in relation to God it is the embodiment of the Divine order, in which the Father rules. On the human side it is the fellowship of those who have responded to God's rule which has respect for men's freedom. Oman entirely rejected the view that the Church can be defined in terms of its organization. While other Free Churchmen criticized the sacerdotalism of the Catholic concept of the Church denying the priesthood of all believers, Oman trained his guns on the

---

[111] For a fuller elaboration of this theme see W. L. Bradley, *P. T. Forsyth, The Man and His Work*, pp. 118ff.

concept of hierarchical authority, since he believed that "the essence of Catholicism is the reintroduction of the law,"[112] and the denial of the relationship of love and trust which was most characteristic of life in the Gospel. The authority of the Church rested on the supernatural Divine order initiated by God Himself and was contrasted with the current liberal conception of God's Kingdom as "the progressive amelioration of humanity."[113] Authority was, however, as in all the writings of Oman, of a personal nature— persuasive, not coercive. Thus God had dealt with men in Christ, and thus they must cooperate with each other. On the face of it this smacks of nominalism, but Oman was not unaware of the importance of tradition and of the need for visible ordinances. He urged that the Christian "will not think it necessary before he can serve the Church to cut himself off from its failures and to endeavour to create a new fellowship corresponding in everything with the ideal, before he can begin."[114] Even more strongly had Forsyth insisted on the danger of the isolationism which cuts off the modern religious community from God's work in history through His Church. "We cannot," he wrote, "just clear two thousand years by a huge somersault and land with a splash in the New Testament, with its polity, practice and habit of mind. . . . It denies historic providence. It repudiates the Kingdom of God in history. It robs us of most of the sainthood, sacrifice, and devotion of the whole Church, and often leaves our public prayers to be but pious journalese."[115]

Oman believed that there was a substantial truth in the Reformed distinction between the "invisible" and the "visible" Church, in that human judgment can never be equated with the Divine judgment and ultimately only God knows who are His. But since the Church is in the world, its existence, though not its purity, must be manifested by institutions, and needs some representative authority. But in principle for the Catholic the *institution* is primary, with its priesthood, bishops, councils, and Pope; while for the Protestant it is the *fellowship* that is primary, with its succession of believers gathered in the bond of love.[116] Moreover, in Protestantism such authority is to be exercised as servant, not master, and is not to appeal to any other motives than for love's sake. "The Church must

112 *The Church and the Divine Order*, p. 107.
113 *Ibid.*, p. 42.
114 *Ibid.*, p. 313.
115 *Congregationalism and Reunion*, p. 10.
116 *The Church and the Divine Order*, pp. 207ff.

live and work as a corporation, but she must not magnify herself as a corporation."[117]

Oman asserted, as a true Protestant, that the institutions of Christianity are secondary to the faith and experience on which they are based. But he gravely underestimated the importance of external authority, and in this respect was not abreast of the most advanced ecumenical thinking of the day. The truth in his view was that no external unity can be expressive of the Christian spirit and that a giant corporation created by the merger of many smaller institutions may be the product of compromise, not of conviction. While the realism of the following citation has relevance for the present, yet its concluding phrase has long been outmoded: "When airs of social superiority ill-becoming those who claim to be the only true successors of the fishermen of Galilee, and resentment and bitterness ill-becoming those who claim to be blessed with the highest ideal of the Church's freedom, pass away, we shall either have outward union, or be so united in heart as to be able to do without it."[118] As over against the political collectivism of his day, and the dangers inherent in the Catholic hierarchical definition of the character of the Church, Oman made a salutary protest in the interest of freedom, fellowship, and "persuasive grace." His weakness was that he was prepared to go to such exaggerated lengths to preserve these values as to declare an external union of the Church to be unnecessary. He had, however, rightly insisted that the Church of Christ is not a merely voluntary organization, but founded firmly upon the rule of God the Father.

Forsyth's ecclesiology was profounder, partly because in reacting from theological liberalism he retained its values while adding to them; partly because he had a much stronger sense of the importance of the historic traditions of the Church, and of the witness of its liturgy and Sacraments; and partly because he did greater justice to the Roman Catholic tradition from which he dissented. It was, to give one famous example, characteristic of his attitude towards a contemporary Protestant cheapening of Holy Communion that he held "a mere memorialism to be a more fatal error than the Mass, and a far less lovely."[119] In the same catholic spirit he wrote: "We have starved ourselves of the rich treasury of Christian devotion in the profound and lovely liturgies of the long past, and of the wealth of example, inspiration, and guidance in the calendar of

[117] *Ibid.*, p. 326f.   [118] *Ibid.*, p. 315.
[119] *The Church and the Sacraments*, p. xvi.

Christian sainthood."[120] It was Forsyth's genius that he combined intellectual insight in his theology with a moral passion and—in a way that has been rare in the Reformed tradition—with a deep appreciation of aesthetic values. The latter was seen in the two perceptive volumes he wrote on art,[121] in his publication of *Intercessory Services for Aid in Public Worship*, and in his important contributions to the *Book of Congregational Worship* (1920), the first to be prepared officially by that denomination.

Forsyth held a very high doctrine of the Church. Occasionally he termed the Church the Body of Christ, but he preferred the image which characterized it as the Bride of Christ, because "it is not only His organ but the object of communion by the Spirit."[122] He would not, however, like Gore, speak of the Church as the "extension of the Incarnation," for that was in his view to commit the idolatry of making Christ and Church equivalent. "The Church is not the continuation of Christ, but His creation and response."[123] Forsyth ever stressed not only the radical dependence of the Church on Christ, but also its continual renewal by the Holy Spirit. Hence it could not be a continuation or extension of Christ, but only a new creation by Christ.

Like Oman, he denied that the Church was constituted by the hierarchy. The true succession of the Apostolate was not the bishopric, as the Roman Catholics and Anglo-Catholics maintained, nor the saints, as Inge declared, but the Bible. "The apostolic succession is the evangelical succession,"[124] he wrote, because the canon of Scripture was written to prolong the voices of the apostles and to replace their vanished witness. But if he was critical of the Catholic conception of the nature and authority of the Church, he was critical of certain Protestant ideas of the Church. He denied the older evangelical view which regarded the Church as a society for saving souls from the Devil, and the view of the social gospellers for whom it was merely an agency for social improvement. He criticized both a Churchless Gospel and the Social Gospel. In the authentic Maurician tradition he claimed "it was a race that Christ redeemed, not a mere bouquet of believers," and thus he admitted the evangelical emphasis on redemption while denying its atomism.

[120] *Ibid.*, p. 37.
[121] These were: *Religion in Recent Art* and *Christ on Parnassus, Lectures on Art, Ethic, and Theology.*
[122] From a symposium, *Different Conceptions of Priesthood and Sacrifice*, pp. 32-33, cited in W. L. Bradley, *P. T. Forsyth . . .* , pp. 221-22.
[123] *The Church and the Sacraments*, pp. 82-83.
[124] *Ibid.*, p. 139.

He insisted that the "same act which sets us in Christ sets us also in the society of Christ. To be in Christ is in the same act to be in the Church. . . . The act of faith which saves us from self would only have a negative meaning if it did not save us at the same time into a society which is a centre of service and sympathy."[125] He warned the protagonists of the social gospel that "the great Church must always be more dogmatic to the social eye than accommodating. . . . It must consent to be unpopular with men that it may be faithful for man's God."[126]

Forsyth was peculiarly perceptive in his understanding of authority. He criticized the Roman Catholics for having set the Church up as equal to or even higher than the Gospel, and his fellow Protestants for having denied the very existence of the Gospel by vindicating their institutions through an appeal to the good works they accomplished. Authority in the Church could only be "the moral holy power of redeeming grace."[127] He recognized the authority of the Bible as primary, but in no literal fashion, and insisted that the Gospel of grace in Christ crucified which produced both Bible and Church was the authoritative principle for interpreting the Bible and testing the life of the Church in every age. He understood why Protestants, with the collapse of the external authorities of Bible and Church, rushed to claim the authority of the individual religious experience. He acknowledged that its value, as a witness to the Spirit, was considerable in delivering the Church from formalism, confessionalism, and literalism. At the same time he insisted that it must never be divorced from the witness to the Word.

Individual experience could never, not even the witness of the conscience, be an adequate authority for the Christian Church. It has, so he maintains, five inherent weaknesses. Experience is judged by intensity, whereas objective facts and the faith they elicit—the contents of belief—are supremely important. Impression becomes more important than regeneration when experience is normative. Its supporters forget that religious experience is sin-distorted and ignore the fact that conscience can condemn but not redeem. A religion of experience casts off the anchors of history and tradition, with the result that such religion degenerates into a

125 *Ibid.*, pp. 61-62.
126 *The British Weekly*, issue of October 9, 1913, p. 43.
127 Address as Chairman of the Congregational Union in 1905, published in *The Congregational Union Year Book*, 1906, p. 59.

reverie. Finally, a religion of experience is not strong enough, because of its subjectivity, to carry a Church.

The authority of the Church is the Gospel of grace. It creates human nature anew, providing forgiveness for estranged man, moral direction and drive leading to conversion and sanctification in the committed company of Christ's people nourished on the Word and Sacraments, and experiencing here and now the assurance of life everlasting. In a remarkable amalgam Forsyth had restated the doctrine of the Church so as to preserve the strengths of the high Anglican and Reformed views, without the tendency towards the idolatry of the institution in the one, and the atomistic individualism of the other.

More deeply than any other Free Church theologian of his day Forsyth understood the significance of the Sacraments, without depreciating the proclamation of the Word. He returned to the Augustinian understanding that the preaching is the *audible* Word and the Sacraments are the *visible* Word. He would not accept any merely symbolic interpretations of the Sacraments. He was scathing about contemporary Congregational practice, with the resulting impression that only the Anglican and Roman Churches took the Sacraments seriously. He wanted to bring the Sacraments to the place that was currently held by clubs as the centre of the social life of the Free Churches. He desired to counteract the cult of the popular preacher, with the reminder that the "chief function of the Church is worship, not preaching, and it is in the supreme and most universal act of worship that we have to show our unity—viz. in Communion."[128] He insisted so strongly on the objectivity of the Sacraments that he did not scruple to write of a Sacrament as an *opus operatum*.[129] By this, however, he did not intend to imply that the objectivity of the Sacrament was due to any change in the bread and wine. Rather, he believed that the gifts of forgiveness and regeneration were conveyed by the real presence of Christ at His Table. Baptism communicates regeneration in title, but the gift has to be appropriated before it becomes actual regeneration. Baptism means that the "stamp of being God's property has been put on the child in a public way" and that "he is born to be born again" and "will be false to his best antecedents and his social committal if he do not become regenerated in the

---

[128] Letter cited in full in W. L. Bradley, *P. T. Forsyth . . .* , pp. 277-78.
[129] *The Church and the Sacraments*, p. 216.

Holy Ghost."[130] He could not believe that Christ was sacrificed afresh in each celebration of the Lord's Supper, but he most certainly held that Christ re-presents His finished sacrifice to His Father on His people's behalf at each Holy Communion.[131] He wrote: "A Church may survive with power errors about its Sacraments as tremendous as those of Rome, but neglect, starvation, and renunciation of Sacraments it cannot survive."[132]

Forsyth insisted upon the theological basis of Churchmanship, on the objective character of the Sacraments as real means of grace; and upon the historic continuity of the Church and the inspiration of its ancient prayers and the witness of the saints. In so doing he led the Free Churches of his own day and a later grateful generation to prize their inheritance in the Gospel and in the Reformation. He also helped to mediate the Catholic tradition to Nonconformity. Anglicans were then in the grip of a Patristic antiquarianism and Free Churchmen extolled the spirit of Christianity oblivious of the need for forms; he taught them to understand each other, and thus accelerated the impetus of the ecumenical movement.

What impact did the teachings of Oman and Forsyth have on the theory and practice of worship? There is no question that their stress on the Divine authority and empowering of the Church served to emphasize the importance of the spiritual discipline of the Christian community, and the immense benefits of gathering for the proclamation of the transforming Word. Forsyth went further in showing that the Sacraments were equally the conveyors of grace, channelling the forgiveness and the regeneration of God. He realized the significance of liturgies as teachers of a reverent approach to God and witnesses to the devotion of the Communion of saints through the long Christian centuries. In due time his emphasis on the objectivity of the Sacraments would lead to their more frequent and more cherished celebration. But, above all, his re-iterated emphasis on the primacy and ultimacy of the supernatural—and it is significant that his last book was entitled *This Life and the Next* (1918)—and on the majestic mercy of a holy God, consummated in the sacrifice of Christ, could only issue in recommending a grateful response to grace. It is in that atmosphere, not in the congratulatory and optimistic mood of immanentalism, that worship thrives.

130 *Ibid.*, p. 168.   131 *Ibid.*, p. 256.   132 *Ibid.*, p. 166.

6. *Conclusion*

We have seen that the history of the English people in the first three decades of the century began with high optimism, but that the balloons of inevitable progress were pricked on the barbed wire of the First World War trenches.[133] Britain's place in the world and her power were reduced, as the British Empire became the British Commonwealth of Nations. The establishment of the Social Welfare State was a proof of the inevitability of collectivism, but also it was an index of social justice, and an achievement of political radicalism and the Christian conscience. The theology of the period is, in part, a reflection of the spirit of the people. Immanentalism was a theology of excessive optimism. We have seen it expressed in the "New Theology" of R. J. Campbell and his followers, which, like Liberal Modernism, was a theology in rebellion against the traditional and historical Christian faith at almost all points. The Bible claimed that salvation came by faith in God's power, but liberalism trusted chiefly in man's own effort.

So liberalism persuaded the Church to seek for popularity by working for social renewal, and by eliminating the other-worldly horizon to concentrate on creating the Socialist utopia on earth. The consequence, as we have seen, was that worship seemed irrelevant to the very artisans whom the new approach hoped to attract. The work in the slums seemed important; the working of the Sacraments seemed antiquarianism and superstition.

Attempts were, indeed, made to dam the floods of theological liberalism. It was hoped that a study of mysticism, as a phenomenon common to many religions besides Christianity, would persuade the world of the universal reality and the reliability of the Christian life. But its techniques were too exotic and strenuous for the common man and it appealed only to the faithful few, despite the sensitive advocacy of Dean Inge, Baron von Hügel, and Evelyn Underhill. But the two latter, in particular, showed that it was an essential part of Christianity and witnessed to the centrality of adoration in public worship, supremely in the Eucharist, as the impetus to the Christian life. They, too, were prophets ahead of their time in witnessing to the faithful. They never let it be for-

[133] C. C. J. Webb believed that World War I had three theological effects. It encouraged the revolt against Christian ethics. It "dealt a mortal blow to . . . optimistic religious immanentalism." It "promoted a revival of interest in the quest of a revelation from without of values which men despaired of finding within a process of civilization which had issued in so tremendous a catastrophe" (*Religious Thought in England from 1850*, p. 149).

gotten that a great abyss, uncrossable on man's part, separates proud man from Almighty God, and that Christ was the bridge and Mediator between the holy and the unholy. They insisted that true religion involves renunciation as the price of immeasurable joy, and is not served by a frantic activism. At least in an era of acute secularism they persuaded the faithful to re-appreciate their heritage in the devotional discipline of the saints and in the supreme corporate act of Christian worship, the Liturgy. Moreover, better than they knew, they were preparing Christians to recognize that they were already one in Christ, however divisive their denominational labels might be.

Neither Gore nor Temple was a particularly mystical man, but each insisted on demonstrating the centrality of the Incarnation, as the supreme example of the immanence of the Transcendent One, with Christ as both the revelation of the Divine design and the perfect exemplar. Both found the Eucharist to be a stimulus to social justice, and Temple, in particular, discerned in it the pattern for the creation of more equitable re-ordering of God's gifts for the creation of true community. For both of them worship was the central need of a truly human life, as the creature's acknowledgment of the Creator and the channel of transforming grace.

Oman affirmed that the supernatural was known through the natural and was, whether man recognized it or not, his background. The Church was a pointer to that Divine order of love, rather than law, which God wills for His earthly children and which manifests His own character. Forsyth went beyond any theologian of his day in realizing that God must be a *holy* Father, and that it is because he hates sin He must judge it, so that judgment is the yonder side of costly and caring love. Further, Forsyth restored the forgotten word "Grace" to the Protestant theological vocabulary, and Oman made it personal again. In concentrating on the Atonement, rather than the Incarnation, as the decisive act of a holy God to redeem the world, Forsyth provided a much needed criterion by which all human aspirations and societies could be judged, and insisted that the Church must be not democracy's tribune, as liberal theologians believed, but its censor. He had a deep understanding of the Catholic and Anglican traditions in their strengths and weaknesses. He particularly valued their devotional and sacramental riches. In so doing he not only prepared Nonconformity to appreciate anew its earlier Reformed sacramental heritage, but also to be in empathetic dialogue with the Catholic tradition. He even prepared the Free Churches to consider the merits of liturgical worship by his teaching and example.

But what Inge, von Hügel, Underhill, Gore, Temple, Oman, and Forsyth had in common, if in differing degrees, was the wit to see that an excessive immanentalism, the apparent friend of religion, was really its enemy. Until they had exposed its pretensions there was no hope for men to return to the recognition of the transcendental God's claim on men, proven by the revelation of His purpose in the Incarnation, sealed by His reconciliation through the Cross, and helped by the Church as the Body and Bride of Christ to inherit eternal life, through the preaching of the Word and the celebration of the Sacraments, and the loving service of humanity prompted by the gratitude of the redeemed. True religion and true worship awaited the recognition by the majority of theologians and ministers that immanentalism was not leading them and their flocks to the earthly paradise, but through the enticing and illusory mists of utopia to the quagmires of despair. The importance of the prophetic seven was to be recognized—if not in their own time—in the latter part of the third decade of the century, when the bitterness of unemployment was followed by the despair of totalitarianism. Then it was that their influence came into its own. They had found their way to the truth by running against the stream.

Four others came by the rocky way of disillusionment with liberal theology, as evinced by their published spiritual biographies. R. J. Campbell recorded the journey in *A Spiritual Pilgrimage* (1917). W. E. Orchard moved from Presbyterianism and Congregationalism to Roman Catholicism as chronicled in *From Faith to Faith* (1933), and C. S. Lewis found his way from an inherited Anglicanism into atheism and back into the fold with many divagations, as retold in *Pilgrim's Regress* (1933). The most enthusiastic devotee of a liberal theology, and also the most excited convert to neo-Orthodoxy was D. R. Davies, whose *On to Orthodoxy* (1939) is the most damaging *exposé* of the shallowness of liberal theology.[134]

[134] Davies, a Congregational minister who left the ministry to devote full time to educational activities on behalf of the Labour movement, and finally became an Anglican vicar, analysed his disillusionment with liberalism in theology as follows: "Christian Liberalism has had four consequences in the social and religious life of our time: (1) a false estimate of human nature; (2) the practical banishment of the other-worldly element in the Christian Ethic; (3) the denial of the uniqueness of Christianity; (4) the secularisation of life and religion" (*On to Orthodoxy*, p. 13).

It seems that a penitential piety becomes credible only when the doctrines of original sin and the holiness of Divine love are stressed. It is only when the Incarnation is stressed that the importance of Sacramental practice is acknowledged. Only when the doctrines of The Cross and Resurrection are emphasized is it felt by faith that "the sufferings of this present world are not to be compared with the joy that shall be revealed." It is a theology of grace alone that elicits the adoration which is the heart-beat of corporate Christian worship and the joyful song of souls in pilgrimage. This was to be more fully appreciated by the theologians of the second three decades of the century.

CHAPTER V

THE LATER DEVELOPMENT OF
THEOLOGY[1] (1933-1965)

IN THE first thirty years of this century theology, with the exception of the exponents of mysticism and the incarnationalists, tended to weaken the role of worship in the life of the Church. In fact, the proponents of immanentalism and of the social gospel virtually equated religion with social duty. In contrast, the theology of the next thirty years strongly supported the centrality of worship in the corporate life of Christians.

It was certainly the case with the first three of the four trends in theology, though dubiously so for the fourth. Successively, these trends were: the return to a Biblical theology which brought with it a revival of orthodoxy in belief; the new ecclesiology which insisted that the Church, far from being a convenience of organization, was part of the gift of the Gospel; and the search for a distinctively Christian Sociology deriving from the incarnational and sacramental nature of the Church. The fourth, and most recent, trend of theology, Cambridge Radicalism, represents the fusion of Bultmann, Bonhoeffer, Tillich, and Freud as filtered through English minds. In its prophetic and critical emphasis it is likelier to stimulate preaching than sacramentalism, but it is significant that all its exponents are Anglicans (and most are clergymen), and they are likelier to demand the reformation of worship than its abolition. The first three theological trends, however, being clearly based upon the uniqueness of the Christian revelation as proclaimed in Word and Sacrament, manifestly strengthened the Liturgical Movement in our time.

[1] There appears to be no comprehensive published account of the interconfessional development of English theology from 1933. Limited help is, however, provided by the following volumes. A good account of Anglican theology up to 1939 only is Archbishop A. M. Ramsey's *From Gore to Temple*. E. L. Allen provides two useful chapters on British theology up to 1950 in G. Stephens Spinks' *Religion in Britain since 1900*. John W. Grant's *Free Churchmanship in England* provides a good account of British Free Church theology until about 1948. John Macquarrie's *Twentieth Century Religious Thought* is an admirable survey of European philosophical and religious thought, but gives little space to British theology. Daniel D. Williams' *What Present-day Theologians are Thinking* treats British theologians, both Anglican and Free Church, with great insight, but too briefly for our purpose. A valuable study is J. K. Mozley, *Some Tendencies in British Theology, From the Publication of* "Lux Mundi" *to the Present Day*.

1. *The Return to Biblical Orthodoxy*

The date given for the beginning of the demise of liberal theology and for its replacement by Biblical theology is 1933. This may seem the less arbitrary when it is remembered that Karl Barth's *Commentary on the Epistle to the Romans* appeared in the English translation by Clement Hoskyns in 1933. That event signalizes the impact on British theology of both Europe's greatest twentieth century theologian and a great English Biblical scholar. Barth was then described variously as a theologian of crisis, a dialectical theologian, and as the theologian of the Word of God. Barth was a Protestant, while his translator, Hoskyns, was an Anglican High Churchman with a deep attachment to Catholic order. Yet both were inveterate foes of any attempt to subordinate the revelation of the living God to the philosophical, scientific, or cultural demands of the spirit of the age. Each in his way was concerned to repristinate the Biblical categories.

Barth's Commentary on Romans waged war upon evolutionary conceptions of the Kingdom of God (that favorite example of liberal doctrinal accommodation), claiming: "Whenever men claim to be able to see the Kingdom of God as a growing organism, or—to describe it more suitably—as a growing building, what they see is not the Kingdom of God but the Tower of Babel."[2] The Divine revelation was not accommodating, nor superficially comforting, but cruelly critical of man's egotism. Hence, thundered Barth, "Religion, when it attacks vigorously, when it is fraught with disturbance, when it is non-aesthetic, non-rhetorical, non-pious, when it is the religion of the 39th Psalm, of Job, and of Luther, and of Kierkegaard, when it is the religion of Paul, bitterly protests against every attempt to make of its grim earnestness some trivial and harmless thing." On the contrary, "Religion is aware that it is in no wise the crown and fulfilment of true humanity; it knows itself rather to be a questionable, disturbing, dangerous thing."[3] Barth emphasized, with Sören Kierkegaard,[4] the infinite qualitative difference between God and man. Hence "the Gospel is not a truth among other truths. Rather it sets a

[2] *Commentary* . . . , p. 432. [3] *Ibid.*, p. 258.
[4] The first English book on Kierkegaard was Dr. E. L. Allen's *Kierkegaard, His Life and Thought*. Existentialism was mediated also by Martin Buber's important *I and Thou* which had a profound influence on H. H. Farmer's thought, and also through a recovery of Pascal and Kierkegaard. See Denzil Patrick's *Pascal and Kierkegaard*. The *Life* by Walter Lowrie and his translations and those of his colleagues made Kierkegaard available to the English-speaking world.

question-mark against all truths."[5] Like Kierkegaard, too, Barth affirmed that faith was existential commitment, and spoke in paradoxes: "for all it is a leap into the void. And it is possible for all, only because it is equally impossible."[6]

The almost forgotten or, at the least, diluted, Biblical terms of Grace and Sin, Justification, Forgiveness, and Resurrection, were interpreted dynamically by Barth. Sin was defined as "that interchanging of God and man, that exalting of men to divinity and depressing of God to humanity, by which we seek to justify and fortify and establish ourselves."[7] "Grace, however, is the fact of forgiveness."[8] Moreover, Grace is not given without a prior judgment of God. Thus "Grace is not grace, if he that receives it is not under judgment. Righteousness is not righteousness if it be not reckoned to the sinner. Life is not life, if it be not life from death. And God is not God, if he be not the End of men."[9] The sole hope for trapped man is the Resurrection of Jesus Christ: "We have seen the old world as a completely closed circle from which we have no means of escape. But, because we have perceived this, we are able to recognize—in the light of the Resurrection of Jesus from the dead—the power and meaning of the Coming Day: the Day of the New World and of the New Man."[10] Here was the return to a strongly Biblical theology, speaking with the existential concern of a Luther and with the magisterial authority of Calvin. "Theology," claimed Barth, "is *ministerium verbi divini*. It is nothing more or less."[11] In Barth's favourite illustration the theologian was like John the Baptist in Grünewald's painting of the Crucifixion, pointing an elongated finger to God the Transcendent in his ineffable majesty. Barth's is a theology of *Krisis* because every human achievement stands under the judgment of God and the Church itself is in constant need of reformation. It is a dialectical theology because it says *Nein* to all attempts to solve human problems apart from God, Creator, Judge, and Redeemer.

Barth's theology did not receive an immediate welcome, and his impact on English theology was never widespread. His paradoxes sounded strange in English ears. His re-assertion of Biblical truth was sometimes misinterpreted as a neo-fundamentalism. His Theology of the Word was thought to be merely the rejuvenescence

<hr>

5 *Commentary* . . . , p. 35.   6 *Ibid.*, p. 99.   7 *Ibid.*, p. 190.
8 *Ibid.*   9 *Ibid.*, p. 187.   10 *Ibid.*

11 *Ibid.*, preface, p. x. The *Römerbrief*, it is interesting to note, has nine references to Luther, five to Calvin, and nineteen to Dostoievsky, as well as seven to Nietzsche and two to Feuerbach.

of Calvinism, though he did not affirm the doctrine of double predestination, and his later exposition of election has strong universalistic overtones. The more serious objections to his earlier theology, however, were his denial of the validity of any natural theology and hence the restriction of revelation to Holy Scripture, and his apparent denigration of man below the level of responsible personality. Nor was there a serious attempt on the part of his critics to follow the brilliant development of his thought in the lengthy volumes of *Die Kirchliche Dogmatik*. But even when Barth's theology was more congenially filtered for English readers through the writings of Emil Brunner, it gave a strong propulsion to the emergence of a Biblical theology in England.

This was provided chiefly by New Testament scholars, of whom the most significant were Sir Edwyn Clement Hoskyns and Professor C. H. Dodd. Both reacted strongly against the futurist eschatology of liberalism which had sometimes been indistinguishable from a future utopia to be brought into being by men. They substituted a "fulfilled" eschatology (the term of Hoskyns) or a "realized" eschatology (in the terminology of Dodd). By this, they meant that the Kingdom of God had been inaugurated by the teaching, the life, death, and resurrection of Jesus Christ, in whom God's new day had dawned.

Hoskyns (1884-1937) had begun a new era in English studies of the New Testament by his brilliant essay, "The Christ of the Synoptic Gospels," in *Essays Catholic and Critical*, edited by E. G. Selwyn (1926). This he followed up with an essay on "Jesus the Messiah" in *Mysterium Christi*, edited by Deissmann and Bell (1930), and *The Riddle of the New Testament* (1931), written in collaboration with F. N. Davey, his pupil at Corpus Christi College, Cambridge. He also left two posthumously published works: the important study, *The Fourth Gospel*, and the volume of *Cambridge Sermons* (1938).

Hoskyns argued in "The Christ of the Synoptic Gospels" that the Gospels were the sacred writings of the infant Christian community; he employed the technique of "Form criticism" to undo the damage created by historical criticism which, as Schweitzer said, had left the reader with "only a tattered copy of the Gospel of Saint Mark" in his hand. The New Testament Epistles were, on this approach, the records connected with the process of building the religious community, and the Gospels should be read in the light of the Epistles, rather than the other and customary way

179

round. The Cross and the Resurrection was the double event that gave them shape. The supernatural element was at least as primitive as the moral element, concluded Hoskyns, and hence "exclusiveness . . . may have its origin in the teaching of Jesus rather than in the theology of St. Paul."[12] His conclusions in this study were revolutionary and warrant extensive citation:

"From this reconstruction it will be seen at once that a whole series of contrasts underlies the Synoptic tradition. . . . The contrast is not between the Jesus of history and the Christ of faith, but between the Christ humiliated and the Christ returning in glory. . . . The contrast is not between a reformed and an unreformed Judaism, but between Judaism and the new supernatural order by which it is at once destroyed and fulfilled: not between the disciples of a Jewish prophet and an ecclesiastically ordered sacramental cultus, but between the disciples of Jesus, who, though translated into the sovereignty of God, are as yet ignorant both of His claims and the significance of their own conversion, and the same disciples, initiated into the mystery of His person and of His life and death, leading the mission to the world, the patriarchs of the new Israel of God. The contrast is not between an ethical teaching and a dreamy eschatology, or between a generous humanitarianism and an emotional religious experience stimulated by mythological beliefs, but between a supernatural order characterized by a radical moral purification involving persistent moral conflict and the endurance of persecution, and a supernatural order in which there is no place either for moral conflict or for persecution."[13] Clearly the Bible and the Church belonged together and Hoskyns had reinterpreted their relevance with new vigour.

More quietly than Barth, but with equal conviction, Hoskyns was preaching to his Corpus Christi students in Cambridge a Christo-centric faith founded on Christ as the inaugurator of God's new regime. In 1926 and 1927 he proclaimed Christ as the fulfilment of the promises of God. He thought it a woeful misunderstanding to conceive of Christianity as awaiting a catastrophe which will overwhelm the present world and usher in the Kingdom of God. "To be a Christian is, rather, the recognition that the great catastrophe lies in the past, that God has acted and is acting energetically, that righteousness has been attained by men and women and is attainable by us through the grace of God."[14]

12 *Essays Catholic and Critical*, p. 169.
13 *Ibid.*, pp. 177-78.   14 *Cambridge Sermons*, p. 27.

Christian discipleship involves, not dreaming, but "plunging head first into the Christian faith and fellowship, believing that the Ecclesia of God is the visible expression in the world of His love and His mercy."[15]

While Hoskyns acknowledged the importance of believing in the role of God in the long history of the human race and in the ordering of Nature, yet "far more important than this is the belief that God acts catastrophically in human affairs, that He works miracles, that men are transformed from sin to righteousness, that prayer calls for an act of God, that it does not merely effect an adaptation to the laws of nature. The God of the Christian religion is a God of miracles."[16] Eschatology, in the view of Hoskyns, exposes, as with a lightning flash, the simplicity of ultimate beliefs, for it "crudely and ruthlessly sweeps away all our little moral busyness, strips us naked of worldly possessions and worldly entanglements, and asks what survives the catastrophe. It is only then that the ultimate moral duties stand alone in their luminous simplicity: Love of God, and Charity to those who, like us, are bereft of that in which they have confidently trusted."[17]

The bracing vigour of Barth's and Hoskyns' Biblical theology can be understood only if we recall the background of European totalitarianism (Nazi, Fascist, and Communist), in which human leaders were claiming an allegiance which belongs only to God, and if we also remember that this theology was making a counter-claim for Christ. This is why Hoskyns preached in these words: "The Church and theology know that they can only sing the glory of God over their own graves and at the place where they have died. . . . And can you wonder that those who know this secret tremble when they see scientists, economists, psychologists, Hitlerites, leaders of the Group Movement, Communists, and all those other confident advisers of men marching with flags flying into the abyss where the Church has already stumbled and fallen?— can you wonder that the Church lifts up its tired, weary warning against human ὕβρις, arrogance?"[18] Like a prophet Hoskyns gives this final warning: "Once again, my brothers in Christ, may I warn you that, as Christians and as men, you are moving along a path narrow and sharp as the edge of a razor, for on one side of you lies the blasphemy of human idolatry, and on the other side yawns the

---

15 *Ibid.*, p. 28.   16 *Ibid.*, p. 35.   17 *Ibid.*, p. 37.
18 *Ibid.*, pp. 147-48. For two studies of the Biblical revival, see William Neil, *The Rediscovery of the Bible* and J. E. Fison, *The Faith of the Bible*.

181

chasm of detachment and cynical aloofness. Between the two walked the Christ."[19] Biblical theology was clearly the iron-ration of the Christian soldier for Hoskyns. And this theology of fulfilled eschatology called the Christian from the balcony view of life into the blood and dust of commitment in the arena, as Barth's theology was to summon the German Confessional Church into being at the Synod of Barmen. In each theologian it was clearly a case of "Choose ye this day whom ye will serve!" The trumpets of liberalism had been muted; those of Biblical orthodoxy gave forth no uncertain sound.

What Hoskyns was accomplishing as an Anglican, Professor C. H. Dodd was achieving as a Free Churchman, and he was later to be assisted by the work of T. W. Manson, R. Newton Flew, and Vincent Taylor. Dodd's *Apostolic Preaching* of 1936 distinguished the basic pattern of apostolic preaching as the *heilsgeschichte*, or history of salvation, the proclamation of the mighty acts of God, as contrasted with moral instruction. The early Christian sermon was *kerygma*, a proclaiming of the Gospel, as contrasted with topical or hortatory preaching which "is teaching, or exhortation (*paraklesis*), or it is what they called *Homilia*, that is, the more or less informal discussion of various aspects of Christian life and thought, addressed to a congregation already established in the faith."[20] The primitive Church was both the creation and the verification of the proclamation of the mighty acts of God: "The primitive Church, in proclaiming its Gospel to the world, offered its own fellowship and experience as the realization of the Gospel. That is the essence of the matter."[21] Thus the Church was created by the proclamation that Jesus Christ crucified was the Messiah of God, as vindicated by the Resurrection, and the Spirit-filled Community—the new Israel of God—in His Name now offered to baptize all who repented of their sins and desired to share their worship and witness to God's new age. Here, again, was a Biblical theology which stressed the interdependence of the Gospel and the Church.

What the New Testament scholars were teaching was soon reflected in the thought of the theologians. A notable restatement of the faith in terms of orthodoxy, on the part of a former distinguished liberal, was Dr. Nathaniel Micklem's *What is the Faith?* (1936). He argued that the Faith is not to be defined by ration-

---

[19] *Ibid.*, p. 149.   [20] *Apostolic Preaching*, p. 5.   [21] *Ibid.*, p. 135.

alism for "the Christian faith is what it is, not what any modern rationalist may like to think it ought to be."[22] Nor is the Faith to be defined in terms of experience, for this assumes "the Christian faith is what I happen to believe."[23] The Incarnation is pivotal, for it is "the recognition that, in Jesus Christ, God has in some way condescended to our low estate and come amongst us."[24] The Trinity is the "only all-comprehensive Christian dogma."[25] He maintained that Protestants should realize that the Blessed Virgin "might be regarded as the patron saint of the Protestant Confession," as the prototype of humble faith.[26] After a discussion of Adoptionist and Kenoticist Christological doctrines, Dr. Micklem decided in favour of the classical Chalcedonian doctrine of the two natures, human and divine. It is also significant that this theological revaluation by a Congregationalist included, as its eleventh chapter, a consideration of "The Church Catholic and Apostolic." Two other events in the life of Dr. Micklem provide surprising evidence of the power of orthodoxy in a Nonconformist theologian. The first is that Dr. Micklem, as Principal of Mansfield College, Oxford, regularly lectured on the theology of St. Thomas Aquinas from the Latin text, and the second, that he was invited by Dr. William Temple, when the latter was Archbishop of Canterbury, to write a Lenten book, which was issued as *The Doctrine of our Redemption*.

It might be supposed that the Free Churches would be readier than Anglicans to devote themselves to the study of a genuinely Biblical theology, since their roots were in the Reformation according to the Word of God, whereas the Anglicans since the days of the Venerable Hooker had insisted that their authority was the three-fold cord of Scripture, Tradition, and right Reason. This supposition would, however, be untrue. Not only the work of Hoskyns, but also the important Biblical and theological studies of Father A. G. Hebert[27] of Kelham and of Father Lionel Thornton of the Community of the Resurrection,[28] are a standing refutation of this view. In fact, the theological faculties at Oxford and Cambridge included many unusually competent Anglican Biblical

---

22 *What is the Faith?*, pp. 31-32.   23 *Ibid.*, p. 32.
24 *Ibid.*, p. 120.   25 *Ibid.*, p. 133.
26 *Ibid.*, p. 146.
27 Notably his typological study, *The Throne of David* and *Fundamentalism and the Church of God*.
28 Notably the series of studies which includes *The Common Life in the Body of Christ*, *Revelation and the Modern World*, *The Dominion of Christ*, and *Christ and the Church*.

scholars, among whom would have to be included Dr. J. A. T. Robinson,[29] before he became Bishop of Woolwich.

The return to orthodoxy took many forms, all witnessing to the inadequacy of liberalism's attempt to accommodate revelation and churchmanship to contemporary culture. The Roman Catholics, after the expulsion of Modernism from their midst, naturally turned for inspiration to the massive synthesis of philosophy and revelation of St. Thomas Aquinas. In this they were supported by the *Aeterni Patris* of Leo XII and the *Doctoris Angelici* of Pius X, as well as by the *Studiorum Ducem* of Pius XI (1923), confirming the primacy of that Doctor of the Church for Christian theology. Maritain and Gilson, the leading French neo-Thomists, concerned themselves with the tragic disunity of modern society which they diagnosed as due to a lack of direction through the divorce of the natural from the supernatural. Their slogan was, in effect, "Back to Thomas Aquinas and from Thomas forward." Widely read in England, they believed that philosophy and art, as well as social justice, had flourished best and could only flourish as the allies of religion. They believed that the Christian faith, with the backing of the Roman Catholic Church, alone provided a world-view in which all these cultural and social activities now atomized could be united, a collectivist ethics such as the times called for, and a source for progress. In England the leading neo-Thomist was the historian Christopher Dawson. But neo-Thomism also appealed to certain Anglican philosophers, notably Austin Farrer and E. L. Mascall, though each was a theologian of considerable independence.

The English Methodists returned to Biblical orthodoxy in part by the rediscovery of Luther's Gospel of Grace, and appropriately so, for John Wesley's heart was strangely warmed by the proclamation of justification by faith through grace when an unknown person read out Luther's Commentary on the Epistle to the Romans in the Aldersgate Society Meeting on what is now regarded as the Methodist Red-letter Day. Luther's stance *coram Deo* was finely recovered in Philip S. Watson's *Let God be God*, as also in Gordon Rupp's *The Righteousness of God*, and a theocentric theology expelled any lingering traces of anthropocentricism among the younger Methodist theologians.

Among both Congregationalists and Baptists there was a return

[29] See especially his study of ecclesiology, *The Body*, and of eschatology, *In the End, God.*

to their Calvinist heritage. This "Genevan revival"[30] of the Reformed tradition was strong in Congregationalism because the liberalism against which it reacted had been extreme in this denomination. The leaders of this new trend were Dr. Nathaniel Micklem (formerly Principal of Mansfield College, Oxford), Dr. J. S. Whale (formerly President of Cheshunt College, Cambridge), and the late Bernard Manning, Senior Tutor of Jesus College, Cambridge.

Dr. Micklem, as Chairman of the Friends of Reunion, was particularly successful in mediating to the Free Churches the devotional heritage of the Universal Church, and appropriately was the editor of *Christian Worship*[31] (1936), while his *A Book of Personal Religion* (1938) showed the continuity of the evangelical tradition in devotion in Bunyan, Calvin, Doddridge, John Newton, Isaac Watts, John Knox, Richard Baxter, and Matthew Henry. Dr. Whale stressed the links of Congregationalism with the Continental Reformed tradition in his chapter on ecclesiology in *Christian Doctrine* (1941), and more fully in *The Protestant Tradition* (1955) which is an admirable assessal of Luther's rediscovery of the Gospel and Calvin's recovery of Churchmanship and discipline. B. L. Manning exhibited the continuity of the Reformed tradition in English Nonconformity with great distinction, in his *Essays in Orthodox Dissent* (1939), in which he showed conclusively that Nonconformists were orthodox in doctrine but dissenters only in churchmanship, refusing any Erastianism that would have compromised their freedom to obey the Gospel. He also wrote *The Hymns of Wesley and Watts* (1942) to demonstrate that the Free Churches sang their orthodox divinity, even if they did not recite it in creeds or confessions. All three insisted in season and out of season that Genevan churchmanship was founded upon the ministry of the Word and Sacraments, which were not to be divided, any more than Gospel and Church were to be divided. This is superbly expressed in Dr. Whale's ecclesiology:

"Christians have never known the Church as a society of man's contriving, and expression of human idealism like a mutual improvement society or a club for recreation, fellowship and goodwill, with the minister of the Word and Sacraments as its competent and salaried secretary. Christians know the Church evangelical and catholic as the sacred gift of God, which no merely naturalistic or evolutionary categories can explain; it is a wonderful and sacred

[30] The term of John W. Grant in *Free Churchmanship in England*, p. 330.
[31] This book is considered in Chap. x *infra*.

185

mystery, the great company of the elect of God stretching beyond the sight of any man across the centuries and the continents; the host of the living God sharing His very life in all places and in all ages, on earth and in heaven; the Church which God loved, Christ purchased, and the Holy Ghost sanctified, and which Christ will present to Himself a glorious Church."[32]

The new insights in Reformed theology and churchmanship were popularized in a series of "Forward Books" under the general editorship of Dr. John Marsh, as well as in the regular meetings of the Congregational "Church Order" Group. Other Congregational theologians who took their Genevan heritage with the utmost seriousness were Principals H. F. Lovell Cocks, H. Cunliffe-Jones, and John Huxtable, and two younger scholars, Daniel T. Jenkins[33] and W. A. Whitehouse.

Among the Baptists, Principals H. Wheeler Robinson, the distinguished Old Testament scholar, and A. C. Underwood, and Dr. Ernest A. Payne,[34] were also protagonists of an orthodox theology combined with Genevan churchmanship. R. C. Walton represented the same trend in the younger generation in *The Gathered Community* (1946). Neville Clark,[35] a young Baptist minister, devoted himself to the task of mediating the Catholic tradition in worship to his denomination.

It was not too much to say that the return to Biblical orthodoxy in England meant the recovery of the Church's soul. The authority of the Biblical revelation, which was both doctrine and life, replaced the uncertainties of human ideals and experiences. The Bible became the source, not the confirmation of religious experience. Theology stressed the objectivity of the Divine deeds for the salvation of the human race. Man learned that the tragedy of his inner civil war was not due to mere ignorance so much as to a Titanism that was the product of human arrogance and self-sufficiency, manifested in rebellion. In the humility of faith, learned after the Divine judgment in history and in the self, God's grace proved effectual for his renovation. His maturation in Christian faith and witness was accomplished in worship, through the preaching of the Word and the celebration of the Sacrament of Holy Communion. His view of life was no longer to be that of

[32] *What is a Living Church?*, p. 28f.

[33] See *The Nature of Catholicity, Tradition and the Spirit*, and *Congregationalism*.

[34] See his *The Fellowship of Believers* and *The Free Church Tradition in the Life of England*.

[35] See *The Call to Worship*.

the bystander, but one of commitment in Christ's mystical Body the Church. Biblical theologians had learned in T. S. Eliot's words that "the way forward is the way back."[36]

A proof of the important impact of the return to orthodoxy in doctrine was that it was far from being the concern only of professional theologians or ministers of religion. This movement caught the imagination of lay apologists for Christianity, among them some of the most distinguished literary figures of the day.

G. K. Chesterton gained a widespread hearing for the traditional Christian faith in his witty essays in *Orthodoxy* and *Heretics*, while *The Everlasting Man* was a devastating polemic against the evolutionary concept which formed the credo of the secularist. Dorothy L. Sayers wrote an intriguing exposition and defence of orthodoxy in her brilliant pamphlet, *The Greatest Drama ever Staged*, and expounded Christian morality in another entitled *The Other Six Deadly Sins*. Her longer book, *The Mind of the Maker*, was an admirable study of the Christian doctrines of the Trinity and of Creation, illustrated from the consideration of artistic creativity. Her *Zeal of Thy House*, written for the Canterbury Festival, was a convincing account of the nature of pride. Her radio cycle, *The Man born to be King* (1953), which is presented by the British Broadcasting Corporation annually, may well be considered the most successful public presentation of the relevance of the Christian drama of salvation in our time.

Another exceedingly successful apologist and Oxford don, also a lecturer in English literature, was Clive Staples Lewis. His most successful broadcast talks were published as *Mere Christianity*, while *The Problem of Pain* and *Miracles* provided answers to the major problems of belief. *The Screwtape Letters* are an exceedingly ingenious imaginative attempt to show the subtlety and demonic nature of evil. Charles Williams, though less well known, was a poet and novelist whose work was a manifestation of traditional theological insights, and whose Oxford lectures on Milton were hammer blows against secularism. He succeeded in making the Christian virtue of chastity exciting,[37] and he also wrote a most perceptive history of the Christian Church, in terms of the attractions of orthodoxy and heresy, entitled *The Descent of the Dove* (1949).

[36] *The Four Quartets: The Dry Salvages*, III, line 6.
[37] See his essay on *Comus*, republished as the introduction to the World's Classics edition of *The English Poems of John Milton*.

The most impressive of the poets, Thomas Stearns Eliot, became a convinced Anglo-Catholic, and his theological insights were subtly expressed in *Ash Wednesday, the Ariel Poems*, and more directly in the play, *Murder in the Cathedral*, and in his apologia, *The Idea of a Christian Society* (1939). He presented Christianity by indirection in the plays, *The Family Reunion* and *The Cocktail Party*. Where Eliot led, other poets have followed—W. H. Auden, Dylan Thomas, Norman Nicholson, Edwin Muir,[38] and Anne Ridler—in appropriating the Christian symbols in their verse.

All these rediscovered the enchantment of orthodoxy and the wonder of the historic Christian faith, communicating it in essays, myths, drama, and poetry.

2. *The Rediscovery of the Church*

The "Back to the Gospel" movement also turned out to be a "Back to the Church" movement. While the Church of England had rediscovered the apostolicity and catholicity of the Church in the Oxford Movement, it did not become fully aware of the world-wide scandal of disunity until its representatives participated in the Ecumenical Movement of the twentieth century, when the "Bridge Church" discovered that its mixed Protestant-Catholic heritage expressed in miniature the whole tension of a Christendom in schism. For the Free Churches which had customarily elevated the Gospel only to depreciate the Church, as a merely convenient organization readily adaptable to the differing demands of different centuries or cultures, the sense of the Church as itself a gift of God, along with the Gospel, was a new and at first a painful discovery.

Perhaps the most exciting aspect of contemporary Church life is that the "Protestant" Churches are emphasizing that they really share in the Catholic character of the Body of Christ; and the "Catholic" Churches are finding that they must stress aspects of faith and worship for which Protestants stand.[39] But this situation has not merely happened, it has been prepared for by the cooperation of Protestants and Orthodox in the World Council of Churches, which was inaugurated at Amsterdam in 1948, and by the unpredictable liberal trends in the Second Vatican Council of the Roman Catholics. Much prejudice on each side of the ecclesiastical divide

---

[38] Muir deserves to be much better known. See *Collected Poems: 1921-1958* (1960), especially "The Transfiguration" and "The Killing."
[39] Daniel D. Williams, *What Present-Day Theologians are Thinking*, p. 152.

had to be overcome before the present *rapprochement* was reached. Moreover, on the Protestant side there were several conflicting conceptions of the nature of the Church. Some held the Pietist view that the true Church consisted of sincerely warmed hearts. Some held so strongly to the Calvinist view of the Church as the invisible number of the elect, and were so critical of the Catholic equation of the Kingdom of God with the Church, that they denied the need of a visible Church, exhibiting an apostolic continuity and a Catholic unity. Others, again, insisted on the local autonomy of the local congregation, as they stressed the importance of "gathered churches."

Inevitably the question arises: What were the forces which compelled the Protestants in general and Free Churchmen in particular to return to a more Catholic understanding of the Church? Undoubtedly, the primary influence was the ecumenical experience itself. The Free Churches, conscious of the scandal of reunion, had been engaged in closing their own ranks. In 1907 the Bible Christians, the Methodist New Connexion, and the United Methodist Free Church were all united. In 1932 the Primitive, the United, and the Wesleyan Methodist denominations were merged to form the Methodist Church. In 1929 the United Free Church joined the established Church of Scotland. Even more significant for the re-understanding of the nature and task of the Church of Christ were trans-denominational unions, such as the establishment of the United Church of Canada by the union of the Methodists, the Congregationalists, and a substantial number of the Presbyterians. Even more remarkable was the creation of the United Church of South India, after thirty years of maturation, which combined Anglicans, Methodists, Congregationalists, and Presbyterians. Furthermore, the Anglican Church was making tentative approaches to the Free Churches, as in the famous Lambeth Quadrilateral proposals of 1920, and to the Roman Catholic Church at the Malines Conversations of 1921 and 1926. All these mergers, attempted or concluded, concentrated attention on the essential character of the Christian Church, and led to discussion of the *esse*, the *bene esse*, and latterly, the *plene esse* of the Church. Moreover, in such a volume as *The Ministry and the Sacraments* edited by Dunkerley and Headlam (1937), representatives of different traditions were learning how much they held in common on even the thorniest issues.

A second factor tending towards the rediscovery of the Church was the conclusion of "Form criticism" that the attempt to reach a "Jesus of History" behind the primitive traditions was quite impossible, since the Gospels and the Epistles are missionary literature, not biography. On this view no distinction was possible between the words and actions of Jesus himself and what was produced by the faith of the Apostolic Church. Hoskyns, as we have seen, insisted that the Gospels must be viewed through the lens of the Epistles. A more radical form critic, Professor R. H. Lightfoot of Oxford, concluded: "For all the inestimable value of the Gospels, they yield us little more than a whisper of his voice; we trace in them but the outskirts of his ways. Only when we see him hereafter in his fulness shall we know him also as he was on earth."[40] If there would have been no Church apart from the Gospel, there would clearly be no Gospels apart from the Church. Therefore, Church and Gospel could not be separated.

Old Testament scholarship was also pointing in the same direction, as Dr. H. Wheeler Robinson and others drew attention to the importance of the concept of "corporate personality" for the Hebrews. According to Professor T. W. Manson, the "Son of Man" is a corporate figure. The Old Testament knew almost nothing of solitary religion, but only of God's covenanted people, or, in days of widespread apostasy, of the "faithful remnant." These were the Old Testament analogues of "the Body of Christ."

In the third place, the political lesson of the need for community was being bitterly learned in these years, as the conflict with totalitarianism let the democracies realize that freedom must be mated with social responsibility, and that any sound interpretation of freedom is based upon tradition and order. The very anxieties of the times called for an authoritative system of belief, a faith communally believed for which to live and to die, if necessary. The very defence of a civilization in time of war demands that its spiritual values shall be made plain, and this undoubtedly spurred the passing of the Butler Education Act of 1944, one of the provisions of which was to provide religious education in all the State-aided schools in Great Britain.

The most considerable attempt on the Anglican side to justify a Catholic form of Church order as required by the Gospel itself was Dr. A. M. Ramsey's *The Gospel and the Catholic Church*. Its underlying conviction was "that the meaning of the Christian Church becomes most clear when it is studied in terms of the

[40] *History and Interpretation of the Gospels*, p. 225.

Death and Resurrection of Jesus Christ."[41] The conclusion was reached that "the structure of the Catholic Church has great significance in the Gospel of God, and that Apostolic succession is important on account of its *evangelical* meaning."[42] Ramsey declared that in the conception of the Church, not as an institution, but as the Body constituted by Christ's Passion and Resurrection, he hoped to see the reconciliation of the Catholic conception of an institution with Creeds, Sacraments, and Episcopacy (which seems legalistic) with the Protestant concept of a gift of the Gospel and justification by faith (which seems individualistic).

Ramsey utterly repudiated individual experience as an adequate norm for the Church, for "the faithful Christian will not draw attention to himself, as an interesting specimen of life in Christ, but dying to all interest in himself and his 'experience' he will focus attention upon the redeeming acts of Christ in history."[43] To insist upon the authority of an individual experience is to commit a double fault—to deny the adequacy of Christ's deeds and to isolate one's self from the redemptive community of the Church. "In later language, the Church is called 'Apostolic' (sent by the one Redeemer in the flesh), and 'Catholic' (living one universal life); and both notes of the Church are essential to its existence as expressing the Lord's death and resurrection, wherein its 'Holiness' consists."[44]

The importance of the apostles, in Dr. Ramsey's view, is that they represent unity and continuity, "being sent by our Lord who Himself was sent by the Father, and declaring, in effect, 'He came, He died, He rose, we are sent and the Body is One.' "[45] "Apostolic succession" is understood in three ways. The succession of bishop to bishop secured a continuity of Christian teaching and tradition in every see. The bishops also succeeded the apostles in the sense that they performed the apostolic functions of preaching, ruling, and ordaining, and this is summed up by the bishop celebrating at the Eucharist, and interceding for his flock and family. Finally, "apostolic succession" is further used to signify "that grace is handed down from the Apostles through each generation of Bishops by the laying on of hands."[46] In the present the bishop sets forth the Gospel of God as the guardian of teaching, as performing the apostolic functions, and as "an organ in the one Body's continuous life in grace."[47]

41 *The Gospel* . . . , p. vi.   42 *Ibid.*, p. vii.   43 *Ibid.*, p. 44.
44 *Ibid.*, pp. 44-45.   45 *Ibid.*, p. 74.   46 *Ibid.*, p. 82.
47 *Ibid.*, p. 83.

Denying the distinction made by Heiler in *Das Gebet*, which divides prayer into prophetic and mystical, Dr. Ramsey insists that in the New Testament prayer is *liturgical*. "It is the sharing by men in the one action of Christ, through their dying to their own egotisms as they are joined in the one Body with His death and resurrection."[48] The Liturgy, as the Ministry and the Creeds, all point to the Gospel and the Church.

The rest of the volume is a penetrating re-examination of Christian history, culminating in the conclusion: "Hence while Catholicism must face the issues of the Gospel and examine itself as to its Pelagianism, Protestantism must ask whether, after all, the historic Church order has not something to do with the Gospel of God. It will not deny its own experience, nor the power of its own ministries; it needs to own, in common with all Christendom the need for one Apostolate, as the organ of unity and continuity, to be made universal for all Christians. At present we are all incomplete: 'In him ye are all made full.' "[49]

The ecumenical approach is all the more impressive because in the final chapter, *"Ecclesia Anglicana,"* Dr. Ramsey criticizes three ways in which some Anglicans have obscured the Catholic meaning of Church Order, by the "Three Branch" theory which claims unity but rationalizes schism; by an Erastianism which regards the Church of England as the moral organ of the nation; and by the clericalist view of some Anglo-Catholics who have conceived the ministry as a channel of grace isolated from the life of the Body. This was an impressive Biblical and theological treatment of its theme, deserving of thorough consideration.

The most systematic analysis from the Free Church side of the meaning of Catholicity was the book of Daniel Jenkins, *The Nature of Catholicity* (1942). Jenkins recognizes that there must be both unity and continuity in the life of the Church, but he believes that the Church's Catholicity or wholeness is its fidelity to God's present, active and demanding Word in Jesus Christ. The foundation of the Church is Jesus Christ, the Word of God, as the Bible bears witness to the Word. The Bible is, indeed, the Church's book, but it holds before the Church that which stands over it in judgment and mercy, God's redemptive grace. It is not necessary for bishops to be guardians of the apostolic testimony, for "the Apostles themselves took care to ensure that we should

---

[48] *Ibid.*, p. 94. [49] *Ibid.*, p. 201.

be left in no doubt as to the nature of their testimony. They left us the Holy Scriptures."[50]

Jenkins does recognize, however, without any lessening of the authority of the Scriptures, that the creeds and traditions of the Catholic Church are also necessary: "the very fact that the Scriptures need exegesis demands such an authority and we can refuse to recognize it only by refusing to admit that the Spirit has been at work in the Church before us, that is, that the Church of our Fathers has been a true Church and our own Baptism a true Baptism."[51] That there is a need for an apostolic ministry is not contested, but only that apostolicity can be guaranteed by any form of ministry. It is contended that it is the Gospel, as mediated and confirmed by the Holy Spirit, which guarantees the continuous life and therefore the unity of the Church, and therefore it cannot be authenticated by anything extraneous to itself.

Free Churchmen were urged to "take episcopacy into their system" by Archbishop Fisher in a Cambridge sermon of 1946, and many of them might be prepared to do so, since for reasons of history and geography this is the likeliest form of Church Order to win the approval of most of Christendom in a fully united Church. Some would concede that episcopacy is an excellent way of fulfilling the necessary function of *episcope* or oversight in the Church. But since there have been heretical bishops and *episcopi vagantes* in history, they could not put their hands on their hearts and state that episcopacy has always guaranteed, to the faithful, continuity in apostolic faith and practice. How can it then be regarded as of the *esse* of the Church of Christ? B. L. Manning expressed this conviction with characteristic pungency: "It is with salvation by bishops, not government by bishops that we quarrel."[52] For our purpose, to note that Free Churchmen were seriously considering the necessity of the Church as a gift along with the Gospel itself is perhaps more important than to be disturbed about the differences in the continuing debate on the essential form of Church order.

Nonetheless, the Anglican claims have forced the Free Churches to consider both the Biblical nature of the Church and the nature of Church order. Dr. R. Newton Flew and Rupert Davies, at the request of Archbishop Fisher, prepared an interesting and valuable report on *The Catholicity of Protestantism* (1950). They insisted,

50 *Ibid.*, p. 28.   51 *Ibid.*, p. 44.
52 *Church Union: The Next Step for Congregationalists*, p. 6.

after a close study of Luther and Calvin, that "it should now be sufficiently clear that belief in the one Holy Catholic and Apostolic Church is integral to the faith of Protestantism. We believe that incorporation into the Church of Christ, the new Israel of God, is not an optional extra which can be dispensed with by those who possess a high degree of spirituality but takes place in the very act of personal faith in Christ."[53]

The crux of the problem of the essential form of Church order is reached in the sixth chapter on "The Ministry and the Sacraments." Here they refer to the Anglican claim, as reasserted in the work *The Apostolic Ministry* edited by Bishop K. E. Kirk, that the "essential ministry" is the Apostolic Ministry, represented by the episcopate in the apostolical succession, as distinguished from all other ministry which is "dependent." They are satisfied that Professor T. W. Manson, the English Presbyterian scholar, has refuted the validity of this distinction between essential and dependent ministry. His words are: "There is one 'essential' ministry, the only ministry that is unchallengeably essential. That is the ministry which the Lord Jesus Christ opened in Galilee after John the Baptist had been put in prison, the ministry which He carried on in Galilee and Judaea, the ministry which He continues to this day in and through the Church, which is His Body. . . . It is in virtue of this presence that it is possible to call the Church the Body of Christ."[54]

Thus, the only conclusion that can be drawn is that the ministry of the Apostles themselves is derivative and dependent. The Apostles were in no sense the "plenipotentiaries" (much play was made by Dr. Kirk's associates with the term *shaliach*,[55] translated "plenipotentiary"); Christ is God's plenipotentiary and the Holy Spirit sent by Christ is His plenipotentiary. Flew and Davies conclude: "To speak of anyone else, or any body of men, as the plenipotentiary of Christ is not only false but blasphemous; for it is virtually to deny, or at least to discount, the continuous activity of the Holy Spirit in the Church."[56]

Hitherto consideration has been limited to the more problematical aspects of the doctrine of the Church; it is now appropriate

[53] P. 91.　　　　　　　　　　　　　[54] *The Church's Ministry*, p. 22f.
[55] Bishop R. R. Williams in *Authority in the Apostolic Age*, p. 139, wrote: "It is hard to believe that the very basis of the Church's life—the 'Essential Ministry,' as Kirk calls it—can be established only by a prolonged and finally ambiguous argument among Rabbinic and Patristic scholars."
[56] *The Catholicity of Protestantism*, p. 105.

to turn to the more positive aspects as exemplified in the studies of a Free Churchman, Dr. Newton Flew, and of an Anglican, Dr. F. W. Dillistone.

Newton Flew's important study was entitled *Jesus and His Church, A Study of the Idea of the Ecclesia in the New Testament* (1938, second edition, 1943). Five main arguments are supplied for the assertion that Jesus intended to found a Church.[57] Jesus directed His preaching to the re-constitution of Israel in view of the advent of God's rule, and the "little flock" which He addresses is the New Israel. The ethical teaching of Jesus can be rightly understood only as directed to this nucleus of the New Israel, and as involving a promise of God's power to enable the disciples to translate the teaching into life; thus the ethical teaching points forward to the gift of the Holy Spirit promised for the Last Days. The very concept of Messiahship, especially as employed by Jesus, implies the gathering of a New Community. The terms "Gospel" or "Word" or "Mystery" employed in the preaching of Jesus refer to the entity which is constitutive of the New Community. (Those who receive the divine "Word" know it as "good news"; for those who reject it, it is a "Mystery" not yet revealed; and the "Gospel" includes the idea of the New Covenant to be established with the newly constituted People of God.) Finally, the Mission of the New Community is declared when Jesus sends forth His disciples. Thus, Flew establishes that the New Community, Ecclesia, or Church, was an original part of the Gospel, and lays to rest the older view that Paul was the real founder of the Church who complicated and institutionalized the "simple" ethical teaching of a Galilean prophet.

Moreover, the Sacraments are seen by Flew to be essential ordinances of the Church. He maintains that there were three decisive moments in the actions of Christ in constituting the Ecclesia. These were: the calling and instruction of the disciples; commissioning them to proclaim the good news that the new era had dawned in both word and deed; and, at the Last Supper, the institution of the new covenant with the disciples as representing the New People of God.

Flew arrives at four conclusions about the nature of the Church. "1. It is God's own creation. . . . The Ecclesia of God is the People of God, with a continuous life which goes back through the history

[57] These are conveniently summarized in the second edition on p. 14 of the Introduction.

of Israel . . . to Abraham . . . to the purpose of God before the world began."[58] "In the second place, the Word of God which called the Church into being has been verified in human experience. . . . The Church . . . has been constituted through the work of the Incarnate Word of God, by sharing in the Spirit, the preaching of the Word and the administration of the Sacraments."[59] Finally, "the principle of authority in the New Testament Church is closely connected with the Word."[60] His point here is that the Apostles were such only as they were eyewitnesses of the Word and witnesses to the Resurrection, and the implication follows that, important as Church order is, it is not as important as the faith.

Among Free Churchmen the acceptance of the authority of a historical Gospel has led to a renewed consideration of the authority of the Church, as God's on-going community of redemption. The Sacraments are no longer regarded as moving spiritual experiences, but as seals of the covenant of promise. The ministry is not a means of self-expression for spiritual philosophers or social reformers, but it is acknowledged unequivocally as "of the Word and Sacraments."[61]

One of the most helpful ecumenical attempts to see the complementary character of the differences between Catholic and Protestant conceptions of the Church is F. W. Dillistone's *The Structure of the Divine Society* (1951). In an exceedingly fresh and clearsighted survey of church history Dillistone isolates six main types of Christian community. The first three of them are Catholic conceptions: the monastic, the imperial, and the organic. The next three are Protestant: the covenantal, the contractual, and the sectarian. Both the monastic and the sectarian types are regarded as tangential to the main concern. The imperial and the contractual concepts are criticized as too static, in that they have become prematurely rigid in their historical formation. The organic and covenantal types, however, are more dynamic, and bear within themselves a vital principle for the on-going life of the Church. Dillistone regards them as the essential types of Catholic and Protestant churchmanship.

The organic conception of the Catholics stresses the common life of Christians in the Body of Christ. It emphasizes the social character of existence. We are born into a family and nation and

---

[58] *Jesus and His Church* . . . , p. 181.
[59] *Ibid.*, p. 182.   [60] *Ibid.*
[61] J. W. Grant, *Free Churchmanship in England, 1870-1940*, p. 397.

from these given relationships we receive the very possibility of personal identity and worth. So it is with our Christian life, for the Sacraments in Catholicism hallow the various stages of our life and are essentially social in character. The covenantal conception of Protestants emphasizes those relations into which we enter voluntarily through personal commitments to God and to one another as we look forward to some common purpose in the future. The organic concept implies that Christians are born, and the covenantal concept that Christians are made. Dillistone believes that both are valid analogies for interpreting the nature of the Church, and that the Christian Church can incorporate and reconcile them. The importance of his study is, indeed, to have recognized that these competitive concepts are ultimately complementary. He believes that "Heirs of the Covenant in One Body" is the most apt expression for the complementary view, since this unites the organic-ontological element with the covenantal-eschatological emphasis.[62]

The thorough-going consideration of the nature of the Church in various reports of the Faith and Order Commission of the World Council of Churches, in which British representatives took part, and of the detailed contributions of individual Churchmen of different ecclesiastical traditions in England, is impossible within this limited space. But enough has been said to indicate that this is a very lively part of contemporary theological conversation, likely to become livelier with the new Catholic-Protestant dialogue. It is of the greatest importance that, despite continuing problems in the sphere of Church order, a considerable consensus has been arrived at between the once mutually suspicious Anglican and Free Church traditions, and this has been made possible by the return to a Biblical theology and by the ecumenical enterprise. On both sides of the divide, it is now recognized that the Church, far from being the club of the religious minded, or the moral uplift department of the nation, or the *ecclesiola* of the pietists, is the Body of Christ, founded by the Messiah through His sacrificial Death and Resurrection and empowered by the Holy Spirit. It is commonly acknowledged that its life is fed by the Word and the Sacraments, and that its two-fold function is "to glorify God

---

[62] This bald summary does not do justice to the complexity and criticisms of Dr. Dillistone's important monograph. A fuller study of Anglican ecclesiology would also have to consider the contributions of Lionel Thornton and E. L. Mascall on the High Church side and the work of F. J. Taylor and others on the Evangelical side. Brief reference to Abbot Christopher Butler's ecclesiology has been made in Chap. VII *infra*.

in adoration and sacrificial service."[63] It is also confessed that the Church must be Apostolic, continuing in the teaching and practice of the Apostles (though there are differences about the nature of the "Apostolic succession"), that it must be Holy, and there is a longing such as has not been felt for centuries that its Catholicity may be made visible and that thus may be fulfilled Christ's High-Priestly Prayer *ut omnes unum sint.*

No further proof of the new consensus on ecclesiology is needed than to cite the following statement from the Report, *Doctrine in the Church of England* (1938), with the assurance that it would be entirely acceptable to all the English Free Churches. The instrumental definition (on p. 112) reads: "The Church exists to worship God made known in Christ, and bears His commission in this world to bear witness to His Gospel, to bring all mankind within the membership, range, and fellowship of the redeemed Society, and to gain for the principles involved in the Gospel application to the conditions of human life from time to time."

This rediscovery of the necessity of the Church has, it need hardly be said, helped to strengthen the conviction of the crucial importance of worship, liturgical and sacramental.

3. *Towards a Christian Sociology*

The third trend during the most recent period of theology has been an attempt, chiefly on the part of High Church Anglicans, to elaborate a distinctively Christian Sociology. Since this is the concern of a very limited group of theologians it warrants only the briefest consideration, especially as the most recent developments of the welfare state in Britain have taken much of the momentum from the movement for the expression of social justice in British society.

The concern to establish a Christian Sociology is no recent phenomenon in the Church of England, which can proudly lay claim to have considered this need as far back as 1848, when F. D. Maurice, Charles Ludlow, and Charles Kingsley cooperated to found the Christian Socialist Movement.[64] This was done as a result of their conviction that unsocial Christians and unChristian Socialists were equally dangerous in that year of revolutions in Europe and the publication of the *Communist Manifesto* by Marx and Engels. The same tradition, based upon the Incarnation and

---

[63] Leonard Hodgson, *The Second World Conference on Faith and Order*, p. 233.
[64] See M. B. Reckitt, *Maurice to Temple.*

its sacramental implications for human society, was taken from the founding Broad Churchmen by the Anglo-Catholics, in the persons of Stewart Headlam, Charles Gore, and Conrad Noel, and a legion of priests in slum parishes who proved to be the protectors of the poor. Its importance in the present century was signalized by the leadership given to the movement by William Temple, successively Bishop of Manchester, Archbishop of York, and Archbishop of Canterbury, who wrote the most popular presentation of its theme in a paperback entitled, *Christianity and Social Order* (1942).[65]

It was Temple's chairmanship of the 1924 Conference on Politics, Economics, and Citizenship (C.O.P.E.C.) in Birmingham, which convinced him of the importance of ecumenical consideration of the reconstruction of society through the social thinking and witness of Christians. In the summer of 1937 Temple was inevitably the leader in the Oxford Life and Work Conference on "Church, Community and State." His most dramatic role, however, was played at the Malvern Anglican Conference of 1941, when England was subject to ruthless bombing, and there was much consideration of the "social reconstruction" which should follow this war in which sacrifices were democratically equal. Papers were to be read by members of the "Christendom group"[66] who, in general, accepted the highly sacramental theology of W. G. Peck and his friends. They included the impressive names of Dorothy L. Sayers, Maurice Reckitt, T. S. Eliot, Middleton Murry, Donald M. Mackinnon, H. A. Hodges, and V. A. Demant.

The most inflammatory papers were, however, given by Sir Richard Acland and Kenneth Ingram. Acland argued that the common ownership of the means of production was a fundamental principle, which received considerable support, and the headlines of the newspapers in England and the United States asserted that the Archbishop and his advisers had capitulated to socialism. In fact, however, Temple got the Conference to agree only that the ultimate private ownership of the resources of the community *may be* a stumbling-block to a just society.[67] The purpose of emphasizing Temple's leadership in this field is simply to demonstrate

[65] A brief summary of this book is provided in Chapter VI. More than 150,000 copies had been sold by 1958 (Joseph Fletcher, *William Temple, Twentieth Century Christian*, p. 282).

[66] See M. B. Reckitt, ed., *Prospect for Christendom*, V. A. Demant, *The Religious Prospect* and W. G. Peck, *An Outline of Christian Sociology*. See also *Malvern, 1941, Proceedings of the Archbishop of York's Conference.*

[67] Fletcher, *William Temple* . . . , pp. 276-79.

that an important body of Anglican thinkers were attempting under his guidance to elaborate a Christian sociology.

What, then, is meant by a Christian sociology? Peck, Demant, and Reckitt have been greatly concerned to develop principles for the Christian interpretation of man in society, and of these the Incarnation is most central. This was made the basis of all Christian evaluation of culture. The foundation of this view is that in Jesus Christ the divine and human natures are united in one person, and Christ represents men before God and incorporates them into a new society of which He is the Head. Thus, in the Incarnation are united the personal and the social principles, which are essential to a true human society. All the positive values of culture are derived from the incarnational principle and judged by it. Art, philosophy, and the socio-political order are all potential values to be incorporated in the new life in Christ.

The Incarnation is, however, to be understood in the light of Christ's Passion, Atonement, and Resurrection. In this way all human values are exposed to the light of the perfect love which judges, forgives and redeems. The redemptive deed of Christ transforms all the partial values of temporal existence by bringing them into a new order of life whose principle is the Divine love in all its depth and inclusiveness.

It could be argued that this approach lacks the definiteness of the Roman Catholic ethical guidance, but it might be retorted that the flexibility possible in the Anglican approach avoids legalism and is free to employ middle axioms and temporary solutions without supposing that they are final. It is clear that no single Christian social philosophy can be derived from this Anglican standpoint, but it provides a dynamic synthesis of faith and human thought. In fact, Anglican social thinkers urge the necessity for both economists and sociologists to supply the scientific data upon which Christian evaluations are founded. These judgments tend to favour a society which combines the maximum of personal freedom compatible with responsible sharing. Generally speaking, Anglican moralists have supported the attempt to find collective solutions for the problems of social security, health, labour conditions, and participation in the decisions of industry and government. As Daniel D. Williams has remarked: "We may appreciate something of the theological integrity and profundity of this school by noting how the doctrine of the Trinity is brought into a new

200

relevance for social problems."[68] The Trinity, in their view, is the Divine Society of Father, Son, and Holy Spirit, which in its own depth understands the mystery of giving and receiving.

In contrast to the liberal "social gospel" teaching of the first two decades of the century, which laid great stress on the "Kingdom of God" as its central concept, the "Christendom group" finds its historical anchorage in the Incarnation, which it makes the paradigm of Divine love and the basis for the sacramental ordering of society. It is, therefore, prepared to see in the Eucharist the pattern for a reconstructed order of society, in which the interdependence of the human society is recognized in its dependence upon God, from whom it receives its human and divine life, a life to be shared.[69]

4. The Thought of the Christian Radicals of Cambridge

The latest development in English theology is the most iconoclastic and therefore the most difficult to evaluate.[70] It is all the more important, therefore, that it should be expounded as far as possible in the words of its proponents, who are less a school than a group of individual theologians in conversation with each other as Cambridge University dons or ex-dons. They are deeply disturbed by the ineffectualness of official Christianity in England, which seems to their view respectable, supine, intellectually irrelevant, and apparently complacent. They are anxious to fracture this stereotype and to present a new image of Christianity, involving a radical recasting of the theology, the piety, and the moral attitudes of the Church.

The new "Christian radicalism"[71] has chiefly found expression

---

68 *What Present-day Theologians are Thinking,* p. 95.

69 No further explanation of these ideas is necessary in view of the social implications of the Eucharist, as expressed by Temple and Dix, which are considered in Chap. IX.

70 Professor E. L. Mascall has provided a pointed critique of *Soundings* in his *Up and Down in Adria,* and Dr. A. M. Ramsey, the Archbishop of Canterbury, a short evaluation of Bishop John A. T. Robinson's *Honest to God* in *Image Old and New.* While the issues raised by the Cambridge radicals have hit the newspaper headlines, they are by no means alone in these concerns or approaches in Britain. Professor R. Gregor Smith provided a pioneer attempt to domesticate Bonhoeffer's thought in *The New Man: Christianity and Man's Coming of Age* and the Rev. Daniel T. Jenkins essayed a similar task, with cautionary qualifications, in *Beyond Religion.* For the Bultmannian approach reference may be made to Professor John Macquarrie's *The Scope of Demythologizing.* Professor Alan Richardson (now Dean of York) and three Nottingham University colleagues have also prepared a brief critique of the movement, *Four Anchors from the Stern.* See also Erik R. Routley, *The Man for Others,* for a more sympathetic approach.

71 The term is used by the Rev. David L. Edwards, co-editor with Bishop

201

in three very recent and unconventional volumes. One, *Honest to God* (1963) is a general and fairly popular account of the re-formulation of Christian faith and life necessary to commend Christianity to the thoughtful agnostic of today and is the work of Dr. John A. T. Robinson, Bishop of Woolwich and former Dean of Clare College, Cambridge. The other two, both of which were edited by Dr. A. R. Vidler, Dean of King's College and former Editor of *Theology*, are *Soundings* (1963) and *Objections to Christian Belief.*[72]

Bishop Robinson of Woolwich is convinced "that there is a growing gulf between the traditional orthodox supranaturalism in which our Faith has been framed and the categories which the 'lay' world (for want of a better term) finds meaningful today."[73] His book is the effort to bridge that gulf. Although this became a best-seller and something of a *succès de scandale*, he ended his introduction with the words: "The one thing of which I am fairly sure is that, in retrospect, it will be seen to have erred in not being nearly radical enough."[74] Dr. Alec Vidler introduces *Soundings* with the declaration, "We can best serve the cause of truth and of the Church by candidly confessing where our perplexities lie, and not by making claims which, so far as we can see, theologians are not at present in a position to justify . . . it is a time for making soundings, not charts or maps."[75] Here then is an exceedingly realistic assessal of the place of Christianity in an age of increasing secularism. Here, too, is an honest, self-critical, tentative and modest essay in re-translating the essentials of Christian belief and practice in a way that will make them relevant in the techno-cratic age.

How is it proposed to recast the traditional structure of theology? Here the first great problem is to find a modern equivalent for the Divine transcendence that does not involve an antiquated cosmology. Robinson inveighs against the survival in theology of a physical conception of a pre-Copernican God "up there" in the sky or a metaphysical idea of a post-Copernican God "out there." In his view an image employing the metaphor of "depth" is better than the customary one of "height" since the latter suggests

---

Robinson of the *Honest to God Debate*, who writes (p. 21): "If I had to put a label on this movement . . . I would call it Christian radicalism."

[72] Originally delivered as four open lectures in Cambridge University in February, 1963. The American edition (J. B. Lippincott and Company, Philadelphia and New York), on which I am dependent, appeared in 1964.

[73] *Honest to God*, p. 8.   [74] *Ibid.*, p. 10.   [75] *Soundings*, p. ix.

remoteness, superficiality, and the lack of profound concern. He is persuaded by modern psychological usage and by the philosophical theology of Paul Tillich that the categories of "ultimate concern" and the "Ground of Being" are preferable.[76] Furthermore, Robinson is convinced that the traditional arguments for the existence of God presuppose that God is an object to be arrived at when man's search or argument is concluded. That, however, would be to conceive of God as a being among beings instead of Being-in-itself, which is the very pre-condition of the search.[77] The Ground of Being is further defined as Love: "Belief in God is the trust, the well-nigh incredible trust, that to give oneself to the uttermost in love is not to be confounded, but to be accepted; that Love is the ground of our being to which ultimately we 'come home.' "[78] Furthermore, God is to be met, not by withdrawal from the world, but "in unconditional concern 'for the other' *seen through to its ultimate depths*."[79] The Rev. G. F. Woods in his "The Idea of the Transcendent,"[80] in presenting a learned philosophical argument, arrives at a similar solution, contending that this essential concept in relation to God is arrived at analogically and is better conceived in personal than in impersonal analogies.

An equally radical attempt at "demythologizing" in theology is applied to the Chalcedonian Christology which affirms that Christ is the union of two natures, divine and human, in the one person. Robinson argues that this implies that God's Son is an intruder into humanity, since "it conjures up the idea of a divine substance being plunged into flesh and coated with it like chocolate or silver plating."[81] He prefers the image of Christ as a window showing God at work,[82] and asserts that Jesus "reveals God by being utterly transparent to him, precisely as he is nothing 'in himself.' "[83] The Rev. Hugh W. Montefiore in "Towards a Christology for Today"[84] finds three difficulties in the Chalcedonian Christology. The Definition assumes that Godhead and manhood are fully known, that they are comparable natures to be juxtaposed, and disregards the functional and dynamic terms in which Jesus spoke of himself. The paradox of grace, which assures man that he is accepted and loved as he is because of God's identification with man in Jesus and by Jesus' loving acceptance of the worst that man can do to him, is the best analogy whereby we can conceive of the union

[76] *Honest to God*, p. 23. [77] *Ibid.*, Chap. 2. [78] *Ibid.*, p. 49.
[79] *Ibid.*, p. 61. [80] Chap. 3 of *Soundings*. [81] *Honest to God*, p. 67.
[82] *Ibid.*, p. 71. [83] *Ibid.*, p. 73. [84] Chap. 7 of *Soundings*.

of the divine and human in Jesus. The Rev. J. S. Bezzant in "Intellectual Objections"[85] claims that the traditional doctrines of the Trinity and the Incarnation are assailed because we do not know a complete human nature which is not a person and Christ is said to combine two natures in his single personality, while the term "person" is unacceptable in reference to the Trinity for it is an entity "which is neither noun nor adjective."[86]

Traditional explanations of the Atonement also come under considerable fire. Professor D. M. Mackinnon in "Moral Objections"[87] objects to the sadistic implication of the penal substitutionary theory, and the fact that this has sometimes led to a daughter's hope of marriage and personal fulfillment being wrongly "sacrificed" to her aged parents on the analogy of following the Cross. The Rev. Professor G. W. H. Lampe in "The Atonement: Law and Love"[88] similarly criticizes all legalistic conceptions of the Atonement that stress man's attempts to make himself acceptable in God's sight, as a misunderstanding of the Gospel which rightly stresses God's love for men at their worst and their most unacceptable. J. S. Bezzant simply states that the substitutionary concept of Christ's Atonement offends the moral sensibilities of today.

What, then, is to be affirmed as the modern equivalent? Bishop Robinson, taking a leaf from Dietrich Bonhoeffer's book, thinks of the redemptive act of Christ as the work of "The Man for others" who challenges men "to participation in the sufferings of God in the life of the world."[89] For the Rev. H. A. Williams in "Theology and Self-Awareness"[90] the principle of Incarnation is essentially the principle of involvement.[91] The practical implications of this revised creed are stated by the Rev. J. S. Bezzant: "I think it is entirely reasonable for any man who studies the spirit of the facing of life as Christ faced it, and his recorded teaching, to decide that by him he will stand through life, death or eternity rather than join in a possible triumph of evil over him."[92]

These attempts to refashion traditional theology have, of course, come under heavy fire, and this criticism should be considered before going on to review the proposed radical revisions of the

[85] Chap. 4 of *Objections to Christian Belief*.   [86] *Ibid.*, p. 103.
[87] Chap. 1 of *Objections to Christian Belief*.   [88] Chap. 8 of *Soundings*.
[89] Cited *Honest to God*, p. 82, from Bethge, ed., Bonhoeffer's *Letters and Papers from Prison* (2nd edn., 1956), p. 166.
[90] Chap. 4 of *Soundings*.   [91] *Ibid.*, p. 73.
[92] *Objections to Christian Belief*, p. 110.

traditional Christian ethic. Archbishop Ramsey believes that Bishop Robinson's preference of the "depth" image is open to the charge that it hardly does justice to the central element of grace in the Gospel, and he asks: "If there is ultimate reality which is love and personal, does not the initiative come not from us but from thence?"[93] Dr. R. P. C. Hanson believes that transcendence is not adequately interpreted, insisting that for the Bible transcendence is not "metaphysical abstraction or separation, but control."[94] The Rev. Professor H. E. W. Turner is doubtful whether the Atonement can be satisfactorily defined in terms of the acceptance of the unacceptable, since it recalls the old subjectivist interpretation of Justification by Faith "or a Lutheranism run to seed." He insists that the "full formula of 'Justification by Grace through Faith' includes precisely what Tillich and Robinson leave out" and thus there is missing "the powerful action of God in Christ which is the ground . . . of the transforming and liberating experience which Tillich describes."[95]

The second major concern of the Cambridge radicals is to rescue Christian ethics from a perfectionistic escape from the world or from a legalism which caricatures the Christian way as "life-denying rather than life-affirming or life-enhancing."[96] Furthermore, it is exceedingly difficult to appeal with confidence to the three historic authorities which formed the grounds for Christian moral choice: the Bible, a system of theological ethics, and the Natural Law.[97] Dr. Robinson is particularly severe on the old supranaturalist ethics which spoke magisterially of the "sanction of Sinai" or "the clear teaching of our Lord."[98] The Sermon on the Mount, he insists, is not a new Leviticus; rather it provides "illustrations of what love may at any moment require of anyone."[99] He favours a "radical 'ethic of the situation,' with nothing prescribed—except love,"[100] but emphasizes that this will make the most searching demands on the depth and integrity of one's concern for the other on the analogy of the "utterly unselfregarding *agape* of Christ."[101]

This "new morality" is, in fact, an attempt to return to the morality of the New Testament, with its command of love, and to

93 *Image Old and New*, p. 8.
94 *The Honest to God Debate*, pp. 108-09.
95 *Ibid.*, p. 151.
96 D. M. Mackinnon in *Objections to Christian Belief*, p. 15.
97 See the careful analysis of these difficulties in G. F. Woods' "The Grounds of Christian Moral Judgments" in *Soundings*, pp. 196ff.
98 *Honest to God*, p. 109.   99 *Ibid.*, pp. 110-11.
100 *Ibid.*, p. 116.   101 *Ibid.*, p. 119.

St. Augustine's *dilige et quod vis fac*. It will require a revaluation of the conservative ecclesiastical attitude to divorce and remarriage. Mackinnon believes that many of these second unions "have been more abundantly justified by their fruits than the frequently tragic human distress they have replaced."[102]

The most radical interpreter of the new morality is the Rev. H. A. Williams, who believes from his studies in psycho-analysis that much conventional Christian morality is a Pharisaic masquerade and a mockery.[103] On this view, if love is self-giving much of what Christians have called virtue is only cowardice. *Per contra*, much apparent immorality may be genuine self-giving. Williams suggests that the prostitute with the golden heart in the Greek film, *Never on Sunday*, who restores confidence to a troubled young sailor by her physical union with him, performs "an act of charity which proclaims the glory of God."[104]

The third area in which a radical reformation is called for is in the institutional life and especially in the cultus of the Church. Here there is considerable difference of opinion, ranging from some theological revisions desirable in the Book of Common Prayer, which are listed by Professor John Burnaby, to the Rev. H. A. Williams's wholesale condemnation of it as "our incomparably unchristian Liturgy."[105]

It is clear, however, that theological revision of the Prayer Book is required by some of the Cambridge radicals. Professor Burnaby claims that many of the Psalms used in the Liturgy are of the type of *klage-lied* complaints and expostulations which are dominated "by a temper which even the most reckless allegorizing can scarcely baptize into Christianity."[106] He finds that the confession of sins seems "inspired rather by fear of God's implacable justice than by sorrow for the wounding of Divine love."[107] He is not less critical of the sentences ("Man that is born of woman . . .") in the Order for the Burial of the Dead which accompany the committal to the grave—he considers them an offence against the Gospel. Yet he believes that the sacrament of Communion rectifies many theologi-

---

[102] *Objections to Christian Belief*, p. 14, where he adds, ironically, that "it is impossible to escape the impression that, to certain sorts of clergy, the effective exclusion from sacramental communion of divorced persons who have remarried is the highest form of the Church's moral witness."

[103] See his "Theology and Self-Awareness" in *Soundings*, Chap. 4.

[104] *Ibid.*, p. 81. Mr. Williams uses extreme instances and citations. See also *ibid.*, p. 82, and the Blake citation in *Objections to Christian Belief*, p. 51.

[105] See H. A. Williams, "Unchristian Liturgy," in *Theology* (October, 1958), pp. 401-04.

[106] *Soundings*, p. 236.   [107] *Ibid.*

cal errors, since "the significance of the sacrament is to represent and realize that oneness of life into which the taking of our nature by the Son of God, its bearing through cross and resurrection into the heavenly places, and the coming of the Holy Spirit to be its strength and stay have brought the Creator and his creatures."[108] Clearly Professor Burnaby has a minimal revision in mind.

Although expressed with moderation, Bishop Robinson's views on worship are more revolutionary in their reinterpretation. He is greatly concerned for a "worldly holiness" which will express the holiness in the communal relationships of life. The real function of worship is "to make us sensitive to these depths [meeting Christ in common relationships]; to focus, sharpen and deepen our response to the world and to other people beyond the point of proximate concern (of liking, self-interest, limited commitment, etc.) to ultimate concern; to purify and correct our loves in the light of Christ's love; and in him to find the grace and power to be the reconciled and reconciling community."[109]

It seems that he wishes to apply an ethical test to worship, and thus to minimize its importance as mediating a sense of the glory of God, as instructional in faith, and creative of loyalty to God and to his Church. What he says is: "The test of worship is how far it makes us *more sensitive* to the 'beyond in our midst,' to the Christ in the hungry, the naked, the homeless, and the prisoner."[110] Nonetheless, Robinson advocates the abolition of worship no more than he advocates the abolition of bishops. He is, in fact, urging that even the reforming of worship will be inadequate unless the correlation of the sanctuary with society is made far more explicit. He deplores an unholy escapism, a withdrawal into another world of the spirit, which is often perpetuated by liturgical worship, even of the most dignified or aesthetic type.

He protests with all his command of language against the idea that "the sacramental moments of communion with God are to be expected in the periods of withdrawal, which, like the camel's water, are to see one through the deserts of the day that must otherwise drain one dry."[111] He even wonders, while recognizing that there must be a rhythm of engagement and disengagement in any active life, "whether Christian prayer . . . is not to be *defined* in terms of penetration through the world to God rather than withdrawal from the world to God."[112] It can be expressed most vividly

---

108 *Ibid.*, p. 237.
110 *Ibid.*, p. 90.
112 *Ibid.*, p. 97.

109 *Honest to God*, pp. 87-88.
111 *Ibid.*, pp. 91-92.

as "preparing in the telephone to meet our God"—that is, to be always open to personal invasion knowing that "persons matter," aware that in our unconditional concern for them we encounter Christ. Such an approach may expose liturgical worship to the most radical revision, provide a prophetic relevance in preaching, and establish a two-way traffic between the Church and the world, as well as encourage much extra-liturgical experimentation in worship and evangelism that would be more natural and less contrived than the present expressions of these perennial tasks of the Christian Community.

All this re-structuring of theology, ethics, and worship, will demand another reformation of the Church of England. Many certainties will have to be given up which were confidently asserted to have been demanded by Christ or the Christian tradition.[113] It is, indeed, a more chastened and charitable Church of England which Dr. Vidler envisions when he speaks of the possibility of a more comprehensive ecclesiastical settlement, which will attempt to satisfy the spiritual, moral, and psychological needs which the state is not competent to meet, and which will "stimulate and defend all those agencies—however little ecclesiastical or ecclesiastical they may be—that minister to the freedom and fulness of man's spiritual life." He concludes his essay on "Religion and the National Church" with a question-mark: "For the Church of England the great question is whether it can be transformed into such a church or is doomed to sink into the position of a religious denomination?"[114] No Church, whether established or disestablished, is likely to gain the loyalty of twentieth century men unless it sees itself in the role not of a master, but of a servant. That clearly is the way the Cambridge Christian radicals visualize the task of the contemporary Community of Christ.

5. Conclusion

As we view the development of theology in England from 1900 to 1965 it may appear to be cyclical rather than linear. For, in the most striking way, the Cambridge radicals are reasserting many of the objections to orthodoxy that Liberal Protestants made at the end of the last and the beginning of the present century. The parallels can be found in the stressing of immanence rather than of transcendence in the doctrine of God, and in the necessity for the Church to be deeply engaged in the struggle for social justice. Dr.

[113] See *Soundings*, pp. 138-39.   [114] *Soundings*, p. 263.

Alec Vidler has rightly paid a belated tribute to the earlier liberals: "Christians in the twentieth century, who on the whole have been less adventurous than the nineteenth century 'liberals' whom they affect to have surpassed, have still much to learn from them."[115] These parallels, however, if alone considered significant, would fail to do justice to the genuine innovations on the theological scene which are distinctive of twentieth century theology in England.

Never has English theology been less insular than in the twentieth century. While it has its own distinctive pragmatism, consonant with the British temper, and in contrast with the more purely theoretical emphasis of non-existential types of theology in Germany, it has been receptive to important foreign influences. German, Scandinavian, French, and American theologians have been read with appreciation. For the point to be appreciated it is necessary only to mention the names of Harnack, Schweitzer, Barth, Otto, Brunner, Bultmann, Bonhoeffer, Kierkegaard, Söderblom, Brilioth, Nygren, Cullmann, the two Niebuhrs, and Paul Tillich. In the process of domestication some of these theological viewpoints lost their sharp and occasionally extreme edges, but the point is that they were taken with very great seriousness and they proved fertile.

In the second place, theology in England has never been so ecumenical as in the present century. This, too, helped to break its insularity, a historic characteristic of English theology, though never of Scottish, which has maintained its links with the Continental Reformed Churches. Thus theology, hammered out in encounter between representatives of different traditions of churchmanship, and published in the form of symposia, has provided a consensus on many major issues that was quite impossible in the nineteenth century.

The third characteristic of the twentieth century in theology, which is true for many other countries besides Britain, is that there is a new-found correlation of Bible, Church, and Liturgy. This is the most significant as well as the most startling phenomenon of the age. It is as if the prodigal intellectual sons who had gone into the far country of culture, and had been dissatisfied with the husks of religious philosophy or the mush of syncretism, returned to appreciate the theocentric faith of the Bible. In rediscovering the Bible, they found it to be the Book of the People of God, and they

---

[115] *The Church in an Age of Revolution*, pp. 270-71.

learned that their intellectual and critical study of it needed to be nourished by devotion through worship. Whatever the explanation, it became clear that Bible, Church, and Liturgy are three witnesses to the re-creating Word of God, Jesus Christ, and that they belong together.

This has been the century when Christian worship has come into its own, although not without a struggle against the supporters of the "social gospel" who found God better served in the slums than in the sanctuary, or the cultivators of "spontaneity" who would have made their own experience the substitute for the richness of Liturgy's testimony to God through twenty centuries as mediated through many cultures and a variety of theologies. There is no question but that the Liturgical Movement has strengthened theology in the service of the Church, and, through drawing out the social implications of the Liturgy, in service to the world. The importance of the organic conception of the Church and of the social sacraments of its life has never been better understood, nor has the instructional and prophetic practice of preaching and the need for a covenanted commitment to Christ been better appreciated. And, equally important, the sense that both Liturgy and witness require the full participation of the laity is recognized in Catholic and Protestant circles as never before. Not least in importance is the dialogue between Catholic and Protestant which has replaced the shouting across a vast abyss of misunderstanding, and which has been made easier by the "new look" and, indeed, new spirit of Roman Catholicism made evident in the Second Vatican Council. In a period when Christian theology has been subject to powerful intellectual attacks and when almost every Christian Communion in England has declined in numbers and influence these are signs of hope in a crepuscular future.

CHAPTER VI

TRENDS AND TYPES OF PREACHING[1]

IF THE Victorian preacher ascended a pulpit as a crown prince his throne, the modern preacher quietly enters it as if it were a witness-box. The era of spellbinders is over. Christianity is the faith of a minority group in contemporary England.

The modern sermon is twice as quiet and half as long as the Victorian pulpit discourse. This can be explained partly by the restriction of the function of the modern pulpit to the communication of the Divine will for men, which eliminates the duty to provide adult education and entertainment in the pulpit; it is also partly explicable from the concision and colloquial directness of speech encouraged by the example of radio and television communication. The tone of the modern sermon, too, is conversational and confidential. Disraeli's approach to Queen Victoria, not Gladstone's, has won the day in pulpit as in Parliament, with the notable exceptions of Sir Winston Churchill's noble war-time eloquence and the verbal jousts between him and Aneurin Bevan.

1. *Changes during the Century*

In the era of the "New Theology"[2] ministers tended to act as if they were social prophets, alternating between compassion and indignant denunciation. In consequence their preaching often owed more to Socialism than to the sacred Scripture. In the succeeding period there was a revulsion from liberalism to neo-orthodoxy.[3] No longer was the Church a social settlement, but a colony of heaven. The Kingdom of God was reconceived, not as a future utopia towards which all decent men and women were striving, but as the rule of God, inaugurated by the Apostolic preaching and in the breaking of bread. This gave a distinctive and elevated status to the preacher, as he became again the herald of God's good news, the announcer of the mighty acts of God accomplishing human salvation. But the preacher also recognized that the Word of God was mediated by the Sacraments, so that he did not become too proud.

---

[1] Those who desire a much fuller treatment of this topic are referred to my *Varieties of English Preaching, 1900-1960* (S. C. M. Press, London, and Prentice-Hall, Inc., Englewood Cliffs, New Jersey, 1963) of which, by the kind permission of the publishers, this chapter is substantially a condensation.

[2] See Chap. IV *supra*.   [3] See Chap. V *supra*.

In the most recent period of our century it became increasingly clear that the highest activity of the Christian Church is worship. This recognition brought three consequences in its train. First, worship was hardly ever, as in Victorian days, conceived as a mere preliminary to preaching; as, so to speak, the fruit-cup before the good red steak or "strong meat of the Gospel." It was valued in its own right as a corporate act of loyalty and renewal. Secondly, the Sacraments—as *verba visibilia*—were seen to be, equally with the Word preached, the iron-rations of the pilgrim rather than the truffles of the unusually pious. Finally, there was in recent years a rediscovery of the social imperatives, not only of the Gospel, but also of the service of Holy Communion. The Eucharist was thus seen to be the stimulus to social service,[4] because it re-enacted the Sacrifice of the Eternal Son of God for all humanity and required the members of Christ's Body to offer themselves for others as "a living sacrifice which is your reasonable service." Thus, for the first time since the sixteenth century both Anglicans and Free Churchmen saw preaching and worship as complementary, not competitive. It is peculiarly in this century that the concept and the practice of "Liturgical Preaching" has been revived, although it was well known in the Patristic Age, as the examples of St. Cyril of Jerusalem, St. John Chrysostom, and St. Ambrose amply prove.

2. *The First Type of Preaching: Apologetical*

It is inevitable that many of the leading preachers in an age when Christianity is under heavy critical fire or even ignored should become apologists. Such clergy and ministers are necessary to expound and defend the tenets of the Christian faith in the light of modern knowledge. Their essential task is to remove the errors and doubts that stand as barriers to belief, whether these be intellectual, moral, or psychological. Thus they can demonstrate that the Gospel as transforming truth fulfils man's nature and destiny. There is, in consequence, hardly a preacher of note in this century who has not, at least in some of his sermons, either recommended the Christian faith as congruent with reason, or attempted to refashion it semantically or in substance in terms acceptable to the modern mind. To preach otherwise would be to play the part of an ostrich.

This apologetical type of preaching, aiming at stilling doubt

---

[4] *The Second World Conference on Faith and Order* (1938), in the report edited by Leonard Hodgson (p. 233) declared: "The function of the Church is to glorify God in adoration and sacrificial service."

and awakening faith, of which Bishop Butler and F. W. Robertson[5] of Brighton were such admirable exemplars in their times, has attracted the talents of many unusual minds. Among them were the following distinguished Anglicans: William Temple,[6] Archbishop of Canterbury, a considerably better lecturer than preacher; Dean Inge[7] of St. Paul's Cathedral (whose matter was as lively as his manner was deadly); Bishop H. Hensley Henson; Dr. Alec Vidler,[8] Dean of King's College Chapel, Cambridge, and formerly Canon of Windsor; and Professor C. S. Lewis,[9] the inspired layman and littérateur, whose sermons were few but profound in thought and imaginative in expression. Two outstanding Roman Catholic apologetical preachers were Fathers C. C. Martindale and M. C. D'Arcy of the Society of Jesus. The distinguished Free Church apologetical preachers include two Methodists, Dr. Donald Soper, famous for his Tower Hill question and answer sessions, and Dr. Leslie D. Weatherhead; Dr. Townley Lord of Bloomsbury Baptist Church; the Congregationalist, Dr. J. S. Whale,[10] formerly President of Cheshunt College, Cambridge; and Dr. H. H. Farmer, a Presbyterian minister, who occupied the Norris-Hulse Chair of Divinity at Cambridge University.

Of this galaxy of apologetical preachers, three have been chosen for more detailed treatment. Bishop Henson is an example of a keenly independent and trenchantly candid mind, with the broad perspective of an historian,[11] who took great care over the writing of his sermons. Dr. Leslie Weatherhead, apart from being the minister of London's City Temple for a quarter of a century, is a pioneer in correlating Christianity and psychology. Dr. Farmer is a distinguished philosopher of religion, who has been acutely aware of critical attacks on the Christian faith and life from many quarters and of theology's need to grapple with them, as well as being a perceptive writer on the art of preaching.

[5] See my *Worship and Theology in England*, Vol. IV, *From Newman to Martineau*, 1850-1900, pp. 311-22, for an estimate.

[6] Temple's theology is discussed in Chap. IV above, and his preaching in my *Varieties of English Preaching*, pp. 235-47.

[7] Inge's preaching is discussed in my *Varieties of English Preaching*, pp. 80-91, and his theology in Chap. IV of the present volume.

[8] See, in particular, Vidler's *Windsor Sermons*.

[9] Lewis's sermons are discussed in my *Varieties of English Preaching*, pp. 164-78; 186-93.

[10] See Whale's *Christian Doctrine* for a superb series of doctrinal addresses which, like Vidler's *Christian Belief* (1950), were delivered to large gatherings of Cambridge undergraduates.

[11] See the three volumes of his *Retrospect of an Unimportant Life* for a religious critique of our century. His shrewd comments on preaching will be found in Vol. III, pp. 15, 114, 312, 327f., and 331.

3. *The Warrior Bishop*: H. Hensley Henson

Herbert Hensley Henson was successively Fellow of All Souls College, Oxford, Head of the Oxford House Settlement in Bethnal Green, Vicar of the vast industrial parish of Barking in Essex, Canon of Westminster and Rector of St. Margaret's (the parish church of the House of Commons), Dean of Durham, Bishop of Hereford, and, finally, from 1920 to 1939, Bishop of Durham. Possessed of a mind of singular independence, which he expressed in the clarity of consummate English prose, he gave himself during a long and distinguished career to the perfecting of his preaching. In consequence, his sermons read better than those of any of his episcopal contemporaries, including William Temple and Charles Gore.

No man was more critical than he of cant and rant in the pulpit. He liked sermons to be lucid demonstrations of central Biblical themes, illuminating the will of God for human duty to which any person of common sense and spiritual insight would immediately respond. Here is sound, solid, clear, reasonable, and practical preaching at its best. Its originality consists in penetrating judgments expressed in pithy and lucid prose.

His sermons are the index of a manly and honest temper, the foe of pretentiousness in Church or State, whether expounded by overweening prelate or arrogant politician. For him the proof of the reality of the creed was the deed done in Christ's name. As Dr. C. A. Alington wrote of him:

> Here, with the warrior bishops of the past
> We lay in peace of that long line the last;
> Unresting soul, predestined from his youth
> To ceaseless combat for the cause of truth . . .
> Still ready to unsheathe against his foes
> The stainless steel of perfect English prose,
> Or launch barbed shafts of epigram and wit
> Which stung to laughter even those they hit: . . . .[12]

His liberality of mind was honoured beyond the confines of the Church of England. He delivered the Lyman Beecher Lectures on Preaching at Yale University in 1909, with the characteristic title, *The Liberty of Prophesying*. In 1935 he delivered the Gifford Lectures at St. Andrews University on Christian Morality.

[12] *Retrospect of an Unimportant Life*, Vol. III, p. vi.

His delay in accepting the yoke of ordination was due to a fear of losing his independence by subscribing to the views of an ecclesiastical party. In this state of mind, he walked to the Norman church of Iffley, stood at the altar of the empty church, and there vowed "that I would never let considerations of my personal reputation and advantage influence my public course." Many years later, reflecting on this decision, he commented: "I was then poor and unknown; I knew that independence, which is the *heritage* of the powerful and wealthy, must be the *trophy* of the poor."[13] Honesty marked every stage of his life. When it was usual to camouflage the acceptance of the principles of Biblical criticism in the pulpit, Henson nailed his colours to the mast, and published the results in *The Creed in the Pulpit*. While fully accepting the Incarnation, he would neither assert nor deny the Virgin Birth, even when the Archbishop of Canterbury pleaded with him to make some statement which would palliate the criticism of his appointment as Bishop of Hereford.

His sermons were prepared with the Greek New Testament open before him. Every word was written out in a careful hand. Even when he preached an old sermon, he almost always rewrote the introduction to make it uniquely applicable to the church he was visiting.[14] In his later years Bishop Henson wondered if, in the midst of his busy administrative life, he had not spent too much time polishing and repolishing his sermons, especially as he had the gift of extemporary speech. His conclusion was that he had no alternative: "Should I be able to face the Judge with a less troubled spirit? Or should I have degenerated into the type, so familiar in the religious world, which is not unfairly described as a WIND-BAG?"[15]

His formidable honesty is tellingly shown in an anecdote. As a retired bishop, Henson was shown to a pew immediately under the pulpit of a fashionable seaside church. Here he had to endure a rhapsodical sermon on the theme that the first Pentecostal experience could be renewed in exact detail, down to experiences of cloven tongues of fire and the gift of speaking in different languages. As Henson left the church, the preacher asked him, "Was I too unorthodox for you?" The bishop replied: "It was not its unorthodoxy which disturbed me, but its incredibility." Later the

---

13 *Retrospect*, Vol. I, p. 76.
14 See the preface by C. J. Stranks to Henson's *Theology and Life*, pp. 7-8.
15 *Retrospect*, Vol. III, p. 312.

following comment appeared in Henson's journal: "I came away from church with a vivid realization of the chasm that separates popular Christianity, whether Catholic or Protestant, from reasonable religion."[16] Henson, and his friend Inge, were the most eminent representatives of "reasonable religion" in the twentieth century English pulpit.

In his view a good sermon has four essentials: interest, intelligibility, relevance and edification.[17] Interest grasps and holds the attention; intelligibility ensures that the message is understood; relevance is a necessity for effectiveness; and edification assures that the hearer is improved. Henson's own sermons are admirable illustrations of his teaching.

A superficial observer might assume from Henson's brusqueness of manner, and occasional asperity, that he was an intellectual snob. The very opposite was the truth. He simply could not stand pretentiousness, but he had a great affection for natural people. He rightly judged of himself that "Nature had endowed me with a sceptical intellect, a sensitive conscience, a considerable power of self-expression in lucid and incisive speech, and a warm heart."[18] How warm that heart was may be gauged from his observation, after he had attained to the highest offices of the Church of England, that "the happiest years of my ministry were those in which, as the vicar of a great industrial parish, I was nearest to the people. Faces look out at me from the past—toil-worn faces radiant with love and confidence. Nothing of what men foolishly call success is worth comparison with the experiences which those faces recall."[19]

Henson had the intuitive capacity of the great preacher to identify himself with the capacities and interests of his hearers, but without playing down to them. He used quite different approaches when preaching at a great commemorative event in a cathedral or university pulpit, when delivering a "political" sermon to the members of Parliament attending St. Margaret's Church, Westminster, and when preaching to a city or country congregation.

His outstanding qualities as a sermon-maker are evident in every sermon. First he would select a text that aptly summarized his message. Then he would fashion a clear plan for the sermon, making two, three or four firm points. The sentences were almost always brief, and the diction was ever lucid. Every now and then

16 *Retrospect*, Vol. III, pp. 326-27.
17 *Church and Parson in England*, p. 140.
18 *Retrospect*, Vol. I, p. 21.   19 *Ad Clerum*, p. 210.

an incisive statement, frequently barbed, would etch itself on the hearer's memory. Occasionally he offers a startling admonition to the clergy: "If a slumberous habit of almost unconscious indolence is the besetting sin of the largely unemployed rural incumbent, a futile and fussy multiplication of engagements which rather obscures than interprets spiritual duty is the besetting sin of his urban brother."[20] On another occasion he stalked bigger game, as when the bishops assembled for the Fifth Lambeth Conference in 1908 were to receive Holy Communion in Westminster Abbey. In his sermon on that occasion, Henson reminded the congregation: "Our prayer for those Bishops at Lambeth will be the prayer that they may be given grace of denominational self-suppression, that is, the power of a true spiritual perspective, the insight which distinguishes between the essentials and the non-essentials of religion, which recognizes the truth even in novel and unwelcome forms and rises to obey the truth it sees."[21]

Even when his theme is Easter, there is no temptation in Henson to smother the message with lilies. A sermon for Easter Day was entitled, "Easter, the Festival of Other Worldism." Its first two points were the enfranchisement and aspiration that Easter releases, but his third was responsibility. "There is," he wrote, "in the Easter message the note of solemn warning. Beyond the grace stands the Judge, and before Him must be laid open all the secrets of human lives."[22] He was shrewd enough to see the dangers of the "Social Gospel" advocated by partisan parsons, while at the same time recognizing that Christianity brings the gift of social hope, and emphasizes that social service is a religious duty and personal righteousness is the prerequisite for performing effective social service.[23]

Henson was not always the austere prophet. He preached as one who could offer consolation and encouragement. He was also a tutor in spirituality, as his ordination charges published in *Church and Parson in England* demonstrate. For the extraordinarily high quality of his average and incidental sermons, a recent admirable collection, edited by C. J. Stranks and entitled *Theology and Life* (1958) should be consulted.

The analysis of one of these, with the rather unpromising title of "Disinterested Service," may be preferred to further general

20 *Retrospect*, Vol. III, p. 15.   21 *Westminster Sermons*, p. 95.
22 *The Creed in the Pulpit*, p. 162.
23 See *Bishoprick Papers*, p. 180, and *Westminster Sermons*, No. XVIII, "The Social Influence of Christianity."

observations. The text is 1 Peter 1:8: "Whom not having seen ye love." Henson starts with a reference to a *Hibbert Journal* article by Claude Montefiore, entitled "What a Jew thinks about Jesus." The article relates that Jowett of Balliol said that he could not understand how Thomas à Kempis could feel a personal attachment to a Jesus who had died many centuries previously. It seems odd to Henson that an ordained minister of Christ should find any difficulty in this respect. The transition is then made to St. Peter, who is also intrigued that thousands who have never seen the earthly Christ can love him even through persecution. The secret of the Master's posthumous influence, experienced through all the Christian centuries, is the Resurrection. "Indeed, nothing else can explain it. For the only condition under which personal influence can survive is contact." The proof of the contact is that Christ stamps on his followers the likeness of his own character, so that men cannot "but take knowledge of them that they have been with Jesus."

The Christian character is therefore fully revealed in Christ and derivatively in his followers. His title is a servant and humility is its hall-mark. Public service appeals to the patriotism and pride of men who receive the homage of their contemporaries. But personal service may be unnoticed, and is often unattractive and even repulsive among the poor, the sick, and the unfortunate. It only appeals to those who are filled with disinterested and serviceable love which perpetuates on earth the spirit of Jesus. Religion cannot be presented as a way of gain, otherwise it is deeply secularized, as has happened in America (as de Tocqueville noticed), and is happening in England. Religion is most fitly symbolized by the Cross. Henson closes by retelling an episode recorded in Joinville's *Life of St. Louis* of France, which Joinville heard of when a prisoner among the Moslems. A religious brother saw an old woman carrying a chafing dish of fire in one hand and a cruse of water in the other. She said that she wanted to burn up heaven with fire and quench hell with water so that no one would do right for the reward of heaven or the fear of hell, but just for the love of God. The concluding words of the sermon are: "May God bless this Church with an unfailing succession of loving, devoted men and women who, in face of all difficulties and discouragements, will witness in character and service to the Presence with them of Jesus Christ, 'Whom not having seen, they love.' "

This is a twenty-minute masterpiece on Christian ethics, inspired by Christ's own example. And how typical the breadth of the reading, from mediaeval and modern historical sources, and encompassing the consideration of both Judaism and Islam, if only incidentally.

Henson's dedication to the truth was total, but he made enemies: his truth sometimes could sting like iodine on an open wound. He offended High Churchmen by his criticism of Tractarian exclusiveness and Low Churchmen by his dislike of their heresy-hunting, which he used to describe as the work of the "Protestant underworld." Both the wily ecclesiastical diplomat and the mealy-mouthed time-server regarded Henson as a dangerous prelate. Sometimes it must be acknowledged that he seemed to equate irritability with inspiration, and that the truth was not always spoken in love. But in an age of religious drift, here was a man who swam against the tide and who never mistook *vox populi* for *vox Dei*. For him Christianity was always light and leaven, the illumination of Divine revelation and the transformation of character through Christ.

4. The Psychological Preacher: Leslie D. Weatherhead

Dr. Leslie D. Weatherhead, who was born in London in 1893, attained his widest fame as minister of City Temple in the same city from 1936 to 1960. One of England's most popular preachers, he is unrivalled as a ministerial physician of souls and preacher of the integration of personality through Christ and the Beloved Community, the Church. He has pioneered in establishing psychological clinics at Brunswick Methodist Church, Leeds, and at City Temple. His experience as a religious psychologist is based upon thousands of case-histories which have laid bare to him the frustrations, fears, anxieties, and civil wars in the human psyche. He has also made a thorough study of all the scientific and spiritual techniques of healing. His crowning work in this area is *Psychology, Religion and Healing* (1951).[24] As preacher, writer and psychologist Weatherhead has exerted a wide influence.

Weatherhead was perceptive in responding positively to the challenge of what was called the "New Psychology." This took considerable courage, since the founder of psycho-analysis, Sigmund Freud, had written of the prospect for religion as *The Future*

[24] It is, as the sub-title indicates, a critical survey "of all the non-physical methods of healing, with an examination of the principles underlying them and the techniques employed to express them, together with some conclusions regarding further investigation and action in this field."

of an Illusion, as if a belief in the Heavenly Father was a symptom of man's unwillingness to stand on his own feet and was only the projection of the comforting illusion of a God on the empty screen of the heavens. Moreover, the assertion of Freud that the sexual instinct was the great driving force in humanity, and the deterministic concepts of the Behaviourists, seem to eliminate the role of religion. Among distinguished psychologists only Jung made place for God. Weatherhead's insight was to turn this potential foe of the faith into an ally.

He has recognized many fruitful insights in psychology with a direct bearing on the Christian life. Both theology and psychoanalysis recognize the paralysing effect of guilt and the unusual importance of confession, but Christianity offers more than acceptance: it offers the forgiveness of God and the restoration of a confident relationship with God and His Church. Weatherhead realizes the positive importance of Christian worship because "in worship, when we express the emotion of admiration for those qualities which God personifies, we are remade in His image, and the more we look away from ourselves to Him, the more we can benefit, paradoxical as it may sound."[25] In true worship the constant emphasis on the unconditional and unchanging love of God to men (as opposed to the hatred that breeds neuroses), the sheer generosity of His grace in Christ (compared with the envy of the sick soul), and the radiant confidence of trust which is faith (contrasted with the suspicion and fear that suppurate in the mind), combine to activate a therapeutic process.

The Christian Church provides a community of altruism as well as a community of appreciation, both of which are essential to the rebuilding of an integrated personality.[26] In sharing the social and missionary work of the Church the introvert becomes outward-looking and the extrovert uses his gifts for the benefit and satisfaction of the needs of others.[27] Weatherhead believes in the great value of intercession for the sick, but complains that this has been exercised in a half-hearted way in the Churches, without imagination and without the confidence of faith.[28] He also holds that preaching aims at providing the very conditions in which a transformation and integration of personality can take place. The Christian com-

[25] *Psychology, Religion and Healing*, p. 453.
[26] *Ibid.*, p. 466. "One of the greatest needs of personality is to be loved."
[27] *Ibid.*
[28] See *ibid.*, p. 241, for the conditions in which this work of the Church in worship can be successfully carried out.

munity hearing God's Word of challenge, consolation, and consecration is the best context for conversion. Here the preacher is enabled by the power of the Holy Spirit to make real the transforming
friendship of Christ.[29]

Finally, Weatherhead is not under any illusion that psychologically trained ministers can become little Christs, for "we shall
not be able to do the things He did by becoming cleverer psychologists."[30] For Christ's was the supernatural power of the eternal
Son of God. In Weatherhead's view the supreme healing power is
the Person of Christ himself, which has not been withheld, but
unappropriated. His conclusion is: "When the Church returns to
her early devotion to Christ and creates united fellowships, even
faintly like the small body of men who went out in the power of the
risen Christ and His Spirit to turn the world upside down, then a
power more potent to heal than any atomic bomb to destroy will
once more surge through sick souls and minds and bodies. It will
be His own power and recognised as such."[31]

It should be made clear that Weatherhead does not often preach
psychological sermons, in the sense that he uses case-studies in the
pulpit. *That Immortal Sea* (1953) is an attractive demonstration
of his versatility in theme and treatment. Four sermons are concerned with practical problems: acquisitiveness, worry, true and
untrue selves, and the confidence necessary to face old age. Four
are acute apologetical sermons, one dealing with the forbidding
topic of "Foreknowledge, Free Will, and Fate" in which a subtle
distinction is made between the direct and the permissive will of
God, and another, titled "Is Life a Matter of Luck?" giving the
reasons for a belief in a superintending Divine providence. A
third is the ironically named "The Advantages of Atheism," which
is superbly argued, and the fourth, "Whose Voice shall I Trust?"
examines critically the counter-claims of the cynic and materialist
in comparison with the claims of the theist. Another group of
sermons are movingly evangelical in character, concerned with
the unconventional love of Christ, the power of Christ risen who
was crucified, and the contrast between human callousness and
Christ's total identification with humanity's needs. Other sermons
are devotional in character, such as the mystical "This Haunted
World."

Another volume of collected sermons, *Over His Own Signature*
(1955), was exclusively devoted to sermons of the devotional

[29] *Ibid.*   [30] *Ibid.*, p. 78.   [31] *Ibid.*, p. 495.

type. Yet in *The Key Next Door and Other City Temple Sermons* (1960), there are eleven doctrinal sermons, six apologetical sermons, and only two sermons on the spiritual life. Dr. Weatherhead is, therefore, a preacher of many different types of sermon, and he proves himself to be a master-craftsman in every one.

His art conceals art. An analysis of citations, references, and illustrations in his sermons reveals the great breadth of his experience, observation, and reading. In *That Immortal Sea*, for example, there are thirty-one references to personal experience and to encounters with a variety of human callings. They range from boyhood memories of the conversation of "dear old ladies" in a boarding-house to army memories of India where he was a padre. The same volume discloses thirty-seven references to twenty-seven different authors, the most frequent being to Tennyson, Browning, Vaughan and Shakespeare. It is entirely appropriate that a preacher who believes that admiration and reverence are at the heart of worship should return so often to the poets who evoke these very qualities. The third largest class of illustrative material consists of anecdotes, of which there are nineteen in this volume. They open up a horizon to the world that prevents worship from being too introverted, and their subjects range from a Hebridean seaman and sacrificial coal-miners to aeronautical pioneers, an American journalist, and a famous artist. The fourth class of references is to foreign lands, of which there are seventeen. These fulfil a double purpose: as traveller's tales they hold the interest and they keep a local congregation alive to the world. Palestine and India have the priority, because Dr. Weatherhead spent three years in the former and visited the latter. The other groups of references are less important, but also interesting. There are nine references to theologians from Augustine to C. H. Dodd, ten to thinkers as different as von Hügel and Bertrand Russell, nine to ministers and preachers, and three to psychologists.

Like Bishop Hensley Henson, Dr. Weatherhead tries to interpret the New Testament from the Greek text. His exegetical carefulness and philological interest are marked. For example, in his book on the parables, *In Quest of a Kingdom* (1934), there are twenty-eight references to sixteen different Biblical commentators.

What is the secret of success in Britain's most popular preacher? One element is certainly his attractive personality, for the preacher of the primacy of Christ's "transforming friendship" (a favourite term) is himself an excellent example of the candid compassion of the disciple. He is and looks friendly, and can "project" this quality in his preaching in several ways. It may be by the conversational casualness with which he introduces the topic of his sermon, or by the vast number of references to his own personal experience, or by the refusal to use technical theological terms without translation. It may be the use of homely analogies, of colloquial English, and the rare employment of a slang term. It may be the ecumenicity of the man, which is wide enough to admit that God uses religions other than Christianity as avenues to Him.[32] It could be the candour with which old prejudices are dismissed. It is certain that his tenderness, combined with a whimsical humour, play a large part in his appeal. Quite typical is his dislike of the offensive pietist with the bland assurance that he is covered by a Divine insurance-policy, as expressed in the following limerick:

There was a young lady of Ryde,
Who was carried away by the tide,
A man-eating shark
Was heard to remark,
"I knew that the Lord would provide!"[33]

Another element in his success is surely his deep sympathy for the difficulties of modern life, his conviction that the dullest lives can have significance through the ennobling grasp of Christ's handshake, and the concentration on understanding and forgiving rather than criticizing. Then, again, Weatherhead has a distinctive quality in his ministry, the insights of the physician of souls, the expert in religious psychology.

His sermons attract in part because they have a clear and memorable structure, and their patterns are very varied. One may be a simple contrast.[34] Another may have a three-fold structure.[35] Yet another will have four points.[36] One, greatly daring, has no less than twelve different conclusions to drive home.[37] This is, whatever the structure, *vertebral* and flexible planning.

---

[32] *The Key Next Door*, pp. 152ff. It may be observed that Dr. Weatherhead in a letter to the author (dated June 19, 1961) kindly indicated that he thought his best sermons were to be found in *The Key Next Door*, *That Immortal Sea*, and *Over His Own Signature*.

[33] *Ibid.*, p. 114.

[34] As in "Babel or Jerusalem?" contrasting the chaos of Babel with the unity of the primitive Christian community at Pentecost.

[35] As in "Whose Voice shall I Trust?" elaborating three competing viewpoints.

[36] As in "Master and Lord" which has four arguments to establish the Divinity of Christ.

[37] "The Advantages of Atheism," where the twelve "incredibles" for the atheist are twelve questions unanswerable on this hypothesis, but credible on the Christian hypothesis.

Another quality of Weatherhead's is a great gift for putting abstract thought into direct speech and into concrete images. Allied to this is his possession of a strong visual imagination, romantically inclined. Almost every book-title of his conveys a clearly defined image. He has an almost Wordsworthian delight in landscape. The attraction (and danger) of this gift may be appreciated by citing one of his passages, describing the vision of the exiled John of Patmos watching the dawn by the seashore:

"Above him the stars flashed like gems in the splendour of the velvet night, at its darkest just before the dawn. It was early on the Lord's day and he longed to worship with those he had been compelled to leave. He turned towards Jerusalem far in the east, and behold the darkness was breaking. He had had his back to it, gazing mournfully at the black, hostile sea as yet unillumined by the dawn. But now the great splendour had begun. The colour spread across the sky. Daffodil first with gleams of pale green and primrose light, then the faintest pastel pink deepening to crimson and gold. John thought of the temple in Jerusalem catching the gleams in its golden dome as God's day of worship began. As a great wave crashed behind him, he turned at the noise and it seemed to shout to him, in a trumpet voice of majesty and assurance, 'I am Alpha and Omega, the first and the last.' "[38]

He is happier in less ambitious effects, and has a talent for vivid, homely analogies. For example, he translates the urgent relevance of the term "Gospel" as follows: " 'Good news,' said a friend of mine, 'is that which can be shouted across a street.' Thus—The war's over! The baby's born! Susan's out of danger! The strike's settled! Here is my bit of good news for you: *God will receive you—Now!*"[39]

Most important of all the secrets of Weatherhead's success is that he selects the central Christian themes and relates them to the daily needs of men and women. Thus psychology's diagnosis and theology's message complement each other perfectly. Weatherhead never fails to see the striking generosity of God's seeking and saving love in Christ for the least and the lost. The Atonement receives full treatment in both *Personalities of the Passion* (1942)

---

[38] *Over His Own Signature*, pp. 142-43. This is all-too-artificial "Vistavision" writing, but suitable for popular purposes. More sensitive writing would have avoided the archaism of "behold," the ugly repetition of "had had," and the commonplace "gazing mournfully," and would have toned down the more blatant "gorgeous Technicolor" effects. But it is thoroughly in line with the Madison Avenue manner of television advertising.

[39] *In Quest of a Kingdom*, p. 73.

and *The Plain Man Looks at the Cross* (1945). It is chiefly as Friend, Healer, and Saviour that Weatherhead interprets Christ, though occasionally as Guide, Revealer, Pioneer, and Teacher.

Despite his undoubted qualities, an honest appraisal of Dr. Weatherhead would have to take into account his occasional falls from tenderness to sentimentality and mawkishness.[40] There is little that is prophetic in his preaching, and almost nothing in the way of announcing a coming kingdom of social justice, or any realization that the very structures of classes and nations and institutions are infected with group egotism. There is, in fact, too much consolation and too little criticism in his preaching.

His greatest achievements are to have pioneered in the religious use of psychology, and to have gathered, held, and sustained so scattered and socially variegated a congregation as that of the City Temple[41] through unusually testing times, and to have commended to them the Gospel with singular freshness, clarity, compassion, and relevance for a quarter of a century.

5. The Preacher as Philosopher and Theologian: Professor H. H. Farmer

Like Bishop Henson, Professor Farmer had the rare distinction of being appointed to a Gifford Lectureship and to the Lyman Beecher Lectureship on Preaching at Yale University. Thus, it is widely acknowledged that he has a profound mind, combined with an enviable gift for terse and vivid expression. His developing thought has mirrored the transition of the century from a philosophical to a Biblical theology.

In his *Servant of the Word* (1941), Professor Farmer has shown how theology in its more recent developments has magnified the responsibility and the privilege of preaching. The importance of the "Christ-event"—the unguessable, historically given, Church-creating event of the advent of Jesus Christ which transforms alienated men and women into the people of God's own purpose— has been re-emphasized by modern theologians. The re-telling of

---

[40] In a Christmas sermon he speaks of the strangeness of the gifts of the Magi for the Christ-child and asks: "I do not mean to be in the least irreverent, but did no one give Him a soft, woolly, cuddly toy, the ancient equivalent of a teddy-bear? Did no one give Him a rattle? Did no one treat Him as a little baby thing?" (*The Key Next Door*, p. 213).

[41] In the preface to *The Significance of Silence*, Dr. Weatherhead writes that his congregation includes "a cabinet minister, and others of rank, position and authority, and also the lowliest and the poorest—people who have been unemployed, people who have been in prison." In days of peace it was not unusual to find fourteen different nationalities represented at one service.

that event, or series of events, accompanied by the power of the Holy Spirit, re-creates the new community, the Church. Such is the recognition of both Bultmann and Tillich.

A second modern emphasis has been on "realized eschatology" and is particularly associated with Dr. C. H. Dodd. This stresses that God's mighty saving act began in Christ's coming, and God's campaign was won in principle in the Cross and Resurrection. In this view all preaching is apostolic, and bearing witness to Christ's saving act is itself part of the act of salvation.

The third modern emphasis is on religion as "encounter" between the "I" of God and the "Thou" of man addressed by God. This has been central to the thought of the distinguished Jewish philosopher, Dr. Martin Buber, and its impact on the thought of Professor Farmer has been deep.[42] Farmer insists that God confronts men as "absolute demand" and "final succour." The necessity of preaching, therefore, is to confront men with God's absolute claim on men whom He has destined to live in eternal fellowship with himself in holy love, and to declare his grace available for their help. Moreover, this assistance comes to human beings, not as isolates, but as interdependent persons, and through the agency of others.

This radical personalism carries notable consequences for the practice of preaching. In the face-to-face encounter between preacher and congregation, the reading of sermons and the use of rhetoric, as of superfluous adjectives and quotations, are to be rejected. And because God's supreme Word to man was the *Word-made-flesh*, who went about doing good, concrete language and vigorous verbs are necessary in preaching, in lieu of cloudy abstractions. The manipulation of personality is wholly to be rejected.

No one has stressed more strongly than Farmer the need to correlate the Gospel to human need.[43] Preaching must awaken men out of their dispirited sense of the futility of human existence by affirming "a divine purpose in history which a man is called to serve here and now and yet which transcends history in its final consummation." Men feel that they are ciphers in the depersonalized industry of today and in the vast ant-like aggregations of apartments and new housing developments. They need the assur-

42 See Farmer's *The World and God, Towards Belief in God, God and Men,* and *Revelation and Religion.*
43 See Chap. 5 of *The Servant of the Word.*

ance of Christ's promises that the eternal purpose is a design of love for the individual. In the third place, modern men long for security and this is satisfied by the Christian doctrine of providence. They also know of the tremendous powers of evil and irrationality. The Christian message asserts that there is a Cross at its heart and yet Divine love wins its way through the horrors of sin and suffering. Finally men need an absolute in conduct and they find it in the call to loyal discipleship by Christ. Farmer rightly concludes that "our preaching has to be strongly doctrinal . . . in such wise that doctrine and life are seen to be inseparably bound up together."[44] But equally "the strongest apologetic, so far as teaching and preaching are concerned, is always a sound dogmatic."[45]

As an apologist there are admirable qualities in Professor Farmer. He never misrepresents the views which he criticizes. He faces with the utmost candour the criticisms levelled against Christian doctrine. But equally he expects his opponents to take Christian views with basic seriousness. He has little time for the critic of Christianity who only brings with him a "casual, flippant, feet-on-the-mantelpiece attitude." The latter attitude, states Farmer, is as irresponsible as if a man should "set up as a judge of dramatic art on the basis of once having seen in his youth a Punch and Judy show."[46]

The value of Professor Farmer's books and sermons is that they take cognizance of the criticisms of Christianity from the side of the physical and social sciences, as well as from the field of the comparative study of religion. These criticisms are elaborated and answered to the full in *Towards Belief in God*. Since God is ultimate reality which is the source and ground of all being, His existence does not admit of *demonstrative* proof. He is always "Eternal Thou" and therefore always "subject" and never "object." Moreover, God is disclosed not in abstract argument but in action and decision.[47] The arguments which he offers in reply to a multitude of criticisms of Christianity are too many to be capable even of summary treatment. It must, therefore, suffice to say that no modern theologian has looked more thoroughly and honestly at the case against Christianity before attempting to state the case for it. Apologetics of this kind enable Professor Farmer to rid the ground of the chief obstacles to faith, and his two vol-

44 *The Servant of the Word*, p. 143. 45 *God and Men*, p. 14.
46 *Ibid.*, p. 17. 47 *Towards Belief in God*, pp. 31-38.

umes of sermons express his positive convictions as to the nature and content of the Christian faith.

The first volume, *Things Not Seen* (1927), reveals the theocentric approach of a religious philosopher, and the second, *The Healing Cross* (1941), the Christocentric approach of a Biblical and systematic theologian. In the first volume religion is considered in terms of adjustment and integration, in the conviction that Christianity "can make men more poised, more harmonious, more strong, more dignified, more hopeful, more at peace with themselves, even in the present restricted and inadequate world."[48] The second volume, however, considers Christianity in theologically pragmatic terms. As the Preface indicates, the Christian message consists in setting forth the Christian way "in the life of individual discipleship, in the faith and hope that those given a new or renewed understanding of that way may be moved by the Spirit of God to make, or remake, their choice to walk therein come what may."[49] The later volume also contains a new, astringent note, calling "to adventure, to danger, to heroic and costing enterprise."[50] The difference between the two volumes corresponds to the change from a revelational and philosophical centre to a redemptional and theological foundation, characteristic of the most thoughtful religious minds of the day.

Farmer, like Inge and Henson, has the gift for incisive statement and he can mint memorable epigrams. As samples, the following may be cited from *Things Not Seen*. "A dumb God spells a dead faith." "Without religion morals easily become manners." "A good character is just as likely to get crucified as to get a peerage." "The Cross was . . . a parable in flesh and blood."[51] *The Healing Cross* includes the following epigrams as true as they are brilliant. "Christ's work is not merely to satisfy need, but to show us what our needs are." "Suffering must be a vocation before it can be a victory." "The Kingdom of God is love, it is not gush." "The temple of faith . . . is only well-built when it is built on the very edge of the pit of self-distrust." And there is the contrast between the Incarnation and the Cross: "The Babe symbolizes the weakness of divine love as it were in repose; the Cross is the weakness of divine love in action."[52]

[48] *Things Not Seen*, p. 23.   [49] *The Healing Cross*, p. x.
[50] *Ibid.*, p. ix.
[51] The citations are to be found, respectively, on pp. 36, 67, 102, and 161.
[52] The citations are to be found, respectively, on pp. 117, 140, 146, 9 (twice), and 100.

It will be recalled that Farmer urged preachers to use concrete and vivid language. Not only his epigrams, but also his metaphors and similes are proof that he keeps his own precepts. There are seventeen images in *Things Not Seen*, and twenty-six in *The Healing Cross*, some of them strikingly original. One of them conceives of God as some transcendent customs officer bidding the soul for the common good to hold nothing back and declare everything, while immortality is distinguished from the radical re-creation involved in Resurrection by being termed a mere "roof-garden" idea, and the Kingdom of God is said to be misconceived as a garden city.

One sermon ought to be analysed to show the depth of thought and admirable expression in Professor Farmer's preaching. It is the eleventh sermon in *The Healing Cross*, and its title is "Justice and the Gospel." The text is Isaiah 45:21, "A just God and a Saviour." The theme is a comparison of the functions, the moods, the directions, and the agents of justice and love and their need of one another.

The sermon begins by a reference to two images on the London skyscape: the great cross surmounting the dome of St. Paul's Cathedral and the figure of Justice, eyes bandaged and scales in her hands, which tops the Central Criminal Court on Ludgate Hill. Both cathedral and court are concerned with sin, but while detection and punishment is the aim of the law, forgiveness is the aim of the Gospel. Justice is coldly impartial in mood, whereas the Gospel is warmly personal. Justice looks to the criminal's past and the Gospel to the sinner's future. Justice compels, while the Gospel persuades.

The second part of the sermon argues that the distance between law and Gospel is too great. It is bad for justice. Justice, separated from the Gospel, isolates the sinner too much from his fellows and the criminal knows that justice is not done. Justice also isolates the guilty man's act from himself, and all his hopes, struggles, and inner bent.

The third section of the sermon insists that the separation is bad for the Gospel. Apart from justice the Gospel is apt to speak of love both divine and human as ignoring and overlooking sin. This is to forget that the divine forgiveness "searches and pursues and tears out and exposes all the evil in us every bit as ruthlessly as the detectives and the prosecuting counsel of the Central Criminal

Court."[53] An admirable illustration follows from G. K. Chesterton's criticism of Jerome's *The Passing of the Third Floor Back* as presenting the Redeemer not as a divine detective, but as a divine dupe. The conclusion is that while the Gospel is always the declaration of the utterly gracious and undeserved goodness of God to us, equally it is an affirmation of the severity of God, eradicating evil from men, "severe because it is good" and "good because it is severe."

This sermon is a model of clarity in profundity and of the making concrete of highly abstract concepts by the use of the two architectural images as symbols. The divisions are clear and logical, and the conclusion is eminently reasonable. It is quite typical of Dr. Farmer's preaching that it nobly fulfils the canons to which he believes modern preaching must conform. The message of the Gospel must have cosmic dimensions or it will be "too small to be true." It must be expressed with a strong agnostic note running through it to emphasize the mystery of God or it will be "too confident to be true." The note of austerity must be heard in challenge and demand or it will be "too easy to be true." Finally, it must be presented in the context of social solidarity and as the Gospel of the Universal Church.[54]

Two relatively minor criticisms are suggested by Dr. Farmer's sermons. The first is that in his determination to avoid all artificiality in diction and in his disdain for rhetoric, he is hiding under a bushel a poet's gift for creating original images. This quality, so evident in his first volume of sermons, is suppressed by a Calvinist hand in the second volume.[55] The same austerity may also be responsible for the marked concision and terseness of his second volume, which hardly allows time for his points to be taken in by the congregation.[56]

The abiding qualities of Professor Farmer's sermons are their explication of a vertebral Biblical theology, their candidness in accepting the pressure of modern day intellectual difficulties, and their relevance in presenting the Gospel to the modern mind.

6. *The Second Type of Preaching: Expository*

If the most typical twentieth century type of preaching is that

[53] *The Healing Cross*, p. 111.

[54] The points made in this paragraph are elaborated by Farmer in the Preface of *The Healing Cross*.

[55] See *Things Not Seen*, p. 53.

[56] This is probably due to the fact that his first volume came from years of experience in the ministry, while the second emerges from the professor's study.

of the apologist, who states the case for Christianity in the light of the criticisms brought against it, the most traditional type of preaching is expository, a sustained exposition of the sacred Scriptures. Its aim is to awaken and confirm faith. It requires of the preacher a disciplined subjection to the authority of revelation so that he may declare the mighty acts of God for the liberation of the human race from its slavery to egotism, anxiety, futility, frustration, suffering, and the fear of death. Through a large part of the present century this type of preaching fell into abeyance, partly because it was associated with an older view of Biblical inspiration, and partly because liberal accommodations of the faith found it more convenient to take a text as a pretext, than to pretend to expound a passage of Scripture. Apologetical, ethical, or topical sermons were the rage. Hence the expository sermon was, for the most part, considered *passé*.

The great exception to the rule was George Campbell Morgan, an autodidact, whose Biblical sermons and lectures were extraordinarily popular on both sides of the Atlantic. First in Westminster Congregational Chapel from 1904 to 1914, and from 1943 to 1953, Campbell preached to crowded morning and evening services, and at his Friday Night Bible School he lectured to between 1,500 and 2,000 eager students of the Scriptures.[57] His conviction was that "the preacher is not merely asking a congregation to discuss a situation, and consider a proposition, or give attention to a theory. We are out to storm the citadel of the will and to capture it for Jesus Christ."[58] He knew the supreme source-book of the Christian faith better than most men of his day. For example, he would never attempt to expound a book of the Bible until he had read it in the original language and in English at least fifty times.[59] He proved conclusively the varied spiritual wealth that is at the disposal of the preacher who mines the deep lodes of the Scriptures. Dr. J. D. Jones, a more gracious preacher, exercised a long and distinguished ministry at Richmond Hill Congregational Church, Bournemouth, by strong exegetical preaching.

What is of special interest is the general return to expository preaching in the last two decades of the period as a result of the Biblical and theological revival. There is no question that this

---

57 See John Harries, *G. Campbell Morgan, The Man and His Ministry*, p. 91.

58 *Ibid.*, p. 245. The alternatives which he rejected were precisely those offered by many a minister in the Liberal Protestant tradition.

59 *Ibid.*, p. 199. The fruits of these lectures were gathered in a series of volumes, collectively entitled *The Analysed Bible* (10 vols.).

is not only deeply necessary but also that it is widely appreciated. At the present time the two largest congregations in London have been gathered by expository preachers. One is the congregation of Westminster Congregational Chapel under the ministry of a former Harley Street physician, Dr. Martyn Lloyd-Jones,[60] and the other is All Souls', Langham Place, where the Rector is the Rev. John R. W. Stott.[61] It is also significant that a College of Preachers was recently established by the Church of England under the directorship of the Rev. D. W. Cleverly Ford, the author of *An Expository Preacher's Notebook* (1960). The latter, indeed, provides a strong justification for the return to expository preaching on the grounds that the Bible is the Church's primary sourcebook, that liturgical worship is essentially Biblically informed, that Biblical preaching "sustains the Pulpit" and the people, and enables the minister "to speak with an authority without which his preaching is insipid."[62]

7. Evangelical Greatheart: Dr. W. E. Sangster[63]

As might be expected, it is the preachers of the evangelical tradition, both in the Anglican Communion and in the Free Churches, who have been the most faithful expository preachers. It is fitting that an outstanding Methodist preacher, Dr. W. E. Sangster, should be selected as a representative of this tradition, because the Methodist Church has a special concern for evangelism. This concern has found splendid expression in the Central Halls of the larger English cities, and Dr. Sangster was from 1939 to 1955 the minister of the Methodist Central Hall, Westminster.

His preaching method was not like that of Campbell Morgan, the running exposition of lengthy passages of Scripture. Rather he explained the central Biblical themes in a breathtakingly rapid and succinct way. He differs from Morgan as telegrams from treatises; his sermons are very like "greetings telegrams," admirably embroidered with imagery which does not detract from the urgency of his communication of the good news. If theologically conservative, he is well read in philosophy, history, and literature.

Born in 1900 of working class parents in the east end of London, he became a local preacher while serving in the British Army dur-

[60] See Lloyd-Jones' *Studies in The Sermon on the Mount.*
[61] See Stott's *Basic Christianity* and *Preacher's Portrait.*
[62] P. 14.
[63] See the excellent biography, *Doctor Sangster,* written by his son, and the vivid pamphlet *W.E.S., A Daughter's Tribute* (1960).

ing the First World War, where his hobby was boxing. The Army taught him admiration for the courage of the average British Tommy and developed his natural gift for friendship. After taking theological training at Richmond Methodist College, affiliated with the University of London, he served various circuits in North Wales, and was called to succeed Leslie Weatherhead at Brunswick Church, Leeds. His most responsible charge was at Westminster, where he succeeded another evangelical preacher, Dr. T. Dinsdale Young. He came to Westminster in the inauspicious month of August, 1939, and exercised a memorably courageous ministry during the Second World War, when London experienced a mass evacuation of population and the ordeal of air-bombardment. He continued in Westminster Central Hall until 1955, when he was appointed to direct the Home Mission Department of the Methodist Church. He died in 1960 after two years of suffering, with exemplary courage, the inexorable approach of muscular atrophy. One Easter Day, at the end of his life, being unable to walk or even to speak, he wrote to his daughter: "It is terrible to wake up on Easter morning and have no voice with which to shout, 'He is risen!'—but it would be still more terrible to have a voice and not want to shout."[64]

Only a few months after Sangster began his work in London the bombing began. Central Hall's vast basement was reinforced and it was then thrown open to the homeless folk from the slums of Pimlico, hundreds of whom were to have no other home for the duration of the war. Sangster and his family insisted on making their home there also and in occupying only one cramped room. This they shared for five long years. It was typical of Sangster's compassion and his realism. His wife organized a canteen and thus supplied economical food each night. Sangster himself moved in and out among the shelter-dwellers, with unfailing zest and interest, telling his anecdotes with incomparable verve. "Service before services" was his motto. He refused to cram religion down the throats of a captive audience. Soon, however, he was asked to conduct evening prayers, and these, with a weekly lecture on current affairs and a Sunday concert, were the highlights in the life of that vast basement shelter.[65] On Sundays Sangster preached to enlarging congregations representative of almost the entire social spectrum. Most surprising among the achievements of these years

[64] W.E.S., *A Daughter's Tribute*, p. 13.
[65] *Ibid.*, pp. 8-9.

was the successful preparation of a doctoral dissertation for the University of London, subsequently published as *The Path to Perfection*, mirror of Sangster's absorbing and catholic interest in spirituality and his conviction that life's supreme quest is for holiness.

If Dr. Sangster was a pietist, he was one with three differences from most others. He knew well enough that men and women needed to be reformed, but he also recognized that economic and social disabilities stunt personality's growth. He had an infectious gaiety and no one could consider this perfect mimic a spoil-sport. Moreover, the range of his reading and hobbies (hill-climbing and visiting ancient abbeys and castles) were those of a man of culture.

He was happy to accept Bernard Manning's definition of a sermon as "a manifestation of the Incarnate Word, from the Written Word by the Spoken Word."[66] He wished to sustain expository preaching because so much of the preaching of the day was marginal, receiving its direction from the daily newspapers rather than from the eternal Good News. He recognized the importance of Christian instruction in doctrinal preaching, but believed that the ultimate task of the preacher was to capture the will. Often his doctrinal sermons ended with an appeal for commitment; but he would be the last to suggest that a preacher should, like an evangelical alarm clock, always be striking for decisions. His most notable sermons fall into two categories: doctrinal and devotional, and, because he used the Christian Year to the full, he was easily able to combine these qualities, as his two volumes of *Westminster Sermons* (1960, 1961) clearly manifest.

One who has read other expository preachers cannot but contrast the crisp, urgent brevity of Sangster's sermons. Other expository preachers, as Pope's characterization of the Alexandrine, are like a wounded snake dragging its slow length along. Sangster's dart, like the snake's tongue, goes directly to the target. He has no prolonged introductions (a failure of that otherwise superb Scottish evangelical preacher, Professor James S. Stewart), or concluding perorations (like the Victorian pulpit orators). Hardly less striking are the vividly fresh and apt illustrations. A New Year sermon, intriguingly titled "Remember to Forget," bids his congregation

---

[66] Sangster cites this definition in his *Craft of the Sermon*, p. 25. It is derived from B. L. Manning's *A Layman in the Ministry*, p. 138.

forget their tactlessness, their sins, and the insults they have received during the past year. It ends thus:

> It was Christmas in my home. One of my guests had come a couple of days early and saw me sending off the last of my Christmas cards. He was startled to see a certain name and address. 'Surely, you're not sending a greeting to *him*,' he said.
> 'Why not?' I asked.
> 'But you remember,' he began, 'eighteen months ago.'
> I remembered, then, the thing the man had publicly said about me, but I remembered also resolving at the same time, with God's help, that I would remember to forget. And God had 'made' me to forget!
> I posted the card.[67]

Sangster has only to announce his text, 2 Corinthians 5:8 (RV), "At home in the Lord," when he immediately captures the hearer's interest with a rapid account of the homing instincts of birds, beasts, fish, and (by analogy) of men. His rich apparatus of references and illustrations derives from such varied sources as biographical incident, visits to antiquities or foreign lands, natural science, classical and romantic English poetry, the great saints of the Christian centuries, and his own observations and experiences. He can comb recondite sources for his illustrations: when he is insisting that the State cannot legislate people into goodness, he cites Bernard Bosanquet's *The Philosophical Theory of the State* with its conclusion that all the State can do is "to hinder the hindrances to the good."[68] A distinctive quality of Sangster's is the frequent citation of a verse from the hymns of Watts or Wesley as an apt summary of belief or avowal of loyalty. This lyrical note is rarely absent from his preaching.

His concentrated sermons are always marked by a clear and memorable structure. In a sermon on Christ as the Master of Time, for example, the sub-divisions and lessons are: the past is not dead; the future is not ours; now is the acceptable time.[69] Another excellent sermon, "Four Judgments on Jesus," is based on four New Testament records of evaluations of Jesus, as devil-possessed, a good man, the Christ, and culminating in the confession of Thomas, "My Lord and my God."[70]

Another quality in Sangster's sermons is the frequent appear-

[67] *Westminster Sermons*, Vol. I, p. 10.   [68] *Ibid.*, p. 29.
[69] *Ibid.*, p. 136.   [70] *Ibid.*, Vol. II, sermon 3.

ance of an inspired phrase, vivid word-picture, or striking epigram. Referring to the parable of the Good Samaritan, Sangster observes, "Jesus took that term [Samaritan] from the vocabulary of the brothel and made it adjectival of the saints."[71] One sentence is all the space he needs to sum up the folly of materialism, describing the man whose skeleton was found in Pompeii's volcanic ash clutching trinkets: "He ran back for the bangles and lost his life."[72] There is also his moving title for a sermon on Christ's going up to Jerusalem: "His Destination is on His Face." Equally characteristic is his terse comment on the right response to the Lordship of Christ: "It isn't cheer; it's discipleship. It isn't admiration; it's consecration."[73] He had a genius for finding a profound message in most unpromising texts.

Considering the gaiety and courage of his life, and the magnetism of his affectionate personality, it is no surprise to read his tribute to his Westminster congregation: "They sit without intellectual pride and their faces light up as your points register in their mind. To serve such people—and God through them—is a privilege of which no man is worthy."[74] Sangster served his people splendidly in his vigour, compassion, and consecration. His weaknesses were an occasional tendency to use highly technical language, without translating it, and on the rarest occasions an insensitive reference.[75] Nor did he always resist the temptation of the popular preacher—sensationalism.

These faults are trivial in comparison with the basic integrity of this preacher of a universal Gospel, his Christian spirituality, and his deep compassion, who in his final illness trod the most difficult steps of the path to perfection. He knew that if he did not submit himself to the Word of God he would be overreaching himself.

8. The Third Type of Preaching: Charismatic

The third function and type of preaching is to teach the holy love of God as to elicit the response of adoration. Many varieties of preaching can be included in this type. Some preachers, like the Congregationalist, Dr. J. H. Jowett,[76] are first and foremost

---

[71] *Ibid.*, Vol. I, sermon 5.   [72] *Ibid.*, Vol. II, p. 40.
[73] *Ibid.*, p. 43.   [74] See *ibid.*, Vol. I, preface.
[75] *Ibid.*, Vol. II, p. 94 for an unexplained reference to the fourth dimension. See also Vol. II, p. 19, for the reference to "mankind crucified on a clock."
[76] For an appreciation of Jowett, see my *Varieties of English Preaching*, pp. 35-63.

exponents of Christ-mysticism. While other ministers noisily debated the reconstruction of doctrine and the so-called "New Theology," or the reconstruction of society according to the imperatives of the "Social Gospel," Jowett emphasized the central importance of the culture and discipline of the spiritual life. His remarkable volume of sermons in this genre, *The Transfigured Church* (1910), was fifty years ahead of its time, for it diagnosed the weakness of the Church as due to a lack of awe in the conception of God, and to a severe limitation in its understanding of the nature of brotherhood which had led to the loss of the artisans. His claim that the Church needed a theological, liturgical, and social reformation showed astonishing foresight. In his way he was a forerunner of Otto and Casel.

Another fine preacher in the same tradition was the Methodist minister, A. E. Whitham, who had a feeling for the Incarnation, the Sacraments, and a Catholic Christianity that was rare in the English Free Churches. Both Jowett and Whitham knew that Christianity has to be caught as well as taught, and they succeeded in conveying some measure of the grace of God in Christ, by the graciousness of their manner.

9. Very Human Divines: "Dick" Sheppard and "Woodbine Willie"

The two most notable charismatic[77] preachers of the twentieth century in England were, however, "Dick" Sheppard, the famous Vicar of St. Martin-in-the-Fields, called "the parish church of the British Empire,"[78] and Geoffrey Studdert Kennedy, the most popular British padre of the First World War, known as "Woodbine Willie."

If Bishop Phillips Brooks' definition of preaching as "truth through personality" is accepted, it follows that the charismatic preacher is a man of absolutely transparent candour, and a striking personality almost wholly subordinated to God. These were, in fact, the outstanding characteristics of Sheppard and Studdert Kennedy. After the fearful disillusionment that set in after the

[77] In the Greek of the New Testament the term *Charis* and its various derivatives refer to the "Grace" of God in Christ and, in a secondary sense, to those persons who are "gracious," because grace-endued. It is in the latter sense that the term is used in this section to mean more than merely dynamic, though Sheppard and Studdert-Kennedy were dynamic.

[78] So called because it is situated in Trafalgar Square where so many Commonwealth countries have the offices of their High Commissioners, and because the overseas religious broadcasts of the British Broadcasting Corporation originated from St. Martin's.

end of the First World War, a merely traditional faith expounded by a complacent Anglican clergyman would have seemed as irrelevant as episcopal gaiters or mediaeval gargoyles. These two men, with perhaps the addition of the co-founder of Toc H, "Tubby" Clayton, and Canon W. H. Elliott, were the only ones who could win and sustain the trust of the disenchanted masses of Englishmen. The fact that Studdert Kennedy was given the bitter-sweet nickname of "Woodbine Willie" by the privates of the British Expeditionary Force in France, and that Hugh Richard Lawrie Sheppard was generally known as "Dick," was proof of their affectionate acceptance by the common man.[79]

Sheppard and Kennedy were in many respects alike. They were colleagues for a time in St. Martin-in-the-Fields. Both were the sons of Anglican clergy. Both had experiences of living among the desperately poor. And both suffered from asthma, and died before their time, exhausted by the spendthrift outpouring of nervous energy required by their ministry to the poor and perplexed. In temperament also, they were alike. Both scorned pretentiousness. Both were intensely generous in time, money, and possessions to the point of quixotry. Both had an irrepressible joy. Both were men of incandescent integrity, genuine humility, and unshakable courage.

They also held a common understanding of their preaching task. They determined to rescue the pulpit from professional or sanctimonious jargon. They were equally concerned to free the teaching of the Church of England from social and political conservatism. Finally, both were eager to present Christ to their people as the companion of men and women in their hardships and sufferings, and as the inspiration for heroic living. Each was a prophet in presenting the Divine revelation as the antidote to popular lies and delusions. Each was also the true priest and confessor, finding his courage, example, and strength in the Sacrament of Holy Communion.

In other ways they differed. Sheppard might be the author of *The Impatience of a Parson*, but he was not half as impatient and impetuous a rebel as Kennedy. Both used colloquialisms in the pulpit, but "Woodbine Willie" never tamed his language, even

[79] It is only a slight exaggeration to state with Ernest H. Jeffs in *Princes of the Modern Pulpit*, p. 155, that "What saved the Church of England, so far as the respect and liking of the masses was concerned, were the personalities and work of two young rebels against ecclesiastical convention—'Dick' Sheppard and 'Woodbine Willie.'"

for the most exquisite or exalted ears. Kennedy used slang, often expletives, and could be counted on to keep the desultory hearer awake by a barrage of explosive terminology. Kennedy was also the more thoughtful radical. He believed that Patripassionism (the doctrine that God the Father suffers) was less a heresy than the essential meaning of the Gospel. While Kennedy used shock tactics, Sheppard tried to coax his hearers into the Kingdom of God.

Sheppard was the model parish priest in St. Martin's for twelve trying years. Kennedy was also an excellent parish priest, but the interruption of the War gave him opportunities as a chaplain which his virile faith coveted most. Sheppard was the successful pioneer of religious broadcasting and his intimate and confidential technique made his ministry at St. Martin's known to thousands upon thousands whom he would never meet. Kennedy, while personally among the most compassionate of men, believed that social justice was the widest possible expression of compassion, and he devoted his post-war years to work as a "Messenger" of the Industrial Christian Fellowship, lecturing up and down the country on the social, economic, and political imperatives of the Gospel.

Kennedy's mind was more acute and his imagination more fertile than were Sheppard's. Indeed, Kennedy was a scholar of great promise and a poet, if a minor one, who became something of a Christian Kipling. Sheppard wanted to make actual Francis Thompson's vision of a new Divine-human encounter in

> . . . the traffic of Jacob's ladder
> Pitched betwixt Heaven and Charing Cross.

On his first Sunday in St. Martin's he imagined the kind of church it might become and set his hand to make that dream come true. This was his ideal:

"I saw a great and splendid church standing in the greatest square of the greatest city of the world. I stood on the west steps and saw what this church would be to the life of the people. There passed me into its warm inside, hundreds and hundreds of all sorts of people, going up to the temple of their Lord with all their difficulties, trials and sorrows. I saw it full of people, dropping in at all hours of the day and the night. It was never dark; it was lighted all night and all day, and often tired bits of humanity swept in. And I said to them as they passed, 'Where are you going?' And they said: 'This is our home. This is where we are going to learn of the love of Jesus Christ. This is the altar of our Lord, where all our peace lies. This is St. Martin's. . . .'

"It was all reverent and all full of love and they never pushed me behind a pillar because I was poor. . . . They spoke to me of two words only, one was the word 'home' and the other was 'love.' "[80]

In due course St. Martin's became the church of Christ's family where class and cultural divisions were irrelevant. Like a true home, ready to welcome the prodigal sons and daughters, the lights were always on and the doors always open. There was always a bed in the crypt and meals in the refectory. Sheppard's marvellous capacity for friendship was the magnet that drew in others dedicated to the catholicity of charity. Art-lovers, and enthusiasts for drama and music and literature, were catered for by the vital services, the Fellowship Guild, the *St. Martin's Review*, and the St. Martin's Players.

Sheppard's sermons radiated the same joyous love of the brethren for Christ's sake, always loving people in their distinctive individuality and never as potential ecclesiastical scalps. His style was as unaffected as the approach to his people. It was marked by man-to-man frankness. As Halford E. Luccock remarks: "Sheppard always talked to a person; he never merely sprayed the solar system with words."[81] Max Beerbohm, that ironic expert in detecting the foibles of men, wrote of the impact of Sheppard upon him when they met at Portofino: "He radiated a youthfulness that was less that of an undergraduate than a schoolboy. Nevertheless he made me feel younger than my years. And better than my character."[82] Sheppard's gift was to see, like his Master, the image of the king, which Christ would renew, in every world-soiled human coin, that others would have discarded as too tarnished for use.

His sermon beginnings were not as unstudied as they seemed. A casual joke can prick the bubble of pride more effectively than a declamation, as he knew, for example, when he narrated the following anecdote: "There was once a fashionable lady who went to a photographer. She was plain but thought she was beautiful. Said she to the photographer, 'Young man, mind you do me justice,' to which he replied, 'Madam, it's not justice but mercy you need!' "[83]

[80] R. Ellis Roberts, *H. R. L. Sheppard, Life and Letters*, pp. 44-45.
[81] *The Best of Dick Sheppard*, p. xix.
[82] *Ibid.*, p. 80.   [83] *Ibid.*, p. 27.

Sentimental as Sheppard often seemed to be, he also had his sterner side. He knew only too well the contrast between the values of Christ and the values of society. He observed that men, looking at Christ with prejudiced eyes, found in Him what they were determined to find—"a revolutionary, a social reformer, a miracle worker, a physician, a kindhearted philanthropist, an Oriental potentate, an upholder of the established order, and, sometimes, apparently, even the first Anglican clergyman."[84] Typical is the whimsical self-depreciation of the remark that "any idea that a round collar is a slipped halo must be once and for all abandoned."[85] Sheppard was not the witty and urbane priest, but neither was he the hail-fellow-well-met muscular type. He was simply and sincerely man's best friend for Christ's sake who had changed the baleful stereotype of the stiff and starchy Anglican incumbent into that of the "human parson."

If Sheppard saw the Anglican priest as friend, Studdert Kennedy viewed him as a fighter for honesty in business and for social justice in economic life. He assumed the great burden of trying to demonstrate in word and deed his conviction of the humanity of God. A double first class honours man at Trinity College, Dublin, and a reader of deep and lengthy books by preference, he had a heart as capacious as his mind. How admirably he filled the duties of a military chaplain is disclosed in his letter of advice to another chaplain:

"Live with the men, go where they go; make up your mind that you will share all their risks and more, if you can do any good. You can take it that the best place for a padre . . . is where there is most danger of death. Our first job is to go beyond the men in self-sacrifice and reckless devotion.

". . . There is very little spiritual work—it is all muddled and mixed—but it is all spiritual. Take a box of fags in your haversack, and a great deal of love in your heart, and go with them, live with them, talk with them. You can pray *with* them sometimes, but pray *for* them always."[86]

His courage, for which he was awarded the Military Cross, and his pungent style made his impact quite unforgettable. In his addresses and his popular rhymes there were two constant

---

[84] *The Human Parson*, p. 98.
[85] Luccock, *The Best of Dick Sheppard*, p. 162.
[86] The citation is from pp. 139-141 of *G. A. Studdert Kennedy By His Friends*, ed. J. K. Mozley. See also the recent biography, William Purcell, *Woodbine Willie*.

emphases. One was that God is involved with humanity in its sufferings. The other was that the Church is to be the spur to social, political, and economic reforms, not the sanctifier of social distinctions.

He was anxious to combat the prevalent idea that the essence of faith was submission; rather it was, in Pauline phrase, to enter into the fellowship of Christ's sufferings. He satirized the older view in the lines:

> This is the Gospel of the Christ.
>   Submit whate'er betides
> You cannot make the wrong world right
>   'Tis God alone decides.

By contrast with this false view, Kennedy pleads for a manlier imitation of Christ:

> O by Thy Cross and Passion, Lord,
>   By broken hearts that pant
> For comfort and for love of Thee
>   Deliver us from cant.[87]

He believed that it was necessary to choose between the omnipotence of God and his love, and he had no qualms in denying the omnipotence to preserve the love. As long as history lasts he is convinced that love must be suffering; only in heaven will it be triumphantly vindicated. The glory of the Christian faith for him was that it proclaimed there was a Cross in the heart of God before there was a Cross on Calvary. Therefore, as his *Rough Rhymes* tell:

> Father, if He, the Christ, be Thy Revealer,
>   Truly the First Begotten of the Lord,
> Then must Thou be a suff'rer and a Healer,
>   Pierced to the heart by the sorrow of the sword. . . .
>
> God, the God I love and worship,
>   Reigns in sorrow on the Tree,
> Broken, bleeding, but unconquered,
>   Very God of God to me.
>
> On my knees I fall and worship
>   That great Cross that shines above.
> For the very God of Heaven is not Power,
>   But Power of Love.

[87] *Lies!* (n.d.), pp. 132-33.

No man protested more strongly than Studdert Kennedy against an Aristotelian conception of God, alone and aloof above the stars, endlessly surveying His own perfections, heedless of men's prayers or curses. For Studdert Kennedy the agony of God was proof of His commitment to the human cause in the Incarnation.

No Anglican clergyman since Canon Scott Holland had sounded the trumpet call for social justice more clamantly than he. He was withering in his condemnation of all who met plans to reduce or abolish poverty with the stale excuse about the impossibility of changing human nature or the misapplication of Christ's words that "the poor are always with you." "There is," he commented, "more real blasphemy in these words than in the most lurid sergeant's speech that ever turned the air of Flanders blue. It is sheer blank atheism."[88] Too religious a man to think that social planners, unassisted by Divine grace which alone transforms the motives of the individual, could build the New Jerusalem out of the dark, Satanic mills of England, he warned the leaders of the Church that its rigid conservatism was forcing men to turn to socialism in place of an unsocial Gospel. The multitude, he cautioned, were revolting from a Church "which damned souls to build churches, sweated workpeople to endow charities, and manufactured prostitutes by low wages to build rescue homes for fallen women and buy a peerage." Furthermore, he claimed that the common people were nauseated by the religion of the upper classes "who patronised God as the best of all policemen, the power that kept the poor people in their places by threats of hell and promises of heaven."[89] He combined the incisive criticisms of Amos with the tenderness of Hosea. As "Messenger" of the Industrial Christian Fellowship, he applied the radical teaching of Christ to war, slums, class-warfare, industrialism, politics, and the problems of marriage. Everywhere his was "the unrestrained utterance of a soul in revolt."[90]

So unconventional a preacher was bound to have many critics as well as thousands of admirers. There is no question that Kennedy upset the balance of the Gospel, which is both criticism and consolation, by often over-emphasizing the judgment of God. It was, perhaps, inevitable when so many clergymen seemed euphoric. Sheppard's defect was the opposite, with the ever present danger of sentimentality. Kennedy's shock tactics ultimately ceased to shock as men became tired of the shepherd who was always crying "Wolf!

[88] Ibid., p. 37.   [89] Ibid., p. 108.
[90] J. K. Mozley, ed., G. A. Studdert Kennedy . . . , p. 167.

Wolf!" His language was too muddied with slang and expletives, so that it distracted from his message. His teaching was lop-sided in another way: he failed to balance sacrifice with hope. Christ was more Victim than Victor for Kennedy. Like the great modern French painter, Georges Rouault, Kennedy's portrait of Jesus depicted a swollen-lipped, blood-smeared and thorn-crowned Christ, against menacing leaden skies. There is suggested only in the faintest golden smudged aureole the risen Christ who tore open the sepulchre and destroyed death. Kennedy was, of course, reacting against the liberal Protestant Christ, the idyllic Galilean teacher of sweetness and light. But the result was that his preaching lacked the serenity of the Christian hope.[91]

The ultimate achievement of Kennedy and of Sheppard was that they enabled thousands of disillusioned men and women to see God, not as a remote and inscrutable Potentate, but as the Father of Christ, who was man's most compassionate Companion involved in their afflictions and agonies and committed to the establishment of a Kingdom of holy love in men's social relationships. And, to the great advantage of the Church of England, they remoulded the image of the Anglican clergyman so that he was seen no longer as a prop of the Establishment, but as a very human and lovable parson.

10. *The Fourth Type of Preaching*: *Liturgical*

Partly in revulsion from the topical sermon which is as up-to-date as the stop-press news in one day's newspaper and out-of-date in the next issue, partly in reaction against the hypothetical discussions of Biblical criticism or social and political issues in the pulpit, our century has pressed for the recognition of the devotional sermon. Dr. J. H. Jowett, the Congregationalist, was the first to recognize the need, for he stated that "When life is a picnic we play with theology: When life is a campaign we grope for a religion."[92] Dr. Russell Maltby and the Reverend A. E. Whitham followed in the same succession in the Methodist Church, as did Dr. James Reid among the English Presbyterians and Dr. F. B. Meyer among the Baptists.

With the recovery of the Christian Year in general among the Free Churches, and of special services for Holy Week, occasions

[91] E. H. Jeffs in *Princes of the Modern Pulpit* wrote that "the wounds and scars of battle were too plainly manifest in the man who stood up, with sad mouth and dark and burning eyes, to tell the people of his hard-won discoveries" (p. 167).

[92] *The Transfigured Christ*, p. 59.

were provided for which devotional preaching was essential and it was deeply appreciated. A proof that even the best Christian minds of the age recognized the limitations of dialectical and even of didactic theology in the pulpit was the mystical quality in Archbishop William Temple's later sermons and particularly in his *Readings in St. John's Gospel.* The final impetus to devotional preaching was, of course, the advent of the Liturgical Movement in all the Churches in England. This made it clear that the Liturgy of the Church is its power-house, at once the focus and dynamo of its unity in Christ, and its impulse to mission and social service.

While other preachers, including Inge, are notable exponents on individual mysticism, the newest type of preaching evokes the corporate mystical response of the congregation. It may therefore justly be termed "Liturgical preaching."[93]

11. *Monsignor Ronald Knox: Wit and Wisdom in Worship*[94]

Donne, Swift, Sydney Smith, Inge, and Knox are all admirable examples of wits in the English pulpit, but Knox's wit is gayer than that of the others. Another master of paradox and whimsy, G. K. Chesterton, has caught the effervescent quality of Knox in his quatrain:

> Mary of Holyrood may smile indeed,
> Knowing what grim historic shade it shocks
> To see wit, laughter and the Popish creed
> Cluster and sparkle in the name of Knox.[95]

Knox's writings are as sparkling as stars on a frosty night.

The son of the Evangelical Bishop of Manchester, he carried all before him at Eton and Balliol College, Oxford. As was to be expected of so nimble a dialectical speaker, he was elected President of the Oxford Union, and had the unique distinction of being quoted in a leading article of *The Times* of London when still an undergraduate. Referring to an inexplicable change in the policy of the government of the day, he quipped: "The honourable gentlemen have turned their backs on their country and now they have the effrontery to say their country is behind them."[96] The same wit,

---

[93] For an Anglican interpretation, see R. H. Fuller, *What is Liturgical Preaching?*
[94] The official biography is Evelyn Waugh's *Ronald Knox.*
[95] *The Collected Poems of G. K. Chesterton*, p. 15.
[96] Nathaniel Micklem, *The Box and the Puppets*, pp. 34-35.

now at the service of religion (for he had been ordained in the Church of England in 1912 and was appointed Chaplain of Trinity College, Oxford), gained him a national reputation with the publication of his satire, *Absolute and Abitofhell*.[97] This protested against the confusion of the traditional Anglican faith with the vapours of philosophical idealism, and its erosion by the acids of Biblical criticism. He had in mind the seven Anglican authors of *Foundations*, who had not yet published the book when he wrote, but with whose views he was all too familiar. The Primate, who preferred decency to dogma, is pilloried thus:

> When suave politeness, temp'ring bigot Zeal,
> Corrected, 'I believe,' to 'One does feel.'

He flays the Biblical critics who dissipate the Divine authority of Scripture by multiplying hypothetical sources, with a powerful contrast between the forefathers in the faith who

> . . . were content MARK, MATTHEW, LUKE and JOHN
> Should bless th' old-fashion'd Beds they lay upon:
> But we, for ev'ry one of theirs have two,
> And trust the Watchfulness of Blessed Q.

Ever a foe to cordial ambiguity, he satirized a polyreligious ecumenism in *Reunion All Around*, with its engaging sub-title, "Or Jael's Hammer Laid Aside and the Milk of Human Kindness Beaten up into Butter and Served in a Lordly Dish, Being a Plea for the Inclusion within the Church of England of all Mahometans, Jews, Buddhists, Brahmins, Papists and Atheists, submitted to the Consideration of the British Public." The disciplinary confusion in the Church of England is reduced to absurdity, as he describes bishops encouraging all unscriptural doctrines, and forbidding high ceremonial, to enable the disobedient clergy "to snatch a fearful joy" and thus taste the spice of martyrdom lacking since the Roman amphitheatre was abolished.

Knox's literary versatility is prodigious. The writer of astute mystery stories, a felicitous translator of Greek and Latin lyrics and epigrams,[98] gifted historian[99] and novelist,[100] he also produced

[97] It first appeared in *The Oxford Magazine* (November 1912) and was reissued in *Essays in Satire* and *In Three Tongues* (1959).

[98] See *In Three Tongues*.

[99] See his *Enthusiasm*, a study of the vagaries of the Christian religion in the seventeenth and eighteenth centuries.

[100] See his *Let Dons Delight*, in which the reader eavesdrops on the fellows of St. Simon Magus college, as they discuss the issues of the day at half century intervals from the Armada to Munich.

the leading modern English translation of the Scriptures authorized by the Roman Catholic Church. The New Testament version appeared in 1945, the Old Testament version in 1949, and both are marvels of clear, precise and idiomatic English. His sermons, too, exhibit great versatility. Polemical sermons were preached in his Anglo-Catholic days,[101] apologetical sermons during his period as Roman Catholic chaplain to Oxford University (1926-1939), and, during his later years, he composed some superb liturgical sermons.

The earliest sermons are often marred by the partisan spirit and by an over-indulgence in facetiousness. One feels that Knox, while capable of writing passages of great beauty, as of religious insight and ardour, is yet chiefly engaged in a hearty bout of ecclesiastical "gamesmanship."

The apologetical and doctrinal sermons offer more substantial fare. They were published under the titles of *In Soft Garments* (1942) and *The Hidden Stream* (1952). He is more impressive in dealing with the day-to-day problems of the Christian life than with abstract doctrine. Contemporary issues give more scope to his irony and psychological insight. He clinches the argument that a plurality of wives or husbands is atavistic today, by insisting that "it is absurd to follow free love unless you follow free hate." Typically Knoxian is an ironical passage about supposedly altruistic bachelors, whom he castigates as "the unselfish people who want to spare several unborn souls the misery of not being brought up at Harrow."[102]

His finest achievements are as a Liturgical preacher. He is ever aware that the revelation of God in Holy Scripture is proclaimed within the context of worship, which aims at the illumination of the mind, the elevation of the heart, and the consecration of the will. Nor does Knox forget that his sermons are also preached within the context of the cycle of the Christian Year, affording opportunities to study the many facets of the Incarnation of the Son of God and to incite the faithful to imitate the saints, themselves the eminent imitators of Christ. Above all, liturgical preaching never allows the congregation to forget that the climax of the Liturgy is the Sacrifice. In all Knox's wit and inventiveness, in his brilliance and aptness of allusion and illustration, the solemn joy of the Liturgy is never forgotten. These sermons enabled the people of God to see that they must *live* the Liturgy in the spirit of glad obedience.

To call Knox a liturgical preacher is not to infer that he was a

---

101 See *The Church in Bondage.*   102 *In Soft Garments*, p. 190.

faddist in matters of ceremonial or vestments. The contrary is the truth: far from feeling that the priest was a very important person, Knox is at pains to insist that the priest is God's *slave* or *tool* in the Mass. One does not decorate a spade or a wrench. It should be recalled that *The Mass in Slow Motion*[103] is a series of meditations on *Low* Mass. Nothing could be more appropriate, since Monsignor Knox might speak like an angel but he sang uncommonly like a rook.[104]

His popular explanation of the Mass ran to nine impressions in eleven years. Not only is it a fresh and moving set of reflections on the successive parts of the Mass, it is also a triumph of communication. For it was, in the form of addresses, delivered to a convent school evacuated from London to Shropshire in time of war. It blends the supernatural sense with a conversational tone and idiom. The measure of the achievement is so great that one is forced to hunt for preposterous parallels to hint at its quality, such as, that this is Ronald Searle supernaturalised, or St. Trinian's sanctified! Theological instruction is inculcated by analogies drawn from ink-stains or laddered stockings. Only Knox could think of Divine revelation and its apparent obscurity as a special kind of hide-and-seek played between God and us.

His profoundest and subtlest liturgical preaching is found in sermons that he delivered to Father Kearney's congregation in London's theatreland each year at the festival of Corpus Christi, which were published as *The Window in the Wall, Reflections on the Holy Eucharist* (1956), and in the addresses which he gave to conferences of priests, published as *The Priestly Life; A Retreat* (1958).

The title of *The Window in the Wall* represents a fine leap of the imagination. Using allegorical exegesis, Knox takes his text from the second chapter of *Canticles* where the lover is said to seek a glimpse of the beloved, "looking through each window in turn." This "brings to mind a fancy which I have often had before now— in looking at the Sacred Host enthroned in the monstrance." The fancy is "that the glittering Disc of whiteness which we see occupying that round opening, is not reflecting the light of the candles in front of it, but shining with a light of its own, a light not of this world. . . ."[105] This is the veiled glory of the Eucharistic

---

103 Further reference is made to this volume in Chapter VII below.

104 *The Mass in Slow Motion,* p. x. When he sang the Mass the only thought he entertained was "a vivid hope that I might die before we got to the Preface."

105 *The Window in the Wall,* p. 2.

Christ, a curtained window, which "lets our world communicate with the world of the supernatural."[106] The call of the Beloved is from the stupefaction of the senses and from anxieties. The medicine of Holy Communion "enables the enfeebled soul to look steadily at the divine light, to breathe deeply of the unfamiliar air," until such time as "God calls us, too, to himself, and makes us glad with the beauty of his unveiled presence."[107] The volume includes a great richness of doctrinal teaching, as the Sacrament is seen successively as the bond of Christian union, the means of Christian renewal, the Bread of the pilgrim, and the channel of Christ's sacrifice and compassion.

The Priestly Life begins with a superb address on "Energy and Repose." It starts with St. Augustine's vivid phrase about the Divine nature, as *semper agens, semper quietus,* always active, yet always at rest. It is mirrored in God's providence in Nature, and still more clearly in the earthly life of Christ, and in his continuing grace in the Sacrament. It is also characteristic of the life of the Church, active in the missionaries, theologians, priests, and great ecclesiastics, yet quietly powerful in the cells of praying celibates. Then there follows a passage of eloquence reminiscent of Cardinal Newman, for its crescendo of rising interest, its dramatic contrast, inevitable images, convincing close, and spiritual penetration:

"For, if you would approach near to the innermost secret of her life, you must go, not to the palaces of Pope or bishop, not to the courts of ecclesiastical tribunals, or the lecture rooms of learned theologians. You must go to the cells of Carthusians and Poor Clares, if you want to know what the Church really is. Shut off from the world and its dusty disputes, sheltered by their protecting walls from public inquisitiveness and from the blare of advertisement, these cloistered souls find a peace which is, if we would but realize it, the breath of the Church's life, the source of her triumphs, the solace of her despair. Look at a man or a horse racing; and then remember that behind all that tremendous display of outward activity there is one tiny valve which beats all unseen, all unheard, within the breast; and if that beating were to cease, all the external activities would cease with it. Something of the same importance belongs to those homes of silence and recollectedness where men and women serve God in holy religion: there lies the heart of the Church. Their restfulness is her secret life; the powerhouse from which all her restless activity must spring. Go elsewhere, and you

106 *Ibid.,* p. 4.   107 *Ibid.,* p. 6.

will see the rippling of her muscles; it is in the hours of contemplation that you will hear the beating of her heart."[108]

In all his later volumes he expresses the "Eucharistic attitude." This he illustrates from Michelangelo's Adam in the Sistine Chapel frescoes—"that recumbent figure, stretching out one hand, at the full length of the arm, towards the Creator, as if in acknowledgment of its utter dependence, its creaturely reliance, on him."[109]

A consummate stylist, Monsignor Knox always preached from a typewritten manuscript but he had a "vocal legerdemain" by which he gave the impression of talking directly to his hearers, when he was, in fact, reading.[110]

His sermons are a product of many virtues. They show the Biblical translator's deep familiarity with Holy Writ, and his submission to its authority. They exhibit a clear and natural structure, lucidity of thought and originality of expression. They have intriguing beginnings and pointed endings. There is a whimsical humanity in the wit and manliness in the monitions. There is also a flexible adaptation of diction and illustration to suit the needs of such different groups as schoolboys at St. Edmund's, Ware, schoolgirls at Aldenham, Oxford undergraduates and priests, and of such special occasions as panegyrics at Westminster Cathedral or society weddings.[111]

For those who like sermons to be a historical and theological exposition of the Scriptures, many of Knox's sermons are too allegorical. The typological exegesis is abused when foreshadowings of the New Testament are found in the Old where there are sometimes only shadows. Even in the Catholic sermons, the easy but fatal transition is sometimes made from light-heartedness to levity, as when Knox writes: "Eastertide is rich in the feasts of martyrs; it was in Spring, perhaps, you got the best bookings for the amphitheatre."[112] For his original and witty mind such a defect was, of course, an occupational hazard.

Our final impression is of a great Roman Catholic preacher, whose brilliant mind and imagination were liberated by grace to make him a most effective cultural attaché of Christ's court and Kingdom. His chief distinction is to have been the unrivalled exponent in England of Liturgical preaching and of the "Eucharistic attitude."

---

[108] *The Priestly Life*, p. 7.   [109] *The Window in the Wall*, p. 34.
[110] See Evelyn Waugh, *Life*, pp. 120 and 242.
[111] See his twenty-four charming wedding addresses collected in *Bridegroom and Bride*.
[112] *Bridegroom and Bride*, p. 69.

12. *A Concluding Survey*

In concluding this survey of twentieth century preaching, two questions must be asked. The first is: What are the distinctive characteristics of the sermons of our day? The second is: What is the effect of contemporary preaching on worship?

In the first place, it is undeniable that the apologetical sermon is more typical of the twentieth than of the nineteenth century. In the last century only the Anglican, Robertson of Brighton, and the Unitarian, James Martineau, spring to mind as pre-eminent apologetical preachers. In the twentieth century reasonable preaching would be a fair description of the sermons of Bishop Hensley Henson, Archbishop William Temple, Professor H. H. Farmer, Dean Inge, and Dr. Alec Vidler, to mention only the most distinguished practitioners of the art. There are several reasons for the popularity of the apologetical sermon. Among them are the increasing secularization of the age; the reduction of the numbers of the Church members of all denominations combined to approximately one fifth of the total population; and the intellectual attacks upon Christianity waged by naturalists, positivists, behaviourists, rationalists, and economists. This meant that a beleaguered Church had to fortify its adherents with reasons for the faith they held.

A second typical twentieth century kind of preaching is the psychological sermon, of which Dr. Leslie Weatherhead has been so notable an exponent. This is likely to be developed with greater sophistication in the future, as it demonstrates how the Gospel relates to the basic psychic needs of the personality, in terms of liberating man from anxiety, alienation, futility, and frustration, and in providing him with a capacity for self-acceptance and transcendence.

In the third place, a clearly distinctive sound of twentieth century preaching has been the ecumenical chorus, as contrasted with the beating of the denominational drum. In this respect the sermons of today mark a great advance over the polemical and partisan philippics that marred many Victorian discourses from the pulpit.

Fourthly, the present century has made an attempt in children's sermons to provide graded religious instruction. It was Dean Inge who observed the educational difficulty involved in the act of preaching to radically diverse individuals in the same congregation, divided by age, temperament, culture, and experience. His term for

251

it was "trying to fill rows of narrow necked vessels by throwing buckets of water over them."[113] One serious twentieth century attempt to lessen this difficulty has been the provision of children's sermons, especially in the English Free Churches.

One of the least satisfactory characteristics of children's sermons is that they seem often to be enjoyed more by the adults than the children. This is possibly because they employ less technical theological terms, but probably because they are better illustrated than sermons for adults. Their most serious defect, however, is that they are often sentimental, and almost always trivial variations on the Pelagian theme, "Be good."[114] Yet, it must be acknowledged that in the hands of such experts as George Macdonald, the novelist, P. T. Forsyth, O. G. Whitfield, and others they have been highly imaginative presentations of the wonder and glory of the Christian Gospel and the exploits of the saints.

In the fifth place, twentieth century sermons have been notably ethical and practical. It was also the perceptive Dean Inge who reminded his hearers of another pressing problem in the communication of Christianity. In a typical epigram he insisted that Christianity "is a way of walking, not talking."[115] It is for this very reason that both in the days of the "Social Gospel" and in the last decade of the present century that "Christian action" sermons have increased in number and significance. It is a recovery of the tradition of the Victorian Christian Socialists, F. D. Maurice and Charles Kingsley, with modern nuances. Theirs was prophetic preaching against the economic exploitation of the artisans by sweated labour. Their successors, like Dr. Donald Soper, Canon John Collins, Bishops Huddleston, Robinson and Stockwood, as well as Archbishop Joost De Blank, have turned their attention to racial discrimination. Several clergymen, notably "Dick" Sheppard, have been notable advocates of Christian pacifism. In these ways the pulpit has often led the people to make practical protests or to give generously to the causes which affirmed the brotherhood of mankind.

Sixthly, the present century has seen a new phenomenon—high quality preaching by laymen. While the Roman Catholic Church has not allowed gifted laymen in its pulpits, several laymen have

---

[113] *Goodness and Truth*, pp. 5-6.

[114] Many that I have heard remind me of the *Punch* cartoon of a harassed mother, shouting to her helper, "Go and find out what Johnny's doing and tell him to stop it."

[115] *Things New and Old*, p. 2.

used books as pulpits for the effective dissemination of apologetics. This was notably the case in the essays of G. K. Chesterton and Hilaire Belloc. Anglicans have been hardly less hesitant to invite their distinguished laymen to preach. This is all the more remarkable in that the three most successful apologists for Christianity in England have all been lay members of the Church of England. They are: T. S. Eliot, the distinguished poet, dramatist, man of letters, and author of *The Idea of a Christian Society*; Dorothy L. Sayers, author of a superb study of the doctrine of Creation entitled *The Mind of the Maker* and of the strikingly successful cycle of radio plays, *The Man Born to be King*; and Professor C. S. Lewis, who held the Chair of Mediaeval and Renaissance Literature in Cambridge University. Lewis seems to be the only Anglican layman whose sermons have been published and are to be found in the volume, *Transposition and Other Addresses* (1949).[116] It is perhaps sufficient to say of Lewis that his *Mere Christianity* was the most successful statement of Christian faith and life ever to be broadcast and that his sermon on "Learning in War-time" was republished as the final and climactic contribution to Ashley Sampson's anthology, *Famous English Sermons*. One has only to recall the preaching of T. R. Glover, the Baptist layman and Public Orator of Cambridge University, and of Bernard L. Manning,[117] the Congregational layman and Senior Tutor of Jesus College, Cambridge, to be aware of the rich contribution that devout and intelligent laymen can make to the pulpit. Such resources will almost certainly be exploited with greater assurance by the Churches in the future.

Our final question as to the effect of preaching on worship can be answered in part by recognizing the importance of Liturgical preaching as practised by Monsignor Ronald Knox, and of devotional preaching as practised by J. H. Jowett and A. E. Whitham. For all three, and for many not as famous as they, preaching was an essential part of the act of worship. As truly as the Sacrament of Holy Communion, preaching was a sacramental communication of the gift of the Gospel mediated by the Holy Spirit to the congregation.

Moreover, the mutual reinforcement of the Biblical and Litur-

---

116 The same volume was published in the United States as *The Weight of Glory* and other addresses. For an appreciation of Lewis as preacher see my *Varieties of English Preaching*, pp. 165-72 and 186-93.

117 See Manning's *A Layman in the Ministry. Varieties of English Preaching* evaluates his role as a preacher on pp. 165-86.

gical Revivals has produced two results. Preachers increasingly recognize their true status as servants of the Word, and less and less do they desire to be the purveyors of idiosyncratic ideas which in their originality often exhibit only original sin in the form of pride. Furthermore, they are more fully aware that the Liturgy, in which the Service of the Word and the Service of the Upper Room are the two essential parts, stimulate mind, heart, and will to the obedience of faith which finds its secular expression in mission and compassion in the workaday world. Both preaching and worship have the same function, the contemporizing of Christ. Preaching today, therefore, is not in competition with worship. Rather it is its complement.

PART II: THE NARROW FOCUS

CHAPTER VII

ROMAN CATHOLIC WORSHIP

THE FIRST part of this volume was devoted to the liturgical, theological, and aesthetic renewal as manifested in general in the religious life in England. The second part, now beginning, will be a detailed study of the development of the theory and practice of worship in *particular* Christian Communions, moving through the spectrum from Roman Catholicism to Unitarianism in the chapters which follow. We start with Roman Catholicism.

The Catholic hierarchy was restored in England in 1850. In the succeeding eleven decades the Roman Catholic Church has made a steady advance both in numbers and in intellectual influence, despite the rising tide of secularism. An administrative index of this growth was the raising of the dioceses of Liverpool and Birmingham to the dignity of archdioceses in 1911.

1. *Roman Catholicism in the Public Life of England*

The most striking advance has been made in the development of an informed and influential Catholic middle and upper middle class in England during the present century. In the last century an influential middle class was needed as the link to bind the older aristocratic Catholic families and the many converts who followed Newman from the Church of England to the Roman allegiance with the thousands upon thousands of impoverished Irish artisans and their families who flocked into Liverpool and Birmingham. Two obstacles stood in the way of the development of such a middle class. The Roman Catholics had not founded Catholic public schools in such numbers and with such academic and social prestige as to compete with the greater Anglican public schools, and the ancient universities, the training ground of most of the nation's leaders, were closed to them by the determinate will of their own hierarchy. Cardinal Manning, the Archbishop of Westminster, though himself an Oxford man, had set his face against the entry of Catholics to Oxford and Cambridge because he believed it would expose them to infidelity. Moreover, he spent the resources of the Church on building parochial schools to retain the masses within the Roman

Catholic fold. In 1895, three years after Manning's death, his successor, Vaughan, was persuaded to agree that Catholics might be permitted, though not encouraged, to attend the ancient universities.

For such an entry into the universities the young Catholics had been prepared at the Catholic public schools. Towards the end of the nineteenth century such institutions as Downside, Douai, Ampleforth, and Stonyhurst, had gained a wide reputation for themselves, which in this century has been considerably increased. The shape of things to come could be seen in the last three decades of the century.

Arthur Conan Doyle was at Stonyhurst and Francis Thompson was at Ushaw. Garner, who was to build the great choir of Downside Abbey, was a partner with G. F. Bodley. Edward Elgar, one of this century's notable composers, was organist of St. George's, Worcester. Richard Terry was at the organ of the English cathedral in Antigua. And, to refer to future converts of distinction, Gilbert Chesterton was a schoolboy at St. Paul's, and Eric Gill was living in the Manse of the Countess of Huntingdon's Chapel in Brighton.[1]

What was lacking in the nineteenth was made good in the twentieth century. The strong and influential English Catholic middle class came into being through the increase and size of the famous Catholic schools, both boarding and day-schools, the latter run chiefly by the Jesuits and the former chiefly by the Benedictines; through the foundation at Oxford and Cambridge of Catholic houses of study for the clergy, who could thus maintain a chaplaincy for Catholic students and fend off agnosticism; and through the vigour of the Catholic literary renaissance. The relevance of these factors for the present chapter is that they helped to promote liturgical and historical scholarship and gained a respect for Catholic culture, which would have been impossible had Catholics been forced to live as in an intellectual ghetto.

At the end of the nineteenth century and in the present century, the Jesuits founded Campion Hall in Oxford and the Dominicans a provincial house of studies in the same university, Blackfriars, while the Ampleforth Benedictines established St. Benet's Hall. In the sister university of Cambridge the Downside Benedictines founded St. Benet's. Their examples were followed by the Capuchins, the Salesians, the Christian Brothers de la Salle, the Irish

---

[1] See ed. G. A. Beck, *The English Catholics, 1850-1950*, Chap. VII.

Christian Brothers, and the Rosminian Fathers, all of whom founded clerical houses for university studies.[2] With this symbolic gesture Catholic scholarship in England came of age. No longer was it the exclusive privilege of those converts to Rome from Anglicanism, like the greatest of them, Newman, who had received an education at the ancient universities as Anglicans, or of those who had been educated abroad, like Lord Acton or Baron von Hügel. It would not be long before the effects of these more generous provisions for higher education would be seen in the publication of learned monographs on Catholic history, liturgy, and spirituality. A welcome and unexpected development, however, would be the resurgence of a Catholic tradition of belles-lettres.

2. *The Catholic Literary Renaissance*

Catholicism has, of course, a very distinguished tradition in English literature from mediaeval times. The roll-call of eminent Catholic men of letters must include Chaucer and Langland, Southwell and Campion, Crashaw, Dryden, and Pope, but it has been greatly increased in the past century. In poetry, sprung rhythms, alliterations, brilliant imagery and passionate religious devotion produced a masterpiece in Gerard Manley Hopkins' *The Wreck of the Deutschland*, which would not have been written without a Jesuit's devotion to St. Ignatius' *Spiritual Exercises*; the poem is a fervent expression of the absolute obedience of faith. Francis Thompson produced another masterpiece in *The Hound of Heaven*, recalling the image of God as the inexorable Divine pursuer, such as St. Augustine had found Him to be in the *Confessions*. Lesser, but far from insignificant poets of the Catholic faith, were Coventry Patmore, the panegyrist of married love, Wilfrid Scawen Blunt, Lionel Johnson, Alice Meynell, Ernest Dowson, Lord Alfred Douglas, Alfred Noyes, and that formidable and antic beast, the "Chester-Belloc."

In the realm of essays G. K. Chesterton proved to be one of the most successful of Catholic propagandists, delighting by his teasing paradoxes and fertile fancy. His religious views were interestingly expressed in *Orthodoxy* (1908) and *The Everlasting Man* (1925), the latter a *tour de force* which presented Christianity as a mystery-novel. Hilaire Belloc, ever a trenchant writer, presumed to antagonize all Protestants by writing a history of the Reformation in which the English variety was written off as "the English Accident."

2 *Ibid.*, pp. 312-13.

Ronald Knox, another great wit and a Jesuit priest, wrote his *Spiritual Aeneid* in 1918 and later a delightful fable, *Let Dons Delight* (1939), where he allows his readers to eavesdrop on the fellows of St. Simon Magus College as they discuss living issues of the day, at half-century intervals, from the time of the Armada to the Munich crisis. The founder of the "Vorticist" movement in literature and art was the greatly gifted D. B. Wyndham Lewis. And Catholic art-criticism has benefited considerably from the expertise of Sir John Rothenstein, John Pope-Hennessy, and E. W. Tristram.

Perhaps the most signal triumphs have come in the art of novel-writing, the most popular and influential of all literary forms in the twentieth century. Compton Mackenzie is the doyen of English Catholic novelists and his trilogy, *The Altar Steps* (1922), *The Parson's Progress*, and *The Heavenly Ladder*, though not his best work, is a polemical study of Anglo-Catholicism as an external and fanatical imitation of Roman Catholicism. It also includes a satirical portrait of Percy Dearmer, the English Nationalist liturgiologist, as the "Rev. J. Q. B. Moxon-Hughes."

The two greatest Catholic novelists, however, are Evelyn Waugh (born 1903) and Graham Greene (born 1904), both Oxford men and converts. They are the English parallels to the Catholic literary renaissance in France which owes so much to Paul Claudel, Georges Bernanos, and François Mauriac. While Waugh's genius runs to satire, as in the superb critique of the escapism and sentimentality of American funeral customs, *The Loved One* (1949), most of his other novels depict, with affection, the idiosyncrasies of life in Catholic country houses where characters are strongly marked, and the faith is strongly held and unembarrassingly discussed. Graham Greene seems to be England's equivalent to Mauriac, and they both depict the conflict between Divine and earthly loves. Greene's *Brighton Rock* (1938) brought back the dimensions of heaven and hell to the flat and garish landscape of Brighton and added depth to the English novel. *The Power and the Glory* (1940) is an astonishing parable of the labyrinthine ways of God's grace in the Augustinian mode. *The Heart of the Matter* (1940) turns on the question of whether a man may be excluded from heaven because he commits a mortal sin for the sake of his wife and illumines grace in squalour, which seems to be Greene's forte.

As Edward Hutton has shown,[3] the Catholic novel has gone through three stages. In the eighteenth century the Catholic faith was treated as ludicrous in England but exotic abroad. In the nineteenth and early twentieth centuries the Catholic novelists had to make the faith appear mysterious and romantic, as Chesterton's novels and "Father Brown" stories show. With Waugh and Greene, however, the gilding is absent and Catholicism is treated as if it were natural and even inevitable. Greene's lack of propaganda is, indeed, the best kind of propaganda and he and Waugh have gained a wide circle of non-Catholic readers.

It is, then, in a cultural context of increased Catholic education, and on the background of an influential Catholic middle class, and in the midst of a Catholic literary renaissance, that important studies in the history of worship and in the meaning of spirituality have been carried out in the present century. Moreover, because Catholicism was swimming against the stream in an age of materialism, deepening doubt, and moral chaos, it made an increasing appeal in a predominantly Protestant country. Its unyielding fidelity to the fulness of the Christian tradition proved alluring to minds that had seen Protestant orthodoxy capitulate to the blandishments of liberalism. Its proclamation of unaccommodating ethical standards also won the grudging admiration of the weaker brethren outside the fold. Its spiritual discipline, as demonstrated by the religious in monasteries and nunneries, who had given up wealth and the joys of family life for the deeper consecration to Christ, as also in the regularity with which the faithful attended Mass, was a proof of Catholicism's continuing power. Its dramatic worship succeeded in eliciting the allegiance and affection of the poor, as no other Communion in England could. It is surely significant that Masterman, an Anglican clergyman, should have given glowing testimony to the popular appeal of the Mass among London's poor: "I have no hesitation in saying that, for the majority of the poor, our services are as incomprehensible as if still performed in the Latin tongue. The central service of the Roman Church, indeed, with its dramatic and appealing character, is far more intelligible even to the humblest worshipper."[4]

---

[3] "Catholic English Literature," being Chap. XVII of G. A. Beck, ed., *The English Catholics*, p. 556.
[4] Richard Mudie Smith, ed., *The Religious Life of London*, cited in G. A. Beck, *The English Catholics*, pp. 419-20.

3. Studies in the History of Worship and Spirituality

Pius XII in his Encyclical, *Mediator Dei* (November 20, 1947), the chief document of the modern Liturgical Movement, paid tribute to "an unprecedented revival of liturgical studies, due in part to the admirable initiative of a number of individuals, but especially to the devoted zeal of certain monasteries of the renowned Benedictine Order." As was seen in the first chapter of this volume, the initiative undoubtedly lay with the Benedictine Abbeys of Solesmes, Mont-César, Beuron, and Maria Laach. In the same tradition, it is unquestionably the Benedictine Abbey of Downside which has pioneered in the development of studies of the history of the Liturgy and of ascetical theology in England. The names of Edmund Bishop, and his friend Cardinal Gasquet, of Abbot John Chapman and Dom Illtyd Trethowan, of Abbot Cuthbert Butler and Dom David Knowles, as well as of Dom Gregory Murray, are sufficient to stake Downside's claim. Other Benedictines in England also made their important contribution, such as Abbot Anscar Vonier of Buckfast, Dom Benedict Steuart of St. Michael's Abbey, Farnborough, and Bishop Hedley, an Ampleforth monk.

In the popular presentation of the lessons of the liturgy the Jesuits were unrivalled, as in Fr. C. C. Martindale's lively *The Mind of the Missal* (1929) and in Fr. Ronald Knox's sparkling account of *The Mass in Slow Motion* (1948). In the person of Fr. Clifford Howell, S.J., they had an indefatigable exponent, both in his writings and his liturgical lectures and missions, of the lessons of the modern Liturgical Movement, including the necessity for lay participation in the Mass by the greater use of the vernacular and, in particular, by the popularization of the Dialogue Mass and the use of commentators, explaining the meaning of the Mass while it was proceeding. The Jesuits also had notable exponents of Eucharistic theology, such as Fr. Bernard Leeming, in his *Principles of Sacramental Theology*, or Fr. Ronald Knox in the less technical group of addresses, *The Window in the Wall* (1956). Yet, significant as these studies were in their effect on the parishes, the most profound studies of Liturgy and spirituality emerged from the Downside cloisters.

The most erudite and original liturgiologist of the century in England was a lay associate of Downside, Edmund Bishop (1846-1917). But for his ailing body and singularity of temperament, he might have been professed as a Benedictine, and he left his library to the Abbey.[5] He developed the passion for study in the original sources and manuscripts in the British Museum, in such hours as could be spared from his duties as a civil servant employed in the Education Department of the Privy Council Office. In 1890 he collaborated with Cardinal Gasquet in producing *Edward VI and the Book of Common Prayer* and they went on to publish *The Bosworth Psalter* in 1908. Francis Aidan Gasquet (1846-1929) had been schooled at Downside, was professed there in 1862, and became the second Abbot in 1900. He was undoubtedly encouraged in the work of scholarship by Edmund Bishop. His greatest work was *Henry VIII and the English Monasteries* (2 vols. 1888-1889), in which he showed that Protestant charges against the state of the monasteries at that period had been greatly exaggerated, amounting to vilification, and demonstrated how much England had lost in spirituality, education, and charity by Henry's seizure of them. As his responsibilities increased, the carefulness of his research and his conclusions unfortunately diminished, but he had shown that an English Abbot could be a distinguished scholar, and many followed the beacon that he and Bishop lit.

Edmund Bishop, to follow the course of the more eminent scholar of the two, though only Gasquet attained the title of "His Eminence," published an important and definitive *Appendix* to the *Liturgical Homilies of Narsai*. His *magnum opus*, which he had contributed in a series of articles to *The Downside Review* over an extended period, was published in 1918 as *Liturgica Historica, Papers on the Liturgy and Religious Life of the Western Church.* His name was known to German scholars, since, for lack of an English publisher, he had gathered the *Collectanea Britannica* and published this collection of about three hundred papal letters of the fifth to the eleventh centuries with annotations in the *Monumenta Germaniae Historica.* In consequence, his latest and posthumous work received international recognition for its vast range, meticulous scholarship, and striking conclusions which, on reconsideration, appeared inevitable.

The opening essay on "The Genius of the Roman Rite" is an index of Bishop's superlative quality. This was reprinted five times, translated into French and German, and was his best known writing. In it Bishop took issue with the common assumption that the Roman Rite is characterized by sensuousness of ritual and

---

[5] See the admirable biography, N. J. Abercrombie, *The Life and Work of Edmund Bishop*, with its detailed account of this pioneer-scholar's contributions to liturgiology.

ceremonial, arguing that this is precisely the element which is not indigenous to it, having been borrowed and adopted through the centuries. Proving his point up to the hilt, he concluded from a study of the early Roman Mass that "the genius of the Roman rite is marked by simplicity, practicality, a great sobriety and self-control, gravity and dignity."[6] He was driven by the determination to trace back to their origins the most venerable components of Catholic worship. Thus the third chapter describes the Gelasian Sacramentary as "The Earliest Roman Mass Book" which was used in Rome at the end of the seventh century. He concludes that it was widely used in Charlemagne's Frankish Kingdom, as a supplement to the *Gregorianum*. The fourth chapter considers some early Mss of the *Gregorianum* and concludes that one group of Mss preserves the book sent by Hadrian to Charlemagne, and that from this can be constructed the authentic texts of the prayers, as well as the rites and formularies used in the Roman Church at the end of the eighth century.[7]

The spirit in which Edmund Bishop approached his work is clearly not that of an antiquarian or rubrician, for he castigates the sterility of much of the liturgical work of the previous century as having been "a study of ritual rather than a study of religion; as a consequence it has seemed to be in touch with professionalism than with life, and appears in its general character to be predominantly of clerical interest."[8] No mere *laudator temporis acti*, he pays tribute to the new devotions which a living Church produces, recognizing that "the source of new forms of private devotion, which become by and by popularized, is in the religious orders."[9] He traces some of the elements of the *Prymer* back to the inspiration of Benedict of Aniane in the ninth century,[10] and he finds the beginnings of the Feast of the Conception of the Blessed Virgin Mary in the devotions of the English monks of Winchester.[11] He provides a history of the development of the Christian Altar from the holy table of cubic shape of the fourth century to the altar-shrine of the eighth, and on to the great reredos altars of the fourteenth and successive centuries, which have become sideboards for the displaying of church treasure and plate on festival days.[12] He is as interesting on the development of the cope, which originally was not a distinctively clerical vestment, to its

[6] *Liturgica Historica*, p. 12.   [7] *Ibid.*, p. 75.
[8] *Ibid.*, p. 166.   [9] *Ibid.*, p. 213.   [10] *Ibid.*, Chap. IX.
[11] *Ibid.*, Chap X.   [12] *Ibid.*, Chap. II.

present eucharistic use;[13] or on the origin and history of the requirement of six candles on the altar.[14]

The first part of his book is devoted to liturgical studies, and the second part (Chapter XVI onwards) to antiquarian studies. Even in the second part he is chiefly interested in the quality of religious life. A comparison of Irish and English devotions, arising from a study of ancient prayer books, leads him to describe Celtic devotions as "all heart, fluency, and little mind," and to define the specifically English quality of piety as "strong feeling controlled and penetrated by good sense."[15] He delights in pointing out that the building of Milan cathedral in the fourteenth century was a testimony to the initiative, public spirit, and self-sacrifice of the citizens themselves, from the richest to the humblest, who gave their most precious possessions or promised to undertake hours of manual labour, as did the civic leader of Milan. On this the humane Bishop comments: "Let us try to fancy for a moment the Mayor (or Lord Mayor, as it is now) and Corporation going out for an afternoon's digging on the Manchester Ship Canal; it is easier to imagine this than to imagine them helping to dig out the foundations of a new cathedral."[16] The realistic and utterly unromantic nature of Bishop's historical reconstructions is well illustrated by this reflection on mediaeval life:

"A truce to all attempts to idealize the middle ages. It was essentially a rough-and-tumble time, insupportable perhaps to our more delicate organisms, a time of plenty of salt beef and salt fish for those who could get it, an age of peas and beans for ever, with a scant stock of clean linen, little furniture and less comfort, an age when a brass pot and half a dozen pewter plates were heirlooms among country people; a day of shambles, and gutters, and narrow streets, and odours and smoky rooms with little ventilation or too much, of bad drainage or none, days of hardness and discomfort; a time when gold and silver-plate enough to ransom a province decked the buffet today and went into the melting-pot of tomorrow. But those ages had, at all events, one great virtue: it was a time when men were wholly convinced that in spite of all drawbacks life was thoroughly worth living; and when they seemed to enter (one way or the other) into the meaning of the words, redeeming the time because the days are evil."[17]

Part of Bishop's genius was seen in his ability to make the most

13 *Ibid.*, Chap. XI.   14 *Ibid.*, Chap. XIII.   15 *Ibid.*, p. 385.
16 *Ibid.*, p. 418.   17 *Ibid.*, pp. 420-21.

educated guesses, and the accuracy of these was to be confirmed by the researches of later scholars. This volume provides two interesting examples. The floridity and even sentimentality of modern ways of devotion are often attributed to Italian origin, but Bishop made the objection, "I will venture to say that much of what is nowadays called Italian in devotions is really German."[18] The researches of the Anglican Benedictine, Gregory Dix, and of Fr. Thurston, the Jesuit scholar, have amply borne out Bishop's contention.[19] Similarly, Bishop was convinced that the remarkable dedication of the Maurist Congregation of Benedictines to historical scholarship must be connected with Richelieu's support of them and his appointment of Dom Grégoire Tarisse to be their Superior.[20] Only two years after Bishop's paper had appeared in the *Downside Review,* the conclusive confirmation of his guesswork appeared in 1913 in Dom Paul Denis' monograph, *Le Cardinal de Richelieu et la Réforme des Monastères Benedictins.* So brilliant a scientific historian, so acute a critic, and so devout a mind, inevitably led not only Cardinal Gasquet but other Benedictine scholars to follow in his footsteps.

His successors, with the exception of Dom Hugh Connolly, have followed him not in the area of liturgical history but in the history of monasticism. The two most eminent are Abbot Cuthbert Butler of Downside, and Dom David Knowles of the same community, former Regius Professor of History in the University of Cambridge. Butler published his lengthy and vivid account of the history of the Benedictine Order and its contribution to the growth of spirituality, education, and charity in Europe as *Benedictine Monachism: Benedictine Life and Rule* in 1922. Perhaps as a result of the frequent visits of Baron Friedrich von Hügel[21] to Downside, and certainly with the active encouragement of Edmund Bishop, Abbot Butler was stimulated to produce his standard history, *Western Mysticism,* in 1922. Dom David Knowles, in a monumental series of volumes, beginning with *The Monastic Order in England* (1940), and continuing with *The Religious Orders in England* (1948) and later volumes, is resuscitating by his historical scholarship and carefully controlled imagination the entire monastic life of mediaeval England. This, too, was a project

---

[18] *Ibid.,* p. 452.
[19] *Ibid.,* see Dix, *A Detection of Aumbries,* pp. 47-60, and Thurston's "Benediction of the Blessed Sacrament" in *The Month,* issues of June-September 1901. Bishop's paper was read in 1893 and published in the *Downside Review* in 1895.
[20] *Ibid.,* Chap. XXVII.   [21] See Chap. V, *supra.*

Bishop had envisioned for Downside Scholars. It is a noble testimony to the *Gesta Dei per monachos* and a tribute to Catholic spirituality through the centuries. Not least interesting is the use of aerial photographs in attempting to reconstruct plans of now ruined and desolate monastic buildings.

Perhaps the most notable work in Eucharistic theology to be essayed by a Benedictine in England was Abbot Anscar Vonier's *A Key to the Doctrine of the Eucharist* (1925).[22] Its most remarkable characteristic is the attempt made to reconcile the teaching of the great Dominican, St. Thomas Aquinas, with the mystery-theology of the Benedictines of Maria Laach Abbey.[23] Vonier was a great supporter of the modern Liturgical Movement and, monk though he was, insisted in his last work, *The People of God* (1937) that it is "a great gain towards our understanding of the Christian mysteries when we are willing to look upon them as being instituted, not for an *élite*, but for a people."[24] His authority for the fullest lay participation in the Mass came from the Canon of the Mass itself, where the Christian multitudes are described as the servants of God, but also as the holy people of God: *Unde et memores, Domine, nos servi tui, sed et plebs tua sancta.* He offers as the key to the Eucharist the emphasis in the teaching of St. Thomas and the Council of Trent on the sacramental character of the Sacrifice of the Altar.

The problem, as he saw it, was: "How am I to be linked up effectively with that great mystery of Christ's death?"[25] The link whereby the benefits of the atonement of Christ (returning to the Father all the glory He had lost through man's transgression) and His redemption (buying back the spiritual liberty of human beings enslaved to sin) were appropriated by humanity was a combination of the Sacraments and faith. He insists that the Sacraments are not symbols but representative signs with power, and calls to his aid the definition of St. Thomas, that "a Sacrament is a commemorative sign of what has gone before, in this case the Passion of Christ, a demonstrative sign of what is being effected in us through the Passion of Christ, that is grace, and a prognostic sign foretelling our future glory."[26]

[22] This was reprinted and published as the second volume of *The Collected Works of Abbot Vonier* to which references are made in this paragraph.
[23] This, the contribution of Abbot Herwegen and Dom Odo Casel, was considered in Chap. I, *supra*.
[24] P. 207.
[25] *A Key to the Doctrine of the Eucharist*, p. 230.
[26] This is a translation of St. Thomas Aquinas, S. Theol. III, Qu. IX, Art. 3:

Vonier argues that these sacramental signs are "not only power-ful in reminding us of the things of God, they have the power to make them live again." They are, that is, "tools in the hands of Christ 'who worketh until now.' "[27] To the Protestant charge that if the Mass is a sacrifice, it would mean that the Sacrifice on Calvary was incomplete, Vonier replies that the two sacrifices belong to entirely different modes of being, the first being a sacri-fice of Christ's own person and the Mass being a sacrifice in the mode of a sacrament. Vonier maintains, as against the immola-tionists, that the Eucharistic Sacrifice is not directly a mystery of Christ's Person, it is primarily a mystery of Christ's Body and Blood.[28] Thus: "Christ, who gave the Body and Blood to the Apostles at the Last Supper, was whole and entire at the head of the festive board. The Christ whose Body and Blood is on the Catholic altar is whole and entire in heaven. But the Eucharistic Body and Blood are representative of Christ in the state in which He was not whole and entire; when He was broken on the Cross at His death."[29] Thus the Eucharistic Body and Blood are the re-presentation not of the Christ who is in heaven, but of the Christ who was broken on Calvary. This doctrine creates some major difficulties, as can readily be seen. In what sense can it be claimed, on Vonier's view, that Christ is the consecrator of the Eucharist?

The difficulties are not lessened when Vonier goes on to insist that "the sacramental presence and the sacramental offering of Christ are not historical events in His career; they do not form new chapters in the book of His life."[30] Confusion becomes greater when he adds: "If there is a repetition of acts, those repetitions are not on the part of Christ, they are on the part of the Church living here on earth."[31] The dilemma which he cannot resolve seems to be: either the completeness of the act on Calvary is maintained, in which case it can hardly be re-presented, or if it is re-presented it is an act of the Church and, therefore, hardly of Christ's. This, indeed, is one of the difficulties of the Platonizing tendency of the mystery-theology, that it can hardly do justice to history's once-for-all character. If the mystery-theology is seeking for a consistent interpretation it might well employ the theology of the Epistle to

"Unde sacramentum est et signum rememorativum ejus quod praecessit, scilicet passionis Christi, et demonstrativum ejus quod in nobis efficitur per Christi passionem, scilicet gratiae, et prognosticum, idest praenuntiativum futurae gloriae."

[27] *A Key to the Doctrine of the Eucharist*, p. 242.
[28] *Ibid.*, p. 282.   [29] *Ibid.*, p. 287.   [30] *Ibid.*, p. 294.
[31] *Ibid.*, p. 295.

the Hebrews and argue that there is one continual sacrifice offered up by Christ as the Great High Priest in Heaven, of which the individual Mass is the local manifestation, but this is decisively rejected by Vonier,[32] possibly because it is customary with High Anglicans.

The most thorough-going criticism of Vonier's sacramental doctrine is provided by Fr. Bernard Leeming in his *Principles of Sacramental Theology* of 1956.[33] The Jesuit theologian, a little unkindly perhaps, regards Vonier's as merely another "moral cause of grace" sacramental theory. He does, however, acknowledge that the theory draws attention to the essentially mysterious character of the Sacraments and to their fuller religious meanings, and provides a salutary warning against trying to define God's awesome dealings with humanity in terms of mere logic-chopping. Furthermore, the theory has the additional merit of emphasizing the essentially personal action of Christ in them, and that they issue in conformity to Christ. Father Leeming criticizes Vonier for obscuring the difference between Christ's presence in the Eucharist from His presence in the other Sacraments. He also urges a clearer exposition of the theological foundations of the sacramental theory. He remarks that even if Christ's death and resurrection are timelessly made present, yet it is never suggested how they cause the mystic death and resurrection, or how the recipient (in Baptism) is made free of original sin and given grace. He considers that the whole theory is based upon an idealist philosophy, but that the Christian faith cannot be accommodated to such a view. Finally, he argues that Vonier confuses a sacrament with a sacrifice, for the symbolism of a sacrifice is man turning to God, and of a sacrament, of God turning to man to sanctify him.

In reply, it might be said that much of Leeming's criticism seems more appropriate to Dom Odo Casel's exposition than to Vonier's, which went as far in a Thomistic direction as was possible, and also, perhaps, that what God does for man in Christ through the sacrifice on the Cross, mediated by the sacrament, is more significant than even the Church's offering to God. It is clear that the mystery-theology has not yet met all the criticisms, but it is equally clear that it has a Patristic basis and an ecumenical importance far surpassing the Tridentine theory. It needs to be reconstructed rather than rejected. Vonier's work had at least the

32 *Ibid.*, p. 344.
33 See pp. 305-13 for the critique of Vonier.

benefit of familiarising English theologians with the new accents of sacramental theology of Maria Laach and its plea for an ecclesiology which would do justice to the supreme process of the Christian's mystical incorporation through the Sacraments. The latter was to find an admirable exposition in the work of the present Abbot of Downside, Dom B. Christopher Butler, in *The Idea of the Church* (1962).[34]

It was hardly to be expected that the Benedictines in the present century would produce a spiritual writer of the quality of Augustine Baker, whose *Sancta Sophia* has been a constant source of guidance for their novices from the seventeenth to the twentieth centuries. In actual fact, though more brilliantly endowed than Baker, Dom (later Abbot) John Chapman's spiritual directions, collected in *Spiritual Letters* (1935), manifest the same balance and sobriety and commitment to the hands of God as Baker's. Where they differ is in the expression of true humility, for Chapman's self-depreciation and utter lack of pretension finds its outlet in whimsy and often in the most Carrollian sense of humour. He deflates himself so that God may be the ultimate director of the souls of his correspondents, but, when necessary, he does not hesitate to delineate the stages of the spiritual life with the utmost clarity, concision, cogency, and practicality. Yet so modest is he that no one would judge from his tone that he was a distinguished New Testament scholar and historian.

What are the sources of his understanding of spirituality? To begin with, the vicissitudes of a varied religious pilgrimage. The son of the Anglican Archdeacon of Sudbury, educated at Christ Church, Oxford (where he took a first in "Greats") and Cuddesdon theological college, he had tried a spell as a deacon in the Anglican Church, then eight months as a Jesuit novice, and finally found his true bent as a Benedictine novice at Maredsous, where he became the pupil of Dom Columba Marmion, among the most distinguished Retreat leaders of modern times. He was professed in 1895 at Erdington, where he ultimately became Prior.

Thereafter his varied duties included the delicate task of acting as Abbot of the Caldey Island community of monks which had left the Anglican Church to submit to the Roman obedience, a period

---

[34] Here it is argued that there have been three theories of the Church in history, as an invisible and purely interior entity, as a visible entity which is potentially a single communion, and essentially a single, visible historical society, and that the third is the only option that does justice to the New Testament and the tribunal of history.

as chaplain at the Front in France and with prisoners of war in Switzerland, and the years from 1919 to 1922 in Rome as a member of the Vulgate Commission. In 1919 he was affiliated to Downside, returning as Claustral Prior in 1922, and eventually becoming Abbot. This versatile man, with a razor-sharp mind and the aesthetic sensitivity of an accomplished pianist, had a wide enough experience of the world to know its allurements and temptations, and to counsel others about that life of contemplation which he had sought with all his devout heart.[35]

Dom John Chapman had learned much from Dom Columba Marmion, but his deepest tutor was St. John of the Cross, the Spanish mystical doctor. As an Anglican he had learned from *The Imitation of Christ*, and as a Roman Catholic from St. Francis de Sales' *On the Love of God*, from Scupoli's *Spiritual Combat*, and from Gay's *Les Vertues Chrétiennes*. In his later years he appreciated St. Theresa, later still St. John of the Cross, and, finally, he was particularly fond of the Jesuit Father, Pierre de Caussade, for his doctrine of *l'abandon*.[36]

Prayer is always emphasized as a privilege, and never as a grim duty. How typical in its practicality and wit is the following direction: ". . . give yourself to prayer when you can, and trust in God that He will lead you, without your choosing your path. Mr. Asquith is an excellent model (not for Cabinet Ministers), but for contemplatives: wait for pressure from without; do not act unless you must; let the *Daily Mail* take the initiative."[37] Equally characteristic is the point that our detractors, like St. Theresa's, may do more good than our flatterers for our spiritual life. This point is humorously illustrated, as follows: "It was like Barry Pain's story of the girl who was told by the great artist that her hair was divine, while the little boys in the street called out 'carrots' as she passed. She was so puzzled that she wanted to die—so she dyed. I can't help believing that St. Theresa got more good from her detractors than from her visions!"[38] There is not a trace of sentimentality or luxuriating in emotion in Dom John Chapman: "We *cannot* call up feelings of love and adoration when we want to; and they would be of little value if we could."[39]

[35] For biographical details, see the second enlarged edition of *The Spiritual Letters of Dom John Chapman, O.S.B., Fourth Abbot of Downside,* edited with an introductory biography by Dom Roger Hudleston. For an appreciation of his spirituality, see Abbot B. C. Butler's evaluation, in Chap. xv of *English Spiritual Writers,* ed. by Charles Davis, S.J.

[36] See Dom Roger Hudleston, ed., *The Spiritual Letters. . .* , p. 24.

[37] *Ibid.,* p. 35.   [38] *Ibid.,* pp. 91-92.   [39] *Ibid.,* p. 150.

The theory of abandonment to God, so exceedingly helpful to souls going through a dry period of their spiritual life, is admirably expressed in the following statement: "Therefore the whole point of the 'Sacrament of the present moment' . . . is that it is a (covering, yet revealing) sacrament; it is God's action, God's will, or it is God."[40] Dom John Chapman believed that as surely as a fish lives in water, so does the soul live each moment in the action of God. Once that conviction is accepted, there is every cause for trusting the Divine love that casts out fear, a sense of which is sometimes given at the beginning of the spiritual pilgrimage, but which is later withdrawn. When it is withdrawn, there should be no desire for extraordinary proofs of the Divine care in visions or other assurances, for such desires are the expressions of disbelief. Such was Dom John Chapman's robust and obedient piety.

A pamphlet on Contemplative Prayer, which is printed as an appendix to the *Spiritual Letters*, had a very wide circulation, and is an extraordinarily clear map of the successive stages in the spiritual pilgrimage of the soul. As conceived by Dom John Chapman, the first kind of mental prayer is Meditation, consisting of three parts: realizing a truth and thus making the Faith real; the drawing out of the imagination from pleasures towards God; and the making of various Acts, either as resolutions or affections. This process leads inevitably to the second kind of mental prayer, namely, the prayer of "Forced Acts." In this second stage, according to Father Augustine Baker, there is only a little thinking, but the making of many Acts. (Abbot Chapman, following St. John of the Cross, does not believe that this is an enduring stage of the soul's pilgrimage, seeing it only as a "wobbly transition state.") The third kind of mental Prayer is Contemplative. In this stage the Acts are not forced, nor are they the prayer, but merely an accompaniment to avoid distractions. (Abbot Chapman adds that many modern writers place the Prayer of Simplicity, that is, continued acts and thoughts, as an introductory stage of contemplative prayer, and often see it as coming after or in "The Obscure Night" of the soul.)

It was not rapture, but the steady direction of the self towards God that Dom John Chapman sought for himself and his pupils in the spiritual life. His manly intellect, unsentimental realism, and inward reserve, as well as his respect for the independence of the souls he directed, combined with the irrepressible humour that

40 *Ibid.*, p. 83.

marked his humanity, made him a most invigorating spiritual director.

The last contribution of spirituality from Downside to be considered is more directly linked with the modern Liturgical Movement. It is Dom Illtyd Trethowan's *Christ in the Liturgy* (1952). It attempts to do for England what Dom Odo Casel did for Austria and Germany, and Père Louis Bouyer did for France, that is, make generally available the newer understanding of the Liturgy as the mystery which incorporates Christians as the Body of Christ. He begins by raising the objection that the Liturgy seems to be a routine for escaping the problems of prayer and that essential religion is surely the union of the *solus cum Solo*. His answer is that "the silent prayer of the heart is a flowering of the soul fructified by the Liturgy" and is itself a preparation for a deeper sharing in the Liturgy. He sees the Liturgy as a "solemn game," for it is "fundamentally the praise of God, entering so far as we can on this earth into his joy (Claudel's *le grand rire divin*)."[41]

In the central third chapter, expounding "Christ's Sacrifice and Ours," the author claims that Christ "has given us his sacrifice under a sacrament, so that we too may sacrifice. We enter in his sacrifice; *our* bread and wine actually become it. Through that sacrifice which is himself, we are incorporated with him."[42] In the Liturgy, which is Christ's sign, "Christ puts the entire Redemptive mystery, not only his Passion and Death, but his Resurrection and his Ascension," and this means that "we have our Lord in all his reality in his consummated, but ever-active glorious state."[43] In consequence, "the past is not repeated, but it is not dead: it remains real in the present."[44]

Successive chapters deal with the various parts of the Mass, with the Liturgical Year, the Singing of the Mass and the Modern Problems, and the Divine Office. Of the Liturgical Year Dom Illtyd says: "the mystery is so rich and so far beyond our comprehension in its totality that it must be spread out for us over the whole year, so that we may gradually assimilate it more and more."[45] He refers, with pride, to the contribution to the liturgical movement made by Dom Gregory Murray of Downside in *A People's Mass*, for this is a very simple setting of the Ordinary of the Mass in which layfolk can easily participate.[46] This has

---

[41] *Christ in the Liturgy*, p. 6.   [42] *Ibid.*, p. 33.
[43] *Ibid.*, p. 34.   [44] *Ibid.*, pp. 35-36.   [45] *Ibid.*, p. 68.
[46] *Ibid.*, p. 109. Dom Gregory Murray has also produced the following important pamphlets: *Accentual Cadences in Gregorian Chant, The Authentic Rhythm of*

won wide success not only in England, but also at Lourdes. He is strongly convinced that it is only by the liturgical use of their own language that the congregation will take their proper part in the liturgical action at Mass. Moreover, "any liturgical culture must be a Biblical culture" and hence "a re-education of the faithful in the Bible must accompany liturgical preaching if our efforts are to produce solid and lasting results."[47]

The strong emphasis on the Liturgy could lead to a depreciation of the role of the Divine Office. This Dom Illtyd Trethowan is anxious to guard against. He strongly recommends that the laity should observe morning and evening prayers, by the use of the Offices for Lauds and Vespers. "These take less than a quarter of an hour to recite with decent reverence, and their general adoption, by the educated laity at least, is something which one can hardly advocate too strongly."[48] The relation of the Divine Office to the Eucharist is finely described: "For the Divine Office is the Church's praise spreading out from its centre, the Mass, over the rest of the day. Properly understood, it is the sanctification of *time*, the drawing of particular periods between the celebration of one day's Mass and the next into the orbit, as it were, of the Eucharist."[49]

The Epilogue, on Christian Perfection and Intellectualism, is all the more impressive because Dom Illtyd Trethowan is an able Christian philosopher.[50] Its conclusion is: ". . . in a decadent age it is easy for us to be infected with the idolatry of scholarship which acts as a substitute for the true culture of the mind. We know that the cure for this and all other disorders is, in a word, the Liturgy, the source of contemplation; the Liturgy is the supreme apostolate; it is the Church herself, whose life is the Liturgy, who is the supreme witness to the Resurrection."[51]

One further Benedictine contribution to thought about the Liturgy needs to be mentioned. That is Dom Benedict Steuart's *The Development of Christian Worship* (1953). It is a sketch or outline of the history of the Liturgy written by a monk of St. Michael's Abbey in Farnborough, Hampshire. It is a most useful attempt "to gather together the results of recent writers on the

Gregorian Chant, Gregorian Rhythm in the Gregorian Centuries, and *Plainsong Rhythm.*

[47] *Ibid.,* p. 117.   [48] *Ibid.,* p. 123.   [49] *Ibid.,* p. 120.
[50] His best known writings in this genre are *Certainty, philosophical and theological* and *An Essay in Christian Philosophy.*
[51] *Christ in the Liturgy,* p. 148.

history of the Liturgy—both abroad and in this country—for the sake of those people who, while anxious to know more about the meaning and history of the worship of the Church, are unable . . . to do so."[52] Carefully and unpretentiously written, it exhibits a fine ecumenical spirit which recognizes the importance of Anglican contributions to liturgiology, and, in particular, the significance of J. H. Srawley's *Early History of the Liturgy* and Dom Gregory Dix's *The Shape of the Liturgy*. It has a particularly helpful account in an appendix of "The Restored Easter Vigil."[53]

The frequency with which the name Downside has dominated the preceding pages is testimony to the leadership of that great Abbey in the understanding of the Liturgy, the Divine Office, and of the spiritual and contemplative life in England. Benedictines from other abbeys also made their own contribution, notably Abbot Vonier and Dom Benedict Steuart, but the claim must be upheld that in the renascence of Catholic intellectual life in England there were three dominating influences: "the importance and influence of Newman, the outstanding place occupied by the great Benedictine Abbey of Downside, and the leading position taken by converts in all this transaction."[54] In fairness, however, to other Orders it should be emphasized that in the popularization of the meaning of the Liturgy among the educated laity distinguished contributions were also made by the Society of Jesus, notably by Fathers C. C. Martindale, Ronald Knox, and Clifford Howell.[55]

4. *The Progress of the Liturgical Movement among English Catholics*

At the outset, it must again be emphasized that the progress of the Liturgical Movement in any country which is predominantly Protestant is bound to be slower than in one predominantly Catholic. It is not a matter of mere numbers, but far more of ethos. The point is that so many features of the Modern Liturgical Movement appear to be so Protestant in character: the emphasis on the vernacular, the importance of Biblical exposition, the aim at greater participation in worship, the central altar around which the people are gathered, have their strong Protestant counterparts. Therefore, it may look as if in a predominantly Protestant

[52] P. xi.
[53] *The Development of Christian Worship*, pp. 273-80.
[54] G. A. Beck, ed., *The English Catholics, 1850-1950*, p. 558.
[55] In the section which follows I am greatly indebted to Father Clifford Howell, S.J., although I take entire responsibility for the statements and judgments there made.

country the advocates of the Liturgical Movement are going to Canterbury or even to Wittenberg or Geneva. This is undoubtedly one factor accounting for the relatively slow progress of the Liturgical Revival among English Catholics. Moreover, a country where Roman Catholicism was reintroduced only a century ago is not likely to be able to allow its Religious Orders to take time off from the task of catechising and evangelising to study such apparently academic matters as the history of the Liturgy. These two reasons would be sufficient to account for the tardiness of the appreciation of the Liturgical Revival in England. It can confidently be supposed that its development will be all the more rapid in the ensuing decade because of the highly important Constitution on Sacred Liturgy which was adopted by the second session of the Vatican Ecumenical Council on December 4, 1963. This important document makes it clear that the Liturgical Revival is not the concern of visionary reformers, but of the whole Church.

Before the Second World War there were several books published on the meaning of the Mass, but extraordinarily few that expressed the view that the laity should be participants rather than spectators. This was, indeed, the era when the dignity and splendour of the Liturgy were chiefly considered, a period of rubrical interest. One of those most influential in spreading the concern for order and dignity was Adrian Fortescue,[56] who published *The Tridentine Missal* in 1916 in an edition, with a prefatory explanation, known as the "Liturgy for Layfolk." Two years later there followed the important book, *The Ceremonies of the Roman Rite Described with Plans and Diagrams*, which had reached a tenth edition by 1958. Father Fortescue also had a deep interest in the Liturgies of the Eastern Church, for in 1908 he had published *The Divine Liturgy of . . . John Chrysostom*, translated into English with introduction and annotation by himself. Liturgy continued to be a matter of the sanctuary and choir-loft, with the people as spectators.

It was beginning to be felt in some quarters, however, that they should at least be intelligent spectators. This was the view of Father C. C. Martindale in *The Mind of the Missal*, in which the distinguished Jesuit expounded the rich piety of the liturgical prayers. A similar concern motivated another brilliant Jesuit, Monsignor Ronald Knox, in his sparkling popular account, *The Mass in Slow Motion*. His Introduction is a breathlessly brilliant

[56] See J. W. Fortescue and John G. Vance, *Adrian Fortescue: A Memoir* (1924).

summary of the Mass. On the clause in the Creed "and was made man," he comments, "and the splendid dramatic moment of *Et homo factus est*, with the noise of kicking and scraping behind you, where rheumatic knees are being laboriously bent in honour of God made Man."[57] There follows the brilliant image of the Preface in the Prayer of Consecration, "with the various ranks of Angels flashing past like the names of suburban stations as we draw closer to the heart of the great capital."[58] Then there follows the amazed wonder of the Consecration itself: "You elevate the Host, the Chalice; or are they trying to fly upwards out of your hands? You hardly know, it is so strange."[59] Finally, there is his pointed conclusion: "So much of drama every day of our lives; and we, how little we are thrilled by it."[60] Moreover, the very clarity of Knox's addresses, and the astonishing fertility of his illustrations, frequently hide the penetration of the thought that went into their making. This is particularly true of his fascinating series of Eucharistic addresses, *The Window in the Wall* (1956), in which he expounds the Eucharist as the focus of the spiritual life where eternity breaks through into time, the spiritual life through the material life, and Christ into human nature. He envisions it as the Sacrament of unity and peace, of our thanksgiving for creation and renewal in Christ, and of Christ's continuing humility. It is the iron-ration of the pilgrim, the Sacrament that prepares for life and for death. Supremely, it is the Sacrament of Christ's love, manifesting his unchanging friendship, his compassion for the multitude, and the Sacrament of Sacrifice.[61] Such enthusiastic and informed introductions to the Mass must, at the very least, have made those who heard them devout and intelligent spectators at Christ's Banquet.

Still in the archaeological and rubrical period between the First and Second World Wars was the foundation by the Benedictine monk, Dom Bernard McElligott, of the Society of St. Gregory. This association of priests and laity was devoted to the study and the spread of Gregorian chanting. However, the Society also had in mind the practical aim of getting the people to sing their own parts of the Mass to the Gregorian settings. By means of Summer Schools, and of a periodical called *Music and Liturgy*, there was some infusion of Abbot Guéranger's ideals among English Catho-

---

57 *The Mass in Slow Motion*, p. xiii.
58 *Ibid.*, p. xv.　　59 *Ibid.*, p. xvii.　　　　60 *Ibid.*, p. xviii.
61 See especially sermons 12, 15, 18, and 20.

lics. On the whole, however, the Society's influence was limited to an educated élite and its chief success has been the introduction of plainsong Masses to schools.

The pioneer in the introduction of the Dialogue Mass was Father Clifford Howell, S.J., who during a study leave in Germany had become familiar with the new Liturgical Movement, but had no opportunity to introduce the Dialogue Mass in England before the Second World War. As a military chaplain, however, he began it among the troops abroad. He had a simple Dialogue Mass booklet printed when in Cyprus, and this proved to be most successful in propagating the idea and the practice of the Dialogue Mass. The idea spread to other chaplains and by the end of the war it was common throughout all the armed forces, and found its way into several parishes.

At about the same time Father Samuel Gosling of Alton, Staffordshire, founded the English Liturgy Society, subsequently renamed the Vernacular Society of Great Britain. Lacking the official support of the hierarchy, it made very slow progress indeed, but its views have slowly spread with the years until they are now very much à la mode, though the founder did not live to see this popularity. Another major influence in spreading the ideals of the Liturgical Movement was Count Michael de la Bedoyere, until 1962 the editor of the *Catholic Herald*, author of *The Life of Baron von Hügel* (1951).[62] He welcomed articles on the liturgical renewal and opened his correspondence columns to the discussion of many aspects of its pastoral significance, and this ultimately persuaded publishers that there would be sufficient interest in books on the same theme.

Father Clifford Howell was not content with pioneering in the use of the Dialogue Mass in England. He felt that a liturgical parish mission should be developed to teach the relevance of the Liturgy to the daily life of folk in the parishes. Early in 1947 he gave the first liturgical mission under the title of "Layfolks' Week." It comprised a series of "leaflet services," made up of material drawn from the Liturgy in the vernacular, arranged so that the laity were given an active part in praying and singing together, and thus would gain the experience of corporate worship. He it was also who introduced the practice of Commentators and Lectors, at first against considerable opposition, but this has dwindled

---

[62] Count Michael de la Bedoyere also wrote *Christianity in the Market-Place*, *The Layman in the Church*, and the biography, *Cardinal Bernard Griffin, Archbishop of Westminster*.

since the Instruction of the Sacred Congregation of Rites approved these customs in 1958. In books, pamphlets, and articles, as in lectures and in the multitude of Dialogue Masses and Layfolks' Weeks he has conducted, Father Clifford Howell has been a veritable dynamo of the Liturgical Movement in England.[63] He has never failed to point out that the participation of the laity in the Liturgy is the practical implication of the doctrine that the Church is the Mystical Body of Christ and that through the Liturgy the Christian is incorporated into Christ.

In recent years there have been several notable protagonists of the Liturgical Movement, and of the catechetical and Biblical movements associated with it. Donald Attwater, an authority on Eastern spirituality, theology, and liturgy, argued for the vernacular in 1944 in his book, *In the Beginning was the Word: a Plea for English Words in the Worship of the Roman Church*. Lancelot Shepherd, an authority on the Roman Rite, gave his blessing to the same project. Others who provided momentum to the Liturgical Movement were Fathers James Crichton and William Raftery, Monsignor Joseph Buckley, and Canon Alban Burrett. They have encouraged the intelligent participation of the laity in the Liturgy in their own parishes, and written articles on the subject for various Roman Catholic periodicals. Theological justifications of the Liturgical Movement of high quality are Dom Illtyd Trethowan's *Christ in the Liturgy* (1952) and Father Charles Davis' *Liturgy and Doctrine*. The latter also edited an important historical volume, *English Spiritual Writers* (1961), tracing the contributions of English Catholic writers on spirituality from Aelfric of Eynsham and Richard Rolle to John Chapman and Ronald Knox.

One consequence of stressing lay participation in the Liturgy was the need to provide simpler settings for the singing of the people's parts in the Mass. Dom Gregory Murray of Downside met this need in his *People's Mass*, as did Dom Laurence Benevot in *The Proper of the Mass*.[64] Both found a widespread welcome, with the result that congregationally sung Masses are now to be heard in many parishes throughout England. Furthermore, Eng-

---

[63] Reference may be made to Father Howell's *The Work of Our Redemption*, and his *Mass Commentaries*, both books that sold widely, and to his booklet *Mass Together* (Chelworth, Malmesbury, Wiltshire) which was phenomenally successful. He has also written *Preparing for Easter*, and translated two important works by J. A. Jungmann, S.J., namely, *Public Worship* and *The Sacrifice of the Church*.
[64] The four settings were published in 1948.

lish enthusiasts for Père Gélineau's vernacular psalm-singing have explored the possibility of attempting to provide an English equivalent. Baroness Bosch van Drakenstein of the Grail Community in Pinner, Middlesex, has sponsored this work, under the musical editorship of Dom Gregory Murray, and the results have been published in two volumes, so far, of *The Grail Version of the Psalms*, the first containing twenty-four and the second thirty Psalms. These have been taken up by several schools, but only in a few parishes.

Most important of all is the linking of the Liturgical Movement with the Catechetical and Biblical Movements. Canon Drinkwater of Lower Gornal, Dudley, the founder and editor of *The Sower*, was the catechetical pioneer who always recognized the teaching value of the Liturgy, and he was most appreciative of the pastoral aspect of the Liturgical Movement. Its two chief publicists are Fathers Alexander Jones and Hubert Richards. The former has written *Unless some Man show me* (1951), an interesting exposition of the Old Testament. The latter was one of the translators of Charlier's *La Lecture Chrétienne à la Bible*, in English *The Christian Approach to the Bible* (1958). Father Richards is also one of the literary editors of *The Grail Version of the Psalms*.

In the slow but steady progress of the Liturgical Movement in English Catholicism, it can be seen that Edmund Bishop followed in the footsteps of Guéranger; Vonier, Trethowan, and Davis passed on the heritage of Casel, Beauduin, and Jungmann; Howell, Jones, and Richards undertook the tasks of Pius Parsch; and Gregory Murray the part of Gélineau. Thus, the Continental Liturgical Movement was channelled to English Catholics.

As for the future, it can be confidently predicted that the Liturgical Movement will grow from strength to strength in English Catholic life. This is guaranteed by the text of the Constitution on Sacred Liturgy adopted by the Vatican Ecumenical Council at its second session on December 4, 1963. Here authoritative approval was given to the concerns of the Liturgical Movement in a noble expression. This document is, in fact, the classical statement of those aims for which the protagonists of the Liturgical Movement have been striving amid much misunderstanding and obloquy, or indifference, in the earlier years of this century. The present chapter will conclude by giving a brief account of it, as outlining the future of Catholic worship in England, and elsewhere.

The Liturgy is Christ's act, "an exercise of the priestly office of Jesus Christ" and in the Liturgy "the whole public worship is performed by the mystical body of Jesus Christ, that is, by the head and His members." For this reason it is "a sacred action surpassing all others."[65] As the participation of the laity is strongly stressed, so also is the eschatological reference: "in the earthly liturgy we take part in a foretaste of that heavenly liturgy which is celebrated in the Holy City of Jerusalem towards which we journey as pilgrims."[66] Pastors are encouraged "to insure that the faithful take part fully aware of what they are doing, actively engaged in the rite, and enriched by its effects."[67] Popular devotions are to be drawn up in accordance with the sacred Liturgy and to lead to it, "since, in fact, the liturgy by its very nature surpasses any of them."[68]

The active participation of the people is required both by the nature of the Liturgy, as also by the status of Christian people as "a chosen race, a royal priesthood, a holy nation, a redeemed people."[69] A liturgically instructed people presupposes a liturgically informed priesthood. Therefore "the study of sacred liturgy is to be ranked among the compulsory and major courses in seminaries and religious houses of study; in theological faculties it is to rank among the principal courses."[70] It is also to be taught in its theological, historical, spiritual, pastoral, and juridical aspects. Also, professors of dogmatic, spiritual, and pastoral theology, and of the holy scriptures are to bring out the connection between their subjects and the Liturgy.[71]

With great care a restoration of the Liturgy is to be attempted. "In this restoration, both texts and rites should be drawn up so that they express more clearly the holy things which they signify; the Christian people, so far as possible, should be enabled to understand them with ease, and take part in them fully, actively, and as befits a community."[72] The investigation of the various parts of the Liturgy to be revised should be theological, historical, and pastoral.[73] Experience gained from recent liturgical reforms is also to be considered. But "there must be no innovations unless the good of the Church genuinely and certainly requires them."[74] Furthermore, "to achieve the restoration, progress, and adaptation of the sacred liturgy, it is essential to promote that warm and living

[65] *Constitution on Sacred Liturgy*, § 7.
[66] *Ibid.*, § 8. [67] *Ibid.*, § 11. [68] *Ibid.*, § 13.
[69] *Ibid.*, § 14, citing I Peter 2:9.
[70] *Ibid.*, § 16. [71] *Ibid.* [72] *Ibid.*, § 21.
[73] *Ibid.*, § 23. [74] *Ibid.*

love for scripture to which the venerable tradition of both eastern and western rites gives testimony."[75]

There is a highly complex consideration of different norms appropriate for the reform of the Liturgy, those of a general character, and those drawn from the hierarchic and communal nature of the Liturgy, and from its didactic and pastoral character, and those for adapting the Liturgy to the culture and traditions of peoples. Certain principles emerge from these considerations. Communal celebrations are to be preferred to private or quasi-private ones. Provision of rubrics to clarify the people's parts is necessary. The rites "should be distinguished by a noble simplicity."[76] The intimate connection between words and rites is to be made clearer in several ways. There is to be more reading from the Scriptures, and it is to be more varied and suitable. The ministry of preaching is to be fulfilled with fidelity. "The sermon, moreover, should draw its content mainly from scriptural and liturgical sources, and its character should be that of a proclamation of God's wonderful works in the history of salvation, the mystery of Christ, ever made present and active within us, especially in the celebration of the liturgy."[77] Bible services are to be encouraged especially on Sundays and feast days, on some weekdays in Advent and Lent, and on the vigils of important festivals.[78]

While the use of the Latin language is to be preserved in the Latin rites, the limits of the employment of the mother tongue may be extended, especially in the readings and directives, as in the prayers and the chants.[79] It is also hoped that in every diocese there will be appointed a liturgical commission for promoting the liturgical apostolate, and also, if possible, commissions for sacred music and sacred art.[80]

Other important parts of the Constitution on Sacred Liturgy are concerned with the reform, restoration, and adaptation of the Eucharist (Chapter II), the other Sacraments and Sacramentals (Chapter III), the Divine Office (Chapter IV), the Liturgical Year (Chapter V), and Sacred Music (Chapter VI). Throughout the aim is that the worship of God may fittingly celebrate the mysteries of salvation, to permit the maximum participation of God's people and thus their edification and sanctification through incorporation in the mystical Body of Christ. To this end there is to be a simplification, clarification, and purification of the rites.

[75] *Ibid.*, § 24. [76] *Ibid.*, § 34. [77] *Ibid.*
[78] *Ibid.* [79] *Ibid.*, § 36. [80] *Ibid.*, §§ 45, 46.

Above all, the great mysteries of salvation are to be emphasized in the Christian Year, as over the sanctoral cycle, and only those saints of truly universal import are to be recalled as pre-eminent servants of God. Scripture is to come into its own as the record of the Divine revelation, and preaching is to be magnified, for Christian worship is the response to revelation. Thus, it may be seen that the Biblical and Liturgical Movements are complementary and mutually re-inforcing. They are both profoundly concerned with the intellectual and spiritual renewal of the life of Christ's Church.

CHAPTER VIII

ANGLICAN WORSHIP TO 1928

FROM THE worship of the Roman Catholic Church we turn to that of the Church of England with its Catholic and Reformed inheritance. Our two chapters on Anglican worship are divided by an important liturgical watershed—the Prayer Book Controversy of 1928. Until 1928, when Parliament rejected the Deposited Prayer Book, against the declared will of the Church of England as expressed through its Church Assembly, the consideration of worship was marked by acrimonious partisanship between High Church and Low. After 1928 a sobering armistice ensued, which was followed by a peace built on mutual understanding. Consequently liturgical experiments flourished in a more united Church.

It is hardly possible to exaggerate the ceremonial chaos which characterized the Church of England in the first three decades. It is wittily detailed in the drawings and commentary of Peter F. Anson, that ecclesiastical Osbert Lancaster of our time, in his *Fashions in Church Furnishings, 1840-1940*.[1] This book is a veritable Christian Diorama! Indeed, the uninitiated reader, consulting only Anson's illustrations of the furnishings of the altar and the vestments of the clergy, might readily suppose that there were three Churches of England, not one. The confusion would be confirmed as he concentrated on the bare and even bleak interiors of Anglican Evangelical churches, on the "British Museum" ceremonial and furnishings of the moderate Anglo-Catholics of the Percy Dearmer school who seemed to think they were living in the late Gothic age of Edward VI and not in the industrial age of Edward VII, and on the Baroque and Rococo altars favoured by the extreme Anglican Papalists of the Society of SS. Peter and Paul which appeared to transport the beholder into seventeenth or eighteenth century Spain or France.

Evangelical Anglican churches had a simple oak Communion-table "either left bare or vested in a stiff frontal of crimson cloth, sometimes embroidered with lilies or passion flowers, but seldom with a cross."[2] The Communion was celebrated from the North

---

1 Published by the Faith Press, London, 1960.
2 Anson, *Fashions in Church Furnishings*, p. 290.

284

end. If there was a reredos, instead of the usual unadorned panel-ling, it often was in the form of Gothic arches with the Decalogue, the Lord's Prayer and the Apostles' Creed painted on the panels. The choir was often composed of women as well as men, and the clergyman would celebrate the Lord's Supper in a surplice with a black scarf. Apart from the surplice and the placing of the Communion-table against the East wall, the service with its well-sung hymns and its unabbreviated sermon might easily be mistaken for the worship of Presbyterians or Congregationalists in a London suburb. It was, in brief, unmistakably Reformed in emphasis.

The moderate Anglo-Catholics took their lead from Percy Dearmer.[3] He, in turn, was trying faithfully to popularize the view of J. T. Micklethwaite as expressed in the first publication of the Alcuin Club in 1897, *The Ornaments of the Rubric*. Micklethwaite, accepting the legal view that all ornaments in use in the sixth year of the reign of Edward VI were perfectly legitimate for continuing Anglican use, surprised the public by the results of his indefatigable researches into Edwardine history. He held that images and pictures, as long as they were not superstitiously abused, were valid ornaments; that curtains, riddels and costers about altars were required by the Ornaments Rubric, and that even a hanging pyx might be used for the reservation of the consecrated elements. He contended that in 1548-1549 there were generally two lights on the high altar and one on each side, but that more might be used for great festivals. All these, therefore, instead of being unwarranted Roman additions to the English Rite perpetrated by Anglo-Catholics, were now declared to be not only authentically Anglican, but to be required by the Ornaments Rubric. Here, indeed, was a turning of the tables on the Evangelicals and Liberals who had hitherto criticized the Anglo-Catholics for disloyalty to the Prayer Book tradition! The triumphant chauvinism of Micklethwaite's conclusion deserves citation: "The substitution of foreign ornaments is mischievous from the countenance it gives to those who profess to see in the present revival in the Church of England only an imitation of the Church of Rome. And we do not want the things, our own are better."[4]

1. *The Popularity of "The English Use"*

Percy Dearmer (1867-1936) publicised these findings both in

---

[3] See Nan Dearmer, *The Life of Percy Dearmer*.
[4] *The Ornaments of the Rubric*, p. 62.

his immensely popular *Parson's Handbook*, which appeared in 1899, re-appeared in a revised and enlarged edition in 1903, and ran to a more profusely illustrated sixth edition in 1907, and in the ceremonial and furnishings of the Church of St. Mary the Virgin in Primrose Hill, London, the living of which he accepted in 1900. His red brick neo-Gothic church, which had been built in 1873, was entirely white-washed, so that the altar which now had riddel curtains and a dorsal stood out for all to see. Three silver lamps of Venetian workmanship were hung in the choir, and in 1914 a rood beam was installed across the chancel arch and a wooden *corona-lucis* was suspended from the rood. All representations of Christ were vested and crowned. The vestments were full and wide, and coloured "apparels" were attached to albs and amices to add to their interest. The ceremonial was elaborate but entirely faithful to the time of Edward VI. The sentimental melodies of Victorian hymn-tunes were abolished and plain-chant was introduced. After 1906 the congregation was introduced to the *English Hymnal*, of which Dearmer was editor-in-chief, and traditional English sacred poetry and melody became familiar.[5] Good music, good craftsmanship, and the beauty of the setting succeeded not only in filling the Church every Sunday, but in widespread interest and imitation. The result was Percy Dearmer turned the "English Use" into an ecclesiastical imperialism. His wife, Nan Dearmer, has not exaggerated in claiming that as a result of his influence the "English Altar" was recovered as the correct official practice of the Church of England and the choir habit of the clergy was restored, as well as the use of the "Lenten Array."[6] His work was forwarded by the Alcuin Club, which by 1912 had published twenty volumes of its "Collections" and almost a dozen "Tracts."

In 1916 Dearmer left Primrose Hill, but four years earlier he and a group of enthusiasts had founded the Warham Guild. This provided a centre in London where those interested in the "English Use" could find the ornaments recommended in the *Parson's Handbook* and be recommended to artists and craftsmen who worked in the sound English tradition. The Guild was assisted by the advice of liturgical and aesthetic experts such as F. E. Brightman, Walter Frere, F. C. Eeles, Geoffrey Lucas, Christopher Webb, and Martin Travers. Its influence was seen not only in parish

[5] Anson, *Fashions in Church Furnishings*, pp. 307-09.
[6] *Life of Percy Dearmer*, p. 115.

churches but in every English cathedral, and even in the churches of the Commonwealth. One of the most famous examples of such furnishings was the Thaxted parish church under Conrad Noel.

Influential as Dearmer's work was, it was not without its critics. His *Parson's Handbook* was successful because it appealed to many different temperaments and types of churchmanship. (The "English Altar" eventually influenced both Liberal and Evangelical Churchmen.) The *Parson's Handbook* had three major characteristics: it was legalistic, strongly nationalistic, and thoroughly antiquarian. At the same time it had a valid artistic approach which demanded good craftsmanship rather than shoddy mass-production. Its legalism strengthened the Anglo-Catholic party because its loyalty was no longer felt to be under suspicion, and there is no question that the stability, growth, and acceptance of Anglo-Catholicism is one of the most significant elements in the twentieth century Anglican Church. At the same time "Dearmer-titis" stiffly turned rubrics into laws, and seemed to believe in the plenary inspiration of the Edwardine settlement. Moreover, its nationalism was insecurely founded, for it failed to recognize that the liturgical and ceremonial customs of England in the reign of King Edward VI, far from being distinctively English, hardly varied from the liturgical and ceremonial customs then current in Italy, Spain, and France. Even more serious was the antiquarianism, for this was a freezing of the current of worship which must change if a Church is to be alive to the art and customs of its own century. As Dom Anselm Hughes remarks, it soon came to be known as "British Museum" religion, "for its insularity in place was coupled with an insularity in time, which was seeking to stereotype all material details by the patterns of the sixteenth century or earlier."[7] Moreover, these liturgical views can hardly have been based on a consistent theological foundation, for Dearmer's restless energy was soon transferring itself to Christian Socialism, Faith Healing, and the Ministry of Women.

2. *The Back to Baroque Movement*

The first challenge to the "English Use" of Dearmer and the Alcuin Club came with the foundation by the extreme Anglo-Catholics of the Society of SS. Peter and Paul. This was another indication of the liturgical chaos in the Anglican Church. On

---

[7] *The Rivers of the Flood, A Personal Account of the Catholic Revival in England in the Twentieth Century*, p. 50.

February 24, 1911, a number of Anglican papalists who were convinced that, but for the freezing effect of Protestantism, English ceremonial would have developed as in the Roman Catholic Church on the continent of Europe, determined to form a society to provide an alternative to the arrested development of the "English Use." A well-to-do layman, Samuel Gurney, was the secretary of the Society of SS. Peter and Paul, which included the brothers Ronald and Wilfrid Knox, N. P. Williams, Cyril Howell, and the Duke of Argyll. Their hope was that their work in familiarising Englishmen with the Catholic liturgical developments on the European continent would ultimately lead to corporate reunion with the Catholic Churches of Eastern and Western Christendom. To this end they were committed not only to introducing Roman Catholic ceremonial to counteract "British Museum" Religion, but also to introducing such Roman devotions as Benediction and the Rosary.

The outward indications of this revolutionary attitude were to be seen in the purchase for their churches of monstrances, thuribles, tabernacles, crucifixes, statues, chalices, and fiddle-back vestments of the Baroque and Rococo styles. As Dearmer started the fashion for Edwardian neo-Gothic, so the extreme Anglo-Catholics popularized the fashion for the theatrical style of the Counter-Reformation, and turned their churches into Spanish or Italian outposts of Ultramontanism. The new fashion was excellently illustrated in the drawings of Martin Travers in *Pictures of the English Liturgy—Low Mass*, exhibiting an Italianate priest celebrating Mass at a Baroque altar, assisted by a server wearing a lace-edged cotta. A companion volume by the same author, entitled *The Celebration of High Mass* was even more extreme, for each illustration depicted a different Baroque or Rococo altar. One, indeed, displayed High Mass with a monstrance enthroned beneath a canopy supported by ample *putti*. For those of undeviating tendencies toward Rome an authoritative volume appeared in Adrian Fortescue's *Ceremonies of the Roman Rite Described*, which provided an official guide following the Decrees of the Sacred Congregation of Rites.

The most enthusiastic renovator of Anglican churches in a Baroque or Rococo manner was Martin Travers the architect. His first striking example of renovation was to be seen in the changes he effected in the Butterfield Church of St. Augustine, Queen's Gate, London, in 1928. He succeeded in eliminating almost every trace of the Gothic Revival in this edifice. The polychromatic brick-work, so characteristic of Butterfield, disappeared under a deluge of white-wash. A huge Baroque gilt *retablo* practically enveloped the East wall. The lowest central panel included a crucifix suspended over a tabernacle; on the panel above a dove floated in a shaft of golden rays; and on the uppermost panel was the emblem of the sacred heart. The sides of this three-tiered altar fairly writhed with scrolls, and enough carved fruit and flowers to have provided a harvest festival of the British Empire. In this, it was not to be compared with the more delicate and lighter Baroque work of his master, Ninian Comper, who, incidentally, could combine Baroque and Gothic by a beauty of inclusion unknown to Travers. His happiest work, perhaps, was accomplished in the renovation of the Palladian church of St. Magnus the Martyr, Lower Thames Street, London, where seventeenth century Baroque was most appropriately added to a seventeenth century church. The refurbishing is fittingly commemorated by T. S. Eliot as the church

> where the walls
> Of Magnus Martyr hold
> Inexplicable splendour of Ionian white and gold.[8]

In this single instance, and it is a notable claim, Travers may be said to have improved upon the original architect, who was none other than Sir Christopher Wren.[9]

Perhaps the extreme to which this imitation and even exaggeration of the Baroque and Rococo styles went is provided by the Holy House, Walsingham. Peter Anson's two drawings admirably point up the contrast between the simple "English Altar" of the Roman Catholic shrine, and the cluttered Baroque of the Anglican Holy House, which is a pure imitation of the *Santa Casa* of Loreto.[10] The Anglican shrine has no less than fifteen altars in honour of the mysteries of the Rosary. It has a plethora of votive candles, *ex voto* tablets and other offerings of grateful visitors, while the atmosphere is saturated with stale incense and the thick fumes of the pendant oil lamps. The crowned and richly costumed Virgin has pride of place on the lace-draped altar. Indeed, as Anson remarks, "the Reformation might never have taken place."[11] The

---

[8] *The Waste Land*, lines 263-65.
[9] Other interesting examples of Travers' work are to be found in St. Matthew's, Westminster; Compton Beauchamp Church, Berkshire; and the Church of the Good Shepherd, Carshalton, Surrey (1930).
[10] These drawings will be found on pp. 325 and 326 of Anson's *Fashions in Church Furnishings*.
[11] *Ibid.*, p. 326.

contrast between the Anglican and Roman shrines at Walsingham show how the wheels of fashion had come full circle, for the Roman Catholics had returned to the Gothic simplicity of Edward VI and the Anglican papalists had almost out-Romanized Rome with their Baroque theatricality. We could hardly have a more impressive testimony of the chaos of ceremonial variations and furnishings in the Anglican Church.

3. *Preparation for Prayer Book Revision*

It was precisely the chaos in Anglicanism, from the left to the right wings, which made a revision of the Prayer Book essential. Without a revision, it was impossible to have unity in the Church of England, for the Prayer Book is the very nexus of Anglican unity. Moreover, without agreed rubrics, it would be impossible for the bishops to discipline the clergy; for in the absence of a ceremonial norm deviations could not be condemned as such. These, indeed, were the conclusions that the *Report of the Royal Commission on Ecclesiastical Discipline* had arrived at in 1906. It had established that there were ten practices current in the Church of England which were illegal and "clearly inconsistent with the teaching of the Church of England as declared in the Prayer Book."

Some were: the interpolation of prayers and ceremonies belonging to the Canon of the Mass, the adoration of the Reserved Sacrament, Corpus Christi processions with the Sacrament, Benediction with the Sacrament, and the observation of the festivals of the Assumption of the Blessed Virgin Mary and of the Sacred Heart. The three volumes of the same report provided ocular evidence of the vast variety of liturgical practices in England. Eucharistic vestments were worn in 113 churches in the Diocese of London and in thirty-seven churches in the Diocese of Rochester. About thirty London churches used incense. St. Columba's, Haggerston, and St. Cuthbert's, Philbeach Gardens (both in the London Diocese), had "public reservation" of the Sacrament, but many churches had altar tabernacles, whether for decoration or use was uncertain. Some churches openly heard confessions, but few had confessional boxes. Statues, almost always of the Madonna, were fairly frequently seen. Many Anglo-Catholic churches displayed the Stations of the Cross. Such was the wide variety, and it may be presumed that where there were illegal ornaments, illegal devotions were also practised.

The Royal Commission came to two principal conclusions of great importance:

"First, the law of public worship in the Church of England is too narrow for the religious life of the present generation. It needlessly condemns much which a great section of Church people, including many of her most devoted members, value; and modern thought and feeling are characterized by a care for ceremonial, a sense of dignity in worship, and an appreciation of the continuity of the Church, which were not similarly felt when the law took its present shape. In an age which has witnessed an extraordinary revival of spiritual life and activity, the Church has had to work under regulations fitted for a different condition of things, without that power of self-adjustment which is inherent in the conception of a living Church. . . .

"Secondly, the machinery for discipline has broken down. The means of enforcing the law in the Ecclesiastical Courts, even on matters which touch the Church's faith and teaching, are defective and in some respects unsuitable. . . ."[12]

This provided the impetus for the long, and as it turned out unsuccessful, process of revising a Prayer Book which had not been changed since 1661. At the outset it was thought that a simple liberalizing of the rubrics was all that would be necessary. The theory was that if the maximum liberty were given there would be no lawbreakers. However, the outbreak of World War I changed the situation in several ways. For one thing, the exigencies of chaplains made it a common practice to reserve the Sacrament. For another, the chaplains themselves became increasingly convinced that the unrevised Book of Common Prayer failed to speak to the needs of the men in khaki to whom they ministered in worship. In particular, the Orders for Morning and Evening Prayer were felt to be too penitential in their approach to worship, the prolix exhortations too dull, and many of the prayers out of touch with the practical needs of their charges. Furthermore, the fellowship of the chaplains had led to the ecumenical interchange of ideas, and many of them admired the American Prayer Book and the Scottish Book of Common Order for their relation of prayers to twentieth century conditions. For these reasons they returned from the Army eager for a more radical revision. Then, again, the *Enabling Act* had given the Church of England in its Church Assembly self-government, subject only to the overriding powers

12 Cited by Alec R. Vidler, *The Church in an Age of Revolution*, p. 163.

of Parliament, and it was felt, particularly by the House of Laity, that Prayer Book revision was a most appropriate subject for discussion by the Assembly.

Furthermore, the two Archbishops had set up Five Committees of Inquiry to feel the pulse of the Church in wartime, and one of these published its report in 1918 under the title, *The Worship of the Church*. This furthered the demand for a thorough reconsideration of worship and for revision of the Prayer Book. The Report began by noting a minatory fact that the instinct for worship had been gravely weakened among the English people. Its causes included the mobility created by the industrial revolution, and the loss of any sense of obligation to attend Divine worship. The tradition of personal prayer and of family prayer was gravely diminished and hence public worship was felt to be less relevant. The Report noted "the spread of materialistic ideals, the overpressure of industrial life, the weakening of home life in general, the denominational differences, and consequent on all these, a deepened reticence about all religious matters."[13]

Further causes of the decline in worship were the lack of any common basis for religious instruction in the national schools, and the failure to bring the laity into the planning and sharing of worship. The Committee of Inquiry emphasized how antagonistic an industrial civilization was to the very values that worship sought to conserve. "The persistent pressure of its competitive processes generated in the people a spirit and temper alien from the very nature of the Church's worship, which, in its turn, divorced from the bitter realities of the people's lives, began to assume in their eyes an artificial character."[14] Aggressive individualism and class warfare militated against the very idea of fellowship in the Body of Christ which is central to worship, and encouraged a rapacity which was in extreme opposition to the simplicity and sacrifice engendered by worship. The same industrialism had alienated the poor from the Church, and hence "the idea of the Church as an institution governed by and administered for comparatively small circles of the well-to-do classes steadily took root in the mind of the people. . . ."[15] This was, indeed, a recognition on the part of the Church of England that the "Social Gospel" was having some impact, not to mention the influence of

[13] *The Worship of the Church, Being the Report of the Archbishops' Second Committee of Inquiry* (London, 1918—"Published for the National Mission by the S.P.C.K."), pp. 6-7.
[14] *Ibid.*, p. 13.　　　　　　　　　[15] *Ibid.*, p. 14.

the strong Christian Socialism of Charles Gore and his Anglo-Catholic supporters.

But this was far more than a party manifesto: the importance of this Report was precisely that its all-party diagnosis of the situation was so probing. The Committee believed, as will be seen, that Prayer Book revision was essential, but they were under no illusions that this was the nostrum that would bring the people flocking back into the Churches. They would, in fact, probably have agreed with Neville Figgis, who told a Cambridge audience in 1909: "In the last generation men were unable to take Jesus as Lord, and were sad. Now they are choosing other masters, and are glad."[16] This is what made the need for relevance in worship and preaching so obligatory, and why the provisions of an essentially sixteenth century Prayer Book could not satisfy the revolutionary situation of the war-racked twentieth century Church.

The Report then proceeded to consider the Prayer Book provisions for worship in detail. The three chaplains on the Committee of Inquiry reported that the men in the armed services had shown a great appreciation for Holy Communion, whereas the rest of the Committee were disturbed to notice that in the parish churches attendance at Matins and Evensong had come to drive the Holy Communion to the position of an exceptional service for committed Christians.

For two reasons this was felt to be a serious misfortune. "In the first place, the Sacrament of the Lord's Supper is definitely ordained by Christ, and has therefore a greater claim on the observance of Christians than any other service that can be devised. Secondly, there seems to be no doubt that the Communion Service makes less demand for intellectual effort and satisfies more directly the spiritual impulses than such services as Morning and Evening Prayer."[17] In the second reason given, it was clear that all the teaching of Inge, von Hügel, and Evelyn Underhill on the primacy of the mystical approach to God had not been wasted. The Committee felt that two difficulties stood in the way of making Holy Communion central: Morning Prayer already occupied the best time for Communion, and the emphasis on fasting before Communion made it impossible to hold it at night. They went on record as favouring a relaxing of the fasting requirement and

16 *The Gospel and Human Need*, p. 8, cited in Roger Lloyd, *The Church of England in the Twentieth Century*, Vol. I, 1900-1918, p. 49.
17 *The Worship of the Church*, p. 15.

therefore of celebrating evening Communions in town parish churches, and they particularly praised the ideal of corporate Communions held at 8 or 9.30 A.M. The preference for the latter hour was prophetic, though they could not have foreseen how exceedingly popular "Parish Communion" about the morning hour of nine was to become two decades later.

There was considerable dissatisfaction with the practice of using Morning Prayer, the Litany, and the Communion Service successively, as being too lengthy and requiring too much reduplication. There was also a sense that the Occasional Offices were too archaic in their phrasing and too lengthy in their exhortations for modern taste, and so might alienate the many outsiders who first attended a church service at a marriage or a burial.

The most radical criticism, however, came from the three serving chaplains who knew how great was the lost ground that had to be recovered. Among them was Neville Talbot, later to become the much loved and unconventional Bishop of Pretoria, who used to introduce himself with a chanted jingle, "I'm the servant of the Lord with my Bible and my Ford!" In a separate appendix they pleaded for "bold and wide experiment," and made no bones about the fact that in their experience the Prayer Book services were "uninstructive and misleading to some, irritating and alienating to others." In their view this was because modern man did not believe in the plenary inspiration of the Scriptures, as did the original compilers of the Book of Common Prayer. They believed the Prayer Book services tended "to authorize and perpetuate a view of Scripture (and of the Christian religion) which is untrue and offensive to any lively conscience and intelligence." Then the ironic addition is made: "No doubt Dean Paget and Dr. Bright on either side of Christ Church choir could make intelligent allowance about, and find mystical meanings in, any part of the lectionary and psalter. Not so the vast majority of people."[18]

It was not all criticism that they offered, but also appreciation and constructive alternatives. Of Holy Communion they wrote: "We think all chaplains will return home anxious to make this service the main, corporate, family, congregational act of worship and fellowship."[19] Moreover, they greatly preferred the Communion Office of the Episcopal Church of Scotland to the English Order for its fulness and plainness of meaning. They strongly recommended W. H. Frere's simplification of Morning Prayer in his

18 *Ibid.*, p. 34.   19 *Ibid.*, p. 35.

Principles of Liturgical Reform as avoiding the repetition of four Lord's Prayers, two Confessions and Absolutions, two Creeds, and four Prayers for the King. They also advised shorter and simpler exhortations, a revised Psalter with the retranslation of obscure passages, the use of Bidding prayers, and the provision of prayers on such topics as the Kingdom of God, Missions, Labour, and Parliament. They were particularly anxious to make services more congregational in character by the avoiding of intonation and the introduction of more hymns, for "In hymns there is a really living and popular interest in British Christianity."[20] They wickedly added: "We should like to see experiments made in the suppression of choirs."[21]

They were, however, most anxious to see the provision of new Acts of Devotion of a more popular kind than the Book of Common Prayer provides. They believed that the trouble with most forms and litanies put out by authority is that they solely emphasize petition (rather than meditation, or adoration), lack the sense of the Christian brotherhood cutting away all barriers of class or nationality, omit the context of worship in the Communion of Saints, and have no interweaving of the devotions with the life of Christ. Satisfactory new Acts of Devotion must be provided in which "for introduction to and maintenance in the presence of God, the picture of Christ (as the Son revealing the Father) must be brought before the mind, and interwoven with the whole devotion, which should proceed from the known life and known desires of Christ and concentrate the mind thereon."[22] They also added the caution that silence should be used to grasp and realize the presence and picture of God.

Second only to this primary stress Godward was the need for an emphasis on fellowship, and appropriately fellowship will be meaningful when the Act of Devotion is shared by all. Also, protesting against the overwhelming immanentalism of their time, they recommended that "services and acts of devotion should end with an act of dedication in which all join—should end on a note of faith rather than of need."[23] Their testimony was not less impressive because they had looked beyond the liturgical confines of the Church of England, and recognized "the worth of the Book of Common Order (Scottish Presbyterian) as a source of prayer which connects worship with 'the daily round,'" and they recom-

[20] *Ibid.*, p. 36. [21] *Ibid.*, p. 37. [22] *Ibid.*, p. 38.
[23] *Ibid.*, p. 39.

mended the Book of Common Worship of the USA for "the wealth of prayer for all occasions" which it contained.[24]

The Committee of Inquiry also considered the need for improvements in Church Music and they were greatly helped by the presence of Dr. Walford Davies on the Committee. Their recommendations in the matter of preaching were, however, insufficiently radical. They strongly criticized the frequent aberrations of Anglican delivery: inaudibility, dullness, long and unintelligible pauses; but omitted that artificiality of tone which Spurgeon characterized as "steeple-in-the-throat grandeur." They suggested that the place of the sermon in the service might be varied to provide interest. They urged that a ten to fifteen minute sermon might "fix and give precision to the lesson of the particular service on any given day."[25]

They approached the real problem and then ran away from it, by suggesting that because the faith of Christ provides a system of thought as well as a rule of life special preaching services should be held (so far so good), but that they should be given in large towns at special seasons in a series. The need for sustained Biblical exegesis for the systematic presentation of the major Christian doctrines in an articulated way, and for an application of Christian ethics to the problems and temptations of the day was no sooner glimpsed by the Committee than glossed over. It is still the most desperate need of the Church of England, as the need for a richer devotional and sacramental life is clamant in the English Free Churches.

However, the deep diagnosis of the weakening of the instinct for worship in this Report and its determination to make Prayer Book revision more relevant to the times is a proof that the revision could not be much longer delayed. If only that national and ecclesiastical unity which had prevailed in time of war had been carried over into the years of peace, or if the Prayer Book revision had been concluded within a year after the Armistice, then Parliament might have recognized this and approved a fairly unanimous revision. One of the effects of the prolonged delay was that it gave more than ample opportunity for bitter factionalism to arise again. It was ultimately the vociferous disagreement of a minority of the Anglo-Catholics and a minority of the Evangelicals that gave Parliament the erroneous impression that the Revised Prayer Book could never be the bond of liturgical concord.

In fairness to the Bishops, however, who come in for consider-

[24] *Ibid.*, p. 38.   [25] *Ibid.*, p. 21.

able criticism later, it must be acknowledged that a serious attempt was made to push through a revision more rapidly. They were seriously proposing consideration of an Alternative Order of Holy Communion in 1918, and had reached agreement on all other matters for revision. They had therefore recommended the Archbishops to call a special conference to deal with this single issue, but the Archbishops were immediately confronted with a Memorial signed by nine Bishops, 3,000 clergy, and 100,000 laymen protesting against any changes in the Communion Service.[26] The Conference did, however, find a compromise Consecration Prayer which was proposed by Dr. Drury, the Evangelical Bishop, and by Dr. Frere, the Anglo-Catholic Bishop. This was to read, immediately after the Words of Institution:

"Wherefore, O Father, we thy humble servants, having in remembrance before Thee the precious death of thy dear Son, his mighty resurrection and glorious ascension, looking also for his coming again, do render unto Thee most hearty thanks for the innumerable benefits which he hath procured unto us; And we pray Thee of thine almighty goodness to send upon us and upon these thy gifts thy holy and blessed Spirit, who is the Sanctifier and the Giver of Life, to whom with Thee and thy Son Jesus Christ be ascribed by every creature in earth and heaven all blessing, honour, glory and power, now henceforth and for evermore. Amen."[27]

The Canterbury Convocation accepted the recommendations on February 11, 1920, although Archbishop Davidson himself would have preferred to have no alternative service. The York Convocation rejected only the Alternative Order for Holy Communion, but accepted all other proposals for revision. The approved proposals were then submitted for the consideration of the Church Assembly (which had come into being through the *Enabling Act* of 1919) and there most of them were ratified. The lay committee, however, was acutely divided on the proposals concerning Holy Communion and Reservation. Five Evangelicals printed a Note objecting to Reservation, and Athelstan Riley printed a dissenting Note questioning features of the Alternative Order for Holy Communion. Partisanship once again became rife, as the dissentients drummed up support for their followers. In October, 1922, the House of Bishops introduced the *Revised Prayer Book (Permissive Use)*

26 G. K. A. Bell, *Randall Davidson, Archbishop of Canterbury*, p. 1326.
27 Cited *ibid.*, footnote 3 on pp. 1326-27.

Measure into the Assembly, attaching the measure to the unaltered Proposals of the Committee. General approval was given to the Proposals in all three Houses, sitting separately, with three dissentients in the House of Bishops. From April, 1923, for the next two years the Houses of Clergy and Laity, sitting separately, went steadily through the herculean task of revision. From the moment that their Report was published, the revisers were deluged with a torrent of rival sets of proposals for further revision. It became clear that this was only adding fuel to the flames of party difference.[28]

At this point in history there appeared three major proposals for revision which were known, from the colours of their bindings, as the Green, the Grey, and the Orange Books. The Green Book was the production of the English Church Union, a vigorously and uncompromisingly Anglo-Catholic group led by Dr. Darwell Stone and Dr. B. J. Kidd, which would have liked an alternative for Holy Communion more closely resembling the traditional Western Rite. N. P. Williams, a founding member of the Society of SS. Peter and Paul, and a future Professor of Divinity at Oxford, was the secretary. In fact, Stone and his supporters were complicating the issue by proposing an additional alternative Order for Holy Communion.[29] The Grey Book was the provision of alternative services and prayers from the central and liberal standpoint and contained a preface by Dr. William Temple, then Bishop of Manchester. The Orange Book was a collection of scholarly pamphlets of the moderate Anglo-Catholics of the Alcuin Club who stood for the English type of Catholicism. By October, 1925, when the House of Bishops began their task of revision, the Archbishop stated that he had received more than eight hundred different memorials on the subject, including a plea for no change from Cambridge University, a petition to the same effect organized by Bishop Knox with over 305,000 signatures, and a statement signed by nine diocesan Bishops opposing any change in the Order of Holy Communion and any alternative service.[30] The revision stage began on October 25, 1925, and sittings were held for fifty full days in Lambeth Palace between then and 1927. From the outset the Bishops of Norwich, Birmingham, and Worcester were known to be in opposition to the entire work.

[28] For this paragraph I have relied on the summary of events in Bell, *ibid.*, pp. 1327-29.

[29] See Chap. VI of F. L. Cross, *Darwell Stone, Churchman and Counsellor.*

[30] Bell, *Randall Davidson . . .* , p. 1329.

The diversity of convictions, the multiplicity of varying proposals, the hardening of party lines, and the canvassing of divergent views in the press and in the local communities, as also the strong conservative opposition to any change which the memorialists had indicated, and the lukewarmness of the Archbishop, presaged a stormy passage for the Ark of the Church of England bearing the Prayer Book Measure through the narrow straits of Parliament. Moreover, even the Church Assembly did not provide that overwhelming vote of confidence in the Revised Prayer Book which might have been expected and which would, perhaps, have impressed Parliament with the firm determination of the Church of England to put its own liturgical house in order. Furthermore, Reservation became an acute problem towards the end of the negotiations. "An Alternative Order for the Communion of the Sick" had attempted to meet the need for those who argued for the necessity of the reserved Sacrament for the sick, while safeguarding it from any attempt at Exposition of the Sacrament leading to the adoration of the consecrated elements. In fact, it satisfied neither the Evangelicals who were dead against reservation in any form and opposed any Alternative Order of Holy Communion, and it alienated the extreme Anglo-Catholics who were entirely opposed to any limitations on Reservation, and the attempt to exclude Tridentine devotions. They, too, were opposed to the Alternative Order of Holy Communion because they regarded the *epiklesis*, or invocation of the Holy Spirit on the elements and on the congregation in the Prayer of Consecration, as an Eastern borrowing and a reversal of the Western tradition of the previous fourteen hundred years. The Evangelicals, led by Sir William Joynson-Hicks, then the Home Secretary, demanded a positive assurance from the Archbishop as to how rigorously the Bishops would treat any clergy who disobeyed the rubrics of the new Revised Prayer Book, supposing it were to become law. The Archbishop would give no other assurance than that he supposed it would work out well, and this sanguine vagueness proved unsatisfactory.

The final debate in the Church Assembly took place on July 5 and 6, 1927, on the measure authorizing the optional use of the Deposited Book. (It should be understood that the 1661 Prayer Book was not superseded and that the Deposited Book was a *composite* Book containing the whole of the existing Book of Common Prayer with the proposed additions and deviations.) No sooner had the measure been moved than it was strongly attacked from the extreme Anglo-Catholic quarter by Dr. Darwell Stone, who alleged that 700 Anglo-Catholic priests were of the same mind as he, in unshakable opposition. From the opposite quarter of the Protestant party, Sir William Joynson-Hicks, Sir Thomas Inskip, and the Bishop of Norwich attacked the measure for the Evangelicals. The final vote was not likely to convince Parliament that the Church Assembly was solidly behind the measure, for the minorities were large enough in each House to presage trouble in enforcing the disciplining of the clergy by the Bishops. The House of Bishops voted 34 for the measure and 4 against it. The House of Clergy voted 253 for and 37 against. The House of Laity voted 230 for and 92 against. In all three Houses 517 positive votes were cast and a formidable 133 negative votes. Thus the minority represented 25 per cent of the opinion.[31] If the ecclesiastical horizon was clouded, the political weather would be tempestuous.

4. *The Revised Prayer Book before Parliament*

The story of the Prayer Book Measure before Parliament is shortly and sadly told, but this blow to the prestige of the Church of England, this frustration of the hopes of liturgical improvement, of a deepened spirituality, and of a closing of the party ranks, was so shattering that opinions differ very greatly as to why it happened and how it might have been averted, and even what it meant for the future of the Church of England. Some objectivity may be reached by the presentation of different viewpoints on this major liturgical controversy of the century.

At the beginning all looked well. The Revised Prayer Book Measure was debated for three days by the House of Lords, beginning on December 12, 1927, and it was approved by 241 votes to 88. The Archbishop of Canterbury (Dr. Randall Davidson) was the mover, who argued that the measure expressed "a united wish officially given by a united Church," representatively arrived at through the Church Assembly, and that it would facilitate the work of the Bishops and "would mean the liberation of the Church from the great mass of those petty strifes which have troubled us up and down the country in the past."[32] He was not conscious of any departure from the Reformed tradition of the Church of England in these proposals, and he reminded the House that the Royal Commission of 1906 had insisted that the law of public worship was too narrow for the religious life of the present generation.

[31] Bell, *ibid.*, pp. 1136ff.   [32] *Ibid.*, p. 1345.

On December 15, 1927, the Measure was considered by the House of Commons. The mover, W. C. Bridgeman, a former First Lord of the Admiralty, was discomposed by interruptions and made the unfortunate concession: "I can imagine those who dislike the Church of England may wish to reject this measure."[33] The Home Secretary, Sir William Joynson-Hicks, a leader of the Low Churchmen, took exception to the Bill as yielding to the Romanising tendencies of the Anglo-Catholics, and admitted (after recalling the Archbishop's written promises to persuade the Bishops to curb illegalities in worship which were not kept) that he found it impossible to trust the Bishops. The most flamboyant speech was that of Mr. Rosslyn Mitchell of Paisley, an ultra-Protestant declamation on the threadbare theme of "No Popery." A quiet but effective speech against the measure was made by Sir John Simon. The Measure was defeated by 238 votes to 205. G. K. A. Bell's laconic comment is: "In a single hectic night the House of Commons had apparently destroyed the work of more than twenty years."[34]

This left the Church in a condition of great confusion. It was thought by the bolder spirits that the chains of Erastian subservience to the State must be broken. In this case their policy would be for the Church to adopt the use of the Deposited Book and let the State terminate the favoured position of the Church if it so desired. At least the Church would then be free to rule its own house as it thought best. The Bishops, however, adopted a temporizing course. If all else failed, then the Church might have to think of asserting its spiritual authority and independence, but for the present they could only assume that Parliament had misunderstood their intentions. They therefore recommended that after some modifications in the measure were made to accommodate Parliament's Protestant fears, the measure should be re-introduced. These were duly prepared.

They consisted chiefly of four changes. The Prayer for the Sovereign, after the third collect in Morning and Evening Prayer, was made compulsory in all circumstances. The statement relating to Fasting Communion was inserted among the Communion Office rubrics. The rules proposed for the regulation of Reservation in the Communion of the Sick were printed in full. Also, the Declaration on Kneeling (the Black Rubric, denying the doctrine of transubstantiation) was reprinted at the end of the Alternative Com-

[33] *Ibid.*   [34] *Ibid.*, p. 1347.

munion Office. In fact, these changes failed to remove Protestant suspicions, and succeeded only in further alienating the Anglo-Catholic wing. This was amply demonstrated by the voting in the Church Assembly, where on March 28 and 29, 1928, 396 votes were cast for the amended Measure and 153 against it.[35] Thus the minority vote had increased from 25 to 38 per cent within a year.

If the Church Assembly's increasing minority demonstrated that it was unconvinced by the changes, it was unlikely that a suspicious House of Commons would be convinced. On June 13, 1928, the measure was re-introduced into the House of Commons and defeated by 266 votes to 220.

The Bishops had failed in their purpose to persuade Parliament to accept their amended proposals. The question then was, whether they would have the courage to recommend the disestablishment of the Church for the sake of the freedom of the Church, a possibility they had hinted at earlier? In fact they pursued a compromising policy again, desiring the advantages of the State connection, without its limitations. They proposed to have their cake and eat it. That is, they issued a statement that the Church must retain its inalienable right to formulate its faith and forms of worship, and they later declared that in administering their dioceses in the present emergency they would allow such deviations from the 1661 Prayer Book as were covered in the 1928 proposals. They were therefore quietly defying Parliament while retaining the State connection.

Perhaps the most objective account of the reasons for the failure of the Prayer Book Measure to gain Parliamentary assent is that of Bishop G. K. A. Bell.[36] He places first in the list the fear of Rome, "the deep Protestantism of the English people," which he considered irrational. Bishop Henson concurred, averring that "Englishmen are not inevitably episcopalian as the Scots are inevitably presbyterian and the Irish inevitably papists, but *au fond* they are Erastian, Bibliolatrous, and always fiercely anti-Papal."[37]

The second cause for failure, as Bishop Bell sees it, was the disunity among the Churchmen. This was undeniably an important factor. Bell felt that the real issue was whether the Low Churchmen were willing to give a sure place in the Church to such a vital religious movement as Anglo-Catholicism undoubtedly was, or

[35] *Crockford Prefaces. The Editor Looks Back*, pp. 79f.
[36] *Randall Davidson . . .*, p. 1354.
[37] *Retrospect of an Unimportant Life, 1920-1939*, Vol. II, p. 153.

whether they wished to drive it out of the Anglican Church as the Methodists had been ejected in the eighteenth century? Henson, too, was critical of the Evangelicals, but he reserved his keenest irony for the fervent Presbyterian, Rosslyn Mitchell. Of that speech which was commonly believed to have swayed the House of Commons, Hensley Henson wrote: "It is, perhaps, rather difficult to understand the process of reasoning by which he was led to engage in the effort to Erastianize an alien church, but the logic of fanaticism is quite unfathomable."[38] While recognizing the deep party divisions in the Church as partly responsible for the debacle, Henson also saw that a great gap divided the learned liturgiologists from the clergy and even more from the laity. Moreover, the liturgiologists were divided among themselves, some desiring a return to the pre-Reformation tradition in the West, others arguing for the Eastern Liturgies as patterns for revision. There is, however, no question that the hardening of extreme Anglo-Catholic and extreme Evangelical opposition to the revised Prayer Book was a major contributory factor to the Parliamentary rejection, especially as they were active lobbyists.

Certainly, also, the lack of real interest in the project on the part of Archbishop Davidson was a significant factor in the defeat. This is a judgment in which Bell and Henson concur. Henson averred that "the Archbishop's heart was not in the work, and, while his influence restrained friction in the discussions at Lambeth, his counsel did little to direct them."[39] Further than this, his failure to provide definite pledges to restrain clerical illegality, if the Prayer Book Measure were to be passed, definitely weakened the cause. Henson believed that the vote of the House of Commons might fairly be described as "*a vote of censure on the Bishops,*" representing the exasperation against the law-breaking clergy, "which has been accumulating all over the country for many years, and has at length found an opportunity of expression, and a Cabinet Minister [Joynson-Hicks] to express it."[40] In his ruthlessly honest fashion Henson stated that the immediate reasons were to be found in "the foolish language of the Bishop of London, the ceremonial absurdities of the Bishop of St. Albans and the bitterness of feeling aroused by the Bishop of Birmingham," adding that the lobbying of Bishop Knox and the Bishop of Norwich inflamed the passion of the House of Commons.

[38] *Ibid.*, p. 166. [39] *Ibid.*, p. 162.
[40] *Ibid.*, p. 167. The italics are Henson's.

It is possible, however, that the inherent defect lay in the attempt to solve two different problems in the Prayer Book Measure, the problem of clerical disobedience and the problem of liturgical revision. Thus two incompatibles were combined: the concern for the spiritual renovation of the Church and the curbing of indiscipline, and the Prayer Book was conceived by the legislators as no more than a more effective stick with which to beat refractory clergy. Henson saw this clearly, arguing that although the restoration of discipline and the revision of formularies were valuable, yet they were irreconcilable, for the former was a popular demand, while the other was chiefly the concern of liturgical scholars.[41] Dr. A. R. Vidler agrees with him and adds: "It might be thought that the right way to revise forms of worship should be by way of experimentation in the parishes rather than as a deal between parties in the Church."[42]

5. The Effects of Parliament's Rejection of the Revised Prayer Book

There is still room for argument as to the long-term effects of the Parliamentary rejection of the Prayer Book Revision Measure, but what its immediate effects were is less controversial.

Unquestionably, as Henson had acknowledged at the time, there was a serious loss of respect for the Bishops. Their scholarship, their pastoral concern, and their administrative abilities were not in doubt, but their sincerity was. They seemed to be politicians rather than prophets, compromisers rather than men of conviction and conscience. Dean Matthews of St. Paul's writing twenty years after the events, felt compelled to criticize their insistence upon the *ius liturgicum* as a piecemeal defiance of Parliament and to "wonder whether calculated and surreptitious illegality is likely to serve spiritual ends."[43] Their policy was even more seriously criticized by Bernard Manning, a Congregationalist historian, in

[41] *Ibid.*, p. 152. But Henson gravely underestimates the desire for revision on the part of chaplains, as indicated in the Report of 1918, *The Worship of the Church*, who were not learned liturgiologists.

[42] *The Church in an Age of Revolution*, p. 167. This also became the official verdict of the Church of England, as may be seen from *Prayer Book Revision, A Memorandum of the Church of England Liturgical Commission.* Its conclusion is: "Finally, we would stress the fundamental lesson of 1927-8 that in all future work of Prayer Book revision *the sole purpose must be the provision of an enriched, worthier and more fitting vehicle for the worship of God in the Church of England.* There is, of course, a rightful place for discipline in the life of the Church, but we do not believe that Prayer Book revision should be taken with disciplinary ends in view."

[43] "The Nation and the Prayer Book," article in *Hibbert Journal*, Vol. XLVII (October 1949–July 1950), p. 22.

giving evidence before the Archbishops' Commission on the relations between Church and State of 1931. He asserted: "We do not believe that Christ's flock can both enjoy the advantages of an Erastian Establishment like Henry VIII's and Elizabeth's and Charles II's *and* ecclesiastical liberty."[44] The clear implication was that the Bishops were running with the hounds and the hare, or, to vary the metaphor, making the best of both worlds. Certainly, as a bench they hardly recovered the respect of the man in the street until Archbishop William Temple went from York to Canterbury in 1942 and proved that a prelate could also be a prophet. The feebleness of the Bishops in refusing either to accept the obedience that an Erastian situation of an Established Church required, or to break the manacles of the State connection and thus free the Church to be liturgical master in its own house, made many think of the advantages of disestablishment. Bishop Hensley Henson, who had been a strong supporter of the national character of the Church of England, was persuaded by the ignominy of the Church's defeat by Parliament to become a supporter of disestablishment.[45] Another loss was of the veneration in which the 1661 Rite had hitherto been held, so vigorous was the argument made for its need of supplementation.

Some, like Dr. Lowther Clarke, the editor of *Liturgy and Worship* (1932) evinced an ostrich outlook by maintaining that there were real advantages in the situation. He was gratified that there was widespread use of the new Occasional Offices and of the additional collects and occasional prayers. He was convinced that "the many years of discussion have not been wasted" because "the English people have received an education in liturgical matters which otherwise would have been impossible," and he showed an incredible chauvinism in believing that continental observers of the British situation envied Englishmen their controversies.[46] The sober and realistic note was sounded by Dr. Matthews, who conceded the need for a revision of the Prayer Book which would leave the main substance of Cranmer's work intact but indicate permissible variations, yet had to conclude: "It is unfortunately most unlikely that the Church will face the necessary task for a

[44] His evidence is reprinted in *Essays in Orthodox Dissent*, pp. 196ff. Manning added that "inasmuch as Establishment curbs Episcopacy I wish it well. That is not the word of a Christian but of an Englishman." For the views of another Free Churchman on the controversy, see P. Carnegie Simpson, *Recollections*, pp. 87-92. Dom Anselm Hughes (*The Rivers of the Flood*, p. 84) refers contemptuously to the "Lambeth Front."

[45] *Retrospect*, Vol. II, p. 151.   [46] *Liturgy and Worship*, pp. 790-91.

long time to come, because the memory of the disaster of 1928 stands in the way."[47] It was thirty-three years before Archbishop Ramsey felt able to recommend that the Church undertake the revision of the Prayer Book and with a clear understanding of the consequences. On June 27, 1961, in his enthronement sermon in Canterbury, he said:

"Here in England the Church and the State are linked together and we use that link in serving the community. But, in that service and in rendering to God the things that are God's, we ask for greater freedom in the ordering and in the urgent revising of our forms of worship. If the link of Church and State were broken, it would not be we who would ask for this freedom who broke it, but those—if there be such—who denied that freedom to us."[48]

Dr. Ramsey's promise to re-institute liturgical reform was implemented in May 1962 when a new Liturgical Commission, representative of all schools in the Church, was appointed. It was not possible to do that until three long decades had helped to bury the bitterness caused by 1928.

[47] *Hibbert Journal*, Vol. XLVII, p. 21.

[48] James B. Simpson, *The Hundredth Archbishop of Canterbury*, pp. 5-6. It is significant that Dr. Hewlett Johnson, the Dean of Canterbury, referred to an interview with Dr. Ramsey in which the latter said: "I want to make man aware of God" (*ibid.*, p. 247).

CHAPTER IX

ANGLICAN WORSHIP AFTER 1928

W HAT WAS happening in the interval between 1928 and the present day? Clearly, a considerable breathing-space was afforded the Church of England to reconsider the relations of Church and State. As we have seen, an Archbishop's Commission was devoted to this purpose in 1931. In more recent years a rigorous attempt has been made to revise the Canons of the Church of England, and it is hoped that this may solve the disciplinary problem, possibly independently of any revision of the liturgy. In the same breathing-space it seems that the folly of divisiveness on the part of parties within the Church of England had been acknowledged, and the improved ecumenical climate has made intra-denominational divisions seem the more scandalous. Certainly there is a charity and even a mutual understanding between the High and Low Church far deeper than existed in 1928. These are significant changes of the Spirit which cannot be tabulated in statistical fashion, but they are readily acknowledged by the clergy.

The next three and a half decades show a remarkable advance in the appreciation of the importance of worship in the life of the Church. This is evident in three notable ways. What was lost at home might be gained overseas, and on this basis, apparently, English liturgical experts had a considerable influence in revising the formularies of the Prayer Books of several other Provinces of the Anglican Communion; to that extent the fruits of twenty years of liturgical research and revision in England were not lost. In the second place, there grew a deeper theological understanding of the place of the Liturgy, and especially of the Eucharist, in the life of the Church, as was to be seen in successive treatises.[1] Thirdly, due in part to the growth of the Continental Liturgical Movement, in part to the revival of a vigorous Biblical theology, and in part to the stimulus of the Ecumenical Movement, there was an unprecedented desire to make unofficial, and largely local, liturgical experiments of great fertility and relevance, as well as originality. The result is that there probably has never been in Anglican history such widespread interest on the part of clergy

[1] See *supra* Chap. I for the consideration of the theory of worship.

and people, or such informed knowledge on worship, as has been shown in the last two decades. To these developments we now turn.

1. Anglican Liturgical Influence Overseas

This is a subject calling for far fuller treatment. Nonetheless, it is important at least to notice how strong a lead was given by the Anglican revisers to Episcopal Churches overseas. One of England's most distinguished liturgiologists, the Rev. Edward C. Ratcliff, collaborated with the Rev. J. C. Winslow in producing the rich *Bombay Liturgy*, which was first printed in *The Eucharist in India, A Plea for a distinctive Liturgy for the Indian Church*, with the approval of the Bishop of Bombay, Dr. E. J. Palmer, in 1920. In 1923 it was authorized for experimental use in the diocese of Bombay, after certain changes were made. In 1933 it was approved, subject to episcopal permission, for the whole Anglican Province in India. After further revision, it was in 1948 incorporated in *A Proposed Prayer Book* of 1951 as "A Liturgy for India." It is to appear in a Supplementary Book. Clearly, this Liturgy has had an important influence on the development of Christian worship in India and its influence is far from spent. The sustained elevation of its language, its profound sense of the Communion of Saints, the large element of adoration it contains, the frequent opportunities provided for responses in the richly varied intercessions, the beauty of the ceremonial, and the preservation of the indigenous atmosphere are its abiding qualities.[2] It is also significant that Dr. E. C. Ratcliff was consulted in the production of the ecumenical Liturgy of the Church of South India,[3] and that the latter includes as a direct borrowing from the Bombay Liturgy the widely admired response in the Prayer of Consecration: "Thy death, O Lord, we commemorate; Thy resurrection we confess; and Thy second coming we await."

This single example has been given prominence, but the pattern of the "Alternative Order for Holy Communion" in the 1928 Prayer Book has undoubtedly played its part in inducing the majority of liturgical revisers in the Anglican Communion to include in their Prayers of Consecration an *epiklesis*,[4] or petition

[2] The texts of the Bombay, the South African, the Indian, the Canadian, and other Anglican Liturgies recently revised are contained in *The Liturgy in English* edited by Bernard Wigan.
[3] See T. S. Garrett, *Worship in the Church of South India*. This former Anglican priest, now a presbyter of the Church of South India, has been the foremost expositor of its ecumenical worship.
[4] The 1928 form of the *epiklesis* was the following: "Hear us, O merciful

for the Holy Spirit's sanctification. It is at least significant that this Eastern importation by way of the Episcopal Church of Scotland, included in the English revision, is a feature of the Liturgies of South Africa[5] (1929), Ceylon (1933), Japan (1953), Canada (1959), the West Indies (1959), and India (1960).

Moreover, there is one other proof of the pervasive influence of Anglican liturgical thought and practice which is so commonplace that it may be taken for granted. That is, that when Congregationalists, Methodists, and Presbyterians have gone into an organic union with Anglicans, as in the Church of South India, or are considering such, as are the Methodists in England, or the three Free Churches in Australia, it is always assumed that the worship will take the form of the Book of Common Prayer. That is, after all, the only Reformed vernacular rite to have remained in continuous use since the mid-sixteenth century in Europe, and is not only an abiding link with the great Western Catholic tradition, but also owes something to the Eastern Church, and in its Psalter goes back to the Hebrew Temple and Synagogue. The denominations that have hitherto united with the Anglican Church have no comparable tradition of worship,[6] important as their theological and pastoral insights are.

2. *The Growing Importance of the Eucharist*

Several reasons may be given for the remarkable witness the Anglican Church has made to the centrality of the Sacrament of the Eucharist in the Christian life. In part it is included in Anglican loyalty to the Patristic tradition both credal and sacramental. It is also allied, at least in the twentieth century,[7] with the strongly incarnational theologies of Charles Gore, William Temple, Lionel Thornton, and O. C. Quick and others. Furthermore, Anglicans have always recognized that there is a deep mystery at its heart,

---

Father, we most humbly beseech Thee, and with thy Holy and Life-giving Spirit vouchsafe to bless and sanctify both us and these thy gifts of Bread and Wine, that they may be unto us the Body and Blood of thy Son, our Saviour Jesus Christ, to the end that we, receiving the same, may be strengthened and refreshed both in body and in soul."

[5] See Professor P. B. Hinchliff's *The South African Liturgy* and *The Anglican Church in South Africa*.

[6] See W. D. Maxwell's *The Book of Common Prayer and the Worship of Non-Anglican Churches*.

[7] Gore and company, however, inherited an incarnational tradition of the nineteenth century based on Maurice, Westcott, and Hort, not to mention the earlier heritage of the Caroline divines and of the Elizabethans, Jewel, and Hooker. Furthermore, the Incarnation was linked with the Atonement in R. C. Moberly's *Atonement and Personality*.

and few have presumed to dissect it (or, what is the same, to define it). They have been content to refer to the "Real Presence." Then, again, their churches have always given a dominant place to the altar, and, in many cases, suggested its numinous quality with altar rails and richly embellished reredos, or given glimpses of it through wrought-iron screens or below massive roods. Even in the newest churches, designed in the light of the Liturgical Movement, the altars may be simpler but they are central and dominating. In many other Communions the altar has been dominated by the pulpit. In Anglicanism this was only true in the eighteenth and rationalizing century, and the Oxford Movement and the Cambridge Ecclesiological Society[8] soon put an end to that. It is hardly to be wondered at, then, that the present century should have produced some admirable Anglican studies of Eucharistic theology. This is so because Holy Communion, for High Churchman and Low Churchman alike, has been the chief means of grace, the application of the benefits of Christ's Passion and Resurrection to His people, and the inspiration and solace of the Christian life.

The century's classic philosophical and theological study of the theme was O. C. Quick's *The Christian Sacraments* (1927) which warrants extended treatment, but this was by no means the only worthy study of its theme. Gore's *The Body of Christ* (1901) attempted to recover the Patristic understanding of the Eucharist for Anglicans, and F. C. N. Hicks emphasized the same understanding in *The Fulness of Sacrifice* (1930). Both stressed the heavenly offering of the great High Priest. A. L. Lilley's *The Sacraments* (1928) was a concise historical study which gave a sympathetic interpretation of the mediaeval understanding of the Sacraments. J. K. Mozley's *The Gospel Sacraments* (1933), while acknowledging its indebtedness to Quick's monograph, was very practical in its emphasis, and in its appreciation of P. T. Forsyth's great book *The Church and the Sacraments* paid a tribute as just as it was unusual from such a quarter on such a theme. Eric L. Mascall's *Corpus Christi, Essays on the Church and the Eucharist* (1953) was another High Church interpretation of its theme, but with singular independence of judgment. It criticized the psychological atomism of mediaeval and post-mediaeval interpretations of the Sacrament, and warned against building upon a sacramental theory of the universe or reducing the meaning of the

[8] See James F. White, *The Cambridge Movement: The Ecclesiologists and the Gothic Revival.*

Eucharist to its social implications.[9] It also introduced many readers to the strengths and weaknesses of recent Roman Catholic Eucharistic interpretations, and re-emphasized the need to recover the eschatological dimension of the Eucharist. J. A. T. Robinson produced a very lively interpretation of the relevance of Holy Communion in his lectures, *On Being the Church in the World* (1960) and a more popular account in *The Liturgy Coming to Life* (1961).

It is a significant fact of the period that the Evangelicals in the English Church made their own contributions. That redoubtable Protestant Bishop E. A. Knox of Manchester produced a characteristically provocative study, entitled *Sacrifice or Sacrament* (1914), a theme to which another Evangelical, A. M. Stibbs, returned in *Sacrament, Sacrifice and Eucharist* (1961). Yet Stibbs' volume, while denying that we should think "we can share in offering the sacrifice which He alone could and did offer,"[10] or that Christ's sacrifice is perpetually offered, moves beyond Memorialism and acknowledges that the benefits received are the remission of sins, the life-giving Spirit, and the invitation to share in the eternal feast.[11]

The great Biblical fidelity and historical understanding of the Evangelical school is, however, more representatively expressed in two other volumes. The one is *The Evangelical Doctrine of Holy Communion*, edited by A. J. Macdonald, with a valuable chapter by its editor; it also includes a penetrating essay on "Anglican Eucharistic Theology Today" by V. F. Storrs, in which he asserts that "In the Evangelical wing of the Church a new feeling for sacramentalism is arising,"[12] and claims that the trend is towards dynamic receptionism and away from memorialism. The other important volume is J. E. L. Oulton's *Holy Communion and Holy Spirit, A Study in Doctrinal Relationship* (1951). This is a most careful exploration of the relationship between these two doctrines, in a detailed New Testament study with illustrative references to the doctrinal exposition and liturgical practice of the Early Church. It criticizes Low Church Memorialism as being "merely self-edification: it offers no grace, it contains no Gospel,"[13] it also criticizes High Church beliefs on the Latin model in the efficacy of a consecratory formula, as being further from the New Testament than the Eastern Church's preference for an *epiklesis*. But even here Oulton is critical of liturgies which invoke the Holy Spirit on the

9 Pp. 42, 45-46. 10 P. 30. 11 *Ibid.*, pp. 52-57.
12 P. 312. 13 P. 128.

people as well as on the elements, for this is to pray "as if He were not already with them and abiding in them."[14] The scholarship of such Evangelicals cannot be dismissed lightly, and, what is more significant, there is no longer any desire to serve a party line, as the independence of the conclusions clearly shows.

Perhaps the most dated position on the Sacraments is the Modernist Anglican interpretation of which F. H. Amphlett Micklewright's *Sacraments and the Modern Man: A Modernist Explanation*[15] is an example, more notable for its negations than its affirmations. Nonetheless, while being concerned to cleanse the Sacrament from superstition and from any connotations of substitution and expiation, he recognizes the symbolic value of the Eucharist, as mystical and didactic. "It is this eternal preaching of the message of the Cross, the example of Jesus, which is presented to the worshipper through the symbolism of the broken bread and the pouring out of the wine."[16] Furthermore, "inasmuch as the Christian Gospel is one of Divine Action, the act of communion appears too as a meeting in a mystic sense of the temporal and the eternal, the reception by the believer, under the form of outward signs of the things which are eternal."[17] A recognition is also made of the social significance of Holy Communion.[18] Its gravest weakness, however, is the product of both the underlying idealist philosophy and of the belief in the uniformity of nature, which means that Micklewright dissociates the spiritual and the material instead of uniting them in the Incarnation and in the Sacrament. This is clearly shown in his pejorative references to "magical" views of Ignatius of Antioch and his approbation of the author of the Fourth Gospel as being the "father of all mystics," because in his thinking "the temporal and material universe stands over against that which is eternal, the world of values."[19] The disjunction is fatal to Micklewright's interpretation of the Christian faith, for Hellenism has overwhelmed the Gospel and the Sacraments.

The classic Anglican interpretation of the Eucharist in our period is O. C. Quick's *The Christian Sacraments*.[20] Quick's plan

---

14 *Ibid.*, p. 133.   15 No date, but clearly post-1933.
16 *Sacraments and the Modern Man* . . . , p. 130.
17 *Ibid.*, p. 132.   18 *Ibid.*, pp. 142-44.   19 *Ibid.*, p. 112.
20 The book was published in 1927; in 1933 A. G. Hebert in *Liturgy and Society* (p. 57) affirmed of Chap. v, "Christ's Life as a Sacrament (2) The Atonement," that it is a classic. J. K. Mozley in the Preface (pp. 9-10) of his *The Gospel Sacraments* wrote of Quick's monograph that it was "the most notable Anglican treatment of the subject within living memory."

was to lay a general philosophical foundation in the first three chapters, and to represent in the fourth and fifth chapters "the historical Incarnation and Atonement as the supreme sacrament and fount of all others,"[21] while subsequent chapters dealt with the operation of the Sacraments, the Church and its unity, and considered Baptism and Holy Communion in detail.

Crucial to his exposition was the distinction between ethical and aesthetic sacramentalism, corresponding to the difference between sacraments as instruments and sacraments as symbols. He contended that each needed the other, "yet no philosophical argument, or carefully drawn analogy, can help the understanding so much as the consideration of the life of Christ in its double aspect as the supreme self-expression of the Godhead within the created world, and as the supreme instrument whereby that world is brought to its fulfilment in eternity."[22] Moving from sacramentalism to sacraments, he affirmed that "for Christians the supreme sacrament, apart from which no other has use or meaning, is the life of Jesus Christ."[23] The fine intervening chapters on the Incarnation, the Atonement, the operation of the Sacraments, the Church and Unity,[24] as well as Baptism, must be ignored in our summary in order to concentrate on his treatment of the Eucharist. It is expressive because all human life, as it realizes its own ideal, is made up of an act of self-offering to God and an act of communion with Him and in Him through Jesus Christ our Lord; yet it is also instrumental as a constantly repeated act from which the soul draws its spiritual food.

The eschatological element is strong in Quick's interpretation,[25] which recognizes that the Messianic Banquet in the Kingdom of God is a central motif but insists that between the Last Supper and its establishment the crucifixion of the Messiah must take place. In the Eucharist Christians "are made partakers of the life offered for them on Calvary, in order that in the end their communion with that life may be fulfilled in the open and glorious vision of their Saviour before the throne of God."[26]

Quick then turns to the two vexed problems of Eucharistic theology, "the problem of the sacrifice offered, and the problem

---

21 *The Christian Sacraments*, pp. xi-xii.
22 *Ibid.*, p. 54.   23 *Ibid.*
24 This includes the fruitful idea that practically all the divisions of Christendom should be considered "as being in principle schisms within the Church" (*ibid.*, p. 147).
25 Quick indicates here his indebtedness to the thought of Hoskyns in *Essays Catholic and Critical*.
26 *Ibid.*, p. 194.

313

of the presence communicated."[27] Christ's sacrifice, it is insisted, is representative, not vicarious. How, then, does the Eucharist become a sacrifice? Quick answers that it does so both mystically and morally. That is, "the life of the truly perfect man, being sacrificed once and for all, is sufficient to cleanse and perfect all those to whom it is really communicated," for "Christ died for us that He might live in us."[28] Thus, Christ's life in men exhibits itself in the same activity of self-sacrifice which He in His own person perfectly fulfilled.

Turning to the mode of Christ's presence in the Eucharist, Quick considers the four traditional theories: Transubstantiation, Consubstantiation, Virtualism, and Receptionism. The first two connect the Presence with the consecration of the elements and the second two affirm the Presence in the hearts and souls of faithful worshippers. Yet in assaying the traditional doctrines, two presuppositions are unacceptable to twentieth century minds. These are: the view that material objects possess a substantiality distinguishable from their accidents or sensible properties and from their value or use; and the concept that heaven is a place where Christ's ascended body is extended in space.

Quick is looking for a theory which will do justice to three factors. The Presence is to be sought, first, in elements not as physical objects but as they are within the process of a certain action which uses them as instruments and expresses itself in them. Secondly, such a theory must not imply a "real absence" of Christ elsewhere, but must insist that the Eucharist is the expressive symbol of the entire process by which the world is made to fulfil God's purpose. Thirdly, the "Real Presence" must be so defined as not to leave the communicant at the mercy of his own flickering introversion. Quick believes that these requirements are satisfied in the following exposition of his theory:

"The Eucharist is the self offering of Christ as externalised in human ritual, so that human lives may be incorporated into its living reality through communion with Him Who offers and is offered. The action of every Eucharist begins in the inward and eternal sphere where Christ is seated at the right hand of God. Christ's action then reaches its first stage of externalisation in His Body the Church, which at a given place and time in the person of its priest solemnly offers the bread and wine in memorial of His passion. The action is thus further externalised and extended

---

[27] *Ibid.*, p. 196. [28] *Ibid.*

into the consecrated bread and wine as themselves representing the offered Body of Christ's manhood. From this furthest or lowest point of externalisation the action of the living Christ returns back and upwards into the members of His Body the Church as they receive Him in communion. In them it brings forth the spiritual fruits of their own self-offering which raises them towards heaven in Christ's power. So the Eucharistic action returns in the end to heaven which was its source. Thus interpreted it consists of a double movement, first downward and outward, then upward and inward. Thus it embodies in ritual and fulfils through the life of the Church that which was at first and perfectly embodied in fact through the historical life of Jesus Christ."[29]

The value of Quick's theory is that it tries to combine both expressive and instrumentalist elements in a mystical and moral combination. His final chapter, "Worship and Morals," warns against both ascetic rigorism and emotional self-indulgence, and reminds the reader that the reconciliation between worship and ethics is found "in the discovery that the true worship of God and the true service of men are alike possible in the one Holy Spirit of love."[30] Yet, with characteristic fidelity to the Bible, Quick says that this union is not commonly achieved—for the Parable of the Good Samaritan records that it was the men of worship (the priest and the levite) who passed by human need on the other side, and that Jesus gave a singularly cold reception to those who professed a sentimental devotion to Him, as in the case of the woman who cried, "Blessed is the womb that bare thee!" Worship, he concludes, is to be the stimulant of the soul, not its narcotic.

It is not the least of the values of Anglican sacramental teaching that it has often stimulated those who most value the Eucharist to undertake the humblest work for Christ in the slums or in the mission-field. No speech at the Anglo-Catholic Congress in 1923 received a stronger ovation than these simple words of the Bishop of Zanzibar: "You have your Mass, you have your altars, you have begun to get your tabernacles. Now go out into the highways and hedges, and look for Jesus in the ragged and the naked, in those who have lost hope, and in those who are struggling to make good. Look for Jesus in them; and when you have found Him, gird yourself with His towel of fellowship and wash His feet in the fellowship of His brethren."[31]

29 *Ibid.*, pp. 223-24.   30 *Ibid.*, p. 240.
31 H. Maynard Smith, *Frank, Bishop of Zanzibar*, p. 302.

The same sense of the social implications of the Eucharist, though expressed in a much more sophisticated way, and with a deeper understanding of the economic and political order, was characteristic of Archbishop William Temple's thinking. In *Personal Religion and the Life of Fellowship* (1926) Temple insisted that the Eucharist was no mystery cult, but the Family Meal where the children gathered round the Table to receive what the Father gives them. Consequently, he insisted, "differences of rank, wealth, learning, intelligence, nationality, race, all disappear; 'we, being many, are one Bread.' "[32]

By the time he wrote *The Hope of a New World* (1940), he saw the Eucharist as also the symbol of a transfigured social order and of the true sanctification of labour for the community. The Holy Communion is, of course, in the traditional sense a means of grace, an effective channel of God's transforming love, but it is also expressive of God's intentions for human community. Bread and wine are the perfect symbols of the economic life of man. Bread is an instance of God's gifts to man made available by human cooperation with God. On God's part there is the gift of seed, soil, sun, and rain. Man's contribution is the labour of ploughing the land, scattering the seed, gathering in of the harvest, threshing the flour, baking the bread and distributing it for the satisfaction of human need. Thus:

"In the Holy Communion service we take the bread and wine—man's industrial and commercial life in symbol—and offer it to God; because we have offered it to Him, He gives it back to us as the means of nurturing us, not in our animal nature alone, but as agents of His purpose, limbs of a body responsive to His will; and as we receive it back from Him, we share it with one another in a true fellowship. If we think of the service in this way, it is a perfect picture of what secular society should be; and a Christian civilization is one where the citizens seek to make their ordered life something of which that service is the symbol."[33] In the Holy Communion so interpreted there is a profound doctrine of man in society. The same theme is most eloquently developed in the

[32] *Personal Religion* . . . , p. 48.
[33] *The Hope of a New World*, pp. 69-70. It is worth recording Temple's notable definition of worship: "What worship means is the submission of the whole being to the object of worship. It is the opening of the heart to receive the love of God; it is the subjection of conscience to be directed by Him; it is the declaration of need to be fulfilled by Him; it is the subjection of desire to be controlled by Him; and as the result of all these together, it is the surrender of the will to be used by Him" (*The Church and Its Teaching To-day*, p. 15).

concluding paragraphs of the introduction to Dom Gregory Dix's *The Shape of the Liturgy* (1948), in which he contrasts "Acquisitive Man" and his successor "Mass-Man" with "Eucharistic Man."[34]

It has been contended that the Anglican Church developed a deepened appreciation of the centrality of the Sacrament of Holy Communion during this period, and the treatises from different schools of thought have borne this out. What is of equal significance, however, is that there has been developing a growing unity of interpretation, in marked contrast with the partisanship of Eucharistic interpretation that characterized the Prayer Book Controversy. The most impressive proof of this assertion is to be found in the remarkable agreement arrived at by a Commission, representative of the chief schools of thought, as it defined in *Doctrine in the Church of England* (1937) its understanding of the hitherto controversial concept of Sacrifice in the Eucharist:

"The Eucharist is a corporate act of the Church towards God, wherein it is united with its Lord, victorious and triumphant, Himself both priest and victim in the sacrifice of the Cross. This connection has been expressed in at least four ways: (1) through stress on the union of ourselves with Christ in the act of communion, and in that union the offering of 'the sacrifice of praise and thanksgiving' and of 'ourselves, our souls and bodies'—a view generally held in the Church of England, many members of which would find here alone the sacrificial element in the rite; (2) through emphasis on the fact that in the Eucharist we repeat the words and acts of Christ at the last supper in words and acts whereby it is held that He invested His approaching death with the character of a sacrifice; (3) through the insistence that the rite is a representation before the Father of the actual sacrifice of the Cross; (4) through the doctrine of the Heavenly Altar, at which we join in the perpetual offering by Christ of Himself and share the life of Christ crucified and risen . . . . There are those who would combine all the views stated, while some of them would be repudiated in certain quarters. We consider that all of them would be regarded as legitimate in the Church of England, and we are agreed in general terms in holding that the Eucharist may be rightly termed a sacrifice—which we have defined as 'an act in which man worships God, the form of the act being an expression of the homage due from the creature to the creator.' But if the Eucharist is thus spoken of as a sacrifice, it must be understood

[34] Pp. xviii-xix, and cited fully in Chap. I.

as a sacrifice in which (to speak as exactly as the subject allows) we do not offer Christ, but where Christ unites us with Himself in the self-offering of the life that was 'obedient unto death, yea the death of the Cross.' "[35]

That statement is an irenic triumph. Even so, there remain important differences of emphasis, as, for example, between those for whom the Eucharist is the Church's supreme *offering*, and those who believe it to be the thankful celebration of God's supreme *gift*.

Archbishop Ramsey has written of the permanent characteristics of Anglican theology as including "the appeal to Scripture and the Fathers, the fondness for Nicene categories, the union of doctrine and liturgy, the isolation from Continental influences."[36] This is a perceptive evaluation, provided that one modification and a significant addition may be made. The modification necessary is that increasingly as the century advanced Anglican theology became subject to Continental influences, both Swedish and French, and the German influence was not negligible.[37] The addition to be made is that Anglican sacramental teaching is inescapably ethical. Holy attitudes must issue in holy actions. One of the glories of the Anglican tradition is that it, like Puritanism, rejected a "cloistered and fugitive virtue." This insistence that the spirit of the sanctuary must be carried into the streets, and that without the humility induced by worship social service becomes mere patronage, is finely stressed by Bishop K. E. Kirk in *The Vision of God*. There he writes: "Yet apart from the atmosphere of worship, every act of service avails only to inflate the agent's sense of patronage. He is the doctor, humanity his patient: he is the Samaritan, his neighbour the crippled wayfarer: He is the instructor, others are merely his pupils. Gratitude (if they show gratitude) only confirms his conviction of his own importance; resentment (if they resent his services) only ministers to the glow of self-

---

[35] *Doctrine in the Church of England*, p. 162.

[36] *From Gore to Temple: the Development of Anglican Theology between Lux Mundi and the Second World War, 1889-1939*, pp. viii-ix.

[37] Anglican Biblical scholarship was indebted to German thought and the Liberal school was influenced by Harnack, Schweitzer, and Otto. A. G. Hebert was, by his translations and his constructive works, a potent mediator of Swedish scholarship, and the influence of Yngve Brilioth, Gustaf Aulen, and Anders Nygren, in particular, was considerable, as English translations of *Eucharistic Faith and Practice*, *Christus Victor*, and *Agape and Eros* were widely read. In Patristics and Liturgics the influence of such French scholars as J. Daniélou, Louis Bouyer, and Cullmann, and of such German scholars as Bultmann and Jungmann was considerable. Barth was appreciated by such Anglican scholars as Hoskyns, Camfield, and Bromiley.

esteem with which he comforts himself in secret."[38] By contrast, the glory of worship is to elicit the grace of humility.

3. *A Fecundity of Experimentation*

The third characteristic of Anglican worship, particularly evident in the last decade of our period, was the fertility of liturgical experimentation. There could be no more vigorous indication of vitality in the Anglican tradition than this, especially as these experiments are marked by imagination and relevance.

Five experiments have evoked unusual interest and therefore deserve detailed consideration. The first is "Parish Communion," associated with A. G. Hebert of Kelham, which began obscurely in 1913, was given publicity in the book[39] which Hebert edited in 1937, and later was even more widely disseminated by the "Parish and People" movement, with its own magazine of that name. The second is the "House Church" associated with Ernest Southcott, who in 1950 or thereabouts attempted to combine the celebration of Holy Communion with evangelism by taking the Church to the homes of his people in the new housing estate of Halton, Leeds. The third experiment, "The Clare College Liturgy," is a liturgical manual of 1954 produced by two chaplains of this Cambridge College, J. A. T. Robinson and C. F. D. Moule. The fourth is "An Experimental Liturgy" of 1958, which was celebrated on the entire Independent Television network in 1959. The fifth and last is the official Report of the Church of England Liturgical Commission, *Baptism and Confirmation*, published in 1959.

4. *"The Parish Communion"*

"By 'the Parish Communion' is meant the celebration of the Holy Eucharist, with the communion of the people in a parish church as the chief service of the day, or better, as the assembly of the Christian community for the worship of God," wrote Hebert, adding "on Sundays the most suitable hour will generally be not long before or after 9.0. A.M."[40] This concern for a simple major celebration of Holy Communion in which most of the confirmed members of the parish would participate was meant to end the current fracturing of the family life and witness of the Church, whereby some parishes had sparsely attended 8 A.M. Communions

[38] P. 184.
[39] *The Parish Communion, A Book of Essays.*
[40] *Ibid.*, p. 3.

followed by a largely attended service of Matins, while other parishes had a High Mass with large attendance and little participation in the Eucharist. It was also believed that the Holy Communion service should be the chief expression of the *koinonia* or fellowship of the Body of Christ in a particular parish and at a convenient hour for entire families to attend. Furthermore, when the worshippers partook of a "Parish breakfast" following the "Parish Communion," they would naturally get to know each other better and become more truly a community in Christ. These were the practical considerations.

There were also significant theological concerns. The Eucharist demonstrates the real nature of the Church when celebrated in the manner of the Parish Communion with full participation. The Church surrounding the altar rehearses "the mystery of the divine *agape* whereby man has been redeemed and the redeemed fellowship constituted as the Body of Christ. The Eucharist sums up the whole Gospel of redemption as the sacramental showing-forth of the one Sacrifice of Christ and of the offering up of the members of Christ through union with Him to be a reasonable, holy, and living sacrifice to God."[41] The Offertory, therefore, must be shown to have much greater relevance to the worshippers. In the early church the bread and wine were brought to the altar by the people themselves and this act then clearly demonstrated their will to offer themselves with their gifts. The modern equivalent, popularized by the Parish Communion, is for representatives of the people to carry the elements in procession from the back of the church, as well as the alms, "each member of the congregation, in some cases, having placed a wafer in the ciborium or on the paten as they came into church."[42] In other ways, too, an attempt is made to involve the congregation more actively in the worship. The Epistle may be read by a layman; and the entire congregation will be instructed to join heartily in the responses and in such parts of the liturgy as are to be sung, where the settings are appropriate for community singing. "Often babies in arms or small children accompany their parents to the communion rail, to be blessed perhaps by the priest as he moves along administering the sacrament."[43] Such care to involve the congregation actively goes a long way to destroy the old mistaken view that the Eucharist was

[41] *Ibid.*, p. 4.
[42] Martin Pierce, *The Parish Communion* (Alcuin Club Pamphlet, undated), p. 4.
[43] *Ibid.*

a theatrical spectacle performed by liturgical experts in the sight of a largely silent and submissive people.

The custom of holding a Parish Communion followed by a Parish Breakfast originated in 1913 in the rural Warwickshire parish of Temple Balsall,[44] where the Eucharist at 8.45 A.M. was the principal service of the day. The Parish Eucharist was initiated at St. John's, Newcastle-upon-Tyne, in 1927 and by 1937, 170 of 250 communicants attended this service regularly each Sunday at 9.15 A.M. It may be of interest to provide a description of the form the Offertory took in this church at that date:

"During the saying of the Offertory Prayer we now have an Offertory Procession. A credence table is placed at the West end of the church, and on it two vessels containing the approximate number of breads that will be required for the communion of the people, and two wine cruets. When the celebrant returns to the altar after the address, four members of the congregation who have been chosen beforehand (if possible, a man and a woman, a boy and a girl) go to this credence table, and while the congregation are saying the offertory Prayer, carry the people's offerings of bread and wine through the congregation to the altar rail, where the offerings are received by the servers and handed to the celebrant for presentation at the altar. Such a procession helps the people to realize the significance of the offertory by giving it a visible dramatic form. It restores the act of offering to its true importance, and marks it as the foundation of the whole Eucharistic action. It has the additional value of giving a share in the action of worship to a greater number of the laity, who need not all be of the male sex."[45]

The Parish Communion has, in subsequent years, become almost the normative celebration of the Eucharist in the Church of England. It has stressed important values, but it has also raised some serious questions. Clearly it is a great gain that, as in the early Church, the Eucharist should have been re-established at the centre of Sunday worship and that it should be widely attended by a devout and committed people. It is also a considerable boon that it is customary in high as well as in low parishes, for it means that the Sacrament of unity is really accomplishing unification. Furthermore, Parish Communion (whether or not it is followed by Parish Breakfast as a kind of equivalent to the love-feast or *agape* of the early Church) undoubtedly helps the local congrega-

44 Hebert, ed., *The Parish Communion*, p. 261.
45 *Ibid.*, pp. 277-78.

tion to understand itself as a true family in Christ. The meaning of Baptism is also more readily apprehended by the people. Not least important is the fact that "the Parish Meeting can discover itself as a fellowship of counsel and evangelism."[46] It has helped to awaken a responsible laity.

Even so, some serious theological questions must be raised by the popularity of the Parish Communion as, indeed, they were by Dr. A. M. Ramsey in his *Durham Essays and Addresses*. The most serious caveat concerns the reduction of instruction inevitable in a service which can allow only about seven minutes for a sermon. Such concision almost compels the preacher to be dogmatic and coercive rather than explanatory and persuasive. Here it is pertinent to recall that one of the attractions of the Elizabethan settlement, according to A. L. Rowse, was the change from the Mass to the sermon which led to "an increase of reflection and edification, a stimulus to education and the active virtues."[47] Is the Parish Communion, then, a second Elizabethan unsettlement? At least, it is a displacement of the Anglican conjoint emphasis on the Word and Sacrament to the advantage of the Sacrament and the disadvantage of the Word.

As Dr. Ramsey has indicated, an exaggerated emphasis on the importance of the Offertory can lead to a Pelagian glorification of man and a forgetfulness that the smaller human offerings are only possible because of the Father's prior acceptance of the perfect sacrifice of the Cross. Dr. E. L. Mascall has also warned that in some circles the idea has gained ground that what makes the liturgy corporate is the fact that many people celebrate it at the same time, yet "whether the communicants be few or many, the liturgy is essentially corporate because it is the act of Christ in the *corpus mysticum*."[48] Moreover, when the note of fellowship is stressed, it must not be forgotten that this is a larger community than the merely local parish community. It is linked with the whole Church militant upon earth and triumphant in Heaven, as the *Sanctus* in the prayer of consecration suggests.[49] The older generation of Churchmen also sense a loss of awe and numinosity in the Parish Communion, which they recall as characterizing the eight

---

[46] Pierce, *The Parish Communion*, p. 16.
[47] *The England of Elizabeth*, p. 485.
[48] *Corpus Christi*, p. 78.
[49] Dr. Ramsey in *Durham Essays and Addresses* (p. 20) suggests this requires a fuller liturgical expression than is provided in the present Communion Office and which was a feature of the First Prayer Book of Edward VI.

o'clock early morning Communions. The provision of a nave altar and the use of the westward posture, not to mention the fidgeting of children, make it harder to concentrate on God and all too easy to focus on man.

It is, of course, possible that the vogue for Parish Communion will pass, especially as for many persons an Evening Communion would be more convenient, and there seems to be little point in Anglican hesitation on such a matter when Roman Catholic permission is readily available for Evening Masses. Moreover, the Evangelical wing of the Church has a long tradition of holding Holy Communion in the evening. Those who will resist such a change are, of course, such clergy as believe that fasting before Communion is an indispensable discipline.

5. The "House Church"

There are two very important features in the worship of the "House Church" as originally developed by Ernest Southcott in Halton, Leeds. The first is that this is an expression of liturgical evangelism, an attempt to supplement the worship and witness of the parish church in the homes of the people. The second is that an appropriate charismatic element enters into the service of Holy Communion when celebrated on the dining-table of a home. This is the interpolation of simple, extempore prayer for or by those in whose home Communion is celebrated.

Southcott's parish comprised some fifteen thousand persons, including the Halton Moor Estate, a slum-clearance area of some six thousand people. His problem was to discover how to make the Church relevant to their daily lives. For this purpose Southcott conceived the idea of *extensive* and *intensive* House Churches.[50] The *extensive* House Churches consist entirely of Bible Study groups of neighbours meeting in a centrally convenient home. The *intensive* House Churches are similar, but more fully instructed and committed cells or groups also meeting in homes, where the Holy Communion is celebrated. The latter is not a substitute for Communion in the parish church, but a supplement to it. It is even an incentive to attend the Parish Communion.

House celebrations have taken place in four different ways.[51] In the case of sick people who were regular communicants, Com-

50 A third occasional type of House Church is interdenominational in character, but this has been little employed. See Malcolm Boyd, *Crisis in Communication: A Christian Examination of the Mass Media*, p. 83.

51 See E. W. Southcott, "The House Church," in *Theology*, Vol. LVI, No. 395 (May 1953), pp. 169-70.

munion is taken to them from the Reserved Sacrament at monthly intervals where it is requested. In the case of elderly people, house celebrations are held monthly for their benefit in different parts of the parish and are attended by friends and neighbours. Twice a year (in a week during Lent and in a week following the Harvest Festival) the Halton clergy hold house celebrations each morning of the week and people are invited to attend by the family after consultation with the clergy. The lapsed are invited to be present, but not to communicate until they have been confirmed. The fourth method followed a month's mission in October, 1952, where the chief technique was to hold house meetings and house celebrations. For an entire month house celebrations were held each morning at 6, 7, and 9.15, and house meetings each day for a fortnight. Nine hundred attended the house celebrations, five hundred the house meetings and over a thousand people entered each other's houses during that short time. Canon Southcott comments: "Here is the Church being the Church. Certainly it is the Eucharist in action."[52]

This is but a sketch—it needs to be filled in with local colour. An American observer described his impressions as follows: "Early on week-day mornings there are house-church meetings with celebrations of Holy Communion in some of the small houses of the Halton Moor Estate. The lights of the house break through the cold and blackness outside and testify to the gatherings of Christians for the breaking of bread together—a very effective form of communication, one is told by certain men and women who first observed the goings on from outside across the street or way, and who are now inside the fold taking part." The account continues with an inside description: "The kitchen table is set up within the living room in one of the compact slum-clearance dwellings. Used candles from the altar at the parish church are placed upon the table that becomes the altar. . . . Home-made bread, the same bread that the family had eaten for tea the night before is used for the service. The Bible and last evening's newspaper are close together; and they will shortly be in the same conversation, too."[53]

Another observer also conveys a vivid impression: "Let it only be said, therefore, that in Halton men who would never otherwise have dreamt of coming to Communion, not in church, and certainly not on a weekday, are coming—at six in the morning—to Communion in the home." The explanation is: "Because here . . . is Christ abiding in the midst of the family. . . . Here is Christ ex-

[52] *Ibid.*, p. 170. [53] Malcolm Boyd, *op.cit.*, p. 83.

posed in the midst of bread and wine and crockery and the table-cloth; and 'Jesus has come to our house!' Here they are, there he is, in the Church! Father reads the epistle. Mother offers up prayers for her home and her street, for her husband's works and the children. '. . . and are in love and charity with your neighbours,' says the Invitation."[54]

Southcott himself has remarked that in the house-celebration there is occasionally time for a short relevant sermon and an opportunity for lay people to intercede in a movingly personal way such as could not be done in the formal worship of the parish. It is clearly one of the values of the house church that it can combine liturgical structure and order with free prayer. Here the Catholic and Puritan traditions are meaningfully combined in a way that has not been experienced in the Church of England since the time of John Wesley and George Whitefield.

What then, is the significance of the House Church experiment? Certainly it has proved to be an effective means of bringing the lapsed or the indifferent back to the Christian community and way of life. But has it any deeper theological significance? There is no doubt that it witnesses significantly to the fact that the Church does not consist of bricks and mortar or concrete, but is the *people* of God. Dr. J. A. T. Robinson believes that the House Church is an approximation to New Testament Christianity, representing the "tap-roots of the Vine, the Church under ground, that of the life of the tree most closely in contact with the clinging soil of everyday existence: it is the tree as it is embedded in the deepest crevices and seams of the secular world."[55] Its great advantage in the modern world is that the cell is a part of the Church with great flexibility and mobility, operating in the area of natural community. It meets in a house: it could as easily meet in an office or a factory or, as it once did, in the catacombs.

It is important to recognize, however, that this is never regarded as an end, complete in itself. The house celebrations are intimately related to Parish Communion at St. Wilfrid's Church, Halton. When Southcott was interviewed and asked about the relationship of the House Church to the Parish Church, he insisted that the House Church was giving roots to the Parish Church, for otherwise the latter's congregation was too large and the membership too

[54] Eric James, "What is going on at Halton?", *Theology, Vol.* LX, No. 440 (February 1957), p. 63.
[55] "The House Church and the Parish Church," *Theology*, Vol. LIII, No. 362 (August 1950), p. 285.

loosely linked together. In the House Church, it was realized that "We don't go to Church, we *are* the Church."[56] Furthermore, it is at these gatherings in the home that a new relationship is sensed between the holy and the common, and everyday life can be offered to God. He ended the interview with a reminder that the Abbé Michonneau said the parable of the hundred sheep should be retold for our own day: Now there are ninety-nine sheep out in the wilderness and only one in the fold.

As might be expected, the Parish Communion at St. Wilfrid's, Halton, is well abreast of the Liturgical Movement's achievements. The celebration is at a table-altar in the nave and the priest faces the congregation as he offers the consecration prayer. The people take bread and place it in the ciborium. Many of the collects in the Order for Holy Communion are said in common. Laymen lead many of the bidding prayers, speaking from different parts of the nave. A true participation of the people links house celebrations and parish celebrations.

What, then, are the values of the House Church experiment? A powerful means has been discovered for demonstrating the potential sanctification of the common life, of the nexus between Christ the Bread of Life and our daily bread, and of every meal as a miniature Eucharist. Here, too, is a Biblical and liturgical mission allowing for the differing stages of commitment. The interested but uncommitted are reached in the extensive house church, and are observers at the Eucharist in the intensive house church. Then, after instruction and confirmation, they share in the parish and House Church Communions, becoming witnesses in turn to their friends and neighbours. Above all, the Eucharist, whether celebrated with splendour or simplicity, is seen to be the pattern of Christian love and service in the world, empowered by the example and the grace of Christ.

There are two potential dangers in the House Church experiment. The first is that the part may be preferred to the whole. The intimate fellowship and the charismatic service in the home may make the formal parish Communion seem impersonal, theatrical, remote, and to that extent less meaningful. The second is a danger inherent in all aggrandizations of the role of the chief Sacrament in the life of the Church—that is the depreciation of the role of the ministry of the Word. To be sure, the Bible is given

[56] The interview is recorded in *Faith at Work* (October–November 1958), pp. 23-27. This magazine is published in Lebanon, Pennsylvania.

a preparatory and instructional role in the extensive house churches. But preaching is reduced to the briefest of talks in the intensive house church; yet the committed Christian needs the iron-ration of Scripture more than the catechumen.

One further hesitation remains. While the example of Ernest Southcott has been followed successfully in a few parishes of the Protestant Episcopal Church of the United States and, with some changes, in a few parishes of the Presbyterian Church of Scotland, it has not been widely imitated in the Church of England. In fact, it has hardly been imitated at all in his own Communion. Is it particularly successful only in the north of England and would it be less successful among the more reserved southerners? Does it only succeed in slum-clearance communities deeply in need of new community roots? Was Southcott unusually fortunate in the sympathy and approval of his diocesan at Ripon and his suffragan at Knaresborough? Or, finally, does the "House Church" experiment need for its successful accomplishment a leader with the courage, drive, imagination, dedication, and warm personality of an Ernest Southcott himself?

6. The "Clare College Manual" for the Liturgy

This experiment in worship attempts to meet the needs of a College House Church. It does not provide a new liturgy. The novelty is to be found in the fact that the Prayer Book Order for Holy Communion is made more meaningful by the use of a specially prepared manual of instruction, with the words of the service on the right-hand pages, and the commentary on the left-hand pages. Furthermore, the ceremonial adds to the relevance of the service in its context in collegiate life, and the exciting preaching of the former Dean, Dr. J. A. T. Robinson, added to the significance of the celebrations.

The manual illuminates the structure of the Liturgy by a helpful introduction and additional preparatory and post-communion prayers, as also by meditations and observations appropriate to the various parts of the Anglican service chosen from the Bible and from several ecumenical sources. Thus the chief gains of the modern Liturgical Movement are transmitted by the manual, which is simply titled, "The Holy Communion, Clare College, Cambridge." In this way members of the College, who comprised a number of Free Churchmen as well as the Anglican majority, became familiar with the coordinate stress on Word and Sacrament, the renewed understanding of the importance of the Offertory, and, in particular, with the "Four Action" pattern of the Eucharist as analysed by Dom Gregory Dix in *The Shape of Liturgy*, and the idea that this is a con-celebration of the whole people of God. In addition, the elements used for consecration consisted of college-baked bread and wine from the college cellars.

The great quality of the manual is that it combines clear theological instruction and spiritual directions with naturalness, and avoids the two commonest perils of manuals of this type, sentimentality and rubrical antiquarianism. A significant sample from the introduction will illustrate the qualities which have been claimed for it. After observing that the service of Holy Communion falls into two distinct parts, it continues:

> The first part, the Liturgy of the Word, has its focus in the Bible, and takes place not at the Table but round the Lecterns. It is a service of prayer, Scripture-reading and preaching, in which the living Christ speaks to his assembled People, as Jesus discoursed with his disciples in the Upper Room, expounding the meaning of his death and promised presence.
>
> In the second part, the Breaking of the Bread, he makes himself known in the Action which he instituted and which ever since has been the central act of the Church on the Lord's Day. In it he makes present to us, through the power of his risen life, all that he wrought on the Cross, till he comes in final victory.
>
> The pattern of this action is four-fold, continuing that of Jesus at the Last Supper, when he took, and blessed, and broke, and gave.[57]

Then there follows a concise exposition of the spiritual meaning of the renewal of these acts in Holy Communion:

> We come, first, to commemorate with thanksgiving that he in his life, death and resurrection offered himself thus to be taken and consecrated, broken and given *for* us;
>
> secondly, to trust his promise that in the bread and wine, taken, blessed, broken and shared as he commanded, he will come *to* us;
>
> thirdly, to let our lives likewise be taken, blessed, broken

[57] Clare College Manual, p. 2. The Clare College Communion Service complete with commentary is published also as an Appendix to J. A. T. Robinson's *The Liturgy Coming to Life*.

and given in union with his, that God's redeeming work and rule may be extended *through* us.[58]

There is special interest in the notes opposite the Offertory. There we read:

> Jesus began by taking the loaf off the supper table. His work now, in us and through us, cannot start until the ordinary material of our lives, just as it is, is turned over entirely to him. In the Offertory we take a loaf baked in the College kitchens and a decanter of wine from the College cellars—symbols of our labour and our leisure, the gifts of God to us as we have worked upon them. They are brought up by laymen, out of the midst of our everyday life, and offered to God, together with our money.[59]

Further interest attaches to a rubric following immediately after the concluding Blessing:

> The ministers go out, a deacon carrying the remainder of the Loaf not set apart for Holy Communion, to be shared at the Breakfast.[60]

The supplementary prayers for private meditation are taken from a wide range of sources, including the Armenian Liturgy, The South India Liturgy,[61] the Liturgy of St. John Chrysostom, the Liturgy of St. James, the Liturgy of St. Basil, the Liturgy of Malabar, and, most interestingly, John Wesley's Covenant Service as used by the English Methodist Church. The citations range from St. Augustine to P. T. Forsyth.

Of the instructional and inspirational value of this unpretentious manual of thirty-one pages there can be no question. But the service must have meant considerably more when Dr. John Robinson was preaching, as may be discovered from his book, *Liturgy Coming to Life* (1960), an account of the Clare College experiment, including some of his Eucharistic addresses. In terms of re-interpreting traditional services with imagination, wit and spirituality, the only parallel I can think of is Monsignor Ronald Knox's *The Mass in Slow Motion* (1948) and that is the highest praise.

The preparation of the Clare College manual was necessary

---

[58] *Ibid.*   [59] *Ibid.*, p. 12.   [60] *Ibid.*, p. 29.
[61] In fact, the citation comes from the Bombay Liturgy used as a source by the South India Liturgy.

because previous ones were the reflection of party ecclesiastical prejudice and of subjective rather than corporate piety, or too obviously written by clergy for clergy. Robinson's manual was prepared in the conviction that "the road to living liturgical reform leads from the bottom upwards, and that is why controlled experiment in the local worshipping community, especially at the sub-parochial or house church level, is so vital to the health of the Body of Christ."[62] There were, of course, serious disadvantages in a college community attempting to live like a church, for it was both an artificial and a highly changing entity; artificial in that there were no women or children apart from those of the teaching and administrative staff, and highly mobile because most undergraduates left after three years. Moreover, the high points of the Christian Year, Christmas and Easter, for example, arrived to find the undergraduates on vacation.

Robinson felt that it was his duty, when Dean of Clare College from 1951 to 1959, to recover the Patristic understanding of the Liturgy as quite literally the *ergon* or work of the *laos*, the people (of God), by which the latter are constituted through the Sacrifice of Christ the very Body of Christ. He was greatly impressed by Gregory Dix's *The Shape of the Liturgy* because it emphasized that the structure of the Liturgy was not based on any pattern of words, but on a four-fold *action*, as performed by Jesus at the Last Supper. He hoped to make it clear in the celebration of the Liturgy that "this is the crucible of the new creation, in which God's new world is continually being fashioned out of the old, as ordinary men and women are renewed and sent out as carriers of Christ's risen life."[63]

He added the preparatory prayers and citations from the great liturgies of Christendom precisely because he felt the exultant note celebrating the mighty acts of God in Christ was missing in the Prayer Book, drowned by the penitential concentration on Calvary, to the neglect of the Creation, Incarnation, and Resurrection. He also magnified the place of the Liturgy of the Word, believing that the sermon is "an indispensable instrument for the regular communication of any through-going theology of the Eucharist and its implications" and that the Word of God must be contemporary, "speaking to every man in his own language, cutting through all

---

[62] *Liturgy coming to Life*, p. 15. The author adds: "Nothing lasting will be achieved, as 1928 showed, by imposition from the top downwards."
[63] *Ibid.*, p. 23.

that muffles and stifles its impact."[64] He found it necessary to stress the four major actions of Taking, Blessing, Breaking, and Sharing, but this was difficult with the Prayer Book Rite of 1661 where the Offertory is separated from the Thanksgiving or Blessing, and the Fraction has been absorbed into the Consecration Prayer.

He also considered it important to accentuate the fact that the action of the Liturgy is social, not individual. If worshippers come to the Eucharist not merely to feed upon the Body of Christ, but to be created the Body of Christ, then this can be emphasized in the common loaf. It is lost in wafers or "breads." In the use of the common loaf there is a second advantage: the importance of the *Fraction* is demonstrated, with its symbolical reminder that the life of God can be given and shared only if it is broken. Moreover, Robinson wished to make it as plain as possible that the Liturgy was con-celebrated, the work of all the worshippers. For this reason he let it be known that any regular communicant was, in turn, to take his part in the communal action to which all were committed. He might be called upon to read the Epistle, to introduce the biddings or requests for prayer, or to make the offering of the bread and wine representing the common life. The western posture for the celebration was adopted, with the president facing the congregation, because it cut across party divisions, and because its psychological function was "to focus attention on a point in the middle, as the Christ comes to stand among his people as the breaker of bread, and to direct their gaze upwards as they lift their hearts to him as their ascended Lord."[65]

Like Archbishop William Temple, Dr. Robinson regards the Eucharist as the stimulus to sacrificial social action. Speaking of the common bread in the Eucharist, he insists that "we cannot without judgment share bread here and acquiesce in a world food distribution that brings plenty to some but malnutrition and starvation to millions more. We cannot without judgment share bread here with men of every race and tolerate a colour bar in restaurants and hotels."[66]

Dr. Robinson has shown that until the Church of England produces a revision of the Prayer Book more suitable both to the insights of our own day and of the early Church, it is possible by re-interpretation, by significant ceremonial, and by the use of an inspiring manual, to make the Liturgy indeed come alive.[67]

[64] *Ibid.*, p. 24.   [65] *Ibid.*, p. 33.   [66] *Ibid.*, p. 43.
[67] There seemed to be no point in offering a critical evaluation, because we

7. *"An Experimental Liturgy"*

In comparison with the previous experiments we have been considering, here is a more daring enterprise, the construction of a new liturgy, which combines the best of the past and the present to provide a more adequate vehicle of worship for the Church of England in an ecumenical century. Ambitious as the project is, finality is not claimed for it. Its three authors, Professor J. Gordon Davies[68] of the University of Birmingham, and two fellow clergy of the same city, Dr. Gilbert Cope[69] and D. A. Tytler, gave it the modest title of "An Experimental Liturgy." Their hope, when this was published in 1958, was that it might lead others to produce their own experimental liturgies or constructively to criticize this one, and thus prepare the Church of England to study the issues that would have to be considered when full-scale liturgical revision should again be contemplated.

Four basic principles have controlled their thinking. The first was the negative decision to avoid depending too much on any existing rite, since all are either too mediaeval or too Reformed in character. They decided, in the next place, to make a comparative study of liturgies preparatory to devising their own, thus ensuring that their rite would have an ecumenical character.[70] Thirdly, they desired to manifest the Biblical foundation of faith as integrated into the Sacrament, and also to demonstrate the Biblical doctrine through the structure of the rite. Finally, this was to be an attempt to make the Liturgy a truly corporate action, thoroughly understood by the people.

---

have already recognized the criticisms of the house church and the parish communion, and this Clare College service of Holy Communion is something of a combination of both related to the special needs of an academic community. In one respect it improves on both—in giving a larger place to preaching. For a criticism of the theology of the Offertory, see Paul Gibson, "Liturgical Revision and a Theology of Incorporation," *Theology*, Vol. LXIII, No. 486 (June 1960), p. 230.

[68] Professor Davies is the founder and head of the Liturgical Institute at the University of Birmingham, the author of *The Origin and Development of Early Christian Architecture* (1952) and of *The Architectural Setting of Baptism*, and is a former Bampton Lecturer.

[69] The Rev. Gilbert Cope wrote *Symbolism in the Bible and the Church* and edited *Making the Building Serve the Liturgy*.

[70] The Independent Television Authority's brochure publicising the transmission of the Experimental Order for Holy Communion on July 27, 1959, contains the following statement in the introduction by J. G. Davies: "the group responsible for producing this experiment did not take any one Order for Communion as its model, but tried, by a comparison of very many, to discover what features are essential in order that the rite should embody the fulness of Christian belief and practice as it is preserved fragmented in the separate branches of the Church."

They accepted the two-fold traditional structure of the Synaxis and the Eucharist, since the basic structure of the Synaxis came from the Synagogue, while that of the Eucharist derived from the Upper Room. Their only modification was to provide an act of Preparation to precede the Synaxis, and thus their rite has three parts.

Part I is *Preparation* and includes four elements: the Entrance, Chant, Greeting (and Collect for Purity), Confession and Prayer for Forgiveness (said by all the people). Part II is *The Ministry of the Word* (corresponding to the Synaxis) and contains ten elements: the Little Entrance (and Salutation), the Collect for the Day, the Old Testament Lesson, a Psalm or Canticle, the Epistle, a Psalm or Canticle, the Gospel (all standing) with *Gloria tibi* and *Laus tibi* optional, a Sermon, the Nicene Creed (with textual emendations), the Grace said by all (and possibly the Announcements and Special Biddings), and the Litany of Intercession. Part III is *The Ministry of the Sacrament*, which consists of five main elements, and many sub-elements. First there is the Offertory (with the *Pax* and presentation of offerings). Then the Thanksgiving follows, with *Sursum corda* and *Sanctus*, the Great Thanksgiving including an ascription to the Trinity said by the people, and the Lord's Prayer said by the people. The Fraction succeeds, including a Sentence and Response, this to be followed by Silence, and possibly by the Prayer of Humble Access. The fourth element is Communion, including the Communion of the clergy, the Invitation to the people and their response (emphasizing the concept of the Messianic Banquet), the Communion of the people, the Post-Communion Thanksgiving. The fifth and final element is the Dismissal.

Such is this interesting rite in skeletal form. There is a logic in the successive order of the various elements. The Preparation follows the shape of Isaiah's vision in the Temple, as the *Gloria in excelsis*—the sublime expression of adoration—leads naturally to the confession of sin and a plea for forgiveness.[71] The Ministry of the Word fittingly begins with a custom borrowed from the Eastern Orthodox Liturgy, the solemn carrying in of the Bible, known as the Little Entrance. This is followed by the reading of the Old Testament, the Epistle, and the Gospel, and the Sermon which expounds the Word of God, which fittingly elicits the response of

[71] It is not an Absolution, since this is to anticipate one of the benefits of the Eucharist itself.

the Creed (in a revised version adopting the first person plural) said by all the people. This part of the service ends with a prayer of intercession in the form of a litany, to enable all to share actively in it. The second main division of the Liturgy, the Ministry of the Sacrament, begins with the bringing forward by the representatives of the people of the gifts of bread, wine, and alms, as tokens of their self-offering. These gifts are then taken and blessed in a prayer of thanksgiving, which offers God gratitude for creation, redemption, and the institution of the Holy Communion, asks for the fruits of communion—forgiveness, unity, renewal and spiritual strength, and recalls the saving acts of Christ to whom the worshippers are linked by the Holy Spirit. Such a prayer fittingly concludes with the recitation by all of the Lord's Prayer, the prayer of the Christian family. The Fraction, or Breaking of the Bread, is followed by a call to Communion. Then a short prayer of thanksgiving is followed by the Dismissal, which reminds the worshippers of their responsibility as representatives of the Church in the world consequent on their union with the risen and ascended Lord of the Church.[72]

The ceremonial of this rite strongly emphasizes the corporate character of the Church. The celebrant faces the people for all are gathered to make a common spiritual sacrifice and to share a common meal at the same altar-table. Members of the congregation take it in turn to bring the Bible to the lectern and to read the Old Testament Lesson and the Epistle. The Litany of Intercession takes the responsive form, but extempore prayer or silence (with or without biddings) may be used, and in each case a member of the congregation may lead the congregation in these prayers. Representatives of the laity bring up to the table-altar the bread, wine, and alms. A single loaf of bread is used for the Fraction to symbolize the unity of all members in the Body of Christ. The Invitation to the people and their response employs the concept of the Messianic Banquet, in which the world-wide fellowship in the Kingdom of God is acknowledged. In all these ways, and in many responses, psalms and canticles throughout the service, the *koinonia* of the Church is re-affirmed and the people really share in the Liturgy.

"An Experimental Liturgy" is therefore marked by a strong consciousness of the fellowship of the Church of Christ, expressed

[72] This is a summary of the meaning of the service using the words of Dr. J. G. Davies as much as possible.

vividly in the ceremonial. The range of Biblical lessons emphasizes the continuity of the people of God throughout history, and the Messianic Banquet the world-wide extension of the Church. The Prayer of Thanksgiving, in which the people have a large vocal part, provides a summary of the holy acts of God from the creation while the Messianic Banquet looks to the consummation of history, and the emphasis is on the once crucified but now risen and ascended Christ. It is a simple, Biblical, joyful, and ecumenical rite. The only question that remains is whether it is sufficiently comprehensive for its purpose, and perhaps whether God's offering to us is minimized and the Church's offering to God overstressed.

In a cogent reply to criticisms,[73] Professor J. G. Davies readily admits that a master of English prose, such as Cranmer was, would be required to provide better rhythms and cadences in the prayers than his group was capable of doing, and that a smoother transition might be effected between the end of the Preparation and the beginning of the Ministry of the Word. He is, however, unwilling to eliminate the Preparation, as some would wish, since he believes this is psychologically necessary for most modern congregations. He concedes, too, that since it is hoped that the sermon will lead to a deeper penitence, the Confession might be taken from the Preparation and inserted between the Sermon and the Creed. A desire was expressed for an action to accompany the versicle and response of the Pax, as is done in the Liturgy of the Church of South India.

More serious criticisms were made of the Thanksgiving. It was said to present two distinct parts instead of a continuous unity. It was also urged that the contention of Professor E. C. Ratcliff that the earliest prayers of consecration had the *Sanctus* as the climax, not the commencement, should have been heeded. Davies, however, remains unconvinced by the evidence, and even if he were, does not feel "that *there was only one pattern*", or that it should be regarded as an ideal form. While admitting that a good rationale has been given by the Rev. A. H. Couratin for the *Sanctus* as the climax of the prayer of consecration, Professor Davies thinks there is an equally good one for retaining it in its usual position, namely, that the focus and setting of Christian worship is in heaven. The position of the Fraction is criticized as coming after and not before the Lord's Prayer, to which Davies replies that it is much more convenient for distribution to follow immediately after frac-

73 *Theology*, Vol. LXII, No. 469 (July 1959), pp. 274-79.

tion and it is more emphatic as a central act in its present position. In keeping with the corporate principles of the revisers it is also suggested that all (not merely the celebrant) should say the Post-Communion Prayer. Finally, Davies concedes that a better form of Dismissal would be: "The Lord be with you. And with thy spirit. Let us depart in peace. In the name of Christ, Amen." And his parting wish is: "May the debate continue to a fruitful conclusion."

From the widespread discussion that the experimental rite evoked, from Canada to Australia, and from India to the United States, it is clear that it has fulfilled its primary purpose of stimulating Anglicans to consider afresh in the light of modern liturgical thinking the principles of Prayer Book revision. It has, moreover, stressed the importance of Biblical theology in liturgical reconstruction, and has dared to treat the English Prayer Book as if it were not sacrosanct and inalterable. Furthermore, while it is not likely to be the *last* word in liturgical revision, it significantly stresses the Eucharist in comprehensive fashion as a memorial, a thanksgiving, a sacrifice, a communion, and an eschatological anticipation of the consummated Kingdom of God. And, as we have suggested, it is an important *first* word in liturgical reform, and one of ecumenical interest precisely because of its attempt at Biblical fidelity. Its borrowings from the Eastern Rites (a Little Entrance, without a Great Entrance, and an *epiklesis*) for a Western Rite are, however, perhaps exotic and not entirely consistent.

8. *The Reconsideration of Baptism and Confirmation*

Hitherto our consideration of worship in the Anglican Church has been almost exclusively concerned with Holy Communion, the central and normative Sacrament of the Christian life. Turning to the initiatory Sacrament, Baptism, and its completion in Confirmation, will give us an opportunity both to study the radical rethinking on Baptism that has occupied Anglican theologians for many years, and to consider the work of the Church of England Liturgical Commission which, after the disappointment of 1928, has after thirty years taken up again the official task of Prayer Book Revision. Its first fruits are to be seen in the report, *Baptism and Confirmation*, presented to the Archbishops of Canterbury and York in November of 1958 and published in 1959.

The subject of Baptism has lately become a storm centre of controversy. For this there are many reasons. Much of the practice of Infant Baptism has obviously become nominal, since a pitifully small number of the children who are baptized ever become confirmed communicant members of the Church. Furthermore, a vigorous denomination, the Baptists, exists to combat the very concept of paedo-Baptism, restricting this Sacrament to believers, and yet many of them believe that there is an advantage in holding a dedication of the child to God within the Christian community. It is also significant that two distinguished Reformed theologians, Karl Barth and Emil Brunner, reject Infant Baptism as a declension from the New Testament insistence upon repentance and faith as prerequisites for entry into the Christian community, while Oscar Cullmann and Joachim Jeremias have defended the traditional practice.[74]

The whole historical question of whether Infant Baptism is an early and primitive practice in the Church or a late excrescence is hotly debated. Moreover, theologians in support of the traditional practice assert that Infant Baptism alone stresses the priority of grace, the finished work of Christ, and the import of the Christian Church as the sphere of the operation of the Holy Spirit. Their Baptist critics, however, assert that faith as the conscious human response to grace must be given its proper role, and that Baptism by immersion is the most dramatic symbolic way of marking the death of the egocentric personality and its rebirth in Christ. Finally, there is commonly felt to be the need for a stronger link binding Baptism to Confirmation and first Communion.

The Church of England was driven to a reconsideration of Baptism by its failure to keep in its community the infants brought to the font. In 1939 it was reported to the Upper House of Canterbury that in the previous twenty-four years 67 per cent of all babies born in England, that is 11½ millions, were baptized in the Church of England, yet the Easter communicants in 1937 numbered only 2¼ millions.[75] Moreover, of the 67 per cent baptized, only 26 per cent were confirmed, and no more than 9 per cent became regular Anglican communicants. It was abundantly clear that the act of Baptism initiated but did not incorporate.

---

[74] See Barth's *Die Kirchliche Lehre von der Taufe* (1953) and Brunner's *Wahrheit als Begegnung* (1938) and the defences in Cullmann's *Die Tauflehre des Neuen Testaments* (1948) and Jeremias' *Hat die Urkirche die Kindertaufe geubt?* (1949). A useful survey of recent ecumenical thinking on Baptism is Ernest A. Payne's contribution to *Christian Baptism, A Fresh Attempt to Understand the Rite in terms of Scripture, History and Theology*, edited by A. Gilmore. See also the Church of Scotland's fine study, *The Biblical Doctrine of Baptism*.

[75] Figures given in Roger Lloyd, *The Church of England in the Twentieth Century*, Vol. II, p. 63.

Dom Gregory Dix in *The Theology of Confirmation in Relation to Baptism* (1946) emphasized that in the Early Church the catechumens underwent a long period of training before Baptism and that after their initiation there followed "Easter Mass in the dawn, and first Communion, as the beginning of Christian life in the exultant Church."[76] He insisted that in those days Baptism, Confirmation and first Communion were three parts of the same rite, and several responsible Churchmen have urged that Baptism should be preceded by instruction and be administered at the age of Confirmation.

On the other hand, two important studies in the early history of Baptism by English scholars supported the view that Infant Baptism was probably known in New Testament times and certainly not later than 80 A.D. W. F. Flemington, a Methodist scholar, made his case in *The New Testament Doctrine of Baptism* (1948). He claimed that "the baptism of infants is a thoroughly legitimate development of New Testament teaching, a practice in full accord with the mind of Christ, and, indeed, one that, rightly interpreted, safeguards certain aspects of evangelical teaching even more effectively than the practice whereby baptism is administered only to 'believers.' "[77] He elucidated the latter point in his claim as meaning that Infant Baptism expresses "the objective givenness of the Gospel."[78]

The other defence of the traditional practice came from the hand of Professor G. W. H. Lampe in *The Seal of the Spirit* (1951). He argued, most eruditely, that in the apostolic Church "Spirit-baptism" and "water-baptism" were indissolubly linked. He concluded that Baptism was the indwelling presence of the Holy Spirit as personal, rather than as a *donum gratiae*, which was given to the believer at this Sacrament of conversion, and that this personal presence would be more fully understood and experienced in the further Christian pilgrimage in the Spirit. This expectation of a fuller apprehension of the meaning of Baptism in the future is clearly as applicable to Infant as to Believers' Baptism. Lampe, however, is critical of some Anglican theologians who associate the special linking of the Holy Spirit with Confirmation and the laying-on of hands, for this denigrates the gift of the Spirit in Baptism.

[76] P. 12. L. S. Thornton, *Confirmation To-day*, should also be consulted, as both Dix and Thornton recognize Confirmation rather than Baptism as the predominant element in Christian initiation.
[77] P. 130.   [78] *Ibid.,* p. 131.

Two further studies which influenced the thought of the Liturgical Commission of the Church of England in its thinking were official reports. The first was *The Theology of Christian Initiation*, the result of a theological commission "appointed by the Archbishops of Canterbury and York to advise on the relations between Baptism, Confirmation and Holy Communion." The Commission emphasized the continuity between the three rites, because "the present-day counterpart to the primitive initiation is not Baptism alone, but Baptism, together with Confirmation, followed by first Communion."[79] Baptism and Confirmation were ultimately separated in the West and were linked in the East only at the expense of administering the complete rite to infants. It was emphasized that the classical order of Christian initiatory rites is "1. Preparation and Examination; 2. Baptism; 3. Confirmation; 4. First Communion." But, it was pointed out, "When Baptism is given in infancy, 1. has to be taken in two parts, (a) by sponsors, (b) in person, so that the new order is 1a, 2, 1b, 3, 4."[80] This situation has arisen not only because of the problems related to Infant Baptism, but also because in the earliest days the abyss dividing the Church and the world was clear-cut, whereas the situation is different in the settled life of the Church centuries later.

Four suggestions are made as warranting careful consideration: "(a) The confining of Infant Baptism to those children of whose Christian upbringing there is some assurance. (b) The establishment of a Catechumenate. (c) The more frequent administration of Baptism within the public Services of the Church. (d) The bringing into prominence of the Baptism and Confirmation of adults as an object-lesson on those aspects of initiation which were prominent in the first age of Christianity and now need to be made prominent again."[81]

The second important official study in this area was the final report of the Joint Committee of the Convocations of Canterbury and York, which was published as *Baptism and Confirmation Today* (1954). It was clearly intended to strike a hard blow against the nominalism associated too frequently with Infant Baptism in the Church of England. Its conclusions were substantially in keeping with the earlier report of 1948. It concluded that "Infant Baptism is only in line with the full teaching of the Church if: (i) it is accepted that it points forward to Confirmation

79 *The Theology of Christian Initiation*, p. 12.
80 *Ibid.*, p. 19.   81 *Ibid.*, p. 22.

and Holy Communion; (ii) there is reasonable chance of the child being taught to 'improve his Baptism'; (iii) the instruction of baptized children in the Christian faith and life be regarded as a matter of the utmost importance."

With this growing unity of opinion in the understanding of initiation, the Liturgical Commission of the Church of England was in a happy condition for commencing the task of Prayer Book revision. It turned its attention first to Baptism and Confirmation, and later was engaged on the reform of the Eucharistic Liturgy.

The first and eagerly awaited report of the Liturgical Commission was submitted to the Archbishops of Canterbury and York in November of 1958 and was printed in 1959 as *Baptism and Confirmation*. Representative of both Anglo-Catholic and Evangelical viewpoints, the Commission was remarkable for its many scholars learned in liturgical lore. Many of them, whom it would be invidious to single out for mention, were known to the wider world through their writings. It may, however, be remarked that it was a little curious that there was no layman in the original membership of the Commission, especially as on all hands the modern stress is on the importance of the laity's part in the Liturgy.

One great novelty, though it was an attempt to recover primitive usage, was the printing first of the Order for the Baptism and Confirmation of Adults, as the "archetypal" service. The Order for Infant Baptism was printed next as a separate service, but directions were appended for its combination, when desirable, with Holy Communion or with Morning or Evening Prayer. The intention was clear that Infant Baptism with its solemn promises made by the sponsors was to be regarded as no "hole and corner" affair, but ought to be administered in the context of full congregational worship. Adult Confirmation was printed third, as a corollary of Infant Baptism. "In this way it is hoped," so the report reads, "to relate each part of the pattern to the archetypal service, while at the same time providing for the maximum of flexibility to meet a variety of pastoral occasions."[82]

A second novelty is the provision for the "Ministry of the Word." That is, a new preface to Adult Baptism, Infant Baptism, and Adult Confirmation is provided, of substantially the same type as the introduction to Holy Communion in the Prayer Book, consisting of a Collect, Scripture Lessons, and a Sermon or Homily framed upon them, in conformity with both Patristic and Reformed

[82] *Baptism and Confirmation*, p. x.

tradition. This, again, was an effective way of combatting mere convention and nominalism in these orders of worship.

An attempt was made to frame orders for Infant and Adult Baptism as much alike as possible. In each order the blessing of the water comes first, then the acts of renunciation and faith, and then the pouring of the water. The principal prayer in each service is the blessing of the water, and in this "an attempt has been made to express the whole Biblical doctrine of Baptism."[83] This prayer offers thanksgiving for Christ as the agent of creation and of redemption, who received the Baptism of repentance and was anointed with the Holy Spirit for man's sake, was delivered up to the suffering of death to purify unto himself a people for his own possession, and who on his ascension poured out the Holy Spirit of promise and renewal. It ends by beseeching God "to sanctify this water to the mystical washing away of sin; and grant that all to be baptized herein may be made members of thy Church, which is the Body of thy Son our Lord; that so, being baptized unto his death, and being made partakers of his resurrection, they may die daily unto sin and rise again unto righteousness; and serving thee faithfully with all thy saints, may inherit the kingdom of thy glory. . . ."[84] This is an admirable summary of the *heilsgeschichte* with special reference to Baptism. In the matter of the promises required there is, however, a different requirement for adults and children. The form for adults is the customary one, while that for infants is briefer and simpler, being thought more apt for godparents at Infant Baptism and for children making promises at Confirmation.

Since it was reported that the ceremony of signing with the Cross was thought by some persons to be the outward and visible sign of Baptism, it was thought wise to place it, along with the optional giving of the lighted candle, under a new heading, "The Ceremonies after Baptism." No provision, however, was made for the giving of a white robe or for the permissive use of oil before Baptism or of chrism after Baptism or Confirmation, since such customs were either impractical or did not command widespread interest.

The Confirmation Rite was drafted with the purpose of "emphasizing the centrality of the prayer for the coming of the Spirit."[85] The Bishop is directed to say this prayer facing the candidates with arms outstretched in their direction according to ancient

[83] *Ibid.*, p. xi.   [84] *Ibid.*, p. 12.   [85] *Ibid.*, p. xii.

custom. Great care was taken in employing the term "confirm" in such a way as to exclude neither of the meanings attached to it, as strengthening or completing.

The important prayer of the Bishop includes responsive "Amens" to stress the significance of the gifts of the Spirit:

> Almighty and everliving God, who hast vouchsafed to regenerate *these* thy *servants* by water and the Holy Ghost, and hast given unto *them* forgiveness of all their sins: Send down from heaven upon *them* thy Holy Ghost the Comforter. *Amen.*
> The Spirit of wisdom and understanding. *Amen.*
> The Spirit of counsel and ghostly strength. *Amen.*
> The Spirit of knowledge and true godliness. *Amen.*
> And fill *them*, O Lord, with the Spirit of thy holy fear. *Amen.*[86]

The formula of confirmation is simple, speedy, and sufficient: "*Confirm*, O Lord, thy servant N. [or, this thy servant] with thy Holy Spirit, that *he* may continue thine for ever."[87]

Three General Rubrics are provided. The first indicates the norm for the administration of these services, namely that the whole congregation shall witness the reception of new members into Christ's Church and be themselves reminded of the promises that they (or their sponsors) made at Baptism and which they made for themselves at Confirmation. The second rubric requires the font to be set up in such a place that the whole congregation shall be able to see and hear the Sacrament of Baptism. The third rubric indicates that Confirmation requires of candidates the ability to say the Creed, the Lord's Prayer, the Decalogue, and the capacity to answer the other questions asked in the Church Catechism.[88]

Finally, the Commission expresses the hope that the report will be welcomed as an attempt to equip the Church with flexible liturgical forms adaptable to changing needs in the pastoral situation, and that it will be recognized as an honest attempt to get behind those controversies which arose out of the late mediaeval period.[89]

The members of the Liturgical Commission must be applauded for their irenic spirit, for the strong Biblical basis of their theology and prayers, for clearly indicating by their rubrics that Baptism is most meaningful as a part of a regular service in the face of a congregation (not a private gathering for family and friends), and

---

[86] *Ibid.*, p. 15. [87] *Ibid.*, p. 16. [88] *Ibid.*, p. xvi.
[89] *Ibid.*

for stressing the solemnity of the promises made (which a sermon or homily will make plain). Moreover, the formal unity of the three services may do much to accustom the mind of the people to a sense of their inter-relationship in the development of the Christian life, while the flexibility allowed for so that they may be incorporated in Morning or Evening Prayer or in the service of Holy Communion will be welcomed by the parish minister. All this represents a considerable achievement and augurs well for the consequent responsibility for providing a revised Order for Holy Communion.

Nonetheless, the Orders already published have not escaped criticism. Indeed, two members of the Commission thought the revision was too radical a departure from the present practice of the Church of England, and disliked the flexibility. Others are disturbed that the Order for Infant Baptism includes no mention of the customary "receive this child into the congregation of Christ's flock." Objection has been raised to the elimination of Mark 10:13-16 and the substitution of Matthew 28:18-30 in the Baptism of Infants since it has nothing to do with infants, to which it might be retorted that the alternative has nothing to do with Baptism. Some exception has been taken to the infelicitous English of the prayers. Perhaps the most controversial feature of the report is to have taken the Adult Baptism and Confirmation as archetypal and primary, when, in fact, Infant Baptism is the commoner mode of present day initiation. On the whole, however, the report has been welcomed.

9. *Retrospect and Prospect*

The historian's task is to record and interpret, not to prophesy, especially in such uncertain times as the present. In comparing the ethos of the Church of England in its internal and external relations at the beginning of the century and in the nadir of its fortunes in 1928, with the present situation, some important and hopeful differences can be observed, and these are promising for the development of its worship.

At the beginning of the century relationships between Anglicans and Free Churchmen were embittered, but there is today a common recognition that England is mission territory for all the denominations. Furthermore, it is common in most universities for Anglican and Free Church ordinands to have been taught by some lecturers of confessional loyalties other than their own, and certainly the best contemporary scholarship in theology is far from being exclusively Anglican. The Student Christian Movement at the universities and local ministers' fraternals in towns and cities have broken down the older alienation. It is commonly admitted that Anglicans have the pre-eminence in worship and Free Churchmen the leadership in preaching, and among the younger generation of clergy and ministers there is a deep longing for reunion. The Ecumenical Movement has changed the whole picture.

The old party exclusiveness which characterized internal relationships at the beginning of the century, and which reappeared in the tragic divisions over Prayer Book revision in 1927 and 1928, has now markedly decreased, with the increase of a great sense of common loyalty to the Church. The Anglo-Catholics are now far less likely to imitate Roman Catholicism than they were and they have entered fully into the recovery of a Biblical theology. Their strenuous spiritual regimen once feared by the Low Churchmen is now admired, as well as their splendid record of service in slum parishes, and their stressing of the social implications of the Eucharist. Anglo-Catholics for their part have come to respect the scholarship and devotion of the Evangelical clergy,[90] and the Evangelicals themselves have acknowledged that they did not pay enough attention to the beauty of holiness in worship or to the importance of the corporate nature of the Church manifested and renewed in the Eucharist. This unity is above all seen in the conjoint stress on Word and Sacrament. Thus an united Church of England is far likelier than the quarrelsome Church of 1928 to impress Parliament with the urgent need for the reform of the Prayer Book. The very fact that the Church of England members of a joint Anglican and Methodist Committee appointed to reconsider the reunion of these Churches were unanimously in favour of union could also prove that the Church of England has more right to speak for the nation spiritually than might previously have been supposed. For, after all, the Methodists are the largest of the English Free Churches.

The almost arrogant sacerdotalism of earlier generations of Anglican clergy is now obsolescent and may shortly become obsolete. Contemporary Anglican worship manifests, through the

90 The Evangelicals have established a research centre at Oxford, named Latimer House, presumably as a complement to the High Church centre at Oxford, Pusey House. In 1960, the Evangelicals established a College of Preachers to which some High Church as well as many Low Church clergy have repaired for refresher courses.

Parish Communion, the House Church, "An Experimental Liturgy," and the Clare College Manual for Holy Communion, a desire to recognize the importance of the laity. It is likely that the apostolate of the laity will be even further developed if the Anglicans and the Methodists unite, for a great strength of Methodism has been the thousands of local preachers who have supplemented the work of the ordained ministers, and who have preached the Gospel in terms understood by the common people. The democratisation of the Church is likelier to lead to even greater relevance in its worship.

Furthermore, we have drawn attention to the more influential examples of liturgical experiment in the Anglican Church in recent years as a sign of new life in a community that reveres tradition. These were, however, only a tithe of the experiments that were being tried. No mention was made of the Rev. Geoffrey Beaumont's *Folk Mass*,[91] an attempt to utilise popular melody in the service of the Church, and thus to bridge the gap between the Church and the world, and between the older and the younger generations. Nor were the renewed importance of services of spiritual healing mentioned. Both experiments are likely to become more common in the future. It is very likely also that the Easter Vigil, a recent Roman Catholic recovery of the practice of the Early Church, may become acclimatised in England in the near future.[92]

From time to time the names of members of Anglican religious communities have appeared in these pages, notably those of Father A. G. Hebert and Dom Gregory Dix, the authors respectively of *Liturgy and Society* and *The Shape of the Liturgy*. It is not without significance that these are among the most significant Anglican treatises on worship in our period. The implication is clear that in such communities of celibates, dedicated to the contemplation of God, deep spirituality may be found, and that its gains are made available for the culture of the spiritual life not of the few, but of the entire Church. The same spirituality engenders the courage of faith as manifested, for example, in Father (now Bishop) Trevor Huddleston's fight against *apartheid* in Southern Africa, so modestly recorded in *Naught for Your Comfort* and so movingly described in the character of Father Vincent in Alan

[91] For a critique see Erik R. Routley, *Church Music and Theology*, pp. 104-07. Also see Chap. III *supra*.
[92] See J. T. Martin, *Christ our Passover*.

Paton's *Cry the Beloved Country.* The Church of England's heritage of worship is immeasurably strengthened by the presence in its midst of communities consecrated to the *opus Dei,* in which there is discipline without deadliness, goodness with gaiety, and faith without fear or favour. The Community of the Resurrection, The Society of the Sacred Mission, the Cowley Fathers, and the Anglican Benedictine Community at Nashdom, must not be forgotten for their contribution to the renewal of worship in England.[93]

We have cited Bishop Hensley Henson's judgment that the Parliamentary rejection of the Revised Prayer Book was in fact less a vote of no confidence in the Book than in the Bishops, for they seemed to be men of expediency rather than of conviction. The same charge could hardly be made of the present Archbishop of Canterbury who, in his enthronement sermon, announced a determination to see Prayer Book revision through and an unwillingness to muzzle the Church at the behest of Parliament. No more could it be made against the present Bishop of Woolwich, whose book *Honest to God*[94] has been satirized as an exposition of the paradox that "the creed of the English is that there is no God and that it is wise to pray to him from time to time," but whose worst enemies could not deny him candour and courage. The bench of Bishops is no longer a synonym for vacillating expediency.

Throughout our period, which has been one of increasing gains for secularism, we have yet seen a genuine ecumenical advance, an improvement in the internal and external relationships of the Church of England, a desire to make far greater use of the talents of the laity, an increase in the courage of the leaders of the Church, a new fertility in liturgical and evangelistic experiment, an increase in the appreciation of monasticism, a deepening concern that society shall manifest the justice that God wills for his people, and a desire to correlate religion with visual art and drama. Above all, there has been growing a clearer and more cogent conviction of the Divine origin and empowering of the Church as manifested in the Eucharist. However strong the forces of secularism and materialism, there is great encouragement in the thought that the

[93] See Peter F. Anson, *The Call of the Cloister* and A. M. Allchin, *The Silent Rebellion* (1958). See also the tribute of an English Presbyterian: "The whole witness of the religious orders is a standing challenge to the values of the present age. The vows to poverty, chastity and obedience are the very opposites of the materialism, sensuality and license which are commonly exalted among us." (Kenneth Slack, *The British Churches Today,* p. 37).
[94] This book was discussed in Chap. V.

Church has never lost sight of her calling to adore God and to serve mankind. And it is precisely this calling which has been renewed in the Church of England through more than half a century's concentration on worship.[95]

[95] One is reminded of the words of Reinhold Niebuhr to Archbishop William Temple: "I told him I thought the Prayer-book had saved the Anglican Communion from rationalism and Pelagianism more than Episcopacy had done" (cited in F. A. Iremonger, *William Temple*, p. 494).

CHAPTER X

THE WORSHIP OF THE
FREE CHURCHES

IKE THE Anglican Church, the English Free Churches—the collective designation for the Baptist, Congregational, Presbyterian, and Methodist Communions—have experienced a renewal in worship. Anglican worship, as we have seen, is an amalgam of Catholic and Reformed elements, with the former predominating. Free Church worship is predominantly Reformed—an amalgam of the Puritan and Pietist traditions within Protestantism—with a recent recovery of some Catholic elements, notably a higher evaluation of liturgical forms and of the Sacraments of Baptism and the Lord's Supper.

The Puritan tradition contributed a strong stress on the sovereignty of God, the authority of Scripture, the primacy of preaching, and a preference for extemporary prayers over set forms. The Pietist tradition modified the idea of Divine sovereignty with an emphatic assertion of the universality of grace, reinforced evangelism and spontaneity in prayer, and added warmth to the covenanted fellowship.

The Catholic influence has been mediated by involvement in the Ecumenical Movement, by the example of Anglican worship (especially strong on the Methodists who were originally a Society within the Church of England), by the admirable service-books of the Church of Scotland, and by a renewed interest in the study of the primitive Church and of the early Fathers.

The worship of the Free Churches is Biblically-based, unpretentious in its simplicity, and not infrequently austere. It is, however, rarely a fugitive piety. Its architecture may occasionally run to an incongruous imitation of Gothic, but there is nothing antiquarian about its ethics. The very ambivalence of its favourite term for worship suggests that there is no hiatus between the "service" of God in the sanctuary and the "service" of men in the street. Its high evaluation of preaching is due to the conviction that when God's Word is faithfully expounded His people receive the Divine promises for consolation, the Divine warnings for correction, and the Divine example and instruction of Christ for their pilgrimage. Especially in recent years aesthetics have not been thought to be inimical to ethics, and symbolism is no longer equated with idolatry. But, as we shall see, aesthetic dilettantism has its own dangers in worship, no less than its opposite, unbuttoned amateurism or calculated casualness.

1. *Three Major Trends in Worship*

"Change and decay in all around I see" was the despairing cry of a Victorian observer. The kaleidoscopic rapidity and variety of change was, however, even more strikingly a characteristic of the twentieth century scene. Anglican worship, as we have already seen, despite the balance and ballast given by the Book of Common Prayer, displayed some giddy vagaries of fashion in ceremonial, vestments, architecture, and music, as it veered from Gothic to Baroque, and from Rococo to Functionalism. The Free Churches, without any norm such as a prescribed Liturgy, were even more at the mercy of modes of taste and interest. In general, however, there were three major trends corresponding to three different theologies and their three different conceptions of the nature of the Church.

The first trend, anti-historical and anti-authoritarian, is hard to define because so inchoate, but it may not unfairly be called "The School of Spontaneity." It was the longest trend, lasting from the beginning of the first to the middle of the fourth decade. It was particularly strong among Congregationalists, and W. B. Selbie, J. Vernon Bartlet, C. J. Cadoux, and Albert Peel were probably its most notable representatives. That it should have attracted the first, a pioneer in the study of the psychology of religion (and a splendid preacher), is not surprising, but it is more than curious that it should have appealed to the other three for they were all distinguished historians.

The second trend was that exhibited by the self-designated "Society of Free Catholics," who admired Catholic mysticism and sacramentalism but disliked Catholic doctrine. This small but influential body included W. E. Orchard, R. J. Campbell, and J. M. Lloyd Thomas, respectively Presbyterian, Congregational, and Unitarian ministers when they joined the Society. It flourished in the second and third decades and then petered out, as Orchard became a Roman Catholic and Campbell an Anglo-Catholic, but not before they had produced two remarkable liturgies of a comprehensive character.

The third trend may be styled "Reformed Churchmanship,"

since it indicates both a strong sense of the Church's continuity and of its re-foundation on the basis of the recovered Gospel in the sixteenth century. It began about 1936, revealing the impact of Karl Barth's Theology of the Word of God, and has continued with great vigour to the present. Its first generation leaders in Congregationalism were Nathaniel Micklem, John S. Whale, and B. L. Manning; in Methodism, R. Newton Flew; and among the Baptists, A. C. Underwood. Its second generation representatives in Congregationalism include John Marsh, Daniel Jenkins, Hubert Cunliffe-Jones, W. A. Whitehouse, and John Huxtable; in Methodism, Gordon Rupp, Philip Watson, and Rupert Davies; and among the Baptists, Ernest A. Payne, R. C. Walton, Neville Clark, and Stephen Winward.

2. The "School of Spontaneity"

Four very powerful influences combined to produce the strongly pervasive impact of this group on the theory and practice of worship, and they are still influential in helping to create a prejudice against liturgical worship as consisting of only "stinted forms." The first was the strong historical memory of the Free Churches, and particularly of the Congregationalists and Presbyterians, for whom the Book of Common Prayer is less a liturgical treasure than an instrument of oppression. It was because the Puritan ministers of these two denominations could not subscribe to the declaration that the Book of Common Prayer was in all things conformable to the Word of God that in 1662 they lost their livings and went out into the wilderness.

The second factor was the strong conviction that forms of prayer are only crutches for beginners in prayer but that when a man has learned how to speak to God in the freedom and intimacy of the Holy Spirit he will cast away all forms; on this view to retain a liturgy is to remain in the adolescent stage of the spiritual life. Hence the easy equivalent is made of sincerity with formlessness. And in making it there was the long tradition of the Society of Friends to support it. Had not the Quakers proved that the adoration of God needs neither ministers, nor altars, nor prayer-books, nor hymn-books, nor even sacraments? As their favourite Johannine text has it: "the Spirit bloweth where it listeth."

The third influence derived from the reigning philosophy and theology of the age, idealism and immanentalism. The former insisted that all objects are ultimately identifiable with ideas, which meant that concept was far more important than concretion; and, as applied to theology, that it is the Logos that counts, not the Incarnation, and that sacraments are, therefore, pictures for simple people. Immanentalism identified God either partly or completely with the world, and the Kingdom of God became little more than the sum total of human idealism. Hence there was a rigid dichotomy between the spiritual and the material, the ideational and the sensate.

The fourth and final influence was the socialistic version of the Christian faith, called either the "new theology" or the "social Gospel," which interpreted love of God almost exclusively in terms of the love of neighbour. The effect of these four influences on traditional Christian worship may be judged from the opposition of categories which its representatives set up. Freedom was contrasted with authority, contemporary experience with the dead hand of tradition, spiritual insight with the life of the senses, sermon with sacrament, social service with formal worship, this-worldly altruism with other-worldly selfishness, creativity with the creeds, the prophetic with the priestly, conceptual with picture-thinking, the Kingdom of God with the Church, and, the favourite antithesis, Spirit with Institution. It will be abundantly clear that the die was heavily loaded against tradition, history, creeds, liturgy, and sacraments, and even against the Church as an institution.[1]

While the general tendency of the "School of Spontaneity" was to derogate from the orderliness and dignity of worship, and even to degenerate in some cases into informality indistinguishable from gaucherie, it also had its merits. Chief among these was the note of contemporary compassion for the underprivileged and a determination to support all workers for social amelioration. These concerns were reflected in Litanies for Labour, in a variety of intercessions for social workers, doctors, nurses, and teachers, and in the rousing hymns of the social gospel which celebrated the establishment of a coming Kingdom of social justice and international peace. In this respect John Hunter's *Devotional Services*,[2] which appeared first in 1882 and in 1901 in its final and greatly

[1] Quite typical is Henry W. Clark's assertion: "According to the Nonconformist view of the Church it is in the idea and in the inner experience of life one is immersed, the idea being formative in the theory of the Church, and the experience formative on the Church's actual meaning—that one does not begin with organisation, but comes to it . . . as to a thing second both in importance and time" (*History of English Nonconformity*, Vol. II, p. 309).

[2] This was treated extensively in my *Worship and Theology in England*, Vol. IV, *From Newman to Martineau, 1850-1900*, pp. 229-37.

enlarged form, set the Free Church standard for the first three decades. It was as influential in Britain as was its American counterpart, Walter Rauschenbusch's *For God and the People: Prayers of the Social Awakening* (1910).

Three disturbing pictures of the gaucherie in worship induced by the cult of informality will be sufficient evidence for the dangers of the approach. Bernard Manning gives an all too vivid account of how some Congregationalists celebrated the Lord's Supper: "Have you never been at a Communion service where the bread and the wine, handed to us from the Upper Room itself, were treated as tiresome, rather unspiritual adjuncts to a service, *impedimenta* to be disposed of as rapidly and inconspicuously as possible, lest they should hinder us (God forgive us) from spiritual flights on our own account? . . . The bread and wine are sometimes huddled round to us before the service proper begins, or perhaps under cover of some hymn. The bread is not broken. The wine is not poured out. Prayer, thanksgiving and the invocation of the Holy Ghost do not precede the distribution of the elements. . . . Let me not be thought to exaggerate. I bring no general charge against our churches, but I say that in some places and at some times these things are done; and everyone knows that that is true."[3]

H. Wheeler Robinson confessed to a similar repugnance when he considered the worship of the Baptists, his own denomination: "An Anglican, entering a Baptist Church for divine worship might often be alienated by the seeming want of reverence. There is no visible altar, and an obtrusive pulpit takes its place. The choir is too visible, and does not seem greatly concerned with anything but its own function. Deacons walk about unnecessarily, and even come to chat with people in the pews. The secretary gives out notices at an alarming length, and may intersperse a few remarks. The preacher, who wears no distinctive dress, follows no particular order in his prayers, and may be wearisomely long in his sermon. People stay about in clusters talking when the service is over, and the minister may come down and join them, or stand in the vestibule shaking hands with people. As for the Communion Service—!"[4]

Apparently some parts of rural Methodism are in a similar case. A reporter in East Anglia, a headmaster and a Free Churchman (but not a Methodist), who has acted for several years as a Methodist local preacher, writes: "The Methodist Church puzzles

---

[3] *Essays in Orthodox Dissent*, pp. 61ff.
[4] *The Baptist View of the Church and Ministry* (1944), p. 23.

me; it is curiously bifurcated. It takes the Baptismal and Communion Service from the Church of England, almost unchanged. But in the ordinary service there seems to be no renascence of worship. Even when ministers take the service, the long rambling prayers persist and the formal informality which never says, 'Hymn no. 666,' but 'Shall we sing no. 666?' Yet if anyone replied: 'Might we have 999 instead?' there would be consternation. I have even heard this summer: 'Shall we read a portion of the Old Testament?' "[5] That these experiences are no longer typical, however commonplace they might have been in the first three decades of the century, is a proof of how far the English Free Churches have come on the road to reverence.

The immanentalism of Liberal Protestant theology in these first thirty years shows other characteristics besides gaucherie in worship. Inheriting the strong stress on experience which marked religious thinking from Schleiermacher to Sabatier, it is not surprising that subjectivity and moody introspection should also leave their marks on the worship of the English Free Churches.

This subjectivity is manifested in egotistical and introspective hymns, the products of lyrical spiders forever spinning from their own insides, and in prayers that concentrate on human feelings and moods rather than on divine deeds or demands.[6] It has become a serious matter when subjectivity even intrudes on the objectivity which denominational directories or manuals of worship are supposed to provide. This happens in the Congregational *Manual for Ministers* of 1936 in two outstanding instances. The sentimental emphasis is dominant in the Order for Holy Communion which places, immediately after the Prayer of Humble Access, John Hunter's invitation: "Come to this sacred Table, not because you

[5] I am indebted to the kindness of the Rev. Dr. Andrew L. Drummond of Alva, Scotland, for this report from the headmaster in East Anglia which he copied in a letter to me dated August 20, 1962. Probably the residual austerity of Calvinism has saved the Presbyterian Church of England from an attitude of "cosiness" towards its Creator. W. E. Orchard suggests as much in *From Faith to Faith*, pp. 48-49.

[6] Among the better hymns that overuse the first person singular, those of George Matheson "Make me a captive, Lord" and "O love that wilt not let me go" might be cited, and among the worst is the erotic "Still, still with Thee, when purple morning breaketh." The state of Christians forever taking their own spiritual temperatures is almost ironically expressed in Shairp's hymn of which the first six lines read:

'Twixt gleams of joy and clouds of doubt
Our feelings come and go;
Our best estate is tossed about
In ceaseless ebb and flow.
No mood of feeling, form of thought,
Is constant for a day.

must, but because you may. . . . Come, not to express an opinion, but to seek a Presence and pray for a Spirit." It also appears in a prayer in the Order of Service for Christmas Day in which familiarity becomes over-familiarity, and fellowship "folksy." "Father of all," it begins well enough, "at this time when the solitary are set in families," then descends to "when children's children gather under the old roof"[7] and ends on a didactic anticlimax. At other times the tenderness is appropriate and restrained, as in the Service for the Burial of a Child. Yet it is a weakness when a Service of Infant Baptism is interpreted to mean, through the Exhortation, that the central fact is that the child is being dedicated to God, not that the Church by virtue of Christ's everlasting Gospel is adding to its membership. This error is contained in the Methodist *Book of Offices* (1936).

In fact the emphasis on children in this period was one of the strongest contributions of an immanentalist theology, presumably as a consequence of its denial of the doctrine of original sin. Here, if anywhere, sentimentality would obtrude, and particularly at Baptist services of the dedication of children or in Congregational "christenings." The minister who refused to make the sign of the Cross on the child's forehead, although this was a venerable custom, was happy enough to plant his own sign, a firm kiss, on the infant's brow. Another proof of the sentimentality of the period and part of its cult of the child was the demand made of Free Church ministers to include a children's sermon as a regular part of the Sunday morning service. This almost inevitably produced a lowering of the seriousness and reverence of worship, when the minister became cute, comic, or painfully condescending. It was even more embarrassing when, in unbuttoned mood, he fell into his anecdotage, recounting the peccadilloes of his youth or of his own children. But, lest we unduly malign one section of the Christian community in England, it should not be forgotten that this was also the period when "Children's Corners" proliferated in Anglican churches. In these would be found miniature chairs and tables, minuscule books, the inevitable Margaret Tarrant picture of an effeminate Jesus surrounded by rabbits, squirrels, and children with perfect manners, but rarely a living child in the Children's Corner!

In this period the sentimentality of children's hymns was so

---

[7] *Manual for Ministers*, pp. 102-03. Yet it was an advance for a Congregational manual of worship to provide prayers for the Christian Year.

treacly that it provoked that sturdy Scottish theologian, A. M. Fairbairn, to the fervent outburst "I am grateful that my childhood was nurtured on the Book of Psalms rather than on the jingling verses that celebrate the 'Sweet Saviour,' or protest how I love 'my Jesus.' "[8] The attitude which Fairbairn criticized led to such astonishing statements as the following, included in an exhortation at a Service of Infant Baptism in a Presbyterian Church: "It has been well said that the most important gospel for a child is not the gospel according to Matthew or Mark, but the gospel according to father and mother."[9] Subjectivity and sentimentality became so strong that Nathaniel Micklem argued that the strongest defence of liturgical forms was that they would rescue both ministers and congregations from being at the mercy of ministerial moods.[10]

Another characteristic of the worship of the "School of Spontaneity" was its near pantheism, to which the wearying didacticism of the "sermons in stones" mentality is closely related. It was as if the Free Churches in their eagerness to run away from the high sacramentalism of the Roman Catholics and the Anglo-Catholics had fallen among Quakers. Certainly the pan-sacramentalism of the Society of Friends was very popular during this period. From this all-spreading root sprang the extempore prayers of thanksgiving that celebrated the scenic wonders of the universe[11] (and the Alps in particular if the minister had just holidayed in Switzerland, or Ben Nevis and Loch Lomond if he were a Presbyterian). It was the origin of the chubby-faced junior choir simpering for the hundredth time through "All things bright and beautiful, all creatures great and small," and because of it the Harvest Festival became the most popular special Sunday of the year, with its annual opportunity for the expression of cupboard love.

Perhaps this pan-sacramentalism was never given a more striking place than in the order for the sanctification of a Church Bazaar in the Congregational *Manual for Ministers* (1936). Such breath-taking liturgical inventiveness should not have been beyond devising a form for the blessing of Bingo or for the con-celebration of Canasta. One cannot but admire the ingenuity of the liturgist, however one may suspect his judgment. The order

8 *Studies in Religion and Theology*, p. 272.

9 Eric Phillip, *Sacramental and Other Services*, p. 2. Phillip was a minister of the Presbyterian Church of England.

10 See the article "Extempore Prayer in the Congregational Tradition," *The Congregational Quarterly*, Vol. XIII (1935), p. 330.

11 See an example of gilded romanticism in D. Tait Patterson's *The Call to Worship*, p. 123.

contains three choice banalities. The first is the Old Testament lesson, with its pointed hint: "And all the women that were wise-hearted did spin with their hands and brought that which they had spun." The second is a specially composed hymn including the apt verse:

> Unveil through deeds which love has wrought
> The Presence wondrous and divine
> That common objects, sold and bought,
> May glow as sacramental sign.

And surely there has never been another liturgical rubric like the one that ends the service: *Then shall follow the Chairman's introduction of the Opener of the Bazaar, the declaration of the opening, and the appropriate votes of thanks.*[12] Bonhoeffer has written of cheap grace, but here were sacraments, glowing ones too, at cut-rates. So pervasive was this pan-sacramentalism that it became necessary for theologians to insist with Archbishop William Temple that if God was everywhere in general then it was difficult to focus on Him anywhere in particular. The sensitive Methodist devotional writer, A. E. Whitham, joined the protest, affirming: "The characteristic truth of Christianity is not that God is everywhere, which may easily mean that he is nowhere, but that God is somewhere—specially, seriously, savingly somewhere—not that He saturates me like a Scotch mist, but that he satisfies me like a warm friend."[13]

The emphasis on the authority of personal experience was retained longest by the Methodist Church. This was not remarkable in view of its Pietistic origins, and of the formalism of the day which John Wesley tried so hard to combat. It is significant that the introduction to the supplementary Methodist book, *Divine Worship* (1935), was most careful to stress that forms were no substitute for experience. Thus: "The glow of a personal experience is necessary to give a sense of reality and the warmth of sincerity to worship, but as the member draws its nourishment from the body, so religious experience finds its strength and renewal as well as its natural expression in fellowship."[14] Indeed, this particular volume demonstrates the very great strengths as well as the weaknesses of Liberal Protestant worship. On the negative side there is the wallowing introversion and self-pity,[15] the

[12] *Manual for Ministers*, p. 173.   [13] *The Catholic Christ*, p. 29.
[14] *Divine Worship*, p. 13.   [15] *Ibid.*, p. 198.

almost interminable catalogue of specific sins and failures,[16] the sentimentalities of the child cult,[17] the pantheism,[18] and the excessive horizontal stress on fellowship.[19] The great values are the recovery of the humanity of Jesus as exemplar,[20] the deep compassion for the handicapped,[21] the stress on the civic and social responsibilities of Christians,[22] and, in particular, on Christian concern for the economic order.[23]

Another characteristic of the worship of the "School of Spontaneity" was that ministers could rarely resist the perils of didacticism in their public prayers. This is perhaps most clearly revealed in a telling direction in the *Directory for Public Worship for use in the Presbyterian Church of England* (1921). This reads: "The Sermon may be placed much earlier in the service, and the teaching which it conveys may then find expression in the prayers and praise that follow, whether in thanksgiving for special mercies, in confession, or in intercession. The Sermon may thus be used to guide the people in their worship."[24] This particular defect has been the historic bane of Protestant worship, not merely of Liberal Protestantism. In effect, it turned the potential priest and mediator in prayer into a boring schoolmaster, who might develop the worship as a series of variations on the one-stringed fiddle of his topic for the day. If the provision of a Liturgy is one way to prevent ministerial tyranny in worship, the use of a lectionary is a similar protective device to spare the congregation from the limited anthology of lections which the minister himself finds helpful.

As early as 1919, Sir John McClure warned in his Chairman's address to the Congregational Union Assembly that preaching had pre-empted all interest in prayer. Indeed, the sermon had become "the golden calf of the denomination" with the result that the earlier parts of the service were merely preliminaries to preaching, and "our assemblies are too often looked upon as the lecture-rooms of popular speakers."[25] The real heart of the problem was succinctly expressed in the assertion that "the preachers of today, who

16 *Ibid.*, pp. 184-87.   17 *Ibid.*, pp. 169-72.
18 *Ibid.*, pp. 217-19.
19 Seen in the first part of the introduction and in the use of popular hymns as prayers (pp. 203ff.).
20 *Ibid.*, pp. 112f., 212, 218.
21 *Ibid.*, p. 177f. for "An Act of Sympathy with Suffering."
22 *Ibid.*, pp. 237-38.
23 *Ibid.*, p. 173f. for "Intercession for Social Life."
24 P. 12.
25 "The Public Worship of God," an address of May 13, 1919, published in *The Congregational Union Year Book* (1920), p. 53.

are ancestored in the Puritans know, in the main, how to present an argument, but not how to create an atmosphere."[26]

Finally, in the "School of Spontaneity" there was a serious devaluation of the Sacraments of Baptism and the Lord's Supper. They were, neither of them, primarily regarded as means of grace, as channels of the transforming Holy Spirit, but as affirmations of fellowship and badges of dedication to the work of Christ. For this reason the stress in Infant Baptism was on the dedication of the child and his parents to God, and in the Lord's Supper on a community memorial rite. The first point may be illustrated from the ambiguity—which was probably deliberate—in the single question put to the parents at Infant Baptism in *The Manual for Ministers* (1936): "You have come to present this child for Christian *baptism and dedication*; do you promise that he shall be brought up as a Christian child in the nurture and admonition of the Lord?" It is equally typical that the expected Pelagian answer was: "We do."[27]

The devaluation of the Lord's Supper was indicated not only by a memorialist doctrine, as we have indicated, but by insisting that a layman had as much right to celebrate it as a minister,[28] and, above all, by the substitution of unfermented for fermented wine and the provision of "diced cubes" of bread, which meant that the great acts of Fraction and Libation hitherto deemed central to the Sacrament were no longer performed. The very term "Sacraments" which had formerly been exclusively reserved for Baptism and the Lord's Supper was now eviscerated of its historic meaning. A tell-tale prayer in the same service book expresses thanksgiving to God at the end of the year "for the sacraments of love and service which have made us conscious of Thy presence in our common life."[29] A final proof that Holy Communion was no longer the greatest privilege of the membership of the Church was seen in the promiscuous invitation issued invariably at most Free Church Communions "to all who love our Lord Jesus Christ to be guests at

[26] Fred Smith in an article, "From Principle to Procedure. A Study concerning modes of Worship," *Congregational Quarterly*, Vol. VIII (1930), p. 482.

[27] P. 74. The italics are mine to indicate where the ambiguity may be found.

[28] In 1931 the Congregational Union asked a layman to preside at the celebration of the Lord's Supper in its Autumn Assembly in the presence of perhaps a hundred ordained ministers. See R. Mackintosh, "The Genius of Congregationalism" in Peel, ed., *Essays Congregational and Catholic* (1931), p. 123. And in 1923 the *Directory of Worship* of the Presbyterian Church of England was amended to allow non-ministerial elders to administer the Lord's Supper in exceptional circumstances at preaching stations.

[29] *Manual for Ministers*, "Order of Service for the Close of the Year."

His table." Since the Methodists had long believed that Communion was a converting[30] as well as a communicating Sacrament, they alone had a theological justification for their position.

All in all, this was perhaps the period of which the Free Churches had least reason to be proud in their theology and in their worship. Previously their worship had been simple, possibly even bare, but also august in its consciousness of a solemn rendezvous with God. The structure and authority of Puritan worship was the Biblical basis which rejected the impure inventions and traditions of men and offered God a New Testament worship marked by purity, spirituality, and fidelity to the Divine ordinances. Its freedom was a freedom in the Holy Spirit under the Word, and never the right of private taste, public fashion, or ministerial predilection. In sheer contrast, the worship of the "School of Spontaneity" was formal about its informality, and gloried in its gaucherie. Its most radical critics established another group.

3. *The Society of Free Catholics*

This Society was never large and it may well have been born fifty years before its time, for it was attempting what then seemed the impossible task of combining Protestantism and Catholicism. Indeed, it never was sure of its objectives. As W. E. Orchard wrote, its comprehensive basis "led to no agreement as to whether 'Free Catholicism' was a new kind of Catholicism, or simply a way of interpreting and commending historic Catholicism, and as a means of preparing for final re-union with Rome."[31] Its founder was the Rev. J. M. Lloyd Thomas, a large-minded and cultivated Unitarian minister who had been greatly influenced by the Modernist Movement on the Continent, and in particular by Loisy and Sabatier, and who gathered about him other Unitarian ministers dissenting from the rationalistic didacticism of their tradition.

His views were publicised in *A Free Catholic Church* (1907). "In a Free Catholic Church," he wrote, "it is believed will ultimately be found an Ideal which, if courageously worked out, will transcend or reconcile the oppositions not merely of Anglicanism and Dissent, but of Romanism and Protestantism."[32] In brief, this was a liberal theology turning back to the devotional and sacramental

---

[30] In June 1740, John Wesley wrote: "But experience shows the gross falsehood of the assertion that the Lord's Supper is not a converting ordinance. For many now present know, the very beginning of your conversion to God . . . was wrought at the Lord's Supper (Wesley's *Works*, Vol. I, p. 262).

[31] *From Faith to Faith*, p. 151.   [32] *A Free Catholic Church*, p. 3.

riches of the historic Church. Its central conviction was that the foundation of the unity of a truly comprehensive Church could never be dogma, but only devotional practice, for it is on doctrine that men are divided, a view which F. D. Maurice had also held. It is only, so they believed, on the basis of symbolic language that men's hearts and imaginations can be brought into unity. Hence, "a Free Catholic Church will accordingly use in its public worship not words of dogmatic precision, but the figurative language of devotional utterance. Its liturgy will not be designed to define opinion like a creed, but to express desire and aspiration like a prayer."[33]

In the course of time, some distinguished recruits from other denominations joined the Society, notably R. J. Campbell, the minister of the City Temple, a controversial Congregationalist, and W. E. Orchard, a Presbyterian minister in charge of the Congregational Church of the King's Weigh House in Mayfair. There were also some Anglican clergy and Roman Catholic laity associated with the Society. Campbell was the first to leave, wholly repudiating his liberalism and becoming an Anglo-Catholic. Lloyd Thomas felt that this desertion was a mortal blow to the Society and that it was quite unnecessary, since devout Free Churchmen were equally sure of the presence of God in their Sacraments. He was constrained to rebuke Campbell with a reminder: "Has he not seen, as I have praised God to see, when Nonconformists have knelt before the altar to receive the Blessed Sacrament how they have sometimes broken down in tears? If that was not the living touch of the living Christ upon their souls and the most holy and real communion—I do not know what it is. I cannot conceive what more even the Roman Mass can be for a sincere and devout Roman."[34] Orchard was to remain the most indefatigable liturgical experimenter of the Free Catholics until he finally submitted to the Roman obedience. Lloyd Thomas alone remained faithful to the Society. He edited its Magazine, and he worshipped with an uncommonly rich ceremonial and ritual borrowed from many Christian centuries in which the very select congregation of the Old Meeting Unitarian Church in Birmingham were privileged to join. But if the Society of Free Catholics did nothing else, it had two accomplishments to its credit. It left behind an intriguing invitation to the ministers of the Free Churches to explore the

[33] *Ibid.,* p. 85.
[34] *Anglo-Catholic or Free Catholic? A Comment on Revd. R. J. Campbell's "Spiritual Pilgrimage,"* p. 11.

liturgies and devotions of historic Christendom as a supplement to their own spare diet of worship, and it provided in the liturgical compilations of Lloyd Thomas and W. E. Orchard brilliant examples of such recoveries.

The Free Catholics disliked the dogmatism of Roman belief but delighted in Roman Catholic sacramental and devotional practice. They were allured by the theological freedom of Protestantism but repelled by the irreverence and unimaginativeness of its contemporary worship. They intended to combine the good features of each tradition, devotional forms with intellectual freedom. In particular, their work was marked by four important characteristics. They proposed to substitute the ardour of mysticism for the chill of didacticism. Instead of the idiosyncratic and all too contemporary prayers of the Free Churches, they proposed to re-establish the historic prayers of Christendom, hallowed by the use of the centuries. In place of the "sacerdotalism" of the single voice of the Free Church minister in his tediously long prayers, they proposed responsive prayers in which the whole congregation could unite with heart and voice. And, finally, the language of their devotions, and the furnishings of their churches, as well as the stained-glass windows and the architecture itself, would be deeply symbolical, and they would restore Holy Communion to the central position it had been given in the earliest age of the Church.

The first fruits of the work of the Society of Free Catholics was Orchard's remarkably comprehensive liturgy, the *Divine Service* of 1919. Brought up as an adolescent in the Presbyterian Church, he was trained at Westminster Theological College in Cambridge, and attained to some local fame as minister of the Enfield Presbyterian Church. Because it was required of him, he prayed extemporaneously, but uncomfortably. At the same time, he was honest enough to admit that it was an apt form of prayer for outsiders and inquirers who might have found liturgical forms artificial and cold, for this kind of prayer "may so strive to interpret the unrealised Godward cravings of others, and give them such expression, as to lead them almost unconsciously into praying themselves."[35] In fact, he produced a superb collection of such prayers in a book called *The Temple*.[36] For the morning service, which was attended by the committed Christian families at Enfield,

---

35 *From Faith to Faith*, p. 90.
36 *Ibid*. Of these prayers Orchard records: "They have converted some to faith, taught many to pray, and been the dying companion of not a few."

Orchard occasionally introduced some simple liturgical forms, which were gradually increased and improved. His tolerant congregation permitted him to remove the organ and rostrum at the "East end" of the sanctuary and to make "a kind of chancel, with the pulpit on one side, and the Communion Table in the centre, behind which, on a sort of reredos, I was allowed to place a brass cross with enamel figures of the four living creatures on the arms, and the *Agnus Dei*, the whole flanked by a brass Alpha and Omega." With pride, he adds: "I think this, too, must have been almost the first Presbyterian Church to have a cross in close association with the Communion Table, at least, South of the Tweed."[37]

In 1914 he was called to succeed Dr. John Hunter, the most eminent Congregational liturgist of his day, as the minister of the historic King's Weigh House which, ever since the time of the renowned Binney, had been the laboratory of the most advanced worship in the Free Churches. The architect of this building was Alfred Waterhouse. It did not please Orchard who called it an "oval shaped boilerette." He thought its locale unfortunate, remarking, "Whatever worship Mayfair may patronize, it is not likely to be Congregational."[38] At the outset of his ministry he agreed to use Hunter's *Devotional Services* for the ordinary services, but not his Communion Order, for "in this he had not only broken away from all historic forms, but had prefaced it with a series of affirmations as to what it did not mean, which I could never take on my lips."[39] Orchard's own Communion Service was on the model of the Book of Common Prayer, except that he became increasingly convinced that transubstantiation was the most satisfactory doctrine for the Eucharist, and that it was appropriate to prepare for the reception of the Eucharist with confession.[40]

His views about this time are expressed with admirable clarity (too clearly for the Congregational Union of England and Wales) in a volume with the challenging title, *The New Catholicism and other Sermons*. The tenth sermon, "The New Catholicism," might well have been printed as the manifesto of the Society of Free Catholics, so excellent a statement is it of their aims. The primary principle is its "desire to reappropriate everything of spiritual value in the historic Catholic system" and the first item to be reappropriated is "its mystic worship." By this Orchard means that the Supernatural reached the soul through the senses. The false

37 *Ibid.*, p. 105.   38 *Ibid.*, p. 117.   39 *Ibid.*, p. 118.
40 *Ibid.*, p. 131.

spirituality of many Free Church thinkers of this period is shrewdly exposed in the charge that to assert body and soul are antagonistic "not only blames the Creator for uniting them, but makes the Incarnation either unthinkable or a mere condescension to a weak human need."[41] He goes on to argue that it is only the perfect reconciliation of the spiritual and the material that "will inspire us to redeem the body from unchastity and grossness, and rescue the material world from ugliness and exploitation. It is no accident that art has reached its highest attainment through Catholic worship."[42]

He insists that Catholicism alone has taken with full seriousness the real presence of Christ in the Sacrament which others have tried to explain away. As for its pageantry, this is inevitable both because of the reality and primacy of the supernatural and also because positive joy demands pageantry for its expression. "The worst enemy of Catholicism," he adds, "could not say it had been a bad school of mysticism; it has been its most prolific soil."[43]

If Orchard were to have been asked at this stage why he did not then leave Nonconformity, in all sincerity he would have replied that he was seeking a Catholicism wide enough to include what Nonconformity had stood for—especially the freedom of prophesying and praying. His generous hospitality would make room for the Baptists because they made the ordinance of initiation significant, for the Methodists because of their zeal for holiness, and for the Quakers because of their stress on silence and spontaneity.[44] Orchard's dissatisfaction with Roman Catholicism is simply that it is not Catholic enough in its comprehensiveness. "If I could not feel that I belonged to the Church which produced Augustine, Francis and Pascal, as well as Luther, Bunyan, and Wesley, I would refuse to belong to any church at all."[45] With such convictions as to the centrality and depth of Eucharistic worship, and as to the inspiration of the saints of the Christian tradition, it was no wonder that he had to frame a Liturgy for the New Catholicism. This is precisely what *Divine Service* is.[46]

The Preface is an interesting statement of the principles upon which Orchard operated. First, in his desire for comprehensive-

---

[41] *The New Catholicism*, p. 147.
[42] *Ibid.*   [43] *Ibid.*, p. 149.   [44] *Ibid.*, p. 154.
[45] *Ibid.*, a sermon, "The Church of Three Dimensions," p. 56.
[46] Its full title is: "The Order of Divine Service for Public Worship, the administration of the Sacraments and other Rites and Ceremonies, and a selection from the Daily Offices compiled from ancient and modern devotions together with an abridged and revised Psalter and Canticles pointed for Chanting."

ness, he was proposing these liturgical forms not as alternatives to free prayer, but as supplements to it. He demands "that room shall be left both for freely uttered and for silent prayer, not only as existing alongside liturgical forms, but as their very crown and consummation."[47] He recognizes that there are differences of practice which will make advanced doctrines and customs acceptable in some quarters, while simpler rites would be more welcome in other quarters. In line with the aim to meet the needs of both Catholic and Protestant temperaments, therefore, he has chosen to provide alternative forms rather than "adopting a colourless and concealed compromise."[48] The most striking evidence of this is the provision for both "A Simple Observance of the Lord's Supper" and "The Order for the celebration of the Eucharist."[49] His autobiography indicates that in one respect he thought he was able to improve on the Book of Common Prayer. That was by providing ten services for Sunday mornings and evenings, "which we found much preferable to the sameness of the Book of Common Prayer; especially as it enabled us to use so much more of the rich and glorious liturgical material in existence."[50]

The chief feature of *Divine Service* is, of course, its use of the great historic liturgies and prayers of Christendom. Its chief sources are: the Book of Common Prayer, Bright's *Ancient Collects*, Selina Fox's *A Chain of Prayer Across the Ages*, Hunter's *Devotional Services*, and Charles Plummer's *Devotions from Ancient and Mediaeval Sources*. He has ransacked the liturgical treasures of the ages to recover such gems as the prayers of Archbishop Laud and of Bishops Andrewes, Hickes, Cosin, and Cotton, the Liturgies of the Western and Eastern Churches, and he utilises the devotions of St. Francis Xavier, Bersier, and Martineau. Here is God's plenty. Orchard was, however, no mere scissors and paste man. He

---

[47] *Ibid.*, p. 5.   [48] *Ibid.*, p. 6.

[49] Both these forms of Communion were regularly celebrated as alternatives by Orchard at the King's Weigh House. It may seem surprising, since Orchard's own preference was so clearly in favour of the high Eucharist, that his conscience allowed him to celebrate the low Lord's Supper. Investigation of the latter rite shows, however, that the rubrics allow both celebrant and communicants to add silent directed petitions which could have the effect of making it more advanced than it appears. For example, when the institution narrative is reached, the president reads, "And as they were eating, Jesus took bread, and blessed," at which point a rubric reads, *Here the Holy Spirit should be silently invoked.* After the Fraction, and delivery, the direction is then given for a *Prayer pleading the sacrifice of Christ and making offering of self to God.* Finally, the reading of the High Priestly Prayer of Christ requires at stated intervals in the silence the remembrance of the saints and the departed, the remembrance of the living, and the prayer for the unity of the Church. Hence, though the ceremonial is simple, the doctrine is, in fact, advanced.

[50] *From Faith to Faith*, p. 134.

was a sensitive editor in looking for translations of ancient collects and litanies that provided the most felicitous cadences, in skilful adaptations, in planning each service so that it had clear architectonic, and in making his own original contributions.

No less than twenty-six prayers are of his own composition, including Litanies of Labour, of Missions, of the Church, of the Sick, of the Holy Ghost, and in the tenth Order of Worship. Some of these prayers are worthy to be compared with the great collects in respect of their Scriptural bases, arrow-like directness, and profound simplicity. In three areas of prayer Orchard excelled: on the great festivals of the Christian Year, in petitions for peace, and in compassionate understanding of the exploited, the degraded, and the dying. In the first category he has sublimely jubilant prayers for Christmas[51] and Easter.[52] In the second, "Christ the only Prince of Peace"[53] is a passionate plea such as only this great pacifist could offer. In the understanding of the problems of the working man, he deserves to be compared for his prophetic ardour with John Hunter, and his collect for Labour Day[54] and his Litany of Labour[55] are incomparable of their kind. His sensitive prayer for St. Mary Magdalene's Day[56] reminds one that it was said during the first World War that his was the only church that prostitutes used to attend, because there was no trace of Pharisaism in Orchard's pure and generous heart or in the inclusive gospel that he preached. His prayers for mourners[57] and especially one at the burial service of a child[58] are epitomes of tenderness.

Where so much is excellent, it is tempting to cite inordinately. It must suffice, however, to illustrate Orchard in joyful and in tender moods. Here is the aspiring adoration of his Easter prayer: "O THOU who makest the stars, and turnest the shadow of death into the morning; on this day of days we meet to render Thee, our Lord and King, the tribute of our praise; for the resurrection of the spring-time, for the everlasting hopes that rise within the human heart, and for the Gospel which hath brought life and immortality to light. Receive our thanksgiving, reveal thy presence, and send forth into our hearts the Spirit of the Risen Christ."[59]

By contrast, here is his prayer at the burial of a child: "HEAVENLY Father, whose face the angels of little children do always

---

[51] *Divine Service*, p. 73. [52] *Ibid.*, p. 91.
[53] *Ibid.*, p. 168. [54] *Ibid.*, p. 162.
[55] *Ibid.*, p. 108. This was included in the Methodist Manual, *Divine Worship*.
[56] *Ibid.*, p. 163. [57] *Ibid.*, p. 186. [58] *Ibid.*, p. 193.
[59] *Ibid.*, p. 91.

behold, and who by thy Son Jesus Christ hast taught us that of such is the kingdom of heaven; we commend unto thy faithful keeping the soul of this little child, whom thou hast gathered with the lambs in thy bosom; beseeching thee that thou wilt accept the innocence of this thy little one, cleansing *him* from all stain of earthly life; that *he* may dwell for ever in thy presence, and find a home in the heavenly Jerusalem, that city which is full of boys and girls playing in the streets thereof; and this we ask through Jesus Christ our Lord."[60]

Subsequent Free Church compilers of worship manuals have learned much from Orchard. In particular, they have followed his comprehensiveness in their borrowings from all centuries and Communions, and benefitted from his gift for expressing contemporary concerns with a strongly Biblical diction in the traditional forms of collect and litany, and, above all, from his genius for collecting a Biblical catena on a particular theme and arranging it responsively as an act of devotion, a declaration of faith, or a reminder of Christian duty.[61] The latter was his most original contribution to liturgical creation.

Ultimately Orchard found that, as his detractors had always prophesied, he had to make his submission to Rome for, despite the naïve belief of the Society of Free Catholics to the contrary, it was impossible to practise Catholic ceremonial and Sacraments without the undergirding of Catholic doctrine on which they rested. Henceforth, as a Roman Catholic priest, he could no longer experiment in compiling revised liturgies, but he did produce a remarkable collection of his own private prayers, the *Sancta Sanctorum: Prayers for the Holy of Holies* (1955). These highly personal meditations recall those of John Henry Newman in their searching self-analysis, deep humility, longing for charity, and in the pruned richness of their imagery. Other themes are Orchard's own, as in a profound prayer that atheists may be delivered from their alluring and evanescent illusions, or in another expressing a prophetic sense of judgment on the Church for its "reluctant yieldings to the pressure of unwelcome truth" and "alliances with worldly powers and the

---

[60] *Ibid.*, p. 193. Each of these prayers shows a tendency to romanticism and sentimentality which is kept in check by the Scriptural citations and the expanded collect form.

[61] Examples are: The Divine Praises or the Declaration of the Divine Nature (2nd Order), the Promises of the Word of God (4th Order), The Commandments of the Lord Jesus (6th Order), New Testament Confession of Faith (7th Order), and Apostolic Exhortations (9th Order).

adoption of earthly armour."[62] They are marked throughout with the deepest spirituality, as of one who sincerely prays "make me like a window of purest glass, which calls no attention to itself by figure, colour, or inscription, but which simply lets the sunshine stream through unhindered and undiminished."[63]

During his controversial ministry at King's Weigh House, when it was said that a Roman Catholic who had been persuaded to attend Orchard's Eucharist expressed the opinion that she much preferred her own simpler services,[64] Orchard was thought to be a peacock. In fact, as his sermons and this last book of personal prayers shows, he was more like a dove, and there was never anything of the pouter pigeon in this deeply spiritual, if impracticable man, ahead of his time.

The last fruits of the Society of Free Catholics was the production of the marvellously comprehensive *Free Church Book of Common Prayer* (1929), chiefly the work of the founder of the movement, J. M. Lloyd Thomas.[65] It was, moreover, regularly in use at his Unitarian Church, the Old Meeting in Birmingham. In many ways it is like Orchard's *Divine Service*, particularly in its raiding of the liturgical treasures of Christendom. However, as the title might suggest, it makes considerable use of Free Church devotional materials, such as Hunter's *Devotional Services*, Orchard's *Divine Service*, and the Unitarian classic in which Martineau contributed some strikingly beautiful prayers, *Common Prayer for Christian Worship*. Furthermore, there is a considerable amount of fresh devotional material composed expressly for the book, including fourteen original prayers. The latter included several prayers to be said with the choir before and after service, and a delicate collect for St. Mary Magdalene's Day. A curious characteristic was the number of prayers for animals.

The book has some unique features, among them the provision in the Fourth Order of a service that could be used by non-Christian

---

[62] *Sancta Sanctorum*, p. 153.   [63] *Ibid.*, p. 69.

[64] Orchard repeats this story in *From Faith to Faith*, p. 139.

[65] A narrative account of this movement is greatly to be desired for it is of considerable ecumenical significance. The Dr. Williams Library has a complete set of the periodical issued by the Free Catholic Society. It is a pity that we do not know definitely which Free Church ministers were associated with J. M. Lloyd Thomas in producing this work of which he was "General Editor." The names of two "High Church" Baptist ministers frequently mentioned in this connection are the Revs. F. C. Spurr, Minister of the Hamstead Road Baptist Church, Birmingham (1922-1936) and G. H. R. Laslett, Spurr's successor in the same church. Spurr's predecessor, R. H. Coats, wrote the admirable *Types of English Piety*, a work on Nonconformist spirituality. (This information I owe to Dr. Ernest A. Payne, General Secretary of the Baptist Union of Great Britain and Ireland in a letter of February 5, 1963.)

theists as well as by Christians, containing adaptations from prayers of the Jewish Liturgy. The First and Fourth Orders of worship were written to promote Christian reunion, as "their use in the Free Churches will enrich their services and promote, through experience of a common devotion, the spirit of re-union and thus hasten the coming of a united Church at home as well as, for example, in South India and the wider mission field."[66] Another characteristic is that allowance is made for periods of silent prayer,[67] for extempore prayer,[68] and for alternatives.[69] Perhaps the chief difference from Orchard's *Divine Service* is in the wider use of modern, post-Reformation prayers. For example, Martineau's *Prayers in Congregation and College*, C. S. Woodward's *The Challenge* (for a children's thanksgiving), Percy Dearmer's *The Sanctuary*, the prayers of the Cambridge Platonists (Whichcote and Norris), Dekker, John Milton, Cardinal Newman, Samuel Johnson, Richard Baxter, Archbishop Benson, John Donne, Robert Nelson, and Bishop Moule, are all laid under debt, in addition to the many authors used by Orchard.

The value of this large compilation of 552 pages, which has the unevenness which might be expected from the work of a committee of individualists, was not that its responsive orders of worship were widely used. In fact, there is no certain evidence that it was used *in toto* anywhere but in Lloyd Thomas's own church. Its value was rather the book's pedagogical importance in introducing to the ministry of the English Free Churches a far wider horizon of devotional practice. The wide sales of the book indicates that it found its way into many ministers' studies and was used as an anthology of devotion. Certainly it proved that the Free Church tradition in Hunter, Orchard, and Lloyd Thomas was making its own contribution to liturgical forms of worship, and that it was employing the classical techniques of the collect and litany, while filling them with modern content. It was, above all, a welcome change from the idiosyncrasies and the dreary didacticism of the school of spontaneity, and it recovered soaring mysticism and sacramental reverence for the Free Churches, and made them part heirs of the Catholic centuries in East and West.

Nonetheless, the Society of Free Catholics was a failure in trying to win the majority of Free Churchmen to its fold. In part, this was because the Society was built upon a flawed foundation—that

---

[66] *Free Church Book of Common Prayer*, preface, p. ix.
[67] *Ibid.*, p. 11.   [68] *Ibid.*, p. 13.   [69] *Ibid.*, p. 20.

Catholic forms of devotion are meaningful to those who repudiate Catholic doctrine. In part, also, this was due to the fact that ministers trained to consider free prayer the finest form of charismatic spirituality could only consider the liturgies of the past as elegant and anachronistic exercises. They were blooms too exotic to be successfully transplanted into the kitchen gardens of Nonconformity. Finally, the Society's members combined too heterogeneous a collection of individuals. But at least in their expression of the sense of the Great Church of the centuries, they provided a bridge to the future for that ecumenism in prayer which now characterizes every Free Church manual of prayer, and in their brief collects and responsive litanies of intercession, they broke the tyranny of the long didactic and extemporaneous prayers which had been traditional in the Free Churches since the Savoy Conference of 1661. They helped also to regain a reverence for the Sacraments.

The *Rodborough Bede Book*, compiled by the Rev. C. Ernest Watson (1869-1942) in 1930, deserves brief consideration here, although he was not a member of the Society of Free Catholics. Nonetheless, he was a friend of Orchard who made considerable use of *Divine Service* and *The Temple* in his own compilation, and was attempting in a less extreme way to supplement the Puritan tradition with the great liturgical devotions of the primitive Church. What gave the *Bede Book* its distinctive character is that Watson preferred, as the title implies, Anglo-Saxon words to those of Latin derivation in the diction of English prayers, and that this anthology of prayers and services was regularly used in the Congregational church of Rodborough in rural Gloucestershire where he had a long and faithful ministry.

Apart from the artificial restriction of its diction, the work suffers a loss of structure from making a fetish of alternative brief exercises for the beginning and ending of worship (of which there are over a hundred). Its other weakness is its attenuated theology which excluded the very concepts which gave the historic liturgies their life and power, as may be seen in his five all too condensed orders for the Eucharist. Its strength is in its anticipation of the influence of the Modern Liturgical Movement in providing so many responsive prayers for the active participation of the congregation in worship, in the various techniques of prayer so generously illustrated, in the use of agricultural imagery, and in making so notable a protest against disordered spontaneity. Watson's achievement is recorded in A. T. S. James, *A Cotswold Minister* (1944).

369

4. *The Return to the Reformed Tradition*

As the Free Catholics had rebelled against the apostles of spontaneity, so the school of Reformed Churchmen rebelled against the liberal theology of both, and against the eclecticism of the Free Catholics. For this attitude there are many reasons. The older immanentalism was giving way under the Continental influence of Karl Barth and Emil Brunner to a repristination of Reformed theology. Furthermore, the early twentieth century phase of indiscriminate enthusiasm for Christian re-union was followed in the mid-thirties by a second phase in which each denomination was looking carefully to its own roots, in the hope of discovering what it distinctively had to contribute to the Ecumenical Movement. This had an inevitable impact on worship. Rattenbury,[70] Bowmer,[71] and Bishop[72] wrote valuable studies of classical Methodist worship, celebrating its combination of evangelical preaching with Anglican sacramental practice, while Newton Flew[73] claimed that Wesley's doctrine of Christian perfection was the product of a long line of development in Christian history. Nathaniel Micklem,[74] John S. Whale,[75] and Bernard L. Manning[76] among the Congregationalists recalled the denomination to its high Genevan origins, and Horton Davies[77] produced the first extensive study of Puritan worship. Ernest Payne[78] reminded the Baptists of their birthright in faith and worship. Carnegie Simpson[79] did the same for the English Presbyterians, while a fine series of studies in the history of Scottish Presbyterian worship emerged from the hands of W. D. Maxwell,[80]

[70] Rattenbury wrote *Vital Elements in Public Worship* and *Eucharistic Hymns of John and Charles Wesley.*
[71] Bowmer was the author of *The Sacrament of the Lord's Supper in Early Methodism* and *The Lord's Supper in Methodism, 1791-1960.*
[72] John Bishop wrote *Methodist Worship in relation to Free Church Worship.*
[73] R. Newton Flew also wrote, with R. E. Davies, *The Catholicity of Protestantism.* His major volume is *The Idea of Perfection.*
[74] Micklem was the editor of *Christian Worship,* the compiler of a fine series of Communion meditations in the Reformed tradition from Calvin downwards, entitled *A Book of Personal Religion,* and the author of *Congregationalism and the Church Catholic.*
[75] J. S. Whale wrote *What is a Living Church?* and the often reprinted *Christian Doctrine.*
[76] B. L. Manning wrote *Essays in Orthodox Dissent, Why not Abandon the Church?,* and *The Hymns of Wesley and Watts.*
[77] The reference is to *The Worship of the English Puritans.*
[78] E. A. Payne wrote *The Fellowship of Believers* and *The Free Church Tradition in the Life of England.*
[79] P. Carnegie Simpson wrote *The Evangelical Church Catholic.*
[80] W. D. Maxwell wrote *An Outline of Christian Worship,* and *A History of Worship in the Church of Scotland.*

William McMillan,[81] and G. B. Burnet.[82] In the movement whose slogan seemed to be "Back to the Reformation," the Methodists[83] were chiefly concerned to recover the theology of Martin Luther. This led to a balanced recovery of the Word and Sacrament, and to the preparation of books of worship that were authentically in the Reformed Tradition.

In the return to this tradition in worship, a splendid lead had been given by the liturgists of the Church of Scotland. Ever since the foundation of the Church Service Society in 1865,[84] the Scottish Church Society of 1892, and the Scottish Ecclesiological Society of 1903, there has been a group of Presbyterian clergymen and laity in Scotland deeply interested in and thoroughly informed on the subject of Reformed and Catholic worship. Even more important, they have produced a type of worship which at its best may be termed "Reformed Catholic," for it avails itself of the Patristic heritage in worship, along with the Reformation emphasis on the importance of preaching and the significance of the two Dominical Sacraments. Two books produced by the Church of Scotland have been deeply influential on the development of an ordered and reverential worship in the Presbyterian, Congregational, and to some extent, Baptist Churches of England. One is *Prayers for Divine Service* (1923) and the other is *The Book of Common Order* (1940), with its superb first Order for Holy Communion, which is the glory of Scottish worship.[85]

The denominational service books published at the beginning of the century had little sense of their own traditions. These, with the exception of those produced by the English Presbyterians, were largely imitations of the Book of Common Prayer and poor imitations at that. This is true of the *Book of Congregational Worship*[86]

---

[81] William McMillan wrote *The Worship of the Scottish Reformed Church.*

[82] G. B. Burnet wrote *The Holy Communion in the Reformed Church of Scotland, 1560-1960.*

[83] See P. S. Watson, *Let God be God* and Gordon Rupp, *The Righteousness of God.*

[84] For the nineteenth century influence of the Church of Scotland on English Free Church worship see *Worship and Theology in England*, Vol. IV, *From Martineau to Newman, 1850-1900*, pp. 100-13.

[85] Its fine consecration prayer has an *epiklesis* like the Eastern Church but the posture is Western and in public view; like the Anglican Rite the language is the vernacular, but unlike it, it refuses to incorporate the Words of Institution and to hide the acts of Fraction and Libation in the consecration prayer. See W. D. Maxwell, *History of Worship in the Church of Scotland*, pp. 181-82.

[86] It is to be noted, for example, in the 1920 book that, while the general order of Holy Communion follows the Book of Common Prayer, and the Consecration Prayer has the *Sursum corda*, the *Sanctus*, and a kind of *anamnesis*, yet there is no

of 1920, even though P. T. Forsyth was included on the committee of compilers. When they departed from Anglican models they relied on Hunter, Orchard, and the like. They did not return to the Reformation or to the Scriptures as their sources. The same judgment could more decisively be made of the Congregation *Manual for Ministers* (1936). The Methodist Church may be forgiven for showing less independence of the Anglican tradition than did the other Free Churches, because when *The Book of Offices* was produced in 1936 the three major divisions of British Methodism had only just been united, and, after all, the Methodists have strong Anglican roots.

The effect of the movement to return to the sources of Reformed Churchmanship was an intimation that the era of Anglican imitations was over. The most recent denominational service-books are more directly related to the history of their own denominations than were either the first service books of the century, or the rather strained and exotic compilations of the Free Catholics. The main concerns of this new school were admirably expressed by John Grant in *Free Churchmanship in England*.

He wrote: "An unfamiliar school of churchmanship appeared, valuing not only the freedom of the Free Churches but also the despised Calvinism that had given rise to English Nonconformity, asserting the necessity of dogma and laying a new emphasis upon the Church visible with its ministry and sacraments. What began as a protest of a few men against the dethronement of the Gospel in certain Nonconformist circles has grown into a widespread revival of Reformed ideals of churchmanship."[87] The new understanding of the Church in terms of the historic Gospel and of the Sacraments in terms of the Word was most vigorously expounded in Principal Nathaniel Micklem's pioneering volume of 1936, entitled *What is the Faith?*

5. Recent Congregational Worship

One of the most impressive contributions in the new mode was that of a group of four "High Genevan" Congregationalists, John Marsh, Romilly Micklem, John Huxtable and James Todd. They prepared *A Book of Public Worship compiled for the use of Congregationalists*.[88] Although the book was not an official com-

---

epiklesis, nor a recapitulation of the mighty acts of God, and, which is an astonishing departure from the Puritan tradition, neither Fraction nor Libation.

[87] *Free Churchmanship in England*, p. 325.

[88] The first edition appeared in 1948. Marsh, now the Principal, was then the

pilation of the Congregational Union of England and Wales, it has probably been more widely used by Congregationalists than any other service book. Its First Communion Order had the distinction of being the sole Free Church Eucharistic Order to be included in Bernard Wigan's important volume, *The Liturgy in English*, along with the Liturgy of the Church of South India, and the Communion Order of the Scottish Book of Common Order, in a volume which otherwise consisted of Anglican liturgies.

A Book of Public Worship contains a long and interesting introduction by John Marsh. Here the basic principles are outlined. The first is that Congregational worship is founded upon a structure which links the Sermon with the Lord's Supper, and the Order for Morning and Evening worship is based on dry Mass, not on such mediaeval offices as Matins or Evensong. Secondly, it was thought desirable to provide orders of service "rightly expressing the place and meaning of Baptism, the Lord's Supper, and Church membership in relation to our own polity."[89] Finally, there was a deliberate search for materials in the Puritan tradition, notably in Baxter's Reformed Liturgy and in the Middelburg Prayer Book, as well as from other similar sources.

The conscious pride in the Reformed tradition is a notable characteristic of the introduction and the contents. Other features are the provision of four different orders of Holy Communion, and even of an abbreviated order for the Lord's Supper "for those who have early Communions on such days as Easter Sunday."[90] Two of the orders keep to the "ancient and reformed practice in placing the sermon before the 'long prayer': often the intercessions will come most appropriately after minds have been stirred by the preaching of the Gospel."[91] The Congregationalists are reminded in the preface that although they love freedom they are not liturgical anarchists, and that their ancestors were convinced that "Standards of worship could not be fixed by the State; they had been determined by the Gospel."[92]

The page of acknowledgements indicates that the compilers

Chaplain, as E. R. Micklem was a former Chaplain of Mansfield College, Oxford, of which Huxtable was a member. Todd learned his Genevanism from J. S. Whale, another Mansfield man who became President of Cheshunt College, Cambridge. Particularly under the inspired liturgical leadership of Nathaniel Micklem, as Principal of Mansfield College, this one institution may be said to have provided in its College Chapel a standard of worship that led all the English Free Churches from 1933 onwards.

[89] *A Book of Public Worship*, Preface, p. xiii.
[90] *Ibid.*
[91] *Ibid.*, Preface, p. xiv.
[92] *Ibid.*, p. vii.

were well acquainted with the Reformed tradition outside their own denomination, for they made use of the Scottish Presbyterian sources of worship (*Euchologion*, and the Books of Common Order of 1928 and 1940), the service books of the American and English Presbyterian Churches, and of the Canadian Book of Common Order. Nor did they forget their own predecessors, as Hunter, Orchard, and Lloyd Thomas, as well as *The Book of Congregational Worship* of 1920, were laid under contribution.

Without question this is the worthiest modern directory of worship produced for the Congregational churches. As a directory, rather than a book of common prayer, it provides a theological structure for worship with an abundance of alternative prayers so that familiarity cannot breed contempt, nor capriciousness lead to congregational confusion. As a supplement to the five basic orders for Sunday worship, there is a valuable collection of ninety-three pages of "Additional Material for Public Worship" consisting of Scripture Sentences; Prayers of Adoration, Invocation, and Confession, with Assurances of Pardon; Prayers of Thanksgiving, Supplication, and for Special Graces; General Intercessions (in one Prayer, in Prayers for Special Subjects, in Prayers with Responses, and in Bidding Prayers); Prayers for Illumination, Dedications of the Offerings, Ascriptions of Glory, and Benedictions.

Furthermore, there are four excellent Orders for the Sacrament of Holy Communion, of which the first is the finest ever produced by Congregationalists and bears the mark of the influence of the Church of Scotland. The Prayer of Thanksgiving worthily commemorates the mighty acts of God in creation, incarnation, redemption, and resurrection, affirms the communion of saints, and includes an *epiklesis* or invocation of the Holy Spirit "to sanctify both us and these thine own gifts of bread and wine which we set before thee."[93] As in the Scottish rite the Words of Institution, with the Fraction, are not absorbed in the Prayer of Consecration, but set solemnly apart.

There are admirable Orders for the Sacrament of Baptism, one for the Baptism of Children and the other for the Baptism of Believers. The theology they express is that Baptism "is both an assertion of the individual application of the benefits of Christ's work, and the act of formal reception into the membership of the Church."[94] This is a great improvement upon preceding Congregational Baptismal rites which were hardly distinguishable from

[93] *Ibid.*, p. 37.　　　　　　　　　　[94] *Ibid.*, Preface, xix.

dedications. The covenant emphasis, characteristic of the Reformed and Puritan heritage, rightly informs the brief but impressive Order "for the Reception of Members into full Communion with the Church" which properly emphasizes the link with Baptism, and requires a profession of faith.

The service for the Ordination of Ministers, which has been approved by the denomination and is now in regular use, definitely requires the laying-on of hands (whereas this was left optional in the 1920 *Book of Congregational Worship* and in the 1936 *Manual for Ministers*). It also requires the solemn presentation of a Bible to the newly-ordained minister, a significant reminder that his authority is founded on the Gospel. The new Reformed emphasis is further stressed in the fourth requirement of the ordinand: "Do you promise to execute your charge with all fidelity, to preach the Word of God, to administer the Sacraments, to fulfil the pastoral office, and to live a godly life, adorning the doctrine of God our Saviour in all things?"[95]

One lack in the book, the absence of any services for the festivals of the Christian Year, was made good by the publication in 1951 of James M. Todd's *Prayers and Services for Christian Festivals*. This, too, availed itself of the chief Reformed sources in English, including the Church of Scotland's *Prayers for the Christian Year* and *Prayers for Use in Time of War*. It also made use of more Anglican sources than the earlier companion volume did, including *The Grey Book*, Eric Milner-White's *Daily Prayer*, and the Book of Common Prayer. This made available to Free Churchmen for the first time the famous Service of Nine Lessons and Carols which Bishop Frere had revived at Truro and Milner-White had popularized in the magnificent setting of King's College Chapel, Cambridge. There were services for Christmas Eve, Epiphany, for each day of Holy Week, Easter, Ascension Day, Whitsuntide, and a Watchnight Service. Furthermore, a collection of sentences and prayers for each festival was prepared for insertion into the five alternative orders of Sunday worship provided by *A Book of Public Worship*, together with short Orders of worship for use at Holy Communion on Christmas Day, Easter Day, and Whitsunday.

The two complementary volumes provided a great enrichment of Congregational worship. They represent a long overdue recognition on the part of concerned Congregationalists that twentieth century worship must fulfil five conditions. First, its variety must be

---

[95] *Ibid.*, p. 202.

a "founded freedom"—that is, based upon a solid Biblical and theological structure. Secondly, that structure must be based upon the central Christian Sacrament, the Lord's Supper or Holy Communion. Within a Free Church tradition this is best recognized by making each service an Ante-Communion, and by providing several Orders of Holy Communion. *A Book of Public Prayer* provides four in full and a shorter order, while *Prayers and Services for Christian Festivals* adds three others. Thirdly, it is acknowledged by the publication of Todd's book that the Christian Year is a witness to the Gospel of the Incarnation, the multi-faceted significance of which is more fully apprehended by dividing it into festivals each with its own integrity. In the fourth place, in an ecumenical age, it is essential that the worshippers should transcend local congregational boundaries and understand that they are, in Forsyth's term, "the local outcrop" of the Holy Catholic Church. This is expressed in the traditional responses of the great Prayer of Thanksgiving in the Order of the Lord's Supper, and in a sense of the Communion of Saints. Finally, there is suitable provision, as there was not in the work of the Free Catholics, for the distinctive services of a single denomination, such as are provided in the services for Ordination and Induction to the Ministry, the Reception of Members into Full Communion, and the Admission of Deacons. Further, it is a great quality of these two volumes that they stress, less the dissidence of Dissent, than the basic unity of the Reformed tradition in worship.

There are two ways in which they might, however, be improved. In their zeal to do justice to the inevitable Biblical basis of worship, they have sometimes assumed that a catena of Scriptures of itself makes a prayer, forgetful of the need for phrases of convenient length and of the rhythms of speech and felicities of cadence that are essential in public prayer. Furthermore, while Biblical thought and a great deal of Biblical diction must be retained, there is an undue preponderance of archaisms.[96] The second defect is the singular absence of responsive prayers, except in one section of the General Intercessions. It is singular because the Congregational churches have insisted that the people, not the ministers alone, make up the community of the redeemed. Yet this service book,

---

[96] In *A Book of Prayer*, p. 47, the petition "*Suffer us* no longer to live unto ourselves . . ." is an example of archaism. A more modern translation of the Scriptures would lead to greater edification than the words (p. 137): "There hath no temptation taken you but such as is common to men." Above all one misses the vividness of Biblical metaphor and simile. Todd's book is almost free of such defects.

ignoring the modern Liturgical Movement's emphasis on the importance of the fullest participation of the laity, condemns them for the most part to be silent in public prayer.

Two recent denominational service books of great merit enable us to see two other Free Church denominations entering into their Reformed heritage with great confidence, while also acknowledging that heritage which they share with the Universal Church of Christ through the centuries. The first is *The Presbyterian Service Book for use in the Presbyterian Churches of England and Wales* and the other is the Baptist production, *Orders and Prayers for Church Worship: A Manual for Ministers.*

6. *Recent Presbyterian Worship*

The Presbyterian Church of England has a distinguished lineage in service books, dating from the famous Westminster *Directory* of 1645 which, for a brief and troubled fifteen years, displaced the Book of Common Prayer as the national formulary for worship. Among the English Free Churches, the Presbyterians claim the distinction of having produced the first official modern denominational service book in 1898. This was significantly revised in 1921, but used the same historic title of a *Director of Public Worship*. The title was reluctantly changed in 1948 only because the new service book was to be used in Wales as well as in England.

The particular interest of *The Presbyterian Service Book* of 1948 is that it combines within the same book two traditions of worship: the older, Puritan type of tradition which is still strong in Wales and the more liturgical tradition characteristic of Scottish and English worship. The Committee responsible for producing the new service book faced a double task: "Firstly, it sought to preserve what was most valuable in the forms of worship of both Churches, which had found expression on the one hand in the Directory of the English Church, and on the other in the freer tradition of the Welsh Church. Secondly, it sought to giver richer expression to the liturgical traditions of the Church Catholic and Reformed."[97] How was this to be done in the same book?

The Committee solved the problem by providing three orders for Sunday worship, the first of which was credal in character, the second non-credal, and the third more congenial to the Welsh tradition. In the same way it provided four orders for the celebration of Holy Communion. The first two were in Reformed liturgical

[97] Preface.

tradition, the third was in the Welsh Puritan tradition, and the fourth was an abbreviated order for the sick. The very considerable debt owed to the Church of Scotland for the liturgical orders is acknowledged. The Scottish influence is manifest in the three-fold prayers of Approach, Confession, and Petition in the first two orders of worship, in the first two orders for Holy Communion, and in the series of prayers for the major Christian festivals.

Where did the English Presbyterians obtain their zest for a worship both Reformed and also Catholic? There is no doubt that one major influence was that of the Iona Community, founded by the Rev. Sir George MacLeod.[98] This is a brotherhood of ministers and craftsmen bound together in a common devotional rule of life. For the three summer months their headquarters is the west-coast island of Iona, the birth-place of Scottish Christianity, where the members of the Community worship, study, learn the new techniques of evangelism, and share in the manual labour necessary to rebuild the Abbey of St. Columba.

MacLeod's theology centres on the Incarnation for the redemption of the spiritual and the material life of man in his totality as socio-politico-economic-cultural being. He is emphatic that the concept of social justice is implicit in the true understanding of Holy Communion, for "the Sacrament, whatever greater things it may declare, at least dictates to men how best to share their Bread. And what is the one remaining problem of this potentially plenteous earth but the problem of how to share the mercies that God would make available for all?"[99] Of chief significance for our purpose is MacLeod's insistence upon the absolute primacy of worship in the Christian life, because it comes before the service of men, because evangelism arises out of worship, and because the Church is the starting point of mission.[100] His understanding of worship is immensely dynamic.[101] No Presbyterian minister has more ardently encouraged the application of the insights of the Continental Liturgical Movement to the Reformed tradition than he, nor inspired more young ministers from his own and many other branches of the Church during their visits to Iona.

In consequence, several of the younger English Presbyterian ministers were the first English enthusiasts for the work of the Iona Community. They met for an annual conference on worship,

---

[98] See George F. MacLeod, *We shall re-build; the work of the Iona Community on Mainland and on Island.*
[99] *Ibid.*, p. 13.   [100] *Ibid.*, p. 23.   [101] See *ibid.*, pp. 29f.

and were called the "Parkgate" group because their first place of meeting was Parkgate in the Wirral, Cheshire. They concentrated their studies on such topics as the nature of the Sacraments, Eucharistic Sacrifice, and Ordination. Through retreats and the keeping of a Common Rule of devotion they kept alive their zeal for the reform of worship. Some of the members of this group were on the Committee which produced the 1948 book. The second important factor was the influence of the Scottish *Book of Common Order* of 1940. It was taken up with great zest by many English Presbyterian ministers, and the use of the First Order of Holy Communion "became the hallmark of the 'progressives.' "[102] For a great many ministers it still is the "norm." And, of course, it is to be found in the English Presbyterian service book.

It is important to notice the convergence of the liturgical ideals of the Congregational and Presbyterian ministers in England, which is so striking a feature of *A Book of Public Worship compiled for the use of Congregationalists* and of *The Presbyterian Service Book*, both of which appeared in 1948. The reasons are not far to seek. Both look back gratefully to Calvin's reformation in Geneva as the pattern of their churchmanship and worship. They were comrades-in-arms in the Westminster Assembly and shared in producing its famous *Directory*, as they have shared the ignominy and glory of the history of English Dissent. Both have benefitted from the splendid researches of the liturgiologists of the Church of Scotland in their attempt to create a Reformed Catholic worship for the twentieth century. Both have had their "ginger groups" of younger ministers dedicated to the promotion of a worthier worship in their own denomination, the "Church Order Group" in Congregationalism and the "Parkgate Group" in English Presbyterianism.

The growing sense of theological and liturgical unity between English Presbyterians and Congregationalists has led the two denominations to affirm a Covenant Relationship with each other in the hope that this may prove to be the penultimate step to organic unity. As a token of this Covenant they jointly publish each year a series of Meditations and Prayers for Holy Week.

---

[102] The information in this paragraph I owe to a lengthy and informative letter, of July 24, 1963, from the Rev. R. Aled Davies, Minister of St. Paul's Presbyterian Church, Croydon, the convener of the Presbyterian Church of England Committee on Public Worship and Aids to Devotion, to whom I am deeply grateful. For the latest revision of the Order for Holy Communion as celebrated in the General Assembly of the Church of Scotland, see the *Ordinal and Service Book for use in Courts of the Church*.

7. *Recent Baptist Worship*

The most intriguing example of the trend to a Reformed Catholic worship is a recent Baptist service book, *Orders and Prayers for Church Worship: A Manual for Ministers*. It shows a considerable theological and liturgical advance on its two predecessors: M. E. Aubrey's *Minister's Manual* and D. Tait Patterson's *The Call to Worship*. It is the work of Ernest A. Payne and Stephen F. Winward. The former is a distinguished historian of Nonconformity, now the General Secretary of the Baptist Union of Great Britain and Ireland, and, significantly, a member of the Central Committee of the World Council of Churches. This manual indicates that the most charismatic of all the English Free Churches, the Baptist, is fully abreast of all the developments of the modern Liturgical Movement, and equally concerned to express Reformed insights within the context and tradition of the Great Church of the centuries.

This may appear, on the surface, a sudden and surprising *volte face* on the part of the English Baptists. Certainly they are far more liturgically advanced than Baptists elsewhere in Europe or in the United States. But for many years they have included in their ranks rebels from the general trend of the "School of Spontaneity." Among these the names of F. B. Meyer, F. C. Spurr, Ruffell Laslett, H. Wheeler Robinson, A. C. Underwood, Hugh Martin, M. E. Aubrey, and more recently Neville Clark would have to be considered. The latter wrote an exciting volume, *Call to Worship* (1960).

The theme of this important essay is "the conviction that the recovery of the Liturgy is the most urgent need of the Free Churches at this time."[103] He offers a radical critique of the worst emphases in the Free Church tradition, including the unbalanced emphasis on preaching, the treatment of the Eucharist as an addendum, the looking for "a blessing" instead of making an offering, and the divorce of worship from life, resulting from the idea of worship as the edification of the elite instead of carrying out a representative action on behalf of a world for which Christ died. He argues for a worship which indissolubly unites Word and Sacrament, and that will be unmistakably corporate and congregational in character. Moreover, he has persuaded his own congregation, after the most careful instruction, to accept the way of renewal he pleads for. It is significant that so much of what Neville Clark hopes to see embodied in the worship of the Baptists is, in

[103] Preface.

fact, provided for in *Orders and Prayers for Church Worship: A Manual for Ministers*, a most courageous publication.

A valuable introduction of fourteen pages provides a theology of worship, as dialogue between God and men, and an account of the two-fold origin of Christian worship combining "synagogue and Upper Room, scripture and sacrament, spoken word and "visible word"—which gives the complete pattern of Christian worship."[104] The influence of the Liturgical Movement is clearly seen in the statement that infrequent celebration of the Lord's Supper, or its relegation to an appendix, is to be deplored, and in the vigorous affirmation that "Christian worship is essentially eucharistic: it is to glory in Christ Jesus, incarnate, crucified, risen, exalted, coming in glory," and in the recognition that even when the Lord's Supper is not celebrated, the service of the Word should retain the pattern of Ante-Communion.[105] There is a firm insistence that the Holy Spirit is the agent in worship but that "he does not only act through 'inspired spontaneity.' "[106] Finally, the compilers desire a flexible liturgy: "In no sense is this book intended to be a Baptist equivalent of the Book of Common Prayer; it is intended rather to serve as a Book of Common Order."[107]

Their model has been the pattern of worship in the Church of Scotland. It is significant that while eight prayers are taken from Congregational sources, and several from the Book of Common Prayer and other Anglican sources, no less than thirty-eight prayers are borrowed from the Church of Scotland's Book of Common Order and eight from the same Church's *Prayers for the Christian Year*. The dependence upon the Scottish Rite is naturally and wisely fullest in the Order for the celebration of the Lord's Supper, for this is incomparably the best Reformed Rite in English-speaking lands, and has, in translation, been adopted for use in Calvin's cathedral church of St. Pierre in Geneva.[108]

It is in the central Prayer of Thanksgiving of the Communion Order that the fullest liturgical advance has been made. The *Sursum corda, Sanctus*, and *Benedictus qui venit*, are followed by the *anamnesis*, and the prayer concludes with an *epiklesis*, but unfortunately omits the note of oblation. Fraction and Libation are separated from the prayer so that their dramatic symbolism may be seen by the congregation. After Communion there is, rather un-

[104] *Orders and Prayers* . . . , Preface, p. x.
[105] *Ibid.*, pp. xi-xii. [106] *Ibid.*, p. xiv. [107] *Ibid.*, p. xv.
[108] W. D. Maxwell, *A History of Worship in the Church of Scotland*, p. 183.

happily, the choice between a read (or extempore) prayer of thanksgiving or a prayer for the Church Universal, including rejoicing in the communion of saints. The choice is unfortunate as the recognition of the communion of saints is an essential, not optional, element in the service. In fact, a general criticism would be that the eschatological element in the Eucharist is insufficiently stressed.[109]

The outstanding qualities of the book are precisely those which we discovered in *A Book of Public Worship compiled for the use of Congregationalists,* which it greatly resembles. The strong Scriptural basis of the Orders, the provision of much additional material to be placed in a theologically-structured service of Ante-Communion, the enhanced importance given to the Sacraments, the celebration of the chief festivals of the Christian Year including All Saints Day, and the place allowed for liturgical, extempore and silent prayer. It has one additional quality: a due recognition of the priesthood of all believers, which is clearly emphasized in the prayer before the laying-on of hands after Baptism: "Enable them as royal priests of Jesus Christ to bring others to Thee in prayer, and to take Thee to others in witness."[110] Yet, it too, fails to provide enough responsive prayers for the priesthood of the laity to become vocal.

Two other interesting characteristics of the book call for comment. One is that provision is made for the laying-on of hands, not only after Baptism and at the Ordination of ministers, but also in cases of sickness, as "was practised in apostolic times and by the early General Baptists of Britain."[111] The other is the all too rare recognition that unless there is family prayer in the homes, there cannot be satisfactory preparation for Sunday worship in Church. Therefore provision is made for prayers that may be helpful in the home.

8. *Recent Methodist Worship*

So far we have chronicled and evaluated the recovery of a Reformed Catholicity in Congregational, Presbyterian, and Baptist worship, but not in Methodist worship. Our difficulty is not any suspicion that such a reform has not taken place in Methodist worship in the last three decades, but the lack of official liturgical

[109] Other rare infelicities are the colloquial "just" in the Exhortation of the Baptismal Order (p. 131), and the unwarrantable changing and weakening of the ending of Ignatius Loyola's famous prayer (p. 134).
[110] *Orders and Prayers* . . . , p. 137.
[111] *Ibid.*, Preface, p. xix.

documents to prove it. For this gap two reasons may be given. The impact of the Modern Liturgical Movement on England arrived too late to have any influence on the official *Methodist Book of Offices* of 1936, and the current negotiations between the Methodist Church and the Church of England would make a revision at present highly inopportune. But if we had a right to expect a fertile soil for such a movement towards a Reformed Catholicism it would be in English Methodism, with its joint Anglican and Free Church inheritance in worship, and its stressing of evangelical witness and Catholic sacramentalism. The renaissance of Luther studies in Methodism would also be a pointer in the same direction, as also the liturgical writings of J. E. Rattenbury, John Bishop, and John C. Bowmer, and the devotional writings of A. E. Whitham, notably *The Catholic Christ*.[112] Indeed, the fullest expression of the theological concept behind the liturgical movement is developed in the work of R. Newton Flew and Rupert Davies, entitled *The Catholicity of Protestantism*.

Fortunately there is more substantial evidence for the trend to Reformed Catholicism than has been hitherto indicated. This is chiefly to be found in the work of the important Methodist Sacramental Fellowship.[113] It was founded in 1935 shortly after the Methodist Union, its first members being "a group of young ministers who were distressed by the growing irreverence of our services and by the humanistic teaching of their day."[114] It came under suspicion for its "high" doctrinal and liturgical views but was cleared in a Conference investigation of 1938. Its Presidents have included A. E. Whitham, J. E. Rattenbury, and Donald Soper, in itself a sufficient claim for distinction. Its triple concern is: the re-affirmation of the historic Faith; the restoration of sacra-

---

112 Whitham wrote (pp. 172-73): "But what I want to emphasize is not the necessity but the grace and kindness towards our infirmities of the Incarnation, the Church, the Sacraments. . . . If the Incarnation, Church and Sacraments mean anything, they do signify that we are not saved *from* the senses but *through* them, and we find God not in spite of the things of time and sense but through their hallowed ministry." Whitham wrote engagingly of the thrill of orthodoxy, the need to combine the evangelical and the sacramental in the Free Churches, the communion of saints past and present, the grace of God needing to be reflected in human charity, and of the gaiety that should characterize goodness.

113 My information is derived from two letters from the Honorary Secretary, Dr. David Sharp of Felixstowe (August 25 and 29, 1957), and two pamphlets which he was kind enough to supply me with: A. S. Gregory, *The Methodist Sacramental Fellowship* (1954) and *What is the M.S.F.?* (5th edn., 1948). J. C. Bowmer refers briefly to its influence in *The Lord's Supper in Methodism, 1790-1960*, pp. 49-50.

114 Pamphlet "In Defence of the M.S.F." by J. E. Rattenbury, p. 7 (cited by J. C. Bowmer, *op.cit.*, p. 49).

mental devotion; and the corporate reunion of believers.[115] It has from time to time been hinted that it is a coterie of sacerdotalists, but nothing could be further from the truth, for in 1939 "the membership stood at 320 in a proportion of one minister to two laymen."[116]

Each member is required to take a pledge, with God's help: "1. To say the Daily Office of prayer adopted by the Fellowship, or to observe some self-imposed discipline of daily devotion. 2. To receive the Holy Communion at least once a month after duly preparing myself. 3. To submit my mind humbly to the Faith of the Church as contained in Holy Scripture and expressed in the Nicene Creed. 4. To support with all loyalty the Methodist Church, and to help forward, as I can, both by prayer and service, the corporate reunion of all believers."[117] No one familiar with Wesley's own conviction of the central importance of the Sacrament, or his desire to restore "primitive Christianity," or his belief in daily devotional discipline, could suppose that the Methodist Sacramental Fellowship would not have gained his entire and hearty approval.

The Methodist Sacramental Fellowship has greatly helped to create an atmosphere favourable to reunion with the Church of England, and, more importantly, to retain in a well-organized and pragmatic denomination, devoted to evangelism and encouraging the vigorous witness of the laity as local preachers, a sense of the Holy Catholic Church as the communion of saints, and of Holy Communion as a "bounden duty and service" as well as the supreme privilege of the Church member. To the Fellowship must be attributed, in large degree, both the increasingly frequency with which the Sacrament is celebrated and the reverence with which it is received in contemporary English Methodism. Furthermore, the annual conferences of the Fellowship has brought to its meetings the rich insights of the modern Liturgical Movement, for its invited speakers have included Father Hebert and Dom Gregory Dix. It has also been in regular contact with parallel organizations in other denominations, such as the Church Service Society of the Church of Scotland, the Free Church Fellowship in the days of Nathaniel Micklem and Malcolm Spencer and its successor the Church Order Group represented by Hubert Cunliffe-Jones, and has encountered Orthodox spirituality in the person of Nicholas Zernov.[118]

[115] A. S. Gregory, *The Methodist Sacramental Fellowship*, pp. 8-9.
[116] *Ibid.*, p. 7.   [117] *What is the M.S.F.?*, p. 23.
[118] A. S. Gregory, *The Methodist Sacramental Fellowship*, p. 12.

While the Methodist Sacramental Fellowship has stressed two most significant parts of Methodism's inheritance, its Nicene faith and its Eucharistic heritage through the Wesleys, there has also been a re-appreciation of two of its distinctive ordinances, the Love-feast and the Covenant Service. The latter is now recognized as the standard observance of British Methodists each New Year and is, therefore, in no need of further attention, more particularly as the inclusion of part of it in the Clare College Manual for Holy Communion means that Anglicans are not likely to forget it either.

The revival of the Love-feast is a project dear to the heart of Frank Baker, as his book, *Methodism and the Love-Feast* amply proves. He suggests that the *agape* disappeared as Methodism became less of a group of revivalistic societies and more of a Church. The advantages of the love-feast were that at a simple meal of bread and water, the converts to the Christian way were able to encourage each other in fervent extemporary prayer and by recounting their testimonies of the goodness of God. Baker is disturbed that "despite the more careful ordering of our worship, in the matter of spontaneous spiritual utterance there has been nothing but decline—in extempore prayer, in prayer meetings, in bands and class meetings and society meetings, and, of course, in the love-feast."[119] But the wider interest of his book is his claim that this service is suitable for ecumenical gatherings for worship at the local level. It is most suitable for expressing unity amongst local congregations where intercommunion cannot yet be practised, as, for example, between Methodists and Anglicans. This was, in fact, the practice at Hilgay in Norfolk, in which the only two churches are Anglican and Methodist.

The Rev. G. I. F. Thomson, Rector of Hilgay, and the Rev. W. Morley Waite, the Methodist minister, shared with their congregations in a joint Agape in the Anglican church on Maundy Thursday evening, 1949. The broken bread was distributed by an Anglican church-warden and a Methodist local preacher. On Wednesday in Holy Week, 1951, another Agape was held at Hilgay, this time in the Methodist chapel, where the new Methodist minister was the Rev. John Lawson. A service was drawn up which was deeply ecumenical in the elements which composed it. The prayers were drawn from the Didache and the Agape of the Eastern Orthodox Churches, and part of the Litany was used to represent the Anglican and Roman traditions. The Methodist contribution

[119] P. 59.

consisted of the hymns for the love-feast, the extemporary prayer, and the offering of testimony. The common loaf was shared in the breaking of the bread and water was drunk, by representatives of the participating group only, from an old two-handled Methodist loving-cup.[120]

In some quarters it was welcomed as a pioneering break-through; in others it was criticized as glossing over the differences between the two denominations, and confusing the Agape and the Eucharist. Whatever may be thought of the ecumenical possibilities of this rite, one can sympathise with Baker for wishing to revive the deeply personal fellowship and charismatic character of worship in love-feasts or similar gatherings as a supplement to the dignified character of Eucharistic worship. The need for this was abundantly manifested in the House Church Communions provided by the present Provost of Southwark, Ernest Southcott, when Vicar of Halton. Moreover, it would be greatly to be lamented if the simplicity, spontaneity, and warmth of free prayer and the sharing of religious experience characteristic of the Puritan and Pietist traditions of devotion were to disappear as a result of the modern Liturgical Movement.[121] Indeed, the diminution of free prayer may in part be responsible for the attraction of some former Free Church members to the Pentecostalist Churches now mushrooming in growth.[122]

Even if the Methodist Church is to unite with the Church of England in the near future, it would be mistaken to suppose that all Methodist ministers would be entirely happy with the unrevised provisions of the Book of Common Prayer, for they are aware of the newer liturgical developments of our time. This is clearly the conviction of John C. Bowmer,[123] the historian of Methodist worship who offers an interesting series of conclusions relative to a revision of the Methodist rites. "There is," he writes, "no intrinsic merit in slavishly adhering to the forms of 1662."[124]

In any Methodist liturgical revision, he holds that much may be learned from *An Experimental Liturgy* and from the *Liturgy of*

---

[120] Details are given in the Appendix, pp. 74-78. Critiques are provided in *The Ecumenical Review* (Summer 1949); *The London Quarterly and Holborn Review* (April 1950); and *The Modern Churchman* (March 1950).

[121] Another Methodist minister aware of the importance of this side of the Methodist heritage is Gordon Wakefield, the author of *Puritan Devotion; its Place in the Development of Christian Piety.*

[122] See Horton Davies, *Christian Deviations.*

[123] *The Lord's Supper in Methodism, 1791-1960,* Chap. 6.

[124] *Ibid.,* p. 57.

the Church of South India,[125] especially in regard to the stress on the participation of all the people in the Eucharistic offering. He is also convinced of the rightness of the Church of Scotland's emphasis in its Communion Order on the manual Acts of Fraction and Libation, which he points out were rubrically required in *The Sunday Service of Methodists* until 1910. He argues for at least the placing of a chalice on the Communion Table, fearing that a germ-conscious people will not willingly give up its individual communion cups. In line with recent liturgical thinking he wishes to see a balance of Word and Sacrament in the Eucharistic celebrations, the provision of a free-standing Holy Table in new churches so that the Manual Acts can be performed in the sight of the people. He rightly wishes that more of the splendid Eucharistic hymns of John and Charles Wesley were revived. His conclusion is that the greatest need is for more instruction in the meaning of the Lord's Supper, and "it may be that this Sacrament which has been the greatest single dividing factor in Christendom shall yet become the means of achieving unity."[126]

Thus, there is no Methodist revision of worship to prove that the Methodist Church has, in fact, recovered the marks of a Reformed Churchmanship which is also sensitive to the Patristic heritage of the Universal Church as rediscovered in the Modern Liturgical Movement. But, as we have tried to show, the writings of Methodists in the related fields of theology and worship, and particularly the aims and interests of the Methodist Sacramental Fellowship, point strongly to a trend in the direction of an evangelical catholicism. And, after all, this would only be to tread in the footsteps of John Wesley himself.[127]

9. *The Summing Up*

In recounting the history of the three major trends—from charismatic spontaneity to Free Catholicism and on to the recovery of the Reformed heritage—the impression may have been given that the transition was a smooth one. That would, in fact, be a wholly erroneous impression. The claims of the proponents of each trend were often bitterly disputed by antagonists. The "School of Spontaneity" regarded the Free Catholics as traitors to Protestantism. The Free Catholics thought the latter no better than

---

[125] See T. S. Garrett, *Worship in the Church of South India.*
[126] Bowmer, *op.cit.*, p. 59.
[127] See the present author's *Worship and Theology in England, From Watts to Wesley and Maurice, 1690-1850*, Vol. III, Chap. VIII.

members of an Ethical Culture Society purveying, in Arnoldian phrase, "morality tinged with emotion." The Reformed Churchmen cried "a plague o' both your houses." Indeed, the antagonism between the advocates of a liberal and an orthodox theology, as between the enthusiasts for free or for liturgical prayer, continued throughout the period.[128]

The tension between the opposed viewpoints ran right through the denominations in the Free Churches, though it was most conspicuous in Congregationalism. The two opposing viewpoints were admirably embodied in the personalities of two well-matched historians of Congregationalism, Albert Peel (1887-1949), the founding editor of *The Congregational Quarterly*, and Bernard Lord Manning (1892-1941), Senior Tutor of Jesus College, Cambridge. In short, it might be described as a battle between the Quaker tendency and the Genevan emphasis on the interpretation of the Sacraments.

Peel's views were chiefly set forth in *Christian Freedom*, where he expressed his dismay that the Society of Friends might be excluded from the Ecumenical Movement because of its repudiation of the Christian Sacraments. His own doubts as to their Dominical institution were reinforced by Lietzmann's *Messe und Herrenmahl*. Peel felt that the Sacraments were obtruded by St. Paul into Christian practice on the analogy of the Gentile mystery religions of the first century. Furthermore, Peel held the view that symbols appeal only to primitive people and to immature minds. For him the natural development of the religion of the Spirit revealed by Christ was away from the use of outward symbols, and he conceived that the Spirit of Truth promised by Jesus demanded ethical obedience and not formal rite or external ceremonial.[129]

In complete contrast to Peel, Manning insisted that the Christian revelation was historically given and that it must be faithfully accepted rather than modernistically modified. The Sacraments, in his view, were given with the Gospel and the Church. He repudiated the notion that the Congregationalists were merely "an unspiritual reproduction of the Society of Friends."[130] In *Essays in Orthodox Dissent* he wrote ironically on this very point: "We have a doctrine of development which is the image of the Pope's.

[128] See Nathaniel Micklem, *The Box and the Puppets.*
[129] P. 81.
[130] *Essays in Orthodox Dissent*, p. 119.

Some of us are inclined to believe in a Spirit that takes the things of Christ to improve upon them. . . . We are disposed to set the rites of the Christian centuries beside those of the Old Testament, useful in their time, but now almost or quite outgrown. We look for an age of the Holy Ghost, when historic Christianity will become only a stage in our redemption. Some of us are almost emancipated from the Sacraments."[131] In such a war there could be no armistice.

These facts have been narrated, not to indicate that the battles between the schools are unending, but rather to show with what difficulties those who sought for improvements in the worship of the Free Churches had to contend. The present achievements are not the gains of the supine, but the rewards of courageous pioneers.

At this vantage of time, when so many liturgical gains have been consolidated, it is appropriate to consider their number and significance and how greatly they have changed the face of worship in the Free Churches.

In the first place, there is no longer any widespread prejudice against the use of set prayers, and there is in many places a welcome for liturgical forms, in the public worship of the Free Churches. The contrary was true at the beginning of this century. Sir John McClure was considered a radical when in 1919 he contended that so-called free prayer was more repetitive and didactic than the name implied; he even castigated it as "preaching with eyes shut."[132] B. M. Peake fourteen years later welcomed the Liturgical Movement because "Christianity is weary of individualism which weakens and divides; it is striving to escape the narrow bondage of the subjective into the freedom of the objective, the universal; from the limitations of the isolated individual to the fulness and strength of the great Community."[133]

It became increasingly recognized that liturgical forms had three advantages over free prayer. They made the preparation for worship less of a strain for the minister and they liberated the congregation from entire dependence upon his moods, feelings, and limitations. They provided a responsive element in devotions entirely suitable for denominations such as the Free Churches which had stressed throughout their history the importance of

---

[131] *Ibid.*, pp. 62-63.

[132] The Chairman's Address delivered in May 1919, and printed in *The Congregational Year Book* (1920), p. 56.

[133] "The Reform of Divine Worship," an article in *The Congregational Quarterly.*

the Reformed principle of the priesthood of all believers. Liturgical prayers also expressed the unity of the local congregation with the Great Church of the world and of the Christian centuries. Generally such prayers were accepted as a great relief after the prolix, diffuse, and repetitive extemporaneous effusions which congregations had often previously endured. The Free Catholics and the denominational service books have performed a useful service.

Today there is perhaps a serious danger that the revolt against spontaneity and free prayer has gone too far. For if the Free Churches were wholly to lose the gift of free prayer, as a supplement to liturgical prayer, they would have lost one of the gifts which they have to bring to the Universal Church. On the lips of a godly and affectionate pastor, who fully shares the hopes and fears of his flock, free prayer is, indeed, a means of grace. Its fervour, immediacy, and relevance to the needs of a local congregation complement the universal and objective qualities of a Liturgy. It is worth recalling the strength and conviction of the charismatic and Bible-centered worship of the seventeenth century Puritans and the eighteenth century Methodists which impressed thousands upon thousands with its unaffected sincerity and joy. Where it survives in village outposts it is still impressive today.[134]

The second gain for Free Church worship is the increasing use of the major festivals of the Christian Year: Advent to Pentecost, with daily services in Holy Week climaxed by the joy of Easter Day Communion. All the denominational service books make provision for these festivals celebrating the mighty acts of God consummated in Christ. Not only do they lead each year to disciplined meditation on the meaning of the Incarnation for the life of the Church and the world, but they have happily ousted many minor secular festivals that once pre-empted Christian interests in England and have become a commercial menace in the United States. In the high days of Puritanism there was a reaction against festivals, partly because the frequency of Saints' Days was an occasion for turning holy days into unholy holidays, but even more because for the Puritan each Sunday was in theory a Pentecost in which the Holy Spirit contemporized all the benefits of the Incarnation and the Atonement for God's covenanted people.

The present declension from Puritan practice in the Free Churches is to be justified as an accommodation to our human

---

[134] See *The Baptist Quarterly*, Vol. XIII (1949-1950), p. 105, for the account of a service conducted by laymen in a Methodist Chapel in a mining village in County Durham.

nature, which sees only in part and can therefore concentrate more readily on separate aspects of the multi-faceted meaning of the Incarnation. The beneficial discipline of Lent, once sneered at as a temporary term of committed discipleship in a year of comparative neglect, is now widely practised in the Free Churches. Holy Week, in particular, is a period when joint services between the local Free Churches are commonly held. Such festival occasions are to be welcomed because they are based upon that holy history which gives theological structure to the New Testament and the earliest creeds, and they prove to be a strengthening of the Christian faith and of spiritual life.

While the recitation of a creed in the Free Churches is not widespread at Sunday services, except in Communion Services in Presbyterian and Methodist churches, there is a much more positive attitude to creeds as summaries of belief, rather than as doctrinal tests. It is part of the decided return to theological orthodoxy in British theology. It is significant that the eminent Baptist Biblical scholar, H. Wheeler Robinson, considered as early as 1924 that the Independent wing of the Free Churches had been unwise in parading its independence of creeds. He was a little tired of ministers quoting Tennyson's half truth:

> There lives more faith in honest doubt,
> Believe me, than in half the creeds.

He preferred his own revised version:

> There lives more faith in honest creeds,
> Believe me, than in half the doubt.[135]

Nathaniel Micklem was not in the least singular in using the Apostles' Creed as a framework for his doctrinal introduction to Christianity in *The Creed of a Christian*, and the proof of the growing orthodoxy in belief of the Free Churches was signally demonstrated by Archbishop William Temple's invitation to Micklem to write a Lenten volume, *The Doctrine of our Redemption*. Any residual doubts about the wisdom of using the creeds in public worship spring from a conviction that the listing of historical and propositional statements about the nature of God is not a very lyrical activity. Indeed, as the perceptive Bernard Manning wrote: "Hymns are for us Dissenters what the Liturgy is for the Anglican. They are the framework, the setting, the

---

[135] *The Baptist Quarterly*, Vol. II (1924-1925), p. 348.

conventional, the traditional part of divine service as we use it. They are, to adopt the language of the liturgiologists, the Dissenting Use. . . . We mark times and seasons, celebrate festivals, express experiences, and expound doctrines by hymns."[136] For this reason Congregationalists and Baptists have historically preferred to use covenants and hymns as substitutes for creeds, for they engage the heart and will in the joyful obedience of faith. But, as a basis for catechetical instruction and as warnings against recurrent heresies, the creeds fulfil a useful purpose. Their use in public worship, however, is as yet too infrequent, irregular, or unenthusiastic to be considered a major achievement.

The third positive gain in Free Church worship is a greatly enhanced appreciation of the Gospel Sacraments of Baptism and the Lord's Supper. It was not always thus. Many ministers in the Free Churches earlier in the century regarded the Sacraments as optional visual aids to preaching, or asserted with C. Ernest Watson that "our divine Master meant life to be sacramental in its common ways and not merely on set or formal occasions."[137] The neglect of infant Baptism was even more common, for as Kenneth Parry observed in 1933: "there are probably men who administer the Lord's Supper amongst us who have never been baptized. And there are certainly more than a few in the membership of our churches who were not baptized as children and have not been baptized as adults."[138] Even among the Baptists there was laxity in the requirement of Believers' Baptism for entrance to membership and Communion, for Principal A. C. Underwood of that denomination complained that it was occasionally administered "at a weeknight service, as though it needed to be tucked away in a corner."[139]

This is all very much *past* history for the present generation of Free Churchmen, and the new apprehension of the value of the Sacraments was gained by such pioneers as P. T. Forsyth. Today the Sacrament of the Lord's Supper is rarely an appendix to the preaching service for the pious few, administered in a perfunctory manner. It is now commonly regarded as the supreme privilege of church members to be guests at Christ's Holy Table and to partici-

---

[136] *The Hymns of Wesley and Watts*, pp. 133, 135.

[137] Article: "The Nature of the Church," in *The Congregational Quarterly*, Vol. VIII, No. 3 (July 1930), p. 344.

[138] Article, "Baptism: Congregational Theory and Practice," *The Congregational Quarterly*, Vol. XI, No. 4 (October 1933), p. 408.

[139] J. H. Rushbrooke, ed., *The Faith of the Baptists*, p. 14.

pate in the Lord's Supper. Every Free Church denomination, as we have seen, has a comprehensive and genuinely ecumenical order for Holy Communion in its official service-book, following the structure and intention of the historic liturgies of Christendom, emphasizing the meaning of this Sacrament as, at once, Sacrifice, Memorial, Communion, Thanksgiving, and anticipation of the eternal Messianic Banquet. Each rite has its great Prayer of Consecration or Blessing, complete with *Sursum corda*, *Sanctus*, *anamnesis*, *epiklesis* and oblation, together with a fitting emphasis on the great symbolic acts of Fraction and Libation. Such unity with the Universal Church of Christ in the chief Sacrament would have been unthinkable, even for the most sanguine of prophets, only fifty years ago. It is the greatest single achievement of the combined Liturgical and Ecumenical Movements.

Gone, too, is the old Memorialism which observed Communion as the memory of a crucified martyr and as primarily the badge of Christian fellowship. On all sides the Lord's Supper is interpreted as a communicating (and also, for Methodists, a converting) ordinance, that conveys to faith the blessedness of forgiveness and the assurance of eternal life. For many it is also the means of our incorporation into the mystical Body of Christ. For some its central act of divine blessing of human labour on the gifts of God prior to equal sharing is the anticipation of and impetus to a juster and more compassionate social order in the world community. For almost all it is a chief means of grace and its more frequent and more reverent celebration is greatly appreciated.

The former nominalism of the administration of Infant and Believers' Baptism has also largely disappeared, as worthier rites of initiation have been prepared in the official Service books of the Free Churches. This is recognized by all to be a Sacrament of the Church and therefore to be administered in the presence of the assembled Christian community. A further implication is that the parents (in the case of Infant Baptism) or believers (in the case of Adult Baptism) are required to give solemn affirmations of their faith and firm adherence to the Church, and this is, in fact, almost the universal practice.

The fourth gain is the great improvement in the solemnity of Ordination Services. We have seen that the Free Churches, with the exception of the Presbyterians, went through a period of anti-sacerdotal amateurishness,[140] when the Ordination of Ministers

---

[140] It was typified by the rejection of dignity in dress as well as ceremonial, as

was rather perfunctorily treated. As an imitation of Quaker pan-sacramentalism weakened the appreciation of the historic Sacraments, so a kind of pan-vocationalism (when it was the fashion to "set apart" social workers to their office in special services) weakened the honour in which the historic ministry was held. Nowadays the ministry is held to be a gift of the ascended Lord to his Church. Consequently, as recent denominational service books show, the rite of Ordination is worthily administered with the laying-on of hands and the invocation of the Holy Spirit. The minister-elect is required to make a statement of faith and to offer solemn promises that he will be diligent in preaching God's Word, administering the Sacraments, and shepherding the flock. Usually there is a sermon in which minister and people are reminded of their responsibilities under God. These can be most moving and effectual in their combination of the Gospel's judgment and consolation.

What depth such a service can plumb is illustrated in Bernard Manning's ordination charge, which suffers greatly in condensation. He is speaking to the congregation of the hardships of the ministry. Then, with holy indignation rising, Manning reaches his tremendous climax, as sword-thrust follows sword-thrust into degenerate consciences:

"But what no young man who has put his whole life on the altar can expect—for until he has experienced it for he can not conceive it—is the coldness, the callousness, and the deadness of those to whom he looks for help, for support both in the work of the Church and in the daily quickening of his own spirit. The gates of hell, the whole world lying in the arms of the evil one, this will not daunt him; but it is when he sees the abomination of desolation standing where it ought not—indifference, worldliness, heartlessness in you the Body of Christ, it is then that the cold fear paralyses his soul, the fear that the whole business is a mockery and the shadow of a name. If this be Christ's Body, it is a dead body, and Christ is dead. You are still in your sins; then He is not risen. The faith is vain; and the man who has renounced all else to preach it is of all men most pitiable. Having preached to others

---

ministers preached in lounge suits (and occasionally flamboyant ties) to express the priesthood of all believers. One recalls the cartoon of Dr. R. F. Horton, distinguished minister of Lyndhurst Road Congregational Church, Hampstead, revealing him in complete nudity, from which the female members of his congregation shielded their eyes, while Horton asserted, "I will wear no clothes to distinguish myself from my brethren." A very considerable number of Free Church ministers wear a clerical collar and, when conducting worship, cassock, Genevan gown and bands.

he feels himself a castaway. In such an hour the Saviour can still save His servant, but do you envy the Church that plunges a man into that pit?"[141]

A fifth gain in Free Church worship is a better balance between Word and Sacrament. It is increasingly realized that the ideal towards which to work is a conjoint celebration of the Word and Sacrament each Sunday as in the Primitive Church. Even if this is a long way from attainment, fortnightly services of the Word and Sacrament are fairly common, especially in the metropolitan area. It is now recognized in the denominational service books that the weekly service on Sunday mornings should preserve the structure of the Liturgy, while stopping short of consecration and communion, relating it clearly to the fuller service of Word *and* *Sacrament* which is its climax and completion.

Of almost equal significance is the gradual realization that preaching and the celebration of the Sacrament reinforce each other powerfully. The values of a Sacramental Liturgy are its universality, its historicity, and its objectivity. These, apart from the proclamation of the Word, may seem antiquarian, generalized, abstract, and remote. Preaching, however, provides the necessary supplementation of particularity, contemporaneity, and existential subjectivity. Unrelated to Liturgy and Sacrament, preaching loses its effectiveness by the unbalanced exaggeration of its qualities. The Liturgy mediates the Gospel which preaching contemporizes.

In addition to these gains achieved during the present century, the Free Churches have not lost (with the possible exception of the charismatic factor now too much depreciated) their own distinctive emphases in worship. For them the authority of the Gospel[142] was and remains primary, to which all worship is the grateful response: the advent of a less philosophical and more Biblical theology in the Roman Catholic and Anglican Churches means only that others share it. Nor have the Free Churches lost the strong moral note which we found alike in Forsyth and Oman, their two chief theologians in this period. It was strongly asserted in the theology of the social gospel. It rings through the intercessory prayers, the offertory prayers, and the hymns of consecration. This was the reason why the footwashing episode from the Fourth Gospel (John 13:3-17) was included as a Post-Com-

141 *A Layman in the Ministry*, pp. 156-57.
142 P. T. Forsyth in the *Soul of Prayer*, p. 120, wrote: "And prayer in Christ's name is prayer inspired by His first interest—the Gospel."

munion lesson in the *Manual for Ministers*. Indeed, the conception of dedication is so all-pervasive that in the most recent Congregational service book there is even provision made for "The Dedication of a Bible"![143]

The authentic Nonconformist note was recently sounded by Principal John Marsh in his address as Chairman of the Congregational Union in 1963. He protested against making church life a religious ghetto: "We should think of the Church offering her worship to God most characteristically in all the life of the world, and of the sacramental, liturgical life we are privileged to share on Sundays as the means by which God has provided for our continual renewal in the attempt to be an obedient people of God in the world."[144] The concept of the Christian life as a covenant between God and His people is still effective in the Free Church tradition and its worship. The Methodists have, of course, an annual Covenant Service, and many Congregational churches and some Baptist churches recite the covenant pledges as new members are received into the full communion of the church, or at the anniversary services celebrating the foundations of their local congregations. Perhaps it is the sense of the local covenanted community which is most significantly missing in a Liturgy which rightly affirms the solidarity of Christians with the Church militant upon earth and triumphant in heaven. And it is this sense of a closely knit and integrated company of Christ which has been characteristic of the warmth of Free Church worship. This, too, must be even more carefully preserved when a more liturgical form of worship is adopted.

It may seem that a more optimistic picture of Free Church worship has been painted than the situation warrants. It is not claimed that congregations are large, or that the preaching is spell-binding, or that all ministers are liturgical enthusiasts. But it is claimed that amid the acute difficulties of preserving the Christian faith in a secular age (and the greater problems of communicating it to the outsider), the worship of the Free Churches today is a more faithful reflection of its heritage in Christ's Gospel than it has been at any time during this century, and that it is no longer the worship of sects but of part of the

---

[143] *A Book of Services and Prayers*, p. 111. This book is a declension from *A Book of Public Worship*, but its copious compilation of classical prayers, its provision of material for the Christian Year, and its comprehensive Eucharistic orders are proof of the immense liturgical advance since *Manual for Ministers*, p. 12.

[144] Published as *Theme with Variations* (1963).

Holy Catholic and Apostolic Church, as its ecumenical-type services of Word and Sacrament demonstrate.

At the same time, it would be dishonest not to indicate a few areas of remaining dissatisfaction. While all the denominational service books in their prefaces claim that they wish to supplement and not to supplant free prayer and the charismatic element in worship, their effect has been the contrary of their avowed intention. Many observers cannot but be disturbed that the gifts of free prayer and the capacity for silent meditation on God's Word seem to be dying out. The cultivation of these is essential if the practices of private prayer and family prayers are to be revived, and without these the renewal of Sunday worship will only be a shadow of what it might be. Along with this loss—so central to the Puritan and Pietist traditions of the Free Churches—is the increasing impersonality and lack of a sense of fellowship as God's covenanted people which the exclusive use of liturgical forms can produce. Finally, for churches which have given the laity so large a share in their government, there is an urgent need to use the gifted laity more prominently in sharing the leadership of worship with the ministry, and in giving them more frequent opportunity to instruct the congregation in the meaning of a Christian's calling in the world. Liturgical worship is intended to give the people a larger part in worship and the priesthood of all believers is negatived by the dominance of a single ministerial voice in lections, prayers, and sermon.

The most serious lack in the Free Church tradition, however, is of a daily discipline of corporate worship such as the Book of Common Prayer provides. It appears to be the single major factor which has caused former Free Church ministers to join the Church of England for that daily continuity in worship which their own denominations lacked.[145] The attempts by the Iona Community in Presbyterianism, the Church Order Group in Congregationalism, and the Methodist Sacramental Fellowship to set up a daily rule of life are witnesses to this profound need and to the temporary way in which it is being met.

All these questions about Free Church worship today are, however, more than counterbalanced by the very important advances made towards a worship that is deeply reverent, sacramentally rich, ecumenically comprehensive, and theologically faithful.

[145] See Dewi Morgan, ed., *They became Anglicans*, and Martin Thornton, *English Spirituality*, p. 4.

CHAPTER XI

THE WORSHIP OF THE SOCIETY
OF FRIENDS

I F FREE CHURCH worship owes most to Calvin and Wesley, it
has also, especially in the current century, acknowledged the
attraction of Fox and his followers. The fascination of the
worship of the Quakers is that it represents the most radical type
of free corporate prayer and expresses the strongest protest
against the restrictions of a liturgy and of sacerdotalism. It is a
strenuous attempt to recover the important charismatic element
in the worship of the apostolic Church.[1] It is a living commentary
on the Johannine text "The Spirit bloweth where it listeth" and
on the Pauline words "Likewise the Spirit also helpeth our infirmities, for we know not what we should pray for as we ought, but
the Spirit maketh intercession for us." It is also a witness to the
Divine initiative and prevenience in all religious experience and to
the need for an expectant and prepared spirit to receive the inti-
mations of the Holy Spirit.

In its quest for corporate mysticism it daringly claims to unite
what has usually been separated in history. The mystic has been
traditionally an isolated soul, representing the flight of the alone
to the Alone, but Quaker mysticism aims to be a squadron in
flight. Yet the Quaker mystics are also prophetic, as their witness
against slavery and war amply demonstrates, so their corporate
mysticism is also intra-mundane. Consequently, to maintain the
metaphor, the squadron in flight touches down on the solid concrete of the runway.

Quaker worship has a peculiar relevance to twentieth century
living conditions. Its emphasis on silence and meditation is most
appropriate for what Aldous Huxley has called "the Age of Noise."
At no other time in history does man seem to have been so assaulted
by noise. The screaming of jet-engines in the skies, the blare of
motor horns and the screeching of skidding tires in the streets,
the ringing of the telephone in the office or home, and the competitive claims of radio, television, and stereophonic recording apparatus, demand silence for the preservation of sanity. The present

[1] Friedrich Heiler, *Prayer, A Study in the History and Psychology of Religion*,
p. 308.

398

century has also seen the most persuasive statements of the Quaker viewpoint in a distinguished series of annual Swarthmore Lectures, subsequently published, and these have shown the significance of the predominantly silent Quaker Meetings as the dynamos of the Quaker testimony.

In addition, the contemporary philosophical movement of linguistic analysis, deriving from Wittgenstein, finds a parallel in the Quaker recognition of the inadequacy of our conventional verbal symbols to mediate the individual apprehension of the claim of God on the soul or the experience of the "inner light."[2] Moreover, in an expanding universe in which the writ of scientific law runs more extensively, contemplation is inevitably preferred to petitionary prayer, so that it is not surprising that distinguished scientists like Sir Arthur Eddington or Dr. Kathleen Lonsdale have found the worship of the Friends congenial. The Quakers claim, as will be seen, a further relevance for their worship in the present century, namely, that silent corporate meditation is the only type of prayer that will unite representatives of different religious faiths in their search for spiritual unity. Finally, both Anglicans and Free Churchmen increasingly allow a place for silent prayer in their forms of worship and thus pay a tribute to the importance of the Quaker concept of worship in the ecumenical movement.

1. The Modern Quaker Renaissance

Since George Fox's foundation of the Society of Friends in the Commonwealth of England in the seventeenth century, there have been many vagaries in its history and even in its worship. At the end of the seventeenth century and continuing through the eighteenth century the mystical trend was exaggerated to the extent of Quietism, and the prophetic witness was eliminated. In this situation passivity and an individualistic introversion were glorified. The nineteenth century brought about a dramatic reversal as Quakerism caught fire from the Evangelical Revival, and the mysticism was almost lost (not to mention the silence of meetings) in a passionate advocacy of preaching. The modern renascence of Quakerism dates from the latter part of the nineteenth century, and is chiefly attributable to the influence of two activistic Quakers who combined the mystical and prophetic strains of original

2 Douglas V. Steere's *Where Words Come From*, a Swarthmore Lecture, is a brilliant and fascinating study of the art of listening to God and man at many levels.

Quakerism as in George Fox and his followers. These were Caroline Stephen, the gracious and cultured sister of Sir Leslie Stephen, and John Wilhelm Rowntree. The former was a convinced Friend, the latter a birthright Friend. Caroline Stephen was primarily the mystic and John Wilhelm Rowntree was primarily the prophet.

As an Anglican in an age of acute doubt, Caroline Stephen found it difficult to worship according to the Book of Common Prayer because the creeds and the traditional theology which that formulary expresses raised questions that reason stifled. The silent worship of the Society of Friends was the healing refuge that she needed: "What I felt I wanted in a place of worship was a refuge, or at least the opening of a doorway towards the refuge, from doubts and controversies; not a fresh encounter with them. Yet it seems to me impossible that anyone harassed by the conflicting views of truth, with which just now the air is thick, should be able to forget controversy while listening to such language as that of the Book of Common Prayer. It seems to me that nothing but silence can heal the wounds made by disputations in the region of the unseen."[3]

Its primary attraction lay "in the fact that it pledged me to nothing and left me altogether undisturbed to seek for help in my own way," but in time she came to recognize that silent worship had the additional benefit of a "strange subduing and softening effect upon my mind."[4] This is what Quakers commonly refer to as "tendering." In due time Caroline Stephen became the foremost interpreter in England of the Friends' way of worship and she had a lasting influence on several generations of Quaker university undergraduates in Cambridge while she was a member of the Meeting there.[5] She gladly testified that "Friends' Meetings have indeed been to me the greatest of outward helps to a fuller and fuller entrance into the Spirit from which they have sprung; the place of the most soul-subduing, faith-restoring, strengthening and peaceful communion, in feeding on the bread of life, that I have ever known."[6] Her influence was cast against any tendency to depreciate the royal priesthood of all believers by the possible introduction of a paid professional ministry on American Quaker lines.[7] She restored to the Quakers a conviction of the rightness of their seventeenth century heritage in a time of acute religious crisis.

---

[3] *Quaker Strongholds*, pp. 44-45.   [4] *Ibid.*
[5] Rufus M. Jones, *The Later Periods of Quakerism*, Vol. II, p. 969.
[6] *Quaker Strongholds*, p. 3.   [7] *Ibid.*, p. 110.

Her work was fully complemented by John Wilhelm Rowntree,[8] who, though a mystic, was less passive in his approach than she. He applauded Fox for having the courage to be logical, since many "other churches profess belief in inward guidance, but they dare not found their constitution on this belief."[9] The heritage of Quietism, forbidding any intellectual or spiritual preparation for worship, was rudely criticized by Rowntree. He was surely behind the conclusion of the Yearly Meeting on Ministry and Oversight which insisted: "True worship is intensely active. It consists in offering ourselves to God—body, mind, and soul—for the doing of His will."[10] He recommended that the children of Friends should be trained in Quaker schools and he was influential in the foundation of Woodbrooke Settlement in 1903 as a study centre for the social questions of the day. For him the preparation of mind and heart for Quaker worship and witness demanded a deep study of the Bible and of psychology.[11] The positive Christian basis of his message is seen in the peroration of his speech at a national Quaker Conference held in Manchester in 1895, when he asked, "Is there indifference to the Higher Life?" and answered:

"Then, O Christ, convince us by thy Spirit, thrill us with Thy Divine passion, drown our selfishness in Thy invading love, lay on us the burden of the world's suffering, drive us forth with the apostolic fervour of the early Church! So only can our message be delivered—'Speak to the children of Israel that they go forward.' "[12]

If Caroline Stephen emphasized the vertical dimension, then the chief importance of John Wilhelm Rowntree was that he linked it with the horizontal dimension of social service and thus prepared the way for the honourable witness of reconciliation and rehabilitation for which the twentieth century Quakers are renowned.

Since his time only one significant change has taken place in the arrangement of Quaker worship. Until 1924 those Friends who had a special gift in vocal ministry were recognized as "Ministers" and recorded as such in the annals of the Society. After this time no such distinction was recorded, and thus expression was given to the desire that the responsibility for vocal min-

8 See Evelyn Underhill's *The Mystics of the Church*, Chap. XIII, for a sympathetic study of Rowntree.
9 *Essays and Addresses*, p. 101.
10 *Worship and Ministry* (1899), the Epistle of the Yearly Meeting.
11 Gladys Wilson, *Quaker Worship*, pp. 89-90.
12 Rufus M. Jones, *op.cit.*, Vol. II, p. 975.

istry should be more widely shared among Friends. As a result, "more Friends do take part in vocal ministry now than formerly; but it has meant that most of their contributions are shorter than those of the earlier 'Ministers,' and that there is rarely any ministry in Meetings today which could accurately be described as preaching and little that could be called exposition."[13]

In general, three successive trends within twentieth century Quakerism may be noted, and each had its parallel in the theological movements of these years. The renaissance of Quakerism was correlated with the re-affirmation of mysticism in the first two decades of this century in the studies of Inge, Evelyn Underhill, and von Hügel. This was also the era of the "new Theology" or the "social Gospel" in which the social witness of the Friends was strengthened, especially during the years of the First World War. Finally, while it cannot be said that the Society, as a whole, has devoted itself to the study of Biblical theology or even to the Ecumenical Movement, it is significant that some of its contemporary exponents have noted these very needs.[14]

2. *The Advantages of Corporate Silent Worship*

From the days of Fox onward the Society of Friends has claimed that the chief advantage of its worship is that stress on inwardness and sincerity, instead of outward profession, which guards against hypocrisy in the Christian life. The claim is made in an unusually belligerent manner by John W. Graham, chiefly by criticizing the "professional prayers" of priests or clergy: "This vast and fruitful error comes from the original mistake in not realising that Prayer is an act of the Inward Man, something different from talking on demand or reading from a prayer book." He continues: "How real prayer can be produced on demand from a platform, or at a fixed point in a service I have never understood. All these devices, made for the help of human weaknesses, increase that weakness. Who can walk with permanent crutches?"[15] Harold Loukes avers that "there is still a need to be reminded that God is not limited by His own means. It is always possible to enjoy a ritual for the wrong reasons and not know one has missed the secret: to be moved by beauty and miss the beauty of holiness, to feed on language and miss the message. But if a man sits in silence with other worshippers, and nothing happens, he knows

---

[13] Gladys Wilson, *op.cit.*, p. 89.
[14] Notably Douglas V. Steere, Thomas F. Green, and Gladys Wilson.
[15] *The Quaker Ministry*, p. 23.

that nothing has happened."[16] Thus, whether stated pugnaciously or pacifically, Quaker worship is first of all a protest against a worship of the lips without the life, a plea for uncoerced spontaneity in the response to the living God in prayer. But in this it does not differ radically from the Anabaptists, the Separatists, or the Puritans, who made the same plea for a sincere Spirit-led worship.

It is in the *corporate* practice of a predominantly silent worship that the distinctive characteristic of Quaker worship is found, and the word "corporate" has to be stressed so that this silent worship may be distinguished from the silence of Trappist monks or of Carthusians, each in his own cell. A constant claim is that this is productive of great serenity of soul, of an inward and healing calm of mind. The fact that this has been partly recognized to be true by many non-Quaker Christians must explain the great popularity among English-speaking Protestant congregations of Whittier's great hymn, "Dear Lord and Father of Mankind," with its closing verses:

> Drop Thy still dews of quietness,
>   Till all our strivings cease:
> Take from our souls the strain and stress,
> And let our ordered lives confess
>   The beauty of Thy peace.
>
> Breathe through the pulses of desire
>   Thy coolness and Thy balm;
> Let sense be dumb, its heats expire:
> Speak through the earthquake, wind, and fire,
>   O still small voice of calm.

Quakers believe that in their worship they find "the silence of eternity interpreted by love."[17]

That historian of modern spirituality and Quaker philosopher, Rufus M. Jones, declares that it is in the quiet that faith grows and faith produces serenity: "Religious faith when it takes us back to the true source of power removes from the mind the peril of bewildering unsettlement. It turns water to wine. It brings prodigals home. It turns sunsets to sunrises. It makes the impossible become possible. The master secret of life is the attainment of the

---

[16] *Friends Face Reality*, p. 119.
[17] Two lines from the second verse of the same hymn.

power of serenity in the midst of stress and action and adventure."[18] Certainly it does not strain the reason to believe that there is too much didacticism, and too many words, possibly too many dogmatic certainties in traditional Catholic and Protestant worship, whereas in corporate silent worship there is the intense relief of moving along at one's own speed of meditation, with the occasional incitation of the spoken ministry.

Another value claimed for corporate silent prayer is that the experience is subtly unitive, for "the group becomes fused into an organic whole through the empowering and enlightening action of the Spirit."[19] So great is this unitive power that Douglas Steere can report: "I have seen this silent worship level a group in which there was an ugly barrier separating two of its members, and I have seen it bring them to ask for forgiveness. I have seen it prepare members in a group to enter into holy obedience against their surface wills on matters in which the whole future course of their lives was at stake."[20] T. Edmund Harvey claims that corporate silent prayer is the most appropriate expression of the priesthood of all believers, whereas in the Free Church tradition the prayer of the minister is the expression of the aspiration of a single representative individual. The advantage of silent worship is that of being "the expression of the needs and longing of one who by a priestly act of the spirit puts himself alongside of his fellow-worshippers, enters in some measure into their spiritual condition, and, feeling their need as his own, prays not only for but with them, as one of them, and borne along by the spirit of prayer, raises with them the hands of a trusting child towards the unseen Father, in whose Presence all together stand."[21]

Several writers have expressed the conviction that silent prayer in a Quaker Meeting has a strongly egalitarian character.[22] No one has caught the distinctive atmosphere more vividly than Christopher Isherwood, the novelist and poet, in a recent work where he contrasts the febrile and frantic air of Hollywood with the recuperative quiet of a Philadelphia Quaker Meeting: "Never-

---

[18] Chap. 7, "Re-thinking Quaker Principles," in Herrymon Maurer, ed., *The Pendle Hill Reader*, p. 180.

[19] P. Edwall, E. Hayman, and W. D. Maxwell, eds., *Ways of Worship, The Report of a Theological Commission on Faith and Order*, p. 171, citation from the Committee on Christian Relationships of the Religious Society of Friends of Great Britain.

[20] *Prayer and Worship*, pp. 83-84.

[21] *Silence and Worship, A Study in Quaker Experience*, p. 51.

[22] Notably John Sykes, *The Quakers*, p. 261 and Howard H. Brinton, *Friends for 300 Years*, Chap. iv.

theless, the Silence, in its odd way, was coming to life. Was steadily filling up the bare white room, like water rising in a tank. Every one of us contributed to it, simply by being present. Togetherness grew and tightly enclosed us until it seemed that we must all be breathing in unison and keeping time with our heart-beats. It was massively alive and somehow unimaginably ancient, like the togetherness of Man in the primeval caves."[23]

As contrasted with the closed character of liturgical worship, the Quakers claim that their type of worship has a germinative quality—an openness to new possibilities of truth and insight. This group mysticism means, according to Howard H. Brinton, that the worshippers are like the spokes of a wheel, for the closer they come to the centre of all Life the nearer they are to each other, and in this unity they experience "the germinating silence of a Quaker Meeting sensitive to the emergence of new life and thought."[24]

A final claim made for Quaker worship is that by its avoidance of the aesthetic distractions of ceremonial and of the dulling repetitiveness of ritual, it leads to a realistic concern for the world. There is thus no temptation, it is asserted, to make worship an escape-hatch from social responsibility. This group-centred, life-affirming worship, built upon the interdependence of men recognizing their creaturehood, means that for Quakers "their customary face is towards the world" and that "their experience of Meeting sends them in search of it."[25]

These, then, are the values claimed for a silent group mysticism: an inwardness that avoids hypocrisy, the creation of serenity and recollectedness, an unitive egalitarianism that truly expresses the priesthood of all believers, an openness to the signals of new truth, and a stimulus to social service.

3. *The Stages of Quaker Worship*

Since the essential character of Quaker worship is that, unlike liturgical worship, it is utterly unpredictable, being dependent upon the sovereign freedom of the direction of the Holy Spirit, it is extraordinarily difficult to describe. The pattern of worship in one Meeting may be entirely different from that of another. The proportions of silence and vocal worship in any Meeting vary greatly.

[23] *The World in the Evening* (New York, Random House, 1954), p. 51.
[24] *Creative Worship*, p. 66.
[25] John Sykes, *The Quakers*, p. 49.

Nonetheless, many leading Quaker writers have attempted to show that it is appropriate to think of various stages or developments taking place in a session of Quaker worship, though, naturally enough, there are diversities in the description. Harold Loukes describes the Quaker Meeting in terms of a deepening of the vertical relationship with God and a deepening of the horizontal relationships between the worshippers.[26] John Sykes defines the separate stages as: settling down, meditative commitment, creativity, "centring down," and a climax of total stillness.[27] Both these accounts are, however, a little vague in their use of terms. Nonetheless, two of the stages they describe are familiar to all students of the Catholic contemplatives, for the "settling down" or concentrating of the attention is the first stage of meditation, and the "centring down" of the self from surface concerns to identity with the Divine will are essential preliminaries for the practice of mystical prayer.[28]

More precise are the analyses of Douglas Steere and Thomas F. Green, because they make fuller use of the familiar categories of traditional Catholic and Protestant prayer. Steere defines the stages as: Preparation, Confession, Adoration, Intercession, and Dedication.[29] Green uses the same categories but in a significantly different order: Adoration, Confession, Dedication, Thanksgiving, Intercession, and a return to Adoration. Green believes that Quaker worship should follow the pattern of the Lord's Prayer which begins and ends on the note of adoration. "It should begin with adoration—for the religious life is a response to a vision of greatness, not a grim drive towards moral virtues."[30]

Such definiteness in elaborating the stages of Quaker devotion may be anathema to other Quakers who might feel that this was to restrict the freedom of worship more subtly than a liturgy can. But it is significant that both Steere and Green are educators, rightly aware of the need of clarity and method in the instruction of the young. Professor Steere has a wide and deep knowledge of the history of Catholic and Protestant spirituality, and is actively engaged in ecumenical theological encounter. Green, the headmaster of Bootham, a distinguished Quaker public school in York, is a former Anglican. "I am deeply grateful," he has written, "for the religious training I received as a boy up to the age of twelve

[26] *Friends Face Reality*, pp. 121-24.   [27] *The Quakers*, pp. 21-33.
[28] Evelyn Underhill, *Worship*, p. 310.
[29] *Where Words Come From*, p. 39.   [30] *Preparation for Worship*, p. 17.

in a village school maintained by the Anglican Church. We learned by heart many psalms, passages from the prophets, the Gospels and the Epistles, and many of the prayers which voice in matchless language the needs of every man. Remembered passages, some, alas, fragmentary, are of inestimable value to me in our silent worship."[31] While Quaker worship has values to contribute to liturgical worship, it seems to be increasingly realized by Quaker leaders that traditional worship has an important theological structure to provide for corporate silent worship. Without an understanding of the discipline of mental prayer and of the Biblical revelation to which every type of *Christian* worship is a response, silent Quaker Meetings may degenerate into "nothing more than an unspoken exercise in the psychological game of free association—a succession of daydreams with a religious flavour."[32]

4. *Quaker Self-Evaluation*

It is a healthy sign in the Religious Society of Friends that thoughtful Quakers are far less defensive about their distinctive type of worship than they used to be, and are willing to recognize that it is open to abuse and in need of reformation.

Friends are no longer content to trust to the unprepared inspiration of spontaneity. The glorification of an impromptu ministry was, according to Rufus Jones, an encouragement of "passivity, not to say mental laziness and emptiness."[33] But what form should that preparation take? Thomas Green believes that the preparation should take a two-fold form—the practice of the techniques of mental prayer and the devotional study of the Bible. He warns that the emancipation of the Quakers from the Bible will lead to an inevitable and steady deterioration in the quality of worship, for "the Quaker, thrown upon his own resources, needs more than anyone a mind well stored with the passages of the Bible."[34] Moreover, he seems to question the wisdom of the traditional Quaker disregard of theological studies.[35] Douglas Steere pleads for a worship and ministry of members who "read and inwardly digest the Bible" and who are informed and "drawn down into the great Christian themes of the love, the joy, and the greatness of God; of suffering, sin, redemption, atonement and resurrection."[36] He even suggests that some of the younger Friends of today have been

[31] *Ibid.*, p. 18.   [32] *Ibid.*, p. 16.
[33] *The Later Periods of Quakerism*, Vol. II, p. 993.
[34] *Preparation for Worship*, p. 18.   [35] *Ibid.*, p. 5.
[36] *Where Words Come From*, pp. 64-65.

drawn into the Society by a passionate theological interest.

There is also an increasing recognition that the technique of silent, expectant worship is extraordinarily difficult to teach to children or to those familiar with the traditional Christian types of corporate prayer. T. Edmund Harvey admits that "it might be held that it would be as unreasonable to teach a child to swim by throwing him into a deep pool of water as to plunge him unprepared into a Quaker Meeting."[37] He further acknowledges that there is the need for an intermediate stage, which, in some cases, has led to the formation of special children's Meetings, in which the children are guided in their meditations and join in hymns. Thomas Hodgkin, in the same vein, recognizes that Quaker worship is "more fitted for those who have made some advance in the Christian life, than for those who are on the threshold," that it needs to be discreetly introduced and that it is not equally well suited to all mental types.[38] Thomas Green frankly admits the strain imposed on those who first attend a Quaker Meeting: "I well remember the first occasion I attended Meeting. After a quarter of an hour or so I felt intense fatigue of mind and body, and the remaining period was a prolonged agony of waiting. . . . Even now, after years of practice, I frequently find my powers of worshipping joyously are exhausted long before the prescribed period of an hour is over." He concludes with the wry observation: "At what varying speeds do the hands of our Meeting House clocks move!"[39]

The most serious criticisms of Quaker worship have yet to be advanced. Both Eric Hayman (who has since left the Society of Friends) and Thomas Green recognize that the absence of creeds, liturgies, sacraments, and of the keeping of the Christian Year, combined with Quakerism's historic indifference to theology, make it peculiarly susceptible to the *Zeitgeist*. The result is that there is a perpetual danger of the ethical dominating the religious motivation and of humanism supplanting devotion to God. Hayman sees this danger arising peculiarly in connection with the appeal that Quakerism makes in the modern world to a constituency wider than the bounds of the Christian Church, and in its becoming a kind of quiet parliament of all the religions.[40] He warns: "It seems that the discovery of a power of response in the human spirit, the realisation

[37] *Silence and Worship*, pp. 56-57.
[38] *The Fellowship of Silence*, p. 87.
[39] *Preparation for Worship*, p. 12.
[40] *Worship and the Common Life*, pp. 77-78.

of a window opening from the soul to eternity, leads some people irresistibly to the conclusion that a power discovered is a power possessed, and then that a power possessed is a power controlled and mastered by the possessor and even deriving from him."[41] Green recognizes the danger, but attributes its prevalence rather to the recovery in 1914 of the historic Quaker testimony to peace and reconciliation. Since that time Friends have been concerned with the unemployed in Britain, refugees from Nazi and Communist oppression, and famine-stricken villages in India. This has proved the sincerity of Quaker belief in the brotherhood of man, but only at the cost of neglecting the prior and primary sense of the Fatherhood of God which constituted them a religious society.[42] Ethics, which for historic Quakerism were theonomous, are becoming autonomous.[43]

Two other criticisms are made of Quakerism, but these are by no means generally accepted. One is Hayman's accusation that an isolationism is growing in Quakerism which insulates the Society of Friends from any desire for contact with the wider Christian Church.[44] It might be said, with more accuracy, that the Quakers will have to make a firm choice between association with the Ecumenical Movement on a firm Biblical and theological basis, and a non-theological immanentalism which might provide the basis for a unity between many religions and ethical humanists. Presumably Steere and Green would choose the first alternative, and perhaps Sykes would select the second.[45] Thomas Green asked a heterodox question which might point to a new style of Quaker architecture: "Is it a reprovable heresy to say that I have often found it easier to get free from the prison of self and catch a glimpse of the majesty of God in a cathedral built to His glory than in some of our drab Meeting Houses?"[46] It hardly seems likely that the Society of Friends would depart so far from their iconoclastic tradition as to build sanctuaries with traditional Christian symbols evocative of the meaning of the Incarnation.

Yet perhaps it is this very iconoclasm, which has amply served to make the historic protest against idolatry, which ought to be reconsidered. It is increasingly clear that in the history of Chris-

[41] *Ibid.*, p. 49. [42] *Preparation for Worship*, p. 8.
[43] *Ibid.*, pp. 5-6, where Green asserts: "I believe that future historians will discern at least a tendency in the thinking of many to replace religion by ethics."
[44] *Worship and the Common Life*, p. 144.
[45] This statement is made on the basis of pp. 29-30 and 261 of Sykes' *The Quakers, a new look at their place in society.*
[46] *Preparation for Worship*, p. 17.

409

tianity there have been two major means of communion with God, the spiritual and the sacramental. Surely they are complementary and not alternative? Evelyn Underhill, who was fully sympathetic to the qualities of Quaker worship and knew that many Catholic mystics had stressed the negative way and the claims of silence,[47] seems reasonable in claiming that the Quaker "exclusive mysticism, making an arbitrary distinction between sense and spirit, could never be adequate to the generous realities of an incarnational faith; or serve the religious needs of a creature poised between the worlds of spirit and sense, and participating in both."[48]

If Quakerism were able to take that step, without denying the importance of silent waiting in worship, or of a genuine interiority and sincerity in the approach to God, and thus find its way more fully into sharing the life of the Universal Church, the other branches would be more likely to take seriously the undoubted gifts which they would receive from the Religious Society of Friends. Thus the claims of both T. Edmund Harvey and Douglas Steere that Quakerism has much to teach the historic Church would be likelier of acceptance. Steere's suggestion is worth pondering, and therefore it is cited almost in full:

"How blessed any Protestant minister might feel if he could have the privilege of sitting for an hour in silent waiting with a little inner company of his congregation. . . . How that message might be clipped, how it might be refocussed, and upon occasion how it might be completely recast as he was swept by a deeper sense of both the needs of his group and of the abundance of God's power to meet the need. In such an experience how it might be charged with power!

"How helpful, too, it might be if this occasion might become the regular spring and source of his ministry, if ministry were required of him that week, or a place where one of the lay group sitting with him might from time to time be inwardly drawn to discharge the vocal ministry of the meeting and on that occasion relieve him of that exercise. If to this little group could in time be added the whole congregation who would all gather with him to wait in this way, with the freedom to minister shared still more widely, and the message come straight from a freshly touched mind and heart, is it impossible to see some, at least, of the steps

---

[47] A point also admitted by Violet Hodgkin in *Silent Worship: The Way of Wonder*, as she compared Quaker silence with that of Carthusian and Trappist monks.

[48] *Worship*, p. 312.

by which this Quaker treasure of a silent waiting ministry could be shared with the whole Free Church family?"[49]

To this query a two-fold answer may be given. The first is that in a remarkable way the Free Churches of England, at least, have recognized the need for silence in worship. This may be seen, for example, in the preface to *Orders of Worship for Use in Unitarian and Free Christian Congregations* (1932), where the editors write: "where there is worship, in spirit and in truth, moments of silence may be of very living and moving power."[50] In the Congregational *Manual for Ministers* (1936) it is specifically enjoined at the climax of the second Order for Holy Communion, when the elements are being received, that there shall be a short period of silence.[51] The Methodist *Divine Worship* (1935) deliberately makes room for "fervent petition and the silent adoration that asks nothing because it possesses all things in God."[52] W. E. Orchard in the Preface to *The Order of Divine Service* demands "that room shall be left both for freely uttered and for silent prayer, not only as existing alongside liturgical forms, but as their very crown and consummation."[53] The Church of Scotland (Presbyterian) customarily allows a period of silence in its prayers of thanksgiving for the faithful departed.[54] In the Church of England it is a frequent custom to have Bidding Prayers, requiring the silent response of the congregation. In all these ways it can be shown that the influence of the Quakers has been very considerable and is not likely to diminish.

Secondly, before it would be reasonable to ask Anglican and Free Church congregations to experiment further in the Quaker mode of worship, as Douglas Steere requests, it might be expected that Quakers would make a gesture of appropriating some of the features of Catholic and Protestant worship on occasion. But, first of all, the Friends themselves must determine whether their real future lies within the Christian orbit or in the direction of a wider religious and ethical syncretism. Certainly many responsible theologians would hold that a truly ecumenical worship must, because of the overwhelming preponderance of Roman Catholics,

---

49 *Where Words Come From*, p. 67. The same suggestion is made by T. Edmund Harvey, *Silence and Worship*, p. 57.
50 P. viii.   51 P. 62.
52 Introduction, p. 15. See also pp. 24, 26, 27, 39, 40, 59, 62, etc.
53 P. 5.
54 *The Book of Common Order*, pp. 22, 28, 35, etc. Provision is also made for a period of silence in the midst of prayers of intercession, as, for example, on pp. 28, 35, 108, etc.

Orthodox, Anglican and Lutheran Christians in the world, move towards a liturgical norm and form, but that within this context a regular place must be found for the immediacy, directness, and warmth of the charismatic elements of free and silent prayer. There is also a need for supplementing liturgical worship, especially among small groups, with occasions of free prayer and silent worship. Indeed, anything less would be to dishonour the varied ways in which men have found a living communion with God.

CHAPTER XII

UNITARIAN WORSHIP[1]

IF THE techniques of Quaker worship are radical, much of the religious thought in Unitarian worship is also radical. No religious communion in England has been more fertile in liturgical experimentation than the Unitarian. If its ancestry is traced back through English Presbyterianism it can point with pride to Richard Baxter's *Reformed Liturgy* of 1661 as the first attempt to provide a scriptural and comprehensive liturgy. If its origins are to be sought in eighteenth century Anglicanism, then they lead to the *Revision of the Liturgy* prepared by Theophilus Lindsey in 1774, itself deriving from Samuel Clarke's private manuscript revision of the Prayer Book.[2] But on either view it has a strong liturgical inheritance, and one which it has not entirely dissipated in the twentieth century. Like Methodism in this single respect, it has affiliations with both the Church of England and with Nonconformity. From the former it derives its appreciation of hallowed forms of prayer and from the latter the conviction that each new age requires its newly-devised prayers, convictions that in their opposition lead to friction.

The eighteenth century Biblical Unitarians did not object to a prayer book; on the contrary, they gave their attention to removing the more objectionable expressions of Trinitarianism in the Book of Common Prayer which they re-issued in theologically bowdlerised fashion. This was to put new wine in the old bottles. The nineteenth century Unitarians were, however, much more adventurous liturgically. Minister after minister of the Unitarian Church produced his own liturgy for his own congregation with astonishing enterprise and fertility of invention. But most were notable for effort rather than for achievement. The great exception was James Martineau's contributions to *Common Prayers for Christian Wor-*

---

[1] The author is happy to acknowledge the assistance given him on modern British Unitarian and Free Christian worship by the late Dr. E. Mortimer Rowe, from 1929 to 1949 the Secretary of the General Assembly of the British Unitarian and Free Christian Churches. Dr. Rowe generously lent copies of liturgical works and pamphlets long out of print and responded to requests for information by letters with generous alacrity. The author also acknowledges help from the Rev. Roger Thomas, Librarian of the Dr. Williams Library of London, and from the Rev. Dr. G. Stephen Spinks, former editor of *The Hibbert Journal*, now an Anglican clergyman.

[2] See the present author's *Worship and Theology in England*, Vol. III, *From Watts and Wesley to Maurice, 1690-1850*, Chap. IV.

ship. Here was choice new wine in the most delicately shaped new bottles. In unforgettable cadences he expressed a blend of Biblical faith and the insights of the day derived from the comparative study of religions, his deeply ethical sense, and from the love of nature and a conviction of the basic unity of mankind emanating from German and American versions of Transcendentalism.[3] Martineau therefore left to the twentieth century a heritage of historic techniques of prayer expressive of the newest insights into the ways of God and men. His influence was felt strongly in his own denomination, but also widely beyond it. It is significant that Martineau's prayers are included in John Hunter's *Devotional Services*, W. E. Orchard's *Divine Service*, *The Free Church Book of Common Prayer*, and the Congregational *Book of Services and Prayers*.

1. *The Anarchy of Eclecticism*

The Unitarian Church has not lacked intelligent and imaginative personalities in the present century, such as L. P. Jacks, the perceptive editor of the *Hibbert Journal* in its golden era and a gifted author, or J. Estlin Carpenter, the expert in the comparative study of religions, each of whom was Principal of Manchester College, Oxford. Both attempted the liturgical task. Jacks produced *Orders of Public Worship* in 1915 for the use of the Manchester College Chapel, "an inspired fusion of the Book of Common Prayer, Martineau's prayers, and of theistic mysticism."[4] A similar verdict might be passed on Estlin Carpenter's *Prayers in Public Worship and in College Chapel* of 1927, though here the inspiration was not as obvious. But neither man had Martineau's liturgical genius; their prayers lacked the balance, the concision, and above all the inevitability of diction that mark classical prayers. In any case, a denomination of highly developed individuals with a keen critical sense is hardly likely to produce or even to value a true liturgy which involves the suppression of idiosyncrasy for the attainment of genuinely *common* prayer.

In all honesty it must be acknowledged that for most of the Free Churches, and particularly for the Unitarians, the twentieth century has brought an ebbing of confidence. The decay of political and cultural liberalism, the disappearance of laissez-faire economics,

---

[3] See the present writer's *Worship and Theology in England*, Vol. IV, *From Newman to Martineau, 1850-1900*, pp. 267-81, for a study of Martineau's prayers.
[4] I take this description from the letter of the Rev. Dr. G. Stephen Spinks (August 3, 1963), a former Unitarian minister and *Hibbert Journal* editor, and the author of the intriguing *Psychology and Worship* (1963).

and the increasing standardisation of life in a social welfare state, have led to the depreciation of that radical independence of mind and prophetic love of freedom so characteristic of classical Unitarianism. In a century when it becomes a source for congratulation for any nation to have escaped from political authoritarianism and economic collectivism, while retaining a concern for social justice, those Communions are best able to survive which have either international ramifications like the Roman Catholic Church, or a national establishment like the Church of England, or a strongly connectional structure like the Methodist Church. It is far harder to command popular allegiance for a loosely-knit group of creedless congregations, such as the Unitarians, the Baptists, or the Congregationalists.

Moreover, as might be expected in the citadel of religious liberty which is Unitarianism, there were opposing trends, with different understandings of the meaning of their fellowship in the Unitarian and Free Christian Churches. Some, like William Whittaker of Manchester, were known as the "Christocentric Group" because they proclaimed the teaching and example of Christ as the basis of Unitarianism. Others, like J. M. Lloyd Thomas of the Society of Free Catholics, wanted to combine modernism in doctrine with the mystical and sacramental practices of the historic Church. A third group wanted to link Unitarianism with the monotheism of the great historic religions like Judaism and Islam in the hope of establishing a fellowship of world-wide theists. Others, again, were barely distinguishable from ethical humanists. Not only were there these different conceptions of the modern mission of Unitarianism, but they naturally resulted in different interpretations of worship. There the division was partly between those who loved liturgical worship and those who maintained that it was in the sermon and in the free prayer of the minister that the spirituality and freedom of Unitarianism were conserved. The inevitable result of these divergent viewpoints was that the anarchy of eclecticism overwhelmed Unitarian worship.

The divisiveness, accentuated by the maximum of local permissiveness, encouraged anarchy, and the chaos that ensued could be paralleled by the "Spontaneity School" in Congregationalism where some, like Orchard, were crypto-Catholics and others, like Peel and Snell, were crypto-Quakers.[5]

5 The author can recall the almost complete loss of the sense of the numinous in Yorkshire Congregationalism. On one occasion, when praying with the choir

This chaotic eclecticism, especially in the years between the First and Second World Wars, could be documented in the experience of many Unitarian ministers. One of them, who naturally desires to remain anonymous, has painted a graphic picture of the situation, in letters and in an interview. When he became the newly-appointed minister of a historic Midlands Unitarian Chapel, with the classic lines and elegant austerity of the eighteenth century, he was surprised to find that the original oak Communion-table was now removed to a side position where it could be used to support ash-trays. In its place in the church was a most unsuitable red, baize-covered, trefoil Communion-table for which a fitted crochet table-cloth, costing many hours of labour, had been made by a devoted lady of the congregation. Utterly out of keeping with the classic simplicity of the building as the shoddy red-covered trinitarian table was, it had to remain. No one could have the heart to discard a really beautiful piece of handiwork made to cover it on Communion Sundays. The same informant tells me that he once visited a Unitarian church on the South coast of England which had three stained-glass windows. On one side was a window inscribed to "Faith"; on the other side a window inscribed to "Hope." In the apse, facing the congregation, was "Charity"—the War Memorial to those who had fallen in the First World War—without any apology or explanation of its incongruity.

It is, however, easier to criticize than to understand the causes of eclecticism. The critic can all too readily poke the finger of scorn at the disparities between theological affirmations and an eclectic symbolism which by its all-inclusiveness negates them. Yet it is often the very catholicity of symbolism which enables worshippers to break out of a theological prison by a leap of faith as well as of aesthetics. It may even be an unconscious protest against theological limitations. And there is no question that the Unitarian supporters of the Society of Free Catholics consciously urged that man was more than a logical mechanism, and that his spirit needed to be fed by the historic Christian symbols.

Yet it was from the very chaos of eclecticism that there arose a demand for ordered worship. The mantle of Martineau fell upon the shoulders of the Rev. J. M. Lloyd Thomas, founder of the

---

before entering the sanctuary, it was necessary to ask a youth to remove a still smoking cigarette which he was dangling from his lips. On another occasion he recalls an organist playing the "Baksheesh" section of Ketelby's "In a Persian Market" as an offertory voluntary. Casualness and even slovenliness were far from being limited to Unitarian gatherings for worship, as these Congregational cautionary incidents show.

Society of Free Catholics and the sensitive and most discriminating general editor of *The Free Church Book of Common Prayer.*[6] He recognized how easily spontaneity could degenerate into slovenliness and in the Old Meeting Unitarian Church in Birmingham, of which he was the minister, he set an example of worship that was both reverent and relevant.[7]

2. *The Reign of Law*

The success of Lloyd Thomas's book proved that Unitarians were ready to reconsider the provision of a denominational liturgy which would do for its day what Sadler and Martineau did for theirs in *Common Prayers for Christian Worship*. The clamant need was for a compilation of orders of worship which would express the aspiration of the denomination as a whole rather than the taste of its most advanced ministers. It became a matter of supreme importance to end the anarchy of eclecticism, to reform casualism, and to recover the sense of the numinous in worship.[8] One remaining difficulty, however, presented itself. That was the fact that while some congregations favoured a liturgical type of service, others were as decidedly supporters of free prayer. Hence the leaders of the denomination, and particularly its wise Secretary, Dr. E. Mortimer Rowe, prepared books of worship to satisfy the needs of both groups of congregations.

The reign of law was introduced by the preparation of three denominational compilations of worship, in each of which Dr. Rowe has taken the chief responsibility. The first to appear, in 1932, was *Orders of Worship for Use in Unitarian and Free Christian Congregations* which was shortly followed by the complementary volume, *A Book of Occasional Services* (1932). An anthology of prayers was prepared by Dr. Rowe and Professor Dorothy Tarrant under the title, *Prayers of Faith and Fellowship*, in 1952. As indicating the present character of Unitarian worship, it is interesting to note that of the 242 Unitarian congregations in England, seventy-five churches use a liturgical type of service and

6 For a study of the Society of Free Catholics see Chap. x, Section 3.
7 The Rev. Roger Thomas informs me that he was confirmed by the Rev. J. M. Lloyd Thomas in Manchester, but that the apostle of catholicity did not bother to ask him if he had been baptized (letter of August 20, 1963).
8 Writing of this period of eclecticism, Dr. Stephen Spinks states: "As the years went by I discovered that Unitarianism was a highly tolerant and sometimes very companionable group of people huddled under a large umbrella labelled 'Free Churches' but whose individualistic forms of worship were often casual and non-reverential" (letter of July 29, 1963).

the rest prefer the free type of prayers.[9] It can be assumed that the worship books prepared in 1932 assist the worship of the former group, and that the one prepared in 1952 assists the worship of the latter group. The degree to which uninhibited individualism has been overcome is shown in an official report of the denomination, which amended Whitehead's famous definition of religion to read: "Thus religion is not only what a man does with his solitariness, but also what he does with his gregariousness."[10]

The preface to *Orders of Worship* tells, in condensed form, the story of Unitarian worship from Theophilus Lindsey to Martineau, and renews the latter's plea to make services "available for the voice of living piety" as the reason for the new compilation. Eight regular orders of worship for Sundays are provided and two of them maintain the legacy of the past. The seventh is a conflation of the famous ninth and tenth orders written by Martineau, and the eighth order is an adaptation of the Orders for Morning and Evening Prayer in the Book of Common Prayer. The other six orders are taken from a wide variety of sources including John Hunter's *Devotional Services*, the compilations of L. P. Jacks and J. Estlin Carpenter previously referred to, the Scottish *Book of Common Order* (1928), Dean Dwelly's *Acts of Devotion* and his *Services of Praise and Prayer for occasional use in Churches* (1924), Hugh Martin's *A Book of Prayers for Students* (3rd edition, 1921), Lloyd Thomas's *Free Church Book of Common Prayer*, and Plummer's compilation of *Devotions from Ancient and Mediaeval Services*. The sources are, therefore, most comprehensive.

The aim was to provide a definite structure and order for worship, but not at the cost of inflexibility.[11] Two admirable characteristics of the book are its provision of several responsive prayers or litanies and the place it makes for meditative silence. Hence the compilers write: "Provision is made in these Orders of Service for a large discretion on the part of the minister, in the alternative

---

[9] See *The Unitarian and Free Christian Churches Year Book of the General Assembly for 1963*, which lists those churches using a liturgy at one or both services on Sundays. Those chiefly in use are: *Orders of Worship, Ten Services of Public Prayer*, and *Seven Services for Public Worship* (p. 37). The *Seven Services*, edited by Bowie, appeared in 1900 and 1917. A better work was J. M. Connell's *Common Prayer in Nine Services*, which was prepared for the Unitarian congregation of Lewes, Sussex, was taken up by a few congregations, and is still in use.

[10] *A Free Religious Faith* (A Report presented to the General Assembly of the Unitarian and Free Christian Churches, 1945) p. 197.

[11] *Orders of Worship*, p. ix, reads: "While a common Order is preserved, in the main, throughout all the Services, the way is left completely open for variety within that order."

use of stated and other prayers, as also of the Litanies and Acts of Devotion. It is further recognised that where there is worship, in spirit and in truth, moments of silence may be of very living and moving power."[12] The latter was a decided innovation in Unitarian worship.

The number and variety of the Litanies and Acts of Devotion are impressive and wholly in conformity with the genius of the Free Church tradition's protest on behalf of the priesthood of all believers in prayer. The first order has a Litany of Thanksgiving, the second one of the Will of God, the third of Intercession, the fifth of Faith, the sixth of Supplication, while the Easter Day Service includes a Litany of Remembrance. Three additional Litanies are also included. Devotional Acts include an Act of Praise (fourth service), and, in the additional forms, Acts of Christian Discipleship, of Christian Remembrance, of Communion, and of Adoration. Furthermore, the orders for the seventh and eighth services include the Beatitudes, responsively affirmed, and the Great Commandments, with the response, "Write these words in our hearts, O Lord, we beseech Thee."[13]

Martineau's prayers clearly carry off the palm, especially his magnificent prayer of consecration, "Eternal God, who committest to us the swift and solemn trust of life," and his concise prayer for Faithfulness: "O GOD, thou hast set us in the train of many martyrs and holy men; and given us, as author and finisher of our faith, one who offered himself as a living and dying sacrifice. We are not our own, but thine. Freely may we crucify our shrinking will, surrender ourselves to the utmost claims of thy Spirit, and seek no peace but in harmony with thee."[14]

The clear serenity and noble obedience of Martineau's faith, the succinct and balanced phrasing, the Biblical content of his diction, and the clean and unrhetorical spirit of his prayers makes them incomparable. The dull didacticism of the "Litany of the Will of God" suffers badly by contrast.

Nonetheless, *Orders of Worship* is a definite advance on its predecessors (Martineau's *Ten Services* excepted) in the variety of its orders, in the rich provision of alternative responsive prayers, in the partial observation of the Christian Year, in the requirement of silent prayer before the concluding collect in each service, and the bidding prefaced to each short prayer in the central part of each service. The book sold over ten thousand copies in the first few

12 *Ibid.*, p. viii.   13 *Ibid.*, p. 93.   14 *Ibid.*, p. 84.

years and contributed to the unification of Unitarian congregations. Its uniquely Unitarian qualities can be found negatively in
the revisions in a monotheistic direction of the *Te Deum Laudamus*
and the modification of the customary Trinitarian Benediction, and,
positively, in some admirable prayers of thanksgiving for the
"Glory of the Outward World"[15] and for human culture.[16]

A Book of Occasional Services was prepared by a committee of
the Church's Ministerial Fellowship. The preface draws attention
to two unique characteristics. It includes an Order of Thanksgiving
for Women after Childbirth, which is "the first published attempt
to provide such an order in conformity with present tendencies of
Liberal Christian Thought."[17] It also bears in mind the need of
laymen by providing specimen addresses for services of worship,
which give an interesting summary of contemporary Unitarian
teaching.

This brief volume consists of an ambiguously phrased "Service
of Christening, Baptism, or Dedication of Children," forms for
Thanksgiving After Childbirth, and for Dedication to Membership
of the Church, as well as orders for the Administration of the
Lord's Supper, Marriage, the Visitation of the Sick, and for the
Burial or Cremation of the Dead. An unusual Appendix provides
a brief anthology of poetry and some prose illustrating liberal
religious thought, including excerpts from Tennyson, Whittier,
Rabindranath Tagore, George Eliot, and Minot Savage, presumably for use as either private meditation or even for lections supplementing the Scriptures.[18]

The Liberal Christian emphasis on experience is strongly to the
forefront in both the Orders for Baptism and the Lord's Supper.
As the minister takes the child in his arms he is to say: "This
water is an emblem of the purity which God desires in the souls
of his children." Then he may use either of the two following
formulae of Baptism: "A.B., I baptize thee in the name of God our
Father, and in the spirit of his son, Jesus Christ" or, "A.B., In the
spirit of Jesus we dedicate thee to his Father and our Father, his
God and our God."[19] The address makes plain that the service is
an act of thanksgiving, and a recognition of the duty of the parents
and of the Church to share in the training of the child in the ways
that lead to God.

[15] *Ibid.*, p. 167.   [16] *Ibid.*, p. 168.   [17] P. v.
[18] The supposition that all may be used for public reading is reinforced by
the reference of p. 66 to Minot Savage's "Children in Heaven" as a suitable
reading for the funeral of a child.
[19] *Ibid.*, p. 5.

The Order for the Administration of the Lord's Supper consists of fourteen elements. The Sentences of invitation are followed by the Lord's Prayer, the Collect for Purity, the Summary of the Commandments, a Prayer of Approach, a Scripture Lesson, an Address or Homily, the recital of the Words of Institution, the Delivery of the Bread, the Delivery of the Wine, a Silent Thanksgiving concluded with the *Gloria*, a Post-Communion Prayer, an optional Hymn, and the final Blessing. The two dominant aspects of the Communion Service are the emphasis on the commemoration of Christ's sacrifice, and the affirmation of discipleship. To that extent the doctrine may be regarded as Memorialist in character. This interpretation is clearly expressed in the Homily, which begins with the declaration that "In this service we commemorate a great friendship and a great sacrifice," and ends, "We should be one in this ministry of the Spirit, in our Christian discipleship, with all faithful men and women of every age and clime who have loved and served humanity in the spirit of Jesus Christ."[20] An identical emphasis marks the words with which the wine is delivered to the people: "In the presence of each other and before God, as a solemn testimony of our discipleship to Jesus Christ, let us take and drink this cup in remembrance of him."[21]

While there are those who might criticize this Communion Order from the standpoint of orthodox Christianity as failing to do justice to the Divinity of Christ, the objective accomplishment of the Atonement, or the eschatological banquet in eternity which should be foreshadowed by this rite, these criticisms are wholly inappropriate to an Unitarian rite, celebrated by those who, while rejecting the doctrine of the Holy Trinity, yet recognize Jesus as exemplar and supreme teacher. If the latter restriction be accepted, it can be seen that this is a moving tribute to Christ and a solemn pledge to follow his leadership.

Criticism may more appropriately be directed to the excessive subjectivity in the words of manducation which imply that it is more important to mention first the presence of participants than the presence of God, or to the words in the homily which state "To-day, whatever our perplexities or difficulties, we still acknowledge the truth and beauty of the Christian principle."[22] Surely a Communion Service is the occasion for the declaration of faith, rather than the confession of difficulty? That blight of so many Free Church services, didacticism, which so easily destroys the

20 *Ibid.*, pp. 21-22.   21 *Ibid.*, p. 23.   22 *Ibid.*, p. 22.

mystical mood of aspiration, is also present in this Order.[23] Nonetheless, the final impression is that this service is a simple but moving testimony to the sacrifice of Christ, a reminder that it is those who follow him in ethical loyalty who are his genuine disciples, and a commemoration of the living and the departed as part of the great cloud of witnesses.

The Lord's Supper is not widely or frequently administered to Unitarian congregations. Some of the older Presbyterian foundations inherited the service, along with their silver Communion-plate, and celebrate the Sacrament quarterly or monthly for a minority of their present congregations. In Great Britain as a whole, however, the majority of Unitarian congregations has either discarded it, or never instituted it. Curiously enough, however, it is always included in the programme of the Annual Meetings of the General Assembly, and attracts a large attendance of ministers and delegates. Several Unitarian ministers have objections to celebrating the service as incompatible with a theism that denies the deity of Jesus Christ.[24]

A Book of Occasional Services deliberately omits any type of Ordination Service or Induction Service, and this was also the case in the Sadler and Martineau book, *Common Prayer for Christian Worship* of 1861. If it is pointed out that this is incompatible with the title of "Reverend" commonly used by Unitarian ministers, it could be replied that this is merely a courtesy title and no more inconsistent than the practice of the famous Victorian Congregationalist divine, R. W. Dale, who was ordained but refused to use the title. More seriously, it is probably a part of the consistent anti-sacramentalism which has characterized all Unitarians not of the Free Catholic type in the present century, and of the anti-sacerdotalism which believes in a "meritocracy" rather than a hierarchy.[25]

The third official worship book to be published in this century by the Unitarians was *Prayers of Faith and Fellowship*, edited by Mortimer Rowe and Dorothy Tarrant. The book was intended to replace the 1910 *Prayers for Church and Home*, long out of print.

---

[23] Particularly in the longest Post-Communion Prayer on p. 25: "May we never forget the kindness that surrounds us in the present. . . ."

[24] I am indebted for the substance of this paragraph to Dr. Mortimer Rowe, as for much of my information on the present practices of the Unitarian and Free Christian Churches. The distinguished American Unitarian, Emerson, it may be recalled, resigned from the ministry because he felt it to be inappropriate to administer the Lord's Supper.

[25] See *Faith and Freedom*, Vol. XIII, No. 38 (Spring 1960), article by E. Mortimer Rowe, "The Historical Development of the Unitarian Ministry in England," pp. 61ff.

It was prepared with the needs of lay preachers prominently in mind, but also as an aid for private devotions. It was further "offered as a contribution to the enrichment of those congregations who do not desire complete liturgical services (such as are provided in *Orders of Worship*), but who prefer the simple and traditional Nonconformist pattern."[26] For that purpose the main contents were arranged in the form of an opening prayer followed by a group of three or four brief prayers in place of the usual prolix and comprehensive intercessory prayer of the minister in the Free Church tradition. With true psychological acumen the editors added that they considered the latter, "whether extempore or written . . . as a less helpful and inspiring type of utterance to-day in public worship."[27]

The sources of the prayers are chiefly those of the Unitarian tradition in Britain and America, so that "the book may be regarded as a treasury of Unitarian and Free Christian religious aspiration."[28] A multitude of nineteenth and twentieth century collections of prayers were carefully examined, and from them were chosen the most relevant and enduring prayers of Martineau, Sadler, Crompton Jones, Carpenter, Armstrong, Tarrant, and others. Specific acknowledgment is made of a prayer from Rauschenbusch's *Prayers for the Social Awakening*, for several prayers from the 1914 and 1937 prayerbooks of the American Unitarian Association, and for two prayers each composed by L. P. Jacks and Samuel A. Eliot. For the restrictive policy of limiting the collection to Unitarian devotions, with the exception of a few brief collects and the prayer of Rauschenbusch, it could be argued that this was an essential temporary measure to provide unity in a denomination suffering from an excess of eclecticism. Furthermore, it enabled the distinctive qualities of Unitarian worship to be observed in pure form. On the other hand, it could be held to be a most myopic policy in an ecumenical century when increasingly both hymn books and prayer books express an inter-confessional indebtedness. In one respect, however, the book broke new ground—in its liturgical "lend-lease" invigoration of English worship with the prayers of American Unitarianism, an example that could well be followed by other denominations.

Prayers of Faith and Fellowship provides a faithful mirror of the two predominant expressions of liberal theology in the twentieth

26 *Prayers of Faith* . . . , p. v.
27 *Ibid.*   28 *Ibid.*, p. vi.

century: in the place given to mysticism and to the social gospel. The calm aspiration of mysticism and its longing for unity with God above the distractions of existence is finely matched with the prophetic concern for justice and compassion. The five evening prayers in this collection and several others breathe the serenity of mysticism, such as the one that pleads for "a heart at rest in the eternal love, and a spirit whose thirst is satisfied with the waters of eternal life."[29] The phrasing is often as felicitous as the spirit of the prayers. Indeed, the great quality of this volume is that it is almost wholly free of dreary didacticism. The emphasis of the social gospel is nobly expressed in five national prayers, with such typically fortifying petitions as the following: "let the need for action arouse us from our indifference to existing evils; let the need of endurance brace our powers and raise our hopes; let the fire of national trial burn up the overgrowth of our luxury, melt away our class-selfishness, fuse our cold hard prudence into a clear-sighted and self-forgetful energy, and make our whole people glow with a common faith in the right and a fervent trust in thee."[30]

At the same time the book is more than a mirror of fleeting twentieth century theological trends. It has three abiding qualities. In the first place, it advances beyond that genial vagueness which has sometimes characterized Unitarian devotions to a definite Christocentric reference in several of the prayers, as in those for Palm Sunday and Good Friday.[31] Secondly, the Unitarians have a strong sense of *pietas*, of the dependence of the living on the labours of their predecessors, which is given memorable expression in four prayers of commemoration.[32] Thirdly, there is the constant recognition that discipleship does not consist in the protestation of loyalty but in the performance of duty. These prayers are ethical through and through.

This conviction accounts for the reality and precision of the prayers of confession, in acknowledging before God that "when thou art nigh, we are weary of our selfish desires, our faithless cares, our unresisted temptations: wasted moments, and bitter words, and vain ambitions rise up in judgment against us: we lay at thy feet with shame the vows we have not kept, and the sorrows we have not sanctified."[33] It sounds through a Harvest Thanksgiving prayer: "May we never be satisfied to enjoy plenty so long as any are in want."[34] This insistence upon ethical honesty in religion

29 *Ibid.*, p. 83.   30 *Ibid.*, p. 103.   31 *Ibid.*, p. 95.
32 *Ibid.*, pp. 99-101.   33 *Ibid.*, pp. 70-71.   34 *Ibid.*, p. 97.

is not stilled even in the closing collects: "O God, may we who have united in worship be fruitful in good works, at one with all on earth who do thy will and one with thy great family in heaven."[35] Here is the authentic Unitarian utterance: "Let the voice of duty ring clear, and the word of conscience be unmistakable."[36]

Nevertheless, the book still suffers from two characteristic weaknesses of liberal theology. There is too much subjectivity and luxuriating in our own attitudes, as in the introspective words: "Yet in this transient moment of devotion we seek to awaken in ourselves some answering sense of humility and love."[37] Here we have the very nadir of Pelagianism in a "do-it-yourself" devotion! Not all the Christocentric references have the rootage in the Gospels of the prayers for Palm Sunday and Good Friday, which would give them objectivity and precision. Generalities do not provide the same ground of assurance in approaching God as do references to the example and teaching of Jesus of Nazareth. It is, for example better to pray "As disciples of the Man of Sorrows, may we steadfastly set our feet to go to our Jerusalem, responsive to all the counsels of thy will; seeking only strength to glorify the cross thou layest upon us, and prepared to be obedient unto death"[38] than to offer the petition, "May the spirit of Christ, the spirit of divine sonship and human brotherhood, be with us, and make us one in faith and love, now and evermore."[39]

3. An Evaluation

The Unitarians, though they have a rich tradition of liturgical worship, seem to have been plagued with the same trouble as were the Quakers in the twentieth century. That is whether their generous spirit and strongly humanitarian interests should lead them to move beyond the Christian orbit into the fellowship with all theists. This has tempted them to cast loose from the Christian historical tradition based upon a specific revelation, of which the Bible is the record and which is consummated in the life of Jesus the Messiah. Until the decision of either Communion is firmly made, whether to be theistic in general, or Christian in particular, their devotions are bound to be characterized by a degree of vagueness, with a consequent loss of power. A newer conception of the authority of the Bible, which conceives it as no longer an armoury

35 *Ibid.*, p. 63.
36 *Ibid.*, p. 20. See also the prayer on p. 11.
37 *Ibid.*, pp. 88-89.
38 *Ibid.*, p. 95, from the Palm Sunday prayer.
39 *Ibid.*, p. 107.

of correct intellectual propositions about God but as the record of the Divine encounters with men, coupled with the recognition that theological orthodoxy has reflected more of the abstractness and speculation of Greek philosophy than of the concreteness of the historically given in the Hebrew understanding of God, should make it possible for those Unitarians and Quakers who deny the Incarnation but affirm the Messiahship of Christ to find a readier welcome in the ambit of the World Church than they did in past centuries. Certainly each denomination has its own insights into the nature of reality in worship to contribute to the Christian Commonwealth. It is interesting, too, that the Unitarians have been readier than any other denomination to concede the importance of the Quaker claim for the place of silence in corporate worship.

What, then, are the values within Unitarian worship which might prove an enrichment of traditional Catholic and Protestant worship? The Unitarians have always welcomed the discoveries of modern science and in this they have exhibited only one important facet of their recognition of the splendour and power of the Creator God. They have emphasized the significance of general revelation, and of the Divine inspiration in thinkers, poets, artists, writers, and philanthropists. They also have been among the first to acknowledge the spirituality of religious thinkers not of the Christian fold. All these insights would give a needed breadth and generosity to traditional Christian worship. In return, they would receive that concentration on the benefits of the historic revelation of Jesus Christ which leads to that adoration of God that stimulates the most sacrificial service in Christ's disciples. In addition, in the tradition of Free Church worship the Unitarians have continually kept alive the importance of responsive prayers stressing the part of the laity in worship. And, not least in importance, they have never allowed aestheticism or antiquarianism to deflect their witness to the need for intellectual and ethical integrity in worship.

CHAPTER XIII

CONCLUDING CRITIQUE

IN THIS epilogue it is proposed to present an evaluation of Christian worship in England in the middle of the seventh decade of the twentieth century, rather than to recapitulate the detailed conclusions of the preceding chapters. In previous volumes it would have been inappropriate to attempt such an assessment because Church traditions in worship were contrasted. In fact, the most that could be attempted in those pre-ecumenical centuries was to delineate the unconsciously complementary character of divergent modes of worship. In this Ecumenical Century, however, the Roman Catholic, Anglican, and Protestant traditions of worship have converged to a remarkable degree. In the first part of this critique there will be an attempt to assess the wide areas of agreement in worship. The second part of the critique will point to the remaining areas of disagreement and to the unsolved problems in worship.

I. AREAS OF AGREEMENT

In the twentieth century worship has come into its own. It is recognized to be integral to the life of the Church and, on the part of many scholars, to be the primary focus and expression of Christianity. In the eighteenth century the intellectual aspects of Christianity were dominant (and the Evangelical Revival did not so much answer the intellectual objections posed by Deism as ignore them). In the nineteenth century there was a violent revulsion from Rationalism to Romanticism and then Moralism, with the result that an exaggerated importance was given first to the aesthetic and then to the ethical aspects of Christianity at the expense of theology. In the twentieth century worship, theology, and ethics are seen to be three essential and inter-related aspects of the Christian life.

This balance was not, however, achieved in the earlier part of this century. The "social Gospel" asserted the ethical element as essential, to the depreciation of the aesthetic, and, to some degree, of the theological.[1] In reaction to this, the exponents of mysticism

---

[1] This immanental theology was superficial because it treated the historical foundation of Christianity lightly and excluded transcendence (and with it the holiness of God).

(von Hügel, Inge and Evelyn Underhill) almost neglected the aspect of social justice, though they did speak of the Divine charity, and they emphasized the aesthetic and ascetic aspects of Christian devotion. Gore and Temple, Forsyth and Oman, were forerunners of the balance which was to arrive finally in the Biblical-theological renaissance and the Liturgical Movement, as well as the concern to frame a "Christian Sociology" in the middle thirties.

1. *Worship as an Inclusive Category*

It is now realized that the Christian religion requires a cultus, a creed, and a code of conduct.[2] It can, indeed, be argued that the primacy of worship is partly due to its all-inclusiveness in providing for the needs of the nature of man-in-community. For worship ministers to his mind (creeds or confessions of faith, lections, and sermons), to his imagination and heart (sacraments, symbols, musical and visual art, hymns, prayers), and reinforces his will by a corporate discipline of inspiration and ethical instruction which is reaffirmed in the entire rite as a communal celebration of life's meaning.

2. *The Primacy of Worship as Encounter with God*

Even more important, however, is the recognition that in worship man's encounter with the living God is basal. The most significant empirical analysis which our century has provided of the distinctive character of religious experience is Rudolf Otto's *The Idea of the Holy*.[3] Here Otto attempts to define the *numinous*, while recognizing that his analysis destroys the complex reality by the very process of breaking it down into its component parts. (What Wordsworth said of poetical experience—"We murder to dissect"—can also be said of piety.) Otto finds in the sense of the numinous an important polarity of attraction and repulsion. The awe and love basic to man's experience of God is a *mysterium tremendum et fascinans*, a mystery which frightens and fascinates. It is the holiness of God which repels and His love which draws man near. Otto also insists that as religion develops it tends to

[2] The studies of such distinguished British anthropologists as Sir James Frazer, Tylor, Marett, Evans-Pritchard, Monica Wilson, and others (including E. O. James), encouraged the historians of Christian worship by demonstrating the importance of the cultus in non-Christian cultures.

[3] Professor Farmer has an admirable seven-fold analysis of man's apprehension of God in worship: as ontologically other, axiologically other, personal, giving all, demanding all, acting intimately within the individual's being, and a unique feeling-tone akin to awe (*Revelation and Religion*, Chaps. III and IV).

interpret the numinous less as eerie than as ethical. The glory of Christianity is that God makes the decisive approach to man in Jesus Christ in such fashion that He binds the world to Himself and Himself to the world. St. Augustine clearly sensed the polarity in the encounter with God, when he wrote: "What is that which gleams through me and smites my heart without wounding it? I am both a-shudder and a-glow. A-shudder in so far as I am unlike it, a-glow in so far as I am like it."[4] Almost fifteen hundred years later G. M. Hopkins expressed the same polarity as "lightning and love."[5] Theology, apart from that polarity regularly renewed in worship, and especially immanental theology, tends to sentimentalize God. Christian ethics, divorced from the experience of worship, loses its authority as it is no longer cosmically teleological.

Thus if worship includes the theological and the ethical, nevertheless its primary claim is that it mediates the sense of the numinous. It manifests, with ever-growing wonder, that the Ultimate has become intimate, the All-holy the All-loving too, in the Incarnation where "the Supreme became servant" (Temple) and in the Cross where Jesus Christ is "The Man for others" (Bonhoeffer), and His entire life demonstrates "the Humanity of God" (Barth). Worship is the response of the personality-in-community to this transforming Revelation, the homage of the Christian Community in the form of a celebration.

3. *Worship and its Social Reference*

Hitherto the vertical dimension has been stressed, but it is an important characteristic of worship in the twentieth century that it also emphasizes the horizontal direction of life. Biblical and liturgical theology insist that the Church is a new race. It is the People of God born not of flesh but of the Spirit, which transcends the centuries and overleaps the barriers of nationality, class, and culture. It is, moreover, not only a saved but a saving community, and as a saving community it is a serving community. While the Church is primarily a worshipping community, this is far from implying that it is a self-preserving society consisting of pious escapists.

The prophetic concern for a juster Christian social order has customarily been voiced from the pulpit, and it should be noted

---

[4] *Confessions*, XI, 9, para. 1. The translation is Professor H. H. Farmer's, as employed in his *Revelation and Religion*.
[5] In *The Wreck of the Deutschland*.

that the twentieth century Anglicans have succeeded to the prophetic role assumed by the "Nonconformist Conscience" in the
nineteenth century. What is new in the twentieth century is the
view that the Eucharist itself (in the interpretations of Archbishop
Temple, Bishop J. A. T. Robinson, and Dom Gregory Dix) is a
prophet, for it announces the Divine demand for sharing those
resources which are the product of God's gifts and man's manufacture and distribution.

Furthermore, it has been realized with great clarity in our age
that social service can easily degenerate into patronage, apart from
that genuine humility which is a by-product of worship, and that
true compassion which is an authentic response to Christ's Passion.
The link between the Eucharist and social service is sacrifice,
Christ's and that of His disciples. Intercession is completed by
action.

We are not likely to establish the equality of men on any
sociological basis. It is not a twentieth century Bill of Rights that
is necessary; it is rather that man viewed from the religious perspective has a Bill of Wrongs. It is only as all human beings
recognize themselves as forgiven and accepted sinners, that they
stand shoulder to shoulder, or better, kneel together *coram Deo*.
It is as shamed accomplices in the Christ-betraying and heart-
breaking inequalities of the world that Christians go forth to serve
their fellows, and not as experts. The note of social penitence is
strong in the confessions and the intercessions of the twentieth
century Church. Moreover, sermons on the Sacrament point out
increasingly that the service of Holy Communion is a blue-print
of a new world order, which is scandalized by the present world
of haves and have-nots in which some eat cake and others furtively
grab crusts from trash-cans.

4. *Worship as the Homage of the Whole People of God*

Increasingly in the present century we have come to realize that
the Church is not properly defined as a hierarchical or sacerdotal
society on the analogy of an army, with clerical officers and lay
privates. Least of all is it to be defined as a worshipping society
with clergymen as actors and the laity as mere spectators. It is,
of course, still true that Churches in the Catholic tradition, with
their emphasis on the apostolical succession, make much of the
difference between the ordained and the unordained members of
the Church; the Free Churches, by contrast, recognize that their

ministers have a special function but insist that they do not have a superior status. It is, however, equally true that in Free Church worship the almost total monopoly of the minister's voice in the prayers has tended toward a virtual sacerdotalism, which denies the priesthood of all believers affirmed in their more democratic forms of Church government. The important point, however, is that in both the Catholic and Protestant traditions there is a new recognition that the Church is the whole People of God and that they must be given a fuller role in worship and in witness. Responsive prayers in the Roman Catholic and Anglican forms of worship have always provided this expression, but there has been an increasing concern to find other ways for liturgical participation on the part of the laity. It is now customary for them to take various parts in the worship, such as reading the lessons, or taking up the Communion Offertory (including the bread and wine with the alms), as an expression of the common priesthood of Christians. Above all, the stress on the vernacular in worship and the use of the Dialogue Mass are the most important recent Roman Catholic incentives to lay participation in the Liturgy. The Halton "House Church" experiment in the Church of England, making the dining-table in the home the temporary altar, and the inclusion of family prayers in the domestic Eucharist, are other aspects of the same concern that the Liturgy shall be the offering of worship by all God's people there present.

Perhaps the most striking proof of the new understanding that worship is *common* worship is the acceptance of the lessons of the Liturgical Movement by the Free Churches, even though this amounted to a revolution on the part of the heirs of the Puritan-Pietist tradition. The Presbyterian Church of England produced its pioneering revision of the Westminster Directory as its official denomination service-book in 1898, entitled *The Directory for Public Worship*, subsequently twice revised. The Congregationalists have produced three denominational service-books in this century, and the Baptists two, the latest being liturgically exceedingly advanced. The Methodists and the Unitarians, because of their Anglican lineage, have never entirely cut themselves off from the liturgical tradition. Coleridge's criticism was applicable in the nineteenth century, but is wholly outmoded today: "Many a proselyte has the Church gained from the Meeting-House through the disgust occasioned by the long-winded preaching prayers of the

Dissenting ministers, and the utter exclusion of the congregation from all active *share* in the public devotion."[6]

5. *Worship as Unitive*

This important trend from charismatic to liturgical worship on the part of denominations which had previously equated formality with insincerity may be an indication of a loss of confidence in their future, and indeed may jeopardize an important element in worship which the Free Church tradition exists to maintain for the coming Great Church—as will be argued later. A more sober, as well as generous evaluation, of this trend is that it represents the conviction that liturgical worship is unitive. It binds the Church of the past[7] with the Church of the present, and it is likelier to bind together the Christians of the future than is a charismatic form of worship. It is a sober recognition of the ecumenical possibilities inherent in liturgical worship which has led the English Free Churches to reconsider their ancient criticism of forms of prayer and, incidentally, to be less hostile to the episcopal form of the ministry. Such a decision is, of course, far from being unanimous, but it is significant that both liturgical worship and episcopacy were accepted by the Free Churches that joined with the Anglicans to form the Church of South India. That more variety is desirable within the structure of liturgical worship, and that no rite should be inalterable, are considerations which do not militate against the fact that a liturgical form of worship can be an important nexus of unity. It is also important to recognize that the Free Church service-books of the past two decades have approximated in their Orders for Holy Communion to the structure of the historic Consecration Prayer of the Western rites, and have incorporated several of its elements.[8]

6. *The Unity of Word and Sacrament*

A recognition of the desirability of liturgical worship, for its historic fidelity and its unitive power, need not imply any derogation of the traditional Protestant emphasis on the importance of

---

[6] S. T. Coleridge, *Notes on English Divines*, Vol. II, p. 33.

[7] G. K. Chesterton wittily argued that the Church "votes by tombstones." It is undeniable that historically the devotees of liturgical worship vastly outnumbered those practising charismatic worship in the primitive and mediaeval Church. Similarly, Roman Catholic and Orthodox Christians in combination greatly outnumber Protestant Christians.

[8] See Huxtable *et alii*, eds., *A Book of Public Worship* . . . , and Payne and Winward, eds., *Orders and Prayers for Church Worship*.

the proclamation of the Word of God in the sermon. Indeed, while Protestants have reconsidered the value of the Sacraments,[9] Roman Catholics have rediscovered the value of preaching, with the result that there is now a conjoint emphasis on the interrelationship of Word and Sacrament.

How is this *rapprochement*, indeed re-marriage, of Word and Sacrament to be accounted for? It is due, at least in part, to an acknowledgment of the dangers inherent in their divorce in past centuries. The over-emphasis on preaching and the depreciation of prayers and sacraments in Protestantism has contributed to four very unfortunate results. As the element of adoration disappeared or was minimized in the Christian life, Christian faith became over-intellectualized. Thus what Jonathan Edwards called the "holy affections" no longer activated the imagination and the will, so that God's will was rather discussed than done. Again, as prayers and sacraments were depreciated, the cult of the popular preacher was magnified. (It should be noted that the twentieth century has not been an era of "spell-binders" in the pulpit.) Finally, an over-emphasis on preaching may well have accelerated the momentum towards splintering so characteristic of the history of Protestantism. Howard Hageman rightly poses the question: "Could the Reformed Churches have proved such fertile soil for the growth of sectarianism, producing one schism after another in their history, if every week they had reminded themselves that 'we being many are one bread and one body: for we are all partakers of that one bread'?"[10]

The *reductio ad absurdum* of this tendency is brilliantly satirized by Peter De Vries in his novel, *The Mackerel Plaza*. He depicts a Protestant Community church, "the People's Liberal," in a wealthy commuters' suburb in Connecticut, the minister of which is known for his taut and sophisticated sermons as the Hemingway of the pulpit. The hilarity of the novel's irony reaches its peak when the Rev. Mr. Mackerel conducts a group of visitors round the church "plant." They are shown the dining-area, kitchen, three parlours for committee and group meetings, as well as two baths on the ground floor. Proceeding upstairs, they are then shown the medical and neuro-psychiatric wings (indefinitely expandable), and the large all-purpose auditorium which can be used

9 See Donald M. Baillie's *The Theology of the Sacraments* as to how far it is possible for a distinguished Presbyterian theologian to go in the Catholic direction in interpreting the Holy Communion as a sacrifice.
10 *Pulpit and Table*, p. 115.

for drama, or as a dance-floor or gymnasium. Almost apologetically Mackerel finally observes: "There is a small worship area at one end. This has a platform cantilevered on both sides, with a free-form pulpit designed by Noguchi. It consists of a slab of marble set on four legs of four delicately differing fruitwoods, to symbolize the Four Gospels, and their failure to harmonize. Behind it dangles a large multi-colored mobile, its interdenominational parts sway-ing, as one might fancy in perpetual reminder of the Pauline stricture against those 'blown about by every wind of doctrine.' . . . Thus the People's Liberal is a church designed to meet the needs of today and to serve the whole man."[11]

Here can be seen the terrible revenge which falls upon those who make didacticism and up-to-date-ness ends in themselves, for the sermon has degenerated into a cultural lecture, and the obedi-ence of faith into uninhibited idiosyncrasy. This is, of course, an extravaganza, but it points to the danger of preaching freed from worship and the sacraments, and both freed from Scripture. There was a period in the early part of this century in England when texts were used as pretexts, and when the chief Sacrament had become no more than a memorial to a heroic Jesus and a token of the allegiance of the pious.

There are equal dangers in the elevation of the Sacrament and the depreciation of the Word in preaching. The Sacrament alone, as the historic Reformers pointed out, could and did degenerate into an attempt to manipulate Divine power, a propitiatory sacrifice renewed instead of an acknowledgment of a gift received anew. It became a meritorious work to be chalked up on the credit side of a vast debit record, and a spectacle to be watched instead of an eucharistic action to be shared. It became the glorification of the priesthood and the depreciation of the role of the layman, and its introspective concentration on immolation eclipsed the holy joy of the Creation and the Resurrection. Moreover, the whole Liturgy was encased in an inalterable and sacrosanct rite of 1570 (Roman Catholic) or of 1661 (Anglican).

Dr. Karl Barth observed with justice that "one might say that the great temptation of Protestantism is Judaism, whereas the great temptation of Catholicism would be paganism."[12] If Protes-tants allowed worship to degenerate into didacticism, Catholics

11 *The Mackerel Plaza* (Little, Brown and Company, Boston, 1958), p. 29.
12 Reported in *The Christian Recorder* (an interdenominational weekly pub-lished in Standerton, Transvaal, South Africa), issue of April 26, 1963, giving as its source, *Réalités*, Paris.

permitted their spectator worship to become hopelessly fossilized until the arrival of the Modern Liturgical Movement. The former stressed ear-gate and the latter eye-gate.

Our century has seen the re-marriage of the Word and Sacrament, the Divine oracle and the Divine drama of salvation, in a conjoint emphasis on the Sermon and the Supper, the Pulpit and the Holy Table. It has recognized that the *verbum audibile* and the *verbum visibile* (to use St. Augustine's terminology) are mutually reinforcing channels or modes of the Divine encounter with humanity in worship. Already the results of this return to the pattern of the primitive Church can be seen in a piety which is Biblical, sacramental, and social.

It has also led the way to the ending of other baleful dichotomies. A comprehensive theology of the Word-made-*flesh* has provided a truer understanding of the nature of man as "ensouled body" instead of that "angelism" (Maritain's term) which depreciated the life of the senses and proposed that men should live as disembodied spirits. A genuine incarnationalism and sacramentalism have proved a spur to Catholic and Protestant concern for religious art and architecture, in which the Church of England has given the lead, with its encouragement of the work of Epstein, Henry Moore, Graham Sutherland, John Piper, Basil Spence, and others. Already there are signs in architecture (if not in art) that the Free Churches are overcoming their aesthetic iconoclasm as a result of their participation in the Ecumenical and Liturgical Movements. While they have never been great admirers of symbolism, there is no reason why they should be insensitive to the artists of the twentieth century, such as Picasso in *The Bombing of Guernica* or Georges Rouault in the *Miserere* series, who arouse a profound pity for or indignation over man's inhumanity to man.

A still further consequence can be seen in the increasing recognition that worship is a celebration of life, as thanksgivings recall the joys of "our creation, preservation, and all the blessings of this life," including the triumphs of technology and the divinely-donated insights of the visual and plastic arts, and the beauty, majesty and mystery of the universe opening out before us today in a vaster perspective. Much more, however, still needs to be done in this area.[13]

13 Van Ogden Vogt in *The Primacy of Worship* has written: "Modern religion needs more expanded actions of praise. There is open opportunity for poetic compositions to celebrate the glory and goodness of life. In city churches, especially, the beauty and bounty of nature should have more frequent and ample

7. *The Recovery of the Christian Year*

Another consequence of the impact of an incarnational theology is the increasing use of the celebrations of the Christian Year by all Christian Communions in England, and not, as formerly, by the Roman Catholics and Anglicans alone. Three reasons account for this significant change. The first is the acknowledgment that the mystery of the Incarnation must be appropriated in episodic manner by distracted human personalities. What God deigns to impart of the mystery of His being and purpose for man is accommodated to man's Lilliputian personality in "God contracted to a span, marvellously made man" (Charles Wesley), and the Christian Year enables God's people to make this annually renewed pilgrimage into the mind and heart of God. Secondly, while men may guess that God's infinite wisdom permits Him to view the Incarnation as a simultaneous whole instead of as a succession of acts, we humans cannot do so. Similarly, a musical composer conceives the three movements of his symphony as an interrelated whole, yet it is necessary for the orchestra to play it and for the audience to listen to it as a succession of bars of music. Thus we learn the Divine Composer's intentions in the Incarnation, act by act, event by event, from the Advent to Pentecost. The Christian Year retells that narrative of transformation with appropriate pauses at the festivals. In the third place, the celebration of the Christian Year is the Church's ultimate defence against the ever-increasing encroachments of the world's calendar. It is the antidote to suffocation by secularism and choking by commercialism. National holidays as well as special days set apart for admirable humanitarian causes can crowd out the absolute claim of God in Christ in the Church. Thus the keeping of the Christian Year makes worship Christ-centred by its rootage in holy history remembered as the creative tradition that renews the corporate life of Christians. In short, the Christian Year is recognized on all sides as an important token of our continuing acknowledgment that the Church, triumphant in heaven[14] and militant on earth,

---

expression. And so many other factors of existence—man in his families, man in his vocational skills and loyalties, man in his civic achievements, man in his apprehensions and arts, man in his struggles for freedom—should be praised in festival and song" (p. 52).

14 One important consequence of the Biblical-theological and Liturgical Renewal is that it has led to a reconsideration of the nature of the Church, and a redis-covery of the doctrine òf the Communion of saints. It is not uncommon nowadays to hear prayers in the Free Churches which remember the faithful departed before

owes everything to the grace of God, which is both stimulus to adoration and propulsion to service.

II. AREAS OF DISAGREEMENT

Considerable as are the areas of agreement, as might be expected in the Ecumenical Century, yet too roseate a picture would have been presented if no reference were to be made to certain unsolved problems in worship which have generated considerable discussion in our period. This will involve the consideration of four important issues.

1. *Liturgical, Free and Silent Prayers*

The increasing recognition by the English Free Churches of the value of theological structure in worship, of the need for more responsive prayers, and, in short, of an increasingly liturgical type of worship is, it was argued, a revolution. It is not, however, an entire abandonment of the tradition of free prayer. While there is less confidence in the value of an entire dependence upon extemporary prayers, and especially of the so-called "long prayer" of intercession which customarily precedes the sermon, there is little indication that Free Churchmen would embrace a single inalterable Liturgy. In this connection it is important to realize that official Presbyterian, Congregational, and Baptist service-books provide *alternative forms* for Morning and Evening worship, as for the celebration of Holy Communion. By so doing, their compilers believe that they can preserve the fulness and fidelity of theological structure, along with such variability in the wording of prayers as will preserve freshness for minister and congregation and also prevent any "liturgical fundamentalism" or literalism. They hesitate to canonize any form of worship so as to give the impression that it is sacrosanct and inalterable. It is a natural expression of the Protestant principle which refuses to absolutize the finite. Furthermore, there is considerable feeling among Free Church ministers that a true doctrine of the Holy Spirit trusts that the Holy Spirit will lead God's people into fuller apprehensions of truth. Nor would they wish to deprive the leader of worship of the opportunity, within the framework of a liturgy, to pray for the particular needs of the gathered congregation as they have become known to him through pastoral visitation, with the immediacy and

God and pray that the congregation may follow their good example. This has been mediated to the Free Churches by the Church of Scotland.

intimacy of free prayer (whether this be prepared, as is customary, or entirely extemporary, which is becoming less common).

The general conclusion of the Free Churches in this matter has been aptly summed up by their greatest twentieth century theologian, P. T. Forsyth: "Public prayer, therefore, should be in the main liturgical, with room for free prayer. The more it really is common prayer, and the more our relations with men extend and deepen . . . the more we need forms which proceed from the common and corporate conscience of the Church."[15] The same writer was equally aware of the defect of even a great Liturgy such as the Book of Common Prayer, namely its tendency to canonize decorum and submissiveness of spirit in worship and life: "We shall think more of order than of effort, more of law than of life, more of fashion than of faith, of good form than of great power."[16]

As yet there seems to be no determined effort on the part of Anglicans to meet the need for the element of the charismatic and the spontaneous in worship to which the Free Church tradition in worship has witnessed. (The "House Church" experiment is a very great exception which proves the rule.) So, while Free Churchmen have come to agree with Anglicans that liturgical worship has very great advantages—notably its universal relevance, its objectivity and independence of ministerial moods and idiosyncrasies, and its ecumenical potentialities—there has been no comparable attempt to appreciate that tradition which Free Churchmen hold dear. Yet it is precisely that element of spontaneity, intimacy, and warmth in the worship of many modern forms of sectarianism in Christianity which has drawn many members away from "mainstream" Christianity. It has, for example, helped to account for the astonishing success of the Pentecostalist Movement.[17] A thoroughly ecumenical Church must seriously attempt to combine complementary qualities of worship in different traditions. The historic Churches stress order in worship, but all too often to the loss of ardour. Both are necessary.

If it cannot be said that there is an agreement to combine liturgical with free prayer, still less is there an over-all appreciation of the value of silent prayer. To be sure, Anglican bidding prayers usually include a short spell of silence after each bidding, but this results in a very "controlled" silence. Free Church orders of worship

---

[15] *The Soul of Prayer*, p. 54.   [16] *Ibid.*, p. 139.
[17] See my *Christian Deviations: The Challenge of the Sects*, Chaps. I and VI.

often include a short period of silence, but this is only a minimal recognition of its role, and the congregation is not trained to use silence to the best advantage. Professor Paul Tillich's words warrant serious consideration: "Contemplation is the step-child in Protestant worship. Only lately has the liturgical silence been introduced into some Protestant Churches and, of course, there is no contemplation without silence."[18] While the Roman Catholic Church has in the religious orders a great tradition of contemplative prayer, it does not yet appear to have taught the laity to practice the art of corporate silence in the Mass. Thus the witness of the Society of Friends still holds in trust for the coming Great Church its own distinctive technique of worship.

It seems a tragedy that the Ecumenical Movement has not yet taught its constituent Churches that all three ways of approach to God are necessary in public worship.

There is another allied and unsolved problem. That is the need to provide a twentieth century discipline for private and familial piety. In part this is being met in the Roman Catholic and Anglican Churches by methods of spiritual discipline which derive from the rather legalistic and ascetic models of the Counter-Reformation, and in part in the Free Church tradition by manuals of prayer, such as John Baillie's fine *Diary of Private Prayer*. But the most disturbing fact is that until there is a discovery of suitable methods for private and family prayer which are Biblical in basis, contemporary in expression, and related to the pattern of public worship, we shall not see praying households of faith which are the essential prerequisite of a lively and expectant gathering of God's people for worship on Sundays. This is an important issue to which, as yet, little attention has been given in either denominational or ecumenical committees or commissions.

The family prayers of the seventeenth century Puritans, the eighteenth century Methodists, the nineteenth century Evangelical Anglicans and instructed Anglo-Catholics, were veritable dynamos of the Christian life. A viable twentieth century equivalent, expressive of the unity of the Universal Church, ought not be an impossibility.

2. *The Sacraments of Baptism and Holy Communion*

Two unresolved problems remain in connection with the under-

18 *Systematic Theology*, Vol. III, p. 192.

standing of the two major Sacraments among different Christian Communions.

One problem is to preserve the emphasis on the Divine initiative in human salvation and on the Church as the community indwelt by the Holy Spirit, in Communions practising Infant Baptism, along with the emphasis of the Baptists and allied denominations on the necessity of expressing faith as a conscious and responsible commitment to Christ and His Church, which they insist is preserved only by the Baptism of Believers. This is still a knotty problem. Some part of the ground of disagreement has been covered, however, in that Churches practising paedo-baptism recognize that greater importance must be given to Confirmation, while Baptists have recognized the importance of Christian education in so-called services of Infant Dedication. Such a compromise, however, is no solution.

The remaining problem is that most of the Free Churches regularly open their Communion-services to members of any branch of Christ's Church, while Anglicans and Roman Catholics insist upon Confirmation in their own Church as the necessary precondition for receiving Holy Communion or Mass. For special ecumenical occasions individual Anglican Bishops are prepared to relax this prohibition, but such exceptions are few. This practice is defended by Anglicans on the ground that indiscriminate admission to Holy Communion masks the scandal of disunity by sentimentalism. The Free Church answer to this criticism is belligerently to accuse Anglicans of believing in "salvation by bishops" or, irenically, to insist that sharing in the Eucharist is itself a great impetus to reunion and a meaningful foretaste of the fruits of unity.

The most hopeful and promising sign in this area is that there is an astonishingly high level of agreement among Christian denominations in England on the meaning of the Holy Communion. This is all the more significant because historically this has so often proved to be the point of greatest contention among Christians. This agreement was high-lighted in the adoption, with a slight emendation, at the Lund Ecumenical Conference of the following definition:

"This dominical sacrament of Christ's Body and Blood, controlled by the words of institution, with the use of the appointed elements of bread and wine, is (a) a memorial of Christ's incarnation and earthly ministry, of His death and resurrection; (b) a sacrament in which He is truly present to give Himself to us, uniting us to Himself, to His eternal Sacrifice, and to one another; and (c) eschatologically, an anticipation of our fellowship with Christ in His eternal Kingdom."[19]

3. *Church Architecture and Art*

While there has been a remarkable renaissance of religious architecture and art in England in the twentieth century, it has raised as many new problems as it has solved. Among them is the extraordinary difficulty of finding satisfactory expressive symbols for Christianity in a secular age, which are neither uncommunicating stereotypes of the past nor broken forms. The situation is aggravated by the fact that the prevailing artistic modes of the twentieth century—naturalism, expressionism, and abstractionism —have no transcendent reference. There is the need for a re-mythologization of Christian art as well as of theology.[20]

In the realm of church architecture there has been a welcome rejection of neo-Gothicism, since this seems to be too obvious an admission of the irrelevance of the traditional Christian faith to contemporary culture. The problem has been to find an authentic Christian style in the twentieth century to replace the antiquarian one. Neither theologians nor architects have made up their minds whether to express numinosity or community. This is evident in the vacillation in modern church architecture between the stream-lined verticality which is the contemporary equivalent of Gothic, evocative of Divine mystery and majesty and of human aspiration, and the functional architecture stressing the central altar with the congregation gathered about it. Perhaps the clue may lie in a combination of asymmetry and intimacy, such as Le Corbusier attained in his masterpiece, Notre Dame du Haut, Ronchamp.[21]

4. *The Link between Worship and Evangelism*

It is a reflection of the loss of contact between the Church and the contemporary world that while the Church has probably become more fully aware of its essential nature as a worshipping community in the twentieth century, yet to the world outside it seems an excessively introverted institution. Its theology and its rites are, as it were, *romans à clef* to the Christian initiates and

19 See the report edited by D. M. Baillie and John Marsh, *Intercommunion,* pp. 29-30.
20 This is well argued by A. C. Bridge, *Images of God.*
21 See G. E. Kidder Smith, *The New Architecture of Europe,* pp. 94-97.

deeply meaningful; to the outsider, however, they appear to be a code hardly worth the trouble of cracking. Despite the frenzied attempt to conduct large-scale preaching missions on the part of the Protestant Churches, and the preference for liturgical missions on the part of the Roman Catholics and the High Anglicans, and even after allowing for the promise of the para-liturgies devised by the Roman Catholic Church to meet the outsider half way, the link between worship and evangelism has yet to be found. Some very serious attempts to find a break-through are in progress, and many such experiments in Europe and in England are worthy of consideration.[22]

An equally discouraging consideration is that congregations using a charismatic type of worship appear to be likelier to produce energetic evangelists than those using liturgical forms. As has been observed before, order does not readily generate ardour.

This failure of communication, so dramatically evident in an England in which only one person in five regularly attends worship, has caused some theologians to call this the "post-Christian" age. It is a token of the bewilderment of Christian thinkers in a secular age. Two types of strategy have been advanced for meeting the situation. One is based on the belief that Christianity must be prepared to enter a new "Dark Age" for which the appropriate mode of Christian existence is withdrawal. For such a strategy a new monasticism seems most appropriate. (It is significant that there are Protestant monastic communities of the French and Swiss Reformed Churches and of the German Lutheran Church, while the Anglican Communion has had its own religious communities for over a century.) These will serve as miniature light-houses in a sea of secularism, ready to welcome the storm-tossed traveller. Then, when a secular world shall have become disillusioned with living as if God were dead, it is affirmed that it will call the Church to its aid. The other strategy believes that withdrawal is, in effect, abandonment. It prefers to find God in the heart of the secular, believing that the more the Church through its committed members is concerned to follow "The Man for others" in identification with the hardships of humanity, the more transparent will its witness to God become.

It is impossible to tell if either of these strategies is right. It would be rash to judge that the lively experimentation of the contemporary Church is a mark either of its present desperation or

[22] See Olive Wyon, *Living Springs.*

of its future vitality. The church historian can only point out that the prospects for the survival of Christianity were darker at the Crucifixion, or in 732 when the Moslem scimitars battered at the gates of Christian France, or on the eve of the sixteenth century Reformation, or in eighteenth century England before Wesley's Aldersgate Street experience, than they are today. The Church is, indeed, an anvil which has worn out many hammers.

Hopefulness for the future is ultimately grounded on faith in the Divine victory, but proximately on the signs of the times. Any prognosis of the future of the Christian Church would have to take account of four very healthy factors. The first, as we have tried to chronicle in this book, is the concentration on the adoration of God in the Modern Liturgical Movement, which is the Church's homage to His self-giving in Christ. The second is the striking expression of the same unitive love in the achievements of the Ecumenical Movement. The third is the massive theological attempt being made in our time to correlate Christianity and culture. The fourth is the ethical recognition that the Church is the servant people of God and that its place is precisely where human need is greatest. In today's world the Church cannot and ought not to compete with the clenched hand of power, but equally the folded hands of pietism are not enough. In the last analysis the pierced hands of compassion alone are adequate for the task and privilege of discipleship.

BIBLIOGRAPHY

1. SELECTED LITURGICAL TEXTS

(Arranged Chronologically by Denomination)

ANGLICAN

The Book of Common Prayer with the Additions and Deviations Proposed in 1928

Arnold, John Henry (ed.). *Anglican Liturgies* (Alcuin Club, London, 1939)

Wigan, Bernard (ed.). *The Liturgy in English* (London, 1962), containing a much wider selection of Anglican Liturgies than the previous volume, with later revisions, together with the Orders for Holy Communion of the Church of South India, the Church of Scotland and the English Congregationalists

BAPTIST

Aubrey, M. E. (ed.). *A Minister's Manual* (London, n.d.)

Patterson, D. Tait (ed.). *The Call to Worship, A Book of Services for the help and guidance of those who minister in the House of God* (London, 1930, revised edn., 1938)

Payne, Ernest A. and Winward, Stephen (eds.). *Orders and Prayers for Church Worship: A Manual for Ministers* (London, 1962)

CONGREGATIONALIST

Hunter, John (ed.). *Devotional Services for Public Worship* (London, 1882, 10th revised edn., 1920)

A Book of Congregational Worship (London, 1920)

Watson, C. Ernest (ed.). *The Rodborough Bede Book* (printed in Woodchester, Glos., 1930, for the use of the Congregational Church in Rodborough)

A Manual for Ministers (London, 1936)

A Book of Public Worship compiled for the use of Congregationalists (by John Huxtable, John Marsh, Romilly Micklem and James Todd, London, 1948)

Todd, James (ed.). *Prayers and Services for Christian Festivals* (London, 1951, a companion to the book listed immediately above)

A Book of Services and Prayers (London, 1959)

METHODIST

Divine Worship, approved by the Conference for Optional Use in Methodist Churches (London, 1935)

The Book of Offices, being the Orders of Worship authorized for use in the Methodist Church together with the Order of Morning Prayer (London, 1936)

PRESBYTERIAN

(English)

Directory of Public Worship (1898; largely revised in 1921)

447

Orchard, W. E. (ed.). *The Order of Divine Service for Public Worship, the administration of the Sacraments and other Rites and Ceremonies, and a selection from the Daily Office, compiled from ancient and modern devotions, together with an abridged and revised Psalter* (London, 1919)

Phillip, Eric (ed.). *Sacramental and other services* (Liverpool and London, 1927)

(English and Welsh)

The Presbyterian Service Book for use in the Presbyterian Churches of England and Wales (London, 1948)

(Scottish)

Prayers for Divine Service (1923, authorized by the Church of Scotland)

The Book of Common Order (1928, authorized by the United Free Church)

The Book of Common Order (1940, authorized by the new and expanded Church of Scotland after reunion)

Ordinal and Service Book for use in the Courts of the Church (1962, in which will be found the latest revision of the Order for Holy Communion as celebrated in the General Assembly of the Church of Scotland)

ROMAN CATHOLIC

Missale Romanum. Editio II juxta typicam Vaticanam amplificata I (New York, 1942)

Rituale Romanum. Desclée ed. (Romae, Typis Soc. S. Joannis Evangelistae, 1914)

UNITARIAN AND FREE CHRISTIAN

Sadler and Martineau (eds.). *Common Prayer for Christian Worship* (1862; revised edn., 1879 with new title, *Ten Services of Public Prayer*)

Jacks, L. P. (ed.). *Orders of Public Worship for use in the Chapel of Manchester College, Oxford* (1915)

Connell, J. M. (ed.). *Common Prayer in Nine Services* (1926, prepared for a congregation in Lewes)

Carpenter, J. Estlin (ed.). *Prayers in Public Worship and in College Chapel* (1927)

Thomas, J. M. Lloyd (general editor). *Free Church Book of Common Prayer* (1929)

Orders of Worship for use in Unitarian and Free Christian Congregations (1932)

A Book of Occasional Services (1932)

Rowe, E. Mortimer and Tarrant, Dorothy (eds.). *Prayers of Faith and Fellowship* (1952)

2. PERIODICALS

DENOMINATIONAL

BIBLIOGRAPHY

ANGLICAN

Anglican World
Church Illustrated
Church Times
Crockford
The Modern Churchman
Parish and People
Prism
Theology

BAPTIST

The Baptist Times
Baptist Quarterly
Transactions of the Baptist Historical Society
Yearbooks of the Baptist Union

CONGREGATIONALIST

Christian World
The Congregational Quarterly
Transactions of the Congregational Historical Society
The Yearbooks of the Congregational Union of England and Wales

METHODIST

The London and Holborn Quarterly Review
The Methodist Recorder
Minutes of the Methodist Conference
Transactions of the Wesley Historical Society

PRESBYTERIAN

The Church Service Society Annuals
The Coracle (Iona Community)
The Presbyterian Messenger
The Scottish Journal of Theology
Theology Today (Princeton, New Jersey)
Yearbooks of the Presbyterian Church of England

QUAKER

The Friend

ROMAN CATHOLIC

Downside Review
The Month
The Tablet

UNITARIAN

Faith and Freedom
The Hibbert Journal (interdenominational liberal quarterly)
Transactions of the Unitarian Historical Society
Yearbooks of the Unitarian and Free Christian Churches

INTERDENOMINATIONAL

British Weekly

Church History (Chicago)

The Ecumenical Review (Geneva; organ of the World Council of
Churches)

Journal of Theological Studies

Journal of Ecclesiastical History

Studia Liturgica (Rotterdam; international and ecumenical liturgical
review)

SECULAR

Architectural Design

Architectural Review

Daily Telegraph

Journal of the Royal Institute of British Architects

The Listener (organ of the British Broadcasting Corporation)

The Manchester Guardian

The Studio

The Times (of London)

3. SOURCES IN ENGLISH LITERATURE

Less direct use of English literature was made in this volume than
in its predecessors, because Christian thought and imagination played
a smaller role in an increasingly secularized century. Incidental references were made to the Jesuit poet, Gerard Manley Hopkins, whose
strangely modern poems conceived in the Victorian age were loosed by
Robert Bridges on the twentieth century sensibility, and to Wilfred
Owen whose realistic account of war—"the poetry is in the pity"—
provided a notable contrast with the chivalric and romantic mood of
Rupert Brooke.

Authors of pronounced Christian commitment often preferred to
express their convictions by indirection, such as Dorothy L. Sayers and
G. K. Chesterton in detective novels. The former's rippled with citations
from metaphysical poetry so as to deserve to be called "Who-Donne-its."
T. S. Eliot's subtle hints of Christianity's clue to the meaning of destiny
were expressed in *The Family Reunion* and *The Cocktail Party*.

It is particularly evident that Catholics and Anglo-Catholics, rather
than Protestants and Free Churchmen, with the exception of Edwin
Muir, found Christianity most stimulating to their imagination. This
may well be because the Incarnation (and its correlate the sacramental
principle) was central to the thought of the former, while the Atonement was central to the thought of the latter.

DRAMA

There has been a notable revival of poetic drama under Christian
auspices in which the Church of England has taken the lead.
T. S. Eliot's *Murder in the Cathedral*, Dorothy L. Sayers' *The Zeal
of Thy House*, and Christopher Fry's *The Sleep of Prisoners* are
three eminent examples. (See Gerald Weales, *Religion in Modern*

English Drama, Philadelphia: University of Pennsylvania Press, 1961.)

Dorothy L. Sayers' *The Man Born to be King* (published 1953) is a dramatic radio cycle of plays regularly broadcast by the British Broadcasting Corporation in Holy Week, which presents Christology without docetism and with great realism.

POETRY

T. S. Eliot's *The Waste Land* and the *Hollow Men* are masterly evocations of the bitter disenchantment and *taedium vitae* of the first two decades of the century, while the *Four Quartets* mirror repentance and return.

Edwin Muir (with pared simplicity) and W. H. Auden (with far greater technical brilliance) walk the same path as Eliot, except that they have committed themselves to the social struggle.

Charles Williams, maker of subtle allegories, preserves a mediaeval sensibility in the modern world.

Dylan Thomas, a later and lesser Donne, reflects the civil war of sense and spirit and has produced some late poems in the metaphysical mode, reminiscent of Herbert.

NOVELS

The twentieth century offers some fascinating portraits of the difficulties of the ministry, ranging from the iconoclasm of W. Somerset Maugham in *Rain* and *Of Human Bondage*, and the polemical accounts of Anglo-Catholic priests in Compton Mackenzie's *The Altar Steps*, to the amused caricatures of Rose Macaulay's *The Towers of Trebizond*, and the sympathetic pictures of Pamela Hansford Johnson's *The Humbler Creation*, Rachel Trickett's *The Return Home*, and Alan Paton's *Cry the Beloved Country*. (See my *A Mirror of the Ministry in Modern Novels*, 1959.)

For an account of Roman Catholicism as it strikes two converts, see the well wrought novels of Graham Greene (especially the eschatological theme in *Brighton Rock* and *The Heart of the Matter* and the labyrinthine mode of grace brilliantly depicted in *The Power and the Glory*) and of that master of satire and eccentricity in character, Evelyn Waugh.

Christopher Isherwood's *The World in the Evening* was used for its subtle evocation of the cool tranquillity and unity of a Quaker meeting.

Peter de Vries' *The Mackerel Plaza* was used for its brilliant critique of a "culture-vulture" parson and for its indictment of a liberal accommodation of Christianity to the demands of the contemporary culture in a "community church."

James Baldwin's *Go Tell it on the Mountain* is a vivid reconstruction of the ardour of fundamentalist faith in an underprivileged social group, and throws light (by analogy) on the early background from which Stanley Spencer's paintings arose. Both novelist and artist are intellectually liberated from, but imaginatively captive to, such an intense religious upbringing.

4. BOOKS

(Except where otherwise indicated, all books were published
in London)

Abba, Raymond. *Principles of Christian Worship* (1957)

Abercrombie, Nigel J. *The Life and Work of Edmund Bishop* (1960)

Acts of the Convocations of Canterbury and York, 1921-60 (1961)

Addleshaw, G. W. O. and Etchells, F. *The Architectural Setting of Anglican Worship* (1948)

Ady, Cecilia M. *The English Church* (1940)

Allen, E. L. *Kierkegaard, His Life and Thought* (1935)

Anson, Peter F. *The Call of the Cloister* (1955)

–––. *Fashions in Church Furnishings, 1840-1940* (1960)

–––. *The Religious Orders and Congregations of Great Britain and Ireland* (Worcester, 1949)

Appleton, L. H. and Bridges, S. *Symbolism in Liturgical Art* (1960)

Argan, Guilio Carlo. *Henry Moore* (Torino, 1948)

Arnold, J. H. (ed.). *Anglican Liturgies* (1938)

Arnold, J. H. and Wyatt, E. G. P. (eds.). *Walter Howard Frere: a collection of papers on liturgical and historical subjects* (1940)

Attwater, Donald. *In the Beginning was the Word: a Plea for English Words in the Worship of the Roman Church* (1944)

Aulén, Gustaf. *Christus Victor* (1931)

Baillie, D. M. *God was in Christ, An Essay in Incarnation and Atonement* (1948, rev. edn., 1955)

–––. *The Theology of the Sacraments* (1957)

Baillie, D. M. and Marsh, John (eds.). *Intercommunion* (1952)

Baillie, John and Martin, H. (eds.). *Revelation* (1937)

Baker, Frank. *Methodism and the Love-Feast* (1957)

Balleine, G. R. *A History of the Evangelical Party in the Church of England* (rev. edn., 1951)

Baptism and Confirmation: A Report submitted by the Church of England Liturgical Commission to the Archbishops of Canterbury and York in November 1958 (1959)

Baptism and Confirmation Today (1954) (The Report of the Joint Committee of the Convocations of Canterbury and York)

Baptist Hymn Book (1962) (The official denominational hymnbook of the British Baptists)

Barth, Karl. *Commentary on the Epistle to the Romans* (trans. E. C. Hoskyns, 1933)

Bate, H. N. (ed.). *Faith and Order* (1927) (Proceedings of the Lausanne Faith and Order Conference)

Batiffol, Pierre. *Histoire du Bréviaire Romain* (Paris, 1893)

Batsford, H. and Fry, C. *The Cathedrals of England* (1960)

Baumstark, Anton. *Comparative Liturgy* (rev. by Bernard Botte, ed. F. L. Cross, 1958)

Beauduin, Lambert. *Liturgy the Life of the Church* (trans. of *La Piété de l'Eglise*, 1914, now issued by Collegeville, Minnesota)

———. *Mélanges liturgiques receuillis parmi les oeuvres de Dom L. Beauduin, O.S.B.* (Louvain, 1954)

Beck, G. A. (ed.). *The English Catholics: 1850-1950* (1950)

Bedoyere, Michael de la. *Cardinal Bernard Griffin, Archbishop of Westminster* (1955)

———. *Christianity in the Market-Place* (1943)

———. *The Layman in the Church* (1954)

———. *The Life of Baron von Hügel* (1951)

["Begbie, Harold" pseud.] *Painted Windows, Studies in Religious Personality* (1922)

Bell, G. K. A. (ed.). *Documents of Christian Unity, Series I-III* (1924-1948)

———. *Randall Davidson, Archbishop of Canterbury* (2nd edn., 1938)

Bennett, Frank. *The Nature of a Cathedral* (London and Chester, 1925)

Bénoît, J-D. *Liturgical Renewal: Studies in Catholic and Protestant Developments in the Continent* (1958)

Benson, E. W. *The Cathedral: Its Necessary Place in the Life and Worship of the Church* (1878)

Benson, Louis F. *The Hymnody of the Christian Church* (New York, 1927, re-issued Richmond, Virginia, 1956)

Betjeman, John. *Collins Guide to English Parish Churches* (1958)

———. *Complete Poems* (1959)

———. *First and Last Loves* (1952)

Bevan, Edwyn. *Symbolism and Belief* (1938)

Biblical Doctrine of Baptism (Edinburgh, 1958) (A Study Document issued by the Special Commission on Baptism of the Church of Scotland)

Biedrzynski, R. *Kirchen unserer Zeit* (Munich, 1958)

Bishop, Edmund. *Liturgica Historica, Papers on the Liturgy and Religious Life of the Western Church* (Oxford, 1918)

Bishop, Edmund and Gasquet, F. A. *Edward VI and the Book of Common Prayer* (1890)

Bishop, John. *Methodist Worship in relation to Free Church Worship* (1950)

Black, Robert. *The Art of Jacob Epstein* (New York and Cleveland, 1942)

Booth, Charles. *Life and Labour of the People of London* (Third Series, 1902)

Bouyer, Louis. *Life and Liturgy* (1956)

Bowmer, John C. *The Lord's Supper in Methodism, 1791-1960* (1961)

———. *The Sacrament of the Lord's Supper in Early Methodism* (1951)

Boyd, Malcolm. *Crisis in Communication: A Christian Examination of the Mass Media* (New York, 1957)

Bradley, William L. *P. T. Forsyth, the man and his work* (1952)

Brémond, H. *Histoire Littéraire du Sentiment Religieux en France* (6 vols., Paris, 1923)

Brenner, Scott Francis. *The Art of Worship* (New York, 1961)
———. *The Way of Worship: A Study in Ecumenical Recovery* (New York, 1944)
Bridge, A. C. *Images of God* (1960)
Bridges, Robert (ed.). *The Yattendon Hymnal* (1899)
Briggs, Martin S. *Goths and Vandals* (1952)
———. *Puritan Architecture and its Future* (1946)
Brilioth, Yngve. *Eucharistic Faith and Practice, Evangelical and Catholic* (1930)
Brinton, H. H. *Creative Worship* (1931)
———. *Friends for 300 Years* (New York, 1952)
———. *Guide to Quaker Practice* (Wallingford, Pennsylvania, n.d.)
Brittain, Fred. *Bernard Lord Manning, A Memoir* (Cambridge, 1942)
Brown, C. K. F. *A History of the English Clergy, 1800-1900* (1953)
Brown, L. A. and Moore, L. T. *The Dual Purpose Church* (1952)
Brown, Robert McAfee. *P. T. Forsyth: Prophet for Today* (Philadelphia, 1952)
Buber, Martin. *I and Thou* (1937)
Buckle, Richard. *Epstein: Drawings* (1962)
———. *Jacob Epstein: Sculptor* (1963)
Burleigh, J. H. S. *A Church History of Scotland* (1960)
Burnet, George B. *The Holy Communion in the Reformed Church of Scotland, 1560-1960* (Edinburgh and London, 1960)
Butler, B. Christopher. *The Idea of the Church* (1962)
Butler, Cuthbert. *Benedictine Monachism* (1922)
———. *Western Mysticism* (1922)
Butterfield, Herbert. *Christianity and History* (1950)
Buttrick, George A. *Prayer* (New York and Nashville, 1942)

Cabrol, Fernand (ed.). *Peregrinatio Silviae* (1895)
Campbell, R. J. *Christianity and the Social Order* (1907)
———. *The New Theology* (1907)
———. *New Theology Sermons* (1907)
———. *A Spiritual Pilgrimage* (1917)
Carpenter, E. (ed.). *The Archbishop Speaks* (1958) (Speeches and addresses of Archbishop Geoffrey F. Fisher)
Carpenter, James. *Gore: A Study in Liberal Catholic Thought* (1960)
Carpenter, S. C. *Prophet and Priest . . .* (1953)
Casel, Odo. *Le Mémorial du Seigneur* (Paris, 1944)
———. *Le Mystère du Culte dans le Christianisme* (Paris, 1946)
Cavert, S. M. *The New Delhi Report* (1962)
Chapman, John. *Spiritual Letters* (1935; 1944 edn. with biography by Roger Hudleston)
Chesterton, G. K. *Autobiography* (1936)
———. *The Collected Poems of . . .* (1927)
———. *The Everlasting Man* (1925)
———. *Heretics* (1909)
———. *Orthodoxy* (1908)
Child, R. L. *The Blessing of Infants and the Dedication of Parents* (1946)

Church Hymnary (revised edition, 1927) (An important Presbyterian Hymnal used in the Church of Scotland and the other British and Commonwealth Churches of the Presbyterian Order)

Clark, Francis. *Eucharistic Sacrifice and the Reformation* (1960)

Clark, Henry W. *History of English Nonconformity* (2 vols., 1913)

Clark, Neville. *Call to Worship* (1960)

Clarke, B. F. L. *Church Buildings of the Nineteenth Century* (1938)

Clarke, W. K. Lowther. *A Hundred Years of Hymns Ancient and Modern* (1961)

———. (ed.). *Liturgy and Worship, A Companion to the Prayer Books of the Anglican Communion* (1932)

Clifford, John. *The Gospel of World Brotherhood according to Jesus* (1920)

———. *The Ultimate Problems of Christianity* (1906)

Collingwood, R. G. *The Principles of Art* (1938)

Collis, Maurice. *Stanley Spencer: A Biography* (1962)

Comper, J. N. *Further Thoughts on the English Altar, or Practical Considerations on the Planning of a Modern Church* (Cambridge, 1933)

———. *Of the Christian Altar and the Buildings which contain it* (1950)

———. *On the Atmosphere of a Church* (1947)

Congregational Praise (1951) (The official hymnal of the Congregational Union of England and Wales)

Constantini, Celso. *L'Istruzione de S'Officio sull' Arte Sacra* (Roma, 1952)

Cook, G. H. *The English Cathedral through the Centuries* (1957)

Cooper, Douglas (ed.). *The Work of Graham Sutherland* (1961)

Cope, Gilbert. *Symbolism in the Bible and the Church* (1959)

———. *Making the Building Serve the Liturgy* (1963)

Cope, G., Davies, J. G. and Tytler, D. A. *An Experimental Liturgy* (1958)

Cox, J. C. *English Church Fittings, Furniture and Accessories* (Oxford, 1915)

———. *Pulpits, Lecterns and Organs in English Churches* (Oxford, 1915)

Cozien, G. *L'oeuvre de Dom Guéranger* (Paris, 1933)

Crockford Prefaces: The Editor Looks Back (1947)

Cropper, Margaret. *Evelyn Underhill* (1958)

Cross, F. L. *Darwell Stone, Churchman and Counsellor* (1943)

——— (ed.). *The Oxford Dictionary of the Christian Church* (rev. edn. 1958)

Cunliffe, C. R. A. (ed.). *English in the Liturgy; a Symposium* (1956)

Dakin, A. *The Baptist View of the Church and Ministry* (1944)

Dale, A. W. W. *The Life of R. W. Dale of Birmingham* (1898)

Daniélou, Jean. *The Bible and the Liturgy* (South Bend, Indiana, 1956)

Dannatt, Trevor. *Modern Architecture in Britain* (1957)

Dark, Sidney. *Five Deans* (1928)

Davies, David Richard. *In search of myself; an autobiography* (1961)
———. *On to Orthodoxy* (1939)

Davies, Horton. *Christian Deviations* (3rd edn., London and Philadelphia, 1965)
———. *The English Free Churches* (rev. edn., 1962)
———. *A Mirror of the Ministry in Modern Novels* (New York, 1959)
———. *Varieties of English Preaching: 1900-1960* (London and Englewood Cliffs, New Jersey, 1963)
———. *Worship and Theology in England* (Vol. III: *From Watts and Wesley to Maurice, 1690-1850*; Vol. IV: *From Newman to Martineau, 1850-1900*; Princeton and London, 1961-1962)
———. *The Worship of the English Puritans* (1948)

Davies, John Gordon. *The Architectural Setting of Baptism* (1962)

Davies, Rupert. *Methodism* (1963)

Davies, Walford and Grace, Harvey. *Music and Worship* (1937)

Davis, Charles (ed.). *English Spiritual Writers* (1962)

Dearmer, Nan. *The Life of Percy Dearmer* (1940)

Dearmer, Percy. *Art and Religion* (1923)
———. *The Art of Public Worship* (1919)
———. *The Ornaments of the Minister* (1920)
———. *The Parson's Handbook* (Oxford, 1899, rev. edn., 1903; 6th edn. with additional matter, 1907)
———. *A Short Handbook of Public Worship* (Oxford, 1931)
———. *Songs of Praise Discussed* (1933)

De Blank, Joost. *The Parish in Action* (1955)

Deissmann, A. and Bell, G. K. A. (eds.). *Mysterium Christi* (1930)

Demant, V. A. *Christian Polity* (1936)
———. *Religion and the Decline of Capitalism* (1952)
———. *The Religious Prospect* (2nd edn., 1941)

Dictionary of National Biography and Supplements (1882–)

Dieci Anni di Architettura Sacra in Italia (Bologna, 1956)

Dillistone, F. W. *Christianity and Symbolism* (1955)
———. *The Structure of the Christian Society* (1951)

Dix, Gregory. *A Detection of Aumbries* (1942)
———. *The Shape of the Liturgy* (1945)
———. *The Theology of Confirmation in Relation to Baptism* (1946)

Doctrine in the Church of England (1938) (The Report of the Commission on Christian Doctrine appointed by the Archbishops of Canterbury and York in 1922)

Douglas, Winfred. *Church Music in History and Practice* (rev. Leonard Ellinwood, New York, 1962)

Driver, Christopher. *A Future for the Free Churches?* (1962)

Drummond, A. L. *The Church Architecture of Protestantism* (Edinburgh, 1934)
———. *The Churches in English Fiction* (Leicester, 1950)
———. *The Churches pictured by 'Punch'* (1947)

Dumoutet, E. *Le désir de voir l'Hostie* (Paris, 1926)

Dunkerley, R. and Headlam, A. C. (eds.). *The Ministry and the Sacraments* (1937)

Dwelly, F. W. *Acts of Devotion* (1923)

———. *Services of Prayer and Praise for occasional use in Churches* (1924)

Edwall, P., Hayman, E., and Maxwell, W. D. (eds.). *Ways of Worship* (1951)

Edwards, David L. and Robinson, J. A. T. *The Honest to God Debate* (1963)

Ekström, Ragnac. *The Theology of Charles Gore, A Study in Modern Anglican Theology* (Lund, 1944)

Eliot, T. S. *The Idea of a Christian Society* (1939)

The English Hymnal (editions of 1906 and 1933) (An important Anglican hymnal)

Ensor, R. C. K. *England: 1870-1914* (Oxford, 1936)

Epstein, Jacob. *Epstein: An Autobiography* (1955)

Epstein, Kathleen. *Epstein at King's Lynn* (1963) (Annotated Exhibition brochure)

Every, George. *The Baptismal Sacrifice* (1959)

——— (ed.). *Herbert Kelly, S.S.M., No Pious Person* (1960)

Farmer, H. H. *God and Men* (1948)

———. *The Healing Cross* (1941)

———. *Revelation and Religion* (1954)

———. *The Servant of the Word* (1941)

———. *Things Not Seen* (1927)

———. *Towards Belief in God* (1942)

———. *The World and God* (1932)

Federer, K. *Liturgie und Glaube: eine theologie-geschichtliche Untersuchung* (Freiburg, 1950)

Fellowes, E. G. *English Cathedral Music from Edward VI to Edward VII* (1945)

Fénelon, François. *Spiritual Letters* (trans. by Sidney Lear, 1880, 1892, 1906)

Fifty Modern Churches (Incorporated Church Building Society, 1947)

Figgis, J. Neville. *The Gospel and Human Need* (1909)

Fison, J. E. *The Faith of the Bible* (1957)

Flemington, W. F. *The New Testament Doctrine of Baptism* (1948)

Fletcher, Joseph. *William Temple, Twentieth Century Christian* (New York, 1963)

Flew, R. Newton. *Jesus and His Church* (1938)

Flew, R. N. and Davies, R. E. *The Catholicity of Protestantism* (1950)

Forman, R. S. (ed.). *Great Christians* (1933)

Ford, D. W. C. *An Expository Preacher's Notebook* (1960)

Forsyth, Peter Taylor. *The Charter of the Church* (1896)

———. *Christ on Parnassus* (1911)

———. *The Church and the Sacraments* (1917)

———. *Congregationalism and Reunion* (1919)

———. *The Cruciality of the Cross* (1909)

———. *Faith, Freedom and the Future* (1912)

457

Forsyth, Peter Taylor. *Intercessory Services for Aid in Public Worship* (London and Heywood, 1896)
———. *The Person and Place of Jesus Christ* (1909)
———. *Positive Preaching and the Modern Mind* (1907)
———. *Religion in Recent Art* (1887, 1905)
———. *The Soul of Prayer* (1916)
———. *Theology in Church and State* (1915)
———. *This Life and the Next* (1918)
———. *The Work of Christ* (1910)
Fortescue, Adrian. *Ceremonies of the Roman Rite Described* (1917, revised edn. of J. B. O'Connell, 1946)
——— (ed.). *The Divine Liturgy of . . . John Chrysostom* (1908)
Foss, Martin. *Symbol and Metaphor in Human Experience* (Princeton, 1949)
Foundations, a statement of Christian belief in terms of modern thought, by Seven Oxford men . . . (Intro. by B. H. Streeter, 1913)
Fox, Adam. *Dean Inge* (1960)
Fox, George. *Journal* (ed. N. Penney, Cambridge, 1911)
A Free Religious Faith (1945). (Report presented to the General Assembly of Unitarian and Free Christian Churches)
Frere, W. H. *English Church Ways* (1914)
———. *Principles of Religious Ceremonial* (1928)
———. *Studies in the Early Roman Liturgy* (3 vols., 1930-1935)
———. *The Use of Sarum* (2 vols., 1898-1901)
Frost, Maurice. *English and Scottish Psalm and Hymn Tunes* (1953)
Fuller, R. H. *What is Liturgical Preaching?* (1957)

Gammie, Alexander. *Preachers I have heard* (n.d., circa 1945)
Garbett, C. F. *The Claims of the Church of England* (1947)
———. *In an Age of Revolution* (1952)
Garrett, T. S. *Christian Worship* (1961)
———. *The Liturgy of the Church of South India, An Introduction to and Commentary on 'The Lord's Supper'* (Madras, 2nd edn., 1954)
———. *Worship in the Church of South India* (1958)
Gasquet, F. A. *Henry VIII and the English Monasteries* (2 vols., 1888-1889)
Gélineau, J. *La Sainte Bible traduite en français sous la direction de l'Ecole biblique de Jérusalem* (Paris, 1956; Engl. trans. Collins Fontana paperbacks, 1963)
George, A. R. *Communion with God in the New Testament* (1952)
Giedion, S. *Space, Time and Architecture* (3rd edn., Cambridge, Mass., and London, 1954)
Gill, Eric. *Autobiography* (1940)
———. *Christianity and Art* (Abergavenny, 1929)
———. *Letters of Eric Gill* (ed. W. Shewring, 1947)
———. *Sacred and Secular* (1940)
Gillman, F. J. *The Evolution of the English Hymn* (1927)

BIBLIOGRAPHY

Gilmore, A. (ed.). *Christian Baptism, A Fresh Attempt to Understand the Rite in terms of Scripture, History and Theology* (1959)

Glazebrook, M. G. *The Faith of a Modern Churchman* (1918)

Glendenning, Frank (ed.). *The Church and the Arts* (1960)

Godfrey, F. M. *Christ and the Apostles, the Changing Forms of Religious Imagery* (1957)

Goodhart-Rendel, H. S. *English Architecture since the Regency* (1953)

Gore, Charles. *Anglo-Catholicism Today* (1925)

———. *The Body of Christ* (1901, 4th edn., 1931)

———. *The Church and the Ministry* (1888, 1919)

———. *The Incarnation of the Son of God* (1891)

———, et alii. *Lux Mundi* (1889)

———. *The New Theology and the Old Religion* (1907)

———. *The Reconstruction of Belief* (1. *Belief in God*, 1922; 2. *Belief in Christ*, 1922; 3. *The Holy Spirit and the Church*, 1924)

Graf, Ernest. *Anscar Vonier, Abbot of Buckfast* (1957)

Graham, John W. *The Quaker Ministry* (1925)

Grant, J. W. *Free Churchmanship in England, 1870-1940, with special reference to Congregationalism* (n.d. but ca. 1951)

Gray, James (ed.). *Studies on Baptism* (Birmingham, 1959)

Green, Thomas F. *Preparation for Worship* (1952)

Green, V. H. H. *Religion at Oxford and Cambridge: A History c. 1160- c. 1960* (1964)

Greene, T. M. *The Arts and the Art of Criticism* (Princeton, 1940)

Greenslade, S. L. *Schism in the Early Church* (1953)

Griffith, G. O. *The Theology of P. T. Forsyth* (London and Redhill, 1948)

Grigson, Geoffrey. *Henry Moore* (1944)

Grohmann, W. *The Art of Henry Moore* (trans. M. Bulloch, 1960)

Guardini, Romano. *Vom Geist der Liturgie* (trans. by A. Lane and published with another work as *The Spirit and the Liturgy*, London and New York, 1940)

Guyon, Madame. *Autobiography* (English trans. by Alpen, 1897)

———. *A Short and Easy Method of Prayer* (English trans. 1901)

Hageman, Howard. *Pulpit and Table* (Richmond, Virginia and London, 1962)

Hales, E. E. Y. *The Catholic Church in the Modern World: A Survey from the French Revolution to the Present* (1958)

Hamilton, H. A. *The Family Church in Principle and Practice* (1941, 3rd edn., 1960)

Hamilton, W. K. *Cathedral Reform. A Letter to Members of his Diocese* (1855)

Hammond, Peter. *Liturgy and Architecture* (1960)

——— (ed.). *Towards a Church Architecture* (1962)

Harnack, A. *Das Wesen des Christentums* (1900; trans. as *What is Christianity?* 1901)

Harries, John. *G. Campbell Morgan, The Man and his Ministry* (1930)

Harrison, A. W. *Church and Sacraments* (1935)

Harvey, J. *The English Cathedrals* (rev. edn., 1956)

Harvey, T. Edmund. *Silence and Worship, A Study in Quaker Experience* (1924)

Hauser, A. *The Social History of Art* (trans. S. Goodman, 2 vols., 1951)

Hay, G. *The Architecture of Scottish Post-Reformation Churches, 1560-1843* (1957)

Hayman, Eric. *Worship and the Common Life* (Cambridge, 1944)

Hazelton, Roger. *New Accents in Contemporary Theology* (New York, 1960)

Hebert, A. G. *The Form of the Church* (1944)

———. *Fundamentalism and the Church of God* (1957)

———. *Liturgy and Society: The Function of the Church in the Modern World* (1935)

———. *The Throne of David* (1941)

——— (ed.). *The Parish Communion, A Book of Essays* (1937; re-issued 1939, 1944, 1954)

Hedley, J. C. *The Holy Eucharist* (1907)

Heenan, John C. *Cardinal Hinsley* (1944)

Heiler, Friedrich. *Prayer* (1932)

———. *The Spirit of Worship* (1926)

Henson, H. Hensley. *Ad Clerum* (1937)

———. *Bishoprick Papers* (1946)

———. *Church and Parson in England* (1927)

———. *The Creed in the Pulpit* (1912)

———. *Letters* (ed. F. E. Braley, 1950)

———. *Retrospect of an Unimportant Life: 1863-1939* (3 vols., 1942, 1943, 1950)

———. *Theology and Life* (ed. G. S. Stranks, 1958)

———. *Westminster Sermons* (1910)

Henze, Anton. *Contemporary Church Art* (London and New York, 1956)

Hervormde Kerkbouw na 1945 (The Hague, 1957)

Hicks, F. C. N. *The Fulness of Sacrifice* (1930, 3rd edn., 1946)

Higham, Florence. *Catholic and Reformed* (1962)

Hinchliff, P. B. *The Anglican Church in South Africa* (1963)

———. *The South African Liturgy* (1960)

Hitchcock, Henry Russell. *Architecture: Nineteenth and Twentieth Centuries* (Harmondsworth and Baltimore, 1962)

Hodgkin, Thomas. *The Fellowship of Silence* (ed. Cyril Hepher, 1920)

Hodgkin, Violet. *Silent Worship: The Way of Wonder* (1919)

Hodgson, Leonard (ed.). *The Second World Conference on Faith and Order* (1938) (Proceedings of the Edinburgh Conference)

Hodin, J. P. *Henry Moore* (Amsterdam, 1956)

Hofman, Werner. *Henry Moore, Schriften und Skulpturen* (Frankfurt A.M., 1959)

Homrighausen, E. G. (ed.). *J. H. Jowett* (New York, 1950)

Horder, Garrett (ed.). *Worship Song* (1905)

Hoskyns, Edwyn Clement. *Cambridge Sermons* (1938)
———. *The Fourth Gospel* (ed. F. N. Davey, 2nd edn., 1947)
Hoskyns, E. C. and Davey, F. N. *The Riddle of the New Testament* (1931)
Howell, Clifford. *Preparing for Easter* (1957)
Howson, J. S. (ed.). *Essays on Cathedrals* (1872)
——— (ed.). *A Week in Chester Cathedral* (London and Chester, 1872)
Hughes, Anselm. *The Rivers of the Flood: a personal account of the Catholic Revival in England in the twentieth century* (1961)
Hunter, Leslie S. *Church Strategy in a Changing World* (1950)
Huxley, Aldous. *On Art and Artists* (New York, 1960)
Hymns Ancient and Modern (1861, 1904, 1950) (A semi-official hymnal of the Church of England)

Inge, William Ralph. *Assessments and Anticipations* (1928)
———. *Christian Mysticism* (1899)
———. *Diary of a Dean, St. Paul's, 1911-1934* (1949)
———. *Faith and Knowledge* (2nd edn., Edinburgh, 1905)
———. *The Gate of Life* (1935)
———. *Goodness and Truth* (1958)
———. *God and the Astronomers* (1933)
———. *Labels and Libels* (New York, 1929)
———. *Outspoken Essays* (1st Series, 1919; 2nd Series, 1922)
———. *Personal Religion and the Life of Devotion* (1924)
———. *The Philosophy of Plotinus* (2 vols., 1918)
———. *Speculum Animae* (1912)
———. *Studies in English Mystics* (1907)
———. *Things New and Old* (1933)
———. *Vale* (1934)
Ireland, Geoffrey. *Epstein: A Camera Study of the Sculptor at Work* (1958)
Iremonger, F. A. *William Temple, Archbishop of Canterbury, His Life and Letters* (1948)
Ireson, G. W. *Church Worship and the Non-Churchgoer* (1945)

James, A. T. S. *A Cotswold Minister* (1940)
James, William. *The Varieties of Religious Experience* (1902)
Jasper, R. A. C. *Headlam, Life and Letters of a Bishop* (1960)
Jefferson, H. A. L. *Hymns in Christian Worship* (1950)
Jeffs, Ernest H. *Princes of the Modern Pulpit* (London, n.d.)
Jenkins, Daniel T. *Beyond Religion* (1962)
———. *Congregationalism* (1954)
———. *Equality and Excellence* (1961)
———. *The Nature of Catholicity* (1942)
———. *Tradition and the Spirit* (1954)
Jones, Alexander. *Unless some Man show me* (1951)
Jones, Cranston. *Architecture Today and Tomorrow* (New York, 1961)

461

Jones, Edgar DeWitt. *The Royalty of the Pulpit; A Survey and Appreciation of the Lyman Beecher Lectures on Preaching founded at Yale Divinity School 1871* (New York, 1951)

Jones, R. P. *Nonconformist Church Architecture* (1914)

Jones, R. Tudur. *Congregationalism in England (1662-1962)* (1962)

Jones, Rufus M. *The Later Periods of Quakerism* (vol. 2, 1921)

———. *Spiritual Reformers in the 16th and 17th Centuries* (1914)

Jordan, E. K. H. *Free Church Unity* (1956)

Jowett, J. H. *The Transfigured Church* (1910)

Joynson-Hicks, W. *The Prayer Book Crisis* (1928)

Julian, John (ed.). *Dictionary of Hymnology* (1890 etc.)

Jungmann, Joseph. *Missarum Solemnia* (Vienna, 1949; trans. *The Mass of the Roman Rite*, 2 vols., New York, 1951)

Jungmann, Joseph. *Public Worship* (trans. Clifford Howell, 1957)

———. *The Sacrifice of the Church* (trans. Clifford Howell, 1956)

Kemp, E. W. *The Life and Letters of K. E. Kirk* (1959)

Kepler, Thomas (ed.). *The Evelyn Underhill Reader* (1962)

Kirk, K. E. (ed.). *The Apostolic Ministry* (1957 edn. with new foreword by A. M. Farrer)

——— (ed.). *The Study of Theology* (1939)

———. *The Vision of God* (abridged edn., 1934)

Klauser, Theodor. *The Western Liturgy and its History: Some Reflections on Recent Studies* (trans. F. L. Cross, 1952)

Knowles, David. *The Monastic Order in England* (Cambridge, 1940)

———. *The Religious Orders in England* (Cambridge, 1948)

Knox, E. A. *Sacrifice or Sacrament?* (1914)

Knox, Ronald A. *The Belief of Catholics* (1927)

———. *Bridegroom and Bride* (1957)

———. *The Church in Bondage* (1914)

———. *Enthusiasm, A Chapter in the History of Religion* (Oxford, 1950)

———. *Essays in Satire* (1928)

———. *The Hidden Stream* (1953)

———. *In Soft Garments* (1942)

———. *Let Dons Delight* (1939)

———. *The Mass in Slow Motion* (1948)

———. *The Priestly Life: A Retreat* (1958)

———. *A Spiritual Aeneid* (1918)

———. *The Window in the Wall* (1956)

Koenker, E. B. *The Liturgical Renaissance in the Roman Catholic Church* (Chicago, 1954)

Korolevskij, C. *Liturgie en langue vivante; Orient et Occident* (Paris, 1955)

Kraemer, Hendrik. *The Christian Message in a Non-Christian World* (1938)

Küng, Hans. *The Council and Reunion* (1962)

Lampe, G. W. H. *The Seal of the Spirit* (1951)

Law, William. *Liberal and Mystical Writings* (ed. W. Scott Palmer, 1908)

Lawrence, Brother. *The Practice of the Presence of God* (English trans. 1906)

Leeming, Bernard. *The Principles of Sacramental Theology* (1956)

Lenwood, Frank. *Jesus—Lord or Leader?* (1930)

Lewis, Clive Staples. *Beyond Personality* (1944)

———. *Broadcast Talks* (1943)

———. *Christian Behaviour* (1943)

———. *The Pilgrim's Regress* (1933, rev. edn., 1944)

———. *The Problem of Pain* (1941)

———. *The Screwtape Letters* (1943)

———. *Surprised by Joy* (1955)

———. *Transposition and Other Addresses* (1949)

L'Hopital, Winifrede de. *Westminster Cathedral and its Architect* (2 vols., 1919)

Lightfoot, R. H. *History and Interpretation of the Gospels* (1935)

Lilley, A. L. *The Sacraments* (1928)

Lloyd, Roger. *The Church of England in the Twentieth Century* (2 vols., 1946, 1950)

Lloyd-Jones, Martyn. *Studies in the Sermon on the Mount* (2 vols., 1959-1960)

Lockhart, J. G. *Cosmo Gordon Lang, Archbishop of Canterbury* (1949)

Louden, R. S. *The True Face of the Kirk* (Edinburgh and London, 1963)

Loukes, Harold. *The Discovery of Quakerism* (1960)

———. *Friends Face Reality* (1954)

Luccock, Halford E. *The Best of Dick Sheppard* (New York, 1951)

McArthur, A. A. *The Christian Year and Lectionary Reform* (1958)

Macdonald, A. J. (ed.). *The Evangelical Doctrine of Holy Communion* (1930)

Mackintosh, Hugh R. *The Doctrine of the Person of Jesus Christ* (Edinburgh, 1912)

———. *Types of Modern Theology: Schleiermacher to Barth* (1937)

MacLeod, George F. *We shall rebuild: the work of the Iona Community on mainland and island* (Philadelphia, 1945)

Macquarrie, John. *The Scope of Demythologizing* (1960)

———. *Twentieth-century Religious Thought* (1963)

Maguire, Robert. *Programme and Idea* (New Churches Group Papers, 1962)

Maitland, C. *Dr. Leslie Weatherhead* (1960)

Major, H. D. A. *English Modernism: its Origin, Methods, Aims* (Cambridge, Mass., 1927)

Malvern, 1941 (1942) (Proceedings of the Archbishop of York's Conference)

Manning, Bernard Lord. *Church Union: The Next Step for Congregationalists* (1933)

463

Manning, Bernard Lord. *Essays in Orthodox Dissent* (1939)
———. *The Hymns of Wesley and Watts* (1942)
———. *A Layman in the Ministry* (1943)
———. *The Making of Modern English Religion* (1929)
———. *The Protestant Dissenting Deputies* (ed. O. J. Greenwood, Cambridge, 1952)
———. *Why not Abandon the Church?* (1939)
Manson, T. W. *The Church's Ministry* (1948)
Marchant, James (ed.). *The coming-of-age of Christianity* (1950)
——— (ed.). *Dr. John Clifford, C.H.: life, letters and reminiscences* (1924)
——— (ed.). *The Wit and Wisdom of Dean Inge* (1927)
Marsh, H. G. *The Origin and Significance of New Testament Baptism* (Manchester, 1941)
Martin, Hugh (ed.). *A Book of Prayers for Students* (3rd edn., 1921)
——— (ed.). *The Baptist Hymn Book Companion* (1962)
Martin, John R. T. *Christ our Passover: The Liturgical Observance of Holy Week* (1958)
Martin, W. B. J. *Acts of Worship* (New York and Nashville, 1960)
Martindale, C. C. *The Mind of the Missal* (1929)
Martineau, James. *Prayers in the Congregation and in the College* (1911)
Mascall, E. L. *Corpus Christi, Essays on the Church and the Eucharist* (1953)
———. *Theology and Images. A Critical Examination of Recent Scholarship* (1963)
———. *Up and Down in Adria* (1963)
Matheson, P. E. *Life of Hastings Rashdall* (1928)
Mathew, David. *Catholicism in England* (1936)
Matthews, W. R. and Atkins, W. M. (eds.). *A History of St. Paul's Cathedral* (1957)
Maufe, Edward. *Modern Church Architecture* (1948)
Maurer, H. and Trueblood, E. (eds.). *The Pendle Hill Reader* (New York, 1950)
Maxwell, William D. *The Book of Common Prayer and the Worship of Non-Anglican Churches* (1950)
———. *Concerning Worship* (1948)
———. *A History of Worship in the Church of Scotland* (1955)
———. *An Outline of Christian Worship, its Development and Forms* (1936)
May, Rollo (ed.). *Symbolism in Religion and Literature* (New York, 1960)
Mellor, Richard. *Modern Church Design* (1948)
Menzies, Lucy (ed.). *The Collected Papers of Evelyn Underhill* (1946)
Mesnard, Pierre. *Le Mouvement liturgique de Klosterneuberg* (Lyon, 1943)
Michell, G. A. *Landmarks in Liturgy* (1961)
Micklem, E. R. *Our Approach to God* (1934)

Micklem, Nathaniel (ed.). *A Book of Personal Religion* (1938)
———. *The Box and the Puppets, 1888-1953* (1957)
——— (ed.). *Christian Worship* (1936, reissued 1955, Oxford)
———. *Congregationalism and the Church Catholic* (1943)
———. *Congregationalism Today* (1937)
——— (ed.). *Officia Breva* (privately printed, n.d.)
———. *What is the Faith?* (1936)
Micklethwaite, J. T. *The Ornaments of the Rubrics* (1897)
Micklewright, F. H. A. *Sacraments for the Modern Man* (n.d., but ca. 1933)
Mills, Edward D. *The Modern Church* (1956)
———. *The New Architecture in Great Britain, 1946-1953* (1954)
Milner-White, E. and Smith, B. T. D. (eds.). *Cambridge Offices and Orisons* (1921)
Minchin, Basil. *The Celebration of the Eucharist facing the People* (1954)
———. *Covenant and Sacrifice* (1958)
———. *Everyman in His Ministry* (1960)
Moberly, R. C. *Atonement and Personality* (1901)
Moffatt, James. *The Presbyterian Churches* (1928)
Moorman, J. R. H. *A History of the Church in England* (1953)
Moore, Henry. *Heads, Figures and Ideas: A Sculptor's Notebook* (1958)
———. *Portfolio of Forty Drawings* (New York, 1946)
———. *Sculptures and Drawings* (intro. by Herbert Read, 3rd edn., 1949)
Morgan, Dewi (ed.). *They Became Anglicans* (1959)
———. *1662 and all that* (1961)
Morison, Stanley. *English Prayer Books, An Introduction to the Literature of Christian Public Worship* (Cambridge, 1943)
Moule, C. F. D. *Worship in the New Testament* (1961)
Mozley, J. K. (ed.). *G. A. Studdert Kennedy By His Friends* (1929)
———. *The Gospel Sacraments* (1933)
———. *Some Tendencies in British Theology, From the Publication of 'Lux Mundi' to the Present Day* (1951)
Mumford, Lewis. *The Culture of Cities* (New York, 1938)
———. *Technics and Civilization* (New York, 1934)
Murray, Gregory. *Accentual Cadences in Gregorian Chant* (Downside Abbey, Bath, 1958)
———. *The Authentic Rhythm of Gregorian Chant* (Bath, 1959)
———. *Gregorian Rhythm in the Gregorian Centuries* (Bath, 1957)
———. *Plainsong Rhythm* (Bath, 1956)

Neil, William. *The Rediscovery of the Bible* (1955)
Neill, Stephen (ed.). *Twentieth-Century Christianity, Modern Religious Trends* (1961)
Neumann, E. *The Archetypal World of Henry Moore* (trans. R. F. C. Hull, New York, 1959)

New Churches Illustrated (Incorporated Church Building Society, 1936)

Newbigin, J. Lesslie. *The Reunion of the Church* (1948)

Newman, John Henry. *Apologia pro vita sua* (1864)

———. *Meditations and Devotions* (1903)

Newton, Eric. *In My View* (1950)

Nichols, J. H. *A History of Christianity, 1650-1950* (New York, 1956)

Nicholls, William. *Jacob's Ladder: The Meaning of Worship* (1958)

Nicholson, Charles and Spooner, C. *Recent English Ecclesiastical Architecture* (2nd edn., ca. 1910)

Niebuhr, H. Richard. *The Kingdom of God in America* (2nd edn., Hamden, Conn., 1956)

Nuttall, G. F. and Chadwick, Owen. *From Unity to Uniformity (1662-1962)* (1962)

Nygren, Anders. *Agape and Eros: A Study of the Christian idea of love* (2 parts, 1937 and 1939, trans. respectively by A. G. Hebert and P. S. Watson)

Oldmeadow, E. *Francis Cardinal Bourne* (2 vols., 1940, 1944)

Ollard, S. L. *The Anglo-Catholic Revival, Some Persons and Principles* (1925)

Oman, John. *The Church and the Divine Order* (1911)

———. *Grace and Personality* (1917)

———. *The Natural and the Supernatural* (1931)

Orchard, W. E. *From Faith to Faith; an Autobiography of Religious Development* (1933)

———. *The New Catholicism and other sermons* (1917)

———. *Order of Divine Service for Public Worship, the Administration of the Sacraments and other Ceremonies . . .* (1921)

———. *Sancta Sanctorum; Prayers for the Holy of Holies . . .* (1955)

———. *The Temple: a Book of Prayers* (1928)

Otto, Rudolf. *The Idea of the Holy* (2nd edn., 1950)

Oulton, J. E. L. *Holy Communion and Holy Spirit, A Study in Doctrinal Relationships* (1951)

Parrinder, Geoffrey. *Worship in the World's Religions* (1961)

Parris, John. *John Wesley's Doctrine of the Sacraments* (1963)

Parry, K. L. and Routley, Erik. *Companion to Congregational Praise* (1953)

Parsch, Pius. *The Breviary Explained* (trans. Naydon and Hoegerl, St. Louis and London, 1952)

———. *The Church's Year of Grace* (3 vols., Collegeville, Minnesota, 1953)

Paton, David M. (ed.). *Essays in Anglican Self-Criticism* (1958)

Patrick, Denzil. *Pascal and Kierkegaard* (2 vols., 1947)

Patrick, Millar. *Four Centuries of Scottish Psalmody* (1949)

Payne, Ernest A. *The Baptist Union, A Short History* (1959)

———. *The Fellowship of Believers* (1944)

———. *The Free Church Tradition in the Life of England* (1944)

Payne, E. A. and Winward, S. (eds.). *Orders and Prayers for Church Worship* (1960)

Peck, W. G. *An Outline of Christian Sociology* (1948)

Peel, Albert. *Christian Freedom* (1937)

———. *These Hundred Years: A History of the Congregational Union, 1831-1931* (1931)

Pepler, C. *The English Religious Heritage* (1958)

Petre, M. D. *von Hügel and Tyrrell* (1937)

Phillips, C. H. *The Singing Church* (1945)

Phillips, C. S. *Hymnody Past and Present* (1937)

Phillips, C. S. et alii. *Walter Howard Frere, Bishop of Truro* (1947)

Pocknee, C. E. *Cross and Crucifix in Christian Worship and Devotion* (1962)

———. *Liturgical Vesture, Its Origins and Development* (1960)

Porritt, Arthur. *John Henry Jowett* (1924)

Prayer Book Revision in the Church of England; a Memorandum of the Church of England Liturgical Commission (1957)

Prestige, G. L. *The Life of Charles Gore* (1935)

———. *St. Paul's in its Glory, A Candid History of the Cathedral* (1955)

Proctor, F. and Frere, W. H. *A New History of the Book of Common Prayer* (1901)

Pullan, L. *Religion since the Reformation* (1923)

Purcell, William. *Woodbine Willie* (1962)

Pusey, E. B. *Remarks on the Prospective and Past Benefits of Cathedral Institutions . . .* (Oxford and London, 1833)

Quick, O. C. *The Christian Sacraments* (1927)

———. *The Doctrines of the Creed* (1938)

———. *Liberalism, Modernism and Tradition* (1922)

Rafferty, W. *Liturgy in the Parish* (1958)

Ramsey, Arthur Michael. *Durham Essays and Addresses* (1956)

———. *From Gore to Temple: The Development of Anglican Theology between Lux Mundi and the Second World War, 1889-1939* (London and New York, 1960)

———. *The Gospel and the Catholic Church* (1936)

———. *Image Old and New* (1963)

Ratcliff, E. C. *The Booke of Common Prayer of the Churche of England: Its making and revisions M.D. xlix-M.D. clxi* (1949)

———. *Three Commemorative Lectures delivered in Lambeth Palace* (1956)

Rattenbury, J. E. *The Eucharistic Hymns of John and Charles Wesley* (1948)

———. *Thoughts on Holy Communion* (1958)

———. *Vital Elements in Public Worship* (1936)

———. *Wesley's Legacy to the World* (1938)

Rauschenbusch, Walter. *For God and the People: Prayers of the Social Awakening* (New York, 1910)

467

Raven, Charles E. *The Creator Spirit* (1927)

Rawlinson, A. E. J. *Christian Initiation* (1947)

Read, Herbert. *Henry Moore, Sculptor* (1934)

———. *Icon and Idea: the Function of Art in the Development of Human Consciousness* (1955)

Reckitt, M. B. *Maurice to Temple: A Century of the Social Movement in the Church of England* (1947)

—— (ed.). *Prospect for Christendom* (1945)

Reed, Luther D. *Worship: A Study of Corporate Devotion* (Philadelphia, 1962)

Régamey, P. R. *Art Sacré au XXᵉ Siècle?* (Paris, 1952)

Reinhold, H. A. *Speaking of Liturgical Architecture* (South Bend, Indiana, 1952)

Relton, H. M. (ed.). *The New Prayer Book* (1927)

Report of the Cathedrals Commission (1961)

Report of the Royal Commission on Ecclesiastical Discipline (3 vols., 1906)

Reynolds, W. J. *A Survey of Christian Hymnody* (New York, 1963)

Richards, J. M. *An Introduction to Modern Architecture* (Harmondsworth and Baltimore, 1959)

Richardson, Alan, *et alii. Four Anchors from the Stern* (1963)

Richardson, R. D. *The Gospel of Modernism* (1933)

Roberts, R. Ellis. *H. R. L. Sheppard, Life and Letters* (1942)

Robinson, H. Wheeler. *The Life and Faith of the Baptists* (1927)

Robinson, John A. T. *The Body* (1961)

———. *Honest to God* (1963)

———. *In the End God* (1950)

———. *Liturgy Coming to Life* (1961)

———. *On Being the Church in the World* (1960)

Robinson, William. *A Companion to the Communion Service; a devotional Manual* (1942)

———. *What the Churches of Christ stand for* (Birmingham, 1926)

Roth, Cecil (ed.). *Jewish Art, An Illustrated History* (New York, 1961)

Rothenstein, Elizabeth. *Stanley Spencer* (1962)

Rothenstein, John. *Epstein: Arts Council Memorial Exhibition* (1961)

———. *Modern English Painters* (2 vols., 1952, 1956)

Rouse, Ruth and Neill, S. C. (eds.). *A History of the Ecumenical Movement, 1517-1948* (1954)

Rousseau, Olivier. *L'Histoire du Mouvement Liturgique* (Paris, 1945; Engl. trans. *The Progress of the Liturgy*, Westminster, Maryland, 1951)

Routley, Erik R. *The Church and Music* (1950)

———. *Church Music and Theology* (1959)

———. *English Religious Dissent* (Cambridge, 1960)

———. *The Gift of Conversion* (1957)

———. *Hymns and Human Life* (2nd edn., 1959)

———. *I'll Praise My Maker* (1951)

———. *The Man for Others* (1964)

———. *The Music of Christian Hymnody, A Study of the development of the hymn tune since the Reformation with special reference to English Protestantism* (1957)
———. *Music Sacred and Profane* (1960)
———. *Twentieth Century Church Music* (1964)
Routley, E. R. and Parry, K. L. *Companion to Congregational Praise* (1953)
Rowntree, John Wilhelm. *Essays and Addresses* (1905)
Rowse, A. L. *The England of Elizabeth* (1950)
Rupp, E. Gordon. *The Righteousness of God* (1953) (Study of Luther's Theology)
Rushbrooke, J. H. (ed.). *The Faith of the Baptists* (1926)

Sales, St. François de. *Introduction to the Devout Life* (Engl. trans. by A. Ross, 1925)
———. *Spiritual Letters* (Engl. trans. Sidney Lear, 1892)
———. *Treatise on the Love of God* (Engl. trans. W. J. Knox Little, 1901)
Sampson, Ashley (ed.). *Famous English Sermons* (Edinburgh and London, 1940)
Sanders, E. K. *Angélique of Port Royal* (1905)
———. *Fénelon, His Friends and Enemies* (1901)
———. *St. Chantal* (1918)
———. *Vincent de Paul* (1913)
Sangster, Paul. *Doctor Sangster* (1962)
Sangster, W. E. *The Craft of the Sermon* (1954)
———. *The Path to Perfection* (1943)
———. *Westminster Sermons* (2 vols., 1960, 1961)
Sayers, Dorothy L. *The Man Born to be King* (1953, 1962)
———. *The Mind of the Maker* (1941)
Schweitzer, Albert. *The Quest of the Historical Jesus* (Engl. trans., 1910)
Selden, John. *Table Talk 1689* (ed. E. Arber, Birmingham, 1868)
Selwyn, E. G. *An Approach to Christianity* (1925)
——— (ed.). *Essays Catholic and Critical* (1926)
Shands, A. R. *The Liturgical Movement and the Local Church* (1959)
Shepherd, Massey H. *The Eucharist and Liturgical Renewal* (New York, 1961)
——— (ed.). *The Liturgical Renewal of the Church* (New York, 1960)
———. *The Living Liturgy* (New York, 1946)
———. *The Reform of Liturgical Worship: Perspectives and Prospects* (New York, 1961)
Sheppard, H. R. L. *The Human Parson* (1924)
———. *Some of My Religion* (New York, 1936)
Shewring, Walter (ed.). *The Letters of Eric Gill* (1947)
Short, E. H. *The House of God* (4th edn., 1955)
Shuster, G. N. *The Catholic Spirit in Modern English Literature* (1922)

Simpson, James B. *The Hundredth Archbishop of Canterbury* (Arthur Michael Ramsey) (New York and Evanston, 1962)

Simpson, P. Carnegie. *Church Principles* (1923)

———. *The Evangelical Church Catholic* (1934)

———. *Recollections* (1943)

Simpson, W. J. Sparrow. *The History of the Anglo-Catholic Revival from 1845* (1932)

Sixty Post-War Churches (Incorporated Church Building Society, 1957)

Skilbeck, Clement O. *Illustrations of the Liturgy* (1912)

Slack, Kenneth. *The British Churches Today* (1961)

Smith, C. Ryder. *The Sacramental Society* (1927)

Smith, G. E. Kidder. *The New Architecture of Europe* (Cleveland and New York, 1961)

Smith, George D. (ed.). *The Teaching of the Catholic Church, A Summary of Catholic Doctrine* (2nd edn., 1952)

Smith, H. Maynard, *Frank, Bishop of Zanzibar* (1926)

Smith, R. Gregor. *The New Man: Christianity and Man's Coming of Age* (1956)

Smith, Richard Mudie (ed.). *The Religious Life of London* (1904)

Smyth, Charles H. *The Art of Preaching; a Practical Survey of Preaching in the Church of England, 747-1939* (1953)

———. *C. F. Garbett* (1959)

Söderblom, Nathan, *The Living God, Basal Forms of Religion* (1933)

Songs of Praise (1925, enlarged 1931)

Studdert-Kennedy, G. A. *Lies!* (n.d.)

———. *Rough Rhymes of a Padre* (1918)

———. *Rough talks by a Padre delivered to Officers and Men of the B.E.F.* (1918)

Southcott, Ernest W. *The Parish Comes Alive* (1956)

Spence, Basil. *A Phoenix at Coventry: The Building of a Cathedral* (1962)

Spinks, G. Stephens *et al. Religion in Britain since 1900* (1952)

Srawley, J. H. *The Early History of the Liturgy* (1913; rev. edn., Cambridge, 1949)

———. *The Liturgical Movement* (1954)

Staley, Vernon. *The Ceremonial of the English Church* (2nd edn., Oxford, 1900)

——— (ed.). *Hierurgia Anglicana* (3 parts, new edn., 1902-1904)

Steere, Douglas V. *Prayer and Worship* (New York, 1938)

———. *Where Words Come From, An Interpretation of the Ground and Practice of Quaker Worship* (1955)

Stephen, Caroline. *Quaker Strongholds* (4th edn., 1907)

Steuart, Benedict. *The Development of Christian Worship* (1953)

Stibbs, A. M. *Sacrament, Sacrifice and Eucharist* (1961)

Stone, Darwell. *History of the Doctrine of the Holy Eucharist* (2 vols., 1910)

Stott, John R. W. *Basic Christianity* (1958)

———. *The Preacher's Portrait* (1962)

470

Stranks, C. J. *Anglican Devotion* (1961)
——— (ed.). *Theology and Life* (1958)
Summerson, John. *Heavenly Mansions* (1949)
Sundkler, B. *The Church of South India: The Movement Towards Union, 1900-1947* (1954)
Sweeney, James Johnson. *Henry Moore* (New York, 1946)
Sykes, John. *The Quakers, a new look at their place in society* (1958)

Taylor, A. E. *The Faith of a Moralist* (2 vols., 1931)
Taylor, Michael J. *The Protestant Liturgical Renewal: a Catholic Viewpoint* (Westminster, Maryland, 1962)
Taylor, J. R. S. *et al. Baptism and Confirmation* (1947)
Temple, William. *Christianity and the Social Order* (1942)
———. *Christus Veritas* (1924)
———. *The Church and its Teaching Today* (1936)
———. *The Hope of a New World* (1940)
———. *Mens Creatrix* (1917)
———. *Nature, Man and God* (1934)
———. *Personal Religion and the Life of Fellowship* (1926)
———. *Readings in St. John's Gospel* (2 vols., 1939, 1940)
———. *Studies in the Spirit and Truth of Christianity* (1917)
The Theology of Christian Initiation (1948) (Report of a Theological Commission "appointed by the Archbishops of Canterbury and York to advise on the relations between Baptism, Confirmation and Holy Communion")
Thomas, J. M. Lloyd. *A Free Catholic Church* (1907)
Thompson, A. Hamilton. *The Cathedral Churches of England* (1928)
Thompson, Bard (ed.). *Liturgies of the Western Church* (Cleveland and New York, 1961)
t'Hooft, W. A. Visser (ed.). *The Evanston Report* (1954)
——— (ed.). *The First Assembly of the World Council of Churches* (1949)
Thornton, Lionel S. *Christ and the Church* (1956)
———. *The Common Life in the Body of Christ* (1942)
———. *Confirmation Today* (1946)
———. *The Dominion of Christ* (1952)
———. *The Incarnate Lord* (1928)
———. *Revelation and the Modern World* (1950)
Thornton, Martin. *English Spirituality* (1963)
Thurian, Max. *Joie du Ciel sur la Terre* (Neuchâtel, 1946)
Tillich, Paul. *The Protestant Era* (Chicago, 1948)
———. *Systematic Theology* (Vol. III, Chicago, 1963)
Todd, James M. (ed.). *Prayers and Services for Christian Festivals* (1951)
Tolles, F. B. *Quakers and the Atlantic Culture* (New York, 1960)
Tomkins, Oliver S. (ed.). *The Third World Conference on Faith and Order* (1953) (Proceedings of the Lund Conference)
Torrance, Thomas F. *Conflict and Agreement in the Church* (2 vols., 1959-1960)

Torrance, Thomas F. *Eschatology and the Eucharist* (1952)
Townsend, H. *The Claims of the Free Churches* (1947)
Townsend, W. T., Workman, H. B. and Eayrs, G. (eds.). *A New History of Methodism* (3 vols., 1909)
Travers, Martin. *The Celebration of High Mass* (1922)
———. *Pictures of the English Liturgy—Low Mass* (1916)
Trethowan, Illtyd. *Certainty, philosophical and theological* (1948)
———. *Christ in the Liturgy* (1952)
———. *An Essay in Christian Philosophy* (1954)
Tribe, F., Rees, A. H. *et al. Worship, its Social Significance* (1939)

Underhill, Evelyn. *The Essentials of Mysticism and other Essays* (1920)
———. *Immanence* (1912)
———. *The Life of the Spirit and the Life of Today* (1922)
———. *The Mystery of the Sacrifice* (1938)
———. *Mysticism* (1911)
———. *The Mystics of the Church* (1925)
———. *Worship* (1936)
Underwood, A. C. *A History of the English Baptists* (1947)

Van der Leeuw, Gerhardus. *Religion in Essence and Manifestation* (1938)
———. *Sacred and Profane Beauty* (New York, 1963)
Vidler, A. R. *The Church in an Age of Revolution, 1789 to the present day* (Vol. 5, Pelican History of the Church, Harmondsworth and Baltimore, Maryland, 1961)
———. *The Modernist Movement in the Roman Church* (Cambridge, 1934)
——— (ed.). *Objections to Christian Belief* (1964)
——— (ed.). *Soundings, Essays concerning Christian Understanding* (Cambridge, 1962)
———. *Windsor Sermons* (1958)
Vine, C. H. (ed.). *The Old Faith and the New Theology* (1907)
Vogt, Von Ogden. *The Primacy of Worship* (Boston, Mass., 1958)
von Hügel, Friedrich. *Essays and Addresses in the Philosophy of Religion* (2 vols., 1921, 1928)
———. *Eternal Life* (1912)
———. *The Mystical Element in Religion as studied in St. Catherine of Genoa and her friends* (2 vols., 1908)
———. *The Reality of God* (1931)
———. *Selected Letters, 1896-1924* (ed. B. Holland, 1933)
Vonier, Anscar. *The Collected Works of Abbot Vonier* (Vol. II; The Church and the Sacraments, 1952)

Wakefield, Gordon S. *Puritan Devotion, its place in the development of Christian piety* (1957)
Walsh, Chad. *C. S. Lewis, Apostle to the Skeptics* (New York, 1949)
Walton, Robert C. *The Gathered Community* (1946)

Wand, J. W. C. *A History of the Modern Church from 1500 to the Present Day* (1946)
Ward, Maisie. *Gilbert Keith Chesterton* (1944)
Ward, Marcus. *The Pilgrim Church* (1953)
Warschauer, J. *The New Evangel* (1907)
Watkin, E. I. *Catholic Art and Culture* (rev. edn., 1947)
———. *Roman Catholicism in England from the Reformation to 1950* (1957)
Watson, Philip S. *Let God be God* (1947) (Study of Luther's thought)
Waugh, Evelyn. *The Life of the Right Reverend Ronald Knox . . .* (1959)
Weales, Gerald. *Religion in Modern English Drama* (Philadelphia, 1961)
Wearmouth, R. F. *The Social and Political Influence of Methodism in the 20th Century* (1957)
Weatherhead, Leslie D. *In Quest of a Kingdom* (1943)
———. *The Key Next Door* (1960)
———. *Over His Own Signature* (1955)
———. *Personalities of the Passion* (1942)
———. *The Plain Man Looks at the Cross* (1945)
———. *Psychology in Service of the Soul* (1929)
———. *Psychology, Religion, and Healing* (1951)
———. *The Significance of Silence* (1945)
———. *That Immortal Sea* (1953)
Webb, C. C. J. *Religion and the Thought of Today* (1929)
———. *Religious Thought in England since 1850* (1933)
Webb, Geoffrey. *The Liturgical Altar* (1939)
Weinbach, Werner. *Der Barok als Kunst der Gegen Reformation* (Berlin, 1921)
Weltkirchen Lexikon Handbuch der Oekumene (Stuttgart, 1959)
Westbrook, F. B. *The Holy Communion Service* (1959)
Westminster Hymnal (rev. edn., 1940) (Official hymnbook of the Roman Catholic Church in Great Britain)
Weyres, Willy; Bartnung, Otto *et al. Kirchen: Handbuch fur den Kirchenbau* (Munich, 1959)
Whale, John Selden. *Christian Doctrine* (Cambridge, 1941)
———. *The Protestant Tradition* (Cambridge, 1955)
———. *Victor and Victim* (Cambridge, 1960)
———. *What is a Living Church?* (1937)
White, James F. *The Cambridge Movement: The Ecclesiologists and the Gothic Revival* (Cambridge, 1962)
Whitehead, A. N. *Science and the Modern World* (Cambridge, 1926)
Whitham, A. E. *The Catholic Christ* (1940)
———. *The Culture and Discipline of the Spiritual Life* (1938)
———. *The Pastures of His Presence* (1939)
Whitley, W. T. *A History of British Baptists* (1923)
Who's Who in Art (12th edn., Eastbourne, 1962)
Wickham, E. R. *Church and People in an Industrial City* (1957)
Wigan, Bernard (ed.). *The Liturgy in English* (1962)

Wilkinson, W. C. *Modern Masters of Pulpit Discourse* (London and New York, 1905)

Williams, Charles. *The Descent of the Dove* (1949)

——— (ed.). *The English Poems of John Milton* (see intro. essay of the World's Classics edn., 1940)

Williams, Daniel Day. *Interpreting Theology, 1918-1952* (1953; see also rev. edn., New York, 1959, entitled, *What Present-day Theologians are Thinking*)

Williams, N. P. and Harris, C. (eds.). *Northern Catholicism, Centenary Studies in the Oxford and Parallel Movements* (1933)

Williams, R. R. *Authority in the Apostolic Age* (1950)

Williams, T. Rhondda. *The New Theology—An Exposition* (1907)

Williams, U. Vaughan and Holst, I. *Heirs and Rebels* (1959)

Wilson, Gladys. *Quaker Worship* (1952)

Witte, Robert. *Das Katholische Gotteshaus* (Mainz, 1951)

Wood, H. G. *Belief and Unbelief since 1850* (Cambridge, 1955)

Woodforde, Christopher. *English Stained and Painted Glass* (1954)

Woodgate, M. V. *Father Benson of Cowley* (1953)

Woodward, G. R. (ed.). *Songs of Syon* (3rd edn., 1910)

Woolman, John. *Journal and Essays* (ed. A. M. Gummere, 1922)

Worship and Ministry (1899) (The Epistle of the Yearly Meeting of the English Society of Friends)

Wotherspoon, H. J. *The Religious Value of the Sacraments* (Edinburgh, 1928)

Wyon, Olive. *Living Springs, New Religious Movements in Europe* (1963)

INDEX

479

WORSHIP AND THEOLOGY IN ENGLAND

VI. *Crisis and Creativity,*
1965–Present

CONTENTS

CONTENTS

ACKNOWLEDGMENTS

A RECENT ERUDITE BOOK by Professor B. A. Gerrish on Calvin's eucharistic theology bore the title *Grace and Gratitude*. This title admirably expresses my own gratitude for the grace shown by so many liturgical scholars to myself in interviews or letters. During a visit to England in June 1993 I was able to interview several Anglican clergymen, two of whom were members of the Liturgical Commission, namely, the Revd. Brian D. Spinks, Chaplain of Churchill College, Cambridge, and University Lecturer in Liturgics; and the Revd. Canon Kenneth Stevenson, Rector of Holy Trinity and St. Mary, Guildford, formerly Lecturer in Liturgics in Manchester University. I also received a useful bibliographical letter from the Right Revd. David Stancliffe, Bishop of Salisbury, also a member of the Liturgical Commission. Another helpful interview of ecumenical import was given me by the Revd. Canon Donald Gray, Rector of St. Margaret's and Canon of Westminster, who is the Chairman of the Joint Liturgical Group. The Revd. Canon Martin Reardon, General Secretary of *Churches Together in England*, also provided useful ecumenical information in a letter. I also received a letter and a most useful enclosure of a catalogue, *Images of Christ*, of which he was the editor, from the Revd. Tom Devonshire Jones, prepared for an exhibition of art in Northampton and St. Paul's Cathedral, London, in 1993.

Monsignor J. D. Crichton, author of several widely read volumes on the recent history of revised Roman Catholic worship, gave me a long interview in his retirement home in Pershore, Worcestershire. The Bishop of Diokleia, His Grace Kallistos (Ware), who is also Spalding Lecturer at Oxford University, sent me a letter on the present status of the Eastern Orthodox Churches in England.

Free Church leaders also gave me valuable advice on their forms of worship in interviews. For Methodist worship I was able to obtain information from the Revd. A. Raymond George, former President of the Methodist Conference, former Moderator of the Free Church Federal Council, and former Chairman of the Joint Liturgical Group. For the worship of the United Reformed Church I had interviews with Dr. David Thompson, Fellow of Fitzwilliam College in Cambridge, and University Lecturer in History, who is the Convenor of the Doctrine and Worship Committee of the United Reformed

Church, and with the Revd. Charles Brock, Chaplain and Fellow of Mansfield College, Oxford. For Baptist worship I was indebted to interviews with the Revd. David Coffey, General Secretary of the Baptist Church at Baptist House, Didcot, and the Revd. Robert Ellis of Bristol.

In addition, I wish to thank the American Philosophical Society of Philadelphia for a generous grant that helped to finance my series of interviews in England in June of 1993, without which it would have been impossible to obtain up-to-date information on the varieties of Christian worship in England as supplementation to my reading.

It is also my privilege to thank my brother and sister-in-law, Dorian and Joan Davies of Woking, and my brother-in-law and sister, Michael and Gloria Scott, for their hospitality during part of my visit.

Marvels still occur, as I have gratefully found, in that the work of over twenty years of liturgical research resulting in six consecutive historical volumes (the last one alone is new) is being re-issued by my generous publisher and friend, Bill Eerdmans, Jr., after a period of from three and a half to two decades since they first appeared in print.

As always, it is a privilege to thank my wife Helen for her editorial and photographic help. I am grateful for much grace, both divine and human.

HORTON DAVIES
Princeton University

INTRODUCTION

THIS VOLUME, sixth in a series, analyzes the development of worship and the theology underlying it in the major Christian denominations of England and also provides a brief account of the hymnody, music, and architecture and art of the contemporary English churches. It is peculiarly difficult for a historian to assess current trends because what seems important may only be a will-of-the-wisp, and what is thought to be only a passing fad may in fact be a promising development.

This particular book has been one of the most taxing to write because, although attendance at divine worship has dropped significantly, the liturgical and hymnodic experiments have been both creative and manifold. Indeed, far more liturgies have been produced in the past three decades than in almost two thousand years of Christian history. The prodigality of the new hymnody has been repeatedly described in terms of an "explosion" of creativity.

The story begins with an account of the present impact on worship of two profound movements, the Modern Liturgical Movement, which began in Solesmes Abbey in France a century and a half ago, and the Ecumenical Movement for the reunion of the divided Churches, which is about half as old. Together they are transforming Christian worship so that Protestant worship seems more Catholic, and Catholic worship since the Second Vatican Council looks more Protestant, the structure of both reflecting an emphasis on *Word* and *Table*.

Chapter II turns to "The Theology of Initiation," which has been the subject of considerable discussion in our period. The Roman Catholic Church has concluded that in the present post-Constantinian situation, where secularism flourishes, Adult rather than Infant Baptism should be considered the norm, while Infant Baptism is offered to believing parents for children that they promise to bring up as Christians. The historical precedents and the arguments for both Infant and Believers' Baptism are considered. It is seen that the climax of initiation into the Body of Christ is the Eucharist or Lord's Supper.

Hence Chapter III considers "The Theology of the Eucharist," detailing the growing convergence in its interpretation across denominational frontiers. The older interpretations stressed the Cross almost exclusively, while the newer interpretations concentrate on the Incarnation, Resurrection, Ascension, and heavenly Intercession of Christ, and the Christian hope of sharing in the eschatological banquet. Other new interests are also expressed, including the demands of social justice, so that all may share bread, and also ecological responsibility.

Chapter IV analyzes "Baptism and Eucharist in the Worship of the Church of England," with citations from its liturgies. Chapter V analyzes "Baptism and Eucharist in Roman Catholic and Eastern Orthodox Worship" and also provides excerpts from their liturgies. Chapter VI analyzes "Baptism and Eucharist in the English Free Churches" — that is, in the worship of the Methodist Church, the United Reformed Church (a union of former Congregationalists, former Presbyterians, and former Disciples of Christ), and the Baptist Union of Churches, with citations from prayers.

Chapter VII is concerned with "Occasional Services." This comprises Marriages, Funerals (Burials and Cremations), and Ordinations in all the denominations mentioned in Chapters IV, V, and VI.

"The Linguistic Controversy" discussed in Chapter VIII has a double focus. One is the heated debate over gender inclusive language as an alternative to traditional religious language with its masculine bias. The second focus, also debated acrimoniously, is the issue dividing conservatives who want to keep the liturgical language of the Book of Common Prayer of 1662 and those who argue for "You" rather than "Thou" language in addressing God.

Chapter IX deals with the issue of liturgical symbolism. Church architecture is the major concern of Chapter X, which includes also a short postscript on church art. In our visual, television age the Church needs far more distinguished religious art than it has received. Chapter XI deals at length with the extraordinary eruption of creative hymnody and, briefly, with church music.

The developments in three decades from 1965 to 1995 herald a great promise for the worship of the Christian Churches at the beginning of the Second Christian Millennium.

CHAPTER I

LITURGICAL ECUMENISM IN THEORY AND PRACTICE

S INCE THE ESTABLISHMENT of the World Council of Churches in 1948, liturgical ecumenism has had a significant impact on English worship. How significant, this chapter hopes to determine. That is why the issue will be discussed in terms of both theory and practice. The theory is outlined clearly in the important statements on *Modern Eucharistic Agreement* published under that title in 1973 by the S.P.C.K. in London, which involved all the main confessional traditions — Roman Catholic, Lutheran, Anglican, and Reformed — and discussed also in other volumes. It is not as easy to determine practice, but there are important pointers,[1] in the general approximation of Churches to each other in recent decades, in the important contributions of the British Joint Liturgical Group to liturgical ecumenism, and in the mutual understanding increasingly witnessed in the vigorous "Local Ecumenical Projects" throughout Britain. Even so, on the pragmatic side, there are still difficulties in assessing the extent of liturgical practice in denominations like the Methodists or the United Reformed Church, for example, for whom a service book is optional, but who rely on one heavily for the sacraments of Baptism and the Lord's Supper. A further difficulty has been stressed by Susan J. White in the reminder that there are a billion television sets currently in operation throughout the world, that "televangelism" is beaming individualistic evangelical services into almost every home, and that this approach is counter to the ecumenical appreciation of corporate worship.[2] A further complica-

---

1. One admirable example is *Baptism and Eucharist: Ecumenical Convergence in Celebration,* edited by Max Thurian and Geoffrey Wainwright, and published jointly by the World Council of Churches, Geneva, and Wm. B. Eerdmans, Grand Rapids, U.S.A., in 1983.

2. See Susan J. White's chapter, "Christian Worship since the Reformation," in P. F. Bradshaw and L. A. Hoffman, *The Changing Face of Jewish and Christian Worship in North America* (Notre Dame: University of Notre Dame Press, 1991), pp. 201-2.

tion is that the charismatic movement can often modify worship even in traditional churches regularly using service books.

If we are to acknowledge the obvious examples of liturgical ecumenism, even if we cannot determine how deeply they have affected every denomination, then the following might be a fair summary of how things seem. Most striking of all is the general sense of the growing importance of a Sunday service incorporating the Word of God in Sermon and the Action of God in the Eucharist. The Roman Catholic Church now insists upon a sermon in the Mass, and the Protestant Churches, which used to regard the Communion as an extra for the pious to be used perhaps once a month or even once a quarter, now emphasize the importance of frequent and regular participation in the Eucharist for the building up of the Body of Christ. And, as we shall see in our study of the eucharistic agreement, denominations have been tutored by the ecumenical movement to interpret the eucharistic rites as combining the contemporary significance of the Christic memorial and its eschatological dimension, and to see the Holy Spirit as the agent of transformation of both the elements and those receiving them in faith.[3]

In the second place, Protestants and Catholics are coming closer together in their expository sermons. Protestants generally have given up their penchant for topical sermons and are more willing to be guided by the far more regularly used lectionaries, such as *The Common Lectionary*. All ministers have been constrained by the impact of this volume to be more thoughtful about the way they make use of Scripture in worship and how they select their texts for reading and preaching. Furthermore, many colleagues in the local ministry, but of different denominations, using the same lectionary, have found community in studying for their sermons. For Roman Catholics there has been a simplification of the Christian Year so that the christological cycle has been emphasized and the sanctoral cycle de-emphasized except for major saints. Protestants have until recently tended to devalue the Christian Year so that commonly only the evangelical feast days of Christmas, Good Friday, Easter, and Pentecost remained; and to these were added civil or denominational celebrations

---

3. I have analyzed the chief ecumenical understandings of theology of the Eucharist in *Bread of Life and Cup of Joy: Newer Ecumenical Perspectives on the Eucharist* (Grand Rapids: Wm. B. Eerdmans; Leominster, England: Gracewing, 1993).

2

which often secularized worship. There is little doubt that the *Common Lectionary* has helped to recover the Christian Year as an annual cycle in which the weekly recurrence of the Lord's Day commemoration occurs, resulting in the celebration of Christ in time. Hence Christ's Incarnation is celebrated in Advent, Christmas, and Epiphany; his Passion, Death, and Resurrection from Lent through Easter; and the continuing presence of Christ affirmed in the Church at Pentecost until he comes again in Advent.

In the third place, Protestants have recovered the sacraments as an integral component of worship on the Lord's Day, thus enhancing their typically Word-oriented worship. Increasingly Baptism is seen as the sacrament of inclusion in the Body of Christ, and parents are no longer allowed to regard this as merely a private family practice, since both parents and godparents are increasingly required to make a public promise to educate their children as Christians in the context of Sunday worship. A movement towards a weekly celebration of the Eucharist is also becoming more common among Methodist and Reformed congregations.

Fourthly, there is a far greater recognition in Protestant and Anglican worship of the role of the congregation, both in providing responsive prayers, and in the importance of the Peace passed from the minister to individuals and thence to others. In addition, it is now common to see lay folk reading the Scripture lessons and assisting in Communion services both by bringing up the bread and wine and monetary offerings to the Table and by delivering the sacrament to recipients. The Roman Catholic Church is recognizing the laity most obviously by allowing worship in the vernacular tongue, by incorporating many responsive prayers and acclamations, and by the use of hymns. Protestants, who have valued hymns since Martin Luther composed them in the sixteenth century, are now being taught new ways in which to sing the Psalms, either in metrical psalmody, or in antiphonal response to a choir or soloist.

In the fifth place, a radical change has been seen in Anglican and Protestant worship with respect to recognition of the role of women, whether they serve as ordained ministers, liturgists, or lay-readers. This has had two benefits: emphasizing in dramatic fashion the importance of the priesthood of all believers, and also sensitizing the Church to the language it uses about God and how it addresses humanity. Gender exclusive language is on the way out in worship, as also is language that demeans ethnic minorities or is militaristic

3

in character. While there are keen supporters even among the priests for the admission of women to the Catholic priesthood, this revolution does not yet seem on the horizon.

Sixthly, there has been an explosion not only of new hymnody, much of it creative in character (as in the hymns produced by Sydney Carter, Fred Pratt Green, Fred Kaan, and Brian Wren), but also of new liturgies, in which different denominations have looked beyond their own borders, and sometimes even shocked their congregations by introducing contemporary language in place of the "thee/thou" utterances of centuries past.

In the seventh place, there has been an increasing recognition of the importance of children in worship, and Catholic Eucharists as well as Protestant services have been devised to seem more relevant to youngsters.

In the eighth place, verbal communication has been increasingly supplemented in Protestant worship by the use of symbolism,[4] by the incorporation of film, drama, and occasional dancing, as well as by processions and banners. Roman Catholic and Anglican worship are already supplied with vivid symbolism.

But this very general account of transdenominational borrowings and ecumenical changes in worship needs to be augmented by actual theological agreements between denominations to which we now turn.

Liturgical Ecumenism in Theory

The book *Modern Eucharistic Agreement* (1973) includes the texts of a remarkable series of transdenominational agreements on the understanding of the Eucharist. The first of these is *The Eucharist: A Lutheran-Roman Catholic Statement.* It has two parts,[5] including "The Eucharist as Sacrifice" and "The Presence of Christ in the Lord's Supper." Both Churches assert the once-for-all character and com-

---

4. See chapter IX in the present volume.
5. The entire document is reprinted in *Modern Eucharistic Agreement* (London: S.P.C.K., 1973), on pp. 33-49. A valuable commentary on the same theme is John Reumann's *The Supper of the Lord* (Philadelphia: Fortress Press, 1985), which considers New Testament origins, ecumenical dialogues, as well as Faith and Order consideration of the Eucharist.

pleteness of the sacrifice on the cross, and both refute a superficial memorialism, insisting that the Eucharist is related to the one sacrifice not by a human recollection of past events, but by a divine re-presenting, through the Holy Spirit, of these events through which the worshippers participate in Christ. The Lutherans reject the dogma of transubstantiation as "a rational attempt to explain the mystery," as also any suggestion of a physical or chemical change, but acknowledge that the Roman dogma "intends to affirm both Christ's presence and the change that has taken place." Those who frame the document conclude:

> It can thus be seen that there is agreement on the "that," the full reality of Christ's presence. What has been disputed is a particular way of stating the "how," the manner in which he becomes present.

A second document printed in the same volume, *Modern Eucharistic Agreement*, is the *Dombes Statement*.[6] The Dombes group was founded in 1937 by the Abbé Paul Couturier, with a French Reformed and Roman Catholic membership. The title of their publication in translation is *Towards a Common Eucharistic Faith? Agreement between Catholics and Protestants*. This includes a "Doctrinal Agreement" and a "Pastoral Agreement." Essentially it is an attempt by members of both sides to share with gratitude the essential gift of Christ in allowing us to share in his being and his life in the sacramental mystery of the Church.

A third document reprinted in the same volume is the important World Council of Churches Statement, *The Eucharist in Ecumenical Thought*, which was produced by the Faith and Order Commission of the World Council of Churches held at Louvain in August 1971.[7] There is a strong family likeness between the Dombes and the World Council Statements. Both insist upon the necessity of faith, although also maintaining that the presence of Christ at the Eucharist does not depend on the faith of the individual, since it is Christ who binds himself in his words and in the Holy Spirit to the sacramental act, which is the sign of the giving of his presence. Both groups also insist on the relation of the Eucharist to the mission of the Church and on the eschatological context of the Eucharist.

6. *Modern Eucharistic Agreement*, pp. 51-78.
7. *Ibid.*, pp. 79-89.

Also included in the book is *An Agreed Statement on Eucharistic Doctrine* coming from the Anglican–Roman Catholic International Commission and issued from Windsor in 1971.[8] The Statement begins by asserting the mystery of the Eucharist — a theme which has been central in the continental Liturgical Movement, emanating originally from the Benedictine Abbey of Maria Laach. It continues with a section on the Eucharist and the Sacrifice of Christ. Here it asserts:

> Christ's redeeming death and resurrection took place once and for all in history. Christ's death on the cross, the culmination of his whole life of obedience, was the one, perfect and sufficient sacrifice for the sins of the world. There can be no repetition of or addition to what was then accomplished once and for all by Christ. Any attempt to establish a nexus between the sacrifice of Christ and the eucharist must not obscure this fundamental fact of the Christian faith. Yet God has given the eucharist to his Church as a means through which the atoning work of Christ on the cross is proclaimed and made effective in the life of the Church. The notion of *memorial* as understood in the passover celebration at the time of Christ — i.e., the making effective in the present of an event in the past — has opened the way to clearer understanding of the relationship between Christ's sacrifice and the eucharist. The eucharistic memorial is no mere calling to mind of a past event or of its significance, but the Church's effectual proclamation of God's mighty acts. Christ instituted the eucharist as a memorial *(anamnesis)* of the totality of God's reconciling action in him. In the eucharistic prayer the Church continues to make a perpetual memorial of Christ's death; and his members, united with God and one another, give thanks for all his mercies, entreat the benefits of his passion on behalf of the whole Church, participate in these benefits, and enter into the movement of his self-offering.[9]

The *Agreed Statement* also expresses that "the elements are not mere signs; Christ's body and blood become really present and are really given." The reference to the consecratory prayer shows the modern understanding of its meaning:

8. *Ibid.*, pp. 82-89.
9. *Ibid.*, pp. 27-28.

According to the traditional order of the liturgy the consecratory prayer *(anaphora)* leads to the communion of the faithful. Through this prayer of thanksgiving, a word of faith addressed to the Father, the bread and wine become the body and blood of Christ by the action of the Holy Spirit, so that in communion we eat the flesh of Christ and drink his blood.[10]

It concludes by emphasizing the eschatological meaning of the Holy Communion:

The Lord who thus comes to his people in the power of the Holy Spirit is the Lord of Glory. In the eucharistic celebration we anticipate the joys of the age to come. By the transforming action of the Spirit of God, earthly bread and wine become the heavenly manna and the new wine, the eschatological banquet of the new man: elements of the first creation become pledges and first fruits of the new heaven and the new earth.[11]

At the end also the participants express the hope that "in view of the agreement which we have reached on eucharistic faith, this doctrine will no longer constitute an obstacle to the unity we seek."[12]

Liturgical Ecumenism in Practice

In this section of this chapter we shall consider the constituent members and, in greater detail, the literary contributions of the Joint Liturgical Group.[13] We shall also examine the workings of the Local Ecumenical Projects.

The British Joint Liturgical Group was founded in 1963 on the initiative of Canon Ronald C. D. Jasper in response to the invitation of Archbishop Ramsey to liturgists from all the mainstream Churches in Great Britain. It began under the chairmanship of a historian of

10. *Ibid.,* p. 29.
11. *Ibid.*
12. *Ibid.*
13. In considering the publications of the Joint Liturgical Group I am greatly indebted to an interview I had with its present Chairman, the Revd. Canon Donald Gray of Westminster Abbey and Rector of St. Margaret's, Westminster, on June 29, 1993, in his study at 1, Little Cloister.

the Book of Common Prayer, the Very Revd. Douglas Harrison, the Dean of Bristol Cathedral. Subsequently the Joint Liturgical Group produced a series of books and booklets which had a significant impact on the Churches of the English-speaking world and in one case even on the calendar planning of the Roman Catholic Church.

Its members at the time of writing include Canon Donald Gray, (Chairman) and the Revd. M. R. Vasey representing the Church of England, the Revds. C. Robertson and A. Scobie representing the Church of Scotland, the Revds. Neville Clark and P. Sheppy representing the Baptist Church of Great Britain and Ireland, the Revds. Dr. Colin Thompson and Susan Durber representing the United Reformed Church, the Revd. Canon Dr. Gianfranco Tellini representing the Scottish Episcopal Church, the Revds. A. Raymond George and Dr. Gordon S. Wakefield representing the Methodist Church, the Revd. P. M. Gallacher and Dr. Donald Whitney representing the Roman Catholic Church, the Revd. E. Greer representing the Fellowship of the Churches of Christ, and the Revd. D. Thomas representing the Church in Wales.[14]

Canon Gray insisted in my interview with him how profoundly involved Ronald Jasper had been with the development of the Joint Liturgical Group and, indeed, with the history of worship of the Church of England and the development of the Church of England's newer rites. He was Secretary of the Joint Liturgical Group from its foundation until his retirement in 1984, and had been Chairman of the Church of England's Liturgical Commission from 1964 to 1981, as well as being an official observer to the *Concilium Liturgicum* which was established to work out the implications of the Second Vatican Council's Constitution on the Sacred Liturgy. In 1969 he was also elected President of the *Societas Liturgica*, the international ecumenical society for liturgical study and research. He was also fully engaged in the revision of the liturgy of the Church of England, resulting in the *Alternative Service Book* of 1980. Canon Donald Gray has written of him: "It is given to few people in the history of the Church of England to have an effect on the day-to-day life of every parish. The 'public face' of any church is its worship and under Jasper's leadership major changes were made. . . ." He adds that Jasper (who became Dean of York) courageously led change "from a historian's knowledge

---

14. The list appears on p. 2 of the J.L.G.'s *A Four Year Lectionary* (Norwich: Canterbury Press, 1990).

of its inevitability and from a liturgist's appreciation of modern scholarship, never forgetting his ministry in the pit-villages of Durham and never allowing the Church's worship to become recherché."[15] A man of such learning and empathy was admirably suited to have guided the J.L.G. through most of its history.

The first product of the J.L.G. was a series of essays on the contemporary understanding of worship, *The Renewal of Worship* (1965), which included essays by Jasper (the Editor), R. D. Whitehorn of the Presbyterian Church of England, J. A. Lamb of the Church of Scotland, S. F. Winward, who as a Baptist wrote a remarkable essay on "embodied Worship" showing how excessively word-dominated much of Protestant worship had become, John Huxtable (Congregationalist), Rupert Davies (Methodist), and R. Aled Davies (Presbyterian Church of England). Jasper's introduction cited a paragraph from the Report of the Faith and Order Conference in Montreal in 1963 as expressing briefly the convictions of the Joint Liturgical Group: "It is heartening to realize that, at a time when Christians are perhaps more aware of the tragic estrangement of the world from the Church, God is so plainly calling us to rediscover together the joy, the depth and the power of Christian Worship."

The second publication of the Group was its *Calendar and Lectionary* of 1967, also published by the Oxford University Press, which included significant essays by the Baptist liturgiologist, Neville Clark. It provided a thematic selection of the Scriptures, three for each Sunday, to be used in ordinary time in the Church Year. This two-year lectionary was adopted by both the Methodists and the Church of Scotland. Its impact on Sunday Schools and other programs was considerable, and would have been greater had Vatican II not committed itself to a three-year lectionary.

Two years later *An Additional Lectionary* was prepared for use at a second Sunday service. It maintained the structure of the earlier book but provided two lections, Old Testament and New Testament. The lections on an average were about 25 verses, and overlap between the two lectionaries was avoided. The importance of these lectionaries is that the thematic approach headed Protestant ministers away from

---

15. This information is contained in *The Dictionary of National Biography, 1968-1989*, ed. C. S. Nicholls (Oxford University Press), in Canon Gray's biography of Jasper.

9

topical and towards exegetical sermons, and presented successively the major themes of the Gospels.

The third production of the Group was *The Daily Office,* jointly published by the S.P.C.K. and the Epworth Press. The introduction was by Stephen Winward, an outstandingly creative Baptist minister. It was a widely purchased book, and filled a gap in Free Church worship, as well as providing a moderate modification of the Prayer Book. Indeed, it became the basis for the Shorter Office in the *Alternative Service Book 1980.* Its defect was, according to Anglican critics, that it had too much Scripture and not enough prayers.

In 1971 there appeared *Holy Week Services,* again edited by Jasper, but with an introduction by the Methodist worship expert, Gordon Wakefield. These services were thematic in character, in which Monday emphasized Penitence; Tuesday, Obedience; and Wednesday, Service. The Thursday service (with a Eucharist) stressed "A New Commandment"; Friday, the Crucifixion; and Saturday consisted of the Vigil of Easter, preceding the Lighting of the Fire or the Candle. These services were revised in 1983 "with flesh added to the bones," according to Canon Gray.

The fifth production of the Joint Liturgical Group was *Initiation and the Eucharist: Essays on their Structure,* published by the S.P.C.K. in 1972. The importance of this book was that it challenged Gregory Dix's long-accepted four-fold structure of the Eucharist. It was a reminder that the Scriptural basis of the Eucharist was seven-fold, and this itself was simply reducible to a two-fold structure since the first and third actions are purely pragmatic, as we "take" to "bless" and "break" to "share." The essentials clearly were Thanksgiving and Communion. This view influenced the *Alternative Service Book.*

1975 saw the publication of the sixth volume, *Worship and the Child,* also published by the S.P.C.K. This dealt with a major problem within the Anglican Church — whether the child who approached the altar rail at the Eucharist should be sent away. The decision was that blessing at the altar rail was better than mere refusal of the consecrated elements. This volume also recognized that the child was, after Baptism, a member of the Church and that at seven or thereabouts had enough sense both of wonder and of meaning to receive the Eucharist.

The seventh production was *The Daily Office Revised with other Prayers and Services,* again published by the S.P.C.K., and with an introduction by Gordon Wakefield. This book contained, besides the revised Daily Office, the following services: a Eucharistic Canon, suitable on ecumenical occasions; a Cycle of Intercessions for the Mission of the Church; and Prayers for Various Occasions, including Baptisms, Weddings, and Funerals. The latter included rites for the Interment of Ashes, and for the Funeral of a Child.

To produce an anaphora of profound depth and simplicity that would be accepted by all the Churches represented in the Joint Liturgical Group was a splendid achievement. Its contemporary relevance is emphasized in the dominant use of the present tense and also in its incorporation of the *Sanctus* with its introduction from the *Te Deum*. It warrants full citation:

> Almighty God, Eternal Father,
> it is our duty and delight
> at all times and in all places
> to give you thanks and praise.
> You are the creator of all things
> and the source of all life,
> in whom we live and move and have our being.
> You have given us your only Son, Jesus Christ,
> to free us from the slavery of sin
> and to make us heirs of eternal life.
> He was born as one of us,
> was obedient to your will,
> and accepted death upon the cross:
> you raised him from the dead
> and have made him Lord of all.
> You send us your Spirit
> to guide us into truth,
> to bring us reconciliation and peace,
> and to renew us as the Body of your Son.
> (And now we give you thanks . . .)
> We praise you, for you are God.
>
> All: *We acclaim you for you are the Lord.*
> *We worship you, eternal Father:*
> *and with the whole company of heaven*
> *we sing in endless praise:*
> *Holy, holy, holy Lord,*

God of power and might.
Heaven and earth are full of your glory.
Hosanna in the highest.
Blessed is he who comes in the name of the Lord.
Hosanna in the highest
Heavenly Father,
we offer you this praise
through Jesus Christ, your only Son, our Lord,
who hallowed your name,
accomplished your will,
established your kingdom,
and gave himself to be our spiritual food.
And now we pray that by the power of your Holy Spirit
these gifts of bread and wine
may be to us his body and his blood.
For on the night when he was betrayed
he took bread, and when he had given thanks,
he broke it and said,
"Take, eat: this is my body which is for you.
Do this in remembrance of me."
In the same way after supper, he took the cup, saying,
"This cup is the new covenant in my blood.
Do this as often as you drink it,
in remembrance of me."
Therefore heavenly Father,
obeying the command of your dear Son,
and looking for his coming again in glory,
we celebrate the perfect sacrifice of his death
upon the cross,
his mighty resurrection and his glorious ascension.

All: *Christ is Victor.*
Christ is King.
Christ is Lord of all.
Father, accept through Christ
our sacrifice of thanks and praise:
and as we eat and drink these holy gifts,
kindle in us the fire of your Spirit
that with the whole Church on earth and in heaven
we may be made one in him.

12

Count us worthy
to stand before you as your people
and to offer without ceasing our adoration and service,
through Jesus Christ our Lord.
Through him, with him and in him,
in the unity of the Holy Spirit,
all honour and glory are yours, Father Almighty,
now and for ever.

All: Amen

The eighth production was reminiscent of the first. Its title was *Getting the Liturgy Right. Practical Liturgical Principles for Today* (S.P.C.K., 1982). It was concerned with the following topics: The Setting of Worship; The Bible and Liturgy; The Content of Preaching; Vocal Parts of Worship; Music and Worship; Silence in Worship; Movement and Drama in Worship; Family Services, and Special Services.

Production number 9 was *Holy Week Revised*, a revision of the previous book on this theme, *Holy Week Services*, issued in 1971.

The next book to appear from the J.L.G. was *The Word in Season. The Use of the Bible in Liturgy*, published by the Canterbury Press, Norwich. The Introduction was by Canon Donald Gray under the title, "Introduction to a Debate." It pointed out how extraordinarily influential had been the J.L.G.'s 1967 *Calendar and Lectionary*, which was used with a few minor modifications in the Anglican *Alternative Service Book 1980*, *The Methodist Service Book* of 1975, The United Reformed Church's *Book of Services* (1980), and The Church of Scotland's *Book of Common Order* (1979). In addition, a number of Provinces of the Anglican Communion also included it in their official worship publications. It is also worth mentioning that the J.L.G. became vitally involved with the English Language Liturgical Consultation, whose Consultation on Common Texts revised the *Common Lectionary. The Revised Common Lectionary* (1992), including the J.L.G. contribution, is used by no less than sixteen Protestant Churches.

The twelfth expression of the work of the Joint Liturgical Group appeared under the Epworth imprint in 1988 under the title *Praying Together*. This also was a joint production of the J.L.G. along with the English Language Liturgical Consultation. Its importance is that its prayers all model inclusive language.

13

1990 saw the publication of *Singing the Faith* (Canterbury Press, Norwich), edited by Charles Robertson of the Church of Scotland; it contains also an article on English art by Dr. Colin Thompson of the United Reformed Church.

In the same year appeared *The Four Year Lectionary,* which, on a trial basis, included regular readings from the Fourth Gospel (as well as the three Synoptic Gospels). Methodists are using this lectionary on an experimental basis, and in a joint essay A. Raymond George (Methodist) and Neville Clark (Baptist) argue that some themes in John's gospel are, if not concealed, at least difficult to discern.

In my very fruitful interview with Canon Gray, in which so much information on the history of the Joint Liturgical Group was provided, I asked him if there had been any impact of American worship on English liturgy. He observed: "Kenneth Stevenson admires the Book of Common Prayer of the Episcopal Church of the U.S.A. because it has *one shape* with variable prayers, whereas the *Alternative Service Book 1980* has *three* shapes with variable prayers and this is more confusing!"

It is manifestly clear that the Joint Liturgical Group in its essays and in its liturgical writings has dealt with the major needs in worship during its existence and filled these gaps admirably. Its cross-denominational approach — evident in its writings and in its members, who have contributed to the liturgical revisions in their own denominations — has made a very significant contribution to liturgical ecumenism.

The same, I believe, will be found to be true of the contributions to liturgical unity made by the growing numbers of Local Ecumenical Projects,[16] although because of their differing denominational links at the local level this impact is difficult to trace. But the fact that Churches with differing denominational worship practices are sharing worship and thus becoming increasingly familiar with the worship of other congregations must, inevitably, lead to wider liturgical unity.

Using the *Register of Local Ecumenical Projects and Sponsoring Bodies* compiled by "Churches Together in England" for 1992, an attempt

---

16. For information on Local Ecumenical Projects I am indebted to Canon Martin Reardon, the General Secretary of "Churches Together in England," for a useful letter dated 23 September 1993, and for an up-to-date *Register of Local Ecumenical Projects and Sponsoring Bodies* prepared by his organization.

will be made to estimate the impact of these local initiatives on a more unitive worship. The *Register* lists the sponsoring bodies in almost every city, town, and village in England, with the date of formation, the depth of association as determined by whether congregations share a common building, congregational life, or, most profoundly, sacramental life, indicating in every case which denominations are involved.

These local ecumenical groups in the majority of cases use the following titles: Council of Churches (388), Churches Together (336), Christian Council (89), Council (35), Fellowship of Churches (34), Interchurch Council, Group, etc. (17), Ecumenical Group (16), Fraternal Association (some are lay, some are clergy) (13), Association of Churches (12). The remaining 232 bodies either use such terms as "Liaison," "Partnership," "Unity," or "Community" in their titles, or their exact title has not been reported.[17]

It is significant that the numbers are growing rapidly. For example, the Revd. Hugh Cross produced a list of 536 Local Ecumenical projects in England in 1988, but by 1993 that number had increased by one third, to 768. How energetic these bodies are is, of course, difficult to determine; but Canon Reardon, the General Secretary of "Churches Together in England" points out that about one third of local ecumenical groupings of churches now call themselves "Churches Together" in a locality. This he interprets as follows:

> Many, perhaps most, of these have adopted that title because it marks a development of the character of their mutual commitment. They are wanting to affirm that they . . . represent a conscious commitment of the decision-making bodies of the local churches to share in one another's life and worship, and to go out into the community together in service and witness.[18]

In the following pages I shall be using this *Register* to indicate as far as I can the impact of Local Ecumenical Projects in large cities such as London, Birmingham, and Bristol, and of more rural areas such as Hampshire and the Isle of Wight, Wiltshire, and Worcestershire. I shall also be examining the growth of ecumenical worship

17. Canon Reardon supplied information on alternative titles on page 2 of a report he had made.
18. See p. 3 of Reardon's report.

in Merseyside in particular because of the general sense that it is further developed there more than anywhere else in England, through the cooperation of the Anglican Bishop of Liverpool and the Roman Catholic Archbishop in Liverpool. In using the valuable information supplied by the *Register*, I make the assumption that the fullest degree of unity in a Local Ecumenical Project is indicated by an agreement to share sacramental ministry in full.

The Greater London Area includes the Barking Area Church Leaders Group, the East London Church Leaders Group, the North and West London Church Leaders Group, and South London Churches Sponsoring Body.

The Barking Area of London includes eleven Local Ecumenical Projects (L.E.P.s), seven of which share their sacramental ministry, of which three were Anglican and Methodist, two were Anglican and Baptist, and at the Newham Docklands in East Beckton there was a shared ministry among Anglicans, Baptists, Methodists, Roman Catholics, and the United Reformed.[19]

In the East London L.E.P.s all three share the sacramental ministry and represent a unity of the Methodist and United Reformed Churches at the local level.[20]

In the North and West London Church Leaders Group there are twenty-one associations in all. Of these fourteen have agreed to share their sacraments, and the United Reformed Church was a partner in each one, while the Methodist Church was linked with them in nine cases, and the Baptist Union in four cases.[21]

In the South London Churches Sponsoring Body there is a total of thirty-four groups. Of these sixteen are committed to sharing the ministry of the sacraments, of which twelve are United Reformed. Seven link the Methodists and the United Reformed, three are a unity of Anglican and Methodist, two join the Anglicans and the United Reformed, and two link the Baptists and United Reformed.[22] In the London area there is a total of sixty-nine L.E.P.s of which twelve share sacramental ministries. Of them ten are expressions of Anglican and Methodist unity; four involve the United Reformed Church, one each with the Anglicans, the Methodists, and the

19. *Register*, pp. 51-52.
20. *Ibid.*, p. 53.
21. *Ibid.*, pp. 54-56.
22. *Ibid.*, pp. 57-60.

Moravians; and one is a union of Anglicans, Methodists, and the United Reformed.[23]

Looking at the statistics for another city, Bristol, and its Council of Christian Churches, we find there are nineteen L.E.P.s, of which twelve agree to share sacramental ministries. Of these the Methodists are involved in nine cases, eight of which are Anglican and Methodist links, and the United Reformed are involved in unions with the Anglicans, the Methodists, the Anglicans and Methodists, and with the Moravians, in one example each.[24]

Next it is important to look at three relatively rural areas, beginning with Churches Together in Hampshire and the Islands. Here L.E.P.s total fifteen, of which only six share a sacramental ministry.[25] What is interesting here is that in five of the six, Anglican congregations are included; and in four cases the United Reformed Church is included. The single most ecumenical union includes the Anglicans, Baptists, Methodists, and the United Reformed Church at Lord's Hill, Southampton.

The second rural area is Wiltshire, with a total of twenty-seven L.E.P.s. Of these no less than seventeen share the sacramental ministry. Eleven represent Methodist and United Reformed unity, two are Anglican and Methodist, and two are remarkable in expressing Anglican, Baptist, Methodist, Roman Catholic, and United Reformed unity. These exceptions are the Devises Partnership of Churches and the Melksham Family of Churches.[26]

The third and last rural area is that of Worcester County Ecumenical Council with 132 L.E.P.s. Here again the proportion of groups sharing the sacramental ministry is high, involving ten groups: eight include Methodists; seven, Anglicans; and six, United Reformed.[27] One clearly notes in the rural areas that the proportion of shared sacramental ministries is higher than in urban areas, and also that Anglicans seem readier for this type of close association in rural rather than in city contexts. But whether in cities or in towns, the impression seems to be that the Methodists and the United Reformed are readier for this closest form of association than Anglicans or Baptists. One cannot,

23. *Ibid.*, pp. 4-5.
24. *Ibid.*, pp. 6-7.
25. *Ibid.*, pp. 31-32.
26. *Ibid.*, pp. 107-9.
27. *Ibid.*, pp. 110-11.

however, ignore the fact that in rural areas the congregations are smaller and less economically independent than in the cities.

In considering the Liverpool area through the Merseyside and Region Ecumenical Assembly, there is a total of forty-five L.E.P.s. Of these less than a half, to be exact only nineteen, have a common sacramental life, which might at first blush indicate that ecumenism in worship was poorly regarded in this neighborhood. In eight of these Anglicans and Methodists are linked, while eight join Methodist and United Reformed congregations. Two of the groups are unusual: the Liverpool City Centre Team uniting Anglican, Methodist, Roman Catholic, and United Reformed associates; and the Skelmersdale Church at the Centre which unites Anglicans, Baptists, Methodists, and United Reformed. But what is even more impressive is that twenty-three ecumenical projects have made local covenants uniting Anglicans, Methodists, and Roman Catholics for regular non-sacramental services, and that Anglicans and Roman Catholics share the same building in two other cases, while at Park Street, Croxteth congregational life is shared between Anglicans, Methodists and Roman Catholics. All this indicates that the Liverpool area deserves its high ecumenical reputation.[28]

One final statistic is deserving of consideration, namely, the degree to which the various Churches as denominations have contributed to liturgical ecumenism. According to the *Register* the Local Ecumenical Projects with Baptist input number 201, with Roman Catholic input 229, with United Reformed input 445, with Anglican input 550, and with Methodist input 572.[29]

Significant as these figures are, they should not be regarded as proof of ecumenical enthusiasm for two reasons. One is that they represent in some cases a realistic recognition of the reduced attendance in worship in all denominations. Another reason for their existence may be the result of a sense of guilt, as was suggested by the influential Anglican Evangelical leader, Bishop Colin Buchanan, in his booklet *Anglicans and Worship in Local Ecumenical Projects,* which appeared in 1987. There he pointed out that on two occasions when the Church of England had attempted to be ecumenical it had failed miserably. From 1963 to 1972 the Church of England was engaged in the projected union of Anglicans and Methodists,

28. *Ibid.,* pp. 66-70.
29. My own additions from the *Register* for 1992.

through which the Methodists becoming episcopal, both Churches would have come into full communion with each other. The scheme collapsed in 1972 when Anglicans voted against it. The very same year, 1972, saw the successful reunion of the Presbyterian Church of England and the Congregational Churches in the creation of the United Reformed Church. A new search for unity led to the publication of "Ten Propositions on Unity" which were accepted by the chief non-Roman Churches in England in 1978. It was then proposed that a scheme for "Covenanting" be enacted in 1980. In 1982 the Methodist and United Reformed Churches accepted the Covenant, but the Anglicans rejected it. The issue is best described in Buchanan's words: "Thus for the second time the Church of England had 'stood up' partners with whom it was in serious ecumenical dialogue, and there was a sense of quandary as to the directions to be taken next. The Archbishop of Canterbury took advice, and decided that the thrust of the new proposals must be towards local ecumenism."[30] This scheme was approved in full Synod in 1984.

The essentials from the Anglican angle are that a diocesan bishop can designate legally whether a parish or an area may become a Local Ecumenical Project. The certificate he supplies will indicate the other denominations taking part, and arrange for ways in which patterns of worship in that location shall be merged or juxtaposed. Buchanan notes that, however reluctantly the Church of England entered into this scheme, this was the first time the Church of England had ever officially recognized in its formularies that other denominations even existed. His ironic conclusion is "The serene (if fictitious) assumption that all the English were Anglican continued until the day before yesterday."[31]

We have seen from the theological agreements between representatives of mainline Churches that the areas of agreement on the Eucharist (hitherto a major basis of differences) far outweigh the differences. We have also observed that the Lima Communion Service devised by the World Council of Churches was widely approved, as witnessed by the Archbishop of Canterbury presiding at one of its celebrations. We have also cited in full the admirable eucharistic canon prepared by the Joint Liturgical Group for use on ecumenical

30. *Anglicans and Worship in Local Ecumenical Projects*, Grove Worship Series, No. 101 (Bramcote, Nottingham, 1987), pp. 3-4.

31. *Ibid.*, p. 5.

occasions. And finally, we have seen through the Joint Ecumenical Projects, unions between Anglicans, Methodists, United Reformed, and Baptists in various combinations working with a shared sacramental ministry; and frequently we have seen, in the Merseyside, for example, local covenanting between congregations including the Roman Catholics. The prospects for greater unity in worship become greater the more Churches are threatened by secularism in the modern world.

CHAPTER II

THE THEOLOGY OF INITIATION

THERE IS A GROWING ecumenical unity in the theology of the Eucharist, as will be seen in the next chapter, but the theology of initiation provides a striking contrast. There are several reasons why the theology of Baptism is a subject of continuing controversy and even of widespread confusion. This has been created in part by the impact of the Liturgical Movement, as the revised edition of *The Study of Liturgy* observed: "Since the concept of the Church as the people of God and body of Christ was at the heart of the movement, the rites were bound to be seen as something more than a private ceremony for the benefit of the individual."[1] Some degree of the confusion in interpreting the rites of initiation can be seen in the fact that "Baptism" can mean the whole process of introduction into the Church or merely the sacramental act of laving with water. Again "Confirmation" can mean chrismation by bishop or priest, the laying on of hands, or two or more of these actions together. Even the point in the process at which a person is said to become a member of the Church varies from denomination to denomination. The Churches disagree as to whether the entire process or a part of it should be necessary for admission to Communion, and even whether the rite of the Eucharist should be the climax of the actions of initiation, or delayed until the age of maturity.

What, then, are the factors that have created confusion and caused a series of different interpretations of the meaning of the rite of Baptism? First, the nature of the earliest Christian initiation in the New Testament is a matter of considerable dispute. There is uncertainty as to (a) the age of those baptized, whether adult or infant, (b) the mode of Baptism and the quantity of water employed (immersion or affusion), (c) the location of initiation (river or in a house), (d) whether it was before or after receiving the gift of the Holy Spirit,[2]

1. Cheslyn Jones, Geoffrey Wainwright, Edward Yarnold, S.J., and Paul Bradshaw, eds., *The Study of Liturgy*, rev. ed. (London: S.P.C.K., 1992), p. 70.
2. Acts 8:15-17 exhibits the laying on of hands detached in time from water

21

(e) whether and when the laying on of hands and chrism were administered, and (f) whether Jesus baptized, since the Synoptic Gospels say "No" and the Fourth Gospel says "Yes"[3] at the start and later "No." It is not even known whether the first apostles were baptized or not.[4]

A second factor has been the radical disagreement between leading European theologians as to whether Infant Baptism is theologically sound or should be abandoned. The latter, for example, is the opinion of Karl Barth,[5] but Kurt Aland and Joachim Jeremias disagree on this matter. Thus, in case of Barth, you have a theologian in the Reformed tradition criticizing Infant Baptism, which is regularly practiced by churches in that tradition. But another significant change is that the Roman Catholic Church now insists that Adult Baptism, following conversion, and a lengthy and disciplined catechumenate, must be regarded as the *norm*.[6] Professor Aidan Kavanagh insists that "*catechesis* begins to appear more as a matter of conversion therapy than an exercise in 'religious education.'" He affirms that the new approach revolutionizes both Baptism and Confirmation:

> *Baptism* begins to appear more as the communal watershed in that it both signifies one having come into communion with Jesus Christ dead and rising among his faithful people and causes that entrance to attain new levels of intensity. . . . *Confirmation* begins to appear less as a brief ceremony of maturity in faith, or of puberty in early adolescence, and more as a solemn pneumatic conclusion to baptism that finally equips one for full sharing in the eucharistic celebration

---

Baptism and administered by different persons. Acts 19:6-7 exhibits Paul laying hands on the candidates immediately after baptizing them at Ephesus.

3. John 3:22 and 4:1-2.

4. See Reginald Fuller's essay entitled "Christian Initiation in the New Testament" in *Made, Not Born: New Perspectives on Christian Initiation and the Catechumenate* (Notre Dame: University of Notre Dame Press, 1976).

5. See Barth, *The Teaching of the Church regarding Baptism,* trans. E. A. Payne (London: S.C.M. Press, 1948), based on a lecture delivered in 1943. Barth's *Church Dogmatics* IV/4 has 288 pages devoted to "Baptism as the sign of the Christian life," with pp. 164-94 directed against Infant Baptism.

6. This is elaborated in the *Rite of Christian Initiation of Adults*, which insists on the unity of Baptism, Eucharist, and Confirmation, calling them "Sacraments of Initiation," and requires pre-catechumenal and catechumenal catechesis and post-baptismal or mystagogic catechesis.

of a people filled with the Spirit of Jesus whom the Father sends as
. that people's living bond of unity.[7]

In the third place, controversy was inevitable because for approximately four hundred years there have existed two radically divergent
ways of being initiated into the Christian Church. While for the
majority it has been entry through Infant Baptism, there are several
Churches which, by the term "Baptist" in their title, demonstrate
that they came into being to demonstrate that Believers' Baptism
was the true mode of entrance. Further, the Disciples of Christ, the
Pentecostals, and several other denominations also practice only
Adult or Believers' Baptism. Its popularity is increasing, and understandably so in an age when secularism, agnosticism and atheism
have taken over, and where the culture no longer supports the faith
as it did in the days of Emperor Constantine. The Revd. Dr. Massey H. Shepherd described the contemporary situation vividly: "We
live in a post-Constantinian, if not a pre-Constantinian era, when
Christian communities and congregations must accept again in a
pluralistic society a status of voluntary groups without special privilege or support from society generally." His conclusion is: "We may
not be persecuted as in the early centuries before Constantine, but
possibly we suffer a worse fate from society as a whole by its indifference. And this indifference is compounded by the larger number of
nominal and uncommitted Christians on our church rolls."[8] This
indicates with the utmost clarity the problem the Church faces in
leading the outsider to its fold, and, by implication, criticizes the
sentimentality and trivialization that have characterized the casual
way infants have often been baptized without requiring any promises
from parents or sponsors in what was all too often a private or family
observance rather than a public celebration of an important and
solemn sacrament.

A fourth area of controversy has been how much of the system of
disciplined training in initiation as envisaged in the fourth to sixth
century of the Church should be introduced into the contemporary
Church. In general, this model has been a valuable corrective to
casualness, and has sparked an important debate in the Roman Catholic and Anglican Churches. Any fruitful consideration of the mean-

7. *Made, Not Born*, p. 4.
8. "The Early Church: Confirmation," *Worship* 46.1 (January 1972): 19-20.

ing of initiation requires this important historical retrospective look at a time when Christian training was at its best. This will be considered later in detail in this chapter. Suffice it to say for the present that the issue has been addressed in England through the scholarly concern of E. C. Whitaker in *Documents of the Baptismal Liturgy* (1960), of J. D. C. Fisher in *Christian Initiation: Baptism in the Medieval West* (1966), and Raymond Burnish in *The Meaning of Baptism. A Comparison of the Teaching and Practice of the Fourth Century with the Present Day* (1985).

A fifth matter that has led to controversy is the interpretation of the multiple Biblical metaphors for Baptism, some of which have been misinterpreted in substantialist or mechanistic ways.

A sixth and practical continuing controversy surrounds the difficulties found in the matter of sequence and how to cope with them. These include the following questions: (a) Is Confirmation really necessary? Doesn't Baptism rather than Confirmation convey the Holy Spirit fully? (b) What function would the elimination of Confirmation leave to bishops other than Ordination? (c) Shouldn't Baptism immediately lead to first Communion, and what is the earliest age a child should receive the Eucharist?

To deal with these six issues would require a lengthy book, but since brevity is the soul of wit, we shall be brief, concentrating on the larger issues. It is not proposed, for example, to reconsider the New Testament evidence for Infant Baptism, for the obvious reason that whether it has a New Testament origin or not, it will continue to be used, even though in our secular situation Adult Baptism is likely to increase, as a result of conversion and sustained and disciplined Christian education. Furthermore, there is a sufficient general awareness of the way Infant Baptism has been trivialized and sentimentalized that the necessary corrections in its observance will be made. In addition, just as Baptist churches in England have recognized the value of Christian parental commitment by services of the Dedication or the Presentation of Infants, so the willingness of the United Reformed Church in England to unite with the Reformed Association of Disciples of Christ, shows that cooperation between those practicing different modes of initiation may well be the way of the future.

Since our primary concern is with the interpretation of Baptism, we shall concentrate on the meanings of Baptism as reflected in the New Testament, as well as during the catechetical instruction given in the fourth to the sixth centuries, and on the enlarged contemporary understanding of its meaning.

The Meaning of Baptism in the New Testament

We have already mentioned the difficulties of determining the exact practice of Baptism in the New Testament, but that should not deter us from trying to understand its significance. Its importance is clear from the multiple references to the sacrament, as well as from the fact of Jesus' own Baptism by John the Baptist, mentioned in all four gospels.

It is clear that originally Christian Baptism was differentiated from that practiced by John the Baptist, although there were parallels. Both forms of Baptism require repentance and ethical transformation. Both are in water. Both are regarded as inaugurating the Messianic community at the end of these days. Both are eschatological events. But the differences are also striking. The gospel writers are embarrassed that Jesus the sinless one should have received Baptism. Christ sees God as infinitely compassionate, not legalistic as John the Baptist did. Christ liberates the disciple from anxiety about his own righteousness so he can concentrate on loving his neighbor. Christ also focusses on his own death as a baptism.[9] This is clear when James and John ask to be seated on Christ's right and his left, and he replies: "Can you drink the cup that I drink, or be baptized with the baptism I am baptized with?"[10]

Christian Baptism from the very beginning is practiced as resting on a command from the risen Lord. In Acts 2:38 Peter on the day of Pentecost declared: "Repent and be baptized every one of you in the name of Jesus Christ for the remission of your sins; and you will receive the gift of the Holy Spirit." It is clear that early Baptism was in the name of Christ,[11] while later the Church baptized in the name of the Holy Trinity, as recorded in Matthew 28:18, 20.

An important clue to the meaning of Baptism in the New Testament can be found in the rich variety of metaphors applied to baptism. Amongst these are taking on the name of the Lord, sealing (or

9. See Luke 12:50.
10. Mark 10:38f.
11. Acts 8:16; 19:5; and 22:16.

25

authenticating), putting on Christ (like donning a garment), and entering the royal priesthood. There are, however, five major metaphors. The first of these involves the most radical assertion that at Baptism the Christian is buried with Christ in death and raised with him in resurrection. This is stressed by Paul in Romans 6:3: "Do you not know that all of us who have been baptized into Christ Jesus were baptized into his death? Therefore we have been buried with him by baptism into death, so that, just as Christ was raised from the dead by the glory of the Father, so we too might walk in newness of life."[12] Baptism involves a radical transformation — an emergence from the tomb.

But baptism is also, to use another striking metaphor, an emergence from the womb, a rebirth. Through Baptism the Christian is incorporated into a new Body, the Church. Titus refers to "the water of rebirth and renewal by the Holy Spirit,"[13] while John 3:5 insists: "No one can enter the kingdom of God without being born of water and the Spirit."

1 Corinthians 12:13 provides another image of intimate union with Christ: "For in the one Spirit we were all baptized into the one body — Jews or Greeks, slaves or free — and we were all made to drink of the one Spirit." In the Body of Christ, the next chapter indicates, the members exhibit the gifts of the Holy Spirit: faith, hope, and supremely, love. Indeed, one of the signs of entering the community is the gift of the Holy Spirit itself. This was experienced dramatically by Christ at his own Baptism in the presence of the dove, the symbol of the Holy Spirit. This gift is sometimes viewed as providing enlightenment or as sanctification.[14]

Also, the baptized are said to be entering a community of the sanctified, for Baptism brings about the forgiveness of sins. Baptism is not only a death, a rebirth, but also obviously a washing in water, a radical cleansing. Paul understood this when he was instructed by Ananias: "Get up, be baptized, and having your sins washed away, call on his name."[15] External washing and internal cleansing are also linked in the New Testament.[16]

12. See the parallel Pauline expression in Colossians 2:12.
13. The reference is to Titus 3:5.
14. Enlightenment in Hebrews 6:4 and sanctification in 1 Corinthians 6:11.
15. Acts 22:16.
16. Outward washing and inward cleansing of a good conscience are correlated in 1 Peter 3:21 and Hebrews 10:22.

While these varied metaphors were held in unity in the New Testament, they became divided historically, with one or another being emphasized more strongly. In the medieval Church it was the connection of Baptism with the cleansing or forgiveness of sins that was emphasized, so much so that Emperor Constantine and many others postponed Baptism almost until death, so that they might go to God blameless. In the Reformation Baptism was for Luther a pledge of a divine promise and therefore a source of great comfort, while for Calvin it was the supreme gift of grace itself, and the symbol of adoption.[17]

Liturgical language is appropriately poetic and incorporates the rich variety of metaphors as we have seen. The only problem is that metaphors can be misinterpreted if treated inappropriately, and this has often happened in the history of Christianity. F. J. Leenhardt[18] asks: What are the causes of the mechanistic rather than personalistic view of the grace of Baptism? He answers that one cause is the human tendency to conceive of personal realities as if they were physical realities. For this reason he argues it is most important to distinguish between the natural element — water in Baptism — and the intention of the service to which the material is devoted. The materials always *mediate* an intention which is conveyed through them. In Baptism water conveys Christ's intention to give his people innocence again as in Eden before the Fall or a new birth in the Spirit of Christ. Leenhardt says the second cause of the error is treating the metaphorical language of the New Testament as if it were literal or physical. For example, the Spirit is often treated as if it were a physical entity. It is indicated by using the word *pneuma*, which delineates the wind or the breath, and it can be said of the wind or the breath that it enters a person, inhabits a person, leaves a person, and that it produces effects perceptible to the eye. Also, in addition, a close connection is established between the Spirit and water from the fact that both descend from heaven. This interpretative error, technically known as reification, has often perverted Biblical meaning.

---

17. See B. A. Gerrish, *Grace and Gratitude: The Eucharistic Theology of John Calvin* (Minneapolis: Fortress Press, 1992), esp. "The Grace of Baptism," pp. 109-23. I have also found helpful James F. White's analysis of the New Testament metaphors of baptism in his *A Brief History of Christian Worship* (Nashville: Abingdon Press, 1992), pp. 20-22.

18. Leenhardt, *Parole Visible* (Neuchâtel: Delachaux and Niestlé, 1971), p. 139.

According to Leenhardt's clarifying exposition, the danger in Roman Catholic sacramental theology is found in the desire for materialization of the communication between God and humanity, and thus a tendency to confuse the personal message with the mechanisms put to work to transmit it. The opposite error is typical in Protestantism, where not enough attention is devoted to these mediations which permit the transmission of the message and the personal relationship between God and humanity. Spoken language and gestural language are both needed in the exposition of the sacraments.[19]

Karl Barth, too, is disturbed by the dangers of reification in the interpretation of the sacrament of Baptism. He finds serious confusion in the Church's understanding of the terminology of "grace." He explains, for example, that the translation of the words of the angel to the Virgin Mary can be "Hail, Mary, full of grace," which is the Roman Catholic view, but it can also be interpreted "Be joyful, you have the favor of God." In the first view, grace is a kind of substance that fills empty space; while in the second view, grace is a favorable disposition given by God.[20]

The Return to the Patristic Practice of Baptism

As we suggested earlier, both Roman Catholics and Anglicans, disturbed by the general failure of the practice of Infant Baptism to bring adult disciples to the Church, have been investigating with great seriousness the practice of Baptism from the third to the sixth centuries A.D. This we must look at from both an explanatory and a pragmatic viewpoint.

If we examine the practice of Baptism in Hippolytus and Tertullian respectively in Rome and in North Africa in the third century, we can see the shape of Christian initiation after catechism in the early Church. It took the form of the baptismal washing, the anointing with chrism (the name for the "oil of thanksgiving"), the laying on of hands, and the reception of the first Eucharist (with a chalice of water and of milk and honey, symbolizing the entry of the candidates into the promised land). According to Leonel L. Mitchell, although

19. *Ibid.*, pp. 140f.
20. *Church Dogmatics* IV/4.

some of the details vary, this "may well be called the ancient pattern."[21]

The three central liturgical actions were closely identified with the Baptism of Jesus by John the Baptist. The Baptism itself was a washing; the anointing signified the gift of the Holy Spirit paralleling the descent of the dove and the voice of the Father declaring Christ's divine Sonship; and the signing of the Cross was identified with the marking of the foreheads of the faithful with a *tau* in Ezekiel 9:4 and the sealing of the servants of God on their foreheads in Revelation 7:3.[22]

In the fourth century, with the recognition of Christianity as the official religion of the Roman Empire, the celebration of Baptism became more complicated.[23] For example, St. Cyril, the Bishop of Jerusalem, elaborated the rites of Baptism in his *Mystagogical Catecheses*. First, the rite of renunciation in the vestibule leading to the baptismal pool required the candidates to turn from the east to the west, reminiscent of Adam turning away from God, and thus anticipating the return to Paradise through baptism. In the inner chamber the candidates were naked — a symbol of primitive innocence. There was also an exorcism and anointing before baptism to produce healing and strength to battle against the devil, as well as insufflation, or breathing upon the faces of the candidates, as an inward sign of spiritual cleansing. The plunging of the candidates three times beneath the water of the pool, with the invocation of the three persons of the Holy Trinity, for Cyril was also symbolic of the three nights and days Christ had spent in the tomb. There were also post-baptismal rites in Jerusalem. A second chrismation was to set the candidates apart as Christ at his Baptism was set apart for God's service. The white garments or tunics stood for purity and the risen life promised to the candidates.

St. John Chrysostom at Antioch in his mystagogical explanation of the rite of Baptism made much of the rite of renunciation, seeing

---

21. Mitchell, *Worship: Initiation and the Churches* (Washington, D.C.: Pastoral Press, 1991), p. 5.

22. *Ibid.*

23. In this paragraph and the two succeeding ones, dealing with the baptismal practices of St. Cyril of Jerusalem, St. John Chrysostom at Antioch, and Bishop Theodore at Mopsuestia, I have benefitted from the admirable analysis of Raymond Burnish in *The Meaning of Baptism: A Comparison of the Teaching and Practice of the Fourth Century with the Present Day* (London: Alcuin Club/S.P.C.K., 1985), chapter 4.

in the kneeling gesture of the candidates that they were in bondage with Satan. This was followed by the act of profession, the candidate promising to enter the service of Christ, after which he or she was anointed with a mixture of olive oil and an unguent. (The golden-tongued orator, for that is the meaning of the name Chrysostom, made much of the symbolism of light, and he envisaged Christ as the Sun of Justice opening the way to Paradise; Baptism took place at Easter *dawn*.) Before the Baptism itself a second anointing took place. The robe was stripped off the candidates by the bishop and others anointed them with olive oil over the entire body. Then the bishop led each candidate down into the flowing water, placing his right hand on the candidate's head, thrusting it down into the water and raising it three times. When the candidates emerged they were embraced, greeted and kissed by all present, indicating that those hitherto slaves and captives to sin were now free sons and daughters invited to the royal table, where they taste of the Master's body and blood and become the dwelling-place of the Holy Spirit.

In the mystagogical lectures of the Bishop Theodore and the Church at Mopsuestia, also in the fourth century, much more was made of the act of renunciation. The candidates were required to stand barefoot on a sackcloth made of goat's hair, and their external garment was removed; then, with outstretched arms, they were to implore the help of God. The engagement to serve God followed on the part of each candidate. The bishop then signed each one with the oil of anointing on the forehead, and the sponsors standing behind each candidate placed a linen shawl over the head of each and raised their candidate to the standing position. Theodore explained the taking off of the garments by pointing out that Adam needed clothes only after he had sinned, and so the removal of clothes symbolized Adam's former state. (The subjective nature of interpretation of symbolism is evident in the divergence between Theodore's explanation and that of St. Cyril of Jerusalem.) As for the symbolism of Baptism itself, Theodore explained that mankind, made in water (in the womb), returned to water, and was dissolved in it waiting to be refashioned. Then recalling the symbol of the potter's vessel from Jeremiah 18:1-6, he urged that the candidate's nature was marred and thus, like a clay vessel, had to be immersed in water to be recreated. Theodore thus linked immersion to both creation and redemption. Concerning the post-Baptismal rites Theodore remarks that the shining garment and the signation of the candidate by the

30

bishop symbolize the presence of the Holy Spirit; the new clothing stands for happiness and joy and is a reminder of the purity required in the candidates' new life, an intermediate step before the General Resurrection.

It is clear that there were not only differences in understanding the multiple meanings of Baptism among the bishops of the fourth century, but even different symbolic actions too. For example, St. Ambrose of Milan introduced the custom of foot-washing immediately after the act of Baptism. Citing John 13:8, he declared: "Accordingly, learn how it is a sacrament and a means of sanctification: 'Unless I wash thy feet, thou wilt have no part with me.'"[24]

Having examined the rites of Baptism in major centers in the fourth century, it is appropriate to consider what their bishops considered the meaning of Christian Baptism to be. St. Cyril of Jerusalem clearly taught that Baptism had a five-fold meaning. In the first place it signified enlightenment, next the adoption as sons and daughters of God, also a holy seal marking God's ownership, and a heaven-bound chariot and thus a passport to the kingdom of heaven, and, in summary form both a tomb and a womb.

For Chrysostom the significance of Baptism was six-fold. It is a bath of regeneration, an act of enlightenment, a burial and resurrection with Christ (as in Galatians 3:27), an act of God through, but not by, human hands, an intimate marriage-like union with Christ, and a liberation and enfranchisement of former slaves and captives. The vividness of his teaching deserves citation. Here is a warning:

> The catechumen is a sheep without a seal [therefore without marking and ownerless]; he is a deserted inn and a hostel without a door, which lies open to all without, a dwelling-place for demons. Yet our Master has decreed that through his loving-kindness this deserted, doorless inn, this robber's refuge should become a royal palace. On this account he sent us, your teachers, and those exorcists to prepare the inn beforehand. And by our instruction, we who teach you are making strong and secure the walls of the inn which were weak and unsound.[25]

24. St. Ambrose, *De Sacramentis* 3.5.

25. *St. John Chrysostom: Baptismal Instructions*, trans. Paul W. Harkins (Westminster, Maryland: Newman Press, 1963), Vol. 31 of Ancient Christian Writers, pp. 17-18.

31

For Theodore the purpose of Baptism is to proclaim eternal life and to instruct polytheists about the One true God. Most important of all Christians learn at Baptism that the Triune God keeps his promises, and this is a solid foundation of assurance for all Christians.

As we review these sets of instruction regarding the rite and the meaning of Baptism, what impressions do they leave? The use of significant gestures such as facing west to deny Satan, kneeling as captives and standing erect as Christ's men and women redeemed from slavery, being anointed with olive oil as athletes and fighters were (implying God's strengthening), and receiving the sign of the cross as the mark of divine ownership, all stress the dramatic nature of Christian initiation. We have also in the mystagogical lectures a profound sense of secrets being unveiled at last. One senses, too, the sheer exhilaration of the experience of Baptism. Finally, one recognizes that the aim is clearly conversion, both ethical and theological. And one realizes that there was an extensive period of catechizing, often involving a commitment of three years. The modern requirements for Baptism seem, by contrast, casual and appallingly minimal.

The system of catechumenate prior to Baptism in the fourth to the sixth-century patristic Church, is worthy of further consideration. Its most striking features were its lengthy duration, strict discipline, and concentration on conversion.

In the first place the candidates could not become catechumens unless brought forward to the leaders of the congregation by sponsors who vouched for their probity and serious intentions. They would be excluded automatically if they were prostitutes or pimps, gladiators, circus performers, actors, or soldiers. All who applied were placed under a most thorough scrutiny. Intending Christians were required to study under careful direction for a period of three years. As Michael Merriman states, "The catechumenate is more process than program."[26] The potential Christian went through four stages. There was first the pre-catechumenal period with a rite for the admission of catechumens, when the leaders were satisfied as to their ethics and keenness. The catechumenate followed, during which time the candidates were present at worship for the Scripture readings and the sermon, when they were dismissed.

After approximately three years catechumens were, if declared to

26. Merriman, ed., *The Baptismal Mystery and the Catechumenate* (New York: The Church Hymnal Corporation, 1990), p. 6.

be *competentes*, admitted by the vote of the congregation to the final stage of the preparation for Baptism, which took place during Lent. It involved them in thorough study, prayer, fasting, and instruction in the meaning of the Creed and the Lord's Prayer. They were also required to submit themselves to repeated acts of exorcism to root out the evil in them; these acts involved insufflation, being anointed with oil like athletes and fighters, and receiving the sign of the cross. The final rites of Baptism were concluded before dawn on Easter Day, and at daybreak they were baptized. In the week following their Baptism they came to be instructed in the meaning of the sacred rites of Baptism and the eucharist.[27]

It is the Eastern Orthodox Churches alone which have retained most of the tradition of the fourth century theologians, and thus they provide a model for today, which the Roman Catholic Church in restoring the catechumenate, and the Anglican Church in admitting children to Holy Communion, are imitating. The best introduction in English to the Baptismal Rite in Orthodox Churches is Alexander Schmemann's *Of Water and the Spirit* (1974).

The Orthodox liturgy remains substantially in its ancient form, although it has had to be telescoped to allow rites that were previously performed on different occasions over a two-month period to be included in a single service. The rite begins with the reception of catechumens and the rite of renunciation and profession, with the priest blowing on the candidate's mouth, brow and breast (insufflation); the candidate makes a three-fold renunciation and is told to breathe and spit upon Satan. The first office ends with the following prayer:

> O Master, Lord our God, call thy servant, N, to thy holy illumination, and grant unto him (her) that great grace of thy holy baptism. Put off from him (her) the old man, and renew him (her) unto life everlasting; and fill him (her) with the powers of thy Holy Spirit, in the unity of thy Christ; and he (she) may be no more a child of the body, but a child of thy kingdom. Through the goodwill and grace of thine only-begotten Son, with whom thou art blessed, together

27. According to Professor Aidan Kavanagh, O.S.B., catechesis is "conversion therapy" (in Merriman, *The Baptismal Mystery*, p. 38). He insists that the restored Roman rites of Christian initiation "presume a leaner and meaner Christianity" (p. 49).

with thy most holy, and good, and life-giving Spirit, now, and ever, and unto ages of ages. Amen.

The second office, that of Baptism, starts with the deacon's solemn blessing of the water. That prayer encapsulates the meanings of Baptism, including the descent of the Holy Spirit, the grace of redemption as in the Jordan, the purity of the Holy Trinity, the illumination of the understanding and the gift of piety from the Holy Spirit, and protection from all enemies. The deacon prays that the recipient may be worthy of the incorruptible kingdom, receiving salvation, becoming a child of light and a partaker in the death and resurrection of Jesus Christ, and preserving the baptismal garment in all purity until the Day of Judgement. He concludes by asking that God may hear this prayer and deliver the one to be baptized from tribulation, wrath, and necessity.

The water having been blessed, the catechumen is finally anointed with oil. The priest dips his fingers in the oil and makes the sign of the cross on the candidate's brow, breast, and between the shoulders for joy and the healing of soul and body, on the ears for the hearing of faith, on the hands because God's hands made the baptizand, and on the feet that he may walk in the way of God's commandments. When the entire body has been anointed, the priest baptizes him, holding him upright and looking toward the east, as he says: "The servant of God, N, is baptized in the name of the Father. Amen. And of the Son. Amen. And of the Holy Spirit. Amen." At each invocation he immerses him and raises him again. The use of the passive voice is especially noteworthy since it is intended to indicate that the action of Baptism is not human but divine.

After this the newly baptized is dressed in his new white robe, which is a symbol of new righteousness. The candidate is also given a lighted candle to hold, emphasizing that Baptism is a sacrament of illumination for the candidate and of the world through the candidate. Then the office of the Holy Chrismation follows, in which the priest anoints the one baptized with chrism, making the sign of the cross on the brow, the eyes, nostrils, lips, ears, breast, hands and feet, saying each time: "The seal of the gift of the Holy Spirit."

Schmemann explains that participation in the Eucharist is the fulfillment of chrismation, for it sums up the union of the candidate with Christ as an adopted child of God the Father. Schmemann writes:

34

Such is the gift of the Holy Spirit, the meaning of our personal Pentecost in the sacrament of the holy anointment. It *seals*, i.e. makes, reveals, confirms, us as members of the Church, the Body of Christ, as citizens of the Kingdom of God, as partakers of the Holy Spirit. And by this *seal*, it truly makes us into ourselves, "ordains" each one of us to be and to become that which God from all eternity wants us to be, revealing our *true personality* and thus our only self-fulfillment.[28]

Then the priest and sponsors, together with the newly-baptized, circle round the front, singing triply, the words: "As many as have been baptized into Christ have put on Christ. Alleluia." The circle symbolizes the endlessness of eternity. Finally, other actions follow on the eighth day after Baptism. First there is the washing off of the holy chrism preparing the newly baptized for the fight which is essential in the Christian life. Then the white garment is removed because it was given to be transformed into the life of the neophyte. The last rite is the tonsure or cutting of the hair, a symbol of total obedience to Christ. Altogether in their profound and dramatic symbolism the Orthodox rites of Baptism are unforgettable in their impact and teaching. The Orthodox Churches, unlike other Christian churches, have not needed to return to the fourth century celebration of Baptism because they never abandoned it.

The Contemporary Understanding of Initiation

We must begin by pointing out the advantages claimed both for Infant and for Adult or Believer's Baptism. At the outset it is clear that the celebration of infant baptism needs to be radically improved. The critique of current practice by Professor William H. Willimon deserves attention. He has written:

> Those who practice infant baptism speak of it euphemistically as "christening," "infant dedication," as a little educative exercise to remind parents to get the child to Sunday School, or as an insipid, cute, rosebud of an affair all full of kisses and talk that "God loves you and we love you,"

28. Schmemann, *Of Water and the Spirit: A Liturgical Study of Baptism* (Crestwood, N.Y.: St. Vladimir's Seminary Press, 1974), p. 107.

hoping that the church can get its real business with the child done later in confirmation class or through an adult conversion experience.... Too long Protestants have believed that such events as Baptism and the Lord's Supper are human actions we perform to help us remember God's acts in the past. Distrusting the ability of the material to be a bearer of the Holy, we have reduced the Sacraments to stimulants to sentiment, occasions for self-commitment, memory exercises that aid us in making ethical decisions or theological insights.[29]

It is clear that Zwingli's influence has overcome the direction of Calvin, who in the *Institutes* (IV.14.3) declared of God: "He condescends to lead us to himself and to set before us in the flesh a mirror of spiritual blessings. . . . He imparts spiritual things under visible ones." P. T. Forsyth supplies the corrective:

Baptism is not primarily an act of the parent nor the child, but of the Church and Christ in the Church. It is our individualism that has done most to ruin the sacrament of Baptism among us. We get the wrong answer because we do not put the right question. We ask, "What good does Baptism do me or that child?" instead of "What is the active witness and service the Church renders to the active Word in Christ's Gospel in the Baptism of the young or old?[30]

This emphasis is now made strongly in most modern rites of initiation. For example, in speaking of the new Roman Catholic rites, Professor Aidan Kavanagh insists:

The document is concretely specific on who a Christian is. He is not merely a set of abstract imponderable good intentions that are essentially incommunicable and subjectively sovereign. Rather, a Christian is a person of faith in Jesus Christ dead and risen among his faithful people. This faith is no mere noetic thing but a way of living together; it is the bond which establishes that reciprocal mutuality of relationships we call communion, and it is this communion which constitutes the ecclesial real presence of Jesus Christ in the world of grace, faith, hope, charity, and character.[31]

29. *Worship as Pastoral Care* (Nashville: Abingdon Press, 1979), pp. 154f.
30. *The Church and the Sacraments* (London: Independent Press, 1949), pp. 177f.
31. Aidan Kavanagh, O.S.B., in *Made, Not Born*, pp. 133f.

It is clear that because Baptism is a celebration of the identity of the Christian community it must never be celebrated privately, and parents and sponsors are nowadays rightly required to confess the Christian faith and solemnly to promise to bring up these children as Christians. It would even be appropriate to celebrate Infant Baptism in the context of the Lord's Supper, since Baptism is the initiating sacrament to the Lord's Table. Increasingly there is a sense that the objectivity of Baptism should be stressed by direct reference to the basic elements, such as water, special clothing, imposition of hands, oil, candles, and the repetition of a creed, to correct subjectivity and excessive verbalism. The significance of Baptism can be stressed also by returning to baptismal vigils and Easter baptismal celebrations. These are all ways by which we are "ineradically identified, signed, sealed, and claimed by God's grace in Baptism."[32] Christians are never born as such: they are made, or strictly speaking, reborn and remade.

If a minister is uncertain whether parents requesting Infant Baptism are Christian or not, then an alternative service, a short Thanksgiving rite for the birth of a child, should perhaps be available, as it is in several religious communities today.[33] Another improvement might be to avoid rebaptism by providing a service of renewal or reaffirmation of faith, which could be used for individuals or could become an annual event in the life of the local church, to be held either on the Sunday when the Baptism of the Lord is remembered or at Pentecost.

What arguments then can be made for Infant Baptism, once its celebration is liberated from sentimentality, subjectivity, and even triviality, and once these practical reforms have been effected? In the first place, it is an excellent witness to the fact that the Church, through Christ, offers the grace of a Christian education from the very beginning of a child's life, not postponing it until adulthood. This stresses the inclusiveness of Christian faith, hope, and love.

In the second place, Infant Baptism is a notable way of emphasizing the divine initiative. The Gospel is there at the very outset of our lives: before we can even speak, God speaks through the Church and its care. The Baptist emphasis is valuable in pointing to the

32. Willimon, *Worship as Pastoral Care*, p. 160.
33. In the English Methodist Church and the United Reformed Church, for examples.

human response necessary for appropriating salvation, but the priority of grace may find a valuable safeguard in the Baptism of infants, for in the Baptism of an infant the grace of God is clearly and unmistakably prior to the individual's response. Every Baptism is to some degree proleptic.

In the third place, it stresses objectivity. As an infant I am not making any claims for myself or patting myself on my own back for my piety or good behavior. There is a complete absence of pride. It could of course be argued that it should be enough to state that children of Christian parents occupy a place in the love of Christ. But, as Geoffrey Wainwright argues: shouldn't infants receive Baptism as a sign of initiation into the Covenant people who acknowledge God's rule?[34]

On the other hand, there is no question but that Believer's Baptism seems appropriate in a time of increasing secularism, agnosticism, and downright atheism, since it requires repentance, faith, and conversion. Furthermore, in its requirement that believers must be submerged three times beneath the water of the baptistry, it is a far more dramatic occasion than the trivial act of sprinkling a few drops of water; and by this action it teaches that the Christian life must be both tomb and womb in its identification with the death and resurrection of Christ. It may be that as non-Baptists look seriously at disciplined instruction leading towards conversion, Baptists might find utility in several of the other gestures of fourth-century practice, and thereby minimize the stress on human achievement.

The wisest course would seem to be to accept both Infant Baptism and Adult Baptism and use far more fully than is now the case those symbolic actions that make Baptism a celebratory event in the life of the individual and the Christian community. The symbolism of cleansing, dying and being born again in Christ (drowning and coming alive), can be effectively communicated with immersion, with use of the white tunic (for both child and adult), the seal of chrismation, the laying on of hands for the gift of the Holy Spirit, and the use of a candle as a witness to Christ who is the Light of the World. Only the discipline of a catechumenate will make possible the recovery of these vivid insights.

There are grounds for hope in the fact that the Faith and Order

---

34. Wainwright, *Christian Initiation* (London: Lutterworth Press, 1969), pp. 53-54.

Committee of the World Council of Churches, in its document *Baptism, Eucharist,* and *Ministry, 1982-1990,* was able to report:

> The most remarkable fact emerging from the responses of the Churches in the baptism section is the degree of convergence that exists in areas of previous dissension, and the willingness of the Churches, in the full face of continuing differences, to seek together a common language and understanding.[35]

After years of controversy, this is a significant achievement.

---

35. *Baptism, Eucharist, and Ministry, 1982-1990* (Geneva: World Council of Churches, 1990), Faith and Order Paper No. 149, p. 54.

CHAPTER III

THE THEOLOGY
OF THE EUCHARIST

THE EUCHARIST, which has long been the centerpiece of worship in Eastern Orthodoxy, Roman Catholicism, and Anglicanism, has begun to attain increasing prominence in the English Free Churches, which previously regarded preaching as the climax of gatherings for worship. Furthermore, the theology of the Eucharist has become richer in its attention to the rite's multiple meanings. Both aspects of the contemporary revaluation of the Eucharist will engage our concern in the present chapter.

One element of the evidence for the growing attention to the Eucharist is the extraordinary proliferation of books on the subject. Two examples only need to be given. One is F. C. Senn's *New Eucharistic Prayers: An Ecumenical Study of their Development and Structure* (New York: Paulist Press, 1987) and the other a collection edited by Max Thurian and Geoffrey Wainwright, *Baptism and Eucharist: Ecumenical Convergence in Celebration* (Geneva: World Council of Churches and Grand Rapids: Eerdmans, 1983). Both are ecumenical in this focus. The second stresses the striking degree of convergence in the interpretation and celebration of the Eucharist.

A second element of the evidence for a deeper appreciation of the Eucharist is found in trans-denominational statements of agreement on the meaning of the Eucharist. A volume entitled *Modern Eucharistic Agreement* (London: S.P.C.K., 1973) documents four significant ecumenical dialogues all produced in 1971. One was between the Roman Catholics and the Lutherans, a second was produced by the Anglican-Roman Catholic International Commission, the third was the Dombes Agreement — *Towards a Common Eucharistic Faith?* — authored by a group of French Roman Catholics and Reformed theologians who had been meeting since 1937 for ecumenical purposes. The fourth document, *The Eucharist in Ecumenical Thought*, is the Louvain Statement of the Faith and Order Commission of the

World Council of Churches. Later we shall consider each of these individual contributions.

The third element of evidence for the growing centrality of the Eucharist is the astonishing proliferation of new eucharistic prayers produced during the past generation. Until thirty years ago it should be recalled that the Roman Catholic Church had a single eucharistic rite unchanged since the Council of Trent, and the Church of England's Holy Communion Service was unchanged since 1662. Anglican revisions of the Eucharist, according to Bishop Colin O. Buchanan's reckoning, totalled no less than sixty-three in the twenty-six years from 1958 to 1984 world-wide.[1] By contrast, the *Alternative Service Book* (1980) contains seven alternative Communion Thanksgivings.

The Free Churches in Britain also produced new orders for their Communion services. The Presbyterian Church in England and Wales issued their Service Book with three orders for Communion in 1968. *The Methodist Service Book* of 1975 had a single service of Holy Communion, but this included the Peace, the Nicene Creed, the Thanksgiving Prayer (including the *Sursum corda*, the *Sanctus*, the ecumenical acclamation, and an invocation of the Holy Spirit), which indicated how ecumenical this service had become. For English Congregationalists *A Book of Public Worship*, compiled by John Huxtable, John Marsh, Romilly Micklem, and James Todd in 1948 included four orders for the Lord's Supper. The former Congregationalists and former Presbyterians produced *A Book of Services* for the new United Reformed Church in 1980, which includes three Communion Prayers of Thanksgiving, all of which contain the *Sursum corda* and the *Sanctus*, as well as the *epiclesis* (invocation of the Holy Spirit). Two include the *Benedictus qui venit*. The addition of the Reformed Association of Churches of Christ to the union of Presbyterians and Congregationalists required that a new book be prepared, and this, the *Service Book*, appeared in 1989 with three Communion Thanksgiving Prayers. The Baptist Union of Great Britain published *Patterns and Prayers for Christian Worship* in 1991. This provides three patterns for the Lord's Supper, only one of which offers, as an alternative, the

---

1. See Buchanan's *Modern Anglican Liturgies, 1958-1968* (Oxford: Oxford University Press, 1968), as well as *Further Anglican Liturgies, 1968-1975* and *Latest Anglican Liturgies, 1976-1984* (1975 and 1987 respectively).

traditional dialogue, with *Sursum corda, Sanctus* and *Benedictus qui venit,* and the invocation of the Holy Spirit.

A fourth element of the evidence for greater appreciation of the centrality of the Eucharist is to be found in the fact that Protestant Churches have demonstrated a growing concensus that the norm of Sunday Services is *Word* and *Table.* It is now recognized that — in the words of Geoffrey Wainwright — "the fullness of Sunday worship requires that the customary preaching service be joined by the Lord's Supper."[2] Moreover, the homily has been re-established in the order of the Mass in the Roman Catholic Church. Wainwright also predicted that the structure of the Sunday Service outlined by the Joint Liturgical Group would gain general acceptance. This included Old Testament Reading; New Testament Readings; Sermon; Intercession; Presentation and Taking of the Bread and Wine; Eucharistic Prayer; Fraction and Communion.[3]

A fifth element of the growing sense of unity in celebrating the Eucharist is owed to the extraordinary influence of Dom Gregory Dix's great book, *The Shape of the Liturgy.* Here Dix emphasized that the Eucharistic Meal has a "four-action shape" which, once the bread and wine are brought together, corresponds to the actions of Christ at the Last Supper: he *took* the bread and wine, he *gave thanks* over them, he *broke* the bread and *gave* wine to the disciples. Nowadays the Fraction is not associated so much with the breaking of Christ's body on the cross as with the many being made one: it is a symbol of restored unity. Of the four actions the two which are seen as fundamental are the Thanksgiving and the Communion.

There has come to be, as a result of modern historical scholarship, a remarkable degree of unity in the interpretation and development of modern eucharistic prayers of thanksgiving.[4] The influence of the

2. In *The Study of Liturgy,* ed. C. Jones, G. Wainwright, E. Yarnold, and P. Bradshaw, rev. ed. (London: S.P.C.K. and Oxford University Press, 1992), p. 331.

3. N. Clark and R. C. D. Jasper, eds., *Initiation and Eucharist: Essays on Their Structure* (London: S.P.C.K., 1972).

4. Amongst important studies of ancient liturgies there have been G. A. Michell, *Eucharistic Consecration in the Primitive Church* (London: S.P.C.K., 1948); J. P. Audet, "Esquisse historique du genre littéraire de la 'Bénédiction' juive et de l'eucharistie," *Revue bénédictine* 65 (1958): 371-99; L. Bouyer, *Eucharist,* and studies by L. Ligier in *Studia Liturgica* 9 (1973): 6-85; G. J. Cuming, *He Gave Thanks: An Introduction to the Eucharistic Prayer,* Grove Liturgical Studies, No. 28 (Bramcote, 1981). Gregory Dix and Henry Chadwick in their translation and edition of Hip-

Apostolic Tradition of Hippolytus has been considerable, although his eucharistic prayer lacks the *Sanctus*. The result is that at the present time it would be generally accepted according to Geoffrey Wainwright[5] that a eucharistic prayer should contain most of the following features: (1) introductory dialogue; (2) preface or first part of the thanksgiving; (3) *Sanctus;* a transition that may either (4) continue the thanksgiving or (5) take the form of a preliminary *epiclesis,* if not both; (6) narrative of the institution; (7) *anamnesis*-oblation (although "oblation" constitutes a difficulty for several Protestant groups).[6]

Among the newer emphases in eucharistic thanksgivings three developments are clear. In the first place, both medieval and Roman emphasis was on the Cross almost exclusively, giving the service the atmosphere of a wake and excluding joy, thereby minimizing the benefits of the Cross in forgiveness of sins and assurance of life beyond the grave, as well as the impact of Christ's own resurrection, ascension, and continuing intercession for the Church. The new thanksgivings include a fuller account of God's mighty acts in Christ, emphasizing the incarnation of our Lord, his life and teaching, as well as his resurrection, ascension and heavenly intercession, and his eventual coming again.

There is also a new theological emphasis on the task and mission of the Church in this world. As we shall see, Liberation Theology clearly envisages Christians sacrificing for social justice. A new and profound sense of ecological responsibility is evidenced in some prayers. Broken bread is our nourishment but also a reminder of the desperately needed bread to feed the world's hungry.

The eschatological dimension of the Eucharist is also clearly adumbrated in the newer prayers of thanksgiving in Holy Communion. This earthly Lord's Supper points to the eschatological banquet, vividly imagined in the book of Revelation, which the worshippers hope to share with the saints in the final kingdom.

---

polytus's *The Apostolic Tradition* (London: S.P.C.K., 1968) have had an important impact on modern revision of the eucharistic prayers.

5. *The Study of Liturgy,* p. 333.

6. It is worth noting W. J. Grisbrooke's article "Anaphora" in *A New Dictionary of Liturgy and Worship,* ed. J. G. Davies (London: S.C.M. Press, 1986). After examining ancient anaphoras and collecting their features and arranging them in a logical order, Grisbrooke came up with the identical arrangement of the three new anaphoras of the 1970 *Ordo Missae.*

It will make our assertions more vivid if we select a few samples of the newer prayers of thanksgiving in the Eucharist. The *Alternative Service Book 1980* includes in one intercession at Communion the following:

> MINISTER: Teach us to use the fruits of the earth to your glory, and for the good of all mankind
> ALL: Hear us, good Lord.[7]

Another requires all to say together:

> Send us out
> in the power of thy Spirit,
> to live and work
> to thy praise and glory. Amen.[8]

Also a preface for Saints' Days proceeds as follows:

> And now we give thee thanks, for the glorious pledge of the hope of our calling which thou has given us in thy saints; that following their example and strengthened by their fellowship, we may run with perseverance the race that is set before us, and with them receive the unfading crown of glory.[9]

The Fourth Eucharistic Prayer of the new Roman rite includes the following petition:

> Father, in your mercy grant also to us, your children,
> to enter into our heavenly inheritance in the company
> of the Virgin Mary, the Mother of God,
> and your apostles and saints.
> Then in your kingdom, freed from corruption of sin and death,
> we shall sing your glory with every creature
> through Christ our Lord,
> through whom you give us everything that is good.[10]

---

7. *ASB*, p. 168.
8. *Ibid.*, p. 199 from Holy Communion B.
9. *Ibid.*, p. 205 from Holy Communion B.
10. *The Sunday Missal: A New Edition* (London: Collins, 1984), p. 55.

One example from the eucharistic prayers of the Free Churches must suffice at this point. It comes from the United Reformed Church's *Service Book* published by Oxford University Press in 1989 and reads as follows:

> Strengthen for service, Lord,
> the hands that have taken holy things.
> May the ears that have heard your word
> be deaf to clamour and dispute.
> May the eyes that have seen your great love
> shine with the light of hope.
> May the tongues that have sung your praise
> also speak the truth.
> May the feet that have walked in your house
> ever walk in the light.
> May the bodies that have tasted your living body be
> restored to newness of life.
> Thanks be to God for his gift beyond words.
> *Amen.*[11]

The Theological Agreements on the Eucharist

Perhaps the most surprising feature in these trans-denominational eucharistic agreements is common interpretation of sacrifice, an issue on which until very recently not only Protestants and Catholics were divided, but also Evangelicals and Catholics within the Church of England.

The Lutherans and Roman Catholics were able to agree that "with contrite hearts we offer ourselves as a living and holy sacrifice which must be expressed in the whole of our daily lives."[12] But the difficulty remained if the worshipping assembly was said to "offer Christ" in the sacrifice of the Eucharist. Lutherans denied such an "offering," believing that only by this means could they preserve the unrepeatable character of the perfect sacrifice of the cross. They added, however, that they could accept the Roman Catholic view that through "this Union between Christ and Christians, the eucharistic assembly 'offers

---

11. See pp. 29-30, a prayer after Communion in the second Order.
12. *Modern Eucharistic Agreement* (London: S.P.C.K., 1973), p. 37.

45

Christ' by consenting in the power of the Holy Spirit to be offered by him to the Father." For it was agreed, "apart from Christ we have no gifts, no worship, no sacrifice of our own to offer to God. All we can plead is Christ, the sacrificial lamb and victim whom the Father himself has given us."

The Anglican–Roman Catholic International Commission meeting at Windsor produced *An Agreed Statement on Eucharistic Doctrine* in 1971. It also affirmed the once-for-all, unique and perfect sacrifice on the cross. The third section, "The Presence of Christ," expresses the conviction that as the great High Priest in eternity Christ intercedes for his people: "It is the Lord present at the right hand of the Father, and therefore transcending the sacramental order, who thus offers to the Church, in the eucharistic signs, the special gift of himself." Unhappily, the issue of the offertory is not mentioned in the *Agreed Statement*.

The Dombes statement, *Towards a Common Eucharistic Faith?*, includes the following affirmation in its definition of the Eucharist: "This meal is the effective sign of the gift Christ made of himself as the bread of life, through the sacrifice of his life and his death and by his resurrection."[13] The third section, "Memorial of Christ," emphasizes that the whole life of Christ was sacrificial and that this sacrifice is re-presented in the Eucharist:

Christ instituted the eucharist as a memorial *(anamnesis)* of his whole life and above all of his cross and resurrection. Christ, with everything he has accomplished for us and for all creation, is present himself in this memorial, which is also a foretaste of his kingdom. The memorial, in which Christ acts through the joyful celebration of his Church, implies this re-presentation and anticipation. Therefore, it is not only a matter of recalling to mind a past event or even its significance. The memorial is the effective proclamation by the Church of the great work of God. By its communion with Christ, the Church participates in this reality from which it draws its life.[14]

The next two paragraphs clearly indicate how the Church offers a sacrifice:

13. *Ibid.*, p. 57.
14. *Ibid.*, p. 58.

46

The memorial, being at once re-presentation and anticipation, is lived out in thanksgiving and intercession. Making the memorial of the passion, resurrection and ascension of Christ, our High Priest and Mediator, the Church presents to the Father the one perfect sacrifice of the Son and asks him to accord every man the benefit of the great work of redemption it proclaims.

Thus united to our Lord, who offers himself to his father, and in communion with the universal Church in heaven and on earth, we are renewed in the covenant sealed with the blood of Christ and we offer ourselves as a living and holy sacrifice which must be expressed in the whole of our daily life.[15]

The parallels between the Dombes Statement and the Louvain Statement prepared by the Faith and Order Committee of the World Council of Churches are very close. The *sacrificum laudis* is expressed thus:

The eucharist is the great sacrifice of praise by which the Church speaks on behalf of the whole creation. For the world which God has reconciled to himself is present in every eucharist: in the bread and wine, in the persons of the faithful, and in the prayers they offer for themselves and for all men. As the faithful and their prayers are united in the Person of our Lord and to his intercession they are transfigured and accepted. Thus the eucharist reveals to the world what it must become.[16]

But the *sacrificium laudis* is certainly not our oblation of Christ's sacrifice.

The Anglican theologian who has devoted most thinking to this issue is the Revd. Canon Kenneth Stevenson, a member of the Church of England Liturgical Commission. The difficulties of the doctrine of eucharistic sacrifice have been carefully and graphically exposed in his important article entitled "Eucharistic Sacrifice — An Insoluble Liturgical Problem?"[17] The first difficulty he considers is the way the offertory is dealt with. When bread and wine are placed

15. *Ibid.*, p. 64.
16. *Ibid.*, p. 84.
17. This appeared in *The Scottish Journal of Theology* 42 (1989): 469-92.

on the table the president may say nothing at all. Or, he may cite 1 Chronicles 29:14, saying "Of your own do we give you." Or he may say words which formally present the gifts to God. One other option is that he may point to Christ as the only offering other than the offering of ourselves. The difficulty, says Stevenson, is caused by the differing and apparently uncertain ways of affirming the offertory, or even by the conviction that an offertory is entirely inappropriate. Stevenson instances the latter objection by citing the words of a friend and fellow-member of the Liturgical Commission, the Revd. Dr. Bryan D. Spinks, who insists: "The Church cannot offer Christ, because the Head and the Body, though one, are united only by the action of the Head. We therefore cannot identify the self offering and the eucharistic memorial with the sacrifice of the Cross."[18]

In a summary of his own book, *Eucharist and Offering,* Canon Stevenson suggests that the liturgies of East and West have adopted three different ways of understanding offering. In one view there is an offering of "story" in which the narrative of salvation is found in the sermon and in the eucharistic prayer. The offering may, on another view, be the people's "response," by which is meant listening to the story in Word and Eucharist, but also acting upon it. The Church is here not a passive recipient, but dares to act boldly in imitation of her Savior. But offering may also be understood in terms of "gift." Here, says Canon Stevenson, we come to the most sensitive issue of all "because of the paradox that in bread and wine God speaks to us in ordinary food that is itself the result of dying and rising, wheat crushed and baked, grapes crushed and fermented. In enacted parable as of old, Jesus plays it slant. The bread and wine are neither formally 'offered' nor ritually 'held back.' They are just there on the table, eloquent testimony of the parable to end all parables, that it is in dying that we live to him."[19]

His exposition of the offertory continues with the observation that there are four ways through the *anamnesis* in the historic and contemporary liturgies. The first is by the formula "remembering . . . we offer," which is used by the West Syrian and Roman liturgies. It has the benefit of proclaiming what the Church is doing, but without any direct relation to Christ's death, which leaves it open to Reformation-style criticisms. The second anamnetic route is used by the Anglican rites of

18. *Ibid.,* p. 484.
19. *Ibid.,* p. 486.

1980: "With this bread and cup . . . we remember." This formula stresses the sacrifice of Calvary but does not explain what the bread and wine are there for. The third option is "in union with Christ we offer," which was employed by both the American United Methodist rite and the ecumenical Lima Liturgy of the World Council of Churches. It relies largely on what Christ is doing now in his intercession, rather than what the Church is doing now in remembering and offering. Its weakness may be that it places too little emphasis on the paradox that both Christ's and the Church's actions are involved. The last anamnetic route is a variation of the third and is used by the Church of Scotland. This ties the eternal sacrifice with the spiritual sacrifice of the church, and with the invocation of the Holy Spirit on the Eucharist; its key phrase is "pleading the eternal sacrifice."

Stevenson's own conviction is that the story should have both vertical and horizontal emphases "so that what God is supposed to have done engages with how human beings are involved." Also, it needs to be spread throughout the anaphora, but focused in the *anamnesis-epiclesis,* because that is where, in traditional texts, the Church says what it thinks it is doing.[20]

Let us turn now to contemporary expressions of "offering" in eucharistic prayers. The Roman Missal of 1970 includes the following offertory prayers:

C: Blessed are you, Lord, God of all creation. Through your goodness we have this bread to offer, which earth has given and human hands have made. It will become for us the bread of life.

P: By the mystery of this water and wine may we come to share in the divinity of Christ, who humbled himself to share in our humanity.

C: Blessed are you Lord, God of all creation. Through your goodness, we have this wine to offer, fruit of the vine and work of the human hands. It will become our spiritual drink.

P: Blessed be God forever.

C: Lord God, we ask you to receive us and be pleased with the sacrifice we offer you with humble and contrite hearts. . . .[21]

20. *Ibid.,* p. 489.
21. Max Thurian and Geoffrey Wainwright, eds., *Baptism and Eucharist: Ecumenical Convergence in Celebration* (Geneva: World Council of Churches; Grand Rapids: Wm. B. Eerdmans, 1983), p. 130.

The fourth eucharistic prayer in the Church of England's *Alternative Service Book 1980* refers, as follows, to sacrifice:

> Therefore, Lord and heavenly Father,
> in remembrance of the precious death and passion,
> the mighty resurrection and glorious ascension
> of your dear Son Jesus Christ,
> we offer you through him this sacrifice of praise and thanksgiving.
> Grant that by his merits and death,
> and through faith in his blood,
> we and all your Church may receive forgiveness of our sins
> and all other benefits of his passion.
> Although we are unworthy, through our many sins,
> to offer you any sacrifice,
> yet we pray that you will accept this,
> our duty and service that we owe. . . .[22]

The Methodist Service Book of 1975 has the simple but meaningful petition:

> Accept us as we offer ourselves to be a living sacrifice, and bring us with the whole creation to your heavenly kingdom.[23]

The *Service Book* of the United Reformed Church of 1989 includes the following communion petition which is reminiscent of the phrasing of the Church of Scotland:

> Therefore remembering the work and passion
> of our Saviour Jesus Christ,
> and pleading his eternal sacrifice,
> we set forth this memorial,
> which he willed us to make.
> Send down your Spirit upon these your gifts
> that they may be for us his body and blood,
> and in receiving them, we may be healed
> and renewed to serve you in the world.[24]

22. *ASB*, p. 141.
23. P. 58, in the fourth order of Communion A.
24. P. 13, from the First Thanksgiving.

The Many Meanings of the Eucharist

Hitherto we have largely limited ourselves to a consideration of sacrifice as one of the many meanings of the Eucharist because it has been a bone of contention between Catholic and Protestant interpreters. In what follows attention will be devoted to other meanings of the Eucharist which have been ecumenically shared in recent years.[25]

It is remarkable that denominations which had hitherto used only the terms of Holy Communion or Lord's Supper have recently adopted the term "Eucharist." Even more intriguing, however, is that the more Catholic denominations, which hitherto employed the term "Prayer of Consecration," now prefer to use the term "Thanksgiving." This calls for some explanation.

The Greek word *eucharistia* means thanksgiving, and was one of the earliest terms used for the Communion liturgy in the Hellenic world. J. P. Audet, in his "Literary Forms and Contents of a Normal Eucharistia in the First Century," has thrown brilliant light on the relationship between the blessing in the primitive Eucharist and the Jewish *berakah* of "benediction."[26] He pointed out, first, that the *berakah* is a solemn act of worship addressed to God, secondly, that it is a strongly communal action, and thirdly that it has a threefold structure. The first component is the "benediction" proper, which is an invitation to divine praise; its second element is the assertion of a motive for the praise, which is always a *miraculum Dei*, a marvellous work of God; and the third element is doxological. It is clear that the parallels between the *berakah* and the thanksgiving prayer in the Eucharist are close. Both are paeans of praise for the mighty works of God.

Contemporary eucharistic prayers express human gratitude, for, as Professor William Barclay, the New Testament scholar, writes: "The Eucharist is the time for thanksgiving to God for his gifts in creation and redemption."[27] An example of the profound and widened sense of gratitude comes from Eucharistic Prayer III of the Anglican *Alternative Service Book 1980:*

25. The present author has expounded at greater length the many meanings of the Eucharist, with worldwide liturgical examples of their use, in *Bread of Life and Cup of Joy: Newer Ecumenical Perspectives on the Eucharist* (Grand Rapids: Wm. B. Eerdmans; Leominster, England: Gracewing, 1993).

26. This article appeared in *Studia Evangelica: Papers Presented to the International Congress on "The Four Gospels" in 1957*, ed. K. Aland *et al.* (Berlin, 1959), pp. 623-62.

27. Barclay, *The Lord's Supper* (London: S.C.M. Press, 1967), p. 108.

Father, we give you thanks and praise,
through your beloved Son Jesus Christ,
your living Word through whom you have created all things;

Who was sent by you, in your great goodness, to be our Saviour;
by the power of the Holy Spirit he took flesh and, as your Son,
born of the blessed Virgin was seen on earth
and went about among us;

He opened wide his arms for us upon the cross;
he put an end to death by dying for us
and revealed the resurrection by rising to new life;
so he fulfilled your will and won for you a holy people.[28]

The Methodist Service Book of 1965 has the following eucharistic Thanksgiving:

Father, all-powerful and ever-living God,
it is indeed right, it is our joy and our salvation,
always and everywhere to give you thanks and praise
    through Jesus Christ your Son and Lord.
You created all things and made us in your own image.
When we had fallen into sin, you gave your only Son
    to be Our Saviour.
He shared our human nature, and died on the cross.
You raised him from the dead and exalted him to your right hand
in glory, where he lives forever to pray for us.
Through him you have sent your holy and life-giving Spirit
and made us your people, a royal priesthood, to stand before you
to proclaim your glory and celebrate your mighty acts.
And so with all the company of heaven we join
    in the unending hymn of praise. . . .[29]

The extended *anamnesis* of the First Thanksgiving of the *Service Book* (1989) of the United Reformed Church is a glorious tribute of gratitude to God:

28. *ASB*, p. 136.
29. Pp. 56-57.

Holy and blessed are you, Lord our God,
King of the universe.
In the beginning you brought light out of darkness,
life out of clay.
When in Adam we disobeyed,
you did not cease loving us.
When we were slaves in Egypt,
you led us to freedom through the Red Sea.
When we wandered in the wilderness,
you gave us bread and revealed the Law to be our guide.
You brought us over Jordan to the promised land,
but we were unfaithful
and would not listen to your prophets.
Yet even in the bitterness of exile
and the harshness of oppression
your faithfulness has always surrounded us.
In the fullness of time, you sent your Son Jesus
to be the living bread and the fulfillment of the Law.
Born of Mary, baptized by John,
he lived among us and proclaimed your kingdom,
bound up the brokenhearted, challenged the proud.
Yet he was betrayed, tortured, and crucified.
In anguish of spirit he opened his arms
and gave up his life.
But out of the depths you raised him up,
broke the power of the enemy,
and won for us forgiveness of our sins
by the power of his cross.
You exalted him as Lord of life
to reign with you eternally,
victorious over sin and death.[30]

As mentioned earlier, modern Eucharists typically have a profound sense of eschatology, of the last things. Hence the Eucharist is understood as an eschatological banquet. As Professor Alasdair Heron has written: "What Christ was, suffered and did for us he makes ever and again contemporary in its completeness for us who are still *in via*. We have to do not only with past and present, but with past,

30. Pp. 11-12.

53

present, *and future* meeting in Him and making Him the ground, accompaniment *and goal* of our journey."[31]

There seem to be three modern sources for the return of the eschatological dimension in understanding the Eucharist. One is the theology of hope which has been exemplified by the German theologians of our time, Jurgen Moltmann, Gerhard Sauter, and Johannes Metz.[32] A second factor is the unusual attention paid in our days to the future, including even the anticipation of political and social revolutions. Some liberals have, in this light, perceived Jesus as less a gentle teacher or model social reformer than as a spiritual revolutionary whose members trusted in the transforming love of God, forgave their enemies, and followed the suffering Christ through martyrdom in the hope of resurrection. The new theologians manifest their distinctiveness in the fact that their direction is expectant and future-oriented. The eschatological dimension of contemporary eucharistic theology is also inspired by a steadfast refusal to succumb to the paralyzing despair so characteristic of our century, caused by two world wars, the Nazi holocaust, the threat of atomic warfare, the plight of millions who die of hunger, and millions more who live a marginalized existence with only crumbs to eat and without shelter. Life without hope is not worth living, and Christian faith galvanizes hope. St. Luke's account of the Last Supper, at 22:29-30, reports Jesus as promising his disciples: "And I appoint unto you a kingdom, even as my Father appointed unto me. That you may eat and drink at my table in my kingdom." Other important eschatological elements in the New Testament are to be found in the Epistle to the Hebrews and the Book of Revelation. Hebrews speaks at length about the eternal, heavenly priesthood of Christ, and Revelation about the marriage feast of the Lamb.

The Epistle, in summary, demonstrates Christ as having a permanent priesthood as the risen and ascended Lord, "wherefore also

31. Heron, *Table and Tradition* (Philadelphia: Westminster Press, 1983), p. 153.

32. Moltmann's work is *Theologie der Hoffnung,* the fifth edition of which appeared in 1965 and was translated as *The Theology of Hope* (New York: Harper & Row, 1967). Gerhard Sauter's book is *Zukunft und Verheissung* (Zürich: Zwingli Verlag, 1965). Johannes Metz has two important essays, "The Church in the World" in *The Church in History,* ed. T. P. Burke (New York: Sheed and Ward, 1966), and "Die Verantwortung der Christlichen Gemeinde," in *Die Neue Gemeinde,* ed. Adolf Exeter (Mainz: Matthias Grünewald Verlag, 1966).

he is able to save to the uttermost those that draw near unto God through him, seeing he ever lives to make intercession for them."[33] The same writer urges his hearers "Through him then let us continually offer up a sacrifice of praise to God, that is, the fruit of lips that acknowledge his name."[34] It is these convictions of the writer of the Epistle to the Hebrews which have found lodging in the historic liturgies because they combine emphasis on the suffering of Christ making his obedience perfect,[35] on the new covenant that his sacrifice to end all other sacrifices made possible, on the Body of Christ's *sacrificium laudis* as its proper response, and, supremely, on the fact that the enthroned Christ lives to make intercession for his people.

The eschatological banquet envisioned by the author of the book of Revelation is a fusion of three rich metaphors, which ocur in concentrated form in a single verse: "And the angel said to me: 'Write this: Blessed are those who are invited to the marriage supper of the Lamb.'"[36] Christ is referred to as Lamb of God twenty-eight times in Revelation, echoing the declaration of John the Baptist in the Fourth Gospel: "Behold, the Lamb of God who takes away the sin of the world!"[37] The image of the paschal lamb is also recalled, for the Lamb bears on his neck the marks of his slaughtering (Rev. 5:6, 9, 12; and 13:8). Yet the Lamb of God overcame death (5:5-6) and rules the world, taking over the book of destiny in the heavenly council (4:2f. and 5:7f.) He also establishes the rule of peace and celebrates his marriage festival with the community (19:9). The image of Christ as bridegroom is found in Paul's letters (Ephesians 5:22f.) as well as in the final chapters of the Book of Revelation where the heavenly city is described as being "prepared as a bride adorned for her husband."[38] The third element in the melange of metaphors is the feast or festival. As a marriage festival it is an occasion of the utmost joy, for it declares the indissoluble union of Christ with his faithful disciples of all the centuries, the communion of saints.

This recovered eschatological and joyful emphasis in the Eucharist

33. Hebrews 7:25.
34. Hebrews 13:15.
35. Hebrews 2:10.
36. Revelation 19:9.
37. John 1:29.
38. Revelation 21:2, a direct echo of Isaiah 61:10.

is a welcome corrective to the pattern of stressing only the agony and death of Christ, and thus treating the marriage feast of the Lamb as a funeral repast.

The most thorough study correlating the Eucharist with the eschatology of the New Testament is the pioneering exposition of Geoffrey Wainwright, *Eucharist and Eschatology*, published in 1971. Wainwright sees the Eucharist as projecting the *parousia* (second coming of Christ) in four major ways: (a) the Eucharist is a memorial of Christ himself as well as a promise of greater things to come; (b) the Church claims that promise in its cry of *Maranatha* in the Eucharist; (c) the Eucharist promises forgiveness of sins and eternal life to the penitent, but judgement to the impenitent; and (d) the Eucharist is a projection in the temporal sense — casting Christ's final advent into the present.[39]

Viewing the Eucharist as an anticipation of the eschatological banquet has several implications, the foremost of which is boundless joy, since Christ will be all in all with his friends. But there are differences between the Eucharist and the final heavenly banquet: whereas the first affords a taste of the Kingdom, the second is the fullness of the Kingdom. Furthermore, whereas the Church now eats at the Table of the Lord at set intervals, the Heavenly Banquet will be unending in its felicity. And whereas the community at the Eucharist is local, that at the final eschatological banquet will be universal.

The great historic liturgies acknowledge that at the Eucharist the Church joins in the worship of heaven in both the acclamation of the *Sanctus,* "Holy, holy, holy, Lord God of hosts; heaven and earth are full of your glory,"[40] and in the recitation of the Lord's Prayer, which anticipates that all the saints will be called children of God. The eschatological character of the Eucharist, in its stress on the completion and perfection of the Kingdom of God in history, affords a further incentive in prosecuting the evangelizing mission of the church, so proving its fidelity to Christ's post-Resurrection command: "Go, therefore, and make disciples of all nations . . ." which was linked to the glowing promise, "Lo, I am with you always, to the close of the age."[41]

39. Wainwright, *Eucharist and Eschatology* (London: Epworth Press, 1971), pp. 91-93.

40. Isaiah's acclamation "the whole earth is full of his glory" (6:3) is amplified to say "Heaven and earth are full of your glory."

41. Matthew 28:19, 20.

The third Roman eucharistic prayer has the following *anamnesis:*

Father, calling to mind the death your Son endured for our salvation, his glorious resurrection and ascension into heaven, and ready to greet him when he comes again, we offer you in thanksgiving this holy and living sacrifice. . . .

May he make us an everlasting gift to you and enable us to share in the inheritance of the saints . . . on whose constant intercession we rely for help. . . .

Welcome into your kingdom our departed brothers and sisters and all who have left this world in your friendship. We hope to enjoy for ever the vision of your glory, through Christ our Lord, from whom all good things come.[42]

The fourth eucharistic prayer of the Roman liturgy is modelled on the Orthodox liturgy of St. John Chrysostom.

The Church of England's *Alternative Service Book 1980* in its first eucharistic prayer proceeds as follows, after the commemoration of creation and redemption:

Therefore, heavenly Father,
we remember his offering of himself
made once for all upon the cross,
and proclaim his mighty resurrection and glorious ascension.
As we look for his coming in glory,
we celebrate with this bread and this cup
his one perfect sacrifice. . . .

and the prayer concludes:

Through him, and with him, and in him,
by the power of the Holy Spirit,
with all who stand before you in earth and in heaven,
we worship you, Father almighty,
in songs of everlasting praise.

42. *Sunday Missal,* pp. 48-50.

All: Blessing and honour and glory and power be yours
      for ever and ever.[43]

The final prayer at the English Methodist Communion refers precisely and appropriately to the eschatological banquet:

We thank you, Lord,
that you have fed us in this sacrament,
united us with Christ,
and given us a foretaste of the heavenly banquet
prepared for all mankind. Amen.[44]

The First Thanksgiving Prayer at the Eucharist of the United Reformed Church's *Service Book* published in 1989 includes the petition:

Bring us together from east and west
and north and south
to sit with Abraham, Isaac, and Jacob,
(and . . . whom we remember this day)
so that at the wedding feast of the Lamb
we may rejoice with all the redeemed. . . .[45]

Having considered the Lord's Supper as Eucharist, Sacrifice, and Eschatological Banquet, we have also now to consider such meanings as Communion, Memorial, Mystery, and Liberation.

The very term "communion" implies a joyful meal of unity, namely that of Christ and the Body of Christ, his friends and followers. St. Paul insisted on the positive necessity of unity at the Lord's Supper in the statement: "The bread which we break, is it not a participation (communion) in the body of Christ? Because there is one bread, we who are many are one body, for we all partake of the one bread."[46] Markus Barth sees three meanings in this term *koinonia* (communion) as employed by St. Paul as he expounds this citation. It means: "(1) to give, in and as a community, thanks to God for the gift of

43. *ASB*, pp. 130-32.
44. *The Methodist Service Book* (1975), p. 61.
45. *Service Book* (1989), p. 13.
46. 1 Corinthians 10:16-17.

Christ, (2) to comfort and strengthen brothers and sisters in demonstrating that Christ's death has created the bond of mutual love, and (3) to signal to all the world that God's work embraces all creatures and that the number of God's people is not yet complete."[47] The same sense of unity is reflected in the earliest Eucharist of the Church. The *Didache* includes the following prayer for the unity of the Church:

> As this broken bread was scattered on the mountains, and gathered together into one, so let your Church be gathered together from the ends of the earth into the kingdom, for yours is the glory and the power through Jesus Christ for ever.[48]

The same image is repeated in Book VII of *The Apostolic Constitutions* in its prayer:

> Almighty Lord and everlasting God, gather your Church from the ends of the earth into your kingdom, as this corn was scattered and is now made one loaf.[49]

In our contemporary world the sense of unity in the Communion should mean that in reasserting our identity with Christ we should be recalled to our true selves again, and experience anew the forgiving love of Christ demanding that we forgive all others. In a time of secularism we should be cheered by recollecting that there is a vast community of the friends of God in Christ spanning the centuries and the continents. We should, whatever our denominational affiliation, regard it as a scandal that the unitive meal is by some denominations refused to other Christians not of their own church. This is clearly a betrayal of the plea of Christ for his followers, "that they may all be one; even as you, Father, are in me, and I in you, that they may also be in us, that the world may believe that you have sent me" (John 17:21).

Eucharistic Prayer II in the modern Roman rite has felicitous references to the unity created by the Holy Spirit, with intercession for the Church, and a plea for unity with the saints:

---

47. Barth, *Rediscovering the Lord's Supper* (Atlanta: John Knox Press, 1988), p. 48.

48. Cited in George Every, *Basic Liturgy* (London: The Faith Press, 1961), p. 72.

49. *Ibid.*

May all of us who share in the body and blood of Christ be brought
together in unity by the Holy Spirit.

Lord, remember your Church throughout the world;
make us to grow in love, together with N. our Pope,
N. our bishop and all the clergy.

Remember our brothers and sisters
who have gone to their rest
in the hope of rising again;
bring them and all the departed
into the light of your presence.

The Anglican *Alternative Service Book 1980* has a final post-Communion Prayer which sees all of us as forgiven prodigals, looking
forward to eternity, and committed to bringing life and light to
others:

Father of all, we give you thanks and praise, that when we were still
far off you met us in your Son and brought us home. Dying and
living, he declared your love, gave us grace, and opened the gate of
glory. May we who share Christ's body live his risen life; we who
drink his cup bring life to others; we in whom the Spirit lights give
light to the world. Keep us firm in the hope you have set before us,
so we and all your children shall be free, and the whole earth live to
praise your name; through Christ our Lord.[50]

The Methodist Service Book (1975) echoes the image of the *Didache*
in its Communion Order:

Though we are many, we are one body
because we all share in the one loaf.[51]

An alternative post-Communion prayer in the United Reformed
Church's *Service Book* of 1989 stresses unity:

50. *ASB*, p. 144.
51. P. B14.

Most gracious God,
we praise you for what you have given
and for what you have promised us here.
You have made us one
with all your people
in heaven and on earth . . .
and we ask . . . that our love may be your love
reaching out into the life of the world;
through Jesus Christ our Lord.[52]

Protestants have always insisted that the New Testament emphasizes that the Lord's Supper is a commemorative meal. Luke 22:19 reports that at the Last Supper when Jesus had broken the bread and given thanks, he said, "This is my body, which is given for you. Do this in remembrance of me." Paul's wording is almost identical, including the statement "that the Lord Jesus on the night when he was betrayed took bread, and when he had given thanks, he broke it and said, 'This is my body which is for you. Do this in remembrance of me'" (1 Corinthians 11:23-24).

Modern scholarship has increasingly recognized that the Last Supper was celebrated during and influenced by the Jewish Passover festival. It has been suggested that there survives even in the present day Passover ritual a detail that demands a strongly Messianic interpretation. Near the commencement of the celebration, after the president or host of the company has called upon God, Creator of the vine and the fruits of the earth, and the guests have drunk a cup of wine and eaten green vegetables, he breaks off a large part from the middle of three pieces of unleavened bread. He then covers it with a napkin and hides it. This action is redolent with Messianic symbolism.

The name of this portion which has been broken off and concealed is *Afikoman*. The name is neither Hebrew nor Aramaic in origin, but Greek. Professor David Daube, a learned orthodox Jew, has affirmed in a London lecture, "*Aphiqoman* is the Greek *aphikomenos* or *ephikomenos*, 'The Coming One,' 'He that Cometh.'"[53] Thomas Cor-

---

52. Pp. 20-21.
53. Daube's lecture, "He That Cometh," was delivered in October of 1966 at St. Paul's Cathedral, London, under the auspices of the Diocesan Council for Christian Jewish Understanding.

bishley views the drama of the Last Supper in the light of the *Afikoman* as follows:

> Picture then the Leader, at the Last Supper, calling for the *Afikoman*, which, we remember, has been hidden since the beginning of the proceedings, and saying to his followers: "The *Afikoman*, He who Comes, who was hitherto hidden, has now come. This piece of bread is my very self, no longer in type but in reality. When, therefore, you eat it, you are eating no longer a symbol, a foreshadowing of a future reality. You are eating my very self. Whenever in days to come, you eat this same *Afikoman*, remember that I am truly present in it and therefore in you."[54]

In the Last Supper Jesus made two striking innovations. The first, as we have seen, was his declaration that he is the Messiah, in the breaking of the bread and references to it as his body. The second was his pronouncement over the cup of wine: "This is my blood which is poured out for many" or, "This cup is the new covenant in my blood." Thus, one can only conclude that Jesus was inaugurating a New Covenant feast that would replace the Passover and the Old Covenant with Israel for his followers in the new expanded Israel, the Church. By these actions Christ was claiming for himself a central and preeminent place in the history of God's chosen people, and the hardest part for the disciples to understand was that he would shortly become a crucified and agonized Messiah. The celebration of the Passover was less the memorial of an historic event than a means of making it actual, an enacted event in which each guest was taking part. In the same way all guests at the Lord's Supper now share a redemption of which they are beneficiaries. No interpretation denies the living contemporary presence of Christ. As Dr. John Huxtable wittily phrased it: "No interpretation of the Eucharist affirms the 'Real Absence.'" Every Eucharist affirms the "Real Presence" of Christ.

Nonetheless, in one sense or another every Eucharist is acknowledged to be a mystery. The Orthodox Church still maintains a central emphasis on mystery. Alexander Schmemann, for example, criticizes the Western Church for having rejected the *musterion*, which he defines as

---

54. Corbishley, *One Body, One Spirit* (Leighton Buzzard: Faith Press; New York: Morehouse-Barlow, 1973), p. 23.

the holding together, in a mystical and existential, rather than rational, synthesis of both the total *transcendence* of God and His genuine *presence*. But this mystery is precisely that of the Kingdom of God, the faith and piety of the Church being rooted in the experience *now* of that which is to *come*, in the communion by means of "this world" with Him who is always "beyond," in truly partaking of the joy and peace of the Holy Spirit.[55]

We may note the necessary use of paradox to maintain the description (*not* a definition) of the mystery. The Eastern Orthodox Church has had an important impact on ecumenical thinking. But two other influences have combined to make mystery theology significant in our day. One is the important analysis and exposition of the *Mysterientheologie* associated with the German Benedictine Abbey of Maria Laach. The second highly significant reason for the importance of the mystery theology is that it had a profound impact on the chief liturgical document to emerge from the Second Vatican Council in Rome. This was the *Constitution on the Sacred Liturgy*, promulgated on December 4, 1963.

Its chief exponent, Dom Odo Casel, distinguished three aspects of Christian mystery.[56] First of all, the supreme mystery is God in his own Being, the utterly Holy and Unapproachable One, Ineffable and Transcendent. Second, the revelation of God in Christ is the personal mystery of God the invisible revealed in the flesh; in his humiliation, Incarnation, sacrificial death upon the cross, as in his Resurrection and Ascension, God marvelously reveals himself in a way that far surpasses all human capacities. The third mystery is that of the cult, which is defined as a liturgical action "in which the redemptive act is rendered in the rite,"[57] and "since the cultic community accomplishes the rite, it shares the saving rite and through it attains redemption."[58]

55. Schmemann, *Church, World, Mission: Reflections on Orthodoxy in the West* (Crestwood, N.Y.: St. Vladimir's Seminary Press, 1979), p. 60.

56. See his *Das christliche Kultmysterium*, 3rd ed. (Regensburg, 1938).

57. The technical terms used are *Repraesentatio* and *Gegenwartigsetzung*.

58. See the present author's *Worship and Theology in England: The Ecumenical Century* (Princeton: Princeton University Press; London: Oxford University Press, 1965), pp. 29f. for a brief consideration of the contribution of the Augustinian canons of Klosterneuberg, Austria, and the *Centre de Pastorale Liturgique* in France, in spreading and supplementing the work of Maria Laach Abbey.

For Casel the entire work of redemption is made present again in the liturgy from the first to the second advent as an objective reality, and not subjective or psychological in character, though it is veiled in symbol or image. In other words, liturgy shares in the reality of God's redemptive action of grace for his people. Another term related to "mystery" in this theology is "transfiguration," an important term also for Eastern Orthodoxy. The purpose of the liturgy is to sanctify, even to deify humankind, bringing transfigured Christians to the Christ of the Transfiguration. Through the bestowal of grace in the liturgy, humanity is raised to the supernatural order and therefore into sharing the divine existence, light, and glory.

Maria Laach's theology is not concerned with any individual meditations on the crucified Christ or devotions to the Christ "imprisoned" in the tabernacle, but only in a proleptic sharing in the life of the glorified Christ. The focal center is Christ in glory, but with the constant recollection that this Christ went "from God to God" by the route of humiliation and suffering and the *via dolorosa*.

As was made plain by Abbot Herwegen in *Kirche und Seele* (Munster, 1928), faith is more than assent to intellectual propositions, since it demands the commitment of the entire person for the whole of life to God. Humanity is no longer regarded in atomistic fashion, but as part of the people of God, mystically incorporated into the *corpus Christi* in the action of the Eucharist, sharing the life, purposes, and divine energy of God. This theology also conceives of daily work as worship, the offering that the Christian in the world brings to the company of the transfigured, to be presented in the offertory of the liturgy, together with the perfect offering of the Atonement renewed. The Eucharist itself is also transformed: it is no longer merely a hierarchical offering in which the laity are passively present, but an action of grace in which the general priesthood of the people of God is exercised in response to the gracious offering and sacrifice of the great High Priest, Christ himself.

There is a four-fold value in recognizing the Eucharist as a mystery. First, the acknowledgment that there is an element of divine transcendence in all God's dealings with humanity, and especially in the self-giving of his eternal Son, which leads us to a very suitable humility. Secondly, the emphasis on mystery makes clear that *lex orandi* is *lex credendi*, and that it is in the surrender of the human mind and will in worship and union with God that God is best known. Thirdly, regard for the mystery in the Eucharist underscores the dominant eschatological experience, which was so prominent in Patristic and Orthodox eucharistic celebration. As Ernst Benz observes: "The Orthodox liturgy has preserved unchanged this early Christian mood of rejoicing and spiritual gladness. In this its character is quite different from the Eucharist in, say, Reformed Christianity, where the early Christian spirit of gladness is clouded over and obscured by the spirit of penitence."[59] One is reminded of the *bon mot* that Christian worship is normally celebrated in a banqueting hall, not a laundry. Fourthly, the sense of mystery keeps alive the recognition that attendance at the Eucharist is the supreme privilege of the members of the Body of Christ. Such a view has been recently recovered in the new Roman Catholic revision of the rite of Initiation, where it is the requirement of a catechumenate to prepare believers for the privilege of the Eucharist.

Perhaps the greatest tribute paid to the Orthodox sense of "the mysteries" is in the adoption, by the Second Vatican Council, of a eucharistic prayer modelled on the Eastern Orthodox Eucharist.[60] The preface to a Eucharistic Prayer IV has a hint of transcendence: "Through all eternity you live in unapproachable light" and "lead all men to the joyful vision of your light." Among the *mirabilia Christi* it declares that "he sent the Holy Spirit from you, Father, as his first gift to those who believe," and it employs a different Invocation of the Holy Spirit *(epiklesis)* as the formula of consecration:

Father, may this Holy Spirit sanctify these offerings.
Let them be the body and blood of Jesus Christ our
Lord as we celebrate the great mystery
which he left us as an everlasting covenant.

Also the memorial acclamation of the people is prefaced by the words:

Let us proclaim the mystery of faith.[61]

---

59. Benz, *The Eastern Orthodox Church: Its Thought and Life* (Chicago: Aldine Publishing Company, 1983), p. 23. The very early Christian rejoicing is recorded in Acts 2:46, where we are informed: "And breaking bread in their homes, they partook of food with glad and generous hearts, praising God."

60. See *Sunday Missal*, where the Eucharistic Prayer is recorded on pp. 52-55.

61. P. 129 from Holy Communion A.

The Church of England's *Alternative Service Book 1980* has the following prayer at the Offertory:

Yours, Lord, is the greatness, the power,
the glory, the splendour, and the majesty;
for everything in heaven and on earth is yours.
All things come from you,
And of your own do we give you.[62]

It also includes the *Gloria in excelsis* sung by all the people as a post-Communion act of praise in Holy Communion A.[63] The third Eucharistic Prayer includes as well this *epiklesis:*

Send the Holy Spirit on your people
and gather into one in your kingdom
all who share this one bread and one cup,
so that we, in the company of all the saints,
may praise and glorify you for ever. . . .[64]

The Methodist Service Book of 1975 also uses the *Gloria in excelsis* as a post-Communion hymn,[65] and in the Thanksgiving affirms:

Father, all-powerful and ever-living God,
it is indeed right, it is our joy and our salvation
everywhere to give you thanks and praise
through Jesus Christ your Son our Lord. . . .
Through him you have sent your holy and life-giving
Spirit and made us your people, a royal priesthood,
to stand before you to proclaim your glory and
celebrate your mighty acts.
And so with all the company of heaven we join in
the unending hymn of praise:[66]

and the *Sanctus* follows.

62. *ASB*, p. 129, also from Holy Communion A.
63. *ASB*, p. 136 from Holy Communion A.
64. *ASB*, p. 138 from Holy Communion A.
65. B 12 (p. 26).
66. B 13 (p. 27).

The United Reformed Church's *Service Book* of 1989 includes the following section in its Thanksgiving II:

> With joy we give you thanks and praise,
> almighty God, Source of all life and love,
> that we live in your world,
> that you are always
> creating and sustaining it by your power,
> and that you have so made us
> that we can know and love you,
> trust and serve you.
>
> We give you thanks
> that you loved the world so much
> that you gave your only Son,
> so that everyone who has faith in him
> may not die but have eternal life.[67]

This simply expressed prayer of genuine gratitude is remarkable in its relative absence of traditional liturgical language.

Our final consideration will be of the revolutionary concept of the Eucharist as the sign of Liberation, a concept which understandably has flourished in the Third World — especially in South and Central America where colonialism, coupled with violent military dictatorship, has maintained a yawning gap between the rich and the poor. Its pioneering theologian is Gustavo Gutiérrez, whose book appeared in an English translation in 1973 with the title, *A Theology of Liberation*. In this volume he correlates the Eucharist with human brotherhood. He sees the life of Christ as a total self-giving for others, vividly recalled in the chief sacrament. He also views the Eucharist as a feast of joy that the Church shares and wishes others to share. Its very reason for being is to create true community. Furthermore, Gutiérrez acknowledges that liberation from sin is at the very root of the need for political liberation and socio-economic justice.

He believes that charity is not enough, and is only palliative. True compassion in his thinking demands revolutionary action. This he sees is a legitimate interpretation of *koinonia*. This term, translated as "community," has a threefold sense. It signifies, first, the common

67. P. 14.

ownership of the goods necessary for human existence, and is backed by the citation "Never forget to show kindness and to share what you have with others, for such are the sacrifices which God approves" (1 Corinthians 10:16). Secondly, *koinonia* means the union of Christians with the Holy Trinity: "The grace of the Lord Jesus Christ, and the love of God, and the fellowship in the Holy Spirit, be with you all" (2 Corinthians: cf. Philippians 2:1). Finally, Gutiérrez warns: "Without a real commitment against exploitation and alienation and for a society of solidarity and justice, the Eucharistic celebration is an empty action, lacking any genuine endorsement by those who participate in it."[68] Such a view endorses "protest Masses" and frequently "prophetic sermons."

Another liberation theologian is Leonardo Boff, whose book, *Faith on the Edge*, subtitled *Religion and Marginalized Existence*, was published in 1989. He envisages Christ as the Liberator, not as the celestial monarch or Suffering Servant. Perhaps the most impressive liberation theologian is Tissa Balasuriya of Sri Lanka, whose illuminating book, entitled *The Eucharist and Human Liberation*, appeared in 1979 under the Orbis imprint.

At the outset one would expect little support for so political an expression of Christianity, since Christianity's Master declared before Pilate: "My kingdom does not belong to this world. If it did, my followers would be fighting to save me from arrest from the Jews; my kingly authority comes from elsewhere" (John 18:36). Balasuriya finds the liberation of the Jews in their Egyptian slavery as a prefiguration of humanity's liberation in Christ. He also emphasizes God's judgement on irrelevant sacrifices in Isaiah 1:11-17 and 58:4-8, and links such religious exercises with blindness to social justice, citing Micah 6:7-8:

> God has told you what is good;
> and what is it that the Lord asks of you?
> Only to act justly, to love loyalty,
> and to walk wisely before your God.

Moreover, the prophetic denunciations of hypocritical or unethical forms of worship were renewed by Jesus when, for example, he overturned the tables of money-changers in the Temple and charged

68. *A Theology of Liberation* (Maryknoll, N.Y.: Orbis Books, 1973), p. 265.

them with turning his Father's house into a den of thieves. The communitarianism of Jesus, say Balasuriya, is further seen in the parable of the Good Samaritan, for Samaritans were looked down upon by the Jews as inferior, yet it is the Samaritan who shows genuine charity by bandaging the wounds of the robbed and stricken man, lifting him on his own horse and paying for him at the inn, while the Jewish priest merely passed by on the other side. Our interpreter also sees the Lord's Prayer as promoting liberation since it teaches Christians to acknowledge God as their Father, rejecting all discrimination in the form of race, gender, or status. Here Balasuriya sees a radical imperative in the Lord's Prayer for it includes a "fine combination of revolutionary commitment and love for all. . . . Forgiveness has to be a liberation of both oppressor and oppressed in a transformed relationship."[69] The petition "Give us this day our daily bread" is clearly communitarian since it stresses not my, but *our* bread.

When liberationists consider the death of Jesus, their exegesis is cloudier. They see it not as a reconciliation between God the Father and humanity or as an act of redemption for the sins of the world, but exclusively, it seems, as an example of radical social injustice in Pilate's willingness to have Christ crucified in the place of a common murderer.[70]

The profound concern of the liberationists for *sharing* is better grounded in the life of the apostolic church, where everybody had everything in common, and where, indeed, there was authentic Christian communalism.[71] In Justin Martyr's *Apology* we see that an important part of the Eucharist was the offertory, when Christians brought offerings, each as generously as he or she could, in order to assist "the orphans and widows, and those who are in want because of sickness or other cause, and those who are in bonds (prisoners), and, in short, . . . all those in need."[72]

Two sympathetic but balanced critics of liberation theology are

69. Balasuriya, *The Eucharist and Human Liberation* (Maryknoll, N.Y: Orbis Books, 1979), p. 71. See also Robert McAfee Brown, *Unexpected News: Reading the Bible with Third World Eyes* (Philadelphia: Westminster Press, 1984).

70. For example, Rafael Avile, *Worship and Politics* (Maryknoll, N.Y: Orbis Books, 1981), p. 48, writes, ". . . the Eucharist . . . is not the proclamation of the natural death of Christ, but of the socio-political injustice by which Christ was put to death."

71. See Acts 2:44-47.

72. *Apology* I.67.6.

Schubert M. Ogden, author of *Faith and Freedom: Toward a Theology of Liberation*, and Durwood Foster, who has a concise essay entitled "A Critical Reflection on the Theologies of Liberation: Assessing their Strengths and Weaknesses."[73] Ogden claims that the liberationists confuse redemption with emancipation, the former being liberation from death, transience, and sin attested by the apostolic witness, while the latter is emancipation from bondage called for by the various movements for human freedom, which are political, economic, cultural, racial, and sexual. Foster also feels that liberationists, in their concern for horizontal justice, have undervalued the vertical and transcendental aspects of the Christian faith.

The liberationist would also like to make changes in the celebration of the Eucharist. These would include a return to prophetic preaching and the occasional use of group meditation[74] with reference to the oppressors of the poor, the marginalized, the stranger, the prisoner, and the sick, in order to awaken the dormant consciences of the affluent and to raise the material hopes of the oppressed. The congregations would also invite the forgotten members of society back again to share the meal of unity and friendship, peace and justice. Justice would also be visibly acknowledged in the offertory, which would include not only the bread and wine to be shared anew in the imminent feast, but also monetary or other expressions of generosity (such as food or flowers or clothing, and similar necessities).

The symbolism of broken bread, as Joseph Grassi reminds us in his book, *Broken Bread and Broken Bodies: The Lord's Supper and World Hunger* (1985), bespeaks both our spiritual nourishment at Christ's table, and our responsibility to provide desperately needed actual bread to feed the world's hungry. The fact that the whole loaf is broken into fragments reminds us that Christ's body on the cross was a broken body — the cost of our redemption. But the bread and wine also signify divine and human cooperation — as God provides the earth, the seed, the sun and the rain, and humanity labors in

---

73. Ogden's book was published in a revised edition by Abingdon Press, Nashville, Tennessee, in 1989, and Foster's essay appeared in *Liberation Theology, North American Style*, ed. Deane William Ferm (New York: Vertizon, 1987), pp. 1-12.

74. For group meditation, see the two-volume work of Fr. Ernesto Cardinal, *El Evangelio in Solentiname* (San Jose, Costa Rica: Departmento Ecumenico de Investigaciones, 1979).

sowing and planting, raising wheat and grapes, as well as transporting, buying and selling, wrapping and bottling them before they reach our holy table or our domestic tables. Thus at the Communion we are all invited to reflect on our responsibility as Christian ecologists.[75]

Now we must end our consideration of the theology of the Eucharist by turning to liturgical expressions of the liberation emphasis. Prayer IV in the new Roman liturgy echoes what might well be the most frequently cited verse of the liberationists:

> Conceived through the power of the Holy Spirit and born of the Virgin Mary, he became like us in all things but sin. To the poor he proclaimed the good news of salvation, to prisoners, freedom, and to those in sorrow, joy. In fulfillment of your will he gave himself up to death.[76]

There is little liberation emphasis in the Church of England's *Alternative Service Book 1980*, except for one of the "Alternative Forms of Intercession" which reads:

> Teach us to use the fruits of the earth to your glory,
> and for the good of all mankind.[77]

The Methodist Service Book of 1975 has one prayer which incorporates a liberation emphasis in the following words:

> We pray for all in sorrow, need, anxiety and sickness, for the lonely and the persecuted, and for all who suffer from cruelty, injustice, and neglect, that in their weakness they may know your strength, and in despair find hope.[78]

The liberation theme rings loudly in a prayer of confession in the *Service Book* of 1989 of the United Reformed Church:

> We have not discerned Christ:
> we have hated when we should have loved,

75. Grassi's publisher is Orbis Books of Maryknoll, New York.
76. *Sunday Missal*, pp. 52-53.
77. *ASB*, p. 168.
78. B 8 (p. 52).

broken when we should have healed;
we have divided the Church
and allowed our brothers and sisters to go hungry
while we have too much.[79]

Thus our contemporary Eucharists are exhibiting a plurality of meanings, most of them held ecumenically. We have considered the Eucharist as Memorial, Thanksgiving, Sacrifice, Eschatological Banquet, Communion (Joyful Meal of Unity), Mystery, and Liberation. I conclude with a citation from Dom Gregory Dix on the importance of the Eucharist:

> Was ever another commandment ("Do this in remembrance of me") so obeyed? Men have found no better thing to do for kings at their crowning and for criminals going to the scaffold; for armies in triumph or a Parliament, or a sick old woman afraid to die.[80]

The many meanings of the Eucharist are a tribute to its continuing relevance and centrality in worship.

79. P. 7.
80. Dix, *The Shape of the Liturgy* (London: Dacre Press, 1945), p. 744.

CHAPTER IV

BAPTISM AND EUCHARIST IN THE WORSHIP OF THE CHURCH OF ENGLAND[1]

THE EXTENT, the variety, and the effects of liturgical experimentation in the Church of England leading up to the production of the *Alternative Service Book* of 1980 and even beyond are so striking that this chapter will require three parts. The first part will provide a summary history of the forms of worship from 1927-8 leading up to 1980. The second part will provide a detailed analysis of the Sacraments of Initiation and of the Eucharist for the *Alternative Service Book* which was given authority for use from 1980 until 2000. The third part will consider proposals for the improvements of the *ASB* (1980).

The Ancestors of the Alternative Service Book 1980

In view of the extraordinary experimentation in many Anglican Provinces throughout the world in recent years, as well as in the new Roman Catholic Communion liturgy, with its four alternative forms of Eucharist, it is hard to believe that the 1662 version of the Book of Common Prayer was for more than three hundred years the single legally approved English form of worship with its one prayer of Consecration for the Eucharist. It was only in 1966 that the Archbishops recommended that the services, Series 1, consisting chiefly

---

1. At the outset it should be made plain that Chapters IV, V, and VI deal only with the two major sacraments of the Church, that of the combined Service of the Word and the Eucharist, and that of Initiation, including Confirmation. Other rites such as Ordinations, Weddings, and Funerals will receive separate treatment in Chapter VII. Such important matters as Inclusive Language, Symbolism, Calendars, and Lectionaries, as well as Church Music and Church Architecture, will also be considered later.

of forms used since 1928 *sub rosa*, should be authorized for experimental use for seven years. These included Morning and Evening Prayer, Infant and Adult Baptism, Marriage, Burial, and Holy Communion. Confirmation was refused recognition since it did not receive the necessary two-thirds majority in the House of Laity. The Eucharistic Prayer of Consecration of 1928 had not been popular and was little used. This was replaced by an "Interim Rite" in shorter or longer form.

In 1965 the Liturgical Commission had already made available the first group of its own proposals in *Alternative Services: Second Series* which contained Morning and Evening Prayer, Thanksgivings and Intercessions, a Thanksgiving after Childbirth, Burial, and an Appendix, which included an incomplete draft of a new rite of Holy Communion. According to R. C. D. Jasper and G. J. Cuming, the latter "met with an enthusiastic reception from the Convocations and the House of Laity which pleaded that it should be completed with speed. This was done and, despite problems over prayer for the departed and the second half of the Eucharistic Prayer, it was authorized for use in 1967."[2] In the following year Baptism and Confirmation, and Morning and Evening Prayer were also approved. Objections from the Evangelicals against the inclusion of prayers for the dead led to the defeat of the proposed Orders for Burial, and the Thanksgiving after Childbirth was also rejected. There was a conservative revision of Morning and Evening Prayer, which excluded many thanksgivings and litanies. Although the first draft of the liturgy for Holy Communion was enthusiastically endorsed, the second draft was found unacceptable, largely because of the objection of the Evangelicals to a single phrase in the *anamnesis*, namely, "We offer unto Thee this bread and this cup. . . ." This was rejected on two grounds by the critics, first because it could be interpreted to mean the sacrifice was renewed at the request of the people, not by the renewed application by Christ of his all-sufficient sacrifice on Calvary; and also because they held that the Christian community's sacrifice can only be a sacrifice of praise. Ultimately the problem was overcome by a compromise formula devised by Canon Ronald Jasper, Chairman of the Liturgical Commission, from 1964. As a leading

2. Cf. R. C. D. Jasper and Paul F. Bradshaw, *A Companion to the Alternative Service Book* (London: S.P.C.K., 1986), p. 25; also cf. G. J. Cuming, *A History of Anglican Liturgy*, 2nd ed. (London & Basingstoke: Macmillan, 1982), p. 208.

Evangelical, Colin O. Buchanan, also then a member of the Liturgical Commission, has expressed the critical view thus: "even self-oblation (whether overtly 'in Christ' or not) has seemed to many to be unsuitable before communion" as suggesting Pelagianism. This would later appear even more objectionable with an offertory procession bringing both bread and wine and monetary offerings to the altar. Buchanan added: "They have not wanted to exclude praise and thanksgiving, but have at the same time desired to keep our Lord's sacrifice in a separate category from any responsive sacrifice of ours."[3] This issue would be a continuing bone of contention between Anglo-Catholics and Evangelicals in the Church of England. Nevertheless, the revised Eucharist was authorized in 1967.

This Second Series Holy Communion had been greatly influenced by two scholars who desired that the Communion Service should follow the structure and contents of Patristic Eucharists. These scholars were Edward Cradock Ratcliff, who taught liturgics successively at Oxford, London, and at Cambridge, and A. H. Couratin, who had taught at Durham University. They saw the Eucharist as a parish Communion with a large congregation, which would include a preliminary Service of the Word (including a sermon), and a succeeding, but not separated, Service of the Sacrament. Part I, including a fifteen-minute sermon, would take thirty minutes and Part II the same. The Communion part of the service has a penitential opening including the Prayer of Humble Access, but the invitation and the confession are new. This section is then completed with the Peace, as in the liturgy of Justin Martyr in 150 A.D. and adopted in all the Eastern liturgies.

Unlike the 1662 Prayer Book, the *ASB* unites the Preface and *Sanctus* in the manner of the Eastern liturgies. The history of salvation is rehearsed in the Preface, before one arrives at the *Sanctus*. As Cuming rightly remarks, the result is that "the bridge-passage from *Sanctus* to Institution Narrative is slight and fails to sustain the feeling of Thanksgiving."[4] That the Four Actions popularized by Dom Gregory Dix, the Anglican Benedictine, in his *The Shape of the Liturgy*, were intended to provide the structure, was made clear from the headings of the four sections thus: "The Preparation of the Bread

---

3. *Modern Anglican Liturgies, 1958-1968* (London: Oxford University Press, 1968), p. 29.
4. Cuming, *History*, p. 211.

and Wine," "The Thanksgiving," "The Breaking of the Bread," and "The Sharing of the Bread." This intention, unfortunately, was obscured by the Church Assembly's requirement of the manual acts. (It should also be added, by way of explanation, why Ratcliff and Couratin had delayed the *Sanctus* until immediately before the Institution Narrative. This was owed to Ratcliff's conviction that the *Sanctus* was the climactic uniting of the praise of the earthly congregation with that of the angelic throngs of heaven.)[5] The insertion of the manual acts into the Institution Narrative also obscured the point that the entire prayer, and not a specific moment in it, effects the Consecration. The final appearance of the Series 2 Communion Order was anti-climactic since it was relegated to an Appendix in Series 3. This included a prayer for the departed and an explicit oblation of bread and wine, written by Bishop Henry de Candole and Canon Arthur Couratin.

The other sacramental contribution to Series 2 was that of Baptism and Confirmation. E. C. Whitaker, a learned historian of Baptism in the Early Church, persuaded the Liturgical Commission in its re-ordering of this sacrament that the act of Baptism should follow immediately after the profession of faith, without the interruption of the Blessing of the Water. The Baptism is succeeded by the signing of the cross, but with the people joining in the words that accompany the crossing. Also, provision is made for two new ceremonies. One is the giving of a lighted candle to the newly-baptized (or the parents or sponsors). The second is a welcome offered by the priest and the people on behalf of the entire Church. At this point the newly-baptized adults leave the font to be confirmed.

When it came time to consider Confirmation there was great difficulty in accommodating the different views about the relation of Baptism to Confirmation. This difficulty is summarized with clarity and concision by Cuming:

Either the Holy Spirit is given once for all in baptism; or baptism is primarily cleansing, and the Holy Spirit comes fully in confirmation; or

---

5. Ratcliff's article propounding his view was "The Sanctus and the Pattern of the Early Anaphora," *Journal of Ecclesiastical History* 1 (1950): 29-36, 125-34. This view is refuted by Dr. Bryan D. Spinks in Chapter 8 of *Worship: Prayers from the East* (Washington, D.C.: Pastoral Press, 1993). The chapter's title is "A Note on the Anaphora Outlined in Narsai's Homily XXXII."

the gift of the Spirit is made in baptism and increased in confirmation. The new prayer, "Send forth upon them thy Holy Spirit," allows the holding of any of these views. So does the formula of confirmation, "Confirm, O Lord, thy servant with thy Holy Spirit." The traditional use of Isaiah 11 is maintained; and finally the old formula, "Defend, O Lord, this thy child," is said by the whole congregation.[6]

Orders for Baptism and Confirmation, as also for Morning and Evening Prayer were authorized, but the services prepared for Burial and Thanksgiving after Childbirth did not gain approval, and no proposals were made for Ordination or Marriage. It is thus clear that Series 2 was strictly limited as a range of services. Difficult as the task of the Liturgical Commission had been in producing it, Series 2 was only an interim step in liturgical reform. Other important influences reinforced the provisional nature of the new rites.

Among these were the publication of the many new translations of the Bible and the dawning of a new era of ecumenical liturgical cooperation. The new translations with their departure from the elegant but anachronistic English of Cranmer and Shakespeare, created the demand for modern liturgical English. The New English Bible New Testament appeared in 1961, and in full in 1971, while the Jerusalem Bible appeared in 1966. The public use of such versions was helped by the passing of The Versions of the Bible Measure in 1965, which approved the Revised Version, the Revised Standard Version, the New English Bible, and the Jerusalem Bible; all were authorized and approved by the Church Assembly. In 1978 the Bible in Todays' English was authorized and in 1979 *The Liturgical Psalter.* All this urged upon liturgiologists and liturgists the need for modern English in all forms of worship.

Stimulated by these new translations of the Bible, the Liturgical Commission, with the assistance of C. Day Lewis, the Poet Laureate, published *Modern Liturgical Texts,* which included contemporary English versions of The Lord's Prayer, the Creeds, and the Canticles, along with modern versions of the Series 2 forms of Baptism, Confirmation, and Holy Communion. To further the concern for contemporary English in liturgies the International Consultation on English Texts (with the acronym ICEL), which represented the major English-speaking Churches throughout the world, came into

6. Cuming, *History,* p. 213.

being. Between 1968 and 1975 it produced three reports on *Prayers We Have in Common*. Its proposals on Creeds and Canticles also received general approbation, but not the Lord's Prayer, because it did not retain the line "Lead us not into temptation." Later still the issue of removing from liturgical language terms deemed offensive because of their exclusively masculine character, their ethnic depreciations, or their militarism came to be important.[7]

The same concern for modern English and for the formation of new liturgies was shared by other Provinces of the Anglican Communion world-wide,[8] and there was special admiration for the newer liturgies of the United States and of Canada.[9] But also nearer home was the stimulus provided by the Joint Liturgical Group, founded in 1963 chiefly by Anglican initiative, but comprised of official representatives of all the main Churches in England, Wales and Scotland. In 1967 and 1968 this Group prepared radical proposals for revising the Calendar, the Lectionary, and the Daily Office, and all were incorporated into the Church of England's program of liturgical reform. *The Calendar and Lectionary* was published by the Oxford University Press in 1967. It was based on a two-year cycle. More familiar, however, is a three-year cycle, as in the Roman Catholic lectionary or in the modification of that scheme known as *The Common Lectionary* prepared by the Consultation on Common Texts, based in the United States of America and Canada.[10]

7. See Chapter VIII below, "The Linguistic Controversy."

8. See Buchanan, *Modern Anglican Liturgies;* also his *Further Anglican Liturgies, 1968-1975* (Bramcote, Nottingham: Grove Books, 1975); and *Latest Anglican Liturgies* (London: S.P.C.K., 1985).

9. Note the comment of the distinguished historian of liturgy G. J. Cuming in *A History of Anglican Liturgy*, p. 228, on *The Book of Common Prayer* (1979) of the U.S.A.: "The outstanding feature of this book is the set of four eucharistic prayers in Rite Two, which fully justify the general view that this is the most distinguished of the new Anglican liturgies. A cursory survey like this cannot do justice to the wealth of learning and careful preparation which went into its making."

10. It should be noted that the Joint Liturgical Group also prepared a *Four Year Lectionary* in 1990 in which the chief work was done by Donald McIlhagga (United Reformed Church), Raymond George (Methodist Church), and Neville Clark (Baptist Church). The lectionary maintains the nine Sundays preparing for Christmas, but now covers four years instead of two, and, apart from a few special days, it devotes one year to each of the Gospels, and a greater element of narrative is included. There is total provision for reading 7092 verses, 2238 from the Old Testament and 4854 from the New. The average lesson is about 30 or 31 verses in length.

Another important contribution of the Joint Liturgical Group to Anglican revision in England was entitled *The Daily Office*. According to the Group's Chairman in 1993, Canon Donald Gray, it was "one of the best sellers of the Joint Liturgical Group."[11] This led to a modest modification of the revision of the Church of England's Daily Office.

An important constitutional change took place within the Church of England in 1970 with the arrival of Synodical Government, thereby simplifying the procedure of revising the liturgy. Instead of the former five Houses which had cumbersomely considered and voted on revisions of services, the three new Houses of Bishops, Clergy, and Laity could consider proposals simultaneously, although they would vote separately, and require a two-thirds majority in each House before a revision could be authorized. A new system permitted the granting of "Provisional Approval" to a service by the show of hands of the entire Synod; if given, such approval would be succeeded by a revision stage, after which "Final Approval" was required by a two-thirds majority in all three Houses. The first great triumph of the Synod was to gain the approval of Parliament for the Church of England's freedom from Parliamentary control for issues of doctrine and worship. This was granted in 1974 by the Church of England (Worship and Doctrine) Measure. As a result the Synod received the power to produce and authorize forms of service when they were thought to be necessary, provided that the unaltered 1662 Book of Common Prayer remained as a regularly available alternative liturgical source.

In this freer and experimental atmosphere of the 1970s, the Liturgical Commission produced its Series 3 forms of service, all of them in contemporary English. In September 1971 the new order for Holy Communion appeared. This was almost unanimously endorsed in 1972, by the General Synod and came into use on February 1, 1973.

This new Communion Rite of Series 3 was in modern language, but it was enriched in several ways. There was more room for silence, more seasonal material, with introductory sentences, Proper Prefaces, post-Communion sentences, blessings, and a two-year thematically organ-

11. This was told me in a fascinating and informative interview with Canon Donald Gray, Chairman of the Joint Liturgical Group, in his study in the cloisters of Westminster Abbey on June 29, 1993.

ized lectionary. The Intercessions were supplemented by Thanksgivings, the confession included a definite act of repentance, the Peace became mandatory, and the Offertory was provided with a sentence from 1 Chronicles 29:14: "Everything comes from you and it is only of your gifts we give you." The rites for Funerals and for Morning and Evening Prayer were published in 1975, while the modernized Collects appeared in 1976, the Order for Marriage in 1977, and in 1978 the Ordinal, the Calendar and Lectionary, and Rules to order the Service. Initiation rites and the Liturgical Psalter appeared in 1979.

Essentially the Service of Holy Communion was a translation and revision of Series 2, using the versions of the *Gloria in Excelsis*, the Nicene Creed, the *Sanctus*, the Lord's Prayer, and the *Agnus Dei* that had been prepared by the International Committee on English Texts. The ICET version of the Lord's Prayer included the petition "Do not put us to the test" but the English Church preferred "Do not bring us to the trial." Scholars protested that the versicle proposed to follow the readings from Scripture, "This is the Word of the Lord" was too simplistic in not allowing for different degrees of authority in different lessons. Another novelty was the frequency of the suggestion of silence, thirteen times in all. The designation of the president as "president" was a clear indication that it is the entire congregation that celebrates. The greatest surprise was the alternative beginning for the prayer for Thanksgiving. The president says: "The Lord is here" to which the response is: "His Spirit is with us."[12]

The Communion as it appears in *The Alternative Service Book 1980* contains no less than seven eucharistic prayers, if 1662 is counted, and Rites A and B take up pp. 113-210. This gives some indication of the rich variations including the many prefaces, the several alternative lessons, intercessions, confessions, and blessings, as well as the six eucharistic prayers in Rites A and B. Basically Rite A is a revision of Series 3, while Rite B is Series 1 and 2 revised. It is worth citing those parts of the eucharistic prayers which touch upon the controverted issues of prayer for the departed and the mode of offering.

In Rite A the first prayer of intercession includes the petition:

---

12. For an explanation and defense of this change, see R. C. D. Jasper, ed., *The Eucharist Today* (London: SPCK, 1974), pp. 101-3.

Hear us as we remember those who have died in the faith of Christ
. . . your eternal kingdom. [P. 125]

Rite A's second Eucharistic Prayer says:

. . . we make with this bread and this cup the memorial of Christ
your Son our Lord. [P. 135]

Rite A's third Eucharistic Prayer proceeds:

And so, Father, calling to mind his death on the cross . . . we celebrate
this memorial of our redemption. . . . We pray you to accept this our
duty and service, a spiritual sacrifice of praise and thanksgiving . . .
[Pp. 137-138]

Rite A's fourth Eucharistic Prayer is worded:

Therefore, Lord and heavenly Father, in remembrance of the precious
death and passion . . . of your dear Son Jesus Christ, we offer you
through him this sacrifice of praise and thanksgiving. . . . Although
we are unworthy, through our many sins, to offer you any sacrifice,
yet we pray that you will accept this, the duty and service that we
owe . . . [P. 141]

In Rite B the Second Intercession pleads:

Hear us as we remember those who have died in faith,
and grant us with them a share in thy eternal kingdom.   [P. 186]

In Rite B the Second Thanksgiving declares:

Wherefore, O Lord and heavenly Father,
with this bread and this cup
we make the memorial of his saving passion   [P. 194]

Also among the Alternative Prayers there is this petition:

yet we beseech thee to accept this our bounden duty and service.
[P. 210]

This series of Communion Services also provides in the Eucharistic Prayer (Rite A) an impressive response or acclamation:

> All: Christ has died:
> Christ is risen:
> Christ will come again.   [Pp. 137, 141]

It is also noteworthy that the inspiration, sanctification and illumination of the Holy Spirit is reflected in several of the Prayers. In the first Eucharistic Prayer of Rite A there is a definite invocation of the Holy Spirit to consecrate the bread and wine *(epiklesis)* immediately following the *Benedictus qui venit:*

> Accept our praises, heavenly Father,
> through your Son and our Saviour Jesus Christ;
> as we follow his example and obey his command,
> grant that by the power of your Holy Spirit
> these gifts of bread and wine
> may be to us his body and his blood.   [P. 131]

Also the *anamnesis* in the second Eucharistic Prayer in Rite A refers to Christ's gift thus:

> Through him you have sent upon us
> your holy and life-giving Spirit,
> and made us a people for your own possession.   [P. 133]

The third Eucharistic Prayer in Rite A, also has an *epiklesis* and a further pleading,

> Send the Holy Spirit on your people
> and gather into one in your kingdom
> all who share this one bread and one cup,
> so that we, in the company of all the saints,
> may praise and glorify you for ever . . . .   [P. 138]

The fourth Eucharistic Prayer in Rite A also has an *epiklesis* (p. 140), as do the two prayers of Thanksgiving in Rite B on pp. 191 and 194.

The theological undergirding of the Eucharist is much stronger than that in the 1662 Book of Common Prayer. In almost every

82

prayer the *anamnesis* is understood as making effective in the present a profoundly significant event of the past, as was the case also in the Jewish Passover. So in the Communion service the Church "continues to make a perpetual memorial of Christ's death, and his members, united with God and one another, give thanks for all his mercies, entreat the benefits of his passion on behalf of the whole Church, participate in those benefits, and enter into the movement of his self-offering."[13] Furthermore, just as the Jewish Passover incorporated a future reference — with four cups of wine, each linked to an Old Testament text, declaring God's judgment against evil and promising final deliverance for his children — the Eucharist anticipates the Second Coming of the Lord and also provides a foretaste of the celestial banquet. This eschatological sense is a notable addition to the *ASB* (1980) Communion Orders.

There is also a third borrowing from Jewish liturgical usage. This is the use of the term "Blessing" or "Thanksgiving" instead of Consecration. It has two advantages. One is that there does not have to be a certain unchangeable formula, as in the case of the traditional Roman eucharistic prayer where the retelling of the institution narrative was the consecratory formula. The second advantage is that with the use of the concept of "blessing" or "thanksgiving" one is less likely to think that the priest consecrates, when it is only God who does so. So in the *ASB* (1980) Rite A lists "Eucharistic Prayer" and Rite B "Thanksgiving."

Similarly, the doctrine of the Holy Trinity comes out clearly not only in the *Sanctus* of the eucharistic prayer, but also in the beginning with the references to the Father, followed by gratitude for the saving actions of the Son, and nowadays, in conformity with the practice of the Eastern Churches, the recognition of the Holy Spirit as the agent of consecration through the final and climactic use of the *epiklesis*.

A fourth notable theological emphasis is on the Eucharist as both forming and expressing the unity of the Body of Christ. This is seen in several ways in the rite itself. In fact, lay members of the congregation are both more audible and more visible as contributors to the action than they used to be. They often read the Old Testament and

---

13. *Modern Eucharistic Agreement* (1973), p. 29, an Anglican-Roman Catholic Agreed Statement on Eucharistic Doctrine of 31 December 1971, cited in Jasper and Bradshaw, eds., *Companion*, p. 118.

Epistle lessons, assist the celebrating priest in conveying the sacred elements to the kneeling members of the congregation, make the triple acclamation, and bring the bread and wine and pecuniary gifts in the offertory procession. They also share the Peace with their hugs or handshakes. Appropriately, too, as they surround the holy table on four sides, faced by the president in their midst (rather than with him or her coming from a distant sanctuary, praying with his or her back towards them), the people sense themselves to be increasingly the people of God and Christ's own adopted brothers and sisters. And they take a larger part in hymns and responsorial chants.

Perhaps the most memorable literary contribution to the Holy Communion Service is Professor D. L. Frost's greatly admired and deeply loved post-Communion prayer:

> Father of all, we give you thanks and praise, that when we were all still far off you met us in your Son and brought us home. Dying and living, he declared your love, gave us grace, and opened the gate of glory. May we who share Christ's body live his risen life; we who drink his cup bring life to others; we whom the Spirit lights give light to the world. Keep us firm in the hope you have set before us, so we and all your children shall be free, and the whole earth live to praise your name; through Christ our Lord. [P. 144]

This prayer unites us all as prodigal sons and daughters in confession, in future hope of life eternal, and propels us into mission.

The same author also provided an alternative Prayer of Humble Access, which makes a point of echoing the start and finish of George Herbert's poem "Love":

> Most merciful Lord,
> your love compels us to come in.
> Our hands were unclean,
> our hearts were unprepared;
> we were not fit
> even to eat the crumbs from under your table.
> But you, Lord, are the God of our salvation,
> and share your bread with sinners.
> So cleanse and feed us
> with the precious body and blood of your Son,

that he may live in us and we in him;
and that we, with the whole company of Christ,
may sit and eat in your kingdom. Amen.   [P. 170]

There has been further thought about the Eucharist since 1980. Some of this is reflected in the innovative *Patterns of Worship* produced by the Liturgical Commission and published in 1989. It also includes four new eucharistic prayers, but these cannot be authorized until the *Alternative Service Book* has run its course of two decades. Eucharistic Prayer A is thoroughly responsive, making it easier for children to maintain interest, while B is a revision of a Roman Catholic original, avoiding a split invocation of the Holy Spirit. Prayer C is a simple, short version, with a clear trinitarian structure, and Prayer D is the briefest, but can be lengthened by use of one of eighteen thanksgivings in the Resource Section. So the Church of England now has an *embarras de richesse* in its many eucharistic prayers of thanksgiving.

The Alternative Service Book 1980 in its Initiation Services has shown itself realistic in the recognition that we live in a dominantly post-Christian era, where only a small proportion of the nation attends worship regularly and where Infant Baptism has often seemed a private family affair, not a commitment of parents and godparents to educate and support the infants in their increasing growth and commitment as faithful disciples of Christ.

This realism can be seen in the provision of a service of Thanksgiving for the Birth of a Child and of a service of Thanksgiving after Adoption. Notes indicate that parents and godparents must be informed by the clergy that neither of these services is Baptism, "which is the sacrament instituted by Christ for those who wish to become members of his Church." These services should normally be used in church but can be used in home or hospital. In addition to parents or adoptive parents and the child, other children should also be present.

The first service begins with the minister's prayer of thanksgiving, followed by that of the parents. The reading of Mark 10:13–16 comes next. The minister may then give a copy of one of the gospels to the parents saying: "This book contains the Good News of God's love. Read it, for it tells how you and your family can share in eternal life, through repentance and faith in Jesus Christ." Then with a simple, apt introduction the Lord's Prayer is repeated. This is followed by one or more of five prayers emphasizing the importance of the home upbringing for the child, and the following prayer is said by all:

85

God our Father
we pray for this child (Name).
that in due time
he may be received by baptism
into the family of your Church
and become an inheritor of your kingdom;
through Jesus Christ our Lord. Amen.

The Thanksgiving after Adoption is much like the previous service except for the sensitive prayer that God will "look down with love on the natural father and mother of *this child;* keep them in your good providence, and give them peace in their hearts," and the declaration of the members of the family that "We receive *this child* into our family with thanksgiving and joy. . . ."

It is recognized that the desirable order is Baptism, Confirmation, and Holy Communion, but this is only possible in an immediate succession for adults who were not baptized as children. In a service in which there is to be Confirmation the bishop must be present; and those who are to be baptized, together with the parents and godparents of children to be baptized and those who are to be confirmed, all stand before the bishop. In explanation of the sacrament, the bishop says that Baptism is the outward sign by which we receive for ourselves what Christ has done for us, and we are united with him in his death, are granted forgiveness of our sins, and are raised by Christ to new life in the Spirit. He then requires that those who have come for Baptism must affirm their allegiance to Christ and their rejection of evil, and parents presenting children for Baptism must bring them up to fight against evil and to follow Christ. Then the bishop asks three questions:

> Do you turn to Christ?
> *Answer:* I turn to Christ.

> Do you repent of your sins?
> *Answer:* I repent of my sins.

> Do you renounce evil?
> *Answer:* I renounce evil.

This part of the Service is termed the Decision.

The bishop then makes the Sign of the Cross on the forehead of each one to be baptized, telling them not to be ashamed to confess the faith of Christ crucified and all respond, "Fight valiantly under the banner of Christ against sin, the world, and the devil, and continue his faithful soldiers and servants to the end of your lives." The bishop then petitions God to lead those to be baptized "in the light and obedience of Christ."

A fine prayer follows reminding all of the Biblical importance of water, which is worth recording in full:

> Almighty God, whose Son Jesus Christ
>   was baptized in the river Jordan:
> we thank you for the gift of water
>   to cleanse us and revive us;
> we thank you that through the deep waters of the
>   Red Sea, you led your people out of slavery
>   to freedom in the promised land;
> we thank you that through the deep waters
>   of death you brought your Son, and raised
>   him to life in triumph.
> Bless this water, that your servants who are
>   washed in it may be made one with Christ
>   in his death and in his resurrection,
>   to be cleansed and delivered from all sin.
> Send your Holy Spirit upon them to bring
>   them to new birth in the family of your
>   Church, and raise them with Christ to full
>   and eternal life.
> For all might, majesty, authority, and power
>   are yours, now and for ever. Amen.

The bishop then requires the adults to be baptized or the parents and godparents of children to be baptized to declare that they believe and trust in God the Father, his Son Jesus Christ, and his Holy Spirit. He then turns to the congregation, saying: "This is our faith." The entire congregation responds:

> This is our faith.
> We believe and trust one God,
> Father, Son, and Holy Spirit. . .

The bishop then baptizes the candidates by dipping each one in the water or by pouring water on each one, and, addressing the person by name, says: "N, I baptize you in the name of the Father, and of the Son, and of the Holy Spirit."

Then the priest may give a lighted candle to each adult who has been baptized and to a parent or godparent for each child, saying to each: "Receive this light." When all have received their candles, he says: "This is to show that you have passed from darkness into light." All the congregation respond:

Shine as a light in the world
to the glory of God the Father.

The Confirmation then follows.

A brief summary will indicate that the bishop prays that God who has given his servants new birth in Baptism by water and the Spirit, and forgiven their sins, now asks that the Holy Spirit may rest on them, "the Spirit of wisdom and understanding; the Spirit of counsel and inward strength; the Spirit of knowledge and true godliness; and let their delight be in the fear of the Lord."

Then laying his hand on the head of each candidate, the bishop says, "Confirm, O Lord, your servant N with your Holy Spirit." Then he invites the congregation to join him in a prayer for the daily increase of the Holy Spirit in those confirmed. Then the service of Confirmation ends with the Welcome. The bishop declares: "God has received you by baptism into his Church." Then the whole congregation responds:

We welcome you into the Lord's Family.
We are members together of the body of Christ;
we are children of the same heavenly Father;
we are inheritors together of the kingdom of God.
We welcome you.

The strengths of the new orders of Baptism and Confirmation are in the clear demand for parental or personal adult commitment, the simple but more effective symbolism, and the welcome given to the newly baptized by the whole congregation. Infant Baptism has ceased to be a hole and corner affair.

Constructive Criticisms

The *Alternative Service Book 1980* was intended to be used for exactly a decade, but its life was extended until the end of the century. The advantage of this decision was that congregations coping with changes in Series 1, 2, and 3 would have a chance to settle down into continuity of liturgy after all this change. But, equally important, it would give time for the liturgical experts to improve the worship of the Church of England as it faced the new millennium. And there is no question that the members of the Liturgical Commission have provided numerous constructive criticisms, based in part on their own historic research, and in part on insights gleaned from Anglican liturgies world-wide, the British Joint Liturgical Group, the new Roman Catholic liturgies, the liturgical movement in Europe, and Patristic liturgies.

Some particularly interesting criticisms directed towards improvement have been made by learned Evangelicals like Bishop Colin Buchanan, who has issued a remarkable series of publications from Bramcote, known as the Grove Series. His fullest account of the changes he considers necessary can be found in *Revising the ASB*. He asserts that the present Liturgical Commission "envisages the use of a 'Directory' — a far more flexible provision of 'liturgical units' . . . than has ever been known officially before."[14] He likens the process to washing the windows of Buckingham Palace, meaning that the process of revision would be never ending. He objects to Section 33 in Rite A where the president can extemporize in praising God for his gifts, to which the people respond with "Blessed be God for ever." This is followed by a prayer emphasizing that the gifts of the people all come from God. He insists that "we ought not to encourage ourselves to believe that the action of the eucharist is about 'offering' bread and wine," adding that "'laying-up' should be without fuss, without liturgical muttering, and without delay." This is the standard Evangelical Group's objection.[15] On this issue, which divides the Anglo-Catholics or High Church Group from the Evangelicals, perhaps the most illuminat-

14. *Revising the ASB*, Grove Worship Series, No. 107 (1989), pp. 10 and 17.
15. See R. T. Beckwith and J. E. Tiller, eds., *The Service of Holy Communion and Its Revision* (Appleford, Abingdon: Marcham Manor Press, 1972), especially pp. 45-47, asserting that the only sacrifice in the Lord's Supper is the giving of thanks.

ing statement has been offered by G. J. Cuming on the interpretation of the eucharistic sacrifice: "For Evangelicals the sacrifice concerned is that of Christ on the cross, made once for all; for the Anglo-Catholics, it is the offering of the consecrated elements."[16] Bishop Colin Buchanan is also strongly critical of the requirement of Confirmation after Adult Baptism, and the oddity that the infant is welcomed into the Church at Baptism, but excommunicated or "ex-corporated a few moments later in the refusal to give the child Communion."[17]

The Liturgical Commission itself in *Patterns of Worship* (1989) was convinced that there was a need for even greater flexibility in worship than the *ASB* had shown. It was felt that family services were necessary that would seem more relevant to children, and especially for folk unfamiliar with traditional worship forms living in the so-called "urban priority areas." Furthermore there was a strong emphasis on the need for prayers characterized by vividness, story telling, and clear relevance, all exhibiting concreteness rather than abstraction in language. It was also felt that worship should stress more strongly the importance of social justice and of ecology.

Other students of liturgy who admired the flexibility of *ASB* (1980) were disturbed that the multiple alternatives recommended had the unhappy result of hiding the structure of worship. This was a concern of both Kenneth Stevenson and Richard Buxton. In Chapter 6 of *The Liturgy Reshaped,* edited by Stevenson, after recounting the changes of shape in the Eucharist in East and West through the centuries, Buxton insists on several relevant principles. The first is that "the underlying shape of the liturgy must be apparent in the way it is performed, so that awareness of it can sink into the unconscious minds of the worshippers and the rite will develop a natural flow of its own." His second principle is that "the shape should not be obscured by the continuing use of ceremonies that arose to give expression to a different understanding of liturgical theology." A prime example of this is the elevation of the elements during the recital of the Institution Narrative, accompanied by the ringing of a gong or bells and censing, which are no longer needed. He is convinced that liturgical scholars must look carefully at the advances in biblical scholarship, as well as changes in theological understanding,

16. Cuming, *A History of Anglican Liturgy,* pp. 218-19.
17. Buchanan, *Revising the ASB,* pp. 22, 23.

90

which can be incorporated into worship where the liturgy has a clear and agreed shape.

Canon Kenneth Stevenson, a member of the Liturgical Commission, provides, in *The Identity of Anglican Worship*, a wide-ranging critique of the *ASB*. He cites its banal, committee-style language, its antiquarianism in producing new prayers too much based on the prayer of bygone ages, especially that of the Fathers, and its ephemerality. He argues, further, that its prayers are too often indebted to the historico-source criticism of liturgiology, which collects units of prayer from many centuries but often at the cost of unity or coherence in prayer. Finally, he argues, there is a politics of revision in which the liturgical establishment is seen as allied with modern synodical bureaucracy.[18] He suggests that much is lost in compromise, which he defines as "horse-trading behind the scenes." Stevenson also finds a contradiction in the twentieth century impulse toward liturgical revision. On the one hand there was pressure to provide variables to suit local conditions, while on the other hand there was a tendency to go back to the roots, whether this was Cranmer or Hippolytus: the first, observes Stevenson, was a Zwinglian memorialist, and the second seems to have had more influence on the twentieth century than he had in the third or fourth.

Elsewhere in the book the Bishop of Monmouth, Dr. Rowan Williams, laments that the preparatory part of the liturgy contains no confession indicating how far short of the Kingdom of God we have come in our political life as Christians, and proposes that, like the Orthodox liturgy and that of Taizé, the liturgy should include the Beatitudes in worship.[19]

Dr. Bryan Spinks, in the same volume claims that it is a serious mistake to compose "Anglican" eucharistic prayers, for this is, in effect, to replace God as the object of theology and liturgy. Hence he writes: "Worship and prayer, like all theology, must resist serving the self-interest of a particular denomination or social class, or an intellectual elite. Anglicans should concern themselves with formu-

---

18. *The Identity of Anglican Worship*, ed. Kenneth Stevenson and Bryan Spinks (London: Mowbray, 1991), chapter 17. The most amusing definition of this committee language I have read comes from Brian Morris's book, *Ritual Murder* (Manchester: Carcanet Press, 1980), p. 72. He calls this lingo "the bureaucracy's idiolect, the consensus-dominated speech of administrative life."

19. *Identity of Anglican Worship*, pp. 10f.

lating good eucharistic prayers rather than specifically 'Anglican' prayers."[20]

Not all Evangelicals are critical of the language and themes of the *ASB* Eucharist. Donald Bridge and David Phypers insist how relevant the *epiklesis* seems to charismatics joining Anglican worship. "To them it seemed to be truly providential that Series 3 Communion and Charismatic Renewal have arrived at the same time."[21] This view is shared by Bishop Colin Buchanan, who has written:

> In the Church of England Series 3 we pray: "Grant that by the power of your Spirit, these gifts of bread and wine may be to us his body and blood," and "Renew us by your Spirit, inspire us with your love, and unite us in the body of your Son, Jesus Christ our Lord." So when charismatics go to the eucharist nowadays where the new words are used, these words vibrate with relevance.[22]

Michael Perham, who edited *Liturgy for a New Century: Further Essays in Preparation for the Revision of the Alternative Service Book*, is anxious that rapid changes in liturgy should not recreate the anxieties that many Anglicans felt in the 1970s at the changes in the Eucharist, and in the 1980s the radical language changes from Cranmerian to contemporary English. Perham, a member of the Liturgical Commission, and presently the Dean of Norwich Cathedral, argues that "the 2000 service book ought to be one that brings much healing to a Church where worship has brought some hurt as well as joyful freshness in the last generation."[23]

Canon Donald Gray in the same volume, while approving of the prominence of the Eucharist in modern Anglican worship, is concerned that Morning and Evening Prayer, which were useful to the inquirers and the uncommitted, need serious revision as para-liturgies or "Family Services" as a result of what he terms "Eucharistic Inflation."

Canon Kenneth Stevenson thinks that in Rite A two penitential prayers are "too much of a good thing,"[24] especially as the Prayer of

20. *Ibid.*, p. 95.
21. Bridge and Phypers, *Communion: The Meal That Unites?* (Wheaton, Illinois: Harold Shaw, 1982), p. 163.
22. Buchanan, *Encountering Charismatic Worship* (Bramcote, 1977), p. 17.
23. *Liturgy for a New Century* (London: S.P.C.K., 1991), pp. xi-xii.
24. *Ibid.*, pp. 33f.

Humble Access comes later. He points out that the dreaded offertory on page 129 is confusing because it can be interpreted in Anglo-Catholic, Roman Catholic, or Evangelical senses. So on this issue of "offering" he suggests that the formula in the American Lutheran *Book of Worship* is clearer if more prolix:

> Blessed are you, O Lord our God
> maker of all things,
> Through your goodness you have blessed us
> with these gifts.
> With them we offer ourselves to your service
> and dedicate our lives to the care and redemption
> of all that you have made, for the sake of him,
> who gave himself for us, Jesus Christ our Lord.[25]

Bishop David Stancliffe, who was a member of the Liturgical Commission as Provost of Portsmouth, has written on "Confirmation and its Future." He begins by admitting that it is difficult to see a way out of the peculiarly Anglican practice of "Baptism, then a gap, then Confirmation, and only then Communion."[26] Since Baptism is our personal Pentecost, as modern liturgical theologians believe, it is difficult to accept the view that Confirmation adds some special ingredient to what was given in water Baptism. He argues for a continuing distinct function for Confirmation, namely that of ecclesial identity, through the renewal of the Covenant. So, Confirmation, based on the Lord's own Baptism, "is a ratification of Baptism, the public recognition of those Messianic gifts, and an empowering for active and conscious service." There is, he argues, authority for a distinct function for Confirmation in the oldest Syriac and Armenian liturgies, which affirm it as an anointing into the Messianic priesthood. This is recognized in the American Book of Common Prayer of 1979, in a prayer which attests:

> . . . by the sealing of your Holy Spirit
> You have bound us in your service;
> Renew in these your covenant. . . .[27]

---

25. *Book of Worship* (Minneapolis: Augsburg Publishing House, 1978), p. 68.
26. *Liturgy for a New Century*, p. 75.
27. *Ibid.*, p. 79.

This change in the understanding of Confirmation, Bishop Stancliffe argues, would have four advantages. It would end the old way of thinking of confirmation as the pneumatic completion of Baptism, and resolve the debate as to whether Baptism is enough for admission to Communion. A distinctively episcopal rite would be maintained, which could be linked with Ordination and the commissioning of particular local ministries. Finally, he concludes, "There now seems to be both liturgical and ecumenical convergence on an understanding of Confirmation which has to do with affirming our Baptism, making public a commitment to the life of the Church, and having the gifts we offer in the service of the Kingdom recognized by the Church's principal minister."[28]

In the same volume, Bryan Spinks, a lecturer in liturgics at Cambridge University and Chaplain at Churchill College, whose historical expertise includes not only the history of the worship of the Reformed tradition in England, but even the early Syrian rites, offers some valuable insights. For example, he sees the proliferation of "Family Services" as a judgment on both the 1662 Prayer Book and the *ASB*, because the former seems quaint and archaic, while the *ASB* appears not only middle class but exclusive, creating a great chasm between those within and those outside the church. He concludes that in the demise of Matins and the proliferation of the Parish Communion, there is a message of "We are the Body of Christ and communicate; you aren't and can't."[29] He, too, is critical of the language of the *ASB* which he faults for its dry didacticism, its woodenness, its lack of evocative imagery, and its *Daily Telegraph* vocabulary.[30] But he is also aware of the contributions made by *ASB* in its relative popularity, its production of a greater theological awareness among worshippers, its provision of a greater sense of belonging to the community, and its improvement of the devotional life of the Church. In short, his is a balanced evaluation rather than a *cri de coeur*.

There is much to be thankful for in these Church of England experiments. We have a Communion rite which links the service of the Word with the Service of the Table. There are, as we have seen, seven different eucharistic prayers, six of which have incorporated

28. *Ibid.*, p. 80.
29. *Ibid.*, p. 104.
30. *Ibid.*, p. 102.

impressive *anamneses* and *epikleses*, and in so doing, have become ecumenical in a way which they were not before. There is a new place for hymnody, for metrical psalmody, and for responsorial chanting of the Psalms. Members of the congregation have more responses to offer, the Peace in which to engage their neighbors, the opportunity to read Old Testament lessons and Epistles as lectors and also to assist in delivering the consecrated bread and wine to the congregation; there are also more prayer responses, and, above all, the liturgy is increasingly celebrated with both understanding and reverence. Unsettling at first, but possibly also stimulating later are other characteristics, including not only the many alternative sentences, calendric changes, various prayers of confession and intercessions but also, surprisingly, a place for extemporal prayer and even for charismatics to use their own distinctive gestures in worship. As Canon Kenneth Stevenson told me in an interview in his study in Guildford,[31] now the Church of England with all its variety would be wide enough to welcome those it had rejected in 1662, namely the Nonconformists such as the Independents and Presbyterians. If, as a result of the foundation of Local Ecumenical Projects, the Church of England is willing for its members to join in common worship celebrated by Catholic, Methodist, United Reformed, and Baptist Churches,[32] and such services include the Lord's Supper, then the rigid denominational divisions may yet be broken down, despite the disappointing failure of the attempt to get the Methodists back in the Church of England. In that case the ecumenical disaster of St. Bartholomew's Day 1662 would be rectified. A Church that can make room for the black Pentecostalist in a charismatic service is one that is taking Christ's wish that all his disciples shall be one with greater seriousness than ever before. There may be a loss of a unified structure in

---

31. This frank and full interview took place in the Rectory of Holy Trinity and St. Mary Church, Guildford Surrey, on June 7, 1993. The extraordinary varieties of worship are documented in visits made to seven Anglican Churches with differing settings and reported in *Anglican Worship Today: Collins Illustrated Guide to the Alternative Service Book 1980*, ed. Colin Buchanan, Trevor Lloyd, and Harold Miller (London: Collins Liturgical Publications, 1980), pp. 59-72.

32. There seemed to be surprising general ignorance in England about the extent of the local Ecumenical Projects. I was informed by Canon Martin Reardon (General Secretary of Churches Together in England, Inter Church House, 35-41 Lower Marsh, London S.E.1. 7LR) that there were 536 Local Ecumenical Projects in England in 1988. In 1993 the number had increased to 768.

liturgy, but the great gain in variety and alternatives more than makes up for it.

Thinking of what will occur after the use of the *ASB* ends in 2000 A.D., I asked Dr. Stevenson how the Liturgical Commission was preparing for the next millennium, and he replied: "It seemed that there should be three books of services: one for the Church as a whole without full Scriptural readings included; one for the diocese including its saints' days; and, thirdly, a book of occasional services and prayers."

There seems to be general agreement that the Eucharist services do not send the worshippers out with a challenge to change the world. Dean Alan Dunstan stresses the importance of the link between worship and the world.[33] Series 2 had a prayer which included the words, "Send us out into the world in the power of the Spirit." The prayer was subsequently abbreviated by eliminating the words "into the world." The United Reformed Church order of worship, Dunstan points out, provides a model prayer of this kind, which begins with thanksgiving for God having fed and renewed his people, and continues:

> Now we give ourselves to you
> and we ask
> that our daily living
> may be part of the life of your kingdom,
> and that our love
> may be your love reaching out into the love of the world.[34]

Perhaps an outsider, who admires the worship of the Church of England and respects the long line of its liturgical scholars, such as Gregory Dix, Edward C. Ratcliff (my own teacher), A. H. Couratin, Colin O. Buchanan, R. C. D. Jasper, G. C. Cuming, E. C. Whitaker, Donald Gray, and Bryan Spinks, from all of whom I have learned so much, may be allowed to suggest that while the Church of England has recovered in its eucharistic prayers the joy of the communion of saints, it has not yet linked the earthly feast with the

33. Dunstan, *Interpreting Worship* (Wilton, Connecticut: Morehouse and Barlow, 1985), p. 100.

34. From *A Book of Services: The United Reformed Church in the United Kingdom* (Edinburgh: The Saint Andrew Press, 1980), p. 40.

marriage feast of the Lamb. This was done admirably, I believe, in the Lima Eucharist, where a concluding prayer of thanksgiving ends:

> Lead us towards the full visible unity of your Church and help us to treasure all the signs of reconciliation you have granted us. Now that we have tasted of the banquet you have prepared for us in the life to come, may we all one day share together the inheritance of the saints in the life of your heavenly city.[35]

35. Cf. Max Thurian and Geoffrey Wainwright, eds., *Baptism and Eucharist: Ecumenical Convergence in Celebration* (Geneva: World Council of Churches; Grand Rapids: Wm. B. Eerdmans, 1983), p. 254. This is the Lima Ecumenical Liturgy prepared by Max Thurian and used in 1982.

CHAPTER V

BAPTISM AND EUCHARIST IN ROMAN CATHOLIC AND ORTHODOX WORSHIP

THE INCLUSION in a single chapter of an analysis of both Roman Catholic and Eastern Orthodox worship in England in the last three decades may appear incongruous: the number of Catholics in England is large, and changes in Catholic worship since Vatican II have been sweeping; by contrast, there are relatively few English members of the Orthodox Church, and these adhere to an ancient, virtually unchanged liturgy. Although they will not receive equal space in this chapter, there are two reasons for their juxtaposition. The first is that doctrinally and liturgically the two churches are close. The second is the fact that there has been an important return in Catholic (and Anglican) liturgical scholarship and revision to fourth century models. Indeed, Roman Catholicism has acknowledged its debt in modelling three of its four major eucharistic prayers on the Orthodox pattern of consecration by the invocation of the operation of the Holy Spirit (the *epiklesis*) on the elements and the recipients.

Roman Catholic Revision

Cardinal Basil Hume, a Benedictine, claims that during recent decades "the emphasis in Catholic worship throughout the world changed. Generally speaking, a ceremonial, strongly rubrical liturgy, celebrated by the priest on behalf of, and in the presence of, the people, has given way to a participatory liturgy expressing the Church as the pilgrim people of God."[1] From 1940 onwards several English Catholics urged use of the English language in the liturgy, among

---

1. Foreword to *English Catholic Worship: Liturgical Renewal in England Since 1900* (London: Geoffrey Chapman, 1979).

them Father S. J. Gosling, who invited a number of priests favoring the vernacular to meet at Stanbrook; this meeting resulted in the formation of The English Liturgy Society (renamed later the Vernacular Society).[2] It was controversial and disapproved of by the hierarchy. Another organization, The Society of St. Gregory, originally interested in music for the liturgy, produced an invaluable educational magazine, successively titled *Music and Liturgy, Liturgy,* and, finally, *Life and Worship* (1970). Its editor, Father J. D. Crichton said its aim was to do "what it could to prepare people for the reform of the liturgy that came with the Council." His more recent writings have re-educated the priests and laity of the Roman Catholic Church in England; these include *Christian Celebration: Understanding the Mass* (1971, 1975, 1993), *Christian Celebration: Understanding the Sacraments* (1973, 1979, 1993), and *Christian Celebration: Understanding The Prayer of the Church* (1976, 1993). Father Crichton himself asserts modestly that the most important native expositor of the liturgy was the Jesuit, Father Clifford Howell, who published what might be called the "first textbook in English on liturgy," *The Work of our Redemption,* which was in its fourth (revised) edition by 1975. Father Howell had, with strenuous effort, prepared his translation of *The Constitution on the Liturgy* by the end of the second session of the Second Vatican Council which had just promulgated it.[3]

Much of the work in liturgical theology in England had, of course, been strongly influenced by continental Catholic theologians, among them Doncoeur, Duployé, Bouyer, Martimort, Masure, and Roguet. Probably the most influential books were Jungmann's two-volume *The Mass of the Roman Rite* (1951 and 1955), and Charles Davis's *Liturgy and Doctrine,* both of them employing, as did the Council itself, the interpretation of the Christian mystery of Odo Casel, whose major work, *Das christliche Kultmysterium,* appeared in English translation in 1962 as *The Mystery of Christian Worship.* This volume distinguished three correlated aspects of the mystery. God in His own Being is the supreme mystery — holy, transcendent and unapproachable. The second aspect of the mystery is the revelation of God in Christ: the Incarnation is the personal mystery of God the Invisible revealed in the flesh, in his humiliation and service to

2. *Ibid.,* p. 63.
3. *Ibid.,* pp. 66, 67.

humanity, and in the utterly undeserved sacrificial death upon the Cross, followed by the Resurrection and Ascension. In these events God reveals himself most marvelously in a manner that surpasses all human capacity or imagination. The third mystery is that of the cult, or worship, defined as a liturgical action "in which the redemptive act is rendered present in the rite."[4] And "since the cultic community accomplishes the rite, it shares the saving rite and through it attains redemption."[5] It is interesting that not only the overall mysticism but also the understanding of its effect, namely, the *transfiguration* or sanctification of the Christian community, are seminal for Eastern Orthodoxy as well. The aim of the liturgy, as of the Christian religion, is to bring transfigured Christians to the Transfiguration. The focal center of this worship is Christ in glory, but one must never lose sight of the fact that this Christ went "from God to God" by the route of humiliation and of the *via dolorosa.*

The liturgical implications of this mystery theology are profound. Faith is much more than an assent to theological propositions as it demands the commitment of the entire individual to God. The individual is not viewed atomistically, but as part of the people of God, mystically incorporated into the Body of Christ in the action of the Mass, sharing the life, purposes, and divine energy of God. Furthermore, daily work must also be seen as worship, the offering the Christian in the world brings to the company of the transfigured, to be presented in the offertory of the Liturgy, together with the perfect offering of the Atonement renewed. Moreover, the Eucharist is no longer conceived as simply a hierarchical offering in which the laity are passively present, but as an action of grace in which the general priesthood of the people of God is exercised in response to the gracious offering and sacrifice of the Great High Priest, Christ himself.[6]

The translation from Latin into the English vernacular has been the truly revolutionary change in Roman Catholic worship in England. The Mass is no longer allowed to be an unmeaning rite,

---

4. The terms used by Casel are *repreaesentatio* and *gegenwartigszetsung.*

5. Odo Casel, O.S.B., *Das christliche Kultmysterium,* 3rd ed. (Regensburg, 1948), p. 121.

6. See the present writer's *Worship and Theology in England,* Vol. 5, for a brief exposition of this theology, and a listing of some criticisms of it, which was decried as Greek antiquarianism and for denying the one-for-allness of history.

aesthetically attractive but linguistically unintelligible. Nor is it necessary any longer to concentrate upon one special moment of time (as at the elevation of the Host) to the comparative neglect of the rest of the action, or to use private meditations as a means of dealing with corporate ignorance of the liturgy's meaning. Now the Eucharist is a continuously significant rite for all participants.

Of almost equal significance is the recognition of the place of the Word of God in the first part of the Mass. Now expository sermons are being regularly preached on the lessons of the day from a four year Biblical lectionary, and the themes stress the temporal cycle of the mighty works of God, culminating in Christ, rather than the sanctoral cycle, which is now considerably reduced in numbers and impact. Several other changes of great significance have followed, including those related to the three-part rites of Initiation, which will be considered in detail later. Meanwhile, the preparation for these changes except among the enthusiastic few was minimal. Father Crichton explains: ". . . there were too few to do too much. England entered the post-conciliar period unprepared."[7]

In order to introduce the new liturgical changes gradually and systematically the Bishops of England and Wales published a leaflet in October 1964 directed to the clergy both secular and religious, introducing the *Instructio ad Exsecutionem Constitutionis de Sacra Liturgia recte ordinandum* ["Instruction for the Execution of the Constitution on the Sacred Liturgy properly ordered"], indicating which parts of the Low, High, and Sung Mass might be said or sung in English. In March 1965 they issued a second leaflet on "The Reform of the Sacred Liturgy, second stage" which was to commence on Palm Sunday, 1975. This instruction extended the use of English at Mass to include all that was said aloud at a Mass with a congregation present, up to the "Secret Prayer" (omitting only the *Kyrie*), and all that was said aloud from the introduction of the Lord's Prayer to the end of the Mass, omitting only the *Domine, non sum dignus*, the concluding *Ite, missa est*, and the blessing. Further concessions were made for parts other than the Ordinary of the Mass in allowing English translations for the services of Holy Week.[8]

The new rites issued in rapid succession from Rome from 1969. On the First Sunday of Advent in 1969 the revised Order of the

---

7. *English Catholic Worship*, p. 78.
8. H. E. Winstone in *English Catholic Worship*, pp. 79ff.

Mass became obligatory in England as from February 15th, along with the new Lectionary. An interim translation of the new rites of Ordination appeared by Easter Sunday of 1969, while the new Calendar came into force on the first day of January, 1970. Easter of the same year saw the introduction of a revised rite for Infant Baptism, and an interim Breviary was published in Rome early in 1969. These were hectic days for translators, especially as Rome had declared its wish for the same English text to be used throughout the English-speaking world. This was the harder to implement because "Thou" language was still used in English worship, while several English-speaking countries had relinquished not only the "Thou" form of address but also the archaic grammatical forms that accompanied it, preferring the direct, if prosaic, "You" form. In addition, there was difficulty with relative clauses referring to the Godhead, and much awkwardness in dealing with adjectives that were pious or even "imperialistic." Ultimately the work was placed in the hands of the *International Committee on English in the Liturgy,* also known by its acronym ICEL.[9]

Worship was no longer exclusively the concern of the priests, but of the laity. In the task of educating the people, there were several instrumentalities. The most helpful commentaries on the new rites were those of Father J. D. Crichton, already referred to, remarkable for their combination of erudition, clarity, and conviction along with the psychology of the human touch. Other help was provided by symposia, such as Lancelot Shepard's *The New Liturgy* (1970), H. E. Winstone's *Pastoral Liturgy* (1975), and the ecumenically produced *The Study of Liturgy* (1978, revised 1992), edited by Cheslyn Jones, Geoffrey Wainwright, and Edward Yarnold, S.J. The Westminster Liturgy Commission, founded in 1969, which established the St. Thomas More Centre for Pastoral Liturgy, had a national impact. The publication in 1975 of the Roman Directory on the Celebration of the Liturgy with Children, on which Edward Matthews wrote a commentary entitled, *Celebrating Mass with Children* (1975), and the authorization of three new children's eucharistic prayers, proved helpful for school chaplains.[10]

Apart from the revolutionary insistence on the vernacular in all rites, together with the recovery of the preliminary service of the

9. *Ibid.,* p. 81.
10. *Ibid.,* pp. 85-86.

Word, including preaching of the Gospel, the most radical revisions were in the rites of Initiation and in the changes simplifying the Calendar. When the *Ordo Baptismi Parvulorum* was issued in 1969 the surprise was double: first, that Baptism, Confirmation and first Communion together form the sacrament of Christian initiation; and second, that in a world which can no longer count on the dominance of Christians in general, and Christian parents in particular, realism demands that solemn promises must be required of parents who wish their children to be baptized. We must, in fact, expect to see many more adult baptisms than has been the case in the past.

Thus for the Baptism of Infants, the questions of the celebrant at the church door require the parents and godparents to declare their own faith and intent to bring up the child as a Christian. The rite begins with a brief service of the Word. No longer in the exorcism is there any direct command for the devil to depart; instead there is a petition that the candidates may be delivered from the power of sin. There follows an anointing of the breast with oil for strength, followed by a blessing of the font which includes an *epiklesis.* Then the parents and godparents make their promises, abjuring Satan and professing their faith in Christ. The baptismal formula is prescribed in the Matthaean form,[11] with a triple immersion or pouring. After Baptism there is the "Messianic" anointing of the head with chrism, and the presentation of the white garment and the candle. These symbolize the purity and fidelity required by the newly washed and newly reborn infant. If desired, the "Effeta" ceremony[12] may be employed. The giving of the salt in the prior rite is eliminated. The emphasis now is on the public entrance into the local Christian community, and on the serious undertaking of the parents to bring the child up in the Christian faith, an obligation which the parish priest is required to obtain from them before agreeing to baptize their child. A serious attempt is made, thus, to avoid indiscriminate Infant Baptism.

The Roman Catholic rite of Confirmation was instituted by the bull *Divinum Consortium Naturae* in 1971. It reaffirms the traditional order of the initiatory sacraments with Baptism and Confirmation leading to first Communion. The purpose of the sacrament of Con-

---

11. Matthew 28:19.

12. This ceremony is derived from Christ's words "Be opened" — referring to both ears and mouth of a man who was deaf and had an impediment in his speech, whom Jesus cured, as recorded in Mark 7:32-37.

firmation is said to be to continue the process of Christian initiation and to equip the candidate with the Holy Spirit for the vocation of sharing in the apostolic witness. This bull appears to reject the view that its function is to provide an opportunity for a mature commitment of faith or to impart the Holy Spirit for the challenges of life for the Christian. Thus "the paradox that was present in Western theology since patristic times is still not resolved: if in baptism we are reborn by the Holy Spirit who comes to dwell within us, in what sense is a new endowment of the Spirit imparted at confirmation?"[13]

It is also important to ask how the traditional three-fold order can be implemented, because in several countries first Communion is delayed until the age of seven and generally precedes Confirmation, which follows during adolescence.

The rite of Confirmation is designed to be performed immediately after the Gospel in the context of the Mass. The permission for priests to be ministers of Confirmation in special circumstances is now extended. Further, if priests assist the bishop, they must receive the chrism they are to use from the hands of the bishop, but both bishop and assisting priests extend their hands collectively over the candidates when the bishop asks God the Father to send down the Holy Spirit with the sevenfold gifts. The act of chrismation is an essential element in the rite and at this point the president makes the sign of the cross on the head of the candidate, with the formula: "N., to be sealed with the gift of the Holy Spirit." These words were chosen, so Paul VI explained, "from the very ancient Byzantine formulary."[14] This was a change from the traditional Latin words translated as "I sign you with the sign of the cross and confirm you with the chrism of salvation in the name. . . ." Its value is that it modestly diminishes the hierarchical component of the older formula by indicating God's Holy Spirit as the donor of grace.

The second surprise occurred in 1972 when the rites of Baptism were completed by the arrival of the Christian Initiation of Adults (RCIA). This was the implementation of the Council's desire, following the practice of the fourth century, to restore the adult catechu-

13. See "Initiation: The Modern Period" by Peter Hinchliff, revised by Charles Brock and the editors of *The Study of Liturgy*, rev. ed. (London: S.P.C.K. and Oxford University Press, 1992). The editors are Cheslyn Jones, Geoffrey Wainwright, Edward Yarnold, S.J., and Paul Bradshaw. The reference is to p. 175.

14. *Ibid.*, p. 176.

menate. This catechumenate is divided into four periods closely following the fourth century pattern. The stages are: pre-catechumenate, catechumenate, enlightenment, and mystagogy, and are entered by three steps. The first is acceptance into the order of catechumens, the second is election or enrollment, preferably at the beginning of Lent, with the celebration of the three sacraments of initiation taking place preferably at the Easter Vigil. The whole period of the catechumenate is conceived not merely as a period of Christian education, but also as a period for the deepening of conversion, maturing of faith, and growing integration into the life of the church, with the assistance of sponsors, godparents, and the entire community. The spiritual development of the candidate for Baptism is measured by the three scrutinies on the third, fourth, and fifth Sundays of Lent, times also of profound self-scrutiny by the candidate for Baptism.

The seriousness of the preparation for Baptism of Adults can be envisaged only if the significance of each of the "stages, steps, or gateways" is explained, and if the wording of parts of the rites are recorded. The document, *Christian Initiation of Adults*, points out that becoming a catechumen "consists of inquiry by the candidate and evangelization of the pre-catechumenate on the part of the Church." It concludes with the candidate entering into the order of catechumens. The second period may last for several years, includes catechesis and rites connected with it, and is completed on the day of election. The third period, briefer, usually occupies the Lenten preparation for the celebration of Easter, and is a time for purification and enlightenment. The fourth and final period proceeds through the whole Easter season and is called post-baptismal catechesis or "mystagogia." It is a time "for deepening the Christian experience, for gaining spiritual fruit, and for entering more closely into the life and unity of the community of the faithful."[15] It is stressed that the candidates will only become "elect," competent, or mature catechumens after a conversion of mind and morals.[16]

Now it is appropriate to examine, if only in summary form, the various rites of the catechumenate, to indicate their great importance, and their attempt to do away with ill-considered Christian initiation.

---

15. R.C.I.A. translated as *The Christian Initiation of Adults*, Introduction, p. 21.
16. *Ibid.*, p. 27.

The Rite of Election or Enrolment of Candidates for Baptism[17]

The candidates are summoned by name, each accompanied by a godparent. The celebrant asks if they are ready for the sacraments: Have they listened to the Word of God, sought to follow it in their lives, associated with their brothers and sisters in prayer? The godparents before God reply in the affirmative. The celebrant then asks the candidates if they wish to receive the sacraments. On their affirmative reply they are asked to give their names for enrolment.

When the celebrant informs the candidates they have been elected or chosen for initiation, they reply: "Thanks be to God."

The celebrant continues:

Now it is your duty and ours to ask the help of God. He is always faithful to those he calls. Be faithful to him in return and strive courageously to reach the goal your calling opens up to you.

Then the celebrant turns to the godparents and reminds them of their duties in these or similar words:

These catechumens have been entrusted to you in the Lord, and you have given us a favorable report. By your loving care and example continue to help them until they receive the sacraments of God's life.

He then invites them to place their hand on the shoulder of the candidate they are presenting. The Prayer for the Elect follows, or in similar words:

Celebrant: My brother and sisters: Today we begin Lent and look forward to the celebration of the life-giving mysteries of our Lord's suffering, death, and resurrection. These chosen men (and women), whom we lead with us to the Easter sacraments look to us for an example of the Christian life. Let us pray to the Lord for them and for ourselves that we may be strengthened by each other's mutual efforts, and so come to share the joys of Easter.

A series of brief prayers for the catechumens follows. Two final prayers follow. The first pleads: "Count these adopted children as sons

17. *The Sunday Missal: A New Edition* (London: Collins, 1989), pp. 173ff.

(and daughters) reborn to your new covenant. Make them children of the promise. Although they cannot reach eternal life by their own nature, may they come to share it by the power of your love."

They are then dismissed with the words:

You have been chosen by God and have entered with us on the way of Lent. May Christ himself be your way, your truth, and your life, especially during the approaching scrutinies when we shall meet with you again. For the present, go in peace.

The elect respond: "Amen."

The Scrutinies

At the first scrutiny the godparents place their hand on the elect person's shoulder, while he/she shows repentance by bowing or kneeling. A prayer asks that they keep the Word of God in their hearts, learn to know Christ, humbly acknowledge their sinfulness, and reject anything in their lives displeasing to Christ or opposed to him and, further, asks that the Holy Spirit may strengthen their weakness and teach them the things of God.

Exorcism then follows. The first prayer asks that the elect stop relying upon themselves, acknowledge their sins and weaknesses, and advance on the way to salvation.

The second prayer says:

Lord Jesus, you are the fountain we thirst for;
You are the teacher we seek;
You alone are the Holy One;
These chosen ones open their hearts honestly
to confess their failures and be forgiven.
In your love, free them from evil,
Restore your health, satisfy their thirst, and give them peace.
By the power of your name which they call upon in faith
stay with them and save them.
Command the spirit of evil to leave them,
for you have conquered that spirit by rising to life.
Show your chosen people the way of life in the Holy Spirit that
they may grow closer to the Father and worship him,
For you are Lord for ever and ever.

Celebrant concludes:
Go in peace until we meet at the next scrutiny.
May the Lord be with you always.

Elect: Amen

The second scrutiny centers on a prayer for fidelity, for preferring the foolishness of the cross to the wisdom of the world.

A final prayer has the celebrant laying his hands on each one of the elect, praying that they be inspired "to become fearless witnesses to the faith," after which he dismisses them until the next scrutiny.

The third scrutiny has a resurrection theme, with a prayer that the elect "may be united to Christ in his death and resurrection and, by the grace of his sacraments, conquer the bitterness of death."

The final prayer ends thus: "Lord Jesus . . . by your Holy Spirit fill them with life; give them faith, hope, and love, that they may live with you always and come to share the glory of your resurrection, for you are Lord for ever and ever. . . ."

Baptism[18]

The importance of the adult rites of Christian initiation can be appreciated only if, after the enrollment and the three scrutinies, we arrive for the Baptism on Easter morning, when the priest begins by saying:

Dear friends in Christ, as our brothers and sisters approach the waters of rebirth, let us help them by our prayers, and ask God, our almighty Father, to support them with his mercy and love.

Then the priest blesses the baptismal water in a prayer making fine use of baptismal imagery.

The Renunciation then follows and the Affirmation of Faith. Each requires the simple response, "I do." I cite the second alternative form.

18. *Ibid.*, p. 308.

Do you reject sin, so as to live in the freedom of God's children?
Do you reject the glamour of evil, and refuse
     to be mastered by sin?
Do you reject Satan, father of sin, and prince of darkness?

The Apostles' Creed, which follows, is divided into three sections for the sake of affirmation of belief in the Trinity.
Then the priest baptizes, saying:

N., I baptize you in the name of the Father, and of the Son, and of the Holy Spirit.

Confirmation

The rite of Confirmation[19] begins as the bishop or priest with the authority to confirm speaks thus:

N. born again in Christ by baptism, you have become a member of Christ and of his priestly people. Now you are to share in the outpouring of the Holy Spirit among us, the Spirit sent by the Lord upon his apostles at Pentecost and given by them and theirs to be baptized. The promised strength of the Holy Spirit which you are to receive will make you more like Christ and help you to be witness to his suffering, death, and resurrection. It will strengthen you to be an active member of the Church and to build up the Body of Christ in faith and love.

Then follows a brief prayer that the Holy Spirit will be poured out on the newly baptized and will anoint him/her to be more like Christ.
After silent prayer, the celebrant lays his hand upon the candidate and says:

All-powerful God, the Father of our Lord Jesus Christ, by water and the Holy Spirit you freed your son/daughter from sin, and gave him/her new life. Send your Holy Spirit upon him/her to be his/her helper and guide. Give him/her the spirit of wisdom and understanding, the spirit of right judgement and courage, the spirit of knowledge

19. *Ibid.*, pp. 309ff.

and reverence. Fill him/her with the spirit of wonder and awe in your presence, we ask this through Christ our Lord. Amen.

The celebrant is then approached by the candidate with the god-parent's hand on his shoulder, and the celebrant dips his right hand in the chrism and makes the sign of the cross on the forehead of the one to be confirmed.

CELEBRANT: N., be sealed with the gift of the Holy Spirit.
NEWLY CONFIRMED: Amen
CELEBRANT: Peace be with you
NEWLY CONFIRMED: And also with you.

All stand present with lighted candles when the rite of Baptism and Confirmation has been completed. All the congregation renew their baptismal profession of faith. During this part of the service the priest sprinkles the people with the blessed water. The newly baptized now take full part in the liturgy of the Eucharist for the first time.

The value of these rites is that the various stages prior to Baptism and Confirmation sort out the serious candidates just as the Scrutinies put the elect to the test also. The emphasis on adopted children is admirable, as also is the wording concerning the gifts of the Holy Spirit. The wording of the Scrutinies seems, to this writer at least, unnecessarily repetitive. But altogether the several rites of initiation are a great improvement on the former private, and apparently casual, family rites. These rites, moreover, use symbolism to the full. The rite of Christian initiation of adults declares that Baptism, whether by pouring or infusion or immersion in water, is "a sign of mystical sharing in the death and rising of Christ" and that "the washing is not merely a rite of purification but a sacrament of union with Christ." Also, it continues, "the anointing with chrism after baptism is a sign of the royal priesthood of the baptized and their enrollment in the fellowship of the people of God." In addition, "the white robe is a symbol of their new dignity, and the lighted candle shows their vocation of living as befits children of light."[20]

20. *The Christian Initiation of Adults,* p. 29.

The Roman Catholic Eucharist

The major striking changes in the celebration of the Mass are the following: the use of the vernacular instead of Latin, the revision of its structure to reflect that of the early church, the provision of four eucharistic prayers to replace the single one, the shifting of the altar from the sanctuary to the nave with the priest facing the congregation from behind the altar, the encouragement of congregational singing, the use of Old Testament lections and prayers of intercession, and a simplification of ceremonial, with concentration on the meaning. These changes require exposition in detail.

While there has been no diminution of the primary sense that the sacraments convey the grace of God to the believing community, there is an increasing stress on the recipients of the sacraments and how they should understand the meaning of the symbols and gestures. For example, real bread is often supplied instead of wafers, and the cup has been restored to the people. Professor James White rightly observes the difference between the old and the revised rite of the Eucharist in summary form: "Many of the devotions which once occupied the people while the lonely priest said the Mass have been pushed aside for a greater sense of corporate involvement in offering thanksgiving together."[21] The new rite, when properly understood, calls for a central altar-table, because it is interpreted as a meal, as well as a sacrifice. Professor Nicholas Lash in an early post-Conciliar discussion of the theology of the Eucharist, *His Presence in the World* (1968), argued that the concept of the meal is a new emphasis; the "food" is the body and blood of Christ, and so the Eucharist is the sacrifice-sign that communicates Christ's crucifixion-resurrection and creates the Church as the Body of Christ. He insists that "the unique and unrepeatable nature of Christ's perfect sacrifice on Calvary" is recalled efficaciously to the Father by Christ through the actions of his Body, the Church.[22] In discussing the need to use sacrificial terminology which can be easily misunderstood, Lash clarifies the situation by stating, "It is misleading to say either that 'we offer Christ to the Father,' or that 'Christ offers us to the Father.'" He urges the more balanced statement that "by the grace

---

21. *A Brief History of Christian Worship* (Nashville: Abingdon Press, 1993), p. 158.
22. Lash, *His Presence in the World: A Study of Eucharistic Worship and Theology* (London and Sydney: Sheed & Ward, 1968), pp. 58-59.

of Christ, our self-offering to the Father, expressed and sealed by our sharing in the meal, is a participation in his self-offering to his Father on Calvary."[23] Professor Lash insists that there are three modes of the presence of Christ: in the gathered community of Christians, in the reading and proclamation of the Word of God in the Scriptures, and in the Eucharist.[24]

A very comprehensive analysis and exposition of the theology of the Conciliar Constitution on the Liturgy was provided by the Oratorian, Father Louis Bouyer.[25] He showed that the interpretation of the Eucharist as the Paschal Mystery was a restoration of its meaning as understood by the Fathers of the Church in both East and West.[26] The Scriptural meaning of mystery, he argues, is not a truth we accept but cannot explain or, like a secret pagan rite something kept for a select coterie. Rather, it is a special revelation of God communicated by the Holy Spirit, undiscoverable by the highest human wisdom and apparent folly to the wise, as expressed in the first two chapters of St. Paul's First Epistle to the Corinthians.[27] It is in Christ alone — in his words and actions and in his passion and resurrection — that the wisdom of God comes to its final realization. Central to the Council's understanding is the paschal mystery of the Christian Passover. The blood of the lamb on the lintel of the doors of the faithful Israelites was a sign of their delivery from Egyptian slavery to freedom. And Christians, through the paschal mystery of the Cross and the Resurrection, become adopted sons and daughters of God through participation in the Eucharist.[28] As Father Bouyer writes: "The memorial of the Paschal mystery, therefore — in the Mass first of all, but through the whole sacramental celebration — is both that great sacrament of the Church through which all grace comes to us from the Father from above, and the perfect Sacrifice of the Whole Christ, through which the Body together with its Divine Head becomes acceptable before the Father. . . ."[29]

This may be the appropriate opportunity to explain two important

23. *Ibid.*, p. 61.
24. *Ibid.*, p. 152.
25. Bouyer, *The Liturgy Revived: A Doctrinal Commentary on the Conciliar Constitution on the Liturgy* (Notre Dame: University of Notre Dame Press, 1964).
26. *Ibid.*, p. 13, especially referring to Hippolytus's *The Apostolic Tradition.*
27. *Ibid.*, pp. 17-18.
28. *Ibid.*, pp. 19-24.
29. *Ibid.*, p. 25.

terms used for elements usually included in the central prayer of consecration or thanksgiving in the Eucharist. One is a Greek word for a Semitic concept, which is often translated into English with a backward rather than a contemporary reference. It is *anamnesis,* usually translated by such words as memorial, commemoration, recalling, or remembrance. But, as Jardine Grisbrooke asserts, these terms suggest the very opposite of what is intended.

> It is an objective act, in and by which the person or event commemorated is actually made present, is brought into the realm of the here and now. And the eucharist, as the early Church understood it, is the "recalling" before God of the one sacrifice of Christ in all its accomplished fullness, so that it is here and now operative in all its effects in the souls of the redeemed.[30]

Grisbrooke borrows this lively definition from Dix's *The Shape of the Liturgy* (p. 243), only adding that "bodies and souls" would have been more a correct rendering for the doctrine of the early Church.[31] The *anamnesis* is that part of the eucharistic prayer which explicitly states that the church is offering the bread and the cup with this meaning, acting in obedience to the command of Christ its Lord. Almost all historic prayers recall the passion, resurrection, and ascension of Christ and include a reference to the Second Coming. Sometimes other aspects of redemption such as the Incarnation and the mediation of the ascended Lord at the right hand of the Father are added, all within the eschatological perspective. In such prayers, to use the graphic terminology of both the Protestant Kierkegaard and the Catholic Casel, Christ becomes our contemporary. As Father J. D. Crichton observes concerning the new Roman liturgy of the Word and Eucharist, ". . . liturgy is a symbolic action that re-enacts the sacred events of saving history and makes God present with his redeeming power."[32]

The second important element in the prayer of consecration or thanksgiving in the Eucharist is called the *epiklesis,* the prayer for the

---

30. *The New Westminster Dictionary of Liturgy and Worship,* ed. J. Gordon Davies (Philadelphia: Westminster, 1983), pp. 18a and b.

31. *Ibid.,* p. 19a.

32. Crichton, *Christian Celebration: Understanding the Mass* (London: Chapman, 1993), pp. 28, 29.

descent of the Holy Spirit, the effect of this descent being the change of bread and wine into the body and blood of Christ, together with a petition that the recipients at Communion may receive the fruits of communion. Three of the four prayers in the new Roman rite have double *epikleses*. The *epiklesis* has been universal in the Eastern liturgies and some Eastern *epikleses* ask for the descent of the Spirit on the people, as well as on the elements. It is particularly interesting that one of the new eucharistic prayers in the Roman rite is definitely modelled on that of the Eastern Orthodox liturgy. It has been argued by some that there is no *epiklesis* in the traditional Roman canon of the Mass, while others such as Grisbrooke claim that it is contained within the *Supra quae* and the *Supplices te* prayers of the canon.

The Eucharistic Prayer IV has the following *epiklesis:*

> Father, may this Holy Spirit sanctify these offerings. Let them become the body and blood of Jesus Christ our Lord as we celebrate the great mystery which he left us as an everlasting covenant.[33]

The same prayer exhibits the two long elements of the *anamnesis* which it employs. The first element recalls God's sending of his only Son in the Incarnation and includes a strong liberation emphasis, referring to Christ thus:

> a man like us in all things but sin.
> To the poor he proclaimed the good news of salvation,
> to prisoners freedom,
> and to those in sorrow, joy.
> In fulfillment of your will
> he gave himself up to death;
> but by rising from the dead,
> he destroyed death and restored life.
> And that we might live no longer for ourselves, but for him,
> He sent the Holy Spirit from you, Father,
> as his first gift to those who believe,
> to complete his work on earth
> and bring us the fullness of grace.[34]

33. *The Sunday Missal*, p. 53.
34. *Ibid.*

The *epiklesis* follows and after that a memorial of Christ's love in establishing the Lord's Supper, ending with an invitation to proclaim the mystery of faith. This is answered by the alternative memorial acclamations of the people:

1. Christ has died,
   Christ is risen,
   Christ will come again.

2. Dying, you destroyed our death,
   rising you restored our life.
   Lord Jesus, come in glory.

3. When we eat this bread and drink this cup,
   we proclaim your death, Lord Jesus,
   until you come in glory.

4. Lord, by your cross and resurrection
   you have set us free.
   You are the Saviour of the world.[35]

It should also be noted that Eucharistic Prayers II and III, but not I, also offer an invocation of the Holy Spirit as an *epiklesis*. And in all four prayers the four alternative acclamations of the people are included. Clearly, the people are given a larger role than in the traditional Eucharist, and the emphasis on the *epiklesis* has deep ecumenical significance since it brings the practice of the Roman Church closer in the supreme sacrament to that of the Eastern Orthodox Churches. The importance of the *epiklesis* is two-fold: it invokes the work of the Holy Spirit in the eucharistic action, and it also asks that the offerings of the people as signs of their self-giving may "be integrated into the offering of Christ which the eucharistic action makes present."[36]

In concluding this section one must admire the thoroughness of

---

35. *Ibid.*, p. 54.

36. Crichton, *Christian Celebration*, p. 101. He also adds: "In the New Testament view (cf. Romans 12:1, 2, etc.), self-offering, the offering of one's whole life and activity, is always associated with sacrifice and here in the eucharist it receives expression."

the revision of the Mass. It is now more intelligible, since the acclamations are added to the *Sanctus* responses, and, by the same token, more of a community action. That permission is given for the cup as well as the bread to be received makes it seem more like a meal and closer to the original Lord's Supper. Finally, the triple emphasis on the sacrificial passion and death, the resurrection, and the Second Coming of Christ, make the celebration more meaningful, hopeful, and more joyful than the traditional rite of Communion.

The radical change in the Calendar (also involving a new Directory for the Lessons in worship) was explained in the Constitution of the Sacred Liturgy (nn. 102-111). It came into being in the 1969 Calendar. The novelty was the decision that the central events in the life of Christ must receive preference over saints' days to allow for suitable recollection of the mysteries of salvation. Hence Sunday takes precedence over every kind of feast in Advent, Lent, and Eastertide, and over all but a few solemnities. Clearly, the Pascal Triduum, commencing with the evening Mass on Maundy Thursday, concentrating on the Easter Vigil and ending with Vespers on Easter Day, forms the climax of the entire liturgical year. By eliminating the octave of Pentecost and making Pentecost itself the last of the holy fifty days, the integrity of the Easter season is emphasized. Also Sundays are named "of Easter" rather than "after Easter." Lent starts with Ash Wednesday and ends on Maundy Thursday. It is clearly a season of preparation for the celebration of the paschal mystery, and the lections are penitential or baptismal in their focus.

The Christmas season too is revised. The celebration of Christmas Epiphany continues from Christmas Eve to the Sunday after Epiphany (or after 6 January if that is kept on a Sunday). That Sunday is the feast of the Baptism of the Lord, while the Sunday after Christmas is the feast of the Holy Family. Advent remains a season of four weeks. It is intended to be kept in a spirit of joy and hopeful expectation; there has been a reduction of the penitential element. The last week, beginning on December 17th, is concerned with the coming of Christ.

The rest of the year is regarded as "Ordinary Time" and lasts for a total of thirty-four weeks, thus emphasizing the extraordinary character and importance of the two seasons of Easter and Christmas.[37]

37. I have availed myself of the summary of recent Catholic calendric change in Peter B. Cobb's article entitled "The History of the Christian Year" in *The Study of Liturgy*, pp. 470-71.

The most striking change is in the simplification of the sanctoral cycle, which distinguishes the recollection of the saints as solemnities, feasts, and memorials. Many of the latter are optional and only saints of universal Christian significance have to be commemorated, while national and regional saints may receive attention. As Professor James White points out, before the reform of 1970 there was a "holy congestion" of saints in the Calendar, "since between 1568 and 1960 171 more saints were added to an already crowded Calendar."[38]

It is interesting to note that many Protestant traditions have begun to take the traditional Christian year more seriously, and to a large extent this has been due to the widespread adoption of versions of the new Roman Catholic Sunday lectionary,[39] with its careful evangelical organization of the thirty-four Sundays in "Ordinary Time."

The three-year Lectionary is built upon the three Synoptic Gospels, with Matthew, Mark, and Luke used in successive years. To give one sample, the Gospel readings from Luke for thirty-four Sundays are divided into eight units. Unit 1 is The figure of Jesus the Messiah, including the baptism of Jesus and the marriage feast at Cana. Unit 2 is Luke's program for Jesus' ministry. Unit 3 includes the call to the first apostles, three readings on the sermon on the plain, the cure of the centurion's servant, the widow of Nain, Jesus' feet anointed by the sinful woman, and Peter's confession of faith. Unit 4 is the first part of the "travel narrative" and the qualities Jesus demands of those who follow him. It includes the start of the journey to Jerusalem, the mission of the seventy-two, the Good Samaritan, Martha and Mary, the importunate friend, the parable of the rich fool, the need for vigilance, "not peace but a division," few will be saved, true humility, and the cost of discipleship. Unit 5 is titled "The Gospel within the Gospel": the message of pardon and reconciliation and the parables of God's mercy, including the lost coin, the lost sheep, and the Prodigal Son. Unit 6 combines the second part of the "travel narrative" with obstacles facing those who follow Jesus. Successively this Unit deals with the unjust steward, the rich man and Lazarus, a lesson on faith, the ten lepers, the unjust judge, the Pharisees and the tax collector, and Zacchaeus. Unit 7 covers the ministry of Jesus in Jerusalem, the debate over the resurrection, signs announcing the end, and Christ the King. It stresses reconciliation,

38. White, *A Brief History of Christian Worship*, pp. 161-62.
39. *Ibid.*

117

and deals with the repentant thief. It is also worth noting that eighteen of the thirty-four Gospel lessons in this sequence are found only in the Gospel of Luke.[40]

Eastern Orthodox Worship

The chief Churches of this world-wide and historic community represent a relatively small number of English worshippers, who are deservedly proud of their historic tradition which their forebears have retained, relatively unchanged[41] through many, many centuries, and in difficult days, and so do not look for change. In our own day, several other churches, both Roman Catholic and Anglican, are in fact looking back to Eastern worship in the fourth century to find models that might warrant imitation. The structure and symbolic actions of baptismal preparation are proving instructive, as are the blessing or consecration of the Eucharist with an *epiklesis* rather than by the mere repetition of the words of the institution of the Lord's Supper, believed to transform the bread and wine into the body and blood of Christ. Furthermore, no form of Christian worship has been as dominantly eschatological with its emphasis on the glory of the Resurrection of Christ and the everlasting joy of the saints in heaven. Nor has any other Church been as effective in the use of symbolism.

Before analyzing their liturgies for Baptism and Eucharist, some account of both Greek and Russian Orthodox congregations in England should be provided. These are still dominantly communities of first generation immigrants who prefer worship in their native Greek or Russian languages; the younger generation brought up in England typically express a preference for an English liturgy. The majority of the clergy in the Greek parishes are not British-born and preach in Greek. As in local parishes in Greece and Cyprus, people often arrive late for the service, move about, and interrupt the service with chatter. The singing is traditional Byzantine chant, without an organ or a mixed choir.

40. *Sunday Missal,* pp. 16-17.
41. Robert Taft, S.J., provides strong evidence for historical change in the Byzantine Liturgy and affirms that the central elements are largely the same, despite additions and subtractions. This is in chapter 11 of his *Beyond East and West: Problems in Liturgical Understanding* (Washington: Pastoral Press, 1984).

The main Russian Orthodox Church in London is the Cathedral of All Saints. There is an English liturgy on one Sunday each month, but otherwise services are in Slavonic. Most of the congregation are English converts. Outside London there are several small parishes, either mission stations or eucharistic centers, with convert priests and chiefly English-speaking congregations. The size of such congregations is generally small, with 20 to 40 persons. On the other hand, the main Greek parishes in London have 500 to 1000 in attendance each Sunday. Statistics reveal how very recent is the expansion of Orthodoxy in Britain. A 1962 Year Book listed 29 Orthodox places of worship, 5 bishops, 37 priests and 8 deacons. A 1989 directory lists 143 places of worship, 12 bishops, 116 priests, and 22 deacons. "This," says Bishop Kallistos (Ware) of Diokleia, "indicates how very recent in origin is the great majority of parishes in this country. Eighty percent of them have existed for less than twenty-five years. Compared with other Christian bodies in this land, the Orthodox Church is indeed a new presence."[42]

Baptism

The first part of the Liturgy for Holy Baptism in the Orthodox Church according to the Greek Rite[43] proceeds as follows. The candidate is first received as a catechumen. The priest removes his clothes except for a single garment and places him with his face towards the east, breathing three times in his face, then makes the sign of the cross upon him thrice, lays his hand on his head, and prays for him. The priest pronounces the three exorcisms, ordering the devil to leave him. Then the priest, after prayers, breathes on his mouth, his brow, and his breast that God may expel all evil and

---

42. This information was kindly sent to me, as that in the previous paragraph, by the Bishop, who is Spalding Lecturer in Religion at Oxford University, in a letter and an enclosed pamphlet on 19/2/1993.

43. I have summarized the Sacrament of Baptism of the Greek Orthodox Church Rite from pp. 9-19 of *Baptism and Eucharist: Ecumenical Convergence in Celebration,* ed. Max Thurian and Geoffrey Wainwright (Geneva: World Council of Churches; Grand Rapids: Wm. B. Eerdmans, 1983). This, in turn was based upon *An Orthodox Prayer Book,* ed. Fr. N. M. Vaporis, translated by Frs. J. von Holtzhausen and Michael Gelsinger (Brookline, Mass.: Holy Cross Orthodox Press, 1977), pp. 55-73. Variations in other Orthodox Churches are relatively few.

impurity, deceit, idolatry and concupiscence from him and make him a reason-endowed sheep in the flock of Christ. The priest then turns him towards the west and thrice asks him if he renounces Satan; the candidate is asked to spit upon Satan. Then the priest turns him towards the east and asks him three times if he unites himself to Christ, and thrice immediately afterwards if he has united himself to Christ. Finally, in receiving three affirmative answers, the priest orders him: "Bow down before Him" and the candidate responds, "I bow down before the Father, and the Son, and the Holy Spirit, the Trinity, one Essence and undivided." A short prayer of intercession follows.

The service of Holy Baptism proper begins with the priest, in white vestments, offering an intercessory prayer including petitions "that this water may be hallowed by the might, and operation, and descent of Holy Spirit" and that it may be "a laver of regeneration," that the baptized may be cleansed and illuminated, may prove to be a child of light, may become a partaker of the death and resurrection of the Lord and be blameless "in the terrible Day of Christ our Lord."

The priest then blesses the baptismal waters with the key words, "Do You Yourself, O Loving King, be present now also through the descent of the Holy Spirit and hallow this water." He makes the sign of the cross thrice, dipping his finger in the water, pleading that the candidate, "being planted in the likeness of Your death through Baptism may become a sharer of your Resurrection."

The Blessing of the Oil follows. The priest breathes thrice upon the oil, and signs it with the cross thrice while it is held in the hand of the godparent. The priest then takes the oil and makes the sign of the cross on the child's forehead, breast, and between his or her shoulders, saying: "The Servant of God (Name) is baptized in the name of the Father. Amen. And of the Son. Amen. And of the Holy Spirit. Amen." As he crosses the breast and between the shoulders, he says, "For healing of soul and body," and on the ears, saying, "For the hearing of faith," and on the feet, saying, "That he (she) may walk in the paths of Your commandments," and on the hands, saying, "Your hands have made me and fashioned me."

After the whole body has been anointed, the priest baptizes the candidate, holding him or her erect, and looking towards the east, saying: "The servant of God (Name) is baptized in the Name of the Father. Amen. And of the Son. Amen. And of the Holy Spirit.

Amen." At each invocation the priest immerses the individual and raises him or her again. Following the baptizing, the priest places the child in a linen sheet held by the godparent.

Confirmation

The choir sings Psalm 31, emphasizing forgiveness and joy, and then the Prayer of Confirmation follows. This blesses God for salvation in Christ, and the gift of "cleansing in Holy Water, and divine sanctification in the Life-effecting Anointing" and begs that God will bestow upon the baptized servant of God also "the Seal of Your omnipotent and adorable Holy Spirit, and the Communion of the Holy Body and Most Precious Blood of Your Christ." Following this prayer the priest gives chrism to the baptized, making the sign of the cross with the chrism (Holy Myron) on the forehead, eyes, nostrils, mouth, ears, breast, hands, and feet. At each anointing and sealing the priest says: "Seal of the gift of the Holy Spirit." The priest invests the baptized in a new clean robe, saying: "Clothed is the servant of God (Name) with the garment of righteousness, in the Name of the Father, and of the Son, and of the Holy Spirit. Amen." Then the priest with the godparent and child circumambulates around the font three times, and the choir sings: "As many of you as have been baptized into Christ, have put on Christ. Alleluia."

Next there ensues the reading of the Epistle from Romans 6:3-11 and the Gospel lection (Matthew 18:16-20). The *ablution* which follows includes a prayer with the petition for the baptized. "Preserve unspotted his (her) pledge of Faith in You." The priest then loosens the child's girdle and garment, and joining the end of these, he soaks them with clean water and sprinkles the child, saying aloud: "You are baptized; you are illuminated; you are anointed with the Holy Myrrh; you are hallowed; you are washed clean, in the Name of Father and of Son, and of Holy Spirit."

The next ceremony is the tonsure. It begins with a prayer indicating that the baptized child "is come now to make offering of the firstlings of hair shorn from his (her) head." A second prayer of the priest, with his hand on the head of the baptized, pleads that as Samuel blessed the head of King David, "so also bless the head of this servant . . . visiting him (her) with Your Holy Spirit, that as he (she) goes forward to the prime of his (her) years, and the grey hairs of old age, he (she) may send up Glory to You, beholding the good things of Jerusalem all the days of his (her) life." The priest shears him (her) in the form of a Cross, snipping off four locks of hair, front, back, and over each ear, saying: "The servant of God (Name) is shorn in the Name of the Father, and of the Son, and of the Holy Spirit."

The rite ends with the *Apolysis* with a blessing on the child and the congregation, through the intercession of the Virgin, John the Baptist, the apostles, the Saint whose name the child has received, and of all the Saints.

The observer of an Eastern Orthodox Baptism is bound to be impressed by the vivid teaching of the symbolism and the gestures which express it. The facing towards the west (the demonic direction) and towards the east (the direction of the Incarnation and so of salvation), the spitting on the devil, the frequent signations with the cross, the cleansing of the water which is also an image of death and entry into the death and Resurrection of Christ, the child's nakedness before Baptism and its later clothing in a clean robe, the anointing of the whole body and its major parts with the healing oil, and the ablution and tonsure stressing cleansing and a simple first offering by the child itself: these all make this sacral rite of passage unforgettable to godparents and to the congregation, and to the brothers and sisters of the child baptized. At a time of extreme variability in many forms of Christian worship, Eastern Orthodox worship is consistently traditional and familiar and reassuring, and it is strongly focussed on the basic theme that Jesus Christ died and rose for our salvation and is our companion to the very end of time. It expresses also the mystery appropriate in the worship of a God who transcends us, but, for all our unworthiness, has given us the supreme gift of the Incarnate Christ, and of the sanctifying Holy Spirit. As the Jesuit Robert Taft expresses it: the liturgy and the architecture, especially in a Byzantine setting, has

> an atmosphere of sacredness and mystery that surrounds its every movement and communicates a sense of reverential awe. . . . Worshipping in this atmosphere of profuse symbolism through which the supernatural splendour of the inaccessible divine majesty is approached, Eastern Christians witness the exaltation and sanctification of creation, the majestic appearance of God who divinizes us through the transfiguring light of his heavenly grace.

He adds that this liturgical atmosphere "stirs us in body and soul in order to transform us before a vision of spiritual beauty and joy."[44] These qualities are, of course, exhibited in the Eucharist as well as in the baptismal rite.

The Orthodox Eucharist

There are three Orthodox liturgies of great significance. These are: *The Liturgy of St. Basil* and its abbreviated form; *The Liturgy of St. John Chrysostom* now in general use among Orthodox Churches; and *The Liturgy of the Pre-Sanctified* used only on Wednesdays and Fridays in Lent. Our analysis will be of the Russian Orthodox liturgy.[45]

It is important at the outset to envision the setting. An Orthodox church is usually built in the shape of an equal-armed Greek cross. It has three main divisions corresponding to the different stages of commitment of the worshippers. The back or western end of the nave is kept for beginners, learners, and penitents. The central part of the nave is kept for the faithful, that is, mature and committed lay members. Both groups are separated from the priesthood by a magnificent screen, the *iconostasis* on which the icons or two-dimensional images of Christ, the Virgin, and the saints are represented. Behind this great screen is the Sanctuary, where the priests say their prayers in secret and prepare the elements of the Eucharist. The *iconostasis* or screen has three doors. The central door, named the Royal Door, has images of Christ and the Virgin on either side, and on the door itself is an icon of the angel of God announcing to the Virgin Mary that she shall conceive the Savior of the world. The opening and closing of this door has great significance in the liturgy as will be seen. There are also two other doors. One is the Deacon's Door, which is for the Deacon who conducts the people's part of the liturgy and who is, as it were,

44. Taft, *Beyond East and West*, p. 44. Fr. Taft, while admiring the qualities of the Orthodox Liturgy, warns against exaggerated enthusiasm, recalling that very few members go to Communion more than a few times each year, and recalls that the Greek Orthodox in the neighborhood of Athens who attend worship regularly number only 9% of the population.

45. *The Orthodox Liturgy, being the Divine Liturgy of S. John Chrysostom and S. Basil the Great according to the Use of the Church of Russia* (London: S.P.C.K. for the Fellowship of SS. Alban and Sergius, 1947), is the text on which our analysis of the Eucharist is based.

both link and interpreter between the people and the priests behind the screen. The third door is the Server's Door, used in the two processions in the course of the liturgy of the Eucharist, known as The Great and The Little Processions.

We must now try to imagine the progress of the liturgy itself, or, to speak accurately, of the two services proceeding simultaneously. The action of the priest or priests goes on behind the screen in the hidden sanctuary, and apart from a few loud exclamations, that service is unheard as well as unseen. For the priests the service begins with the *Prothesis* — that is, the elaborate preparation of the elements of bread and wine. Five small loaves are used by the priest to typify the five loaves in Christ's miracle of feeding the five thousand. Meanwhile the Reader proceeds outside the Sanctuary with the Prayers of the People.

Then follows The Service of the Catechumens or Learners which is led by the deacon. It is very like the liturgy of the Word in Anglican or Free Church worship, with prayers, psalms, and Scripture lessons. When this is completed, the Deacon enters the choir to read the prayers which take the form of litanies, requiring the responses of the people. When he has entered the nave, all three doors of the screen are opened to symbolize the opening of the heavens at the Baptism. There is great sensitivity in the wording of Orthodox prayers:

> In peace let us make our supplications to the Lord:
> For the peace that is from above and the salvation of our souls;
> For the peace of the whole world, the welfare
>   of God's Holy Church, for the unity of all;
> For this holy house, for those that in devotion, faith,
>   and the fear of God do enter therein;
> For this city, for this holy Church, for every city and land,
>   and for those who dwell in faith therein;
> For healthful seasons, for abundance of the earth's fruits,
>   and for peaceful days;
> For those who travel by sea or land, for the sick and suffering,
>   for those that are in bonds and their safety.
> That we may be preserved from all tribulation, wrath,
>   and necessity, assist, preserve, pity and keep us, O God,
>   by thy grace; . . .
> With all saints let us commend ourselves and each other
>   and our lives unto Christ our God.[46]

46. *Ibid.*, pp. 32-34.

When these prayers are ended, the first climax of the service is reached. This is the Little Entrance. The deacon, bearing the Gospel book, and the priest come from the Sanctuary into the nave, preceded by a reader carrying a lighted taper. This symbolizes Christ's entry with the divine Gospel from the sanctuary of heaven into the world's darkness. It dramatizes the Light of the World. Then follow the readings of the Epistle and Gospel and, in turn, the Litany of the Catechumens. The latter are then dismissed.

The third part of the service — known as the Liturgy of the Faithful — now begins. After the prayers of the faithful are concluded, the Hymn of the Cherubim is sung, during which the Great Entrance takes place. In this procession all the clergy and assistants take part. The acolytes bear lights, while the thurifers swing the incense, and the clergy carry replicas of the Passion of Christ: the Cross, the Spear, the Scourge, and the Thorns. The procession enters by the Server's Door and returns to the Sanctuary by the Royal Door enveloped by clouds of incense. The Royal Door is then closed until the priest and deacon have made their communion. Thereafter, as the priest and deacon come through the Royal Door bearing the gifts of bread and wine to the faithful, the other two doors are flung open wide.

Following the Great Entrance, there is a noble prayer of consecration. It begins with the *Sursum corda*, continues with the *Sanctus* and with thanksgiving for God's revelation to and redemption of humanity, narrates the Words of Institution, and concludes with an *epiklesis*, or prayer that the Holy Spirit may consecrate the bread and wine that they may convey the most sacred benefits of Christ's sacrifice to the assembled faithful. Perhaps the most moving words in the prayers are those said by the priest for himself and the communicants: "Of thy mysterious supper, Son of God, today admit me a partaker: for I will not tell the secret to thine enemies, nor give thee a kiss like Judas, but like the thief I will acknowledge Thee: Remember me, Lord, in Your Kingdom."[47]

The leading characteristic of Orthodox worship is that it is a vivid expression of the mystery of the Christian revelation, linking heaven and earth. The sanctuary symbolizes heaven — the domain of the Holy Trinity and the hosts of angels and the saints — and the nave, earth. The entrances in the liturgy are celestial descents, expressing the condescension of the Incarnation and the Lord's great humility

47. *Ibid.,* p. 91.

in laying aside his heavenly privileges to dwell in the darkness of the earth to which he brings the Gospel of light, being himself "The Light of the World."

Most Western Communion services, whether Roman, Anglican, or Free Church, until very recently lacked a profound eschatological emphasis or sense of joy. If the Western Churches concentrated on the Cross — the supreme means of grace, the Orthodox Churches focussed on the end of grace — eternal life. The timeless emphasis of the icons means that time stands still; the worshippers long for mystic union with God, the world forgotten. If Roman Catholic worship is essentially concerned with the Effectual Sacrifice, and older Protestant worship was that of the Divine Oracle, then Orthodox worship is basically a theological Mystery Drama.

One must also admire the highly inventive and poetic wording of many of the Orthodox prayers which enable the imaginations of the worshippers to take wing. Most Western prayers, by contrast, are precise and pragmatic, with the typical directness and concision of collects. Moreover, allowance is made in Orthodox worship for silence.

Finally, some Orthodox Christians have begun to question wondering whether the conservatism of the liturgy may not appear to support the violation of human rights inside and outside the Christian community. There is agreement among Orthodox leaders that however few those attending worship may be, a sermon should always be included in the worship. Even this admirable liturgy, it appears, may be improved by a concern for human justice in the here and now.[48]

48. See Ion Bria, ed., *Martyria/Mission: The Witness of the Orthodox Churches* (Geneva: World Council of Churches, 1980) for consideration of "The liturgy after the liturgy."

CHAPTER VI

BAPTISM AND EUCHARIST
IN THE WORSHIP OF THE
ENGLISH FREE CHURCHES

THIS CHAPTER will concentrate on the liturgical revision since 1965 undertaken by the Baptist Union of Churches, the United Reformed Church, and the Methodist Church in the re-ordering of the Gospel sacraments of Baptism and the Lord's Supper or Holy Communion.

The Baptist Union of Churches

Since this is a union of local churches, allowing a great deal of freedom to ministers and to local congregations for experimentation in worship, one encounters the greatest difficulty in assessing its worship. Two indications of the variety were provided by Baptist ministers themselves. The first comes from the introduction to *Praise God: A Collection of Resource Material for Christian Worship* published by the Baptist Union in London in 1980, and compiled by Alec Gilmore, Edward Smalley, and Michael Walker. It refers to "diversity within our fellowship" and the difficulty of providing at the same time "for the minister who wanted to retain much of what he would regard as the beauty and dignity of older forms as well as for the minister who wanted to address God and his people in today's language and thought forms." Here they deal with a common problem in worship; the difficulty, they rightly say, is "to achieve revision without abandoning much that was good from the past or climbing on a bandwagon that would be gone in five years' time."[1]

---

1. *Praise God,* p. xiii. The compilers add (p. xiv): "Our attempts to find contemporary prayers written by Baptists was disappointing. After approaching several ministers to say we would be interested to consider some of their prayers for inclusion, we concluded that few Baptist ministers ever actually wrote prayers, some

The second witness to the difficulties of catering to both tradition-alists and innovationists was provided in a most helpful interview I had with the Revd. David Coffey, General Secretary of the Baptist Union at Baptist House, Didcot on June 22nd, 1993. He made it clear that there were not merely two but three types of Baptist churches at the local level. There were the traditionalists, who had been influenced by the Liturgical Movement in the direction of using set prayers, especially for the celebration of the sacraments, and of using notes for their regular prayers. There were also Baptist ministers and congregations that retained the tradition of extempore prayers and appreciated variety in their services. And, thirdly, there was an incursion of charismatics into many Baptist congregations, which has led to a greater informality and spontaneity in worship, along with popular songs and choruses and more dramatic gestures for expressing enthusiasm in worship. When I asked the General Secretary what impact the charismatics had on the worship of the Baptist Church, he replied that "aspects of their hym-nody reflect a more relevant culture today" and pointed out that whereas the older forms of worship used a pipe organ (which he dubbed "a single person orchestra"), the charismatics use full orchestra contain-ing trumpet, trombone, piano, drums, saxophone and xylophone to produce music which is both relevant and cheerful. While few Baptist churches have accepted such charismatic manifestations as speaking in tongues and prophesying, churches that have welcomed the milder forms of charismatic expression might number 25%. An equal percent-age have embraced a more formal or "high church" model. Such churches would have a robed minister, a robed choir, a side pulpit, three Scripture lessons read from a side lectern, responsive readings, and processions to the Communion Table.

The main body of Baptists, however, were neither charismatic nor high church, but used extemporary prayers, as had been charac-teristic of them for over three hundred years. The only significant change had been in the general increasing attention to celebration of the Christian Year — at Christmas, Lent, Holy Week, Easter and Pentecost. David Coffey's greatest anxiety was his sense of the weakening of contemporary preaching, where instead of Biblical exegesis there was often only what he termed "Biblical psychology sermons" on how to get in touch with your feelings, lacking theo-

---

clearly relying fairly solidly on books of contemporary prayers already in existence, and some presumably using extempore prayer only."

logically based conviction solidly founded on the exposition of the Scriptures.

The Revd. Robert Ellis,[2] belonging to the liturgical group of Baptist ministers, whom I also interviewed, pointed out how helpful the praise and prayers of the French Reformed Movement at Taizé and those of the Iona Community of the Church of Scotland had been for the traditional liturgical churches among the Baptists. He was disappointed that traditional Anglican chants had been replaced by metrical psalmody in his group, but was pleased that among Baptists generally the presentation or Blessing of Infants continues to be a significant feature of worship. He gave a very frank answer to my question: "Do you read prayers or extemporize?" He replied that he used notes for intercessions, "but I use no notes for the historic type of eucharistic prayer in the Communion Service using the structure of the *anamnesis, epiklesis,* and climactic *Sanctus.*" He also observed that the status of the Communion had grown across all theological and ecclesiological levels; that it is now less common for the central prayer of thanksgiving to be offered by deacons; that while individual cups are still used, chalices are employed in house Communions; and that the Northern Baptist College calls its weekly Communion "The Eucharist."

The official Baptist Service Book is *Patterns and Prayers for Christian Worship,* published by the Baptist Union in 1991, with a corrected edition a year later, printed also by the Oxford University Press. It bears the symbol of the Cross above waves, a sign of Baptism, with a fish beneath, the sign of IXΘUS, meaning "Jesus Christ, God's Son, Saviour." The content of this service book will be discussed after we survey its predecessors.

Orders and Prayers for Worship: A Manual for Ministers was compiled in 1960 by E. A. Payne and Stephen Winward, both of them ecumenical enthusiasts who were sympathetic to the Liturgical Movement. Its influential successor was the expression of a desire for less traditional worship in both language and thought forms. This was *Praise God: A Collection of Resource Material for Christian Worship.* Its Preface by David Russell, then the General Secretary of the denom-

---

2. The Revd. David Coffey had also brought in for the interview the Revd. Robert Ellis so that I would be aware of the right wing or high church group among English Baptist ministers, who graciously drove me from Didcot to Oxford while he answered my questions.

ination, states that it "takes into account the fact of different translations of the Bible available to worshippers and the change that has taken place in the language of prayer, particularly in the mode of addressing God, and has observed carefully the liturgical practice of a wide range of Christian expression."[3] The breadth of the borrowing is indicated in the Acknowledgements, which cite many translations of the Bible, prayers from the Gelasian and Leonine Sacramentaries, Anglican, Roman Catholic, and Church of Scotland sources, the Joint Liturgical Group, and even Dag Hammarskjold's *Markings*, translated by W. H. Auden and Leif Sjoberg.

The structure of *Praise God* is three-fold. First there are forty-six pages devoted to Scripture and Prayers for the Christian Year. The second section provides Sentences and Prayers for Adoration and Invocation, Confession, Thanksgiving, Petition, Intercession, Prayers for the Opening and Closing of Worship, Benedictions, Ascriptions of Glory, and for Special Days, being Occasions of Thanksgiving, Remembrance, Dedication, and Mission. This section comprises seventy-three pages. The final section is concerned with Sacraments and Ordinances, including Sunday Worship, Word and Sacrament, Infant Dedication and Thanksgiving, Christian Initiation, Christian Marriage, and Christian Burial. This comprises forty-three pages.

Its sources are widely ecumenical and its choices seem admirable. At the same time its compilers have not lacked in inventiveness, as four examples of their own prayers will demonstrate. For Pentecost they have prepared the following prayer:

> Holy Spirit, we ask that our characters may bear evidence of your presence within us. May the patient toil of the years produce the harvest of your love. May people see in our lives the signs that you are with us — love, joy, peace, patience, kindness, goodness, fidelity, gentleness and self-control. In Christ's name. Amen.[4]

One petition deserves citation:

> Teach us to live
> As Jesus lived
> Who took the hopes of men

---

3. *Praise God*, p. v.
4. *Ibid.*, p. 39.

And made them real
by stepping out of safe convention
Into love.[5]

Two examples of intercession now follow:

> Loving Father, we pray for those who work by night, to guard and
> serve us while we are sleeping: the miners, industrial workers, light-
> housemen, nurses, doctors, and all the others who cannot rest at night.
> Watch over them, we pray, and keep them safe from danger and
> loneliness, for the sake of our guardian and saviour, Jesus.[6]

Another intercession "For the Under-privileged" proceeds thus:

> Hasten the time, O Lord, when no man shall live in contentment
> while he knows that others have need. Inspire in us and in people of
> all nations the desire for social justice that the hungry may be fed,
> the homeless welcomed, the sick healed, and a just order established
> in the world, according to your gracious will made known in Jesus
> Christ, our Lord. Amen.[7]

All the prayers borrowed, adapted, or original are marked by great
naturalness, simplicity, and empathy, and if used regularly would have
improved the range of extemporary prayer in Baptist congregations.

As previously noted, the most recent Baptist directory for worship
appeared in 1991, under the title *Patterns and Prayers for Christian
Worship*. The Committee responsible comprised the Revds. Bernard
Green (Chairman, also then General Secretary of the denomination),
Christopher Ellis, Rachel Harrison, Stuart Jenkins, Michael Nicholls,
and Tony Turner. The Preface indicates that while "Baptist have their
roots deep within the Free Church tradition" and "Therefore the
freedom of the Holy Spirit is a significant factor in their worship,
and they do not have a fixed liturgy or approved prayer-book" yet
the conclusion cannot be drawn "that worship has no shape or basic
content, or that preparation and forms are despised." It is observed
that "There is now a wide variety of practice from liturgical formality

5. *Ibid.*, p. 82.
6. *Ibid.*, pp. 87-88.
7. *Ibid.*, p. 93.

to charismatic exuberance, from reformed traditionalism to ecumenical experiment."[8] While the previous volume *Praise God* had moved away from liturgical forms, a more moderate viewpoint is expressed in this volume: "Experience shows that it is wrong to assume that the Spirit is necessarily more manifest in a free form of worship than in a structured form."[9] The point is also made that "within the latter years of the twentieth century the Lord's Supper has generally become an integral part of the Service. Responsive participation by the congregation has become a prominent feature. The liturgical movement has had widespread influence on Baptist churches through ecumenical contact."[10] Further, it is clearly acknowledged that Baptist worship has a structure of Word and Sacrament, and that it combines "a catholic emphasis on tradition and fellowship, and a charismatic stress on gifting and participation."[11]

The greatest change in Baptist worship, apart from the new emphasis on the Christian Year, has been a more profound appreciation of the Gospel sacraments. This is strongly emphasized in a paragraph that warrants citation:

> Since the nineteen-sixties there has been a perceptible shift in Baptist concepts of Baptism and the Lord's Supper. Our denomination has been delivered from seeing these ordinances as symbolical actions, personal confessions of faith, or times of individual praise. Baptism has become far more an act of obedience in which God meets with men and women as they demonstrate the reality of their repentance and identify with Christ in membership of his body, participate in his Supper, and the life of his Spirit. The Lord's Supper has become a much more central act of worship in which there is a looking back to the Cross, forward to the Coming, upward to the Risen Christ, inward for personal salvation, and outward for the personal dimension of fellowship."[12]

It is curious that the outward dimension is not for Mission!

The prayers in this volume have a noteworthy simplicity combined with vividness, as the following example indicates:

8. *Patterns and Prayers,* pp. v and vi.
9. *Ibid.,* p. 1.
10. *Ibid.,* p. 3.
11. *Ibid.,* p. 4.
12. *Ibid.,* p. 5.

Creator God, we worship you. In the beginning you said,
"Let there be light" and the light shone, piercing the darkness.
You have made the vast universe and amidst its movements
    and glories your Spirit is at work.
Scattering the stars and moulding the hills,
    you have made a world full of beauty.
You have made humankind in your own image,
    stewards of the earth, partners in creation.
We are here because of you: that we exist is your doing.
You are our God, our parent, giving us life,
    lavishing gifts upon your children.
The distances of space praise you. The depths of our being
    acknowledge your creating power.
Creator God, we praise you.

In this prayer we note both the inclusive word "humankind" instead of "mankind" and the strong ecological stress of our being partners in creation rather than its masters.

There is also an excellent Pentecostal Prayer of Confession, which begins with "Spirit of God, you are . . . the wind of change . . . opening us up to new dreams and new hopes, new life in Jesus Christ," and which continues:

Forgive us our closed minds
which barricade themselves against new ideas,
preferring the past to what you might want to do
through us tomorrow.
    Forgive our closed eyes
which fail to see the needs of your world,
blind to opportunities of service and love.
    Forgive us our closed hands
which clutch our gifts and our wealth
for our own use alone.
    Forgive us our closed hearts
which limit our affections to ourselves and our own.
    Spirit of newlife
forgive us and break down the prison walls
of our selfishness. . . .[13]

13. *Ibid.*, pp. 55-56.

Here the repetitive structure is a strength equal to the demand for individual change.

It is interesting that patterns are offered for the celebration of the Lord's Supper. There is also a stress on its varied meanings: "It may be seen as the necessary preparation for sharing, a sign of the violent cost of our salvation, or the completeness of Christ's self-offering and the complete self-offering to which we are called." It is suggested that the symbolism of the action will be increased if one loaf is used, with a reminder of 1 Corinthians 10:17. It is also recommended that the lifting of the cup in full view of the congregation corresponds to the breaking of the bread, and it is of particular importance in those fellowships which have returned to the use of a chalice or common cup.[14]

A significant stress on the meaning of the Lord's Supper is provided in the alternative Invitation to the Table:

> Brothers and Sisters in Christ, it is right we call to mind the meaning of this Supper. It is a remembrance of the sacrifice of Christ for the sins of the world; an encounter with the risen Lord; a feeding on him in faith; a communion with one another in his body, the Church; and a looking forward to the day when he will come again. Therefore, we need to come in faith, conscious of our weakness, renouncing our sin, humbly putting our trust in Christ, and seeking his grace.[15]

The second pattern for the Lord's Supper includes responses, the Peace, the traditional *Sursum corda,* the *Sanctus,* and the words of Acclamation.[16]

For the Baptism of Believers and Reception into Membership two patterns are provided. One provides an introduction, followed by questions to the candidate(s), a prayer, and the Baptism itself. This is followed by a hymn, prayers of response and intercession, offering, Invitation to the Lord's Supper, a hymn, prayer of approach and/or sharing of the Peace, reception into membership, with questions to the newly baptized and church members, the offering of the right hand of fellowship, the laying on of hands, the Communion, a hymn, and the Benediction. These are bare bones and need for the Baptism, at least, the addition of flesh.

14. *Ibid.,* pp. 67-68.
15. *Ibid.,* p. 76.
16. *Ibid.,* pp. 80-91.

The Baptism is itself preceded by the Declaration of Faith.

LEADER: Do you believe in one God, Father, Son, and Holy Spirit?
CANDIDATE: I do.
LEADER: In obedience to the call of our risen Lord Jesus Christ, do you repent of your sins, and come to be baptized?
CANDIDATE: I do.
LEADER: With the help of the Holy Spirit, do you offer your life in service to God wherever he may call you to go?
CANDIDATE: I do.
LEADER: Then come and be baptized.

Each candidate then enters the baptistery, to be baptized with the following words:

Having heard of your repentance and your faith, I now baptize you, — my brother/sister — in the name of God the Father, God the Son, and God the Holy Spirit.[17]

The Baptism is followed by candidates sometimes crying, "Jesus is Lord!" and the congregation responding with "Hallelujah!"

Next follows The Laying on of Hands.[18] The Minister declares: "We are now to lay hands on (Names), who have been baptized, as a sign of blessing and an act of commissioning, and to ask that they may be fully equipped for their vocation as servants of Jesus Christ in the Church and in the world.

Each candidate kneels and the leader(s) lay(s) hands on each, offering prayer such as:

Lord, bless these your servants and strengthen them by your Holy Spirit as we commission them for service in the Church and the world in the name of the Lord Jesus Christ.

Then the candidate(s) stand(s) as the leader says:

You are no longer aliens in a foreign land, but fellow-citizens with God's people, members of God's household. You are built on the

17. *Ibid.*, pp. 100-101.
18. See *ibid.*, pp. 102-4.

foundation of the apostles and prophets, with Christ Jesus himself as the cornerstone. Ephesians 2:19-20.

The service of Reception into Membership[19] commences with an introductory statement indicating that the congregation is entering into a covenant with the new member. A profession of faith is required, which includes a statement of belief in the Holy Trinity, a vocation to serve Christ in the local Baptist church, a commitment to serve Christ according to Baptist principles, and an acceptance of responsibility as a church member.

Then, after inviting church members to stand, the minister asks them: "Do you welcome (Name) into the family of God in this local church?" and the members reply: "We do." They are also required to encourage the new members.

The leader then offers the hand of fellowship to the new member(s), and says, for example: "In the name of the Lord Jesus Christ, and on behalf of this fellowship, I welcome you into the membership." Then the new members may be asked to sign the church roll. The Reception into Membership concludes with a Prayer of striking relevance:

> Lord our God, you have joined us together in Christ and from each to the other you will speak your Word of comfort and challenge. Make us ready to listen and swift to act, both church and new member(s). May they not fail you, nor we fail them.[20]

The service then continues with the Lord's Supper.

In considering the flexibility of the alternates, the diversity of styles, the Biblical authority of the ordinances, and the high level of commitment expected of future members, one sees the strengths of Baptist worship.

The United Reformed Church

Like the Baptists, the Congregationalists, who form the largest segment of the United Reformed Church, and the Presbyterians that joined them, suffered as Dissenters from the Church of England from

---

19. *Ibid.,* pp. 104-7.
20. *Ibid.,* p. 106. This is the first of two alternative prayers.

the seventeenth century onwards. Both Congregationalists and Presbyterians collaborated in the Westminster Assembly of Cromwellian days, and also preferred a directory of worship, providing the structure and topics of prayers, without determining the words. The Reformed Association of the Churches of Christ which joined them combined, with a tradition of free prayer, the practice of Believers' Baptism and a celebration of the Lord's Supper every Lord's Day. The new United Reformed Church is a remarkable ecumenical amalgam.

In recent years the United Reformed Church has produced two directories of worship. The first, entitled *A Book of Services*, published by the Saint Andrew Press of Edinburgh in 1980, was produced by a Committee chaired by the Revd. John Huxtable. The brief preface states, with respect to the former Congregationalists and former Presbyterians in the union at that point: "Both the traditions which came together to form the United Reformed Church cherished freedom in worship. The publication of this book does not impugn that freedom. The orders found here are not prescribed. It is not expected that they will be used in our churches to the exclusion of others. Yet we believe most of these services reflect the ethos of our Church and of its inherited traditions."[21]

The structure of worship is clearly that of The Word and the Prayers, for the first part, and of The Thanksgiving and the Communion for the second part. The Word and the Prayers includes the following items in the following order:

1. Scripture Sentences
2. Prayer of Approach
3. Hymn or Psalm
4. Confession of Sin
5. Assurance of Pardon
6. *Gloria* or *Kyries*
7. Prayer for Grace
8. Theme Introduction
9. Old Testament and/or New Testament Reading(s)
10. Psalm, Canticle, Hymn, or Anthem
11. New Testament Reading (or Epistle and Gospel)
12. Sermon
13. Creed

21. *A Book of Services*, p. 7.

14. Notices
15. Special Acts (e.g. Baptism, Confirmation, Ordination, etc.)
16. Prayers for the Church of the World

The second section, The Thanksgiving and the Communion, includes the following items in the following order:

17. The Invitation and the Gracious Words
18. The Peace
19. Offertory
20. Hymn
21. The Narrative of the Institution
22. The Taking of the Bread and Wine
23. The Thanksgiving
24. The Lord's Prayer
25. The Breaking of the Bread
26. The Sharing of the Bread and Wine
27. Acclamation
28. Prayer
29. Hymn or Doxology
30. Dismissal and Blessing[22]

In reference to the Entry there is an interesting note to the effect that in several churches the Bible is carried into the church at the start of worship "to remind the people that we can only meet God because he has first come to us. The record of his coming is the Bible. It is appropriate for someone who is going to read from it to carry it in" and it is suggested that "the preacher, a servant of the Word, should follow."[23] Great stress is laid on the importance of the Assurance of Pardon, and it is maintained that the best balance of readings is one from the Old Testament and a Gospel and Epistle from the New. The "Theme Introduction" will link the lessons and the sermon. This is a relatively new development in the Free Churches and, with the use of a lectionary, almost guarantees that sermons become less varied topically and more exegetical in character. It is rightly said that "the message in the readings is made contemporary in the sermon" but other forms of

22. *Ibid.*, pp. 7 and 8.
23. *Ibid.*, p. 10.

proclamation are also allowed, such as a dialogue, a drama, or a film.[24]

Directions for the Peace make it clear that the minister may add to his saying of the words of the Peace a handclasp to one of the persons near him, and this action can then be passed through the entire congregation.[25]

A full communion service requires:

The recital of the mighty acts of God in creation and redemption, often with special thanksgivings according to the season of the year.

The commemoration with bread and wine of the sacrificial death and resurrection of Christ "until he come"; invocation of the Holy Spirit, praying that what we do in obedience to Christ may be united to his perfect sacrifice and that we may be made one in him and receive the benefits of his passion and victory.[26]

It is emphasized that the bread and wine should be passed through the congregation, so that each person serves his neighbor and the corporate character of the Communion is thus emphasized, and the sharing is most effectively expressed when a single loaf and a common cup are used.

It is also stressed that the service ends symbolically "if the Bible, the gifts of money and the communion vessels are carried out of the church, the minister and people following. In this way we proclaim that our service continues in God's world."[27]

The Assurance of Pardon is given significance in the first of its alternative expressions:

In repentance and faith
receive the promise of grace
and the assurance of pardon:

Here are words you may trust,
words that merit full acceptance:

24. *Ibid.*, p. 12.
25. *Ibid.*, p. 13.
26. *Ibid.*, p. 14.
27. *Ibid.*, p. 15.

"Christ Jesus came into the world to save sinners."
Your sins are forgiven for his sake.

Thanks be to God.[28]

The Prayers for the Church and the World are notable for their comprehensiveness and their simplicity. One example is a prayer "for those in trade and industry, members of the professions, and all who serve the community." Its petition is as follows:

Grant that men and women in their various callings may have
grace to do their work well;
and may the resources of the earth be wisely used,
truth honored and preserved,
and the quality of our life enriched.[29]

Another prayer prays for "the sick and the suffering, victims of injustice, the lonely and the bereaved."[30] These brief samples of prayer manifest both an ecological awareness and a reflection of liberation theology.

For the Communion part of the service there are three Thanksgiving Prayers provided. The first offers the traditional *Sursum corda*, with seasonal prefaces, an *anamnesis* or recollection of God's creation and Christ's self-giving, followed by the *Sanctus*, the *Benedictus qui venit* and a clear *epiklesis*, namely,

We pray that
through your Holy Spirit
this bread may be for us
    the body of Christ
and this wine
    the blood of Christ.[31]

The second Thanksgiving also includes the traditional elements, with *anamnesis* and *epiklesis*, and includes the Acclamation:

28. *Ibid.*, p. 20.
29. *Ibid.*, p. 24.
30. *Ibid.*, p. 24.
31. *Ibid.*, p. 31.

Christ is Victor.
Christ is King.
Christ is Lord of all.[32]

The Third Thanksgiving includes the traditional responses with a touching *anamnesis:*

We thank you, holy father,
Lord our God
for Jesus Christ
your beloved son,
whom you called and sent
to serve us and give us light,
to bring your kingdom to the poor,
to bring redemption to captives
and to be for ever
and for us all
the likeness and embodiment
of your constant love and goodness.
We thank you
for this unforgettable man
who has fulfilled everything that is human —
our life, our death.[33]

The petition for the Holy Spirit does not take the usual form of an *epiklesis:*

We beseech you
send among us your Holy Spirit
and give a new face
to this earth that is dear to us.
Let there be peace
wherever people live,
the peace that we cannot make ourselves
and that is more powerful than all violence,
your peace like a bond,
a new covenant between us all,

32. *Ibid.,* p. 33.
33. *Ibid.,* p. 35.

the power of Jesus Christ
here among us.[34]

The Dismissal and Blessings are provided with seasonal alternatives; the one for Passiontide, for example, says:

Go in peace to serve the Lord
remembering that you are not your own,
but were bought at a price;
and the blessing. . . .[35]

A Book of Services also provides orders for the Baptism of Infants and for the Baptism of Believers and Confirmation. These will be summarized briefly.

The order for the Baptism of Infants begins with an introduction indicating the New Testament authority for Baptism, and making use of Mark 10:14 as evidence for Jesus welcoming children. Then parents are required to promise that they affirm the Trinity, that they will bring their child up in the Gospel and the fellowship of the Church, in addition to providing a Christian home. Godparents, if any, make the same promises.

Two alternate prayers follow, asking that the Holy Spirit may use the water for Baptism and our own obedience to Christ. The Baptism requires the minister to pour or sprinkle water on the child's head, saying:

N . . . I baptize you in the Name of the Father and of the Son and of the Holy Spirit.

The minister then presents the newly-baptized child to the people and calls on them to witness that this child has been received into the family and household of God, and calls the people to pray and care for the child that he/she may grow in Christian faith and life and continue in Christ's service all his/her days. A concluding prayer sums up all that has taken place in gratitude and a reminder of obligations towards the child.[36]

34. *Ibid.*, p. 37.
35. *Ibid.*, p. 41.
36. *Ibid.*, pp. 44-49.

The introduction to the order for the Baptism of Believers reminds the believers that Christ was baptized by John at the start of his ministry, and after his resurrection commanded his disciples to preach the Gospel to all nations and to baptize, adding that this sacrament is "a sign and seal of the covenant of grace which God has made with us in Christ."

The candidates for Baptism are then required to make not only solemn but highly realistic promises to God, including the following:

> Do you repent of your sin, renounce evil and turn to Christ?
>
> and Do you confess your faith in one God, Father, Son and Holy Spirit?
>
> and Do you promise, in dependence on God's grace,
> to be faithful in private and public worship;
> to live in the fellowship of the Church and to share in its work;
> and to give and serve,
> as God enables you, for the
> advancement of his kingdom in the world?
>
> and Do you promise, by that same grace, to follow Christ and to seek to do and to bear his will all the days of your life?
>
> and And do you trust to his mercy alone to bring you into the fullness of the life of the world to come?

The expected answer to all these promises is "I do."

After a prayer, following the words of Infant Baptism, the adult believer is baptized while the minister pours or sprinkles water on his/her head with the Triune formula. A final prayer begs that the candidates may be enabled to keep the promises they have made.[37]

In the rite of Confirmation the minister lays his hand on the head of each candidate in turn or raises his hand in blessing over each, and says:

A . . . The God of all grace,
who has called you to Christian faith and service,
confirm and strengthen you with the Holy Spirit
and keep you faithful to Christ all your days, Amen.

37. *Ibid.*, pp. 50-54.

Then the minister reminds the congregation that they are witnesses that those confirmed have been received into the family and household of God and to membership of this congregation, and then he says to the new members: "In the Name of the Lord Jesus Christ, welcome." Then the minister and one or more of the elders give the right hand of fellowship to the new members, saying, "May your joining us be a blessing to you and to all of us, and may our one Lord keep us one with all his people, for ever." A final prayer asks for God to keep those confirmed faithful to Christ and for his blessing to rest on the work and witness of this church.

After this Herculean effort to combine the traditions of the Congregational Church and of the Presbyterian Church in England, incorporating the insights of the Liturgical Movement, it must have seemed excessive labor to have to produce a new directory of worship in 1985, only five years later. This revision was deemed necessary for two reasons. The first was the need for inclusive language, and the second was a change in the constitution of the United Reformed Church "to whose numbers were added in 1981 members of the Reformed Association of Churches of Christ in Great Britain and Ireland." Additionally, it was stated in the Preface, "To such consideration can be added the influence of cross-fertilization between the separated Christian traditions as they increasingly join in worship, action and study."[38]

The title of the new directory was *The Service Book: The United Reformed Church in the United Kingdom*. It was published by the Oxford University Press in 1989. It contains several innovations, among them an order for the renewal of baptismal promises which should deepen the seriousness with which the sacrament of Baptism is regarded, and give an opportunity for those who need a public reaffirmation of their belonging to the Body of Christ, without a re-Baptism. The second order of worship is provided for those who were former members of the Churches of Christ. A new service of healing is also provided. Perhaps the most striking contribution is the parallel placement of the promises of parents for Infant Baptism along with the promises of believers in Adult Baptism.

The Committee responsible for this work was chaired by Professor Colin Gunton, a theologian teaching at King's College in the University of London, together with J. C. Brock, David M. Thompson,

38. *The Service Book* (1989), p. 6.

K. C. Fabricius, C. A. McIlhagga, Justine S. Wyatt, Colin P. Thompson, M. H. Cressey, J. H. Taylor, and Susan Durber, who is also a member of the Joint Liturgical Group.[39]

The structure provides the same thirty items and the same division between the Ministry of the Word and The Sacrament of the Lord's Supper that was first given in *A Book of Services* of 1980. Commentary here is restricted to the innovations in the newer book. In the first place there is an admirably brief but comprehensive Offertory Prayer:

> Almighty and most merciful God, out of the fullness of your gifts we bring before you this bread and wine, our money, and our lives. Blessed be your holy Name forever, through Jesus Christ our Lord. Amen.[40]

Alternate prayers come from the new Roman Catholic Rite, with its valuable recognition of divine-human partnership:

> Blessed are you, God of all creation,
> Through your goodness we have this bread to offer
> which earth has given and human hands have made.
> It will become for us the bread of life.

But to this a marvelous stanza has been added:

> Blessed are you, God of all creation.
> Through your goodness we have ourselves to offer,
> fruit of the womb and formed by your love.
> We will become your people in the world.[41]

An ingenious set of Scriptures for the Institution Narrative of the Lord's Supper provides an opportunity for a number of readers to be used, and thus express the corporate character of the Eucharist.

---

39. I had the advantage of an illuminating interview concerning the preparation of this book with Dr. David Thompson, Fellow of Fitzwilliam College, Cambridge, and University Lecturer in History, who served on the Committee responsible for *The Service Book* and is now convenor of the Doctrine and Worship Committee of the United Reformed Church. The interview was held on June 11, 1993, in his college study.

40. *The Service Book,* p. 9.

41. *Ibid.,* p. 9.

There are three Thanksgiving Prayers. The first is the work of Dr. David Thompson, formerly of the Reformed Association of Churches of Christ. It has a concentrated remembrance of the mighty acts of God expressed with vivid verbs, and it has a notable conclusion:

> Bring us together from east and west
> and north and south
> to sit with Abraham, Isaac, and Jacob,
> (and . . . whom we remember this day)
> so that at the wedding feast of the Lamb
> we may rejoice with all the redeemed.
> This we ask through Jesus Christ,
> your Son, our Lord,
> who with you, Father, and the Holy Spirit,
> reigns now and forever.
> Amen.[42]

The second Thanksgiving is a reproduction of the first in the earlier volume, *A Book of Services* (1980). The third Thanksgiving contains an important ecological emphasis:

> Your universe you put into our care;
> your creation you entrust into our hands,
> with all its wonder and its travail.
> You make us partners in your labours
> and invite us to share in your peace.[43]

The same prayer has a vivid *epiklesis:*

> Lord send on us
> and on this thanksgiving meal the Spirit of life,
> who spoke through Moses and the prophets,
> who descended on Jesus at the river Jordan,
> and on the apostles on the first day of Pentecost.
> Send this same Spirit of fire
> that its coming may transfigure our humanity
> by the power of Christ's blood.[44]

42. *Ibid.,* p. 13.
43. *Ibid.,* p. 15.
44. *Ibid.,* p. 16.

It should be observed that all three rites include the traditional responses, and the second order ends with an admirably constructed prayer:

> Strengthen for service, Lord,
> the hands that have taken holy things.
> May the ears that have heard your word
> be deaf to clamor and dispute.
> May the eyes that have seen your great love
> shine with the light of hope.
> May the tongues that have sung your praise
> also speak the truth.
> May the feet that have walked in your house
> ever walk in the light.
> May the bodies that have tasted your living body be
> restored to newness of life.
> Thanks be to God for his gift beyond words.
>   Amen.[45]

The Baptismal Service[46] does not differ greatly from that in the 1980 book. It has a similar fivefold structure comprising Introduction, the Promises, the Baptismal Prayer, the Baptism, and final Prayer. The Introduction, however, provides the New Testament authorities for this sacrament, and explains briefly its significance, thus: "Baptism unites us to Christ, and to all that God accomplishes for all people and all time. In Baptism we are buried with Christ and are raised with him to new life; our sins are washed away, and we are brought into the covenant of grace; we receive the Spirit to equip us as members of Christ's body, the Church."[47]

The Promises are almost identical whether made by parents and sponsors or by believers, requiring faith in the Trinity, repenting and turning to Christ, fidelity in private and public worship and in the life of the local church, following Christ for life, and trusting that he will bring the candidate into the fullness of the world to come.

The Baptism, as always, is in the name of the Father, the Son, and the Holy Spirit, and is followed by admission (if a believer) to

---

45. *Ibid.*, pp. 29-30.
46. *Ibid.*, pp. 31-36.
47. *Ibid.*, p. 31.

the membership of the local church, with the offering of the right hand of fellowship. The concluding prayer gives thanks for the newly baptized and that he/she and the church members may be found faithful.

There is also, as in the earlier volume, Thanksgiving for the Birth of a Child. Its purpose is to provide for parents who do not wish to have their children baptized, or who cannot make the promises required at the Baptism of Infants. But it is stated at the outset: "In either case the act looks forward to baptism at a point in the future, and is not therefore a substitute for baptism."[48] It is a thanksgiving, dedication, and blessing for church members who thank God for the gift of the child, and promise to provide a Christian home for the child and to bring him or her up in the faith of the Gospel and the fellowship of the church. For parents who are not church members the promise required is "so to live that your child will be surrounded by love and goodness."[49] This substitute for Infant Baptism has a double advantage: it does not cheapen Infant Baptism, and gives those who believe in Believers' Baptism an occasion for expressing their gratitude to God for the gift of a child and for their own rededication.

The last of the rites of initiation is the Confirmation Service. The Introduction makes it clear that the purpose of Confirmation is "to seek now the gift of the Holy Spirit in confirming and strengthening the faith"[50] of the candidates. It is also a profession of faith and an acceptance of the responsibilities and privileges of church membership.

One or more candidates may then make their own personal act of witness, by an account of their own conversion, the reading of parts of Scripture that are particularly meaningful to them, or a hymn or poem. This is probably an innovation brought about by the former Churches of Christ members, since it was an integral element in Believers Baptism in the Baptist Union of Churches, as we saw in their rite. The actual formula of Confirmation is very close to that of the Church of England: "Send your Holy Spirit upon him/her/them: the spirit of Wisdom and understanding; the spirit of counsel and power; the spirit of knowledge and the fear of the

48. *Ibid.*, p. 37.
49. *Ibid.*, p. 39.
50. *Ibid.*, p. 41.

Lord." To which is added as the minister and elders lay their hands on each candidate: "By your holy spirit, confirm and strengthen, Lord, your servant A (candidate). Amen."[51] Two other alternate formulas are provided as well. Finally, the service ends with the Welcome made by the minister in the following words: "In the name of the Lord Jesus Christ, and in accordance with the decision of the church meeting, I declare you to be admitted to the full privileges and responsibilities of membership of the one, holy, catholic, and apostolic Church, and in particular to the exercise of that membership in this congregation of Christ's people."[52] In the Baptist as well as in the United Reformed Church, this assertion of the privilege and responsibility of membership in the local church is a significant expression of Christian democracy, for the new members have a vote at all church meetings they attend.

Considering the production of two directories of worship within the space of a decade, with such admirable clarity of focus, expression, and exposition, not to mention relevance, one can only be enthusiastic about the results. If one wanted proof of Free Church relevance and inventiveness in prayers, one composite book alone would provide the evidence: *A Call to Prayer* (1993), edited by Caryl Micklem.

The Methodist Church

The Methodist Service Book first appeared in 1975 and was revised and expanded in its edition of 1992. Like the service books of the Baptist Union and the United Reformed Church, it is a directory. The Preface insists that "these forms are not intended . . . to curb creative freedom, but rather to provide norms for its guidance."[53] David Kennedy and Philip Tovey indicate the different ways the book is used in English Methodism as follows: "Some Methodist congregations do use *The Methodist Service Book* as a 'pew book'; for some, it is a 'ministerial manual'; for others, it is totally peripheral."[54]

---

51. *Ibid.* p. 42.
52. *Ibid.*, p. 43.
53. *The Methodist Service Book* (Peterborough: Methodist Publishing House [1975], 1992), Preface.
54. *Methodist and United Reformed Church Worship: Baptism and Communion in Two "Free" Churches*, Grove Worship Series, No. 120 (Bramcote, Nottingham, 1992), p. 4.

A new book is in active preparation, delayed probably because of the breakdown of the projected Anglican-Methodist union.[55]

The importance of Methodist worship can be gauged in three ways. The Methodists, in the first place, are more numerous than Baptists and the United Reformed Church members combined. They have, owing to the impress of their founder John Wesley, retained his profound respect for the service of Holy Communion. It is significant that a Communion service closely resembling that of the 1662 Book of Common Prayer, with the "thou" language retained, is included in the 1975 *Methodist Service Book*. Furthermore, no church in England has made greater use than the Methodist Church of local preachers, and they have pioneered in the recognition of the role of the laity in worship, which is a very recent phenomenon in Churches with a more formal liturgy.

The most recent edition of *The Methodist Service Book* contains two orders for Holy Communion — the Book of Common Prayer form of 1662, and a modern rite. The compilers of the Service Book desired that the Eucharist should be given a more central place in their worship and this is indicated in the general directions: "The Worship of the Church is the offering of praise and prayer in which God's Word is read and preached, and in its fullness it includes the Lord's Supper, or Holy Communion."

The structure of Holy Communion, with the mandatory sections asterisked, is as follows:

The Preparation
1. Hymn
2. Collect for purity
3. The Commandments
4. Confession

55. In a fruitful interview with the Revd. A. Raymond George, former President of the Methodist Conference, former Moderator of the Free Church Federal Council, and former Chairman of the Joint Liturgical Group, on June 15, 1993, at the John Wesley Chapel, Bristol, he mentioned that the proposed union with the Anglicans was supported by 75%, and that, according to the Bishop of Bristol, was a higher majority than the vote that permitted the British to enter the European Union. It was Mr. George who had prepared the all-important Ordinal.

5. Assurance of Pardon
6. Collect or other prayer
7. Hymn or *Gloria*

The Ministry of the Word
*8. Scripture Lesson (Old Testament, Epistle, or both)
*9. Hymn
*10. Gospel Reading
*11. Sermon
*12. Intercessions
*13. The Lord's Prayer
14. Blessing and Dismissal of 'those who leave'

The Lord's Supper
*15. The Peace
16. The Nicene Creed
17. Hymn
*18. Bread and Wine are brought to the minister or uncovered
*19. Taking of the Bread and Wine
*20. The Thanksgiving
*21. The Breaking of the Bread
*22. Silence
23. Prayer of Humble Access (revised form)
*24. The Invitation to Communion
*25. The Communion
*26. The minister covers the remains.
*27. Silence
*28. Post-Communion Prayer
29. Hymn
30. Blessing
*31. Dismissal

Of the thirty-one items seventeen are obligatory, including the two places where silence is required.

There are several noteworthy characteristics in this rite. The penitential section comes at the very beginning rather than after the intercessions as in Series 3 in the Anglican form in 1974. The Declaration of Pardon is such, and not a petition. It goes thus:

Christ Jesus came into the world to save sinners.
Hear then the word of grace:
Your sins are forgiven.
Amen. Thanks be to God.[56]

Because some ministers or local preachers sense a lingering hierarchical arrogance in these words, there is a tendency to change "your" to "our sins."[57] The *anamnesis* is briefer than usual:

Therefore, Father, as he has commanded us,
we do this in remembrance of him,
and we ask you to accept our sacrifice of praise
and thanksgiving.[58]

The *epiklesis* also is brief and concentrates on the recipients rather than on the elements:

'Grant that by the power of the Holy Spirit
we who receive your gifts of bread and wine may share in
the body and blood of Christ.[59]

Probably the greater centrality of the Eucharist in Methodism is found, as David Kennedy and Philip Tovey observe, in the fact that while *The Methodist Hymn-Book* (1933) contained 18 eucharistic hymns in a collection of 984, *Hymns and Psalms* (1983) provides 38 out of a total of 832.[60]

The Final Prayers are expressions of a simple, very concise, and deep devotion in which all can easily join:

We thank you, Lord,
that you have fed us in this sacrament,
united us with Christ,
and given us a foretaste of the heavenly banquet
prepared for all mankind. Amen.

56. *Methodist Service Book,* p. B6.
57. See Kennedy and Tovey, *Methodist and United Reformed Church Worship,* p. 18.
58. *Methodist Service Book,* p. B14.
59. *Ibid.*
60. Kennedy and Tovey, *Methodist and United Reformed Church Worship,* p. 20.

The Dismissal is equally concise and relevant:

Go in peace in the power of the Spirit
to live and work to God's praise and glory.

The congregation responds:

Thanks be to God.[61]

The 1991 texts provide four orders of service for Baptism and Confirmation. The first is for the Baptism of those who are able to answer for themselves, and the second is for the Baptism of Young Children. The third combines the first and second, and the fourth is a service of Public Recognition and Confirmation of Full Members. There is a significant change from the 1975 book, where Infant Baptism was placed first, as if it were the norm. The later texts begin with Baptism of Believers, a reflection of the missionary task of the Church in the late twentieth century.[62]

The first form for those who can answer for themselves contains the following parts: The Preparation, The Ministry of the Word, The Baptismal Prayer, The Promises and Profession of Faith, The Baptism, and The Final Prayers. The general directions indicate that the font should stand apart in a prominent place, and recommend that water should be sprinkled or poured on the candidate three times, or that he should be dipped in the water thrice.

The Preparation includes a hymn and a Collect, and the Ministry of the Word of the regular pre-Communion Service. The statement in the Declaration has been revised and desires to put Baptism in a wider context "as a means, but not necessarily the only means, of becoming part of the people of God." The first three lines read:

Brothers and sisters in Christ,
through grace,
through the sign and seal of baptism,

61. *Methodist Service Book*, p. B17.
62. The later texts are Entry into the Church (4 Services) and were approved by the Methodist Conference of 1991 as Alternative Services. My citations will be from Kennedy and Tovey, *Methodist and United Reformed Church Worship*.

and through the power of the Holy Spirit
we become God's people, the Church.[63]

The most important part of the service, the Baptism itself excepted, is the Decision, where there is a triple interrogation of the
candidates, as in the Anglican *Alternative Service Book* of 1980,
demanding affirmation of the Christian faith and commitment to
Christ, with a triple profession of faith. There is also an interrogation
of the congregation.

The prayer immediately before the act of Baptism includes the
words,

> Look now in love upon your church,
> and grant that these your servants,
> now to be baptized in this water,
> may die to sin, be raised up to new life in Christ,
> and be born again from above by the power of the Holy Spirit.[64]

The rite for young children is parallel to that for believers, with three
major differences. In the new service the promises are introduced as
follows: "Dear friends in Christ, young children are baptized on the
understanding that they will be brought up in the fellowship of Christ's
Church and taught the Christian faith; and with prayer that they will
confess Christ as Lord, enter into the fullness of the Church's life, share
in the Communion of the Lord's Supper and serve Christ in the world."
Here there is no way that parents can be unaware of their responsibilities. The second change is that the element of water is given greater
attention in the new rite for Baptism, for the new prayer is rich in water
imagery and direction 4 refers to the possibility of being baptized in a
baptistery, river, lake, or the sea. The third change is the inclusion of a
text based on a prayer from the French Reformed Church offered
immediately prior to Baptism:

> N,
> for you Jesus Christ has come,
> has lived, has suffered;
> for you he endured the agony of Gethsemane

63. *Ibid.*, p. 9.
64. *Ibid.*, p. 8.

and the darkness of Calvary;
for you he has uttered the cry, "It is accomplished!"
For you he has triumphed over death;
for you he prays at God's right hand;
all for you, little child,
even though you do not know it.
In your baptism, the word of the apostle is fulfilled:
"We love, because God first loved us."[65]

It would be hard to find better words to stress the divine initiative in human salvation: this *is* prevenient grace.

At the service of Confirmation in the 1975 book, those who are to be confirmed kneel, while the congregation remains standing, and the minister prays:

Heavenly Father, all-powerful God, who in Baptism
    received these your children into your family,
    establish them now in faith by the Holy Spirit,
    and day by day increase in them your gifts of grace;
the spirit of wisdom and understanding; Amen.
the spirit of counsel and might; Amen.
the spirit of knowledge and true godliness and the fear
of the Lord; Amen.
and keep them in your mercy for ever. *Amen.*

It is clear that there has been considerable liturgical revision in the Methodist Church, and there will be more to come before the next Service Book is completed, supposedly in 1995. Its ecumenical import, with its Anglican and Free Church links, promises to make it a very attractive book.

What we have not been able to include, the Baptists excepted, is an account of how the newly initiated, like the charismatics, like to simplify the more traditional elements of the worship of the Free Churches. But I cherish the Revd. Raymond George's reminder to me that popularization can often lead to trivialization, in the memorable words, "People now want chatty, claphappy services or liturgical dances, though the latter are only a development of processions." It is a warning worth remembering.

65. *Methodist Service Book*, p. A38.

CHAPTER VII

OCCASIONAL SERVICES

I N THIS CHAPTER we shall be concerned with what may be termed occasional or pastoral services. These are, in the order in which they will be treated, weddings, burial or cremation rites, and ordinations. Significant changes in all these services over the last three decades will be noted.

Marriages

Probably no other human relation reflects so quickly or so decisively the powerful psychical currents within than does marriage. For both joy or misery the stakes run high in the modern world. Protective sanctions have been eroded by modern means of avoiding pregnancy, and by attitudes countenancing deviations or even the absence of norms. Marriage may be viewed, on the one hand, as a bond that is divinely tied and intended to last a lifetime, and, on the other hand, as a casual or tentative link to be broken when, for example, one of the parties finds another more alluring partner.

The *Collins Illustrated Guide to the Alternative Service Book 1980* of the Church of England rightly indicates that the Christian Marriage Service projects an ideal in contemporary society; it is a beacon of light in the shadows of secularism:

> In a secularizing society the ideal of monogamy is slowly disappearing around the Church of England. Premarital sexual relationships, casual sexual relationships, various forms of "group marriages," and forms of homosexual pairings: these both witness to the slow disappearance of the ideal, and also help it to disappear. The question for the Church itself is how far it can adapt its own practice to show compassionate understanding for those for whom the ideal has seemed impossible or not worked out — and still retain credibility for the ideal itself.[1]

1. *Anglican Worship Today: Collins Illustrated Guide to the Alternative Service Book 1980* (London: Collins Liturgical Publications, 1980), p. 187.

The marriage order in the *Alternative Service Book 1980* emphasizes the centrality of self-giving and self-transcending love, without
depreciating the sexual impulse. Its opening sentence is: "God is love,
and those who live in love live in God: and God lives in them."[2] The
first prayer rightly stresses the intended permanence of Christian
marriage:

Grant to your servants
that, loving one another,
they may continue in your love
until their lives' end. . .[3]

It is significant that the reasons given for marriage in the newer
rite have been reversed, so that living together for the sake of each
other is mentioned first, then the sexual union, and only thirdly the
begetting of children. The second reason is delightfully expressed: "It
is given, that with delight and tenderness, they may know each other
in love, and, through the joy of their bodily union, may strengthen
the union of their hearts and lives."[4]

The mutuality of the self-giving on the part of the two partners
is vividly seen in the exchange of rings, whereas formerly the giving
of the ring was a unilateral act. One improvement proposed by the
Liturgical Commission but rejected by the Synod was the mention
of the bride and bridegroom "belonging to one another's families."
This was the particular concern of Mrs. Jean Mayland, wife of a vicar
and member of the Commission.[5]

It is interesting that the Methodist Marriage Service includes this
emphasis in its comprehensive intercession with responses:

All grace comes from you, O God
and you alone are the source of eternal life.
Bless your servants A. and C.
That they may faithfully live together
to the end of their lives.

2. *ASB*, p. 287, citing 1 John 4:16.
3. *Ibid.*
4. *Ibid.*, p. 288.
5. See *Anglican Worship Today*, p. 187.

Be with them in all their happiness
that your joy may be in them, and their joy may be full.

Strengthen them in every time of trouble
that they may carry each other's burdens
and so fulfil the law of Christ.

Let your blessing be on their home
that your peace may dwell there.

Let it be a place of welcome
that its happiness may be freely shared.

Bless the families and friends of A. and C.
that we may be united in love and friendship. . . .[6]

The opening words of the minister rightly addresses a variegated group in the congregation, making all feel at home: "We are gathered here in the presence of God to witness the marriage of A.B. and C.D., to support them with our prayers, and to share their joy."[7]

The Wedding Service of the United Reformed Church changes the traditional word of the promises made by the partners thus:

A, will you take C to be your wife in Christian marriage?
Will you love her, comfort her,
honour and protect her,
in times of prosperity and health,
and in times of trouble and suffering,
and be faithful to her
as long as you both shall live?[8]

But it also uses the time-honored vows so familiar from the Book of Common Prayer. The prayers in the service also have refreshing realism and absence of sentimentality. For example, there is the

6. *The Methodist Service Book* (Peterborough: Methodist Publishing House, 1975), pp. E11-12.
7. *Ibid.,* p. E4.
8. *Service Book: The United Reformed Churh in the United Kingdom* (Oxford University Press, 1989), p. 54.

following petition: "And give them grace when they hurt each other to recognize and acknowledge their fault, and ask each other's forgiveness and yours."[9]

Patterns and Prayers for Christian Worship, the manual produced by the Baptist Union of Great Britain in 1991, points out in the introduction to the service of Christian Marriage that various customs attached to the wedding service "may well be questioned in the light of contemporary views of marriage." It continues:

> For example, the custom of the bride arriving after the bridegroom may be varied by both the man and the woman entering the church at the beginning of the service and walking down either side to meet at the front. The custom of the bride being given away by her father may be omitted, repeated for the groom, or extended by including other members of the couple's families and the whole congregation. Alternatives are offered in the following material.[10]

The promises made by groom and bride have a touching simplicity: "I will love you in good times and bad. I will love you when it is easy and when it is not. I will love you when love brings us close, and when love pushes us apart. I will love you when my love is obvious and when it is hidden by my faults. Please go on trusting me." The answer each makes is the same and equally touching: "I will. Rich or poor, well or ill, strong or weak: I will, till death parts us. It is God's intention. I give my word."[11]

The Roman Catholic Church has a variety of Wedding Masses, but our consideration will be limited to Formula A, from which the rich Nuptial Blessing deserves full citation:

> Father,
> by your power you have made everything out of nothing.
> In the beginning you created the universe
> and made mankind in your own likeness.
>
> You gave man the constant help of woman
> so that man and woman should no longer be two, but one flesh,

9. *Ibid.*, p. 58.
10. *Patterns and Prayers* (London: Oxford University Press, 1991), pp. 120-21.
11. *Ibid.*, p. 132.

159

and you teach us that what you have united
should never be divided.

Father,
by your plan man and woman are united,
and married life has been established
as the one blessing that was not forfeited by original sin or
washed away in the flood.

Look with love upon this woman, your daughter,
now joined to her husband in marriage.
She asks your blessing.
Give her the grace of love and peace.
May she always follow the example of the holy women
whose praises are sung in the scriptures.

May her husband put his trust in her
and recognize that she is his equal
and the heir with him to the life of grace.

May he always honour her and love her
as Christ loves his bride, the Church.

Father,
keep them always true to your commandments.
Keep them faithful in marriage
and let them be living examples of Christian life.
Give them the strength which comes from the gospel
so that they may be witnesses of Christ to others.
[Bless them with children
and help them to be good parents.
May they live to see their children's children.]
And, after a happy old age,
grant them fullness of life with the saints
in the kingdom of heaven.
We ask this through Christ our Lord.[12]

12. *The Sunday Missal: A New Edition* (London: Collins Liturgical Publications, 1984), pp. 1015-16.

The Solemn Blessing and Dismissal after the Eucharist includes fine petitions, such as: "God the eternal Father keep you in love with each other, so that the peace of Christ may stay with you and be always in your home" and "May you always bear witness to the love of God in this world so that the afflicted and the needy will find in you generous friends and welcome you into the joys of heaven."[13]

Perhaps the most notable change in recent Roman Catholic wedding rites is the stress on the equality of the partners in the marriage. The old rite included a prayer for the bride that she be "faithful to one embrace, . . . honorable in her chastity" without any parallel demand from the bridegroom. This rightly has been rectified.

Funeral Services

When the Liturgical Commission of the Church of England began to work on a revised funeral service, the members were convinced that three factors would have to be taken into account. The first was the clear need for a more joyful and less lugubrious service, the second need was to provide for the modern use of cremation in lieu of burial, and the third requisite was to devise a service for the funeral of a child. There was also additional pressure from the Anglo-Catholics to provide prayers for the dead.

In their 1973 introduction to the service the Liturgical Commission claimed that their aims were as follows: "a. to secure the reverent disposal of the corpse; b. to commend the deceased to the care of our heavenly Father; c. to proclaim the glory of our risen life in Christ here and hereafter; d. to remind us of the certainty of our own coming death and judgement; e. to make plain the eternal unity of Christian people, living and departed, in the risen and ascended Christ; and f. to offer some consolation to the mourners."[14] This analytical proposal could well be used as a test of the adequacy of all modern Christian funeral services.

The Anglican Funeral Service is full of joy, recalling the promises of Christ and making use of the 23rd Psalm and the *Te Deum;* immediately before the Committal the minister cites the following words:

13. *Ibid.,* p. 1016.
14. *Anglican Worship Today,* pp. 214-15.

I heard a voice from heaven, saying, Write this: "Happy are the dead, who die in the faith of Christ! Henceforth," says the Spirit, "they may rest from their labours; for they take with them the record of their deeds."[15]

The Committal takes the following alternative forms:

We have entrusted our brother/sister N to God's merciful keeping, and we now commit his/her body to the ground (*or* to be cremated): [earth to earth, ashes to ashes, dust to dust;] in sure and certain hope of the resurrection to eternal life through our Lord Jesus Christ, who died, was buried, and rose again for us. To him be glory for ever and ever.[16]

There is also a separate service for the Funeral of a Child. This service cites Mark 10:13-16 as a reminder that Christ said, "Let the children come to me; do not try to stop them; for the kingdom of God belongs to such as these. I tell you, whoever does not accept the kingdom of God like a child will never enter it" (NEB). The Committal begins with the declaration: "We have entrusted N. to God's merciful keeping." There are also special prayers to be used after the birth of a still-born child or the death of a newly-born child. A sensitive prayer commends a still-born or newly-born child to the love of God:

Heavenly Father, by your mighty power you gave us life, and in your love you have given us new life in Christ Jesus. We entrust this child to your merciful keeping, in the faith of Jesus Christ your Son our Lord, who died and rose again to save us, and is now alive and reigns with you and the Holy Spirit in glory for ever.[17]

The only serious weakness in the funeral rite is the lack of a blessing when the mourners are dismissed.

The English Methodists have a Funeral Service with a wide series of readings to bring comfort to Christians. It also includes several empathetic prayers for mourners, including the following:

15. *ASB*, p. 315.
16. *Ibid.*, p. 316.
17. *Ibid.*, p. 323.

Grant, Father, to the bereaved, the Spirit of faith, that they may receive your promised grace to help in time of need. May they look to Jesus, the pioneer and perfecter of the faith, who for the joy set before him endured the Cross, despising the shame, and is seated at your right hand in glory. As they return to the duties of life, let your peace protect them and the risen victorious Lord sustain them in your service all the days of their life.[18]

The *Service Book* of the United Reformed Church in the United Kingdom of 1989 subtitles its Funeral Service "A Witness to the Resurrection." It begins positively with the minister's Preface: "We have come together to worship God and to give thanks and praise for the life of AB. . . . We have come to pray for the comfort and strength that God promises to us. We have come to affirm the Christian conviction that death is not the end — but a new beginning."[19] One prayer includes the petition: "Show us now your grace, that as we face the mystery of death we may see the light of eternity. Speak to us once more your joyful message of life and death overcome. Help us to live as those who are prepared to die, and when our days here are ended, enable us to die as those who go forth and live, so that living or dying our life may be in Jesus Christ our risen saviour."[20] It is a service full of psychological understanding of grief, and even of the guilt of mourners. This is seen in various alternative commendations of the departed, including the following:

Eternal God, before whose face the generations rise and pass away: we praise you for all your servants departed this life in your faith and love, especially for A . . . , whom today we commend into your sure keeping; each of us recalling in a moment of silence what she/he has meant to her/his loved ones, friends, and colleagues. We give thanks for all your goodness to her/him; all she/he accomplished by your grace; and all that she/he was to those who loved her/him. And now we praise you that for her/him sorrow and sickness are ended, death itself is past, and she/he lives for ever in your love and care; through Jesus Christ our Lord.[21]

18. *The Methodist Service Book,* p. F19.
19. *Service Book,* p. 68.
20. *Ibid.,* p. 69.
21. *Ibid.,* p. 75.

The Committal is brief and profoundly reassuring in one example: "Now that the earthly life of A . . . has come to an end, we commit her/his body to be buried/cremated confident of the resurrection to eternal life."[22] Additional prayers are provided for the funeral of a child, and for the funeral of a still-born child, and for use in particularly distressing circumstances.

It is impressive that so many revisions of the funeral or cremation orders of service help the mourners to accept death, to give thanks for their happy memories of those who have died, while insisting in Scriptural citations and prayers that, through the resurrection of Christ, there is hope for life beyond death.

The Baptists in their *Patterns and Prayers for Christian Worship* (1991) subtitle the Funeral Service "A Service of Hope." They, too, have created memorable services combining the characteristics we have already seen in other modern funeral services. Two prayers deserve citation. The first is:

Father your love is stronger than death; by you we are all being brought to life. Help us, as we hear the promises of your Word, to believe them and to receive the comfort they offer. You are the giver of hope: fill us with joy and peace in believing, that our fears may be dispelled, our loneliness eased, and our hope re-awakened; through Jesus Christ our Lord.[23]

The following commendation is theologically sound and also reassuring:

Depart, O Christian soul, out of this world,
in the name of God the Father almighty who created you,
in the name of the Holy Spirit who sanctifies you.
May your rest be this day in peace and your dwelling in the paradise of God.[24]

The Baptists have also special prayers for the Death of a Child, as well as for Sudden or Violent Death, and also After a Suicide.

22. *Ibid.*, p. 79.
23. *Patterns and Prayers*, p. 146.
24. *Ibid.*, p. 150. I have omitted the final petition of the Commendation because I considered it complete as it stands.

One prayer has doubtless provided solace for many mourners in such a situation:

> Lord Jesus Christ, you spoke of your Father's love for all people; help us to know that your love will never be withdrawn from ——— or from us. Lord Jesus Christ, you wrestled with the questions of life and death in Gethsemane; help us to know that you understand and are present where there is anguish of mind.[25]

The older Roman Catholic Order of a Christian Funeral was dominated by the thought of purgatory, but the new *Order of Christian Funerals* that appeared in 1990 represents a substantial revision and reordering. The General Introduction to that document declares: "In the face of death, the Church confidently proclaims that God has created each person for eternal life, and that Jesus, the Son of God, by his death and resurrection, has broken the chains of sin and death . . ." and that he "achieved his task of redeeming humanity by the paschal mystery of his blessed passion, resurrection from the dead and glorious ascension."[26] The effects of these events are mediated by the Church through the proclaimed Word of God and the liturgy. In the Church's funeral rites, praise and gratitude are offered to God for the gift of a life which has now been returned to him. At the same time the Church also recognizes that Christians sin and so the Church commends the dead to God's merciful love and pleads for the forgiveness of their sins. In the third place, the Church in the Mass for the Dead joins the Church in heaven, as part of the one great communion of saints. Finally, this Communion celebration also brings hope and consolation to the mourners, as well as insisting on the need for forgiveness. As Father Crichton adds tartly, this is all the more necessary "in our time when one would think . . . the celebration of the death of someone is sort of a premature canonization."[27]

As for the rite itself, it takes place in three principal stations: the home, the church, and the cemetery (cremation chapel). On the day before or on the day of the funeral liturgy, family and friends usually

---

25. *Ibid.*, p. 165.
26. Cited in J. D. Crichton's *Christian Celebration: Understanding the Sacraments,* 3rd ed. (London: Geoffrey Chapman, 1993), p. 203.
27. *Ibid.*, p. 203.

gather in the home for a brief service of prayers, Scripture lessons, and a blessing. Then follows the Vigil or the Wake held in the church (or home) with the reception of the body, including the sprinkling with holy water, the entrance procession, the placing of the pall and Christian symbols on the coffin, an opening prayer, Scripture lessons, a short homily, intercessions, the Lord's Prayer, and the final prayer and blessing. The climax is the Funeral liturgy itself with the Mass and the final Commendation. And the most important part of the liturgy after the reception of the eucharistic elements is the final Commendation. The conclusion of the funeral rites is the Committal; this is the last act of the community of faith in caring for the body of its deceased member and it inevitably puts great strain on family members. There are five alternative prayers, one of which is familiar from the Book of Common Prayer. It starts with "In sure and certain hope" and includes the words known to most English Christians, "we commit his/her body to the ground, earth to earth, ashes to ashes, dust to dust." Monsignor Crichton suggests that the prayers proposed, to say nothing of the elaborate symbolical gestures, take far too long to be included in the twenty minutes which is customarily allowed at cremations.[28]

This twenty-minute restriction in crematoria is not the only objection that is made to services of cremation. While burial is difficult for mourners, especially in bad weather, cremation is found by many to be "psychologically unsatisfying as the coffin slides away on rollers while the words of committal are said: it disappears, but there is no true committal to the fire, as there is to the earth in burial when the earth is cast on the coffin."[29] A further difficulty is that there is often a time lapse of several weeks between the cremation and the short service for the burial of the ashes, and this causes a repetition of sadness for mourners. Dean Michael Perham in his *Liturgy Parochial and Pastoral* refers to "all the undesirable elements of cremation — rotas, 'canned' music, and the sense of a conveyor belt service, with another funeral every twenty minutes. . . ." He proposes that cremation no longer be considered as the equivalent of burial, which it cannot be, but that it be regarded only as part of the process of preparing the body for burial. The casket of ashes would then become the focus and equivalent of the coffin for the funeral which could

28. *Ibid.*, pp. 210-11.
29. *Anglican Worship Today*, p. 219.

then take place in a church, followed by the local interment of ashes. The advantage would be that the bereaved could both have the funeral within their own community and thereafter be able to visit the buried remains without making a journey away.[30]

Michael Perham has contributed greatly to a clearer understanding of the Christian meaning of death and the afterlife in his book *The Communion of Saints*. He rightly cautions that "all eschatological talk must be symbolic."[31] He cites with approval Professor John Macquarrie's dictum that "belief in a final judgement is the hope that what is now ambiguous will resolve itself and the advance of good over evil will decisively prevail."[32] Perham claims that nearly all Christians today reject the idea of a hell where God everlastingly punishes the wicked without any hope of deliverance, for this would reduce God's mercy and compassion to subhuman level.[33] He prefers to restate the traditional understanding of Purgatory in order to indicate new growth on the part of those men and women who are going in the right direction but with obstacles to overcome, and who need patience and perseverance.[34] Citing Archbishop Michael Ramsey, he views heaven as "the grasp of perfection granted to those who have made the final choice" — a perfection of beauty, wisdom, and love.[35] He approves of the prayer in the *Alternative Service Book 1980* which reads:

> May God in his infinite love and mercy bring the whole Church, living and departed in the Lord Jesus, to a joyful resurrection and the fulfillment of his eternal kingdom.[36]

---

30. Perham, *Liturgy Pastoral and Parochial* (London: S.P.C.K., 1984), pp. 142-43. Gilbert Cope in *Dying, Death and Disposal* writes: "At least it is my opinion that in the process of bereavement it is psychologically desirable for most people that the 'departed' should not only depart, but should be seen to depart ceremonially, and not mysteriously disappear — down a hole or through a wall or behind a curtain — to the sound of indeterminate music and incomprehensible utterance."

31. *The Communion of Saints: An Examination of the Place of the Christian Dead in the Belief, Worship, and Calendars of the Church* (London: S.P.C.K., 1980), p. 91.

32. From Macquarrie's *Principles of Christian Theology* (London, 1960), p. 325.

33. Perham, *Communion of Saints*, pp. 101-2.

34. *Ibid.*, p. 104.

35. *Ibid.*, p. 107.

36. *ASB*, p. 315.

Presumably this is because it does not presuppose a static rest but fulfillment, implying continual growth in God's love and service.

Ordination

This is clearly an occasional service, but not in any regular sense to be grouped among the pastoral services. It is, however, an important index to the role of a pastor or a chief pastor, such as a bishop.

Two modern factors have changed the forms of Ordination in the Church of England. One is the influence of the Church of Scotland via its impact on the Church of South India, and the other is the preparation of ordination rites in 1968 as part of the unsuccessful attempt at Anglican-Methodist unity in England. In the words of Professor Paul Bradshaw: ". . . the imperative formula accompanying the imposition of hands that had been characteristic of the Anglican rites was abandoned in favour of an ordination prayer with the imposition of hands being performed during its central petition, which was an invocation of the Holy Spirit on the ordinand for the particular ministry being conferred."[37] Also, when more than one are being ordained, instead of repeating the whole prayer over each, the prayer is said first collectively over all, and when the central petition is reached, that only is repeated for each ordinand, while hands are laid over the ordinand, and the prayer is concluded.

Essentially there is a different prayer for each of the three orders — bishops, priests, and deacons — and that prayer clearly defines the identity of each order of the ministry. In each case the structure of the rite is identical. It begins with the presentation of the candidates with the assent of the people, followed by the Ministry of the Word. Next follows the examination of the candidates, a time of silent prayer, and the hymn, "Come, Holy Ghost. . . ." The climax is the ordination prayer with the laying on of hands. The concluding ceremonies include the handing over of a Bible (and a pastoral staff in the case of a bishop) with the giving of the right hand of fellowship

37. Bradshaw in *The Study of Liturgy*, rev. ed. (London: OUP, 1992), p. 391. Bradshaw argues elsewhere that the use of imperative formulas in ordination rites is indefensible because they induce erroneous ideas about Ordination; "they suggest, for example, that the grace of order is something that can be bestowed by command rather than sought in prayer" (*The Anglican Ordinal: Its History and Development from the Reformation to the Present Day* [London: S.P.C.K., 1971], p. 208).

and the formal declaration that the candidates are ordained. Some provinces within the Anglican Communion give deacons a New Testament and allow for the giving of a chalice and paten as well as a Bible for priests.[38]

As might be expected, the English Methodist Church follows the structure of the Anglican rite, with an opening collect, and Old Testament, Epistle, and Gospel readings. A sermon and the recitation of the Nicene Creed follows. Then the Secretary of the Methodist Conference presents to the president those who are to be ordained as presbyters, indicating that each has been examined for fitness, and each candidate rises as his or her name is called; the people also stand and acknowledge their worthiness. A public examination follows, requiring acknowledgement of a call, acceptance of the Scriptures and the doctrines of the Christian faith, acceptance of the discipline of the Church, and a promise of fidelity in prayer and studying the Scriptures. The actual Ordination follows with the hymn, "Come, Holy Ghost . . ." The president prays, while the candidates kneel, and he lays his hand on each of the candidates in turn, saying over each one:

> Father, send the Holy Spirit upon N., for the office and work of a Minister in the Church of Christ[39]

There is also a form for the Ordination of Deacons and Deaconesses, which has the same ritual structure as the Ordination of Presbyters. Both forms of Ordination require the giving of the same promises and take place in the context of the Lord's Supper.

The structure of a service of Ordination in the United Reformed Church differs from the Anglican and Methodist orders. The "ordination to the Ministry of the Word and Sacraments" and of induction to a pastorate "is held under the authority of a District Council. The Moderator of the Synod is invited by the Council to preside, and the service is normally held in the pastorate to which the minister is inducted."[40]

After Scripture sentences and prayers, the Act of Ordination

---

38. *ASB*, p. 393.

39. The entire service of Ordination is printed in *The Methodist Service Book*, pp. G1–G15. The ordination formula appears on G11.

40. *Service Book*, pp. 85-96.

begins with statements relating briefly the circumstances leading to the call, and the minister-elect may make a statement about his or her faith and sense of calling, and a statement concerning the Nature, Faith and Order of the United Reformed Church. Then Affirmations follow to the questions about the faith of the minister-elect, and members of the congregation are invited to reaffirm their faith and their promises to support the minister-to-be. The act of Ordination proceeds as follows: the congregation is invited to stand, the ordinand kneels, and the presiding minister offers a prayer of profound gratitude for Christ and the Church, and for the minister-to-be. Then those appointed by the District Council lay their hands on the ordinand's head, as the performative words are said: "Fill your servant AB . . . with your Holy Spirit, as in Your Name and in obedience to Your Will we ordain him/her to be a minister in Your Church."[41] Then a Declaration is made by a representative of the District Council that AB has been ordained to the ministry and inducted to the pastorate of this congregation. The presentation of a Bible to the minister follows, and the presiding minister offers the new minister the right hand of fellowship. Prayers of Intercession and the Lord's Prayer follow; the Lord's Supper may also follow. There are in the same *Service Book* also forms for the Commissioning of Church-related Community Workers, and for the Ordination and Induction of Elders. The latter is an excellent expression of the priesthood of all believers.

The Baptist Union of Great Britain in its *Patterns and Prayers for Christian Worship* offers two sets of services for ordination to the ministry and two sets of services for induction to a local church. We shall focus on describing and analyzing the two ordination forms. The introduction states that

> In ordination a person's call from God to the pastoral ministry of Word and Sacrament is given public recognition as he or she is set apart to serve and to lead. The ordination service acts as a focal point after years of prayerful preparation. . . . In the ordination service the importance of the preparation process is generally reflected by the involvement of a College Principal or Tutor, or other person concerned with ministerial training.[42]

41. *Ibid.,* p. 89.
42. *Patterns and Prayers,* pp. 170-71.

In these respects the Ordination of the ministers of the United Reformed Church is similar.

The First Pattern of Ordination may take the form of statements from the ordinand, the church secretary of the ordinand's home church, an officer from the commending association, or a representative from his or her college, and the church secretary of the calling church. Or the leader may ask each of these persons if they believe the ordinand has received a call from God. This is followed by questions to the ordinand, concerning the ordinand's faith in the Triune God, a promise to teach Christ's Gospel, to nourish the flock of Christ, to ensure that the local church will be welcoming, and to take up the cross.

Then a Bible is presented to the ordinand normally by a college representative, with the words: "Receive this copy of the Scriptures. Study them so that you may grow in Christ and help the Church to proclaim the whole truth of God for the world."[43] Then the ordinand kneels holding the Bible, and laying on of hands and the ordination prayer follow. The prayer proceeds thus:

> Almighty Father, we praise and glorify you because you sent your only Son Jesus Christ to be the servant of all, and because Jesus who has died is risen and reigning and calls women and men to follow him today.
>
> Now we ask you to anoint this your servant ——— with your Holy Spirit as we ordain him/her in your name to share in the ministry of Christ. Send upon him/her the Spirit of Wisdom to proclaim the good news of forgiveness of sins through Jesus; send upon him/her the Spirit of love to bring healing to those who are broken; send upon him/her the Spirit of power to challenge all who oppress the weak. Keep him/her faithful in times of trial and testing, always abounding in hope and filled with the grace of Jesus Christ our Lord, to whom be glory for ever and ever.[44]

The service ends with the Declaration of Ordination and the blessing of the congregation on the new minister.

The pattern of the second order for Ordination begins with a call to worship, a time of praise, Scripture readings, and prayers for God's

43. *Ibid.*, p. 180.
44. *Ibid.*, pp. 180-81.

blessing on the service. Then there follow a statement concerning the service of ordination and induction, questions to the ordinand, presentation of the ordinand, laying on of hands and prayer, the presentation of the ordination Bible, and a hymn or song. The Ordination Prayer is as follows:

> Our Father God, we now set apart your servant —— in the name of Jesus for the work of ministry. We ask that he/she may know the presence and power of your Spirit. Guide and direct him/her as he/she seeks to lead your people. Make him/her a wise and able teacher, fill him/her with your love that he/she may be a good pastor, and enable him/her to lead in mission and ministry that your name be glorified. Keep him/her faithful in times of testing, humble in times of success, and joyful in your service; through Jesus Christ our Lord.[45]

In considering these Baptist rites one is impressed by their flexibility and variety, as well as solemnity, particularly as they frequently allow ministers to offer extempore prayers as alternatives.

The Roman Catholic liturgy for Holy Orders has, since the deliberations of Vatican II, been greatly revised and simplified. Three major changes have taken place: the complexity of the old order with vestings, anointings and the handing over of various cultic articles, has been greatly reduced; the role of the episcopate has been restored to its ancient dignity in the hierarchy of order; and the diaconate is no longer a stage on the way to the priesthood, but is restored as a permanent ministry in the Church.

The three services of orders for the episcopate, the priesthood or presbyterate, and the diaconate, have a common structure. Ordination is conferred within the Eucharist, after the ministry of the Word, with many alternative readings. In each case the service comprises the following features:

(1) The candidates are presented to the bishop and the congregation declares its assent to them;

(2) the bishop describes the duties of each particular order and briefly examines the candidates;

(3) the prayer of the people follows, including a bidding, a litany, and a collect;

45. *Ibid.*, p. 189.

(4) the laying on of hands upon each candidate takes place in silence followed by the Prayer of Ordination;

(5) the symbols of office are duly delivered followed by a kiss, and the newly ordained fulfill the liturgical functions of their order in the Eucharist.[46]

The signs of office are vividly symbolical. A bishop receives a Gospel-book, which is imposed on his head presumably that he may live under the yoke of the Gospel; a ring as a symbol of his marriage to his diocese; the mitre, which is placed on his head with a new formula: "Receive the mitre and may the light of holiness shine in you . . . ." Finally he is given the pastoral staff or crozier as a sign of his task to rule and care for the flock of Christ committed to his charge.[47] In the ordination of priests, members of the clergy who are present rearrange the stole and put on the chasuble of the elect. The paten and chalice containing the bread and wine which the people have offered are also given, with the formula: "Receive the offering of the holy people which is to be offered to God. Realize what you are to do, imitate the mystery you are going to handle and conform your life to the mystery of the Lord's cross." The deacons are vested with stole and dalmatic and receive a book of the Gospels.

The theology of the ordination of bishops can be derived from two sources, the homily and the prayer of consecration. The former is largely a summary of the Constitution on the Church of Vatican II, and it stresses that bishops, as successors of the apostles, are to continue Christ's work of preaching, sanctifying, and ruling the flock entrusted to them. They receive the gift of the Holy Spirit by the imposition of hands. It is significant that the gift or *charisma* is emphasized, removing the entire idea of holy order away from the juridical and legal sphere.[48] The bishop's rule in the Church is admirably summarized in the conclusion of the homily:

Give your care to the whole flock in which the Holy Spirit has set you to rule the church of God in the name of the Father whose image you show forth in the church, in the name of his Son, Jesus Christ

46. I am indebted for analyses of the Roman Catholic Holy Orders to Crichton's *Christian Celebration*, chapter 8, and Bradshaw in *The Study of Liturgy*, pp. 397ff.
47. Crichton, *Christian Celebration*, p. 151.
48. *Ibid.*, p. 143.

whose function of teacher, priest and pastor you perform, and in the name of the Holy Spirit who gives life to the church and strength to you in your weakness.[49]

The consecration prayer is derived from the *Apostolic Tradition*[50] of Hippolytus, which originated in about 215 A.D. but bears traces of later additions. Since this prayer underlies all the rites of ordination in the Eastern church, its inclusion was intended as a notable ecumenical gesture. The central part of the prayer petitions: "Pour out now on this your Elect that strength which is from you, the sovereign Spirit, which you gave to your beloved Son (Child = Servant) Jesus Christ, the Spirit he himself gave to the holy apostles who established the church in different places to the unceasing praise and glory of your name."[51] The final part of the prayer sums up the functions of the bishop, as shepherd of God's flock, as exercising the high priesthood, as offering the forgiveness of sins; he is to be gentle and clean of heart, and his life is to be the offering of a sweet savour to the Father, through the Son and the Holy Spirit.

The ordination prayer with the laying on of hands by the bishop and presbyters is the climax of the rite for ordaining priests. The formula used in the anointing expresses succinctly the meaning of the ordination prayer: "May our Lord Jesus Christ whom the Father anointed with power and the Holy Spirit keep you that you may sanctify the Christian people and offer sacrifices to God." The meaning of the ordination is expressed with great clarity in the questions the bishop puts to the candidates for priesthood. The priest has, under the bishop, a pastoral care for the people of God. He has the duty to proclaim the faith and to celebrate the sacraments, and he promises with God's help each day to enter into a closer union with Christ and with him to consecrate himself to God for the salvation of the people.

The homily in the ordination of the diaconate indicates that the deacon has a threefold ministry, of liturgy, of the Word, and of charity. In the liturgy he reads the Gospel, prepares the offerings, and also administers Communion. He also administers Baptism, assists at marriages, takes Communion to the sick and dying, and presides at

49. *Ibid.*, p. 144.
50. *Apostolic Tradition*, 3, p. 9.
51. Cited in Crichton, *Christian Celebration*, p. 145.

funeral services. He teaches the faithful and non-faithful alike and preaches at liturgical and non-liturgical services. In his ministry of charity he assists the bishop and the priests, though the duties are not specified. The ordination prayer, recalling the institution of the seven deacons of Acts 6:1-6, includes the invocation of the Holy Spirit: "Send, Lord, your Holy Spirit on these (candidates) that they may be strengthened by the gift of your sevenfold grace for the faithful execution of their ministry." The prayer ends by reminding the deacons that they are to care for the sick and the poor, to bear themselves modestly, and to lead a life of innocence and purity. Also since married deacons are included in the rite the previous commitment to chastity has been replaced by an injunction regarding "appropriate behaviour." The prayer ends with a view to mission: the deacon is to be like Christ, who came not to be served but to serve.

These are all impressive services notable for their Biblical references, their effective use of symbolism, their requirement of fidelity to Christ and continuing dependence upon the Holy Spirit. Only two criticisms that I am aware of have been offered about them. J. D. Crichton thinks that the Order for the priesthood, while rightly correlating the priest's role and putting it in the context of life and service, still lacks "sufficient emphasis on mission" because "there are few, if any countries in the world where the church is not in a missionary posture and vast numbers of priests are looking for inspiration and help to enable them to carry out the mission they believe is theirs."[52] Professor Paul Bradshaw approves in principle the ecumenical gesture of using a Hippolytus prayer from the *Apostolic Tradition* which is still used in the ordination rites of the Coptic and East Syrian Churches. He points out, however, that it is actually an expanded version of Hippolytus that is used in Eastern ordination rites (and, in the West Syrian case, in the consecration of a patriarch). He believes that it would have been a more effective ecumenical gesture to adopt the second Byzantine prayer for a bishop which is found in most other Eastern churches. He offers also another more serious criticism:

It is also regrettable that in every case the imposition of hands remains detached from the ordination prayer even when the rite is used for

52. *Ibid.,* p. 154.

only one person, and that ordination is still viewed largely as a purely clerical act: the lay people present at the ordination are explicitly described in the bishop's address as "the relatives and friends" of the ordinands and are not included in the exchange of the kiss at the end, though they do express assent to the bishop's choice of the candidates at the beginning of the rite.[53]

Dr. Bradshaw's criticisms are not picayune because he is the author of an important historical study of *The Anglican Ordinal,* published in 1971 and he teaches in a notable Roman Catholic University, Notre Dame, as a professor of liturgics.

If, however, one measures the new Roman rites of ordination as a whole, one can only admire the rescue of these rites from what Father J. D. Crichton described as "the topsy-turvy theology of orders which had been current since the early Middle Ages."[54] He also cites a Catholic liturgical scholar who described the former liturgy of the presbyterate as a *maquis presque impénétrable* (an almost impenetrable thicket).[55] The reduction to simplicity is an important achievement.

---

53. Bradshaw in *The Study of Liturgy,* pp. 397-98.
54. Crichton, *Christian Celebration,* p. 146.
55. *Ibid.,* p. 151.

CHAPTER VIII

THE LINGUISTIC CONTROVERSY

RECENT DECADES have witnessed much liturgical experimentation and consequently much controversy, but the most vehement arguments have been associated with two linguistic issues — inclusive language and contemporary language. Inclusive language has been made an issue by women who believe that both the patriarchal society from which the Biblical documents emerge, and the masculine names of two Persons of the Trinity in Christian theology have rendered women "invisible." The rallying cry of this group was formulated by Mary Daly in 1974 in the catch phrase: "Since God is male, the male is God."[1] This, says Professor Roland M. Frye, includes "the implied conclusion that the liberation of women requires the emasculation of God."[2] Professor Teresa Berger claims that "The background to this struggle is the androcentrism of the traditional (liturgical) language which rendered women invisible. This is now seen and recognized as incompatible with the equal dignity of women and men as created in the image of God." She adds: "As a consequence of this realization, we now refer, on a very basic level, to "brothers and sisters" instead of 'brothers'; we say 'men and women' instead of 'men' and 'mankind'; we speak of the 'sons and daughters' or 'the children of God' instead of the 'sons of God.'"[3] As we shall see, the inclusiveness is primarily concerned with gender, but not wholly so.

The second acute controversy is concerned with the struggle between advocates of the retention of the seventeenth century language of both the 1662 Book of Common Prayer and of the King James Bible and the passionate advocates of contemporary language in the

1. Daly, "The Qualitative Leap Beyond Patriarchal Religion," *Quest* 1 (1974): 21.

2. Frye, *Language for God and Feminist Language: Problems and Principles*, Report No. 3 (Princeton, N.J.: Center of Theological Inquiry, 1988), p. 3.

3. Berger, "Liturgical Language: Inclusivity and Exclusivity," *Studia Liturgica* 18 (1988): 132-33.

liturgy. As David and Ronald Jasper write in the introduction to their book, *Language and the Worship of the Church* (1980):

> Few things in recent years have engendered more passion than liturgical change in the various Christian Churches. What has become clear is the importance of familiar and well-loved forms of language to people. Words often repeated or sung in the context of particular liturgical actions represent a stability and a relationship with God and things of ultimate concern, to disturb which arouses the deepest passions.[4]

We shall consider these two problems of language in worship, inclusive language and contemporary language, in greater detail successively.

Inclusive Language

The bitterness of the inclusive language controversy has been caused to a large extent by the corrections which have been proposed by the feminists. Some feminists desire to substitute such terms as Creator, Liberator, and Comforter for the three Persons, Father, Son, and Holy Spirit, but these are functional not personal terms and therefore not equivalents. Yet others have suggested that Father and Mother should replace Father or that the terms be alternated, but this is not biblically acceptable and is also confusing.[5] Other feminists dislike references to the historic Jesus as Son of God or Son of Man and would prefer Child of God, which is, however, a rejection of the particularity of the Incarnation and substitutes vagueness for concreteness. It is also important to recognize that Judaism and Christianity, in contrast with other religions of their time, deny sexuality in their conception of God. Numbers 23:19 specifically denies sexuality in God in the phrase "God is not a man. . . ." Deuteronomy 4:15-16 clearly denies sexuality in God as it records the teaching of Moses: "On the day when the Lord spoke to you out of the fire on

---

4. Jasper and Jasper, *Language and the Worship of the Church* (London and New York: St. Martin's Press, 1990), p. vii.
5. See Gail Ramshaw Schmidt, "Lutheran Liturgical Prayer and God as Mother," *Worship* 52 (November 1978): 517-18.

Horeb you saw no figure of any kind; so take good care not to fall into the degrading practice of making figures carved in relief, in the form of a man or a woman : . ." (NEB).

Furthermore, Roland Frye rightly argues: "Combined words such as Father and Mother, Mother-Father, God-she, and he/she suggest a grotesque hermaphrodite god or androgynous divinity."[6] When it is proposed that God the Mother be added to the invocation of the Holy Trinity we have already become polytheistic and changed the Trinity to a Quadrinity.

Feminists have been quick to point out that the Bible does have passages where God is described in terms of motherhood, but these are all similes. In Isaiah 42:14 God is made to say: "Long have I lain still, I have kept silence and held myself in check; now I will cry like a woman in labour, whimpering, panting, and gasping . . ." (NEB). But there is no suggestion that God is a woman. Indeed, the previous verse had imaged him as a warrior. Also Isaiah 66:13 demonstrates the Lord in a simile as compassionate: "As one whom his mother comforteth, so will I comfort you; and you shall be comforted in Jerusalem." Other Biblical similes are avian in character, yet any suggestion that God is a bird would be blasphemous. For example, Deuteronomy 32:11 affirms that God's care for Israel is "as an eagle that stirs up her nest, that flutters over her young, he spread abroad his wings, he took them, he bore them on his pinions." The most moving of all such similes is used by Jesus as he expresses his profound compassion for Jerusalem: "How often would I have gathered your children together as a hen gathers her brood under her wings, but you would not."[7] This is a wonderful image of protection.

It is profoundly significant that God and Christ are said to be like a mother, but they are never called Mother in either Testament. Roland Frye reminds the reader: "References to God as Father . . . occur in every New Testament book with the sole exception of the brief epistle of III John. God is considered as Father about two hundred and fifty times in the two Testaments, and most often of course in the New."[8]

Yet while there is no need to change the orthodox theology of the Christian faith, there is an amplitude of reasons for changing the

6. Frye, *Language for God*, p. 7.
7. Matthew 23:37 and Luke 13:34.
8. Frye, *Language for God*, p. 6.

179

image of women in the language of liturgy, and this can be done with the appropriate use of inclusive language. For example, in the book written by Vivienne Faull and Jane Sinclair, *Count Us In — Inclusive Language in Liturgy*, the authors indicate that "A woman is a daughter of God, yet Romans 8:23 anticipates her adoption as a son."[9] They claim that although it is stated that God is "without body, parts, or passions" our God-language is overwhelmingly masculine. They properly affirm that Genesis 1:26-28 says that God created both male and female in his own image, and this stresses common humanity as prior to gender differences. Further, they add that according to Paul a Christianly animated society must always seek to ensure that "in Christ there is neither Jew nor Greek, slave nor free, male nor female."[10] They note that the Church of England has been slow to notice the inclusive revisions of liturgical texts that have already taken place in the U.S.A., Canada, and New Zealand, and point out, further, that in 1983 at the World Council of Churches Assembly in Vancouver, the language of the liturgy was notably inclusive. They do, however, acknowledge that in the Church of England's Lent, Holy Week, and Easter services there is evidence of avoiding the excessive use of masculine language; the congregation in the Easter Vigil is addressed as "brothers and sisters in Christ."[11] The rest of the book produces an admirable series of guidelines for the correction of excessively masculine affirmation in liturgy.

Dr. Brian Wren is one of the few men with the necessary empathy to analyze the destructive impact of excessive masculinity in God-language. He notes two elements in flawed maleness which cloud our picture of God. One is the importance of being in control, whether of emotion, people, events, the body, nature, ideas, or the feminine. The other is that maleness is often defined in terms that are scornful of femaleness and qualities thought of as feminine are downgraded and despised.[12] He elaborates the cost of control created by a patriarchate. "Patriarchate is characterized by divisions and oppositions based not on equality but subordination, not this-*with*-that but this-*over*-that: reason over emotion, soul over body, spirit over

---

9. Grove Liturgical Study No. 26 (Bramcote, Nottingham, 1986), p. 22.

10. *Ibid.*, p. 20.

11. *Ibid.*, p. 22.

12. *Wren, What Language Shall I Borrow? God-Talk in Worship: A Male Response to Feminist Theology* (New York: Crossroad, 1989), p. 13.

flesh, mind over matter, 'man' over nature, and men over women."[13] Wren continues his analysis by claiming that much of the traditional language of prayer emphasizes God's absolute control, as the King, God Almighty, Father, and Protector, to the neglect both of God's love and of human autonomy. He adds that the Christian experience of God is implicitly anti-patriarchal, since it sees God not as a single isolated Being but as complex co-equal unity in relatedness.[14] But he rightly warns against substituting neutral terms for inclusive language purposes. Amusingly, he proves his point by suggesting that "Parent me, O Great Sustainer, as I traverse the alienating institutions of industrial society" is a pathetic substitute for "Guide me, O Thou great Jehovah, pilgrim through this barren land."[15]

One of his hymns, "Bring Many Names,"[16] is more ingenious than convincing in that in successive verses he uses not similes but metaphors for God as Mother and God as Father. The second verse runs:

Strong mother God, working night and day,
planning all the wonders of creation,
    setting each equation,
    genius at play:
Hail and Hosanna,
strong mother God!

The third verse proceeds:

Warm father God, hugging every child,
feeling all the strains of human living,
    caring and forgiving
    till we're reconciled:
Hail and Hosanna,
warm father God!

It is ingenious in letting us see what we normally consider as masculine activities undertaken by the strong mother God, and normally

13. *Ibid.*, p. 32.
14. *Ibid.*, p. 134.
15. *Ibid.*, p. 135.
16. The hymn cited can be found in Wren's *What Language Shall I Borrow?* p. 169.

feminine concerns as marks of the warm Father God. But such calculated revision of Biblical metaphors is destructive of the Trinitarian theology he claims to believe in.

Having looked at the problem from the viewpoint of a very sympathetic man, we should now see it from the standpoint of a distinguished woman theologian, who first correlated exclusivity with creating the invisibility of women. She is Professor Susan Brooks Thistlethwaite, who writes:

> Inclusive language is born in the struggle of those who are linguistically invisible as they come to the recognition that their invisibility reflects and perpetuates the exclusivist basis of their society. When a corporation head decides to hire "the best man for the job," women have stopped wondering why they are not hired. Economic exclusivity depends on linguistic exclusivity. And lest we think that this is a problem of excluding only women, consider who the "man" is in the black community. The "man" is the white male boss. In terms of use, "man" is not only male; he's white and of the managerial class.[17]

Liturgical language clearly has to render women visible, but how can this be done? Professor Teresa Berger suggests that three means have been used in the attempt to produce inclusive God-talk. "The first is an attempt to rediscover and reclaim female 'counterparts' within the dominantly male tradition in order to create a balance of male and female pronouns and imagery." She cites one example of this in the following benediction: "The blessing of the God of Sarah and of Abraham, the blessing of the Son, born of the woman Mary, the blessing of the Holy Spirit who broods over us as a mother with her children, be with you all."[18] A second means excludes all male terminology in reference to God, which is, of course, based on a reversed exclusivity. But, as we shall see, there are better ways of creating inclusivity than this. The third means is to abstain completely from using male or female pronouns when referring to God. "The liturgy then speaks of God giving God's only Son (more

17. Thistlethwaite, "Inclusive Language and Linguistic Blindness," *Theology Today*, January 1987, p. 534.

18. Berger in "Liturgical Language," p. 134, where she cites the blessing included in I. Gjerding and E. Kinnamon, *No Longer Strangers: A Resource for Women and Worship* (Geneva: World Council of Churches, 1984), p. 45.

radically: God's only Child) or of God Godself delivering God's people out of bondage."[19] This, however, is dully repetitious and lacks specificity. Less radical ways must be found to repair the damage, which will avoid reverse exclusivity.

It may be constructive to consider what a single Communion, the Church of England, did about removing masculine exclusivity from its liturgy. It was first alerted to the invisibility of women in worship by Vivienne Faull and Jane Sinclair in *Count Us In* (1986). They pointed out that other Anglican Provinces were already removing male exclusivity from their liturgies. For example in 1985 the Canadian Church had modified the *Sursum Corda* by omitting the masculine pronoun so that it read "to give thanks and praise" omitting the customary "him." A year earlier the New Zealand Church made much the same kind of change. Then they suggested guidelines, which will be summarized. The first proposal was to use generic language for masculine terms (such as "people" or "all people" for "man" and instead of "he, him, his" to use "we," "their," "one," "the one," "the person," "the individual" or "someone"). They also proposed to avoid masculine terminology in generic groupings, recasting "clergymen" to read "ministers," "clergymen and women," or simply "clergy," and for "laymen" to substitute "laity" or "laypeople." They also proposed the use of "ancestors" or "forebears" for "forefathers" and suggested that "friends of Christ" or "brothers and sisters in Christ" replace "brothers in Christ." They also recommended avoidance of stereotyping with such terms as "the fair sex," "the weaker sex," or "the girls" when adult women are referred to, substituting "woman" or "the women." They particularly stressed the need to use women's names and not to refer to a woman as someone's wife, mother or daughter, for example, "Mr. Smith and his wife" might be rephrased as "Paul and Janet Smith."

These writers pointed out, also, the appalling paucity of female role models in the Calendar of greater and lesser festivals in *The Alternative Service Book* of 1980, which remembers eleven women and eighty-five men. They recommend using Scripture translations that avoid generic masculine terminology, such as the *New Jerusalem Bible*. Finally, they point out how depressing it is for a dominantly female congregation at the Eucharist to see several male celebrants and not a single woman is visible in the sanctuary area. In this single

19. Berger, "Liturgical Language," p. 134.

respect things will be assuredly better now that women can become priests in the Church of England.[20]

Two years later there was an official response from the Church of England in a report by its Liturgical Commission entitled *Making Women Visible: The Use of Inclusive Language with the ASB*.[21] The Introduction to this 1988 publication pointed out that over the previous decade sensitivity concerning the use of male terms to include both genders had arisen, with the result that the term "humanity" is preferred to "mankind," "astronaut" to "spaceman" and "chair" to "chairman," and so on. The word "sexist" now "applied to features of a given language that exclude, insult or trivialise women."[22] The report acknowledged that *The Alternative Service Book* uses exclusive language at three points: in the Nicene Creed where it reads "for us men and our salvation," and in two prayers in Rite A. The first asks "that men may honour one another and seek the common good" and the second that we be enabled "to live in love and peace with all men." Also the oddity in the Wedding service is mentioned where one prays that God would "give them grace to minister to others as you have ministered to men."

The book has a fine paragraph on the Gospel's affirmation on women:

Do not be afraid, Mary, for you have found favour with God (Luke 1:30). The incarnation itself depended for a moment on the response of a woman to God's declaration of grace. Jesus' first resurrection appearance was to another Mary, and in the way St. John's Gospel tells the story she stands for every Christian in their personal encounter with the risen Christ. It was to women that Jesus first entrusted the message of the Resurrection. Jesus gave women and children a status in the community of the people of God that was often denied them by the practice and teaching of his day.[23]

Later it is added that on the Day of Pentecost St. Peter provided striking evidence of the inclusive nature of Christ's Gospel in his use

---

20. These suggestions appear on pp. 26 and 27 of *Count Us In*.

21. *Making Women Visible*, issued by Church House Publishing of London.

22. This definition is taken from Deborah Cameron, *Feminism and Linguistic Theory* (New York: St. Martin's Press, 1985), p. 72.

23. *Making Women Visible*, p. 6.

of Joel 2:28-32, for it embraces not only the gender difference but distinctions of race, age, and social status. The book also welcomes the exploration of the Episcopal Church of the U.S.A. into identifying passages in Scripture and tradition that lay less emphasis on the masculine and also provide alternative names for God. One striking example is Psalm 18, which has many such alternatives names for God, each indicating a close personal relationship. There God is perceived by the Psalmist as: My Rock; My Stronghold; My Deliverer; My God; My Mountain; My Suzerain; My Redoubt; My Refuge; My Saviour; and the Horn of My Salvation.[24]

Because the issue of inclusive language is so controversial, the report asserts that it is "not reporting changes which *must* be made but aiming to provide the best alternatives in each case."[25] Pages 29 to 55 list "Suggested Alternatives" which might be adopted eventually at the local level. Some examples may be worth citing, not for being remarkable, but for being typical. In the Order for Holy Communion Rite A, the prayer that offers to God "thanks for all your goodness and loving kindness to us and to all men" simply omits "to us and all men." Another prayer confessing that "we have sinned against you and against all men" is altered to "against you and against our neighbour."[26] In the order for Holy Communion Rite B, the text "Glory be to God on high, and in earth peace, goodwill towards men" becomes "Glory be to God on high, and in earth peace to those of good will." The report suggests that other references to "all men" in Rite B Communion be changed to "everyone" and "the world," showing genuine flexibility in the alternatives.[27]

The book concludes with six pages of supplementary texts which use feminine images in introductory sentences, post-Communion texts, collects, canticles, and a responsive prayer. The latter is entitled A Litany of New Birth and warrants citation:

O gracious God of life and birth.
How you labour, how you suffer, to bring forth the new creation!
Indeed, you cry out like a woman in childbirth.
And your Spirit groans within us.

24. *Ibid.*, p. 7.
25. *Ibid.*, p. 23.
26. *Ibid.*, p. 30.
27. *Ibid.*, pp. 31 and 35-36.

But your cries become cries of joy,
as you behold fragile new life there before you.
All creation waits with eager longing for the revealing
of your daughters and sons;
We ourselves long to take part in the glorious liberty
of your children.
Who can separate us from the love of God?
Even a mother might forsake us!
O God our God, how wonderful is your name in all the earth![28]

Inclusive language changes, as we have seen, have largely concerned themselves with de-emphasizing masculinity, but other kinds
of "exclusivity" have also been challenged. True inclusivity requires
the elimination of racial slurs, insensitive references to handicapped
persons, and concepts such as imperialism that are at odds with
Christian commitment to peace. Professor Robert A. Bennett, a
member of the Inclusive Language Lectionary Committee issued a
significant warning. He claimed that church tradition, allied with
culture and theology, forges another link in the chain of exclusivity
in emphasizing male dominance and female subordination, light and
dark color symbolism, and the acceptance of physical impairment as
indicators of sinfulness. This becomes even more fixed when certain
texts are associated with special occasions in the liturgy, "such as the
reading of Ephesians 5 on female submission as part of the marriage
liturgy or the reading of Proverbs 31:10-31 on the dutiful housewife
for female religious figures."[29] In the same way we must be careful
not to encourage anti-Semitism by giving the impression that the
Jewish nation betrayed and crucified Christ. Norms in language and
in racial or ethnic self-identification change and must be carefully
watched by a Church wishing to be truly inclusive.

Archaic vs. Contemporary Language

Another hotly disputed issue in the sphere of language is that which
divides linguistic conservatives, deeply attached to the traditional
language of the Book of Common Prayer of 1662, from the mod-

28. *Ibid.*, p. 62, adapted from *No Longer Strangers*.
29. "The Power of Language in Worship," *Theology Today*, January 1987, p. 549.

186

ernists who are convinced that such archaic language will prevent the young and the outsiders from ever becoming insiders. There is also a group in the middle which believes in the use of modern language, but finds much of recent liturgical composition prosaic, dull, unrhythmical and lacking in images.

A most interesting observation on this issue was made by the Dean of Norwich, the Very Revd. Michael Perham. He holds that the contestants in the "Thou/You" controversy have different views about God: "One who wants to address God in a special language, to make him separate and, by implication, 'above' all others, is saying something about his theology. His view of God is different from one who wants to address God more intimately, to regard him as a readily approachable being. It is clear that the latter view accords more with the pattern Jesus gave...."[30] The Dean, while insisting that language and theology should be contemporary, warns that it should avoid being merely conversational or like that of a modern tabloid newspaper. Of the language of *The Alternative Service Book 1980* he writes that it has "a distinctive style, crisp and clear, as attractive and compelling as any" and he points out that most of its unhappy phrases are the consequences of "instant amendments by revision committees and on the floor of Synod, sometimes destroying the painstakingly creative work of the authors."[31]

David Crystal, in a fascinating essay on "Liturgical Language in a Sociolinguistic Perspective," declares that "no imposed liturgical change has ever affected so many people at once as when Latin was replaced by the vernacular in Roman Catholic Christianity. A similar impact, but on a smaller scale was felt when the Series III texts were introduced into the liturgy of the Church of England." The main difference was to stress the perceived difference of liturgical language, which in the new productions was objected to as "everyday," "mundane," and "lacking in variety." Actually, the change was very considerable. It involved, in Crystal's analysis, special grammatical words and inflections, such as: "thou," "thee," "ye," "art," "wilt," "unto," "-(e)th," "-(e)st," "spake," "brethren," etc. There were also special lexical words: "thrice," "behold," "vouchsafe," "whence," "henceforth," "thence," etc. There were also vocative namings with O, such as "O God, who . . ." as well as vocative structures, without O, especially in direct address with adjective plus noun in direct

30. Perham, *Liturgy Pastoral and Parochial* (London: S.P.C.K., 1984), p. 22.
31. *Ibid.*, p. 23.

address, such as "eternal Father" or "dear Lord," or a noun with a postmodifying relative clause, as in "Lamb of God, who takest away the sins of the world. . . ." Also there were imperative or subjunctive verbs, such as "go thou," "glory be to the Father," or "praise be. . . ." Then there was also unusual word order, frequently following an archaic or Latin construction, such as: "he having eaten went . . ." and "whom, when he saw, he walked." Furthermore, there were distinctive idioms such as "who livest and reignest" and "through the same Jesus Christ. . . ." In the new rites they have almost entirely disappeared, with the single vocative construction remaining as a relic and testimonial of the previous linguistic age.[32] This analysis makes liturgical language of the Book of Common Prayer seem extraordinarily archaic, as to be only intelligible to insiders and to be clearly a missionary obstacle in the way of commending the Christian faith.

The Church of England's Commission on Worship, acutely aware of the problem of dated language, provided the following guidelines in its report, *Patterns for Worship:*

1. Use concrete visual images rather than language which is conceptual and full of ideas.
2. Avoid Latin-style construction with dependent clauses.
3. If there is a choice, prefer the word with fewer syllables.
4. Address God as You.
5. Keep sentences as short as possible. Use full stops rather than semicolons.
6. Use language that includes women as well as men.
7. Watch the rhythm. The language should be rhythmic and flow easily, but take care not to have a repetitive poetic 'dum-de-dum'.
8. Liturgical language should not be stark or empty. It is not wrong to repeat ideas or say the same thing twice in different words. Cranmer realized that people need time and repetition to make the liturgy their own. We need to do it, however, without a string of dependent clauses.
9. Be prepared to throw it away after using it, and to do it differently next time.[33]

32. Jasper and Jasper, *Language and the Worship of the Church*, pp. 132-33.
33. *Patterns for Worship* (London: Church House Publishing, 1989), p. 49.

This was excellent advice, but like all the best advice it was difficult to accept.

Dean Ronald Jasper in his *Development of the Anglican Liturgy, 1662-1980* included in Chapter 13 the history of the modernizing of liturgical language. The difficulty of the issue had been presented in *The Language of the Book of Common Prayer* (1965) by Dr. Stella Brook who saw the difficulty as caused by the divorce between the spoken and written styles of twentieth century English. The written style had deteriorated into an artificial stylized idiom and used a vocabulary which was no longer a genuine part of living speech. Spoken English had deteriorated also and in the process it had become slipshod, using vague catchwords and a very restricted vocabulary. All this would make a good liturgical style difficult to develop, for liturgy needed to reach the heart and mind of the worshipper and to express profundities in a style combining dignity and comeliness.

In 1968 *Modern Liturgical Texts* was published as a document for discussion, with alternatives provided for some texts. It comprised four sets of materials. First there were the Common Texts: the Lord's Prayer, the *Gloria in excelsis*, the Nicene and Apostles' Creeds, and the four main Canticles. Secondly were added the metrical canticles and their tunes, which had been prepared by C. Day Lewis, the poet, and Alan Ridout. Thirdly, there was a "You" form of the Series Two Baptism and Confirmation Services, chiefly the work of David Ayerst, Elisabeth Montefiore, and Stella Brook. Fourthly, there was a "You" form of the Series Two Holy Communion Service which was completely the work of Geoffrey Cuming.[34] Perhaps the most important contribution for the future was the inclusion in the booklet of six principles governing the approach of the Liturgical Commission to modern liturgical language. These were as follows:

1. Translation of *sense* is prior to translation of words.
2. Modern language requires the removal of all archaic words and, in most cases, of esoteric words.
3. "Thou" and its cognates have been eliminated.
4. Subject to the requirements of theological accuracy, Anglo-Saxon words have been preferred to Latin ones.

34. Jasper, *Development of the Anglican Liturgy, 1662-1980* (London: S.P.C.K., 1989), pp. 291-92.

5. Relative and other dependent clauses have been avoided in favour of co-ordinate main clauses.

6. Self-consistency between the . . . texts has been kept in view.[35]

The reception given by the Lambeth Conference of 1968 to these texts was extremely encouraging, since it was generally acknowledged that "You" forms marked an "irresistible trend." Indeed, after 1968 "You" forms became invariable in all the new rites in the Anglican Communion.[36]

The task was both long and difficult, but helped by the fact that it was undertaken not only by the Liturgical Commission of the Church of England, but also by the Joint Liturgical Group, and Jasper was the Chairman of both groups. Perhaps relative clauses in the Collects provided the greatest obstacles to revision and it is worth mentioning the solutions which were adopted. These were four:

1. The use of a different kind of relative clause — "Almighty God, whose Son Jesus Christ fasted" (Lent 1).
2. The use of the past definite tense — "Almighty God, who anointed Jesus at his Baptism" (Epiphany 1).
3. The substitution of a statement — "Almighty God, you have knit together your elect" (All Saints).
4. The substitution of a noun in apposition — "Lord of all power and might, the author and giver" (Pentecost 17).[37]

As a result some seventy of the Prayer Book Collects were revised in such a way as to retain in whole or in part their familiar wording.

Almost all this considerable work of revision found its way into the *Alternative Service Book 1980*. As an example of its dignity, simplicity, and comeliness I cite the following words from its First Eucharistic Prayer:

As we eat and drink these holy gifts
in the presence of your divine majesty,
renew us by your Spirit,
inspire us with your love,

35. *Modern Liturgical Texts*, p. 4.
36. Jasper, *Development of the Anglican Liturgy, 1662-1980*, p. 293.
37. *Ibid.*, p. 305.

and unite us in the body of your Son,
Jesus Christ our Lord.

Through him, and with him, and in him,
by the power of the Holy Spirit,
with all who stand before you in earth and heaven,
we worship you, Father almighty,
in songs of everlasting praise:

All: Blessing and honour and glory and power be yours
for ever and ever. Amen.[38]

In conclusion, this chapter has unveiled for us not only the patriarchal context of the society in which the Bible was produced, but also the magisterial figure of a Christ, who demonstrated respect for the dignity of women and children. We have witnessed a struggle to rectify masculine exclusivity in Christian liturgy as in life and have also seen the Liturgical Commission of the Church of England striving to modernize the language of the liturgy. This latter task has been ecumenically assisted by the work of the Joint Liturgical Group for the benefit of all the English-speaking Churches, many of which, unlike the Church of England, have had women ministers for decades. Above all, in the repairing of liturgical insensitivity to persons of other races, to the physically and socially handicapped, and to the dispossessed, as well as to women stereotyped, scorned, or ignored to the point of invisibility, we see the rectifying and compassionate power of *agape*, the very love of Christ himself animating his modern disciples in improving their liturgy.

Perhaps a hopeful indication of the shape of things to come may be the citation of two inclusive eucharistic prayers which admirably illustrate their desire for active verbs instead of cerebral propositions, multiple short responses or acclamations, and the use of feminine approaches in language:

The president declares:

Can a mother forget her own children?
Tenderly she gathers them to herself.
So again Lord you have embraced us. . . .

38. *ASB*, p. 132.

and a little later the president continues:

Glorious God,
Your bride awaits
in loyalty and faith!
With all who serve you,
with all who have gone before,
with apostles, prophets,
saints and martyrs,
we unite to praise and thank you.[39]

---

39. David J. Kennedy and David Mann, *Making the Eucharistic Prayer Work*, Grove Worship Series, No. 103 (Bramcote, Nottingham, 1988), p. 24. The prayer was prepared by both authors.

CHAPTER IX

LITURGICAL SYMBOLISM

THERE ARE THREE main reasons why liturgical symbolism has in recent decades become a subject of major concern. The first is that the Liturgical Movement has awakened many Protestant denominations to the poverty of symbols in their worship; worship reduced to the exchange of spoken words, excluding the material and the sensory, has often produced verbose, abstract, intellectualistic, or merely notional services. The second reason for reconsideration has been the radical revision of the worship of the Roman Catholic Church since Vatican II with the acknowledgment that several of their rites were cluttered with irrelevant secondary symbolism that overshadowed the significance of the primary symbols. The third reason relates to the remarkably widespread cultural reaction against the rationalism of the Enlightenment and the domination of science; psychologists, sociologists, anthropologists, philosophers, and historians of religion have begun to re-evaluate symbolism as a means of conveying truth.

The poverty of symbolism of Protestant worship was brilliantly exposed by a Baptist minister, Stephen F. Winward, in an essay entitled "Embodied Worship."[1] He starts by pointing out that our Christian worship derives its distinctive character from the Incarnation of the Word of God (John 1:14) and that embodied worship responds to the nature of humans who are not pure but embodied spirits. Their inner devotion requires outward expression in words and deeds which include the body, make use of matter, and are perceptible to the senses. He suggests that a saying of Christ to the woman at the well of Sychar — "God is spirit and those who worship him must worship him in spirit and in truth" — is misinterpreted to suggest the Hellenistic contrast between the material and the spiritual, and in consequence true Christian worship is thought to be immaterial. From the outset he claims that "two acts,

---

1. In *The Renewal of Worship: Essays by Members of the Joint Liturgical Group,* ed. R. C. D. Jasper (London: Oxford University Press, 1965), pp. 42-57.

193

baptism and the Lord's Supper, instituted by the Lord himself, were at the heart of primitive Christian worship. Incorporation, and the renewal of life in Christ were inseparably associated with the material (water, bread, wine), with action (washing, eating, drinking), with symbol, ceremony and sacrament."[2] Historically Protestantism reacted against the excessive elaboration of ceremony in medieval Catholicism with its extensive processions, multiplied gestures and bows, crossings and genuflections, so that especially under Zwingli in Zurich, art and beauty, symbol and image, lights and eucharistic vestments, instrumental music and choirs, gestures and ceremonies were totally abolished. Winward urges, "Open eyes as well as open ears may be engaged in the worship of God."[3] He then turns to the ceremonial element in worship, pointing out that a symbol is not necessarily a material object but may be an action. If a crucifix is a symbol, so also is the breaking of a loaf at the Lord's Supper. The appropriate gestures for prayer are kneeling or standing. Christ stood to pray (Mark 11:25) and assumed that his disciples would imitate him. In the early Church bowing to an object or a person was a silent sign of submission and respect. "The kiss of peace" now common in many churches is the symbol of friendship and involves the clasping of hands. Other examples of symbolic gestures in worship include at the beginning of worship the carrying of the Bible by a church officer, preceding the minister appointed to read and expound it in the service of the Word, and the offertory as the stewards bring forward the gifts symbolizing the gratitude of God's people. The most important elements in embodied worship, the sacraments, are both symbol and ceremony. He pleads for the recovery of the unity of Word and Sacrament, now generally accepted in Protestantism, but also insists on the correlation of the fellowship, the action, and the material elements in worship.[4] In denying the material we diminish the sacrament of Communion, for the action of breaking the bread is important and "the use of manufactured wafers and tiny cubes of bread is to be deplored." Similarly the sprinkling of a few drops of water on the face denudes the sacrament of Baptism. His conclusion is: "The false antithesis between the spiritual and the material, the soul and the body, must be overcome,

2. *Ibid.*, p. 44.
3. *Ibid.*, p. 50.
4. *Ibid.*, p. 55.

if we are to recover biblical wholeness. The inward and the outward components of worship must not by man be put asunder, for God himself has joined them together."[5]

The exaggeration of the ceremonial and the over-extension of secondary symbolism in Roman Catholic worship has been corrected in the Church's most recent rites. Monsignor Crichton in his book *Christian Celebration: Understanding the Sacraments* finds the maintenance of the symbolism of oil dubious, since while olive oil may be an important component of life in some areas, in most parts of the world it is not. "It does not help very much to be told that Greek athletes anointed themselves with olive oil to give strength and suppleness to their limbs. For as soon as you have to be told that this 'signified' that, you are being told at the same time that the symbol is dead."[6] He adds that it is difficult to see any justification for the continued use of anointing before baptism. "As we have seen," he adds, "originally it meant an anointing for the struggle against Satan and the whole body was anointed. What significance can a dab of oil on the chest of a wriggling infant have?"[7] The same author insists that both the institution (the church) and the rite in worship can become opaque:

> The one can be complicated, weighed down with legalism appearing to be an end in itself and, since the institution is a people, it can be defaced by all the sins and follies of humankind. The rite can become encrusted with non-functional elements, it can degenerate into the meaningless performance that is called ritualism, it too can appear to be an end in itself.[8]

The third reason for the positive re-evaluation of symbolism has been provided by philosophers, psychologists, sociologists, anthropologists, and historians of religion, and it requires fuller consideration than this chapter has room to provide. Hence it will be treated with the utmost reasonable brevity. In the Biblical world it is clear that a symbol was understood as a vehicle that mediated to the

5. *Ibid.,* p. 55.
6. J. D. Crichton, *Christian Celebration: Understanding the Sacraments,* 3rd ed. (London: Geoffrey Chapman, 1993), p. 21.
7. *Ibid.,* p. 25.
8. *Ibid.,* p. 10.

community the significance of life in society, and even in the entire cosmos. The symbol was also understood to participate in the reality that it represented and even also to mediate that reality to those who participated in the symbol. Some sense of this complex interrelationship has been recovered in the late nineteenth and the twentieth century.

Among the pioneers in this recovery were Ernst Cassirer and Susanne Langer among philosophers,[9] and more recently Paul Ricoeur, a phenomenologist.[10] Mircea Eliade, a historian of religion, highlighted the importance of the symbolic in ancient and modern religion.[11] The psychoanalysts, such as Freud and Jung, showed how in the unconscious symbols had a profound impact in forming human personality.[12] Social anthropologists such as Clifford Geertz, Victor Turner, and Mary Douglas, demonstrated the importance of symbols for understanding human society.[13] Outstanding social thinkers such as Max Weber, Emile Durkheim, and Karl Marx as well as a recent thinker Robert Bellah, have explored the relationship of symbols and society.[14] The implications of the contribution of these thinkers for worship have been admirably shown in Professor William R. Crockett's *Eucharist: Symbol of Transformation.*[15] According to his analysis these writers deal with two aspects of symbolism: one is the *meaning*

9. See Ernst Cassirer, *The Philosophy of Symbolic Forms,* 3 vols. (New Haven: Yale University Press, 1953-1957); Susanne K. Langer, *Philosophy in a New Key: A Study in the Symbolism of Reason, Rite, and Art,* 3rd ed. (Cambridge, Massachusetts: Harvard University Press, 1957).

10. See Ricoeur, "The Symbol . . . Food for Thought," *Philosophy Today* 5 (1960): 196-207; and *The Symbolism of Evil* (New York: Harper & Row, 1967).

11. Eliade, *Images and Symbols* (London: Harvill, 1961); and *The Sacred and the Profane: The Nature of Religion* (New York: Harcourt Brace & World, 1959).

12. See Sigmund Freud, *A General Introduction to Psychoanalysis* (New York: Washington Square Press, 1952), chapter 10. See also Carl G. Jung, *Man and His Symbols* (New York: Dell Publishing Co., 1968).

13. See Clifford Geertz, "Ethos, World-View and the Analysis of Sacred Symbols," *Antioch Review* 17 (1957-1958): 421-37; and "Religion as a Cultural System," in *Anthropological Approaches to the Study of Religion,* ed. M. Banton (London: Tavistock, 1966). For an introduction to Turner with primary bibliography, see Mary Collins, "Ritual Symbols and the Ritual Process: The Work of Victor W. Turner," *Worship* 50 (1976): 336-46.

14. See Robert N. Bellah, "Christianity and Symbolic Realism," *Journal for the Scientific Study of Religion* 9 (1970): 89-96.

15. William R. Crockett, *Eucharist: Symbol of Transformation* (New York: Pueblo Publishing Co., 1989). See especially chapter 7, "Contemporary Perspectives."

of symbols as a phenomenon in human culture, and the other the psychological or social *function* of symbols; Crockett names these aspects, respectively, the "symbolic-realist" and the "sociological."[16]

The "symbolic realists" insist that symbolism has an integrity of its own and must not be subsumed into other categories because they function in different ways. Symbols may contain religious, philosophical, esthetic, psychological, and socio-political meanings, but cannot be reduced to any of these meanings or functions. Among the sociologists and functionalists Durkheim and Weber saw that religious symbolism has a transforming power. They recognized, as Bloch did, that religion with its charismatic leaders, proposes an utopian and transformative power for the amelioration of society.[17]

Definitions

In order for liturgy to become intelligible it uses actions or gestures as well as words to convey multiple messages. These are sometimes suggested by the objects themselves and their uses; the gestures and actions and their associations also convey meanings, and the terms for these are usually named "signs" or "symbols."

At the outset of this section it may be worth pointing out that the human language through which we communicate with one another differs when used in different contexts. In the context of everyday use, our aim is to avoid any ambiguity; and in this setting a knife is solely a cutting instrument, a chair is intended to be sat upon, or a glass is a container of liquid. In the context of natural science, mathematical symbols, the table of chemical elements, and other related terminology all eradicate multiplicity of meanings for the sake of exactitude and clarity. In a third context, to which poetry and liturgy both belong, delight is taken in polysemous language, because it is capable of enriching thought and affections as well as indicating ethical values. A simple non-theological example of such language would be the description of the Union Jack flying over the Houses of Parliament in London. It recalls past history, gives the

16. *Ibid.*, pp. 237-38.

17. It is interesting to learn from William Crockett (p. 247) that Jurgen Moltmann was greatly influenced by the "warm Communist" Ernst Bloch in the writing of his important *Theology of Hope.*

passers-by some sense of national pride, and reveals that the governing body is still in session.

The central symbols of the sacraments, as we shall see, are also polysemous, which lends them richness, but can also contribute to both confusion and obfuscation of their central significance. Liturgy incorporates a melange of metaphors. Many of its understandings are metaphoric, expressing likenesses where there are also significant differences between the two objects or actions combined. This is necessarily so because of the fact that God, who is utterly other and transcendent, has made us in his own image. He has, furthermore, in the second person of the Trinity, become incarnate, identifying radically with humanity. It is his own incarnation, his "embodiment," that grounds the central series of convictions in Christian worship and Christian life, as embodied faith.

One example of the polysemous nature of liturgical metaphor is provided by the manifold significance of "bread" in the Eucharist as analyzed by Father David Power:

> In the eucharist the word and thing "bread" must have a demonstrable reference to what common sense recognizes as such a substance, but the meaning depends on its cultural and traditional polysemy. Bread feeds, but it also gathers. It may be taken or it may be given. There is the bread that nourishes, the bread that delights, and the bread of affliction. In the tradition there is the bread that David took from the tabernacle, the bread of manna in the desert, the bread of the Jewish Pasch, the bread that Jesus broke with the disciples, and the bread that he promised for the life of the world. When the bread of the Lord's Supper functioned only as a thing to be swallowed, but not broken, chewed or shared, when the semantic context referred to it only as the body of Christ to be eaten or adored, the richness of multiple meanings was lost.[18]

There is a radical difference between signs that are used for organizational and functional purposes, and those which touch on the meanings of things. The former are usually termed "signs" and the latter are termed "symbols."

It is worth considering the definition of sacred symbols provided

18. Power, *Unsearchable Riches: The Symbolic Nature of Liturgy* (New York: Pueblo Publishing Co., 1984), p. 65.

by Professor Clifford Geertz, a social anthropologist deeply interested in religion. "Sacred symbols," he writes, "relate an ontology and a cosmology to an aesthetics and a morality; their peculiar power comes from their presumed ability to identify fact and value at the most fundamental level, to give what is otherwise merely actual a comprehensive moral import."[19] Father David Power observes that there are two levels of signification involved in the designation of places and times, persons or actions as "holy." At one level (to adopt terms made famous by Rudolph Otto in his *The Idea of the Holy*) the holy is represented as *wholly* other, a *mysterium tremendum et fascinans*, repelling because it inspires awe and even dread and fear, but also attracting because it enraptures and promises happiness through communion with it. At another level, according to Power, the holy offers and evokes through its symbols its ultimacy and its ability to grant *wholeness* to persons and societies who acknowledge it as the ultimately supreme power in human life.[20]

It is worth noting that while other religions are profoundly concerned with cosmic events, such as the struggle of a primeval god or divine hero, or of battles between gods and demons, Christianity on the contrary is content to explain its significance in terms of everyday objects and often commonplace experiences. It refuses to accept the Greek's radical contrast between the spiritual and the physical or material. Indeed, as Archbishop William Temple claimed:

> Christianity is the most materialistic of all great religions. The others hope to achieve spiritual reality by ignoring matter — calling it illusion *(maya)* or saying that it does not exist . . . Christianity, based as it is on the Incarnation, regards matter as destined to be the vehicle and instrument of spirit, and spirit as fully actual as far as it controls and directs matter.[21]

Both in the teaching of Jesus and in the sacraments of initiation and Eucharist which he transmitted to his disciples, Christian symbolism utilizes everyday objects and common experiences in the majority of cases. The things used are commonplace: bread, wine, water, and oil.

19. Geertz, *The Interpretation of Cultures* (New York: Basic Books, 1973), pp. 127-28.

20. Power, *Unsearchable Riches*, p. 75.

21. *Readings in St. John's Gospel* (London: Macmillan, 1955), pp. xx-xxi.

Even the actions associated with them are diurnal and homely, indications of concern, caring, and nurturing. These include breaking bread, pouring out wine, bathing, touching, and salving with oil (in the sacraments of initiation and healing). Father Power warns that they lose their effectiveness and their significance in the liturgy when they are instrumentalized — when they are seen as a means only of guaranteeing grace (in the *ex opera operantis* approach) or even as a means only of establishing community order, such as when the cup is not freely given to all participants.[22]

Using Susanne Langer's clarification in part, Robert Browning and Roy Reed in their book, *The Sacraments in Religious Education and Liturgy: An Ecumenical Model* (1985), observe that in trying to communicate about God's actions we use both signs and symbols, but at the deepest level we use symbols. Generally speaking, signs need to be very precise — like the blowing of a whistle or waving of a flag to indicate that a train is ready to leave the station. But in the case of symbols, according to Professor Langer, what is conveyed is the conception of the thing, not the thing itself.[23] Langer believed that there was no one-to-one correspondence between the symbol and the conception, but to prevent the conception being purely arbitrary there are patterns of correspondence between the symbol and the conception.

Paul Tillich, however, asserted that it is the very essence of a religious symbol that it actually participates in the power it symbolizes. He held very firmly that "symbols open us, so to speak, in two directions — in the direction of reality and in the direction of the mind."[24] Dr. F. W. Dillistone in his important book, *Christianity and Symbolism,* dealt with Carl Jung's view of the power of symbols — heroes, child prodigies, the virgin, the witch, the force of evil, and the saving element — and their power to reach the unconscious depths of the human psyche. He agreed that the power of the archetypes was too intense to be rendered negative by any process of deliberate exclusion. His conclusion was: "If they are not sanctified with the Christian context they will almost certainly present themselves in demonic forms."[25]

22. Power, *Unsearchable Riches,* p. 96.
23. Langer, *Philosophy in a New Key* (Cambridge, Massachusetts: Harvard University Press, 1942), p. 25.
24. Tillich, "Theology and Symbolism," in *Religious Symbolism,* ed. F. Ernest Johnson (Port Washington, New York: Kennikat Press, 1955), p. 110.
25. Dillistone, *Christianity and Symbolism* (London: Collins, 1955), p. 187.

200

It is important to realize how significant symbolic gestures are. Professor Franz Leenhardt of the University of Geneva in his thoughtful book, *Parole Visible,* contrasts spoken and gestural language in the context of the Sacraments.[26] He observes that while words have preeminence in communication, words are not always understood by all. They are also slow and analytic and important words are often lost in phraseology. Furthermore, the very precision of words can sometimes cut or mutilate reality. By contrast, the gesture is rapid and synthetic and frequently suggests more than it says.

Just as the word distinguishes itself from noise by means of certain locutions and grammar, so does the gesture transmit meaning with reference to a code translating an intention. Much of the gestural code is comparable to onomatopoeia; it borrows its meaning directly from the gesture itself. A raised fist is a threat; a vigorous gesture in the direction of the door says "Get out" more quickly than words. Open arms invite and express the attitude of union and communion.[27] In the liturgy (as in a concert or a stage performance) standing for the reading of the Gospel is a sign of profound respect, while kneeling at the altar for reception of the sacred elements is a sign of deep reverence, as is making the sign of the cross — the token of our redemption through Christ.

Professor Franz Leenhardt insists that the sacraments of the Gospel, Baptism, and the Lord's Supper are tied to the life of Christ Jesus. "One could say," he adds, "that they are the continuation, also like the preaching of the Church, of the life of Christ, but they raise more directly the register of the visible, the sensible, the corporeal."[28] He also adds that the two sacraments of Baptism and the Supper take their meaning from the sacrament par excellence — the incarnate life of the Word of God in Jesus of Nazareth. The two decisive moments of this life are found in their sacramental translation: the initial hour of the baptism of Jesus by John founds the baptismal sacrament; the last hour of the last meal of Jesus with his disciples is the foundation of the eucharistic sacrament. Leenhardt powerfully

---

26. Leenhardt, *Parole Visible* (Neuchâtel: Delachaux et Niestlé, 1972).

27. *Ibid.,* p. 28.

28. *Ibid.,* p. 75. The French original reads: "on pourrait dire qu'ils en sont le prolongement, comme l'est aussi la prédication de l'Eglise, mais ils relèvent plus directement du registre du visible, du sensible, du corporel."

201

insists that "beside the saying of the sermon, there is place for a gestural statement, which goes back to the same historic act of God in Jesus Christ, and which expresses the same intention with regard to the destiny of humankind. As Jesus is the author of the Word, so Jesus the founder of the sacramental gestures is today the actor of these gestures." He regrets that in the contemporary church the assurance that Jesus performs these gestures to associate believers more closely with himself has been weakened and often totally effaced.[29]

Leenhardt believes that these sacraments of Baptism and Eucharist should not be regarded as the cause of grace but rather as channels for the mediation of grace. Otherwise serious misinterpretations occur. A common error made by both Catholics and Protestants is to conceive of grace as a kind of substance, a sort of spiritual fluid to be poured into a waiting receptacle. Such a view may be attributed to two common causes. One is the natural and all too common tendency to conceive personal realities in the mode of physical realities. As Leenhardt points out, it can be corrected by distinguishing what the natural element is and the service to which it is devoted in the sacramental action. It is essential to acknowledge that the material *mediates* an intention conveyed through the material employed.[30] The second common error is to treat the metaphorical language of the New Testament as if it were literal or physical in meaning. For example, the Holy Spirit is invisible, but is likened to the wind or the breath in the use of the term *pneuma*. It is important to recognize that as the Spirit is the Holy Spirit, no man can ever control, channel, or divert it. If it has been in the past the error of Roman Catholicism to confound the personal message with the concrete mechanisms which permit the transmission of the message and to give the credit for the transmission of grace to the Church or the hierarchy or the priesthood, the error of Protestantism, always so concerned for the Word, is that it has often forgotten that the Word is always incarnated or embodied in some manner. Other ways of weakening the power of the sacraments, such as the incorporation of too much secondary symbolism, will be considered later. Meanwhile the multiple meanings of the major sacraments will be investigated.

29. *Ibid.,* pp. 79-80.
30. *Ibid.,* p. 31.

The Polysemous Sacraments

The richness of the significance of the sacraments is in their visual and dramatic character and the many meanings that they suggest to the devoted and attentive worshipper.

Consider, for example, the significance of water in Baptism. In the world of the New Testament water was seen as the very source of life, especially critical because of the arid desert landscape of the Middle East. As Monsignor J. D. Crichton writes: "Until comparatively recently water was an element whose significance was understood by everyone. But since it has been tamed, tanked, and tapped and is available at will, people treat it as they do electric power. It is always there: you just turn the tap and it comes."[31] Yet for thousands of years in Palestine it was the source and symbol of life; without it men and women and children would surely die.

But water had other meanings, too. In several other cultures water has been seen as a symbol of regeneration and new life — whether it was the sacred river Lethe, or a spring, or a sacred bath. The latter is clearly the image behind Ephesians 5:25-27: "Husbands love your wives, as Christ also loved the church and gave himself up for it, to consecrate it, cleansing it by water and word, so that he might present the church to himself all glorious, with no stain or wrinkle or anything of the sort, but holy and without blemish" (NEB). Its cleansing and purifying power has led the candidate of Baptism into a new life. And the same concept lies behind Romans 6:3-4 which asserts a change from death into life: "Have you forgotten that when we were baptized into union with Christ Jesus we were baptized into his death? By baptism we were buried with him, and lay dead, in order that as Christ was raised from the dead in the splendour of the Father, so we might also set our feet upon the new path of life" (NEB). In the last citation St. Paul clearly seems to be assuming Baptism by immersion and that suggests a further symbolism in Baptism, namely drowning, for water brings death. The Christian symbolically follows Christ from death to life in the immersion of Baptism. The symbolism of death and rebirth is very powerful also in the Synoptic Gospels, which recognize total immersion as a sign of the death of the old ego, as in Mark 10:38 and Luke 12:49, where Christ declares:

---

31. Crichton, *Christian Celebration: Understanding the Sacraments*, 3rd ed. (London: Geoffrey Chapman, 1993), p. 16.

"I have come to set fire to the earth, and how I wish it were already kindled! I have a baptism to undergo, and what constraint I am under until the ordeal is over!" Baptism meant for Christ and his disciples a radical revolution in their values, the death of egotism, and the commitment to walk in the paths of the Beatitudes. Baptism was the tomb of the old life and the womb of the new life.

Many baptismal prayers mention the religious importance of water in salvation history. For example, the United Reformed Church in its first major Baptismal prayer begins thus:

> Almighty God,
> through water you bring us bountiful love.
> In the beginning
> your Spirit moved over the face of the waters
> bringing order out of chaos;
> with the waters of the flood
> you cleansed the world,
> and through the Red Sea and across the Jordan
> you led your people to the land of promise.
> By the life and death of your Son
> and by his mighty resurrection and ascension
> you have given us the assurance
> that healing waters will flow from him for all nations.

The prayer continues with images of cleansing and new birth:

> We pray that A . . . , who is washed in this water,
> may be made one with Christ in his death,
> cleansed from all sin
> and delivered from all evil.
> Send your Holy Spirit upon A . . .
> for new birth in the family of your Church,
> and raise him/her with Christ to full and eternal life.[32]

It is important to contrast the act of Baptism in the first century A.D. with its contemporary celebration. Primitive Christians hearing the word "baptize" immediately thought of being plunged into the water, being immersed and submerged, and thereby being cleansed

---

32. *Service Book: The United Reformed Church*, p. 33.

and transformed so that the old state of the person disappeared and the person was completely new. Consider, says Dr. Franz Leenhardt, the eastern neophyte of the first century who descended into the water with his limbs burnt by the sun and soiled by the dust stuck to his sweat, and the new vitality and sparkling cleanliness he would experience. By contrast contemporary Infant Baptism, in which only a few drops of water are sprinkled on the forehead of the baby, is so ludicrously inadequate that Professor Leenhardt thinks a new name should be found for Baptism, such as "the sacrament of the new life," "the sacrament of the new birth," "the birth of the life of the Spirit," or "the sacrament of the (vital) union with Christ."[33]

It is clear that the very action of baptizing in the contemporary churches has been profoundly enfeebled and that the significance of water has been largely lost. By contrast, Baptism in the earliest Christian years meant life.

And we would do well to remember, and attempt to recapture its fourfold symbolic significance. First, it meant washing or cleansing and purification. Second, it meant a transformation into a completely new being in which the ego had begun to be transformed through union with Christ. Third, it meant being drowned and rising again as a parallel to the death and resurrection of Christ whose union with the candidate was symbolized in Baptism. Fourth, this union with Christ effected incorporation into the community of the Church.

The symbolism of the Eucharist is even richer than that of Baptism. One of the most useful discussions of eucharistic symbolism is provided by Bishop Hugh Montefiore in *Thinking about the Eucharist*, a volume of essays by members of the English Archbishops' Commission on Christian Doctrine in 1972.[34] Montefiore points out that this is a table meal, as was the Last Supper, and the presence of the holy table in the modern church with the bread and wine clearly suggests God's hospitality. "It is a very deeply felt and almost universal instinct that a true welcome shows itself in offering food and drink. And so the very fact that a sacred meal lies at the center of the rite demonstrates the generous acceptance by God of his people. We eat and drink as his guests.[35] But the table is holy because it also has

33. Leenhardt, *Parole Visible*, p. 85.
34. Published by the S.C.M. of London. Hugh Montefiore's essay, chapter 5, is entitled "Symbols and the Eucharist."
35. *Ibid.*, p. 75.

205

religious associations with sacrifice: this is the table of the crucified and risen Christ, as expressed in the hymn:

> And so we show thy death, O Lord,
>   Till Thou again appear,
> And feel when we approach thy board
>   We have an altar here.

The vivid symbolism of the Eucharist is also eschatological. In the major traditional eucharistic prayer of thanksgiving, we recall that we celebrate together "with angels, and archangels, and the whole company of heaven" and we recall the communion of saints already beside Christ and the heavenly banquet which we hope to share in the future. But, of course, the two basic symbols in the Eucharist are bread and wine. Food is a basic human need, and bread and wine are natural and universal symbols as well as liturgical symbols. Bread is everyday nourishment and sustenance. We acknowledge this every time we pray the Lord's Prayer: "Give us this day our daily bread." But, after the consecratory prayer of thanksgiving, the bread on the altar becomes everlasting bread, for it is Christ himself, and life-imparting heavenly manna, transmitting the benefits of Christ's Passion.

Wine too, is a natural symbol of nourishment, drunk daily in many countries, but it is "a natural symbol of feast and festival . . . Wine is the token of the special occasion. It expresses and encourages cheerfulness and conviviality: it is 'wine that maketh glad the heart of man.'"[36] Wine is not customarily drunk alone, so the cup suggests a party, and at the Lord's Supper symbolizes (especially with a common cup) the unity of believers in Christ.

This cup, however, does not only symbolize joy and felicity, but also suffering and pain. The eucharistic wine, normally red, is a symbol of the blood of Christ. Here, as Montefiore affirms, there is a fusion of images.

> Blood symbolizes life, for without blood we cannot live. To drink the blood is a symbolic act of sharing in the life-blood of Christ. Blood, however, symbolizes not only life but death; for blood outpoured, unless staunched, leads to death. And so to drink the consecrated

36. *Ibid.*, p. 77. The biblical citation comes from Psalm 104:15, and Judges 9:13 refers to "wine, which cheers God and man."

wine is not merely to share in the life-blood of Christ but also to assert his sacrificial death.[37]

Thus the image of the chalice at the Eucharist generates feelings of joyful celebration, of friendship and unity, but it also generates feelings of cleansing, reconciliation, and sanctification.

Two modern images have added to the polysemous character of the Eucharist as celebrated in our own day. The first is the recognition that in a restricted sense, each Eucharist is a miniature Harvest Festival. In thinking of the bread and wine, one recognizes that God has provided the sun and the soil and the seed for both wheat and vine, and humanity has cooperated with God to make the end product, by preparing the ground, sowing the seed or the vine, gathering the products, and transporting them so that we can receive them at our daily as well as at our holy table. This symbolism can teach us an ecological lesson as well.

The second image, brought to our attention especially by the courageous Roman Catholic priests of South America and Sri Lanka who minister to the dispossessed and the marginalized is that in remembering the sufferings of Christ we should also be recalling the sufferings of the poor and disadvantaged for whom Christ in his Incarnation showed such concern. They ought to be sitting with us at Christ's table. As Professor Raymundo Panikkar expresses it:

> The great challenge today is to convert the sacred bread into real bread, the liturgical peace into political peace, the worship of the Creator into the reverence for the Creation, the Christian praying community into an authentic human fellowship. It is risky to celebrate the Eucharist. We may have to leave it unfinished, having gone first to give back to the poor what belongs to them.[38]

It is important also to be reminded of the larger symbols implicit in the sacraments, quite apart from the water, bread, wine, and oil, and this has been done with remarkable empathy and deep learning by Dr. F. W. Dillistone in his *Christianity and Symbolism*.[39] Two such symbols are sacrifice and covenant. Behind the immemorial

37. *Ibid.*
38. Cited by William R. Crockett in *Eucharist: Symbol of Transformation*, p. 263.
39. Published by Collins of London in 1955.

expressions of sacrifice in many cultures and multiple religions there have been two fundamental impulses, the first being to accept death that life may flow, and the second, to grasp life and slay a victim symbolically that its life may be made available.[40] The second symbol — covenant — is of equal antiquity and universality, and was often accompanied by sacrifice. Both sacrifice and covenant are involved in the two major Christian sacraments. In Baptism, as we have repeatedly emphasized, there is the symbolism not only of the womb, but also of the tomb, and Baptism is into the redeeming death of the crucified and resurrected Messiah Christ. Moreover, as Scripture indicates (Mark 10:38), Christ underwent two Baptisms, the first a Baptism of water by John the Baptist and the second the Baptism of suffering. In the Eucharist the symbolism is even more direct, for by it Christians become incorporated into the body of Christ, or, as C. H. Dodd phrased it, "are given the freedom of the city of God,"[41] and become beneficiaries of the New Covenant between God and themselves ratified by the death of Christ and recalled in the sacrificial symbols of his Body and Blood, the consecrated bread and wine.

The concept of covenant, a solemn bond or engagement entered into by God with the people of Israel under Abraham and later under Moses on Mount Sinai, and the new covenant prophesied by Jeremiah based on the inward righteousness of the heart (Jeremiah 31:31) and ethical rather than legalistic in character, was believed by Christians to have arrived in Christ Jesus. Its solemnity was stressed by Christ himself as he instituted the Lord's Supper. As recorded by Matthew in his Gospel, as Jesus gave his disciples the cup of wine, he said: "Drink ye all of it; For this is my blood of the new covenant, which is shed for many unto the remission of sins."[42] These solemn words uttered just prior to his Passion are Christ's inauguration of the New Covenant, no longer restricted to a single nation but available to the whole world for all time; they are proleptically his sacrifice, and they promise the forgiveness of sins and reconciliation with God.

Protestant Churches, especially those in the Reformed tradition, have also adopted the symbolism of the "seal" with respect to the

40. Dillistone, *Christianity and Symbolism*, p. 247.
41. *The Bible of Today* (Cambridge: Cambridge University Press, 1947), p. 160.
42. Matthew 26:27-28. Also see Mark 14:24.

two "Gospel Sacraments." Baptism and the Lord's Supper are "seals" of God's promises, proofs that we are his possessions. The Shorter Catechism of the seventeenth century defines the sacrament as "an holy ordinance instituted by Christ; whereas, by sensible signs, Christ, and the benefits of the new covenant, are represented, sealed, and applied to believers."

Other symbols, important in their way although they are hardly central to the sacraments, should at least be mentioned. Oil, which is used in some rites of initiation and in sacred rites of healing, is symbolic of health and strength. The laying on of hands is used in Confirmation and Ordination as a symbol of the descent of the Holy Spirit, and an invitation to God to send his grace on those on whom the hands are imposed. Another symbolic gesture of increasing popularity in the Eucharist is the Pax or Peace, in which one grasps the hands of neighbors in the congregation, declaring, "The peace of Christ be with you" or a similar phrase betokening the union of Christians in Holy Communion.

Difficulties with Symbolism

These have been hinted at earlier in the consideration of reification and the danger of taking metaphors literally, but now require further elaboration.

To begin with there can be excessive elaboration of symbols, as was explained in *Episcopal Services* by a group of Anglican clergy describing the services according to the revised rites of the Church of England.[43] The authors begin by stating that the contemporary concept of a bishop is that of servant and shepherd rather than as ruler, and that this view should be reflected in the liturgy. The bishop's seat should no longer be referred to as "throne" but as his "chair." For simplicity's sake they urge that a bishop should refrain from putting on or taking off a mitre frequently, and from taking short walks in the sanctuary carrying both mitre and staff. Nor should those who attend to the bishop bow to him "every time they make a movement." It is also unnecessary, they argue, "for objects passed

43. The authors are Paul Bradshaw, Robert Jennings, Brian Bundle, and George Timms. The volume was co-published by The Church Literature Association, the Alcuin Club, and the S.P.C.K. in 1980.

to or from a bishop to be handed down a long hierarchical chain."[44] The book further lists objects no longer required, such as the gremial veil (except when chrism is used at confirmation), the hand candle, a cushion for genuflection, the shorter rochet under the alb, and the tunicle in addition to the dalmatic beneath the chasuble. Furthermore, they list two customs that no longer need to be observed: the bishop need not wear the mitre during the lection of the Gospel or when washing his hands or being censed.[45] This book's authors rightly remind their right reverences that contemporary ritual is simpler, less fussy, and humbler than it used to be.

Another difficulty in liturgical symbolism is the unnecessary profusion of secondary symbolism, which only obfuscates the primary symbols. According to Fr. Ted Guzie most of the symbolism of the old Roman rite was calculated to draw attention to the objects of bread and wine, while the new rites eliminate secondary symbolism and stress the *action* of the faith community which in the Eucharist is celebrating its redemption.[46] It is in the sharing of the meal that we are reminded of our dependence upon people and forces other than ourselves from whom the bread and wine come. Christ's first disciples as Jews were familiar with the ritual of a Jewish meal with blessings of bread and wine, and thanksgiving prayers during the meal. Consequently, when Jesus said, "Do this in memory of me" he was reminding them of union with God, with one another, and all creation, which he had brought alive for them and the entire world.[47]

The most thorough analysis of the misappropriation of symbols known to me is that of Professor David Noel Power in his book, *Unsearchable Riches: The Symbolic Nature of Liturgy*.[48] He lists five categories of misappropriation as follows: (1) naive realism, (2) allegorization, (3) rationalization, (4) support for ideology, and (5) leaving lives sacramentally empty. By naive realism is meant an overelaboration of the visual so that the interiority of the symbol's meaning is lost. Allegorization's error is the precise opposite — a

44. *Ibid.*, pp. 7-8.
45. *Ibid.*, p. 27.
46. Guzie, *Jesus and the Eucharist* (New York: Paulist Press, 1974), p. 110.
47. R. L. Browning and R. A. Reed, *The Sacraments in Religious Education and Liturgy: An Ecumenical Model* (Birmingham, Alabama: Religious Education Press, 1985), pp. 79-80.
48. Issued in 1984 by the Pueblo Publishing Company of New York.

kind of excessive neo-Platonism in which, for example, the priest washing his hands is interpreted in light of the action of Pontius Pilate. The third error — the rationalization of symbols — means that their polysemous quality is reduced to a single conception. Such concepts as original sin, causality, transubstantiation, and institution, says Fr. Power have their role to play, but can be overworked. Emphasis on them can diminish one's experience of the celebration and its immediate symbolical meanings. The fourth error is to use liturgical symbolism as a support for ideology, for example, to buttress the ecclesiastical hierarchy. While organizations need a stable structure, "the current organization of the Roman patriarchate has become stabilized and sacralized beyond necessity. The manner of celebration has been given a divine quality that is illusory." Fr. David Power also argues that basic Christian communities allow for a more divergent ministry and "express [through their liturgical symbolism] a more politically conscious sense of God's actions in human affairs"; "In a number of communities," he observes, "women take a prominent and even a presidential, ministerial role."[49] Finally, he says that the sacralization of the hierarchy has led to many lives becoming semantically deprived. Instead of representing community and the power of God as alive in the people, symbols of power and ministry have been diverted to the priesthood and the hierarchy whose activity liturgy almost exclusively represents. The result is that other gifts and services within the community go unacknowledged and their apostolate is silenced.

His book leads to a most moving conclusion. He argues that the last criterion of sacramental truth is the experience of the Cross and solidarity with those who suffer. Such truth, he urges, depends upon a conjunction between liturgy and ethics,

> since taking up one's cross identifies one with Jesus Christ, the experience is that of solidarity with the suffering of the world. Within that solidarity is the experience of hope. The believer knows that in the darkness one is not abandoned by God and it is possible to expect the kingdom divinely promised. . . . It is the experience of those who in the name of Jesus Christ live lives inspired by the Beatitudes. In a period of liturgical crisis, it is important for the whole Church to look to the contrast experiences and the contrast liturgical models

49. Power, *Unsearchable Riches*, p. 178.

provided by those communities that live the struggle for freedom in faith and hope. The orthodoxy of the sacramental canon is verified and authenticated by the orthopraxis of solidarity with victims and of hope in suffering.[50]

It is clear that ethically and symbolically contemporary churches have far to go. But it is cheering that Catholics "have succeeded in disencumbering the liturgy from much of the minor ceremonial, in such a way that the great, constant, elemental symbols now stand out in all their power" while "on the Protestant side, some steps have been taken to enrich the material and dramatic symbolism of a long denuded cultus. . . ."[51]

Such changes have involved acute struggles between the reformers and the conservatives in Catholicism, Anglicanism, and Protestantism. The Roman Catholics rediscovered the power of the basic symbols of water, bread, wine, and oil, and the centrality of the Eucharist as a meal and an emblem of joy and hospitality, and the ears of the laity were opened to their own vernacular language. Further, the new Roman services delivered the laity from the hierarchical legalism that forgot that it was God and not the priest who was the source of grace. The new simplicity was easily pilloried, as when an English Archbishop, concurring with Evelyn Waugh's Catholic conservatism, wrote: "Of course, you are right. That is why they are playing up the People of God and the Priesthood of the Laity. The Mass is no longer the Holy Sacrifice but the Meal; at which the priest is the waiter. The bishop, I suppose, is the head waiter and the Pope the Patron."[52] On the Protestant side of the divide, the worshippers began to develop visual sensitivity to supplement their verbal and aural acuity. For both Catholics and Protestants unity was discovered in the coordinate stress on Word and Sacrament.

50. *Ibid.*, p. 216.
51. Geoffrey Wainwright in *The Study of Liturgy* (London: OUP, 1992), p. 559.
52. Martin Stannard, *Evelyn Waugh: The Later Years, 1939-1966* (New York and London: W. W. Norton & Company, 1992), p. 480.

CHAPTER X

CHURCH ARCHITECTURE
AND ART

T HE LATTER HALF of the twentieth century has witnessed a radical change in church architecture from the neo-Gothic style popularized by the nineteenth century Tractarians, which the Anglo-Catholics continued to employ until World War II, to the more functional style of contemporary building. This can be described as a change from the *domus Dei* to the *domus ecclesiae*, from the symbolic and monumental house of God to the efficient house of the church, combining spaces for worship, as well as for social, charitable, and educational activities.

This contrast has been most vividly interpreted by the architectural historian, Peter Hammond, who defends modern functional churches. He writes:

> To treat the eucharistic liturgy as a solemn spectacle performed on a distant stage by a handful of professional actors for the edification of an amorphous crowd of spectators is to misconceive its essential character. A church is essentially a place for *doing*, for corporate *action*, in which all the people participate and each has his appropriate function to perform; it is not a sort of jewelled cave in which the solitary individual may find some kind of worship experience, and where his emotions may be kindled by the contemplation of a remote spectacle. . . .

It is outmoded, he argues, to regard the church building as a house of God; it is rather the house of the people of God. Hammond continues: "It is still necessary to insist that the building exists for the people who are themselves the temple of the living God; that it is not a shrine or a monument to some abstract conception of religion, but a liturgical and pastoral instrument for the furtherance of the Church's apostolic task."[1] Hammond's impatience at the older style

---

1. *Towards a Church Architecture* (London: Architectural Press, 1962), pp. 28-29.

213

of ecclesial architecture is expressed thus: "Christendom is dead. It is high time that we recognized the fact and stopped building churches which are no more than extravagant essays in romanticism, wholly unrelated to the social realities of the modern world."[2]

The traditional form of establishment churches reinforced the criticism that churches were oblivious to the social needs of the times. Other-worldly, detaching themselves from the architecture surrounding them, their triumphal monumentality magnified their authority, or, in the words of E. A. Sovik, "their saccharine charm insulated their habitues from the realities of the world, or their 'dim religious light' provided a sentimental and esoteric escape." The same author says bluntly: "What this ultimately means is that there can be no more church building in the sense that is meant when we talk about 'houses of God,' shrines, temples, naves, chancels, or sacred edifices. We need to return to the non-church."[3] It is hardly surprising that those worshippers who are comfortable with the symbolical, monumental church, describe the new buildings as starkly, nakedly, and clinically simplistic in their functionalism. Few realize that they mark a return to the house-churches of primitive Christianity.

One of the prime reasons for the change has been the impact of the Liturgical Movement which has been operative for just over a century. This has changed the liturgy from being regarded as a hierarchical performance with the congregation as spectators into a communal, domestic celebration of worship requiring maximum visibility and audibility for the Christian community. In the 1960s the major principles of the Liturgical Movement affected church architecture in several ways. First, a long linear building with the nave and distant chancel was to be replaced by a single chamber to be used for the liturgical action. In the second place, it was thought essential to encourage maximum participation by the congregation to express the corporate character of the Eucharist. Thirdly, it was important to have significant and dignified (rather than casual) arrangements for Baptism. This could be done by placing a font near the entry of the church symbolizing Baptism as entry into the Christian life, or by putting the font near the center of the church or adjacent to the altar and pulpit, thus ensuring the visibility of the

2. *Ibid.*, p. 166.
3. Sovik, *Architecture for Worship* (Minneapolis: Augsburg Publishing House, 1973), pp. 38-39.

action. It was also important to provide a central place for the ministry of the Word in lections and proclamation. It was essential that the people leading services should be close to those sharing in the worship.

Church architecture was also influenced by the remarkable revision of worship effected by the Second Vatican Council. Gone was a form of worship dominated by rubrics, wittily described by Maurice Lavanoux as "like barnacles on the barque of Peter."[4] As Professor James F. White pointed out, the *Instruction on Implementing the Constitution on the Sacred Liturgy* which appeared on September 26, 1964, led to many changes, the chief of which, apart from the use of the vernacular instead of Latin, was mandating the moving of the altar-table to a free-standing position to allow the priest to face the people across it. Other changes included: the removal of side altars and the tabernacle; the provision of a more prominent pulpit or ambo, and a presidential chair so that the priest could sit down while portions of the Mass were delegated to a variety of ministers; and "the wholesale destruction of much art that had provided for personal devotions." His conclusion is: "So ascetic are many of these churches that one can now speak of a 'Catholic plain style.'"[5] The central word in contemporary church architecture as in present day worship is "participation." It is expressed in Vatican II's call for "that full, conscious, and active participation" which, say the Whites, "could well be the slogan for all the changes we have seen in worship in the last twenty years."[6] Fr. J. D. Crichton comments on the changed situation in Roman Catholicism: "There are those who say we have entered an age of new Puritanism, that our modern churches are stark, without colour, without statues or pictures. There is some truth in this, though the reason for it is that Catholic churches until recently were such a clutter of miscellaneous objects obscuring the basic liturgical function of the building that priests and architects have been glad to get rid of them."[7]

---

4. Lavanoux was editor of the *Liturgical Arts Magazine*. The citation comes from Susan J. White, *Art, Architecture and Liturgical Reform: The Liturgical Arts Society, 1928-1972* (New York: Pueblo Publishing Company, 1982), p. 153.

5. James F. White, *A Brief History of Christian Worship* (Nashville: Abingdon Press, 1993), p. 176.

6. James F. White and Susan J. White, *Church Architecture: Building & Renovation for Christian Worship* (Nashville: Abingdon Press, 1988), p. 17.

7. Crichton, *Christian Celebration: Understanding the Mass*, 3rd ed. (London:

Important philosophers and theologians also contributed indirectly to a rethinking of church architecture. Influential existentialists emphasized the primacy of being and befriending over having; the Jewish thinker Martin Buber showed how an "I-Thou" relationship could degenerate easily into an "I-It" relationship, while Gabriel Marcel emphasized the commitment that characterizes deep relationships with persons and with God. Dietrich Bonhoeffer, a radical theologian who revolutionized the interpretation of Christianity, insisted on the importance of following Christ by means of a new worldliness, sharing in Christ's sufferings with the marginalized and excluded, whom he chose as his friends. This imperative is strikingly expressed in Bonhoeffer's *Letters and Papers from Prison,* particularly in the following citation:

> The Church is her true self only when she exists for humanity. As a fresh start she should give away all her endowments to the poor and needy. The clergy should live solely on the free-will offerings of their congregations, or possibly be engaged in some secular calling. She must take part in the social life of the world, not lording it over men, but helping and serving them. She must tell men, whatever their calling, what it means to live in Christ, to exist for others. . . . She must not underestimate the importance of human example, which has its origin in the humanity of Jesus. . . . It is not abstract argument, but concrete example which gives her word emphasis and power.[8]

Such considerations demanded the provision of rooms in which eleemosynary concerns for the poor, the sick, and the old, as well as youth, could be expressed practically.

It is Peter Smith who as an architect and a Christian has seen most clearly perhaps the implications of the radical view of Christianity for church buildings. In his eyes it means an architecture which gives up exterior impressiveness and hierarchical power. "There is," he insists, "something distinctive about Christ's attitude to 'the multitude,' or rank and file. He ascribed ultimate value to ordinary people."[9] Peter Smith thinks an altar of sacrifice has to be eliminated

---

Geoffrey Chapman, 1993), p. 184. See A. Bugnini, *The Reform of the Liturgy, 1948-1975,* trans. J. O. Connell (Collegeville, Minnesota: Liturgical Press, 1990).

8. Bonhoeffer, *Prisoner for God: Letters and Papers from Prison,* trans. Reginald H. Fuller (New York: Macmillan Company, 1960), pp. 180-81.

9. Smith, *Third Millennium Churches* (London: Galliard, 1972), pp. 26, 35.

from the Eucharist. In his view Communion was instituted for three reasons. It was established primarily as an act of remembrance of the whole life of Christ, and thus the occasion of an *anamnesis* of joy and celebration. Secondly, he holds, it is a metaphoric symbol of the unity between Christ and his people. The meal is a sign of fellowship, "with infinite potential for love when Christ himself is the spiritual food which nourishes the *koinonia*." In the third place, Smith maintains that the Last Supper marked the threshold of the new age; it heralded dramatic change necessary for a pilgrim people: an interior change accomplished by the Holy Spirit and a transformed relationship between the Church and society. Lastly, urges Peter Smith, the Eucharist ratifies an identity of purpose between Christ and his people. "Christ enjoined his followers to be motivated in all things by love, offering himself as the definition of that love — 'as I have loved you.'"[10] Apart from his unwillingness to accept the recalling of the sacrifice of Christ on the Cross as a primary meaning of the Eucharist, Smith's interpretation seems sound and orthodox. The implications of his theological understanding are straightforward. He urges simplicity and flexibility, both of which require the elimination of pews and altars. "The basic criterion is that people should be so disposed around a centre that they are in good auditory and visual contact with the speaker or performer."[11] He also believes in an irregular heptagonal plan for the worship space, and used such a design in three churches which he built — St. Martin's Anglican Church, Higher Poynton, Cheshire, and the United Reformed Churches of Stoke Newington and St. Andrew's in Reading. He believes in economical building and erected one church at Stanwood in Sheffield for well under £18,000.

In a "Diakonic Postscript" Peter Smith adds that three years after it was built, Stoke Newington Church was being used for a plethora of community-care responsibilities, including providing lunch each day for about forty pensioners, who meet at the same time as a pre-school play group. Several nights a week the church serves as a counselling center, and it also provides meetings for the wives of prisoners. It is proposed to use the worship space for Workers Educational Association and other extramural lectures, debates, day conferences, etc.

10. *Ibid.*, pp. 35-36.
11. *Ibid.*, pp. 78, 89.

We have already noted the fourth reason for functional designs — namely, economic limitations. The impressive monumentality of the older churches with their "sermons in stone" attitude, their high verticality, and their lancet windows filled with stained glass was costly. The new churches are made of brick and are modest in size as well as expense.

A fifth and final reason for the shift to more functional architecture is pragmatic and secular. It seems particularly appropriate in newer housing areas, where several denominations may combine to use the same worship and social activities. Also, if the congregation disappears the building can be more easily converted into school or office facilities. And the rooms not used for worship will be exactly like the rooms used in schools or offices, with educational and dining facilities. A church providing social services does not need to proclaim its relevance.

New Churches and Their Architects

Any account of modern church buildings in England would have to include the contribution of George Pace, described by Archbishop Coggan as "God's man for the hour" because his architecture for churches sprang from mastery of his craft and from his own Christian faith and theological understanding. He was consultant architect to nine cathedrals of the Church of England. He built 30 new churches and carried out new works and restorations in well over 700 churches.[12] Nonetheless his architecture is midway between neo-Gothic and functional modern. His son says his churches were "Gothic in character but not form" as he wanted an architecture "capable of expressing wonder, worship, magic, and symbolism" and wished to provide spatial relationships, solids and voids, in the Western traditional style.

A typical church of Pace's creation is that at Thornaby-on-Tees completed in 1970. This shows a central altar in one corner and a font in the opposite corner, an inclining timber roof, a thick limestone altar, simple well-lit windows, a dominant stainless steel hanging cross, tall wrought-iron candlesticks, and ash pews that were stained red. Other

12. See Peter G. Pace, *The Architecture of George Pace, 1915-1975* (London: Batsford, 1990), p. 143.

churches that he built in this style in the 1970's were at Woolston; James the Deacon, York; and Bransholme Church Center, Hull. His major work was the restoration of Llandaff Cathedral, completed in 1957, with its impressive central pulpitum bearing Sir Jacob Epstein's *Majestas* sculpture of the crucified and risen Christ in unpolished aluminum. The sixty-eight pre-Raphaelite figures from the old choir stalls are gilded and arranged in niches gathered round the figure of Christ as witnesses to the power of Christ's risen life. This pulpitum with the magnificent Christ figure on it was intended to break up the vista from the West door and make the nave look less like a parish church and more like a cathedral.[13] He had a special gift for designing symbolic objects, including crosses, tombs, windows, altars, fonts, and particularly candlesticks and organ cases, all of which stress simplicity, elevation, and strength, and usually employ wood and wrought iron.[14] He was internationally known for building the Chapel of the Resurrection at Ibadan University to be used by many denominations as well as the Cathedral at Ibadan. He also erected the University of Keele Chapel for the ecumenical use of Anglican, Roman Catholic, and Free Church members. His work could be simple but it was never stark, and he valued the play of color and the elevation of a building that also elevated the spirit.

The two architects who first introduced modern functional churches into England were Robert Maguire and Keith Murray, who erected St. Paul's, Bow Common, Stepney in 1960. This can indeed be termed "the first modern church in England" since the altar was moved well forward, close to the worshipping community. "Outside the building leaves a sober impression, but inside the central main room rises up from a low encircling side aisle, and culminates in a white lantern providing the direct source of light for the room."[15] The architects have written about the liturgical meaning of the building, that it expresses

> a liturgy seen as a movement towards the place of the altar and the communion, a movement towards the light. In this church the move-

13. I worshipped in Llandaff Cathedral in June 1993, and I genuinely admired the vista and the small, high stained-glass window by John Piper.

14. Pace, *Architecture of George Pace*, p. 149.

15. This is the description provided by the editor of *Christliche Kunstblatter* 2 (1970), and reported on p. 61 of *English Parish Churches*, with introductory texts by Graham Hutton (London: Thames and Hudson, 1976). It fails to do justice to the impression of an illuminated fort given by the exterior with its lantern roof.

ment is inwards through the dark porch, past the font, through the procession to the place of the Ministry of the Word — synaxis — into the light of the sanctuary. In this the colonnade and hanging corona of lights around the sanctuary, and the ciborium define the spaces without preventing free movement between them.[16]

The flexibility is provided by its three-sided forms looking towards the central altar. The architects also explain that although the church had to be able to seat 500 people, its normal congregation would be smaller, so they erected columns which they painted white and brightly lit on their inner faces to enclose but not to threaten the small congregation.

Another of their churches was All Saints, Crewe, completed in 1965 with space for 350 worshippers. This was illuminated by strip lighting close to the roof and all around, and thinner strip lighting also at a height of about 12 feet and between the windows. A dramatic tent-like covering or ciborium was provided above the central altar.

Perhaps the most successful of all their churches was St. Matthew's, Perry Beeches, Birmingham. It is located near a busy roundabout in an undistinguished suburb of Birmingham. The outward form provides a sense of enclosure and protection from the noise and bustle of traffic. Concrete bands separate the blocks of pale grey bricks, and outside and inside are well matched. The hexagonal tower is enclosed by a larger hexagon.

The interior is lit from the gables and the structure is lighted by the thin glazed slits that separate each roof from the walls — so that each seems to float out from the massive cross-beam spanning each corner. The square sanctuary projects from one wall, with an open-frame pulpit to one side, and the brick font beyond, just inside the porch. Floors are of glazed red brick; ceilings are boarded. Spotlights illumine the tower over the altar, and lamps suspended from the cross beam light on the congregation, whose pews are angled on the altar in three blocks ... and though the church seats 400 the vicar enjoys an almost conversational proximity with his congregation.[17]

16. Maguire and Murray, *Modern Churches in the World* (London: Studio Vista, 1965), p. 90.

17. Michael Webb, *Architecture in Britain Today* (Feltham: Country Life, 1969), pp. 227-28.

Their most dramatic building is St. Mary's Abbey, West Malling built for a community of Anglican sisters, combining a church, a cloister, and a new residential range. The church has an open-frame roof resembling an upturned ship's hull with its ribs and beams of leaf green and boards of dark blue. The chapel is floodlit with a central altar facing the nuns.

Another early and innovative building was the St. Philip and St. James multi-purpose Church Center at Hodge Hill, Birmingham, erected in 1968, whose architect was Martin Purdy. The worship room is a rectangle; in one corner there is a raised platform for the altar and lectern, and the choir stalls are in a corner to the right of the platform. The rest of the space is flexible because the seating consists of movable chairs for the use of the congregation. The many other rooms are used for educational, social, and charitable purposes.

Other new and striking churches were built by other denominations, such as the Waterlooville Baptist Church in Hampshire in 1967 by Michael Manser Associates. This church employs exposed steel, glass and brick in a well-proportioned manner. The interior, which is almost square, is flooded with light from glazed side walls and a rooflight over the communion-table. The plan includes a badminton hall, a creche, and meeting rooms. The outside exhibits a dominant Cross.[18]

A modern and more functional Roman Catholic church, erected on the plans of Richard Mahoney and Partners is St. Michael and All Angels, Birkenhead. Like the Perry Beeches church of Maguire and Murray, it was intended to provide a focus in a featureless housing estate, and in the interior to create a close and intimate relationship between the altar and a congregation of 600, with pews surrounding the altar on three sides. Its exterior presents a dramatically high triangle.[19]

Another noteworthy Roman Catholic church is Sacred Heart in Leeds, built on the plan of Derek Walker which Michael Webb describes as "uninhibitedly theatrical, raised above street level and set back on three sides, combining a fully-glazed baptistery, a church whose facades are composed by bays and projecting out between slit windows and massively ridged sacristy and confessionals." He adds that

18. Peter Hammond and Stephen Twombley, eds., *British Modern Architecture* (London: Frederick Muller, 1984), p. 112.

19. Webb, *Architecture in Britain Today*, p. 230.

the baptistery is exciting, with its "roof supported by four slim mush-room-headed columns with aluminum-framed glazing hung around three sides. Over the central font is suspended a cross." The sanctuary contains a low stained-glass window by Laurie Lee, which resembles a mosaic because of the excessive brilliance of the lighting.[20]

The same Derek Walker also built St. Benedict's Roman Catholic church in Leeds on a new housing estate. This is constructed of Douglas fir. The church includes a sanctuary, a Lady chapel, a bap-tistery and bookstall. Michael Webb observes that "a sense of enclo-sure is subtly achieved by the white-tiled panels . . . set into glazing down the long sides, but in contrast to the urban Sacred Heart this is an outwards-looking building." This interior is also flooded with light, and white brick walls keep the space in.[21]

Two recent Roman Catholic churches have been built to the plans of a Protestant architect, Dr. Michael Blee of Lewes. He won the design in a competition for the new Holy Innocents Catholic Church at Orpington, Kent, in the English equivalent of the Silicon Valley. This is described as an "exciting, efficient and cost-effective solution" which the priests consider much too "Protestant"! The sanctuary is thought by them to be too crowded, there are no communion rails, and the pews are said to be spaced so close to each other that kneeling is practically impossible. This church has dynamic roof forms pointing to the heavens. Blee's other Catholic church is the Priory of Good Counsel at Hassocks in Sussex and was completed in 1981. This too has a remarkable roof, in this case conical and high surmounting the extended lower ground story. The fact that a Protestant architect can be chosen to design Roman Catholic churches shows how far the Ecumenical Movement and the Liturgical Movement have come; indeed they have almost coin-cided in their impact on architecture.[22]

The most striking Roman Catholic building of our period is the Cathedral of Christ the King in Liverpool built in five years by the architect Sir Frank Gibberd. According to Michael Webb its form was determined by three factors: to enclose a unified space around the central altar, to exploit the natural drama of the rocky outcrop

20. *Ibid.*, p. 232.
21. *Ibid.*
22. Randall Lindstrom, *Creativity and Contradiction* (Washington, D.C.: The American Institute of Architects Press, 1988), pp. 71-75.

on which it stands, and, thirdly, to complement the other crown on the skyline of the city, the Anglican Cathedral.[23] Its elevation is striking, with a cone-shaped vault ending in a round tower, extending to a height of 290 feet. It is a great achievement to have created a building which can seat 2000 worshippers around a central altar. The tower and vault are supported by sixteen conical trusses evenly spaced around the circle, and they are projected like flying buttresses to take the diagonal thrust. Like Spencer at Coventry, Gibberd employed distinguished artists. Piper and Reyntiens filled the ribs in the cylindrical tower with stained glass, with three bursts of light symbolizing the Trinity. The nave floor was designed by David Atkins with a foundation of black and dark grey marble for the intricate motifs he supplies. The massive ninety feet high entrance porch and the sliding doors bear William Mitchell's symbolic designs, the three crosses, crowns, and the four evangelists, wholly appropriate for a cathedral dedicated to Christ the King.

The architect was faced by two problems. First, how was the new building to be related to the massive crypt erected by Lutyens, a radically different architect? Next, how could Gibberd find a way of providing secondary foci beside the central altar so that 2000 people would not feel belittled and minimized? Rather than solving the first problem he chose to ignore it; the second was solved by providing at opposite edges of the massive circle the subordinate foci of the choir and organ and the entrance porch. The most remarkable feature is the symbolism of the design, which provides a massive crowned tent, an apt image of the nature of the Christian Church in the twentieth century as engaged in the pilgrimage of faith under the royal guidance of Christ, the King of kings, and the Lord of lords. Here also is a modern cathedral where the liturgical design was paramount: to associate the congregation ever more closely to the celebrants of the Mass so that the ministers at the altar could be clearly seen and heard by the vast congregation.

Another early and interesting, though much smaller, building is the Chapel of Churchill College, Cambridge, whose chaplain is the Revd. Dr. Bryan D. Spinks, a distinguished liturgiologist. This was built between 1963 and 1967 by the architects Richard Sheppard, Robson and Partners. Originally it was decided that the chapel should be placed directly at the college entrance so that all students would

23. Webb, *Architecture in Britain Today*, p. 232.

have to pass it on entering or leaving the college. A later committee, probably scientists considering religion fanatical or *passé*, placed it in a remote position, not far from the living quarters of married students. Now it is oddly located next to the noisy sports fields. For this reason the building seems more enclosed than is appropriate for a church. It is, however, an intriguing building. The plan is that of a Greek Cross. Four concrete columns carry four concrete beams of great depth, and the roof of the central bay amid the nine bays formed by the beams is glazed. This is where the portable altar table stands, along with a reader's desk and four candelabras. The brick walls are illuminated by ribbons of windows at a high level. Four vertical slot windows are the only ones in the lower part of the room. The building serves as a social and cultural center as well as a place of worship, and is used by students of all denominations. In the over-enclosed and darkened space, one is grateful for the joyful coloring in the stained glass provided by John Piper.[24]

Thus far we have mentioned only one modern Baptist church and a few United Reformed churches. This relative silence reflects not only the diminishing membership in these congregations, but also the fact that the ministers of the Free Churches have always adopted the basilican posture at the Communion services and stressed the maximum participation of the people of God in their sacred ordinances. Thus what was being contended for in terms of sharing, accessibility, and intelligibility by the Roman and Anglo-Catholic proponents of the Liturgical Movement was a privilege never forfeited by the churches stemming from the Reformation. The plain fact is also that for much of their history the Baptists, Congregationalists and Presbyterians (now The United Reformed Church), and the Methodists sacrificed generously of their pounds and pennies to build their churches since they were, unlike the Church of England, unestablished; but what might have been spent on elegant sanctuaries was given, rather, to the maintenance of the ministry and of missionaries in foreign lands. Such a tradition, with a sound recognition that it is the people who constitute the Church, not a building, and that ethical obedience and charity to the needy are proofs of their covenant-relationship to God and to the wider Body

24. For the description I am indebted to Reinhard Gieselmann, *Contemporary Church Architecture* (London: Thames and Hudson, 1972), and my own visit in June 1993, when I was the guest of the chaplain, Dr. Spinks.

of Christ, is rightly cherished. One's only regret is that these congregations seem to be almost color-blind and I do not know a single one which has invited a distinguished modern artist, either painter or sculptor, to enrich its building by his or her work.

Many churches built a century or more ago have been updated to fit them for modern functional use. Peter Cobb writes: "Most Christian communities have inherited treasured medieval or Gothic Revival buildings from the past, but many of these have been successfully re-ordered in accordance with the insights of the Liturgical Movement without vandalism. Usually the chancel has constituted the greatest problem: either it has been turned into a virtually separate chapel for weekday worship or it has been cleared of choir stalls and the altar brought nearer to the people."[25] Kenneth White's booklet, *The Attractive Church*,[26] contains plans of seven Anglican churches which have been successfully adapted to modern conditions either by reducing the worship area and focussing it, or by adding space for other activities. These adapted churches are St. Thomas, Kendal; St. Mark, Watford; Christ Church, Islington; Christ Church, Highbury; Christ Church, Surbiton; St. Mark, Binfield; St. James, Streatham; and Emmanuel, Wimbledon.

The American architect E. A. Sovik acknowledges that there can be impediments to wise reparation. The major difficulty would be dealing with a sound and intractable structure, and he remarks how courageous the sixteenth century Reformers were in making drastic changes such as closing off the ancient choirs, which they preferred to use for small assemblies or for instructional rooms. Sometimes they even set the seating so that it faced the pulpit half way down the nave; the same possibilities, he observes, are open to some parish churches today.[27] He encourages the building of a *centrum,* a central space used for several purposes such as a musical gathering or a cinema with a rear screen projection not needing a darkened room. He recommends chairs instead of pews for flexibility, a table rather than an altar, and a reading desk rather than pulpit which suits the

25. *The Study of the Liturgy* (1992), p. 541. For a fuller account see *Making the Building Serve the Liturgy,* ed. Gilbert Cope (London: Mowbray, 1962).

26. This was published in 1979 as No. 69 of the Grove Worship Series, in Bramcote, Nottingham.

27. Sovik, *Architecture for Worship* (Minneapolis, Minnesota: Augsburg Publishing House, 1973), p. 116.

more conversational (rather than oratory) style used by modern preachers. Fonts and bowls are easily provided, but if the rite of Baptism requires immersion arrangements are more difficult, though not impossible. He observes: "Some of the most pleasant amenities in public rooms all over the world are fountains of running water" and a permanent feature in a *centrum* could be a fountain built into a wall or free-standing.[28]

Randall Lindstrom reported on a visit to England that "England's most pressing religious issue now may be the fate of its redundant churches — churches that no longer serve a purpose or that serve so few people as to be a financial burden. Medieval and Gothic churches (usually rural or in small towns) are being reincarnated, sometimes awkwardly, as apartments, restaurants, and offices. Many are falling victim to the wrecking ball."[29] He reports on the way a United Reformed church in Windsor was spared from demolition. The congregation sold most of its center-city property to a commercial developer, who razed the old Victorian church and erected a complex of office buildings on the site. The proceeds from the sale allowed the congregation to fund new construction for a church, and they built this in the style of a two-story office building, with the church rooms and worship space on the first floor, and rental office space on the upper floor. The tenant providing the income from the office is ironically a government tax office. Windsor's United Reformed Church has survived. Christ Church and its Crown House Offices were completed in 1980; the architectural firm responsible was Garnett, Cloughley, Blakemore and Associates.[30]

The change we have witnessed in church architecture has kept pace with the increasing development in English social life, where democracy is beginning to overcome radical class distinctions. It has also paralleled the change in forms of worship that goes on inside church buildings. We have observed a transition from hierarchical worship to more democratic worship, from a priest and deacon celebrating alone to worship in considerable part deputed by the chief celebrant to his (and recently her) assistants who read the lessons (apart from the Gospel) and who offer the consecrated elements to the faithful and occasionally read the people's prayers. This process

28. *Ibid.*, pp. 71f., 77, and 93f.
29. Lindstrom, *Creativity and Contradiction*, p. 86.
30. *Ibid.*.

of democratization has been replicated in the very design of the churches themselves. The hierarchical worship demanded neo-Gothic churches with a distant chancel beyond the nave, elevated walls and windows filled with stained-glass, general chiaroscuro suggesting mystery as well as majesty; the democratic, shared, essentially participatory worship requires edifices that are efficient, multi-purpose, simple to the point of stark nakedness (in some cases), and devoid of symbolism. One would not expect such architecture to stimulate the creativity of artists. But the marvel is that the demand for Christian art is growing, especially in the Anglican and Roman Catholic churches.

Church Art[31]

Although this chapter is entitled "Church Architecture and Art," our consideration of church art can be no more than an extended footnote. The English Churches as a whole have not encouraged the use of distinguished contemporary art. Only two English denominations, the Church of England and the Roman Catholic Church, have supported Christian art. With one small qualification, one can include the Methodist Church with the Baptist Union and United Reformed Church in the judgment of near-blindness to symbolism and art. The Methodists have a better reputation simply through their travelling exhibition, *Church and Artist,* which toured thirty urban locations in the early 1960s and is now, thirty years later, on the road again. One of their members, it should be noted, was an outstanding painter, if an unorthodox interpreter of Christianity. This was Sir Stanley Spencer, whose work was never accepted by any English church. One painting, at least, is a masterpiece, locating *The Last Supper* in Spencer's own local milieu, Cookham on the Thames. This 1920 canvas depicts the thirteen figures at the climactic moment when the disciples realize that the bread broken by Christ is his *flesh,* and as St. John examines the divided loaf

31. In the following pages I am greatly indebted to the kindness of two Anglican clergymen, Bishop David Stancliffe of Salisbury, who provided bibliographical assistance, and the Revd. Tom Devonshire Jones, the esthetically erudite Vicar of the parish church of St. Mark, Regent's Park, London, and editor of the superb catalogue entitled *Images of Christ: Religious Iconography in Twentieth-Century British Art* (1993), published by St. Matthew's (Northampton) Centenary Art Committee, Tanners, Moulton Lane, Boughton, Northampton.

his mouth is open with stupefaction. The originality of the painting is partly in the triform table, but uniquely in the fact that the broken loaf in Christ's hand is heart-shaped, a symbol of his transforming love. Already there is a sense that the disciples are saints, for they have wing-shapes at their backs and at their feet. It is unfortunate that no church ever chose to show a single Spencer painting. Today they are exhibited in a memorial chapel at Burghclere in Berkshire, as well as in the Tate Gallery.

It is cathedrals of the Church of England that have most encouraged religious art, and of them all Chichester has been outstanding. Its support of the arts was made possible by the backing of Bishop George Bell and the patronage of the Dean, Walter Hussey, who was renowned for art patronage in St. Matthew's Church, Northampton where he was previously Vicar. Hussey had persuaded Henry Moore to sculpt his masterpiece the *Madonna and Child* (1943-1944) for that church, and also contracted Graham Sutherland's poignant and awe-inspiring painting, *Crucifixion* (1946), which was partly prepared for by examining photographs of the Holocaust. At Chichester Cathedral Dean Hussey persuaded Graham Sutherland to paint an image of the risen Christ meeting St. Mary Magdalene, entitled *Noli me tangere* ("Do not touch me"). He employed John Piper and arranged for a Chagall window (1978) and a mural by Hans Feibusch called *The Baptism of Christ* (1951). The Dean of King's College, Cambridge, George Pattison, declares that Hussey "was possibly the most successful 'patron of art' operating within the Church of England in this century."[32]

Salisbury Cathedral has a new east window of five lancets known as the Prisoners of Conscience Window, produced by Gabriel and Jacques Loire of Chartres, appropriately including the face of Dietrich Bonhoeffer. In its colors of blue, yellow, black, and red, it is the recent glory of the cathedral. Also in the cathedral close can be seen the *Walking Madonna* (1981) of Elisabeth Frink, which shows the Mother of Christ aged by pity.

St. Paul's Cathedral in London exhibits a Henry Moore *Madonna and Child* whose technique is like that of the earlier Moore and indicates both the dependence and independence of the Child in

---

32. Jones, *Images of Christ*, p. 13. For some indication of the extent of Church patronage of religious art in the twentieth century, consult Michael Day, *Modern Art in English Churches* (Oxford: Mowbray, 1984).

relation to the Mother. It also exhibits a *Virgin and Child* (1957) by Josepha de Vasconcellos. St. Paul's, moreover, showed the Northampton exhibition, *Images of Christ*, in the summer of 1993. According to the Revd. Tom Devonshire Jones, Lincoln Cathedral put on a superior exhibition in 1990.[33]

The modern Coventry Cathedral is, of course, the most impressive example of an architect in full collaboration with his artists, Sir Basil Spence encouraging Sir Jacob Epstein, John Piper, Graham Sutherland, and John Hutton. On the exterior is the sculpture by Epstein of the victorious St. Michael above the defeated devil, and the high glazed doors on which Hutton engraved thirty-five angels and thirty-one saints. In the vast zig-zagged nave on the right is the glowing abstract window of John Piper for the baptistery, and beyond and above the high altar there is Graham Sutherland's green and gold tapestry representing Jesus Christ the Redeemer in the Glory of the Father, and there are four lateral panel images of the four evangelists as witnesses of Christ. There is a lower panel which, with its blacks and greys, strikes the right sombre notes for the Christ who passed to his glory through the anguish and desolation of the Cross. This crucifixion, like the Northampton representation of the same event, evokes memories of Grünewald's agonized Christ and of the victims of Belsen, Buchenwald, and Auschwitz.[34]

Ely Cathedral in its south transept has a sculpture of *Christ and Mary* (1963) by David Wynne, a large *Christus* by Hans Feibusch (1981), who left murals for sculpture after a serious illness, as well as a sculpture by Simon Verity. Verity is well represented in Anglican cathedrals; in addition to Ely, there are two of his works on Exeter cathedral's west front, one of an angel (1980) and the other of St. Peter (1985), and he also has a sculpture at Wells Cathedral.

Peter Eugene Ball, the sculptor, has works in five cathedrals. These are *Crucifix* (1984) in Birmingham, *Crucifix* (1987) at Portsmouth, *Christus Rex* (1980) and *Light of the World* (1990) at Southwell Minster, *Crucifix* (1989) and *Pieta* (1990) at Winchester, and *Madonna and Child* at Southwark. Worcester Cathedral displays a Pieta sculpture by Glynn Williams.

33. Jones, *Images of Christ*, p. 29.
34. I have provided a much fuller account of the art and architecture of Coventry Cathedral in *Worship and Theology in England: The Ecumenical Century, 1900-1965* (Princeton and Oxford University Press, 1965), pp. 56-69.

To these one must add a brief catalogue of English parish churches with competent objects of Christian art. St. Paul, Haringay has an inventive reredos in travertine marble by Stephen Cox to cheer this community whose previous church was burnt by fire in 1986 and was subsequently redesigned by Peter Jenkins. St. Matthew's, Northampton has works by John Piper, and murals by Feibusch, as well as masterpieces mentioned earlier. Among Feibusch's other church murals are *Crucifixion* in St. Martin, Dagenham (1948); *Resurrection* in St. James, Merton; *The Trinity in Glory* in St. Alban, Holborn; and *Christ in Glory* in Christ Church Priory, Bournemouth. St. Mary, Hadleigh, Suffolk has a *Head of Christ*, and an oil painting by Maggi Hambling. All Saints, Basingstoke displays with pride *The Holy Spirit*, a window designed by Cecil Collins. The new church of St. Mary, Peterborough has a striking sculpture by Lee Grandjean entitled *Resurrection* (1990-1991), which depicts the risen Christ with upheld arms walking away from the wall to which is attached the Cross.

Roman Catholic Cathedrals with important art works include Westminster Cathedral with two outstanding representations of the fourteen *Stations of the Cross*. One was done by Eric Gill early in this century, and Roy de Maistre's painting of the same devotional theme is in the Grand Corridor. Liverpool Metropolitan Cathedral has the *Altar Cross* of Elisabeth Frink, along with works by Piper and Reyntiens, David Atkins, and William Mitchell.

Perhaps Catholicism's greatest modern work of art is displayed outside the Convent of the Holy Child Jesus. This is Sir Jacob Epstein's noble *Madonna and Child* (1953). Laurie Lee has described this sculpture as follows:

> The Christ child is not the customary babe but a lean lad of some five or six years. The mantled Mother with open hands reveals and offers him to the world. And the child both in expression and design is all prophecy: the robe that wraps his narrow body is also the robe of the tomb; the arms outstretched to embrace the world also assume the attitude of crucifixion; and the face with its large wide eyes and serene brow, looks out with love and knows what that love will cost him.[35]

35. This citation is from the volume Lee edited with Geoffrey Ireland, *Epstein: A Camera Study of the Artist at Work* (London: André Deutsch, 1958).

Gifted in many media, Norman Adams has produced murals at St. Anselm, Kennington in 1971, *Stations of the Cross* (1975-1979) at Our Lady of Lourdes in ceramics, and stained glass for St. Anthony, Durham.

Artistic promise for the future can be seen in the fact that several of the artists whose work was exhibited in 1993 in Northampton and St. Paul's Cathedral are relatively young. Stephen Cox and Lee Grandjean are under fifty; Sarah Raphael, Jean Lamb, Roger Wagner, and Richard Kenton Webb are in their thirties; and Mark Cazalet and Tim Shaw are under thirty.

The puzzle is that the English Free Churches have not been supportive of modern Christian art. Why is this? I would suggest that there are three reasons. In the first place, their worship until very recently was auditory rather than visual, emphasizing the importance of preaching, and depreciating the sacraments. This has changed greatly in recent decades, but the tradition of four hundred years is not easily overcome. Secondly, their ministers and members were taught the dangers of idolatry and took with utter seriousness the second commandment which forbade making any likeness of God, apparently forgetting that St. Paul in the Epistle to the Colossians 1:15, referred to Christ as "the image of the invisible God." It has been more characteristic of Anglican doctrine to stress the Incarnation and of Free Church doctrine to emphasize the atonement. Thirdly, within the Puritan ethical tradition of the Free Churches there is a suspicion of the senses as if any esthetic or sensory stimulation necessarily involve sensuality. The Liturgical Movement with its joint stress on Word and Sacrament may prompt a new esthetic consciousness in the years to come.

CHAPTER XI

HYMNODY AND CHURCH MUSIC

T HE GROWTH OF HYMNODY and church music in the last generation has been called by some an "explosion" and by others a "flowering." But the liveliest metaphor I have read to explain the variety is sylvan. Dr. Robin Leaver has observed:

> . . . today many new hymnodical trees blossom at our services, such as: the many-branched standard hymn books with their all-embracing coverage; the sapling supplements to the established books, which have grown rapidly but now look somewhat unsteady in the wind of change; the collections of charismatic conifers waving their hands in the air and celebrating Christmas all the year round; and the multiplicity of home-grown parish pot-plants, highly original hybrids which have a propensity to shed their autumnal loose-leaves at every service.[1]

There has also been a revolution in music styles, as described by Jane Sinclair:

> The period of liturgical experiment in the 1960s and 1970s, culminating in the publication of *The Alternative Service Book* in 1980, ran concurrently with a revolution in popular music styles and the burgeoning of the charismatic movement in some Anglican churches. In some churches musicians and ministers wholeheartedly embraced new musical styles: out went the organ and the robed choir, in came the band with amplification and overhead projector or parish song book.[2]

---

1. Leaver, *A Hymn Book Survey, 1962-1980*, Grove Worship Series, No. 71 (Bramcote, Nottingham: Grove, 1980), p. 3.
2. Sinclair, *Keeping in Tune with Heaven: A Response to the Report of the Archbishops' Commission on Church Music*, Grove Worship Series, No. 122 (Bramcote, Nottingham: Grove, 1993), p. 4. The Archbishops' Commission on Church Music published its report entitled *In Tune with Heaven* in 1992; it provides a fascinating account of the musical variety, changes, and conditions in both urban and rural Anglican parish churches.

The same author declares that the forty recent years of rapid change have had a deleterious effect on music. The relevant factors include the "crippling cost of the upkeep of organs, the demise of corporate singing in schools and the consequent lack of children trained in and used to singing," and "the gradual decline in church attendance since 1945." She adds that these difficulties are felt most acutely in the inner city or under-resourced rural areas.[3]

Our plan in this chapter will be to examine briefly the supplements and the revised standard hymn books, then to sample the most creative products of the new hymn writers and to note the contemporary topics which their hymns illustrate, and, finally, to refer to the new melodies accompanying the words.

Supplements and New Hymn Books

Perhaps at the outset it should be made clear that hymnody plays a more significant role in Free Church worship than in Anglican worship, a fact acknowledged by both groups. For example, the importance of hymns is claimed by Leslie E. Cooke, a distinguished minister in the Congregational churches. He wrote:

> The noblest hymns of the church are its theology. If we were to ask what more than anything has preserved the faith and kept the Church true to it, the answer would be not the classic statements of the faith, not the work of scholars, important as they are, but the Church's hymns. There is a real sense in which it is true to say that a theology which does not issue in praise and adoration, which cannot be sung, is a bad theology. No statement of the Christian gospel is adequate which does not make a man want to praise and glorify God.[4]

There is a difference here between the Anglican tradition where the hymn is essentially an accompaniment to the liturgy (perhaps a commentary on it or an adornment of it) and the conventional Free Church pattern where it is seen as integral to the liturgy itself. This, indeed, may be one of the chief reasons why it is within Methodism and in the United Reformed Church that the most creative hymn

---

3. Sinclair, *Keeping in Tune with Heaven*, p. 4.
4. Cooke, *Above Every Name* (London: Independent Press, 1962), p. 88.

writers can be found, as was the case in the eighteenth century with Isaac Watts and Charles Wesley. The most significant expositor of the function of hymns in Free Church worship was Bernard Lord Manning, who wrote: "Hymns are for Dissenters what the liturgy is for the Anglican. They are the framework, the setting, the conventional, the traditional part of divine service as we use it. They are, to adopt the language of the liturgiologist, the Dissenting Use."[5]

The greater importance of hymnody for the Free Churches is further certified by the fact that no Anglican Prayer Book had any provision for hymns in its rubric until *The Alternative Service Book* of 1980. Furthermore, there was no single official hymn book for the use of Anglicans, since Evangelicals and Catholics in the Church preferred hymn books which emphasized their own theological preferences and emphases.

The years from 1964 to 1975 are the start of the age of supplements. As Erik Routley wrote, "the red light of inflation had already begun to glow," for there was in these years a growing store of new material. It was difficult to judge the durability of such material. Hurried inclusion in a revised hymn book seemed unwise, especially since this might also empty the hymn books of valuable classical material that ought not to be jettisoned.[6] The result was that the major denominations decided to produce updating supplements for use alongside existing hymnals. Supplements were relatively inexpensive and could be renewed in a shorter time. Two major collections forming supplements appeared in 1969. These were *Hymns and Songs,* a Methodist publication, and *100 Hymns for Today,* which was an Anglican product and primarily a supplement for *Hymns Ancient and Modern.* The latter had first appeared in 1861 and was the best known and most durable collection of hymns for Anglican use. The new supplements reflected generally the new social concerns implicit in the Gospel as well as in the growing ecumenical sense of the centrality of Holy Communion. Moreover, whereas the older hymnals were written in anachronistic "thou" language, the newer songs utilized contemporary "you" language.

Professor J. R. Watson of the Department of English in the Uni-

---

5. Manning, *The Hymns of Wesley and Watts* (rpt. London: Epworth Press, 1988), p. 133.

6. Routley, *A Panorama of Christian Hymnody* (Collegeville, Minnesota: The Liturgical Press, 1979), p. 188.

versity of Durham remarked of hymn writers that "they are perpetually working in the shadow of their predecessors, and especially that of the compilers of *Hymns Ancient and Modern*. . . ."[7] This collection dominated hymn writing for over a century despite what Bernard Manning described as its "wretched versification, doubtful grammar, and questionable theology"; the same critic thought badly of the *English Hymnal,* which, in his view, was "stuffed out with second-rate creaking translations of Greek and Latin hymns, fusty as a second-hand Lewis and Short, more like the meritorious exercises of the Classical Sixth than Poetry, the handmaid of Piety."[8]

The Methodist *Hymns & Songs,* according to Robin Leaver, was unrivalled among supplements both for its breadth of coverage and its sense of adventure.[9] New hymn writers included were Fred Pratt Green, himself a Methodist, Fred Kaan, and Erik Routley. Four of Sydney Carter's songs are represented here, and several tunes provided by the 20th Century Church Light Music Group.

The compilers of the Anglican supplement, *100 Hymns for Today,* explain in the editorial preface: "We have tried to steer a middle course . . . between restatements of traditional and ephemeral or 'pot' productions." The result is that the book contains hymns by Doddridge and Wesley as well as by newcomers like Sydney Carter, Fred Kaan, Timothy Dudley-Smith, and Patrick Appleford. On the musical side there is a perfect union of words and tune in the Bayly-Routley hymn "What Does the Lord Require."

Yet another supplement, an addition to *The Baptist Hymn Book* (1962), was entitled *Praise for Today.* It appeared in 1974. Of its total of 104 hymns, 31 texts and 51 tunes appear here for the first time. Both themes and tunes are contemporary, and many of the new hymn writers are included.

A fourth supplement to standard hymn books is the child of two hymnodic parents, namely, *Congregational Praise* and *The Church Hymnary: Third Edition,* a hymn book used by the Presbyterian Church in England but mainly the production of the Church of Scotland. The parents united to found the United Reformed Church in the United Kingdom. The supplement is entitled *New Church*

---

7. In *Language and the Worship of the Church,* ed. David Jasper and R. C. D. Jasper (London and New York: St. Martin's Press, 1990), pp. 174-75.

8. Manning, *The Hymns of Wesley and Watts,* pp. 33-34.

9. Leaver, *Hymn Book Survey,* p. 12.

Praise and was published in Edinburgh in 1975. On the textual side it is remarkable for the developed hymnody of Brian Wren, while musically it owes much to the compositions of Peter Cutts and Caryl Micklem, the latter of whom has eight texts and fourteen tunes in the book. A high proportion of the new material is unique to this supplement. It includes the provocative hymn of Brian Wren, which begins:

> Here hangs a man discarded,
>   a scarecrow hoisted high,
> a nonsense pointing nowhere
>   to all who hurry by.

as well as Sydney Carter's even more provocative folk song "Friday Morning" with its stinging refrain:

> It's God they ought to crucify instead of you and me
> I said to the carpenter a-hanging on the tree.

The aim seems to be to strike the conscience of the casual or the inattentive worshipper.

In 1976 *English Praise: A Supplement to the English Hymnal* appeared as the fifth supplement. This generally undistinguished work has, however, followed Gelineau in providing eight responsorial psalms. Its hymn writers include Brian Wren, Michael Hewlett, G. B. Timms, and Hilary Greenwood of the Kelham Community. The latter has an Easter hymn, the ending of which reads:

> Mary asked the gardener
>   Where the body lay;
> but he turned towards her,
>   Smiled at her and said:
> "Mary, Spring is here to stay,
>   Only death is dead."

In an interesting survey of the general characteristics of modern supplemental hymnals, Robin Leaver points out that they include many hymns that are theologically unorthodox: ". . . in the struggle to express modern concerns of urban life, social responsibility, and the everyday things of supermarket and television, basic theological

236

truths have been distorted. For example, many a modern 'creation' hymn praises the creativity of man rather than the creativity of God."[10] On the other hand, while the musical offerings of the charismatics cannot be accused of unorthodoxy, they often seem trivial and trite. It is perhaps wrongly supposed that simple evangelistic hymns, suitable for revivals, are appropriate for regular congregational use. The hymnologist Erik Routley has rightly warned: "I do not believe that souls will be won for Christ by the use of texts and music that call for no discipline, to which asceticism is a stranger, and that communicate everything that they have to say at the first impact."[11] The repetition over and over again of simplistic charismatic choruses can be a strain on the patience of long-term churchgoers.

Next we turn from the consideration of the supplements to standard hymn books to other kinds of supplements. The need for these arose in part from evangelical crusades, and in part from youth clubs associated with churches which took up the 20th Century Church Light Music Group and who were drawn to the religious protest songs of Sydney Carter and others. The growing charismatic movement created its own songs, as well as borrowing from revivalists like Sankey and his successors. Finally, family services, less formal and less structured than traditional liturgical services, required a new kind of music, which meant, in the unflattering words of Robin Leaver, "happy hymns with jiggy tunes."[12] Only the most popular of these collections can be listed here. *Youth Praise* (2 volumes, 1966 and 1969) was designed to meet the need of youth groups as its title suggested. *New Life: Songs and Hymns for Assemblies, Clubs and Churches* was edited by J. Bailey and published by Galliard in 1970. It was a lively book with excessively colloquial terminology — unsuitable to induce reverence in worship and dubiously orthodox in content. *Family Worship*, appearing in 1971 with a revised edition in 1975, provided an order of service for family worship to which were added twenty metrical psalms and canticles and ninety-two hymns, songs, and choruses. These are unpretentious hymns which might well appeal to those without experience of traditional liturgical services. *New Orbit: Songs and Hymns* was written for seven- to twelve-year-old children, in the same way that *New Life* had been prepared for

10. *Ibid.,* p. 20.
11. Cited by Leaver in *Hymn Book Survey*, p. 20.
12. Leaver, *Hymn Book Survey*, p. 16.

teenagers. *Sound of Living Waters* and *Fresh Sounds: A Companion Volume to Sound of Living Waters* appeared successively in 1974 and 1976; these volumes were clearly aimed at charismatic worshippers and their sounds, according to its editors, Betty Pulkingham and Jeanne Harper, reflect "the cascade of joyous praise, of awesome wonder, of sincerity and hope, which accompany the Holy Spirit's renewal in the Church today." The second volume has much that is new and its music is more widely representative. *New Horizons* is the third Galliard book for the young, but seems more humanist in its themes and interpretation than the earlier volumes. Another Galliard production, shared by the Youth Division of the Methodist church, is called *Partners in Praise,* 1979. It tries to supply hymns and songs which will attract both adults and children, and like prior Galliard books, it provides suggestions for optional musical accompaniments and descants.

From supplements we now turn to revised standard hymnals. The most widely used revised Anglican hymnal is *Hymns Ancient and Modern, New Standard,* which was first published in 1983, but has since appeared in its thirteenth impression in 1989. This, as might be expected in serving *via media* Anglicanism, combines a fine selection of traditional music with a judicious selection of modern hymns. It includes seven hymns by A. F. Bayly, whose gift is for combining Christian faith with modern science, as is expressed in the fifth stanza of the hymn beginning "Lord of the boundless curves of space." This proceeds as follows:

> Science explores your reason's ways,
> and faith can this impart
> that in the face of Christ our gaze
> looks deep within your heart.[13]

Erik Routley has a joyful hymn based on Psalm 98. Its second verse skips along:

> Joyfully, heartily resounding,
>   let every instrument and voice
> peal out the praise of grace abounding,
>   calling the whole world to rejoice.

13. Hymn 493, verse 5.

Trumpets and organs, set in motion
    such sounds as make the heavens ring;
all things that live in earth and ocean,
    make music for your mighty King.[14]

Routley's tunes are also employed.

The most daring inclusion is of a satirical song by Sydney Carter. Its title is "House full" and in it those who reject the needy while comfortable in their beds also reject Jesus, the excluded infant Christ forced to be born in a manger. Two verses express the pointed irony in full:

No, we haven't got a manger,
no, we haven't got a stable.
We are Christian men and women
always willing, never able.

Jesus Christ has gone to heaven;
One day he'll be coming back, sir.
In this house he will be welcome,
but we hope he won't be black, sir.[15]

One valuable addition is a series of hymns written by John E. Bowers. These welcome folk to church and indicate the purposes of worship.[16]

Fred Pratt Green has eleven of his hymns included; one makes memorable use of the insignia of Christ's Passion, the crown of thorns, the purple cloak, and the sceptred reed.[17] A characteristic hymn celebrates Christ as the world's light, peace, and life. In its third verse:

Christ is the world's life, he and none other;
Sold once for silver, murdered here, our brother —
He, who redeems us, reigns with God the Father:
    Glory to God on high.[18]

14. "New Songs of Celebration Render," verse 2.
15. Hymn 400.
16. These are Hymns 444, 445, 446, and 447.
17. Hymn 517.
18. Hymn 440.

All of this Methodist minister's hymns are Biblically based, clear, relevant, intelligible, and well rhymed.

The official English Baptist hymn book is *Baptist Praise and Worship*, which appeared in 1991. A committee was appointed in 1984 to produce a hymn book by the early nineties. The editorial committee was under the chairmanship of Alec Gilmore, while the music committee was chaired by Michael Ball, and the worship committee was led by Michael J. Walker. The Preface recognized that "Experimental forms of worship and changed emphases in theology had taken place as early as the mid-1960s. The ecumenical and charismatic movements had challenged many of the more rigid traditions of worship, and there had been an explosion of hymn writing."[19] There was also an acknowledgment of the need for inclusive language, and for a fuller recognition of the Christian Year. The book combines classical hymns with modern hymns and even includes popular songs and choruses for those who prefer informal worship.

One liturgical novelty for Baptists is the inclusion of responsive readings for ministers and congregations. Because chants are not widely used today, it was thought wise to include some sixty psalms for responsive reading.

Since it was discovered that less than half of the hymns of *The Baptist Hymn Book* of 1962 were in regular use, roughly this proportion of regular hymns was retained. *Hymns for Family Worship Services* includes hymns suitable for children as well as adults. The charismatics have also left their impact on the new book. When I asked the Revd. David Coffey, General Secretary of the Baptist Union, to describe the impact of the charismatics on Baptist worship, he answered that their impact had been positive, since "aspects of their hymnody reflect a more relevant culture today." He instanced the fact that "the older worship used a pipe organ (a single person orchestra), but the charismatics typically have an orchestra containing trumpet, trombone, piano, drums, saxophone, and xylophone, and this orchestral accompaniment is both cheerful and relevant." His only criticism was that "their impact was divisive on a congregation where their introduction had not been prepared for."[20]

---

19. *Baptist Praise and Worship* (Oxford: Oxford University Press, 1991), p. v.

20. I had a most courteous and informative interview with the Revd. David Coffey at Baptist House, Didcot, on June 22, 1993.

The book contains ten hymns by Fred Pratt Green, fifteen by the Anglican Evangelical Timothy Dudley-Smith, and seven by Graham Kendrick which are marked by Biblical fidelity and vivid lyrics, as in the following example:

Meekness and majesty,
manhood and deity
in perfect harmony —
the man who is God:
Lord of eternity
dwells in humanity,
kneels in humility
and washes our feet.[21]

Two of Sydney Carter's songs are also included, neither of them provocative. The wisdom of the editors is seen in their determination to keep twenty-three of Charles Wesley's hymns and nineteen of those by Isaac Watts.

The former Congregationalists, Presbyterians, and members of the Reformed Churches of Christ had a difficult task in shaping a hymn book which would unite these three traditions. Their efforts eventually resulted in *Rejoice and Sing*. In analyzing this book I have benefitted from a most informative interview given me by Dr. David Thompson, Convener of the Doctrine and Worship Committee of the United Reformed Church.[22]

The resources the committee had were *Hymns and Psalms*, a Methodist publication of 1981 prepared by an interdenominational group; *With One Voice*, produced by the predecessors of the Uniting Church in Australia in 1977; *Mission Praise*, an Evangelical production intended for the ecumenical "Mission in England"; and *Jubilate Hymns*, a late twentieth-century Evangelical compilation with many hymns by Graham Kendrick. Routley's survey, *A Panorama of Christian Hymnody* (1979), was also of great use. An indication of the difficulties the committee faced is the statement by Dr. Colin Thompson, a member of it, that "Over 2,000 unpublished texts alone were submitted to the Committee."[23] The task was given to a Com-

21. Hymn 58.
22. The interview with Dr. David Thompson took place on June 11, 1993, in his study at Fitzwilliam College, Cambridge.
23. Charles Robertson, ed., *Singing the Faith: Essays by Members of the Joint*

mittee of sixteen, with a subcommittee on word and music. The experts included Fred Kaan, Caryl Micklem (a hymnwriter as well as musician), and Alan Gaunt, an able translator of classical hymns into modern English.

The method employed was the following. First, there was a need to construct an ecumenical core — that is, a list of hymns that any hymn book should have. Each member of the committee was invited to produce his or her own list, resulting in approximately 1,000 hymns, later reduced to 200. A parallel exercise was to get a list of essential hymns from representatives of the three uniting traditions, which led to pruning down a total of 30 hymns. The criterion was theological, so that Watts and Binney represented Congregationalism, metrical psalmody served for Presbyterians, and hymns related to Believers' Baptism and frequent Communion benefitted the Churches of Christ. The third task was to send members of the Committee to find a total of 250 hymns from current English language hymn books. The fourth stage of the work was to consider the new materials which were obtained either by consulting supplemental collections of hymns or hymns invited by the Committee. About 5000 were examined and about 300 agreed upon. In the fifth stage, there was a concentration on hymns and topics that were missing, some for particular and rare occasions. It was agreed, as a principle, not to include children's hymns, since many children enjoy singing adult hymns. Dr. David Thompson in expounding this point added: "They don't have to be satisfied with 'All things bright and beautiful, All creatures great and small.'" The sixth stage was reached when it was decided to publish a list of hymns the committee had decided to use and to invite church members to add what they thought was missing from the list. At this stage "All Things Bright and Beautiful" was omitted, as also was "At the Name of Jesus," which was regarded as both too antiquated and too long.

Some of the more difficult issues related not only to the elimination of popular but antiquated hymns, but to maintaining a balance of topics, and of the old and new. The wealth of eucharistic hymns was overwhelming and required pruning. The same was true of twentieth-century hymns on justice and peace.

Liturgical Group on the Use of Hymns in Worship (Norwich: Canterbury Press, 1990), p. 108.

The original intention was to produce a collection of 600 hymns, together with liturgical Psalms and Canticles. Considerable time was spent on how to arrange the hymns; the organizing principle was to reflect, first of all, God's initiative toward humanity, and then move into the response of humanity to God. In the first section songs to and about the Trinity — the Creator, the Incarnate Christ, and the Holy Spirit — reveal God's movement towards humanity. Then follows our human response in worship, the sacraments, and witness in the wider world, until, finally, humanity is united in eternal praise of God ("There Is a Land of Pure Delight"). The first section is more reflective in character, the last more eschatological in emphasis.

Some difficulty was found in trying to fit the Psalms and Canticles into the structure used for the hymnody. The psalmody was defined as psalms set for chanting, and the United States Episcopal Church versions were used; the Psalms were not Christianized. But since "All People That on Earth Do Dwell" was wanted, it was included as a metrical psalm to encourage people to look in the psalmody section. The Canticles section included those in the Anglican *Alternative Service Book 1980*, the traditional metrical versions of the *Te Deum*, and Timothy Dudley-Smith's immensely popular "Tell Out My Soul the Greatness of the Lord." Responses for the people to use in Communion and other services occupied the first twenty items in the book.

The committee made the decision to use inclusive language wherever possible. Military metaphors were softened wherever possible: hence "Fight the Good Fight" was kept, but "Onward Christian Soldiers" was excluded. Attempts were also made to exclude racism, to avoid the indiscriminate mention of leprosy (at the behest of LEPRA), and to avoid use of the word "dumb" with reference to the handicap of being speechless. Earlier missionary hymns with imperialist trappings like "From Greenland's Icy Mountains" or "Hills of the North Rejoice" — which referred to "shores of the utmost west" (California) as "unvisited, unblest"[24] — were all passed over.

The resulting volume is a first-rate hymnal which justifies the considerable time and expertise spent on its production. My own single objection is to a few hymns that are simplistic, naive, and repetitious, such as No. 29, where the word "glorified" appeared nine times in three stanzas of three lines each. The committee argument,

24. *Ibid.*, p. 109, a point wittily made by Dr. Colin Thompson.

according to Dr. David Thompson, was that the book should reflect the whole range of material to be inclusive. He added that Nos. 392 to 404 derived from Iona Community use, that these function in the Evangelical tradition as one liners, and might do away with projectors and scraps of paper.[25] The book has turned out to be one of Oxford University Press's best sellers in its category because of its popularity.

The final revised standard hymnal to be considered is *Hymns and Psalms: A Methodist and Ecumenical Hymn Book,* which was published by the Methodist Publishing House in 1983, with a second edition in 1988. It was an ecumenical product prepared by representatives of the British Methodist Conference and by members of the Baptist Union, Churches of Christ, Church of England, Congregational Federation, Methodist Church in Ireland, United Reformed Church, and the Wesleyan Reform Union. The committee responsible for the book claims in the Preface that it has "sought to respond to our changing times, and to produce a book which articulates the needs, the joys, and the fears of the contemporary world." This stated intention was implemented in two ways: firstly, by including a considerable number of hymns written in the previous twenty or thirty years, and secondly, by including a large section entitled "God's World." The latter deals with "the natural world and the human use of creation, with the social order, and with the human condition." The music of the book was selected to encourage congregational singing. The Preface concludes with the committee's claim that it tried to make available "the riches of classical, evangelical, catholic and charismatic hymnody of the past and the present."

The collection includes 823 hymns, the major Christian canticles, and 54 Psalms. Its ecumenical breadth can be seen in its inclusion of 28 hymns by Fred Pratt Green, 12 by Albert Bayly, 10 by Brian Wren, 9 by Percy Dearmer and by Timothy Dudley-Smith, 8 by Fred H. Kaan, 6 by G. W. Briggs, 5 by R. E. Davies, 4 each by Caryl Micklem, Brian Foley, Timothy Rees, F. Bland Tucker, and Alan Luff, and 3 each by D. T. Niles and Bryn Rees. Inevitably and rightly there are many hymns by Charles Wesley. This was a noteworthy ecumenical effort and achievement, and it is unfortunate that it did not deter denominations that had combined with the

---

25. The extensive analysis of the difficulties, the methods employed, and the achievement of *Rejoice and Sing* was provided almost entirely by Dr. David Thompson, and should be useful to other compilers of modern hymnals.

Methodists in this effort from preparing their own denominational hymnals.

In our survey it remains only to consider the publication of Roman Catholic hymnals, which were not needed before the changes brought by Vatican Council II. Catholic writers themselves declare: "The first difficulty that faced the Catholic community was that we had few, very few hymns that could be appropriately used at Mass and the need for such hymns led to the making of new hymnals, the editors of which were able 'to spoil the Egyptians.' It was thus that much of the English tradition of hymnody came into common use among us."[26]

The urgent demand for new hymns for Catholics was met first by two cautious volumes, *Praise the Lord* (1966), edited by Wilfrid Trotman, and two years later by the *Parish Hymnal.* The *New Catholic Hymnal* (1971) was the joint work of Anthony Petti, a Professor of English in Canada, and Geoffrey Laycock, the Director of Music in a Teachers' Training College in Norwich. According to the judgment of Erik Routley, "it is an original and demanding collection" and "is conceived in a mood of violent opposition to the consenting standards of the *Parish Hymn Book.*" Many of the older texts substituted "you" for "thou," and the rhythms and harmonies of the music editor, who contributed eighteen items, are "free-ranging and adapted to the variety of texts he was required to set."[27] Among the impressive composers were Michael Dawney, Elizabeth Poston, Geoffrey Laycock, Edmund Rubbra, Lennox Berkely, William Tamblyn, and Benjamin Britten.

The New Hymnwriters

It is time that we considered the authors of new hymns and sampled some of their most attractive wares. One is struck, at the outset, by how many of the most inventive new composers are Free Church ministers, and in particular how many of their number are or were alumni of Mansfield College, Oxford, where Dr. Erik Routley was for many years organist, choirmaster, and Lecturer in Ecclesiastical

26. J. D. Crichton, H. E. Winstone, and J. K. Ainslie, eds., *English Catholic Worship: Liturgical Renewal in England since 1900* (London: Chapman, 1979), p. 86.

27. Routley, *The Music of Christian Hymns* (Chicago: G.I.A. Publications, 1981), p. 169.

History. Routley was a great encourager of hymnodists, whether writers or composers, or, as he was, both.

The earliest of the new hymnwriters was A. F. Bayly, and those following him were Erik Routley himself, G. B. Caird, Caryl Micklem, R. T. Brooks, John Gregory, and Brian Wren. Other former Congregationalist hymnwriters, now ministers of the United Reformed Church, are Fred Kaan and Alan Gaunt. The only Free Church minister whose impact is comparable with theirs is the Methodist minister Fred Pratt Green, a fine poet.

The gift of A. F. Bayly is to commend the Christian faith and to link it with the latest scientific achievements. For example, the opening line of a hymn, "Lord of the boundless curves of space," reminds us immediately of Einstein's theory of relativity. One of the best in this manner begins:

> O Lord of every shining constellation
>   that wheels in splendour through the midnight sky,
> grant us your Spirit's true illumination
>   to read the secrets of your work on high.

It continues:

> You, Lord, have made the atom's hidden forces,
>   your laws its mighty energies fulfil;
> teach us, to whom you give such rich resources,
>   in all we use, to serve your holy will.

After tracing God's creative will in all creation, the hymn ends:

> Great Lord of nature, shaping and renewing,
>   you made us more than nature's sons to be;
> you help us tread, with grace our souls enduing,
>   the road to life and immortality.

Another distinguished hymn, "Lord, Your Kingdom Bring Triumphant," shows how God can be served in a variety of contemporary vocations. Two consecutive verses will indicate its empathetic approach:

> Consecrate your people's labour
>   at the airfield, mill, and port;

with the gladness of your presence
    bless our homes and grace our sport.

Let your mercy and your wisdom
    rule our courts and parliament,
and to soldier, sage and scholar
    may your light and truth be sent.

As a hymnodist, Erik Routley's[28] gift was to make psalms speak with a contemporary voice, as he did with Psalm 98 in the hymn "New Songs of Celebration Render" and Psalm 33 in the hymn "God Speaks and All Things Come to Be." He was the leading English-speaking hymnologist in the world, and his influence was felt through the insightful books he wrote as well as the melodious tunes he composed.

George Caird was a distinguished Professor of New Testament in Montreal's McGill University as well as at Oxford University, where he had also been Principal of Mansfield College. One of his widely anthologized hymns, entitled "Almighty Father, Who for Us Thy Son Didst Give," contains the memorable lines:

In mercy guard us, lest by sloth and selfish pride
we cause to stumble those for whom the Saviour died.

Another verse affirms that:

On just and unjust thou thy care dost freely shower;
make us thy children, free from greed and lust for power,
lest human justice, yoked with man's unequal laws,
oppress the needy, and neglect the humble cause.

The best known of the United Reformed hymnologists is undoubtedly Brian Wren, who has, for example, ten hymns included in the Methodist compilation *Hymns and Psalms* (1985) and six in *Baptist Praise and Worship* (1991). The best anthology of his hymnody is *Faith Looking Forward: The Hymns & Songs of Brian Wren*,[29] which

---

28. A fine tribute to Dr. Routley's influence is *Duty and Delight: Erik Routley Remembered*, ed. Robin Leaver, James H. Litton, and Carlton R. Young (Norwich: Hope Publishing Company and Canterbury Press, 1985).

29. Wren's hymns are cited from *Faith Looking Forward: The Hymns and Songs*

was published with many tunes by Peter Cutts, another Mansfield College alumnus, in 1983. God's plenty is found here; the difficulty is in restricting oneself to a few citations. One can only admire the fine Communion hymn "Great God, Your Love Has Called Us Here," with its admirable fourth verse:

> Then take the towel, and break the bread,
> and humble us, and call us friends.
> Suffer and serve till all are fed,
> and show how grandly love intends
>> to work till all creation sings,
>> to fill all worlds, to crown all things.

Typical of Wren's insightful writing is a fine ecological hymn, which begins:

> Thank you, God, for water, soil and air,
> large gifts supporting everything that lives.
>> Forgive our spoiling and abuse of them.
>> Help us renew the face of the earth.

The fifth verse continues:

> Thank you, God, for making planet earth
> a home for us, and ages yet unborn.
>> Help us to share, consider, save and store.
>> Come and renew the face of the earth.

Another of his hymns, which celebrates both divine and human love in touching ways, includes this verse:

> Love is great! — the love of lovers,
> whispered words and longing eyes;
> love that gazes at the cradle
> where a child of loving lies;
>> love that lasts when youth has faded,
>> bends with age, but never dies.

---

of *Brian Wren* (Carol Stream, Illinois: Hope Publishing Company; London: Stainer and Bell, 1983); and Wren's *Faith Renewed : 33 Hymns Re-Issued and Revised* (Carol Stream, Illinois: Hope Publishing Company, 1995).

As a result of his shocked experience at an S.C.M. meeting, where while worshipping with Anglicans and Orthodox he was prevented from sharing Communion with them, he wrote a fine hymn on Christian unity:

Lord Christ, the Father's mighty Son
whose work upon the Cross was done
    to give and receive,
make all our scattered churches One
    that the world may believe.

One of his most provocative hymns is also one of the greatest. It was partly inspired by Paul Tillich's *The Courage to Be*, in which three endemic anxieties are treated: fate and death, guilt and condemnation, and a sense of emptiness and meaninglessness. This hymn considers those states and shows how Christ can, through his human experience, enter into such suffering with healing. All six verses of the hymn entitled "Here Hangs a Man Discarded" will be cited:

1. Here hangs a man discarded,
    a scarecrow hoisted high,
a nonsense pointing nowhere
    to all who hurry by.

2. Can such a clown of sorrows
    still bring a useful word
when faith and love seem phantoms
    and every hope absurd?

3. Yet here is help and comfort
    for lives by comfort bound,
when drums of dazzling progress
    give strangely hollow sound:

4. Life, emptied of all meaning,
    drained out in bleak distress,
can share in broken silence
    our deepest emptiness;

5. And love that freely entered
    the pit of life's despair,

249

can name our hidden darkness
and suffer with us there.

6. Christ, in our darkness risen,
   help all who long for light
to hold the hand of promise,
   till faith receives its sight.

This is one of the profoundest religious poems I have ever read, and
it must have comforted many among the comfortless.

Like all contemporary hymnologists of standing, Wren has composed ecologically sensitive hymns. One, called "Come, Cradle All
the Future Generations," begs:

Come, cradle all the future generations,
   and guard their right to live upon this earth,
lest human deeds, by stealth or conflagration,
   snuff out all life and put an end to birth.

Its sixth and concluding verse pleads:

Come, let us guard the gateway to existence,
   that thousands yet may stand where we have stood,
give thanks for life and, praising our persistence,
   enjoy this lovely earth, and call it good.

Another realistic hymn is titled "The Horrors of Our History." It
begins:

The horrors of our history
   are vast, beyond belief.
We greet each new atrocity
   with bafflement, or grief,
yet all the evil energies
   that haunt the human race
come, not from alien galaxies,
   but from our inner space,
and terror, pain and genocide
   intrude on every prayer

with shades that whisper,
   "Where is God?
   If only God were there!"

The closing verse:

The fruits of knowledge, plucked and prized,
   have scattered wide their seed:
we are as gods, with open eyes,
   for shame or glory freed,
and share, as midwives to our God,
   the work of giving birth
to faith's fulfillment, mercy's child:
   new heavens and new earth.
Come blow, great wind of Pentecost,
   till all the churches dare
   to bear the horrors,
     heal the wounds,
      and show that God is there!

Here is a very inventive hymn writer, with a gift for vivid verbs and excellent rhyme, and a capacity to convey the truths of the Gospel in all their rude but radiant relevance.

Brian Wren has even dared to write a hymn eliminating the usual reference to God as masculine. The first verse proceeds thus:

Dear Mother God,
   you held me at my birth.
You sang my name, were glad to see my face.
   You are my sky, my shining sun,
and in your love there's always room
   to be, and grow, yet find a home,
   a settled place.

For Fred Pratt Green,[30] another widely respected contemporary hymnwriter, the issue of inclusive language has not been so easily resolved. In 1981, it prompted this witty bit of doggerel:

30. All hymns are cited from *The Hymns and Ballads of Fred Pratt Green* (Carol Stream, Illinois: Hope Publishing Company; London: Stainer and Bell, 1982).

How can we sing the praise of Him
　　Who is no longer He?
With bated breath we wait to know
　　The sex of Deity.

Our Father is our Mother now
　　And Cousin, too, no doubt.
Must worship wait for hymnodists
　　To get things sorted out?

O rise not up, you men of God!
　　The church must learn to wait
Till Brotherhood is sisterised,
　　And Mankind out-of-date.

O may the You-know-who forgive
　　Our stunned ambivalence,
And in our sexist anguishings
　　Preserve our common-sense.[31]

Such tongue-in-cheek humor is not, of course, characteristic of the hymns for which he is widely known and appreciated.

Green's sense of the need of ecological responsibility is aptly expressed in "Harvest Hymn," which reads:

For the fruits of his creation,
Thanks be to God;
For his gifts to every nation,
Thanks be to God;
For the ploughing, sowing, reaping,
Silent growth while we are sleeping,
Future needs in earth's safe-keeping,
Thanks be to God.

The second verse is concerned with social justice:

In the just reward of labour,
God's will is done;

31. *Ibid.*, p. xvii.

In the help we give our neighbour,
God's will is done;
In our world-wide task of caring
For the hungry and despairing,
In the harvests we are sharing,
God's will is done.

Of this hymnodist Erik Routley justly wrote: "It is safe to say that no hymnal that ignores him can claim to be fully literate."[32]

Consider, for example, how vividly Green paints the scene in Gethsemane beside the twisted olive trees:

Jesus in the olive grove,
Waiting for a traitor's kiss,
Rises free from bitterness.

As he wakes his comrades up,
Torches flicker in the glen;
Shadows turn to marching men.

In that dawn of blows and lies
Church and State conspire to kill,
Hang three rebels on a hill.

Innocent and guilty drown
In a flood of blood and sweat,
How much darker can it get?

It concludes:

It is God himself who dies!
God in man shall set us free:
God as Man — and only he.

Let him claim us as his own;
We will serve as best we can
Such a God and such a Man!

32. Routley, *A Panorama of Christian Hymnody*, p. 193.

253

Like all sensitive hymnodists, he insists that Christians concern themselves actively with social justice:

> The Church of Christ in every age
> Beset by change but Spirit-led
> Must claim and test its heritage
> And keep on rising from the dead.

> Across the world, across the street,
> The victims of injustice cry
> For shelter and for bread to eat,
> And never live until they die.

The same gifted author can rejoice in music:

> When, in our music, God is glorified,
> And adoration leaves no room for pride,
> It is as though the whole creation cried:
>   Alleluia!

No one but Fred Pratt Green has expressed in one hymn the whole meaning of worship, and this warrants full citation:

> God is here! As we his people
>   Meet to offer praise and prayer,
> May we find in fuller measure
>   What it is in Christ we share.
> Here, as in the world around us,
>   All our varied skills and arts
> Wait the coming of his Spirit
>   Into open minds and hearts.

> Here are symbols to remind us
>   Of our lifelong need of grace;
> Here are table, font, and pulpit;
>   Here the cross has central place.
> Here in honesty of preaching,
>   Here in silence, as in speech,
> Here, in newness and renewal,
>   God the Spirit comes to each.

254

Here our children find a welcome
In the Shepherd's flock and fold;
Here as bread and wine are taken,
Christ sustains us as of old;
Here the servants of the Servant
Seek in worship to explore
What it means in daily living
To believe and to adore.

Lord of all, of Church and Kingdom,
In an age of change and doubt,
Keep us faithful to the gospel,
Help us work your purpose out.
Here in this day's dedication,
All we have to give, receive:
We, who cannot live without you,
We adore you! We believe!

Fred H. Kaan, for whom English is a second language, exploits the language memorably, and his hymns, eschewing blandness, cut deep into our consciences.[33] One hymn, beginning "For the healing of the nations," contains this challenging verse:

All that kills abundant living,
let it from the earth be banned:
pride of status, race, or schooling,
dogmas that obscure your plan.
In our common quest for justice
may we hallow life's brief span.

The same author can provide an admirable hymn for Infant Baptism:

Now in the name of him, who sent
to preach by word and sacrament,
upon this new-born child we pray
the strength of God in doubtful day.

33. All citations are from Fred Kaan's hymns included in *Hymns and Psalms* (The Methodist Publishing House, [1983], 1988); Hymns 402, 590, and 348.

Our names are written in his hand;
he leads us to the promised land.
We rise in wonder from the flood
and love becomes our livelihood.

With Noah, through disaster borne,
with Moses, from the river drawn,
with Jonah, from the sea released,
we celebrate this rising feast.

The strongest note that Kaan strikes is realism. For example, in a hymn for harvest thanksgiving, with the opening line "Now join we, to praise the creator," he also remembers:

But also of need and starvation
we sing with concern and despair,
of skills that are used for destruction,
of land that is burnt and laid bare.

We cry for the plight of the hungry
while harvests are left on the field,
for orchards neglected and wasting,
for produce from markets withheld.

The hymn ends with an eloquent plea:

Then teach us, O Lord of the harvest,
to be humble in all that we claim;
to share what we have with the nations,
to care for the world in your name.

His theological inspiration comes from Bonhoeffer and J. A. T. Robinson. It is tempting to cite from his other bold hymns, such as "Sing We a Song of High Revolt" or "Sing We of the Modern City" but limitation of space forbids this. His "We Meet You, O Christ, in Many a Guise" is found both in the 1975 hymnal of the Southern Baptists of the U.S.A. and in the *New Catholic Hymnal* of 1971, so wide is his reach.

In addition to the Free Church hymnodists already cited, it is important to recognize the contribution of Timothy Dudley-Smith, an Evangelical Anglican, whose hymns are solidly grounded on Scripture. But he can weave wonder, as he does at Christmas:

> Child of the stable's secret birth,
> the Lord by right of the lords of earth,
> let angels sing of a King new-born —
> the world is weaving a crown of thorn:
>> a crown of thorn for that infant head
>> cradled soft in the manger bed.
>
> Eyes that shine in the lantern's ray;
> a face so small in its nest of hay —
> face of a child, who is born to scan
> the world of men through the eyes of man:
>> and from that face in the final day
>> earth and heaven shall flee away.

Omitting the fine third and fourth verses, we reach the finale:

> Child of the stable's secret birth,
> the Father's gift to a wayward earth,
> to drain the cup in a few short years
> of all our sorrows, our sins and tears —
>> ours the prize for the road he trod:
>> risen with Christ; at peace with God.[34]

Church Music

This is a vast topic and will be covered briefly because as Professor N. Temperley points out, we live at a time when the public knows much more about musical history and musical styles than used to be the case. Indeed, church choirs are finding it daunting in the presence of sophisticated congregations to sing anthems. Temperley concludes that "this side of parish church music is on the way out" and hence "the real function of parish church music as an opportunity for people

---

34. *Hymns and Psalms*, No. 124. This is one among nine of Timothy Dudley-Smith's hymns to appear in this volume.

to sing in worship, has re-emerged from torpor."[35] Jane Sinclair, in *Keeping in Tune with Heaven* (1992), points out that forty years ago the organ and the robed choir dominated the music life of churches, but that for the most part this has changed radically, except in cathedrals and well-to-do city churches. Now the chorus culture has spread widely, and the congregation is much more vigorously involved in worship. The standards and the quality of music have not been maintained in general, even as regards hymnody.

She concludes that "the statistical survey and oral evidence received by the *Archbishops' Commission on Church Music* strongly suggests that either organ and hymn book, or music group and song book (or a combination of the two) dominate the styles of music available in the average parish church today."[36] If good modern hymns with good tunes are chosen, one hopes that this may educate those who prefer the chorus type of singing, and thus hymnody can perform a serious instructional task. The unassailable advantage of hymn-singing is that it can unite the hearts and minds of a congregation marvelously.

Erik Routley in his *The Music of Christian Hymns* argued that the radical revision in church musical taste could be dated from Sunday, October 14, 1956, when the televised Sunday Evening Hymn Singing Programme came from the Somerset parish church of Martock. After three or four conventional hymns, sung to organ accompaniment, a piano was substituted and the congregation sang the tune "Chesterton," which had been composed by Geoffrey Beaumont. The next year Beaumont's *Folk Mass* appeared and the Twentieth Century Church Light Music Group was formed, which produced several hymn tunes that became exceedingly popular. This music included mild syncopation, and it had close parallels with so-called gospel songs; both, according to Routley, were characterized by "conformity, manufactured enthusiasm, the complete shutting out of any message but its own, and the fatal ease of composing music. . . ."[37]

One composer who hoped to improve this situation was Malcolm Williamson, whose great gift of composing for children is evident in his short chancel-operas, *Genesis* and *The Winter Star*. About the same

---

35. Temperley, *The Music of the English Parish Church* (Cambridge: Cambridge University Press, 1979), p. 374.

36. Sinclair, *Keeping in Tune with Heaven*, p. 4.

37. Routley, *The Music of Christian Hymns*, pp. 158-59.

time Sydney Carter emerged as a new type of Christian folk-singer who remarkably managed to link the "folk underground" with the more conventional society with which it was at odds. His complete collection can be found in *Green Print in Song* (London: Stainer and Bell, 1973). His most famous song is "Lord of the Dance," which criticizes static conventional Christian morality, and is set to an old Quaker melody of considerable cheerfulness. This kind of song has two qualities that recommend it: the author is usually also the composer, which guarantees stylistic unity; it is also, typically, informal and intriguing. Its weakness is that it encourages an uncritical simplicity.

Such songs are generally written for solo voice and chorus, and can be accompanied unpretentiously with a single guitar. Stainer and Bell have published several books of gospel songs of which the best may well be *One World Songs* of 1979. One unusual and promising song collection, called in England *The Gospel Song Book*, included compositions by Malcolm Stewart, a theologically educated Roman Catholic whose biblical songs are impressive. Roman Catholic composers who provided suitable liturgical settings were Laurence Bevenot, Gregory Murray, and Wilfrid Trotman. Composers of hymn tunes above the ordinary among Roman Catholics were Geoffrey Bouton-Smith, Philip Duffy, Christopher Walker, Bernadette Farrell, David Saint, and Ernest Sands.[38]

Amongst organ composers Herbert Howells has produced two sets of popular Psalm Preludes, and Percy Whitlock has written Four Extemporisations for Organ. Peter Hurford composed Five Short Choral Preludes; Francis Jackson, The Archbishop's Fanfare; and Eric Thiman, two sets of eight Interludes for the Organ. Kenneth Leighton produced Paran, and G. T. Thalben-Ball, an Elegy. Among Anglican composers of hymn tunes are William Llewellyn and Peggy Spencer-Palmer. The leading creators of good quality hymn tunes among the Free Churches have been Erik Routley, Peter Cutts, John Wilson, and Caryl Micklem.

Perhaps the most utterly unexpected development was the arrival on the scene of an internationally renowned composer in the person of John Taverner, whose mystical music, similar in some respects to Messaien, found its inspiration in the liturgy of the Eastern Orthodox Church.

---

38. A list provided by the Revd. Edward Matthews on pp. 153 and 155 of *Singing the Faith*, ed. Charles Robertson.

In sum, there have been the astonishing changes in church hymnody and music in the past three or four decades — all of which are exhibited in a plethora of hymnbook supplements. The hymns have often adopted language which is inclusive of both genders, eliminates racial exclusiveness, and extends sensitivity towards the handicapped. They have also opted for contemporary language, preferring "you" to "thou" and avoiding archaic or anachronistic formulations. The subject matter of contemporary hymnody has been enlarged to include the correlation of science and faith, the variety of modern vocations, the obligations imposed by ecology and social justice, and the celebration of human love. Some hymns pierce the conscience in strikingly provocative ways, and a few are banal in their repetitions and sentiments. As far as the music itself is concerned, many organs and robed choirs have disappeared except in the cathedrals and large city churches, and anthems are much rarer. But on the whole hymnody and music — the latter often accompanied by an amateur orchestra — is sung with greater gusto and more profound relevance.

CONCLUSION

ONTEMPORARY ENGLISH CHURCHES face the twenty-first century with both anxiety and hope. Part of the anxiety stems from the shared concerns of all people in this uncertain and violent age. And part of it concerns the evident secularization of English culture, as reflected in declining church attendance. It is estimated (perhaps 'guesstimated' is a better word) that in England only one person in five regularly attends worship on Sundays, except on festal or family occasions such as Christmas, Easter, Weddings, Baptisms or Funerals.

Confidence in the importance of preaching the Word has clearly diminished. Perhaps the use of microphones in the pulpit has led to a chattier and more casual rather than to a more proclamatory mode of address.[1] Yet on the other hand the use of common lectionaries crossing denominational frontiers, and in some communities the ecumenical gathering of ministers to study common lections, has revived the practice of consecutive Biblical instruction rather than the topical sermons formerly preferred by many Free Church ministers.

Unquestionably the major Gospel sacraments, Baptism and Holy Communion, have become more reverently and carefully administered, especially among the English Free Churches. The Baptists and the Disciples of Christ, of course, have always made use of Believers' Baptism, both in the action of immersion and in the requirements of promises of discipleship and of support by the local community of Christians. But in an increasingly secular world, even the Roman Catholic Church has now made Adult Baptism, with a strenuous and lengthy process of education and testing aimed at conversion, the norm.

Infant Baptism, meanwhile, is regarded in all English churches as an offering of a child to God by the parents; the requirement of making a solemn and public promise to bring the child up as a faithful Christian is exacted at all such Baptisms, as it is at the Baptist service of Dedication of Infants. Both the symbolism of Baptism and the promises required of parents and godparents are most emphatic in the Church of England and the Roman Catholic Church. There is an increased tendency for Confirmation in Roman Catholic and

---

1. In the words of Christopher Driver, the contemporary sermons have become "muted oracles, conversational, and defensive."

Anglican Churches and full church membership in the Free Churches to take place in early adolescence.

As far as the Eucharist (or Holy Communion) is concerned, this has always been central in Catholicism and Anglicanism. The service has become less "magical" and more meaningful for Roman Catholic worshippers with the translation from Latin into the vernacular English, and less stultified (as also in the case of Anglican Communion) with the use of various alternative prayers of consecration. In some Free Churches, a growing respect for the Lord's Supper is seen in the elongation and greater frequency of its celebration and in the use of traditional prayers of Consecration or Thanksgiving, including the traditional responses.

A new emphasis on the people of God has contributed to a role played by the laity in worship. It is now common to see men, women, and even occasionally children, carrying the monetary gifts to the Communion table, and also, occasionally, the bread and wine to be used in the consecration of the elements. In some Anglican Churches, we see laymen and women assisting the priest in delivering the consecrated bread (or wafers) and wine to the congregation kneeling or standing at the altar rails.

"The priesthood of all believers" is affirmed in practical ways in the increasing role of the laity in the Free Churches. Methodists have recognized the value of lay preachers from the days of their origin, the other Free Churches less so. This is beginning to change. For many years elders and deacons in the Free Churches, both male and female, have carried the consecrated elements of the Communion from the table to the members in the pews. What is perhaps new is that reverence is replacing casualness in the laity's role in this sacrament.

The role of women in worship has increased dramatically. For many years there have been ordained women serving as ministers in the Free Churches of England, but the Church of England has only very recently, after considerable contention, followed the example of most other Anglican Provinces overseas in ordaining women. This change has not been accepted by the Roman Catholic Church, despite its long list of women saints and the devout members of so many of its religious communities, but the idea has notable defenders among priests and even monks,[2] as well as an occasional prophetic bishop.

---

2. One prophetic monk who believed in the ultimate ordination of women in the Roman Catholic Church and was a *peritus* at Vatican II Council is Father

The content of prayers in Sunday worship seems to have improved in at least four ways. It is much more inclusive, and more sensitive to feminine needs. It emphasizes increasingly the need for ecological responsibility toward all of creation. The immediacy, range and ecumenicity of prayers has increased. Finally, a linguistic revival has renewed the language of prayers: archaic forms of English are being exchanged for contemporary, but one hopes, still literary English. The virtue of silence, long valued by the Quakers, has in this cacophonous age, been rediscovered and consciously reintroduced in English prayer.

There is cause for rejoicing in the increasing use of innovative and creative art (paintings, tapestries, sculptures, and stained-glass) by the famous and yet-to-be renowned in the Anglican and Roman Catholic Cathedrals in England and in other individual churches whose rectors are oriented towards the arts. One cannot but celebrate, as well, the travelling Art Exhibition of the Methodists. The other Free Churches, for the most part, still retain Puritan iconoclastic tendencies which prevent them from displaying religious art or symbolism.

There is also hope to be found in the flowering of excellent new hymns. Some celebrate human love, others link faith with modern science, still others recall the poor and the social implications of the Gospel and seem — in some cases — strikingly relevant to everyday life in the factory and the supermarket. There has, however, been a lowering of the quality of words and music in several popular collections of hymns. For splendid new or traditional religious music one has to attend the cathedrals or larger churches.

While the new functional style of church architecture has improved the audibility and the visibility of the elders in worship, given congregations a deeper sense of unity, and often provided useful extra rooms to be used for social, educational, and charitable purposes, the strong and almost dominantly horizontal lines leave, with some exceptions, little room for the verticals of aspiration.

However deep the anxiety may be in an increasingly secular age, there are also solid grounds for exercising the second theological virtue — hope. If one recalls the resources of the Triune God, who

Godfrey Diekmann, O.S.B., of the Benedictine Abbey and University in Collegeville, Minnesota, U.S.A.

263

is Creator, Redeemer and Renovator; if one remembers that the Bible is the Divine Word for our instruction and inspiration; if one recollects that prayers spoken and silent are an open communication with God; if one calls to mind the infinite love of God in the self-giving of the sacraments and the billions of Christians past and present who, like a cloud of witnesses, testified to the integrity, the truth, the love, and the forgiveness of God and the promise of life everlasting through Christ. . . then there are solid grounds for hope.

Finally, if one considers the situation of the infant Church on what seemed to be Bad and not Good Friday, or the prospects for Christianity when the Muslims in 732, overrunning Europe, had reached the heart of France at Tours, or how, at the Reformation and Counter-Reformation, the Western Church was fractured beyond recognition; then we can recall that the Church of Christ has worn out many hammers, and we can join in the opening exchange of the Communion Prayer of Thanksgiving:

Lift up your hearts.
We lift them up to the Lord.

BIBLIOGRAPHY

BIBLIOGRAPHY

1. LITURGICAL TEXTS

(Arranged chronologically and denominationally)

ANGLICAN (at home and abroad)

The Alternative Service Book (of the Church of England, 1980)
See also the following, edited by C. O. Buchanan:
  Modern Anglican Liturgies, 1958-1968
  Further Anglican Liturgies, 1968-1975
  Latest Anglican Liturgies, 1976-1984

THE FREE CHURCHES

BAPTIST
Praise God: A Collection of Resource Material for Christian Worship (Baptist Union, 1980)
Patterns and Prayers for Christian Worship (Baptist Union, 1991; revised edition, 1992)

METHODIST
The Methodist Service Book (1975)
The Methodist Service Book (1992)

PRESBYTERIAN
The Presbyterian Service Book (1975)

THE UNITED REFORMED (a union of ex-Congregationalists, ex-Presbyterians, and subsequently ex-Disciples of Christ)
A Book of Services: The United Church in the United Kingdom (Edinburgh, 1989)

ORTHODOX CHURCHES

An Orthodox Prayer Book (Greek ed. by Fr. N. M. Vaporis, trans. by Frs. J. von Holtzhausen and Michael Gelsinger, Brookline, Massachusetts, 1977)
The Orthodox Liturgy, being the Divine Liturgy of S. John Chrysostom and S. Basil the Great according to the Use of the Church of Russia (S.P.C.K. for the Fellowship of SS. Alban and Sergius, London, 1947)

THE ROMAN CATHOLIC CHURCH

Ordo Missae (1970) (The Roman Missal as approved by Vatican II)

267

The Christian Initiation of Adults (1970)
The Sunday Missal: A New Edition (Collins, 1984)
The Sunday Mass (Collins, 1989)

2. HYMN BOOKS

THE ANGLICAN CHURCH

Hymns Ancient and Modern (1861)
100 Hymns for Today (Supplement to above in 1950)
The English Hymnal (*English Praise: A Supplement to the English Hymnal*, 1976)
Hymns Ancient and Modern, New Standard (1983, 13th impression, 1989)

THE FREE CHURCHES

BAPTIST UNION OF CHURCHES

The Baptist Hymn Book (1962, with the Supplement *Praise for Today*, 1974)
Baptist Praise and Worship (1991)

METHODIST

Partners in Praise (for youth, 1979)
Hymns and Psalms: A Methodist and Ecumenical Hymn Book (1983)

UNITED REFORMED

Rejoice and Sing (1991)

THE ROMAN CATHOLIC CHURCH

Praise the Lord (1966)
Parish Hymnal (1968)
The New Catholic Hymnal (1971)

3. PERIODICALS

Journal of Ecclesiastical History
Journal for the Scientific Study of Religion
Liturgical Arts Magazine
Philosophy Today

Revue bénédictine
Scottish Journal of Theology
Studia Liturgica
Theology Today
Worship

4. BOOKS

(published in London unless otherwise indicated)

Aland, K., *et al.* (eds.). *Studia Evangelica: Papers Presented to the International Congress on "The Four Gospels" in 1957* (Berlin, 1959).

Anglican Archbishops' Commission on Doctrine. *In Tune with Heaven* (1992).

―――. *Thinking about the Eucharist* (1972).

Anglican Liturgical Commission. *Alternative Services: Second Series* (1965).

―――. *Making Women Visible* (1982).

―――. *Modern Liturgical Texts* (1968).

―――. *Patterns for Worship* (1989).

―――. *Series Three*, forms of services (1971-1979).

Avila, Rafael. *Worship and Politics* (Maryknoll, N.Y., 1981).

Balasuriya, Tissa. *The Eucharist and Human Liberation* (Maryknoll, N.Y., 1979).

Banton, M. (ed.). *Anthropological Approaches to the Study of Religion* (1966).

Barclay, William. *The Lord's Supper* (1967).

Barth, Karl. *Church Dogmatics* (1936-1969).

―――. *The Teaching of the Church regarding Baptism* (1948).

Barth, Markus. *Rediscovering the Lord's Supper* (Atlanta, 1988).

Beckwith, R. T., and J. E. Tiller (eds.). *The Service of Holy Communion and Its Revision* (Abingdon, 1972).

Benz, Ernst. *The Eastern Orthodox Church: Its Thought and Life* (Chicago, 1983).

Boff, Leonardo. *Faith on the Edge: Religion and Marginalized Existence* (Maryknoll, N.Y., 1989).

Bonhoeffer, Dietrich. *Prisoner for God: Letters and Papers from Prison* (New York, 1960).

Bouyer, Louis. *The Liturgy Revived: A Doctrinal Commentary on the Conciliar Constitution on the Liturgy* (South Bend, Indiana, 1964).

Bradshaw, Paul, and Lawrence Hoffman. *The Changing Face of Jewish and Christian Worship in North America* (South Bend, Indiana, 1991).

Bradshaw, Jennings, Bundle, and Timms. *Episcopal Services* (1980).

Bria, Ion (ed.). *Martyria/Mission: The Witness of the Orthodox Churches* (Geneva, 1980).

Bridge, Donald, and David Phypers. *Communion: The Meal that Unites?* (Wheaton, Illinois, 1982).

Brook, Stella. *The Language of the Book of Common Prayer* (1965).

Brown, Robert McAfee. *Unexpected News: Reading the Bible with Third World Eyes* (Philadelphia, 1984).

Browning, R. L., and R. A. Reed. *The Sacraments in Religious Education and Liturgy: An Ecumenical Model* (Birmingham, Alabama, 1985).

Buchanan, C. O. *Anglicans and Worship in Local Ecumenical Projects* (Bramcote, 1987).

———. *Encountering Charismatic Worship* (Bramcote, 1977).

———. *Revising the A.S.B.* (Bramcote, 1989).

Bugnini, A. *The Reform of the Liturgy, 1948-1975* (Collegeville, 1990).

Burke, T. P. (ed.). *The Church in History* (New York, 1966).

Burnish, R. *The Meaning of Baptism: A Comparison of the Teaching and Practice of the Fourth Century with the Present Day* (1985).

Cameron, Deborah. *Feminism and Linguistic Theory* (New York, 1985).

Cardinal, Ernesto. *El Evangelio in Solentiname* (San Jose, Costa Rica, 1979).

Casel, Odo. *Das christliche Kultmysterium* (Regensburg, 3rd ed.; English trans.: *The Mystery of Christian Worship*, 1962).

Chrysostom, St. John. *Baptismal Instructions*, trans. Paul W. Harkins (Westminster, Maryland, 1963).

Clark, N., and R. C. D. Jasper (eds.). *Initiation and Eucharist: Essays on Their Structure* (1972).

Cooke, L. E. *Above Every Name* (1962).

Cope, Gilbert (ed.). *Making the Building Serve the Liturgy* (1962).

Corbishley, Thomas. *One Body, One Spirit* (Leighton Buzzard, 1973).

Crichton, J. D. *Christian Celebration: Understanding the Mass*, 3rd ed. (1993).

———. *Christian Celebration: Understanding the Sacraments*, 3rd ed. (1993).

———. *Understanding the Prayer of the Church* (1976, 1993).

Crichton, J. D., Winstone, and Ainslie (eds.). *English Catholic Worship: Liturgical Renewal in England since 1900* (1979).

Crockett, W. R. *Eucharist: Symbol of Transformation* (New York, 1989).

Cuming, G. J. *He Gave Thanks: An Introduction to the Eucharistic Prayer* (Bramcote, 1981).

———. *A History of Anglican Liturgy*, 2nd ed. (1982).

Davies, Horton. *Bread of Life and Cup of Joy: Newer Ecumenical Perspectives on the Eucharist* (Grand Rapids, Michigan, 1993).

Davies, J. Gordon (ed.). *A New Dictionary of Liturgy and Worship* (1986).

270

Davis, Charles. *Liturgy and Doctrine* (1960).

Day, Michael. *Modern Art in English Churches* (Oxford, 1984).

Dillistone, F. W. *Christianity and Symbolism* (1955).

Dix, Gregory. *The Shape of the Liturgy* (1945).

Dunstan, Alan. *Interpreting Worship* (Wilton, Connecticut, 1985).

Eliade, Mircea. *Images and Symbols* (1961).

————. *The Sacred and the Profane: The Nature of Religion* (New York, 1959).

Every, George. *Basic Liturgy* (1961).

Exeter, Adolph (ed.). *Die Neue Gemeinde* (Mainz, 1966).

Faull, Vivienne, and Jane Sinclair. *Count Us In — Inclusive Language in Liturgy* (Bramcote, 1986).

Ferm, D. W. (ed.). *Liberation Theology, North American Style* (New York, 1987).

Fisher, J. D. C. *Christian Initiation: Baptism in the Mediaeval West* (1966).

Ford, David F. (ed.). *An Introduction to Christian Theology in the Twentieth Century* (Oxford, 1989).

Frye, R. M. *Language for God and Feminist Language: Problems and Principles* (Center of Theological Inquiry, Princeton, 1988).

Geertz, Clifford. *The Interpretation of Cultures* (New York, 1973).

Gerrish, B. A. *Grace and Gratitude: The Eucharistic Theology of John Calvin* (Minneapolis, 1992).

Gieselmann, Reinhard. *Contemporary Church Architecture* (1972).

Gjerding, I., and E. Kinnamon. *No Longer Strangers: A Resource for Women and Worship* (Geneva, 1984).

Grassi, J. *Broken Bread and Broken Bodies: The Lord's Supper and World Hunger* (Maryknoll, N.Y., 1985).

Green, F. P. *The Hymns and Ballads of Fred Pratt Green* (Carol Stream, Illinois, 1982).

Gutiérrez, Gustavo. *A Theology of Liberation* (Maryknoll, N.Y., 1973).

Hammond, Peter. *Towards a Church Architecture* (1962).

Heron, A. I. C. *Table and Tradition* (Philadelphia, 1983).

Hippolytus. *The Apostolic Tradition,* trans. and ed. Gregory Dix and Henry Chadwick (1968).

Howell, Clifford. *The Work of Our Redemption,* 4th ed. (1975).

————, trans. *The Constitution on the Liturgy* (1965).

International Consultation on English Texts. *Prayers We Have in Common* (and reports on this theme between 1968 and 1975).

Ireland, Geoffrey, and Laurie Lee (eds.). *Epstein: A Camera Study of the Artist at Work* (1958).

Jasper, D., and R. C. D. Jasper (eds.). *Language and the Worship of the Church* (New York, 1990).

Jasper, R. C. D. *The Development of the Anglican Liturgy, 1662-1980* (1989).

———. *The Eucharist Today* (1974).

Jasper, R. C. D., and Paul Bradshaw. *A Companion to the Alternative Service Book* (1986).

Joint Liturgical Group. *An Additional Lectionary* (1969).

———. *Calendar and Lectionary* (1967).

———. *The Daily Office* (1968).

———. *Four Year Lectionary* (1990).

———. *Getting the Liturgy Right* (1982).

———. *Holy Week Services* (1971).

———. *Initiation and the Eucharist . . .* (1972).

———. *Praying Together* (1988).

———. *The Renewal of Worship* (1965).

———. *Singing the Faith* (Norwich, 1990).

———. *The Word in Season: The Use of the Bible in Liturgy* (Norwich, 1988).

———. *Worship and the Child* (1975).

Jones, Wainwright, Yarnold, and Bradshaw (eds.). *The Study of Liturgy*, rev. ed. (1992).

Jones, Tom Devonshire. *Images of Christ: Religious Iconography in Twentieth-Century British Art* (Northampton, U.K., 1993).

Jung, Carl. *Man and His Symbols* (New York, 1968).

Jungmann, J. *Missarum Solemnia* (Vienna, 1949; English trans.: *The Mass of the Roman Rite*, New York, 1968).

Kennedy, David, and David Mann. *Making the Eucharistic Prayer Work* (Bramcote, 1988).

Kennedy, David, and Philip Tovey. *Methodist and United Reformed Church Worship* (Bramcote, 1992).

Langer, Susanne K. *Philosophy in a New Key: A Study in the Symbolism of Reason, Rite, and Art*, 3rd ed. (Cambridge, Massachusetts, 1957).

Lash, Nicholas. *His Presence in the World: A Study of Eucharistic Worship and Theology* (1968).

Leaver, Robin. *A Hymn Book Survey, 1962-1980* (Bramcote, 1980).

Leaver, Litton, and Young. *Duty and Delight: Erik Routley Remembered* (Norwich, 1985).

Leenhardt, F. J. *Parole Visible* (Neuchâtel, 1972).

Lindstrom, R. *Creativity and Contradiction* (Washington, D.C., 1988).

Macquarrie, J. *Principles of Christian Theology* (1960).

Made, Not Born: New Perspectives on Christian Initiation and the Catechumenate (South Bend, Indiana, 1976).

Maguire, Robert, and Keith Murray. *Modern Churches in the World* (1965).

Manning, B. L. *The Hymns of Wesley and Watts* (1988 reprint).

Matthews, E. *Celebrating Mass with Children* (1975).

Merriman, M. W. (ed.). *The Baptismal Mystery and the Catechumenate* (New York, 1990).

Michell, G. A. *Eucharistic Consecration in the Primitive Church* (1948).

Micklem, Caryl (ed.). *A Call to Prayer* (1993).

Mitchell, L. L. *Worship: Initiation and the Churches* (Washington, D.C., 1991).

Modern Eucharistic Agreement (London, 1973).

Moltmann, Jürgen. *Theologie der Hoffnung*, 5th ed., trans. as *The Theology of Hope* (New York, 1967).

Morris, Brian. *Ritual Murder* (Manchester, 1980).

Ogden, Schubert M. *Faith and Freedom: Toward a Theology of Liberation* (Nashville, 1989).

Pace, Peter G. *The Architecture of George Pace, 1915-1975* (1990).

Perham, M. *The Communion of Saints: An Examination of the Place of the Christian Dead in the Belief, Worship, and Calendars of the Church* (1980).

————. *Liturgy Pastoral and Parochial* (1984).

———— (ed.). *Liturgy for a New Century: Further Essays in Preparation for the Revision of the Alternative Service Book* (1991).

Power, David. *Unsearchable Riches: The Symbolic Nature of Liturgy* (New York, 1984).

Register of Local Ecumenical Projects and Sponsoring Bodies (compiled by "Churches Together in Britain," 1992).

Reumann, John. *The Supper of the Lord* (Philadelphia, 1985).

Roman Catholic Bishops of England and Wales. *The Christian Initiation of Adults* (R.C.I.A. — its Latin abbreviation, for the authorization had arrived in 1972).

————. *Instructio ad Exsecutionem Constitutionis de Sacra Liturgia recte ordinanum* (1964).

————. *Ordo Baptismi Parvulorum* (Order for the Baptism of Infants, 1969).

————. *The Reform of the Sacred Liturgy* (second stage, 1965).

Routley, Erik. *The Music of Christian Hymns* (Chicago, 1981).

————. *A Panorama of Christian Hymnody* (Collegeville, Minnesota, 1979).

Sauter, Gerhardt. *Zukunft und Verheissung* (Zürich, 1965).

Schmemann, Alexander. *Church, World, Mission: Reflections on Orthodoxy in the West* (Crestwood, N.Y., 1979).

————. *Of Water and the Spirit: A Liturgical Study of Baptism* (Crestwood, N.Y., 1974).

273

Senn, F. C. *New Eucharistic Prayers: An Ecumenical Study of Their Development and Structure* (New York, 1987).

Shepard, L. *The New Liturgy* (1970).

Sinclair, Jane. *Keeping in Tune with Heaven: A Response to the Report of the Archbishops' Commission on Church Music* (Bramcote, 1993).

Smith, Peter. *Third Millennium Churches* (1972).

Sovik, E. A. *Architecture for Worship* (Minneapolis, 1973).

Spence, Basil. *A Phoenix at Coventry: The Building of a Cathedral* (1962).

Spinks, Bryan D. *Worship: Prayers from the East* (Washington, D.C., 1993).

Stannard, Martin. *Evelyn Waugh: The Later Years, 1939-1966* (1992).

Stevenson, Kenneth W. *Eucharist and Offering* (New York, 1986).

—————. *Liturgy for a New Century* (1991).

—————. (ed.) *The Liturgy Reshaped* (1992).

Stevenson, K. W., and B. D. Spinks (eds.). *The Identity of Anglican Worship* (1991).

Taft, Robert. *Beyond East and West: Problems in Liturgical Understanding* (Washington, D.C., 1984).

Temperley, N. *The Music of the English Parish Church* (Cambridge, 1979).

Temple, William. *Readings in St. John's Gospel* (1955).

Thurian, Max, and G. Wainwright (eds.). *Baptism and Eucharist: Ecumenical Convergence in Celebration* (Geneva and Grand Rapids, 1983).

Wainwright, Geoffrey. *Christian Initiation* (1969).

—————. *Eucharist and Eschatology* (1971).

Webb, Michael. *Architecture in Britain Today* (1969).

Whitaker, E. C. *Documents of the Baptismal Liturgy* (1960).

White, James F. *A Brief History of Christian Worship* (Nashville, 1993).

White, James, and Susan White. *Church Architecture: Building & Renovation for Christian Worship* (Nashville, 1988).

White, Kenneth. *The Attractive Church* (Bramcote, 1979).

White, Susan J. *Art, Architecture and Liturgical Reform: The Liturgical Arts Society, 1928-1972* (New York, 1982).

Willimon, William H. *Worship as Pastoral Care* (Nashville, 1979).

Winstone, H. E. *Pastoral Liturgy* (1975).

World Council of Churches. *Baptism, Eucharist, and Ministry, 1982-1990* (Geneva, 1990).

Wren, Brian. *Faith Looking Forward: The Hymns and Songs of Brian Wren* (Carol Stream, Illinois, 1983).

—————. *What Language Shall I Borrow? God-Talk in Worship: A Male Response to Feminist Theology* (New York, 1989).

PERMISSIONS FOR HYMNS CITED

INDEX

INDEX

INDEX OF NAMES

INDEX

INDEX OF SUBJECTS